Global Society

THIRD EDITION

Global Society
The World Since 1900

Pamela Kyle Crossley
DARTMOUTH COLLEGE

Lynn Hollen Lees
UNIVERSITY OF PENNSYLVANIA

John W. Servos
AMHERST COLLEGE

WADSWORTH
CENGAGE Learning·

Australia · Brazil · Japan · Korea · Mexico · Singapore · Spain · United Kingdom · United States

WADSWORTH
CENGAGE Learning·

**Global Society:
The World Since 1900,
Third Edition**
Pamela Kyle Crossley,
Lynn Hollen Lees and
John W. Servos

Senior Publisher: Suzanne Jeans

Acquisitions Editor: Barbier
Brooke

Development Editor: Larry
Goldberg

Editorial Assistant: Katie
Coaster

Media Editor: Lisa Ciccolo

Marketing Program Manager:
Michael Ledesma

Design Direction, Production
Management, and Composition:
PreMediaGlobal

Manufacturing Planner: Sandee
Milewski

Rights Acquisition Specialist:
Jennifer Meyer Dare

Cover Image: Copyright Ng
Hock How/Getty Images

For product information and technology assistance, contact us at
Cengage Learning Customer & Sales Support, 1-800-354-9706

For permission to use material from this text or product,
submit all requests online at **www.cengage.com/permissions**.
Further permissions questions can be emailed to
permissionrequest@cengage.com.

Library of Congress Control Number: 2012900098

ISBN-13: 978-1-111-83537-8

ISBN-10: 1-111-83537-3

Wadsworth
20 Channel Center Street
Boston, MA 02210
USA

Cengage Learning is a leading provider of customized learning
solutions with office locations around the globe, including
Singapore, the United Kingdom, Australia, Mexico, Brazil and Japan.
Locate your local office at **international.cengage.com/region**

Cengage Learning products are represented in Canada by
Nelson Education, Ltd.

For your course and learning solutions, visit **www.cengage.com**.

Purchase any of our products at your local college store or at our
preferred online store **www.cengagebrain.com**.

Instructors: Please visit **login.cengage.com** and log in to access
instructor-specific resources.

Printed in the United States of America
2 3 4 5 6 7 16 15 14 13 12

Contents

Global Technologies

Preface

We wrote the first edition of this book when the twenty-first century was barely a year old. The patterns of the late twentieth century were clear enough to us and inspired the themes of this book: Maturing international management programs for credit and finance, rudimentary institutions of international law and justice, and global venues of communication and influence had made unilateral national actions problematic and often ineffective. These trends also limited the scope of national governments and qualified previously absolute notions of national sovereignty. Some of the developments so obvious in the late twentieth century were confirmed in the first decade of the twenty-first. The concentration of wealth in a small global elite while a third of the world languishes with inadequate income, health care, housing, and education threatens the stability of nations, regions, and continents. The need for scientific innovation and industrial entrepreneurship is more urgent than at any time in the past half century, yet the conundrum of widespread, rapidly compounding global debt hampers initiatives to maintain and modernize systems of communications and support. The need for private competition and innovation is weighed against a history of unregulated irresponsibility that has brought grief to the world's most advanced economies. The ability of governments to address problems of huge magnitude is weighed against increasing discomfort with the tendency of governments toward intrusive surveillance and mounting defense expenditures. The threat of major environmental and resource failure is gathering faster than expected, and the global response so far is inadequate. Thinking creatively about these problems benefits from knowledge of their history.

In trying to balance the general and specific, we seek to apply a globally-integrated approach in our treatment of the twentieth and early twenty-first centuries. We emphasize the transnational dynamics of environmental change, the development and distribution of technologies, and broad cultural shifts such as the growing awareness of gender and ethnicity. Instead of seeing "nations"—whether governments or populations—as discrete units, we look, when appropriate, within and beyond nation-states to identify those groups and institutions that operate on a transnational level. We also acknowledge the importance of individuals in shaping the history of their societies and regions. Competition and accommodation, stratification and equalization, distribution and maldistribution, cultural convergence and cultural differentiation are all at work within a global—rather than a national or regional—context. Global processes work themselves out differently in different regions, shaping and reshaping distributions of power. The globe does not produce homogeneity any more than does a single society. On the contrary, contact and exchange result in constant cultural production, ending some traditions and creating others, destroying some elites and elevating new contenders, exhausting some resources and generating new ones.

New to This Edition

In revising this text we have discovered that most of our themes have withstood the test of time, our readers, and our reviewers. In the third edition, we have deepened our treatment of some themes and introduced others that help connect the past century with the ongoing developments of the current one. The process of globalization, which underlies the transnational connections we explore, is given more explicit attention as are the environmental impacts of political, economic changes. We have new narrative and analysis of the history of global debt. The theme of Islam in politics shapes our discussion of recent developments in the Middle East and of changing ideological debates in the past decade. We have five new features on technology, and all features have been revised for broader coverage and tighter integration with the text. At appropriate points, we deepened our coverage of Southeast Asia and Latin America. And, of course, we have brought our coverage up to 2011-2012. Along with these improvements comes a leaner text and new maps to amplify the book's narrative. We hope readers will welcome our continuing focus on global society and its transformations in the twentieth century, and that the innovations in this edition will be useful to teachers and students.

Organization

Because we have resisted allowing a single national history or a succession of constructed political eras to control the narrative, the structure of our book is chronological but not rigid in the assignment of specific years to specific chapters. Broadly, our part structure is built around different phases of globalization.

Part I: Old and New Empires, 1900–1919 explores the systems of imperialism, world trade, and politics that prevailed at the beginning of the twentieth century. It covers not only the slow chaos of the disintegration of the great empires based in Europe and Asia but also the emerging cultural sensibility of the "modern," the "international," and the "progressive" as people learned of a wider world through rapidly changing technologies. Well beyond Europe, societies had to adapt to multiple importations as new elites came to power and nationalist demands mounted. For the first time in history, the Pacific region became a focus of strategic calculation by the world's most powerful emerging empires.

Part II: Struggles for Supremacy, 1919–1945 treats the tumultuous attempts to restore global order following World War I. We see nation-states not only struggling to control parts of the world left ungoverned or unexploited by the decline of the empires but also dealing with waves of economic dislocation. Powerful new technologies for the production of goods spread globally, and old patterns of exchange and distribution began to break down. The loss of a largely unified world market in a period of depression pressured political elites to innovate for their own survival. New ideologies unsettled political relationships and nourished aggressive nationalisms. At the conclusion of the Second World War, the elements were in place for restructuring global patterns of power and distribution and tackling environmental problems.

Part III: Rise and Fall of the Bipolar Order, 1946–1981 deals with the politics, economics, and culture of the Cold War. We point out that even while the bipolar order was being established by the United States and the USSR, it was being subverted by leaders in Latin America, Africa, and Asia who were seeking a fuller independence from former or current colonial masters. Unlike the imperial systems still in place at the beginning of the century, the superpowers of the Cold War era regarded emerging states as sovereign nations, to be enlisted as clients either through persuasion or coercion. For their part, the new nations negotiated the narrow path between the superpowers as best they could. China and India, in particular, struggled for leadership of this "Third World" of nations, hoping for safety and prosperity outside domination of the superpowers. By the time of Nixon's visit to China in 1971, the bipolar order was markedly weakened and was soon to be superseded by new patterns of competition for dominance. Globalization of both production and consumption changed ways of life on all continents.

Part IV: Emergence of New Global Systems from 1981 contains the final two chapters. Neither summaries nor predictions, these chapters consider the "global society" that has emerged from the previous parts of the story at work. The bipolar international system was replaced by a multicentered order operating within a highly competitive, global economy whose defining characteristic is rapid change. Yet new challenges of the twenty-first century are undermining that international system, as nations and regions attempt to shelter their economies or seek individual market advantages. While new electronic technologies have opened unprecedented access to information and international communication, differentials in the distribution of wealth and well-being continue to widen. Dissidence and resistance also take on new global forms, exploiting the same avenues of media and technology used by the more formal powers. While some groups, and indeed some nations, still influence world political and economic development disproportionately, in the global society effective change is increasingly the result of coalitions and compromise.

In the third edition we have enhanced our discussion in the concluding section of the mechanisms of global indebtedness and the implications of the toward extreme concentrations of wealth at the top of the scale and pools of extreme poverty at the bottom, whether globally and in individual societies. As our earlier chapters make clear, extreme curvatures in distribution of income, wealth, and services are not unprecedented, and the consequences are not unknown. This issue is distinct from the cultural and ethical critiques of modernity coming not only from the Islamic world but also from other sectors, which we explore at appropriate points throughout the text. Whether the new patterns of global society will enhance or degrade general welfare are not yet known, but we hope we have illuminated the reasons for the dramatic transformations that have affected so many of us in the twentieth and early twenty-first centuries.

Features

To build on the book's coverage of the environment and technology, we have included a feature called Global Technologies. This feature now appears in every chapter and explains the development of technologies in broad economic, social and environmental context. Five new topics have been introduced, and topics carried over from the second edition have been revised to broaden their coverage.

Instructor Companion Website

This website provides a variety of resources to help you teach your students, including primary sources, weblinks, and an Instructor Resource Manual by Sarah Nytroe, DeSales University, with chapter outlines, lecture suggestions, class activities, and global technology questions. It also includes HistoryFinder for World Civilization, a quick and easy way to add sparkle to your presentations. Thousands of images, audio clips, maps, interactive maps, and primary sources are all easily downloadable as PowerPoint slides.

Acknowledgments

The authors express warm thanks to Larry Goldberg, who has kept the third edition on track with well-timed reminders, quick and clear answers to our questions, steady encouragement, and good cheer. We remain grateful to Nancy Blaine for bringing us together, to Jean Woy for her support of the project, and to Julie Dunn Swasey and Jeff Greene, whose editorial suggestions improved earlier editions and live on in this one.

Marysa Navarro was an important figure in helping to shape the concept of the book. Her expert advice on coverage of Latin America and Africa made the book stronger. The authors wish to thank her for these contributions. John Servos would like to thank Peter Czap, Sean Redding, and Jerry Dennerline at Amherst College for their advice and suggestions.

Finally, this book also benefited from the careful reading and suggestions of the following instructors, to whom the authors express their appreciation:

Peter Guardino, Indiana University

Anthony Gulig, University of Wisconsin–Whitewater

Steven A. Leibo, The Sage Colleges and SUNY Albany

Kevin P. McDonald, University of California, Santa Cruz

David Rayson, Normandale Community College

Melissa Sartore, University of Wisconsin-Waukesha

Arthur Schmidt, Temple University

Joseph P. Smaldone, Georgetown University

Gregory Vitarbo, Meredith College

Sarah Nytroe, DeSales University

— P.K.C.

— L.H.L.

— J.W.S.

PART I

Old and New Empires, 1900–1919

CHAPTER 1

The World in 1900

On April 14, 1900, the president of France, Emile Loubet, and the leaders of the French government rode through the Paris streets in golden carriages to the gala opening of the *Exposition Universelle Internationale*, a world's fair designed to celebrate both modern technology and European power. Led by soldiers on horseback and saluted by cannon fire, they rode to Festival Hall, where they were greeted by thousands of people. Loubet called the fair a "work of harmony, peace, and progress,"[1] and he offered the hope that the twentieth century would see an increase in human happiness and well-being. Alexander Millerand, the minister of commerce, emphasized how science and industry had transformed everyday life: "Machinery has become the queen of the world." Telephones and railways had conquered distance, just as medical research had been victorious over diseases. "We have seen the forces of nature serve and adapt themselves to our hands," he said.[2] Millerand's optimism was boundless, and he hoped for a glorious future of good health and prosperity. For the next six months, the fair preached its message of progress to forty-seven million visitors.

The hallmark of the fair was its lighting. In the cellars of the Palace of Electricity, ninety-two boilers turned water into steam; engines then transformed the steam into motion, driving dynamos that produced electric current. The Eiffel Tower, a new bridge over the Seine, and the fair's exhibition halls were all illuminated by

[1] *The Nineteen Hundred: Paris Exposition Illustrated*, Vol. 10, #5 (1900), p. 9.
[2] Ibid.

electric lights. On the fairgrounds, electricity powered a moving sidewalk, an electric train, and a gigantic Ferris wheel. Visitors could see the spectacular results of industrialization firsthand as they toured the fair's exhibits.

At the fair, European machinery overshadowed the exhibition spaces allotted to colonized peoples. Despite the fair's attempt to describe other cultures authentically, the pavilions in which Africans pounded nuts and Asians danced, carved, and performed were built with mass-produced metal and glass, plaster and cement. Mud huts, mosques, and temples were illuminated by electric lights. First-aid stations, post offices, and telephone booths for fair visitors were only a few steps away from these newly constructed images of the exotic. Asian and African cultures were represented as foreign, primitive, and natural, in sharp contrast to the conveniences of the industrialized world that surrounded them. Europeans saw themselves as being modern because of their new science and technology. Modernity meant machinery and electricity; their absence signaled inferiority and dependence. The fair sent the message that Europeans were different from the colonized peoples of Asia and Africa.

The male organizers of the fair also emphasized the differences between men and women. The official medal of the exhibition showed a man with a torch in his hand resting on the back of a woman, the representation of France. The man's light illuminated the fairgrounds, while the woman provided support for him.

During the Paris Exhibition of 1900, strings of electric lights illuminated the Eiffel Tower and spotlights swept the sky, drawing visitors to the site. Evening crowds could tour the exhibits as if it were daylight.

Award certificates idealized women as mothers and exalted men for their physical strength and skill. Most of the fair's featured artists, architects, and designers were male, as were the judges. The fair also trivialized women's social and cultural contributions: A small Palace of Women was filled with recent fashions and a restaurant. In contrast, male military might was celebrated in pavilions stretched along the Seine and sports fields in the Bois de Vincennes.

The Paris fair took the side of social and cultural conservatism. Much of the architecture echoed historical European styles; virtually no "modern" art was displayed. The featured painters and sculptors presented familiar, sentimental images of an idealized social order: Men were strong and heroic; women were beautiful and passive.

The Paris World's Fair offers a good starting point for this history of global society. The exposition displayed the world of 1900 as its rulers understood it and presented it to their citizens. The fair's European organizers planned it around nation-states and around those industries and activities in which Europeans excelled. Countries sponsored shows of their best contributions to science, fine arts, civil engineering, military weapons, mining, and machinery. In 1900 modernity was measured in Western European terms.

The most striking qualities of the world in 1900 were evident at the Paris Exposition. Technological change on a global scale had been the hallmark of the nineteenth century, when industrialization had transformed parts of Europe, Russia, Japan, and North America. In those countries an economic revolution had taken place. When fossil fuels such as coal and oil replaced animals and humans as sources of power, it made possible a vast expansion of production. Large factories replaced many small-scale workshops. Wages rose, drawing migrants into rapidly expanding cities to fill new jobs. A wealth of increasingly cheaper consumer goods increased standards of living for ordinary workers. Opportunities changed for both women and men as technology transformed the nature of work in offices, plants, and homes.

Technological change also had powerful and unintended environmental impacts. Steam engines and motorcars triggered dramatic increases in energy consumption. An abundance of coal, oil, and natural gas provided cheap power, and humans began to use more and more energy. The smoke from burning coal and oil poisoned the air, and paper mills consumed forests and polluted rivers with toxic discharges. As invention liberated people from earlier constraints on production and movement, it also degraded the environment. An awareness of the environmental consequences of energy choices became a theme of growing importance in twentieth-century global history.

In the twentieth century, the boundaries of the nation-state became increasingly irrelevant to social movements and social processes. Borders do not stop the flow of ideas and peoples. Commodities are produced internationally and move easily among continents. Today the air we breathe and the water we drink bear traces of distant places. In the modern world, no individual can remain isolated from the impact of policies and actions undertaken by strangers on other continents.

This book interweaves the central themes of technology, environment, and gender with an analysis of the political and economic history of the twentieth century. Our story begins with a look at the world in the late nineteenth century to establish a baseline against which changes can be measured. Although this book moves chronologically, a strict time line is sometimes abandoned to set a particular theme in context. Every chapter moves among regions and states to show the widespread and often different impacts of historical events. The history of the twentieth and early twenty-first centuries demands a global treatment.

Nation-States and Their Resources

Only countries that were independent in 1900 (a total of fifty-five) received an invitation to the fair, but colonial territories were also represented. The fair mirrored world politics. The most powerful European nations—Britain, France, and Germany—dominated the fairgrounds, just as they did international relationships.

But Japan provided the real surprise. Along with its anticipated exhibits of flowers and tea ceremonies, the Japanese displayed steel, engines, and military hardware. The first Asian country to industrialize, Japan shocked the Europeans with its manufacturing skills. Some of them recognized the Japanese commercial domination of Asia for the first time and worried about Japan's potential strength. A new player had joined the international lineup of economic and military powerhouses.

Modern states emerged out of warfare. States built centralized bureaucracies, taxed land and incomes, and developed strong armies in order to fight one another and to make sure their inhabitants remained loyal. In North Africa and Asia, modern state forms multiplied in the area between Egypt and Japan in response to European expansion. To remain independent, kingdoms such as Egypt, Ethiopia, Persia, and Thailand studied European institutions, bought arms, and established schools, attempting to graft new methods of governance onto older sets of institutions. State-making was a global process, although its precise contours varied in relation to local resources and circumstances.

States and Colonies

By 1900, most of Africa and large parts of Asia and the South Pacific had fallen under the control of more powerful states. Britain, Russia, China, France, the Netherlands, Austria-Hungary, and the Ottomans controlled vast multiethnic, multilingual empires, each uniting several territories under one ruler; other European powers had smaller, less diverse sets of colonial possessions. Joining in the rush for empire, in 1898 the United States had acquired the Philippines and Puerto Rico through victory in the Spanish-American War. Empires, whether composed of contiguous territories or scattered around the globe, dominated the map of the world in 1900, as Map 1.1 shows. European political and social theories justified imperial rule as a force for human progress and civilization. Empires, Europeans believed, benefited both the ruler and the ruled, who would be

MAP 1.1 Independent States of Latin America, c. 1890.
The date at which each territory became an independent country is listed on the map.
Direct European control was limited to British, French, and Dutch Guiana, British
Honduras, and most islands of the Caribbean.

uplifted by the religion, technology, and education exported by the imperial power. Independence was not viewed as a legitimate political goal for non-European populations.

In 1900, only one part of the world had thrown off rule by foreign kings and emperors. Combining armed revolution with a philosophy of democracy and natural rights, after 1776 the peoples of the lands south of Canada quickly established their liberty from European control. Soon after the British armies were driven out by the thirteen colonies, a revolt by slaves and freedmen ended French power in Haiti. In the years between 1810 and 1826, virtually all of Latin America fought successfully for independence from Spain and Portugal. Popular movements led by powerful colonial-born whites, or Creoles, overthrew Spanish armies and substituted constitutional regimes for dynastic control by European monarchs. In the following decades, new rulers worked to build national identities within the boundaries that resulted from the anticolonial wars and local conflicts within Central and South America.

Visualizing democratic regimes in which individual rights and liberties were guaranteed, the leaders of the new American states designed legislatures, judiciaries, and elections, through which voters would control national policy. Liberals, who wanted free trade, religious freedom, and parliamentary rule, dominated in the early governments. But visualizing republics of virtue was easier than establishing them in countries where the army, the Catholic Church, and the wealthy proved unwilling to cede power to democratically elected officials. In much of Latin America, military strongmen, called caudillos, took control of regional or national governments, paying little attention to the rule of law. States in Latin America combined the democratic ideologies of the American and French revolutions with the hierarchical and conservative traditions of Spain and Portugal in an unstable mix that continued to erupt into political conflict throughout the twentieth century (Map 1.1). Differences of political ideology, of ethnic background and language, of social class, and of regional origin undermined the unity of these states. Although Indians had citizenship rights in Latin America, they did not participate fully in their national communities because minority populations were effectively excluded from political and economic power.

The development of the Mexican state illustrates the continuing inequalities within that society. Although a majority of the Mexican population was *mestizo* (mixed European, Indian, and African), a substantial minority clung to an Indian identity, expressed through dress, language, and community of residence. At the same time, a small group of families of European descent monopolized the country's wealth and power. Not only did those elite families hold a large share of the land, they also dominated the government, the Catholic Church, and the military. The mass of the Mexican population remained illiterate and poor, living in isolated communities or working as peasant-laborers on large estates or in the towns. European descent was prestigious, whereas an Indian identity signaled backwardness.

In 1900, the dictatorial ruler of Mexico, Porfirio Díaz, looked to Europe for inspiration as well as for investment capital. Díaz portrayed himself in his speeches as a modern, reforming leader, while using strongmen to keep the country quiet and rigging elections to keep himself in power. Several of his key advisers were nicknamed the *científicos* because of their interest in using science to modernize the economy. Under Díaz, foreign investors were enticed into building railroads and textile factories and expanding export agriculture and mining. The state worked to improve infrastructures, at least in the cities. It drained swamps, constructed sewer systems, and founded hospitals. It boasted of lowering death rates and improving education.

Despite the high prestige of European technology and culture, many Mexicans still took pride in the nation's Indian past. As liberal historians wrote the history of the new Mexican nation, they recognized the contributions of pre-colonial Indian cultures. For the Paris Exhibition of 1889, the state had built a replica of an Aztec temple, with statues of Aztec gods and heroes decorating the facade. Early designs for the pavilion at the 1900 fair also included references to Mexico's pre-Hispanic past. As Mexicans began to define a modern Mexican identity, they included Indian themes and examples. By the time of the Mexican Revolution of 1910, artists as well as politicians had integrated an Indian heritage into the image of the nation. Nevertheless, the indigenous population continued to be exploited and denigrated.

The Mexican fusion of a self-confident modernity with emphasis on a pre-Hispanic heritage distinguished it sharply from neighboring states in Central America, where Indian populations were smaller and more repressed. Not only did Guatemala, El Salvador, Nicaragua, and Costa Rica lack modernizing governments and industrial sectors, but their economies depended almost exclusively on agriculture, both for subsistence and for export. Moreover, migrants from the West Indies and from China, imported to work on plantations, complicated the ethnic landscape. Unlike Mexico, states in Central America fell into a quasi-colonial relationship with the United States. An expansion of United States power in that region, which began in the late nineteenth century, rested on both U.S. ownership of profitable banana companies and its purchase of a concession to build a canal across the Panamanian Isthmus. When the new state of Panama became independent in 1903, U.S. influence was confirmed by its ownership of a ten-mile-wide strip of land on which the canal would be built. This enclave economy gave the United States a base in Central America, which would last through most of the twentieth century.

Transforming states into nations is a slow process. In classic nationalist theory, "nations" rest upon a pre-existing culture and common language; they are historically created communities of people who identify with one another, and who therefore have the right to a government all their own. Nations, in effect, are made up of people who consider themselves part of a nation. Today we recognize that in many, if not most, areas such ties do not arise naturally from past history but are created by state institutions, such as schools and armies, and by print culture. Individuals are taught to imagine themselves as part of a wider community, whose boundaries are said to be the nation. Nationalism is the feeling of loyalty to and belonging within a nation, which has arisen historically under

different sorts of conditions. By the late nineteenth century, nationalist sentiments had arisen all over the world; however, they had been most effectively
channeled and strongly expressed in the nation-states of Europe.

In Europe, during the second half of the nineteenth century, two new nations
were created through the combination of successful military action and diplomacy
backed up with nationalist ideologies: The monarchy of Piedmont Sardinia consolidated territory on the Italian peninsula to form the Kingdom of Italy, and
in Central Europe, the Prussian state engineered the federation of multiple city-
states, duchies, and kingdoms into the powerful German Empire. It took much
longer to transform individuals into self-identified Italians and into Germans than
it did to create new structures of government.

When new states are created, two problems emerge: boundaries and minorities. How should the territories ruled by "the people" be demarcated on the
ground? In a world in which individuals spoke different languages and accepted
various ethnic, caste, and tribal identities, what constituted "a nation"? This
second question at first seemed the simpler. Some people assumed that with
education and economic development, minorities would merge into the majority, and their distinctiveness would disappear. Others saw minorities as outsiders
who threatened the nation and therefore had to be treated differently. The
minority problem, of course, was related to the boundary problem. Should
land be the defining characteristic of a nation, or should it be shaped around
particular inhabitants? What should be done if the potential members of different "nations" live intermixed with one another, as they did, and do today, in much
of Latin America, Africa, Asia, Europe, and the United States? What should be done
about "nations" whose members are scattered among multiple countries? The settlement of Germans in Eastern Europe and Russia, of South Asians in Africa and the
Caribbean, and of Chinese throughout Southeast Asia fueled conflict throughout
the twentieth century, and minority populations continue to be resented in many
societies today. Nation-states promised homogeneity, but empires bred differences.
The promise of national self-government could not be kept when states were not
willing to rearrange their boundaries or to cede territory to accommodate the wishes
of minorities. One of the major problems of the twentieth century, easily visible in
1900, was the tension between the claims of nationalism and the claims of ethnicity
and culture.

By 1900, nationalism had successfully defeated the claims of empire in the
Americas and in some parts of Europe, and it was gaining recruits in colonies
around the world. In the United States, political rhetoric linked nationalism and
democracy, making these two ideologies available for use against the empires
of the world. To champion nationalism at home but imperialism abroad was
an inconsistent position, and ultimately Europe and the United States found it
an indefensible one. Within multiethnic Britain, Russia, Austria-Hungary, and
the Ottoman state, nationalists had moved beyond loyalty to their dynastic rulers,
and by 1900 they were seeking independence for their particular group or territory.
Ethnic nationalism energized many Serbs, Armenians, Hungarians, and Lebanese.
Active nationalist organizations operated in Ireland, Egypt, and in India. The contest

of strength between nationalism and imperialism lasted for most of the twentieth century, producing murderous conflicts. By 1900, it was well launched.

Population and Natural Resources

The wealth of nations can be measured in several ways—production, population, land, and natural resources, for example. Because comparable economic statistics for much of the world are not available before recent decades, it is impossible to compare the relative wealth of nations in 1900 with any precision. Yet estimates of the gross domestic product, the total value of the goods and services produced by a state, in the early twentieth century easily identify a few economic giants: Britain, France, Germany, the United States, China, and Russia. If population is taken into account and per capita wealth is measured, European countries, along with the United States, Australia, and Argentina, led the pack in 1900. In Asia, large populations meant low average incomes, but even there production was rising faster than the size of the population. In the early twentieth century, needed resources were growing faster than the world population. Certainly many people were poor and many went hungry, but widespread economic development meant that on average the amount of the world's goods potentially available to each person was rising. The problem of distribution of goods was as important as the level of production.

Population is an essential resource for a society. As workers, soldiers, taxpayers, and parents, people provide the goods and services that are needed to keep states strong. Demographers estimate that there were about 1.6 billion people living on the earth in 1900, about a third the number there are in the world today. Well over half of them resided in Asia. During the nineteenth century, Africa's share of the world's population decreased, while that of the Americas and Europe increased sharply. The industrializing regions managed to reproduce their populations more successfully than those whose economies were based primarily on agriculture and trade.

These rising numbers represented a growth in human capital. At this time, the industrialized states began to invest much more heavily in their populations, in the belief that healthy, educated citizens made states strong. Where states provided clean water supplies and efficient sewage disposal, people lived longer. Cities such as Paris, London, and Philadelphia had hospitals, public baths, and medical clinics for the poor. City governments inspected housing, immunized children, and quarantined the sick so that by 1900 the major cities in North America and Western Europe had higher birth rates than death rates.

European governments brought some of these technologies to the large cities of their empires. The British built a sewage system in Calcutta and huge reservoirs in Hong Kong, and the French made similar efforts in the capitals of Senegal and Morocco. Nevertheless, the vast expansion of public health and sanitation services brought by imperial governments went primarily to European settlers, who generally lived apart from local populations. In Kampala, Uganda, British officials used tax money to supply water, roads, and sewers to the urban areas they controlled; the sections of the city that were administered by the chief of the Buganda people had neither services nor taxes. Since most Africans were too poor to pay the British city taxes or to build homes that met British building codes, income differences increased racial segregation. Death rates were also much higher in the Bugandan sections of the town, largely because of differences in sanitation.

Populations were becoming more densely settled in many regions. During the nineteenth century, the pace of urbanization accelerated in industrializing areas, where more jobs and higher wages could be found. Railroad systems centralized migration into the larger towns, and city-based bureaucracies grew as states consolidated. The urban proportion of different countries and continents varied widely, as shown in Figure 1.1. About two-thirds of Britain's residents lived in cities with more than five thousand people, but less than one-fifth of the Latin American, Australian, and Asian populations had moved into settlements of that size. Differences in levels of urbanization correlated well with differences in incomes because rural wage levels were usually lower than urban ones. Nevertheless, some of the world's largest cities were in Asia and the Middle East. In 1900, Peking and Calcutta had more than one million residents. Bombay, Constantinople, and Shanghai numbered more than seven hundred fifty thousand. Northern Africa had a belt of big cities stretching

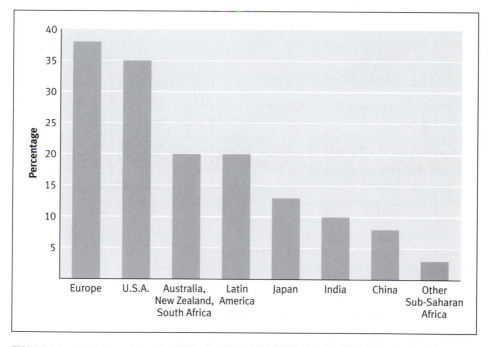

FIGURE 1.1 Percentage of total population living in settlements over five thousand people in 1900.
Although cities could be found on every continent, urbanization was much more extensive in Europe and North America than it was in India, China, or sub-Saharan Africa, where the vast majority of people lived in rural areas.
Source: Paul Bairoch, *De Jérico a México* (Paris: Gallimard, 1985), pp. 375, 522, 531, 542.

from Algiers to Cairo. Cities had been the centers of state power and control for centuries, and they continued to serve that function.

Luckily, no single country or region has a monopoly on all resources, but valuable commodities such as water, oil, and minerals are scarce in many areas. Differences in distribution help to explain differences in power. Most islands in the Pacific Ocean, for example, lack oil and mineral deposits, extremely important commodities for industrialization. The amount of good agricultural land varies widely among regions. Of the thirty-six billion acres of land on earth, no more than 10 percent is currently cultivated. Mountains, deserts, glaciers, snow, and rocks make most land unfit for agriculture. In places like Arizona, Egypt, and China, irrigation can make dry areas fertile, but water is scarce in the Middle East and in parts of Africa and South Asia. Without water, farmers' productivity is low. Although rural people on every continent have managed to feed themselves, the difficulty in many areas has been to generate a surplus beyond the needs of local farm workers. For complex societies to grow, food must be produced for city dwellers and for those who do not farm. In 1900, well-developed agriculture provided a strong basis for economies in industrializing areas, as well as rich countries, such as China. Moreover, if not enough food was produced, it could be imported using railways and steamships. Technologies were exported from one region to another. In 1900, land remained a source of wealth, but it no longer automatically constrained population size in parts of the world that were linked by trade and good transportation.

Production Around the Globe

The international economy was thriving at the turn of the century. On January 1, 1900, the *New York Times* announced that 1899 had been "a year of wonders.... Prosperity left scarcely any of our industries untouched and touched nothing it did not enrich."[3] The U.S. economy, it judged, was "the envy of the world." Business forecasters in other capitals were similarly happy. Economic growth occurred in Canada, Australia, Europe, and much of Latin America as well. The Asian economies grew more slowly, but China, India, the Philippines, Indonesia, Malaya, and Vietnam increased production, exporting more and more goods to Europe and North America, as well as regionally, and importing increasing amounts in return. Although sub-Saharan Africa was less deeply linked to international markets than most of Asia, Rhodesia, the Belgian Congo, Nigeria, Ghana, and Cape Colony had important export industries. Hopes for future economic development in Africa ran high. A widening circle of investment, production, distribution, and exchange linked the continents together ever more tightly.

At this time the core of the world's industrial enterprise was in Europe: in the north of Britain and France, in Belgium, in the Ruhr area of the German Empire,

---

[3]The *New York Times*, January 1, 1900, financial supplement, p. 2.

and in Berlin. Textile and metallurgical production had been transformed in these areas, starting in England in the later eighteenth century. A series of inventions—steam engines, spinning machines, mechanical looms, and new styles of smelting furnaces—led to mass production of cheap textiles, coal, and cast iron, which soon flooded world markets. Moreover, steam engines could power railways and steamships, pump deep mines, and run dozens of machines from a single source. Within a few decades, a cascade of new technologies transformed the steel, chemical, and electrical industries. The net effect on production was dubbed the Industrial Revolution.

Heavily urbanized industrial zones had grown up around coal mines and iron ore deposits throughout Western and Central Europe, their factories financed from capital cities and staffed by migrant workers. The products of these factories moved to other continents in ships and were traded for food and raw materials. Europe's stiffest competitor was the United States, whose coal and steel industries in the Midwest were booming and whose ships traded in the Pacific and in Latin America.

Meanwhile, the Russian and Japanese governments had begun to industrialize their economies, and Chinese and Indian entrepreneurs were building factories using European technology. The term *globalization* accurately describes the multi-centered world economy of the late nineteenth century. Integrated by the combination of free trade, imperialism, and industrialization, states and colonies around the world were tightly linked to one another. Economic exchanges reinforced political and cultural ones produced by mass migration and the export of religions, constitutions, and laws.

Economists describe the years 1900 to 1914 as "liberal capitalist," to signal the commanding role of markets and the limited interference of governments in the economy. Economic outcomes resulted primarily from the uncoordinated decisions of individuals working to promote their own interests and to earn profits. Most governments had few functions: They provided law and order, national defense, and the regulation of trade, but few spent much money on social activities other than primary education. States set the rules of the economic game but interfered only in selected industries, such as railways and banks. Governments made their major contribution to economic growth through the regulation of international finance and trade. With the exception of Japan, governments regulated most industries only in rudimentary ways, and few businesses were state owned. Taxes were low and citizens' obligations small, although people protested the few burdens that did exist.

Under the protective umbrella of stable exchange rates, European investors sent money around the globe. Although most of their money went to other industrial or industrializing regions, significant amounts flowed into the railways, public utilities, plantations, and mines of Europe's colonies. Moreover, the barriers to trade were low. Although the United States, Russia, and much of South America levied protectionist taxes on foreign imports, Western Europe, China, and Japan imposed only moderate tariffs or were free traders. Commodities of every sort had easily set monetary values: steam engines and sugar, bicycles and bananas. European factories needed cotton from the United States and Egypt, copper from the Belgian Congo and Canada, and tin and rubber from Malaya. European consumers demanded sugar from Cuba and Java, wheat from Russia and the United States, sheep from Australia, and cattle from Argentina. The gold standard and relatively low tariffs encouraged international trade.

The increased exploitation of land and natural resources had serious, unforeseen consequences. Industrialization on a large scale degraded local environments. The smoke from burning large amounts of coal polluted the air, and rivers suffered from the increased dumping of industrial wastes. Copper smelters released arsenic as a byproduct. Strip mining scarred hillsides, and upland areas were deforested, decreasing rainfall and intensifying erosion. In 1900, however, few worried about the long-term environmental effects of technological change.

Technology and Power

A state's power rested on its geographical position, population, land, and productivity, which were closely linked to its technological expertise. Differences in resources reinforced huge inequalities, which the globalized economy and communication system did little to mitigate in this period.

Global Communications

By 1900, the world was unified by communications technology and by the relentless desire of many Europeans to see the peoples of the earth and to write about them. Explorers hiked along the rivers of Africa and into the mountains of Tibet, "discovering" what for them were new places. European expeditions raced, as yet unsuccessfully, to reach the South Pole, while Americans and Scandinavians mapped Greenland, moving ever farther into the northern polar region. Everywhere distances had shrunk as governments or private corporations built railroads and canals. By 1914, the best and fastest steamers could speed from London to Calcutta via the Suez Canal in two weeks. The availability of cheap steel and the continued refinement of steam engines led to lighter, larger, and faster ships, which were cheaper to run. As the cost of transporting goods and people fell, circles of trade and movement widened. Telegraph and telephone lines multiplied to speed up the exchange of information over land.

To permit the speedy exchange of information by telegraph, hundreds of thousands of miles of thick copper cable had been laid under the world's oceans. Around 1900, messages could move from the London stock exchange to New York in under three minutes and to Bombay in about half an hour. The British government thought it so important that all its colonies and naval bases have secure cable connections with London that it arranged for an "all-red," or all-British, cable line circling the globe from one subject territory to another. Thus government messages

GLOBAL Technologies

Horseless Carriages

By 1900, horseless carriages were becoming familiar sights on city streets around the globe. Some were driven by steam and others by electrical batteries, but gasoline engines were increasingly popular because of their combination of light weight, responsive throttles, and range between refueling. Inventors had long played with the idea of deriving motive power from the controlled ignition of gunpowder or other explosive materials but practicable engine designs did not appear until the 1870s and 1880s when engineers, most notably Germany's Nikolaus August Otto and Gottlieb Daimler, developed ways to regulate the combustion of petroleum-based fuels with precision. Early fears of the clatter and speed of gasoline-driven autos soon gave way to fascination, not just among pioneer motorists but also among city planners eager to find a solution to the problem of horse manure on city streets. World output of motor vehicles, about 9,500 units in 1900, climbed to over a million units in 1915 and two million in 1919.

Internal combustion engines, and the vehicles they powered, revolutionized transportation—and much more. Their ceaseless hunger for fuel helped make petroleum a critical global resource. Their manufacture demanded capital, abundant quantities of steel, glass, and rubber, and networks of roads and service stations. Automobiles thus came to drive economic growth, most dramatically the United States in the 1920s, Germany in the 1960s, and Japan in the 1970s. Automobiles thus gave rise to many of the world's largest corporations during the twentieth century and supplied livelihoods to millions of workers. They also catalyzed social change—affording their owners new mobility, new leisure pursuits, and even new sites for courtship. The changes came with substantial costs. Exhaust gases fouled the air, asphalt highways and parking lots scarred landscapes, and automobile accidents became a major cause of premature death in industrial societies.

could move from London to Johannesburg or Sydney without fear of blockage or snooping by the French or the Germans.

The combination of steel, steam engines, and the telegraph brought most of the world into easy intercommunication. Even if villagers in inland Borneo and Brazil remained relatively isolated, town dwellers in the South Pacific and South America were part of a network of services, commerce, and information flows that stretched from local to national to international centers. Governments' efforts to know about the people and the lands they administered had produced a deepening technology of knowledge, which was put into place around the globe.

Transportation and Migration

Faster means of travel and knowledge of a wider world encouraged migration at unprecedented levels and speeded up daily journeys. After development of the internal combustion engine, bus services among towns soon followed in North America and Europe. The wealthy took advantage of cars for trips between home and office or for outings into the countryside. Railways permitted commuting into central cities from suburbs.

Hundreds of steamships regularly crossed the Atlantic and Pacific oceans, facilitating east-west travel. Most of the major shipping companies were British-owned in 1900. German, French, and Japanese firms also operated particular routes. The Suez Canal shortened trips to Asia, and, after 1914, the Panama Canal did the same in the Americas. Railways linked major cities in Argentina and Brazil with coastal towns in Peru, Bolivia, and Chile. In addition, several transcontinental lines joined the east and west coasts of Canada and the United States. In 1905 the trans-Siberian railway opened and was connected to railways across Europe. When Jules Verne, the French novelist, imagined a race around the world in the late nineteenth century, he calculated that it could be completed in only eighty days using railways, steamships, and elephants!

The paths around the globe provided by rail and ship lured not only the rich and the adventurous but also ordinary folk who were trying to find jobs or to avoid problems at home. In the century before the First World War, more than thirty million Europeans migrated to the United States. Russian and Polish Jews traveled west to Hamburg, Germany, then on to London and New York. French, Spanish, and Maltese settled along the North African coast in Algeria, while Portuguese, Dutch, and British moved into Angola and Cape Colony. Millions of Chinese moved into Southeast Asia via Singapore, into Peru via Macao, and into the United States and Canada, where they helped to build the transcontinental railroads. Over a million South Asians went to Africa, the Caribbean, and the Pacific islands as indentured laborers during the nineteenth and early twentieth centuries, and millions more went to Burma and Malaya to work on European-owned plantations. Some were lured by prepaid tickets and golden promises; others were coerced by kinsmen or clever recruiters. Even the very poor could migrate. Although initially much of this Asian exodus was male, single women and families soon followed. By the late nineteenth century, young women were crossing the Atlantic and Indian oceans in large numbers. Long before the era of the airplane, both free and forced migration had created multicultural communities around the world.

In its long nineteenth-century phase of expansion, the world industrial economy depended on cheap labor. If local populations were either unwilling or insufficient, employers had the financial and technological resources to bring in workers from a long distance away, and workers had multiple incentives to move on their own. Hundreds of thousands of young people moved from villages into the towns to work as factory hands, laborers, or servants. Others moved to plantations, mines, railways, and dockyards. International and national labor markets

Henry Guttmann/Hulton Archive/Getty Images

A procession of sailing- and steamships passes through the Suez Canal around 1874. The vessels are watched by crowds of Egyptians, some of whom might well have helped to dig the one-hundred-mile-long canal that linked the Mediterranean and Red seas. The canal permitted a vast expansion of world trade and eased travel between Europe and Asia.

thrived as news about areas with a high demand for labor spread to regions where there was underemployment. Letters from New York to Ireland told of high wages and low trans-Atlantic fares; recruiters' advertisements in India offered free passage to Guyana or Mauritius for those willing to harvest sugar cane or to Southeast Asia for work on rubber and tobacco plantations. Employment in many industries became international, and many people moved from jobs on one continent to jobs on another.

Migration mixed the populations and cultures of the world. By the early twentieth century, many people crossed the oceans regularly, bringing with them large amounts of cultural baggage. Consider the case of Miguel Alfredo Martinez de Hoz. Born in Argentina, he spoke Spanish, a world language that linked him to the rest of Latin America and to Spain, but his mother was English, and he spoke that language too. The manager of several railways in Argentina, he regularly imported goods from England, and he traveled to London to represent Argentina at international expositions. Martinez lived in Buenos Aires, where the major buildings copied European models and where dozens of bookstores sold newspapers and books in several European languages and in Arabic.

It was not just the Argentinian elite that had international connections. In 1901, Oreste Sola, a textile worker's son, moved from Biella, Italy, to Buenos Aires. At first he lived with his godfather and other friends, remaining for some time within an Italian emigrant community. Through letters, he and his parents exchanged news and told of upcoming visits by kin and friends. Hundreds of thousands of Europeans chose to relocate to Argentina during the early twentieth century. By 1914, 30 percent of the Argentine population was foreign-born, making that country strikingly multicultural.

In 1900, movement from country to country was relatively unrestricted. The lack of tight border controls and a system of passports meant that most people who could pay could move freely. Nevertheless, a few states differentiated foreigners from citizens and limited the entry of some groups. The United States excluded Chinese laborers and regulated all immigration after 1891 to block people that the government considered undesirable. During the First World War, several European countries required aliens who wanted admission to present passports, and they kept that system in place after the end of the war. As international tensions exploded during the 1920s and 1930s, states shut down easy avenues of global exchange. Concern for boundaries and for ownership of resources replaced the more fluid nineteenth-century arrangements.

Colonialism and the British Empire

The main vehicle for European control of world resources in 1900 was, of course, empire. At the Paris fair, pavilions paraded the variety of territories owned by the major colonial powers. Russia built a Siberian Palace. The Netherlands displayed replicas of Sumatran houses and a Javanese temple, and filled them with dancers and crafts workers imported from the Dutch Indies. The French state constructed separate halls for its many colonies— Cambodia, Cochin-China, Tonkin, Annam, the Ivory Coast, Tunisia, French Congo, Madagascar, Senegal, Dahomey, Guinea, Algeria, New Caledonia, and its islands in the Caribbean. The colonial areas of the fair, which were among the fair's most popular attractions, demonstrated the extreme dependence of much of Asia and Africa upon its European rulers. Visitors came to gawk at exotically dressed "natives" who were confined within their pavilions like animals in a zoo. In Paris, colonies existed for the entertainment and profit of their European hosts.

Two sorts of empires coexisted in 1900. The territorial empires of Russia, China, Austria-Hungary, and the Ottomans had been built over centuries by the conquest of lands and peoples surrounding a core region. In these states, hereditary monarchs ruled autocratically over their subjects, whatever those subjects' ethnicity or religion might be. By 1920 each of these empires had been dismantled by the dual impacts of war and revolution. A second type of empire had emerged during the eighteenth and nineteenth centuries as the result of European conquest of land in the Americas, Asia, and Africa. In these sea-linked empires, Western and Central European countries—Britain, France, the

Netherlands, Belgium, Germany, and Portugal—exercised political authority over territories on other continents. Political relationships within these empires had a dual character, however. Although the colonial powers had organized representative institutions at home and held elections in which a range of political parties contested policies, they denied these same freedoms to most populations overseas. At home, residents were citizens; in the colonies, they were subjects. This double standard defined colonial relations in the twentieth century. Europeans invoked differences of race, culture, and education to justify the inequalities of the colonial condition, which were designed to maintain the prestige of the controlling power. Relationships within the British Empire illustrate the strategies and impacts of colonial rule.

By the end of the nineteenth century, the tiny British Isles ruled more than one-quarter of the earth's land and one-quarter of its population, the largest empire in history. As they traveled, captains, soldiers, scientists, merchants, and missionaries had regularly claimed territories for the British Crown. This expansion, which had begun in the Americas in the early seventeenth century, reached its peak in the early twentieth century when Queen Victoria claimed rule over approximately one hundred different colonies, ranging in size from barren piles of rock—for example, some of the Falkland Islands—to the vast expanses of India. Settler colonies that had large European populations, such as Australia and Canada, had by 1900 gained substantial powers of home rule. In contrast, colonies with primarily non-European populations were not considered capable of self-government. In dependencies such as Malaya, Nigeria, and Egypt, the British used techniques of indirect rule, permitting indigenous leaders limited powers and functions. In 1900, the British Empire stretched around the globe, linking multiple peoples to the rulers in London. A look at its strategies of administration, at its imperial ties to India and Africa, and then at its informal empire in Latin America will bring the problems of colonial governance in 1900 into clearer focus.

Running the Empire

In 1897, the British Empire celebrated the sixtieth anniversary of Queen Victoria's rule. Throughout the colonies, politicians unveiled statues of the elderly queen while bands played and soldiers marched. In a display of loyalty, the colonies sent impressive delegations to London. More than fifty thousand troops in splendid uniforms paraded through London streets, led by victorious generals and dozens of princesses, rajahs, chiefs, and potentates who had cast their lot with the empire. The admiring crowds showed that empire had an enthusiastic audience in Britain.

The attitudes of Victoria's subjects outside of Britain toward her and toward British administration are much more difficult to determine. The British Empire rested on formal claims of sovereignty that were unknown to many of its subjects and opposed by others. Imperial institutions generated solidarity and mutual interests, but it is important not to overemphasize the impact that the empire had on ordinary people in the colonies. Most citizens of the empire had probably never seen a British official. Pictures of the queen in post offices and statues of her in city squares gave Victoria a symbolic presence in her colonies but did little to override cultural and linguistic differences.

The unity of the empire, such as it was, came from its rulers in London. In theory, the British Parliament made imperial policy, which was to be overseen by the secretaries of state for India and for the colonies. In practice, civil servants working within the India Office and the Colonial Office set the rules of the game, and these policies were then carried out overseas in some fashion by dozens of governors, viceroys, secretaries, and residents and their assistants. Since the central, quite conservative aims of British rule remained the same—the maintenance of British sovereignty, the strengthening of law and order, the collecting of taxes, and the securing of trade—British officialdom looked roughly the same wherever it appeared. Judges, generals, district officers, police chiefs, and customs inspectors had similar functions wherever they worked, although the specific rules and therefore the outcomes differed. Under these expatriate British, thousands of local employees worked as policemen, clerks, surveyors, soldiers, and tax collectors. The empire depended on the cooperation of those it governed for its operation. This group of men who chose to work for the British personified both the success and the failure of the empire. On one hand, they showed how the empire incorporated and trained colonial peoples. They functioned as a local elite who had bridged some of the divide between colonizer and colonized. On the other hand, the British considered indigenous peoples inferior and used the argument of racial difference to keep even the literate and wealthy at a social distance.

India, the Jewel in the Crown

If London operated as the core of the British Empire, India was its second center. Its size and wealth made Britain a major political and economic power in Asia, and its enormous population could be employed as soldiers and workers around the globe. The British were determined to maintain their Indian territories, warning away the Russians and Chinese from border areas and crushing any internal rebellions.

India was acquired in stages during the later eighteenth and early nineteenth centuries by the East India Company, a group of traders given monopoly rights by the British king. Most of India came under British government rule in 1858. There was neither a constitution nor the machinery of representative government to secure the rights of the Indian population. Then, in 1876, Parliament named Queen Victoria Empress of India. Her appointed governor, the viceroy, managed India with the help of a British-led civil service and provincial legislative councils, whose members were for the most part appointed. Effective units of Indian self-government stopped at the village level. Indirect rule was confined to the states where Indian princes retained formal power, such as Hyderabad, Kashmir, and much of Rajastan, but in those areas the British government oversaw foreign policy and also appointed resident British councilors to give advice on internal administration. Whether it was exercised directly or indirectly, British power was considerable.

The army maintained British rule in India. Thousands of young Indian men from the Punjab, Nepal, and the northwest frontier joined army regiments, where they were commanded by British officers and stationed around the country. After a major revolt by South Asian soldiers in 1857, large numbers of British troops also came to India in rotation as extra insurance of military loyalty there. By the late nineteenth century, India had a unified, apolitical, professional army paid for by Indians that was used by the British not only in colonial wars but in Europe during the world wars of the twentieth century.

Extracting taxes was the main function of British government in India. Collecting this money efficiently was a monumental job that brought the British into conflict with local practices throughout all the directly ruled areas. Claiming to have rights over all the land, the British levied heavy taxes on it, which then had to be assessed. The effort to establish private, individual ownership and tax responsibility undermined communal rights, markedly changing village societies. Even if the aims of British governance were conservative, its impact was not. Because India was an agricultural society, the attempt to itemize and tap land revenue brought civil servants into the heart of the Indian economy.

What did the British bring to India? Colonial officials saw India as a static, "oriental" society in which religion and tradition dictated behavior. This gave them multiple excuses for ignoring social problems, as well as Indian arguments for reform, on the ground that the government did not want to interfere with Indian customs. The result was the selective, limited importation of British institutions and resources. Western-style schools developed for the elite, who were taught English along with European political ideals. Lawyers produced new legal codes and administrative regulations. Christian missions operated hospitals, schools, and churches. In the larger cities, private companies provided telephones, telegraphs, and electricity, using European equipment. Parts of Calcutta had water mains connected to the houses and underground sewage disposal systems. Yet the impact of such changes in 1900 was limited. The mass of the population was illiterate in any language and too poor to use the courts. Whether Hindu or Muslim, they largely ignored the Christian missions in favor of their own temples and mosques. The new urban technologies of sanitation and communication benefited mostly Europeans and a handful of wealthy Indians.

Britain also provided investment capital. By 1900 about a tenth of British capital overseas went to India and Ceylon, most of it to provide a modern infrastructure—railways, docks, canals, and public utilities in the cities. By 1900, India had the most extensive railway network in Asia and more miles of track than either Britain or France. Improved communications, along with the imposition of free trade, integrated India into the international economy, sometimes in destructive ways. During the nineteenth century, the country shifted away from manufacturing to the production of raw materials. Cotton, tea, and jute were raised in large quantities for export. Its industrial sector, unprotected

Mary Evans Picture Library/The Image Works

A tea plantation in the hills of Bengal, India, in 1880. Female workers picked tea leaves and carried them back to sheds for sorting and curing while male European managers looked on. This scene was sketched for an illustrated London newspaper, *The Graphic*, which regularly reported on the British Empire.

by tariffs, remained small. In 1900, India was a country with limited urbanization, low per capita income and productivity, and high death and birth rates.

Africa

Europeans gradually encroached on African territories, moving inland from the coast during the nineteenth century as technological changes permitted easy entry and safe return. Adventurers claimed "discovery," arranged concessions, and eventually got government support. Politicians justified their ill-gotten gains in multiple ways: They argued that the tropics required economic development, that populations needed to be civilized and their souls saved, and that trade needed to be safeguarded against European competitors. David Livingstone, the British explorer-missionary, used the slogan "Christianity, Commerce, and Civilization" to defend his activities. In addition, widely accepted anthropological theories convinced most Europeans that they were more intelligent and moral than the peoples of Africa and Asia. Science justified their racism and legitimized European rule.

In the 1880s and 1890s a crass scramble for Africa accelerated, and quick annexation became the preferred technique of conquest. Machine guns and automatic rifles gave European troops decisive advantages in the short military campaigns and rebellions. The major European states met in Berlin in 1884 to carve up Africa into separate spheres of influence for Britain, France, Italy, and Germany. They also reaffirmed the abolition of the international slave trade, although slavery itself continued in several parts of Africa. The Congo Free State was made the private property of the Congo Company, owned by Léopold II of Belgium. Only Liberia, Ethiopia, and Libya remained independent in 1900, and Italy was to conquer Libya in 1912 and Ethiopia in 1936. The French expanded their territories in West Africa to include much of the land from Algeria south through what are now Chad, the Central African Republic, and the Republic of Congo. The British controlled most of the land from Cape Colony to Cairo in the east and south, as well as Nigeria, Gold Coast, and Sierra Leone in the west (see Map 1.2).

No matter what lines were drawn on maps or what divisions were made in European capitals, Europeans effectively administered very little of the land south of the Sahara in 1900. Although European governments worked to abolish the international slave trade, they had neither the power nor a strong inclination to abolish slavery within Africa, where slaves were used to produce commodity exports and to provide household service through the nineteenth century. Not only Africa's vast size and varied landscape, but its dozens of different political units ranging from well-organized kingdoms to stateless kinship groups made the continent difficult to conquer and impossible to occupy. How could a few thousand Europeans control the nomads of the desert, the hunting and gathering societies of the southwest, the herding societies of the east, or the thriving plantation economy of Zanzibar? The growth of international commerce in ground nuts, cocoa, ivory, and cloves brought resources to many rulers and to peasant producers. Europeans had to deal with hundreds of different languages, many subdivisions of authority, and migratory peoples whose political loyalties were fluid. African peoples, in fact, had some bargaining power in determining how they were ruled because European countries were not willing to pay for effective governance and control. Moreover, during the late nineteenth and early twentieth centuries, African populations mounted major rebellions against European rule in Egypt, the Sudan, French West Africa, German Southwest Africa, Rhodesia, and parts of South Africa. Imposition of colonial rule in Africa came late and met regular challenges.

Indirect rule through African leaders was the preferred solution to the challenges of colonial rule in most of the continent. The British used the fiction of the "protectorate" to reward collaboration and cooperation by the leaders of several African kingdoms, much of whose authority was left intact. Newly Christianized chiefs exercised power in the territory of Uganda through an advisory council. British interference was greatest in South Africa, where the discovery of gold and diamonds, combined with the temperate climate, drew thousands of settlers, and in Kenya, where European farmers took over highland areas. In

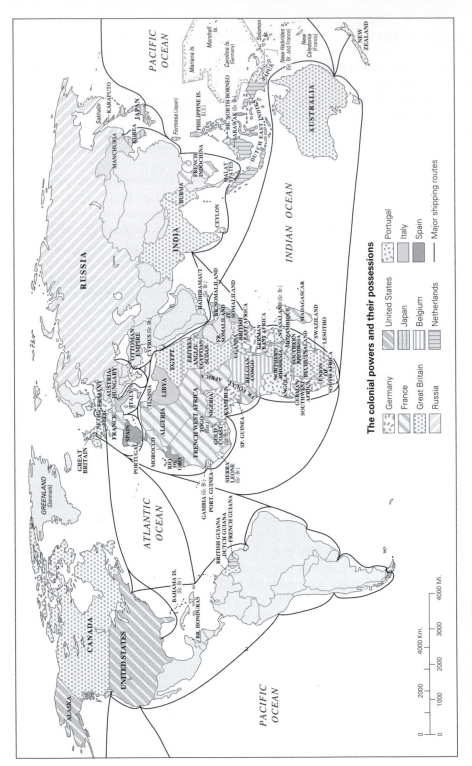

MAP 1.2 Colonial Empires in 1914.

Steamships and railways tied together the far-flung empires of Eurasia and the Americas. While the Spanish and Portuguese empires had shrunk during the nineteenth century, those of Britain, France, Germany, and Belgium had grown as a result of the division of Africa. Japan had acquired colonial territory in Korea.

The colonial powers and their possessions

- Germany
- France
- Great Britain
- Russia
- United States
- Japan
- Belgium
- Netherlands
- Portugal
- Italy
- Spain
- Major shipping routes

1900, the British government assumed political control of Nigeria, hoping to strike it rich through investment and trade. Colonial officials gave local rulers in its northern regions a virtually free hand, discouraged Christian missionaries from interfering with the predominately Muslim population, and restrained the building of Western-style schools. Even in the more closely controlled southern part of the country, there was only one resident British political officer for every seventy thousand people as late as 1925. Under these conditions, much of the pre-colonial African social and political order survived intact.

The position of African political leaders and the survival of African control over land varied dramatically from colony to colony, however. The situation in several states of southern Africa offers a contrast to the situation in Nigeria. Cecil Rhodes, who rose to political power in Cape Colony on the basis of money earned from local diamond and gold mines, used his British South Africa Company to fight the Shona and Ndebele people in the area, taking their land in the process. The result was the creation in 1895 of Rhodesia, named in his honor, which was administered by British officials. Historians consider the states of the Cape region to be "settlement colonies" because of their large British and migrant Dutch, or Boer, populations. Nevertheless, the coastal towns, where Arab traders, Muslims from Southeast Asia, Indians, and former slaves lived, were culturally diverse. The British and Boer rulers coped with this ethnic diversity by insisting on racial privilege and moving toward rigid segregation of town populations. In 1902, the Cape Native Reserve Location Act marked out areas within Cape Town and Port Elizabeth as locations for African residence; the governments of Natal and Transvaal soon made similar provisions. Zulus, Xhosa, and other local peoples were legally excluded from migrating within the cities.

In 1900, the British defeated the Boers in a struggle to consolidate British control over South Africa, but they soon turned political control over to their former enemies, ignoring the issue of African political and social rights. After the Union of South Africa was formed from several Boer and British-run states in the area, not only Africans but Asians and people of mixed race were prohibited from serving in Parliament, and their limited rights to vote were gradually eliminated.

Conquest by the British set in motion two major processes that ultimately transformed African societies. First, Europeans and their animals brought in epidemic diseases, and the new colonial patterns of residence and migration permitted the diseases to spread. Rinderpest devastated African herds. Smallpox epidemics killed thousands of people. Mistaken disease-control policies allowed sleeping sickness to ravage parts of Uganda and to become endemic in eastern regions. African populations declined substantially in size from the time of conquest until the mid-1920s. Although European death rates were also high, greater access to quinine, vaccinations, and safe drinking water gave Europeans more protection against infectious diseases.

Demographic devastation was accompanied by ideological revolution. Dismissing the religion, education, and science of the sub-Saharan peoples as primitive, the colonialists brought in substitutes and in the process slowly undermined the civilizations of tropical Africa. Encouraged by European governments, mission

Christianity mounted large, successful campaigns of conversion in the later nineteenth century. Doctors introduced Western medicine and theories of disease. Mission schools brought literacy into formerly oral cultures, turning their pupils into an educated elite. The cultural break with the past, which came during the early twentieth century, was extreme.

What did the British bring to Africa? Arbitrarily grouping together collections of hostile neighbors and separate ethnic groups, administrators slowly imposed the machinery of a modern secular state and a capitalist economy. In the early twentieth century, colonies acquired civil services, police forces, armies, and Western-style judicial systems. English-language primary and secondary school systems were built, and modern hospitals and methods of disease control were introduced. As export crops were cultivated for sale in Europe, an infrastructure of banks, roads, railways, harbors, and telegraph lines grew in the largest towns to encourage economic development. The impact of French colonial rule was similar. The Suez Canal, built by a French engineer with Egyptian labor during the 1860s before being bought by the British government, served as the main passage from Europe to India and East Asia, linking northern Africa even more tightly into global networks of commerce and travel.

Informal Empire and Challenges to Colonial Rule

The export of capital and culture gave the British power far beyond the borders of their formal possessions. Some scholars use the term *informal empire* to identify countries such as Argentina that were not legally or politically controlled by another state but were heavily influenced by that state. Certainly, power comes in multiple forms and can be exercised in ways other than by political dominion. British bankers helped to shape financial policies in Latin America; British merchants and trade decisions changed East Asian economies. Informal empire was less a matter of direct government intervention than of negotiation between two unequal parties. Because of its navy, its capital investments, and its industrialized economy, Britain was the only superpower in the world from 1812 to the late nineteenth century, when Germany and the United States became economically and militarily competitive. When the British government spoke, other countries listened, even if they did not obey.

European countries dominated the international system of the later nineteenth century. Europe was the core of a world in which the Americas, Africa, and Asia then counted as the periphery. Nevertheless, certain places on that periphery exercised a great deal of independence. During the nineteenth century, the United States progressed from being a weak former colony to being a potential superpower and rival, staking out the Americas as its first sphere of influence. By the early twentieth century, the British Parliament and the Colonial Office had conceded political liberty with few strings attached to both Canada and Australia, and the same route was followed with New Zealand and the Union of South Africa. None of these so-called areas of white settlement hesitated to challenge British policies when they felt that their self-interest was at stake. Virtually all of Latin America was politically sovereign and acted accordingly. As Japan industrialized, its economic, military, and political challenges to Europeans mounted. Moreover, even within the European empires, the methods of indirect rule and the limited resources of governments necessarily left much initiative in the hands of local elites and distant populations. European domination did not mean tight European control.

Educational institutions also spread the skills and types of knowledge that were needed to challenge colonial rulers. In Egypt, European-style technical schools, which began in the early nineteenth century, had produced several hundred graduates by 1900, most of whom worked as engineers. A handful of Africans managed to get technical training in Senegal and Sierra Leone before 1900. A more impressive effort took place in India, where several engineering colleges were founded during the nineteenth century, alongside many arts faculties. Raffles College in Singapore and scholarships to Cambridge permitted small numbers of Singaporeans to train in the professions. By the early twentieth century, European universities had opened their doors to a few children of the imperial elites. As a result, Western knowledge was exported from the European center to the periphery, where it passed into the minds and hands of people who adapted it for their own purposes.

By 1900, some educated Indians, Chinese, Indonesians, and Egyptians were demanding greater privileges for themselves and more power within the colonial structures. Through the press and through political institutions and organizations, local elites asked for more rights. For them, globalization brought widened contacts and awareness of other challengers of imperial authority. The new technologies of communication and of transport allowed these local elites to travel to London, Paris, or Berlin. As they learned more about their colonial rulers, they also learned about nationalism and representative government. Moreover, local populations sometimes rebelled or refused to pay their taxes, forcing colonial authorities to reexamine the terms on which colonial rule took place. By 1900, imperial rulers in Asia and North Africa had to contend with an articulate opposition to colonial regimes.

Struggles for Recognition

The Paris fair not only provided a setting for national governments to display their achievements, it also provided a forum for those with different political and social visions to meet and make their case before an international audience. During the six months of the fair, more than 130 groups came to Paris to discuss economic and political topics, as well as technological or practical ones. Socialists, feminists, and opponents of slavery used their right to free speech to rally support for their points of view.

Socialists

In September 1900, more than a thousand delegates from twenty countries came to the Socialist Congress, where they hotly debated questions of social policy and political tactics. In general, they advocated collective or governmental control of the means of production of goods, and they called for economic cooperation instead of the competition of capitalism. Angered by the poverty that they saw around them, socialists argued that income had to be redistributed and social privileges ended. The question of whether violence should be used to capture control of nation-states divided socialists deeply. Many were inspired by the writings of the German socialist and theoretician Karl Marx, who called for the workers of the world to unite and to overthrow rule by aristocrats and the bourgeoisie, or middle classes.

By 1900, socialists had established large, active political parties in Germany, France, and Belgium; smaller parties existed in Britain, Italy, and several other European countries. But the audience for socialism had already spread to Russia, South Africa, and Australia. Fledgling socialist groups from North and South America sent delegates to the fair. The first Japanese socialist, although unable to afford the trip to Paris, sent a letter of support to the Congress's organizers.

Resolutions passed at the Paris meetings revealed socialists' concerns. Some focused on practical reforms to improve workers' lives: minimum wages and maximum labor hours, better housing and education. Other groups insisted on the need for radical measures—general strikes by all workers, for example—to encourage social revolution. In Russia, militants retained their commitment to Marxist doctrine and to the use of violence to overthrow governments. The Congress put most of its energy into debating future political strategies. Should socialists cooperate with nonsocialist parties and serve in governments with them? Most thought not, but by 1900 a growing number of socialists had rejected revolution in favor of reform and democracy, as it became clear that capitalism was neither collapsing nor impoverishing the mass of the population.

Women

Women's political activities operated through different channels from men's political activities because so few countries permitted females to vote or to serve in elected offices. At the turn of the century, only New Zealand and several states in Australia and the western United States had established female suffrage. In Europe, the issue of votes for women divided females and frightened conservative males. Many argued that women's proper public roles were maternal and did not require direct participation in electoral politics. When the International Council of Women (ICW), launched by U.S. suffrage activists in 1888, spread to European countries, it declined to take a position on women's voting rights to avoid alienating its members. Instead, in its early years, the ICW concentrated on the issues of peace and the legal rights of married women. Although it claimed to include "representatives of all churches, and all sections, races, and parties," ICW members were generally elite, white, Christian women who were relatively conservative in their politics. Led by a Scottish aristocrat, Ishbel Hamilton-Gordon, Lady Aberdeen, the ICW used international meetings to lobby for peace and to dramatize the broad appeal of social issues such as child welfare and opposition to prostitution. Women organized to defend maternal obligations could get a hearing for their claims as long as their practical politics were nonthreatening.

At the same time, many politically active women believed that the lack of equal political rights for women had to be combated directly. Feminist socialists, such as the Polish political organizer Rosa Luxemburg and the Russian Alexandra Kollontai, argued for universal suffrage. The strongest defenders of women's equality founded the Socialist Women's International in 1907, and worked through it to publicize women's contributions to the political struggles of the period.

The fair's Palace of Women dramatized some of the contradictions of late-nineteenth-century attitudes toward the place of women in society. The first floor housed a library of works by women on women's issues and a lecture hall for their meetings, while the basement held an exhibit showing a typical day for a Parisian woman—riding in the park, visiting, dressing for dinner, and an evening party. When the images of women in the colonial pavilions were added to the mix, the range of definitions of the female widened much further. In the Dahomey exhibit, women could be seen grinding grain and producing food. In the Japanese pavilion, they appeared as hostesses in kimonos. The fair made it clear that there was no single international condition of "the female," despite the efforts of feminists to proclaim international sisterhood. In 1900, well-educated North American and European women dominated women's political organizations, and they brought with them a particular set of class interests and political concerns that fit people like themselves.

The interests of uneducated rural women had as yet few supporters. In most of the world, men maintained patriarchal control over their wives and daughters, with women's dependence being sanctioned by religion, custom, and law. In much of Africa, Asia, and the Middle East, parents married off their daughters as teenagers, sometimes to much older men who already had other wives or concubines. Daughters were valued less than sons and were less likely to be educated. Cultural practices such as foot binding in China and genital cutting or clitoridectomy in Africa accentuated female inferiority by limiting women's mobility and sexual pleasure. Even in Europe and North America, where in the nineteenth century changes in the laws had given women legal rights over their children and their own property, most women remained within domestic settings and had only limited education. Nevertheless, age brought respect and dependents to control. Mothers directed their daughters and daughters-in-law. Within the household, women's multiple functions as producers of goods and reproducers of labor could give them leverage and resources to command. Where women raised food and animals, they could market any surpluses, earning money for themselves and their families. The problems of rural households and villages bore little resemblance to the concerns advanced by feminists at the Paris fair.

Pan-Africanists and the Opposition to Colonialism

The support for colonialism at the Paris fair marginalized but did not silence opposing points of view. In the sociology hall, W. E. B. Dubois, the African American social scientist and crusader for racial justice, had organized part of the "American Negro Exhibit," which focused on material from African American schools in the American South. Dubois compiled an impressive array of books, patents, models, and photographs documenting the achievements of educated African Americans and their institutions, thus challenging the prevailing racist assumptions about Africans' abilities.

After winning a gold medal for his work, Dubois traveled to London to attend the first Pan-African Congress for people of African descent and discuss the "present condition and outlook of the darker races of mankind." The ending of slavery in Brazil in 1888 completed the emancipation of slaves in the Americas, continuing a process begun by the British for the West Indies in 1833. An assessment of the status of African migrant populations and their descendants was long overdue.

Delegates and speakers at the Pan-African Congress held in London during the summer of 1900. Representatives came from four African countries, the West Indies, Canada, the United States, and Britain. Bishop Turner of the African Methodist Episcopal Church, U.S.A., chaired the meeting, which brought together middle-class men and women of different races and religions.

Henry Sylvester Williams, a lawyer from Trinidad who had been trained in Canada and was practicing in London, had developed the idea of Pan-Africanism in 1899. His own global wanderings had convinced him of the need for African unity and for solidarity among migrant Africans. The London meeting brought together more than thirty professionals of African ancestry, who were joined by antislavery advocates, Quakers, and other supporters to exchange ideas about the future of Africa and its peoples.

Although the meeting did not openly challenge colonial rule, Williams's assertion of a Pan-African identity that would override the claims of empire and ethnicity was a revolutionary idea. In his later writings, Dubois used the idea of Pan-Africanism to support his calls for justice for "the black world" and an end to colonial rule both in Africa and in the Caribbean. By 1903, when Dubois published *The Souls of Black Folk,* he pointed to the creative equality of white and black populations to argue for racial justice and political freedom for African peoples. "The problem of the Twentieth Century is the problem of the color-line,"[4] Dubois proclaimed. Even if an immediate end to colonial rule seemed far distant in 1900, some of the people who would become its active opponents had already moved into the public eye.

CONCLUSION

In his opening speech at the Paris World's Fair, the French minister of commerce stressed the unity of humankind: "All, sons of different races, citizens of diverse nationalities, belong to the same family." Alexander Millerand stressed fraternity, the brotherhood of all peoples. But what did fraternity mean in the context of 1900? Missing from his analysis were the other great principles of the French republic, liberty and equality, each of which was denied by the basic premises of empires. The spirit of the French revolution had bypassed the Paris exhibition. Nevertheless, visitors to the fair had challenged then dominant notions of class, gender, and race. Although their attacks were muted, they had made strong cases for social change.

The fair displayed a world that was profoundly divided between industrialized nation-states and their colonies. The relative power of each could be seen in the size and scope of the exhibits. When the organizers of the fair discussed the future, they could not even imagine a world in which colonized peoples would win their independence. In their predictions of the future, the United States and Japan loomed as rivals, but not Australia, Canada, China, South Africa, Brazil, or Korea.

The fair gave its visitors a false sense of security and global harmony. At the fair, the peoples of the world seemed easy to understand and to appreciate. Their wants seemed limited to consumer goods. Moreover, the fair's image of progress ignored the destructive potential of many technologies. Within recent European

---

[4]W. E. B. Dubois, *The Souls of Black Folk* (New York: W. W. Norton & Co., 1999), p. 5.

memory, conflicts had been confined to colonies, where the imbalance of weaponry generally guaranteed European victory. Visitors to the fair saw the benefits of relatively free trade, open migration, and international peace. These conditions were soon to disappear.

For Further Reading

Samuel L. Baily and Franco Ramella, eds., *One Family, Two Worlds: An Italian Family's Correspondence across the Atlantic, 1901–1922* (New Brunswick, N.J.: Rutgers University Press, 1988). Letters recount how members of one family migrated to Argentina and how they constructed a life there.

C. A. Bayly, *The Birth of the Modern World, 1780–1914* (Oxford: Blackwell Publishing, Ltd., 2004). A thematic discussion of the changes in states, societies, and cultures under the pressure of globalization.

Jared Diamond, *Guns, Germs, and Steel* (New York: W. W. Norton, 1997). An original interpretation, grounded in biology and geography, of why parts of the world developed differently.

Bill Freund, *The Making of Contemporary Africa*, Second Edition (London: MacMillan Press, 1998). A discussion of African society in the twentieth century.

Daniel Headrick, *The Tentacles of Progress: Technology Transfer in the Age of Imperialism, 1850–1940* (New York: Oxford University Press, 1988). A discussion of how empires developed and underdeveloped their colonies as they built railways, telegraphs, schools, and botanic gardens.

Peter Marshall, *The Cambridge Illustrated History of the British Empire* (New York: Cambridge University Press, 1996). A topically organized, beautifully illustrated analysis of the British Empire.

Thomas R. Metcalf, *Imperial Connections: India in the Indian Ocean Arena, 1860–1920* (Berkeley: University of California Press, 2007). The British Empire from the vantage point of a colony that expanded.

Joel Mokyr, *The Lever of Riches: Technological Creativity and Economic Progress* (New York: Oxford University Press, 1990). Analysis of the impact of inventions on social and economic change.

Jonathan Schneer, *London 1900: The Imperial Metropolis* (New Haven, Conn., and London: Yale University Press, 1999). A portrait of a multicultural city's links to the British Empire.

Related Websites

The British Empire
http://www.victorianweb.org/history/empire/index.html
Industrialization in Britain
http://www.victorianweb.org/technology/index.html
Thomas Edison and the Electrical Industry
http://americanhistory.si.edu/lighting/19thcent/prec19.htm
World Expositions: Paris, 1900
http://www.expo2000.de/expo2000/geschichte/detail.php?wa_id=8&lang=1&s_typ=13

CHAPTER 2

Imperialism Encompasses the Pacific, 1900–1914

I n the summer of 1905, representatives of Tsar Nicholas II of Russia and the Meiji Emperor of Japan spent a month in Portsmouth, New Hampshire, negotiating the terms on which their recent war would end. The Russian delegation was led by Count Sergei Yulyanovich Witte. At nearly seven feet in height, Count Witte was a man of extraordinary personal authority, and his entourage was given the primary place in all ceremonial processions in Portsmouth. His adversary in the negotiations was Baron Jitaro Kimura, barely five feet tall, whose entourage followed politely in Witte's wake, accepted more modest hotel accommodations and was more restrained in demanding privileges and attention from the local hosts. But Kimura was a determined advocate for Japan, and he had an advantage that the prestige of imperial Russia and the imposing presence of Count Witte could not erase: Japan had won the war.

The Russo-Japanese War of 1905 was the first modern conflict in which an Asian power had defeated a European one, and the world's governments and media had some difficulty adjusting to the news. Japan's victory had depended in part the country's rapid centralization and industrialization in the late nineteenth century, producing the startling development and deployment of imperial Japan's modern navy. President Theodore Roosevelt, who hosted the peace conference, hoped to restrain the demands of victorious Japan and to soften the blow to Russia's pride. He succeeded in both. But Russia's loss of the war, and subsequently of the treaty negotiations, discredited the tsarist government at home. Witte's personal loss of prestige also dampened enthusiasm for the modernization programs he had sponsored in industry and the military.

La battaglia navale del 27 maggio nello stretto di Corea terminata con la sconfitta della flotta russa.

Courtesy of MIKASA Preservation Society

The great Japanese admiral Togo Heihachiro and his flagship *Mikasa* were celebrated in this contemporary magazine illustration. In the Battle of Tsushima Bay, the Japanese fleet sank or disabled twenty-eight of thirty-eight Russian ships while losing only three torpedo boats of their own. The *Mikasa* was built in Great Britain by Vickers but carried the much stronger Krupp armor that would later be used by the dreadnoughts (see Chapter 3). At various times the ship's destruction was demanded by Britain, the United States, and the Soviet Union. It was instead preserved and restored through international cooperation and is today a museum ship in Yokosuka, Japan.

This was the second time Japan had defeated a land-based empire that had expended enormous resources on naval development. The first victory, in 1895–1896, had ended the hopes of the Qing Empire, based in China, of building a modern navy. European and American journalists and statesmen derided the Japanese victory over the Qing Empire as an easy defeat of a weak and incompetent regime, but they could not dismiss the Russian defeat so easily. In defeating Russia on land and sea, Japan challenged the assumptions of the time concerning the inferiority of nonwhite peoples and their inability to industrialize, lead successful nationalist movements, or to become international leaders.

The Russo-Japanese War of 1904–1905 also marked the emergence of the Pacific Ocean as a new arena of imperial competition. Despite the tensions between the new empires of Japan and the United States for domination of the Pacific, there were great parallels in their emergence as sea powers. Both were impatient with the old practices of Britain and France, which emphasized colonization of the land and diplomatic control of the economies of Asia. They also brought with them vigorous new ideologies of empire, claiming to bring prosperity and advancement to the peoples they dominated. Together, they ended both the long age of the land-based empires and the century of British hegemony on the sea.

Twilight of the Land-Based Empires

Although many historians cite the British Empire as the model for understanding how imperialism worked in the nineteenth century, it is important to remember that the British Empire was only one kind of imperial system. In 1900, much of the world— indeed, its most populous parts—was still controlled by empires such as Russia, the Qing Empire based in China, and the Ottoman Empire based in Anatolia, that had existed for centuries and functioned differently from the British Empire. The greatest similarity among these older empires was that they were built on overland expansion. They had expanded in previous centuries by gaining control of strategically important territories that touched their borders. In many cases these territories—such as the steppes of Central Asia, the deserts of the Middle East and North Africa, the inhospitable tundra of northern Asia, and the profitless jungles of southern China and Southeast Asia—demanded higher expenditures for conquest and defense than could be recouped from their development. These empires neither expanded overseas nor created sufficient naval power to defend themselves successfully from foreign assault.

They depended primarily on agriculture for their wealth, but over the centuries the traditional elites had concentrated their riches in the cities. Since the eighteenth century, these empires also supplied Europe with profitable raw and finished goods, bringing the proceeds home and further stimulating their well-established market cities such as Beijing, Guangzhou, Istanbul, and Cairo, which in the nineteenth century continued to generate wealth through their integration with new overseas trade enterprises. Long after the military might of the land-based empires had waned, they remained critical actors in the world economy because their capitals were often great pools of wealth that attracted the newer empires of Europe and the rising commercial interests of the United States of America.

In 1900 the Ottoman, Russian, and Qing empires were in varying degrees of decline. In the mid nineteenth century, the leaders of these empires realized the importance of naval power. But a lack of capital for investment and a lack of native expertise kept their naval development programs from succeeding. The Ottomans in the nineteenth century had made some progress with naval deployment, but they were dependent on Europe to build modern ships for them. Russia still had not made itself a naval power even in the Black Sea. The Qing did not have a navy or any plans for one before the 1870s, and in 1895, when they were easily defeated by Japan, they had to face the fact that their attempts to build a modern navy had been a disaster.

The Ottoman Empire

The oldest of these land-based empires was the Ottoman Empire, ruled by Muslims of Turkic descent, whose capital was at Istanbul (in earlier centuries this had been Constantinople, capital of the Byzantine Empire). The Ottoman Empire had wrested control of Anatolia from the moribund Byzantine Empire and competed with Russia and Hungary for control of Eastern Europe. By the 1700s, the Ottomans were also governing Greece, the Middle East, and much of North Africa. Tensions with the Austro-Hungarian Empire and with Russia were constant. France and Britain were sometimes allies of the Ottomans and sometimes their enemies. But in the middle of the nineteenth century, Britain and France backed the Ottomans against Russia in the Crimean War (1854–1856), which resulted in the halt of Russian expansion into Ottoman lands.

In the later nineteenth century, European culture had a strong impact on the great Ottoman cities. French and German languages were used in the new schools and universities, and for medical, technical, and scientific studies. Newspapers in French kept the Ottoman urban elites informed of current events and international affairs, and many Turks traveled to Europe for education or entertainment. The latest European political ideas reached the Ottoman cities very rapidly. European military reforms in organization and weaponry were introduced into the Ottoman armies in the early 1800s, and European nationalism, constitutionalism, and civil rights were well known in the Ottoman Empire by the 1860s.

These foreign ideas had supporters in the Ottoman Empire, but they also had many opponents. Rebellions by the traditional Ottoman soldiers often brought extreme and widespread violence to the Balkans and frequently to Istanbul itself. Muslim religious leaders were outspoken in condemning the liberalizing influence of European political thought. Nevertheless, by fits and starts, the Ottoman government underwent a very dramatic transformation during the 1800s. By the end of the century, two important ideas had become accepted by a significant number of political leaders in Istanbul: that the Ottoman government should continue to move toward a liberal constitutional monarchy of the British and German kind, and that within the Ottoman Empire there existed a coherent nation of Turkey that had a future of its own, independent of that of the empire. The "Young Turk" party of students, bureaucrats, soldiers, and merchants assumed that in the future the Turkish-speaking portion of the Ottoman Empire would live under its own laws and values, but the areas of the empire that were predominantly inhabited by Europeans or Arabs would have to determine their own fates.

Some of those fates were already easy to guess before 1900. In the Balkans, Serbia and Montenegro had been recognized as independent at the Congress of Vienna of 1878, although they had no way of defending or governing themselves. Russia had become a military protector of both and was expected to absorb or colonize them. Bulgaria had been granted home rule but was also without a government or an army. Bosnia and Herzegovina were coming under the economic and military thrall of the Austro-Hungarian Empire. Syria, Lebanon, Palestine, and Jordan were all known to be coveted by both Britain and France. Though

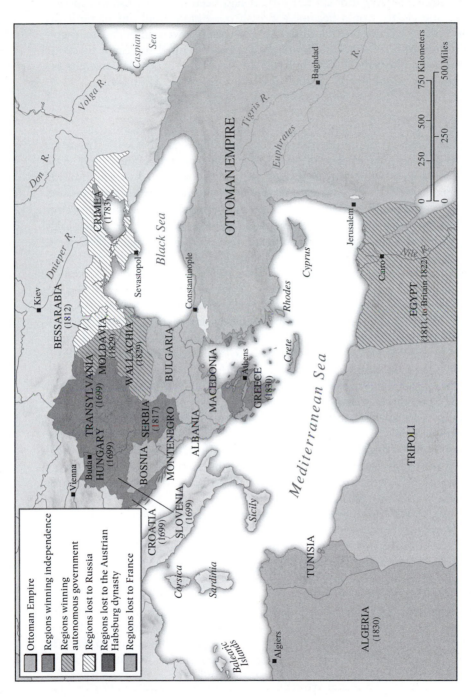

MAP 2.1   Ottoman Territorial Losses, 1699–1912.

The tensions between Russia and the Ottomans contributed to the erosion of Ottoman control over Egypt and the eastern Balkans, and independence for Greece and Serbia. Russia and Austria-Hungary expanded at Ottoman expense. Algeria was lost to France.

Legend (map key):
- Ottoman Empire
- Regions winning independence
- Regions winning autonomous government
- Regions lost to Russia
- Regions lost to the Austrian Habsburg dynasty
- Regions lost to France

Map labels:
Caspian Sea, Volga R., Don R., Dnieper R., CRIMEA (1783), Black Sea, BESSARABIA (1812), Kiev, Sevastopol, Constantinople, OTTOMAN EMPIRE, Tigris R., Euphrates R., Baghdad, Jerusalem, Cyprus, Rhodes, Crete, Cairo, Nile R., EGYPT (1811, to Britain 1822), MOLDAVIA (1829), WALLACHIA (1829), TRANSYLVANIA (1699), BULGARIA, MACEDONIA, SERBIA (1817), BOSNIA, MONTENEGRO, ALBANIA, GREECE (1830), Athens, HUNGARY (1699), Buda, Vienna, CROATIA (1699), SLOVENIA (1699), Sicily, Corsica, Sardinia, Balearic Islands, Mediterranean Sea, TUNISIA, TRIPOLI, ALGERIA (1830), Algiers

Scale: 0 250 500 750 Kilometers; 0 250 500 Miles

Egypt was nominally an Ottoman territory, it had been under British occupation since 1882 and clearly would become a British possession in all but name if the Ottoman Empire collapsed. And while the European powers intended to dominate many territories of the old empire, local peoples hoped to regain or create independence for themselves. The tensions among rising nationalist movements created long-term instability in the Balkans and parts of the Middle East.

The Russian Empire

The story of Russia in the nineteenth century had many parallels with that of its old enemy, the Ottoman Empire. Russia had begun to examine and adopt some European ideas well before the 1800s. As in the case of the Ottoman Empire, many in Russia—including aristocrats, landowners, and religious leaders—resisted these proposals. Reformers in Russia did not have the gradual success that reformers in the Ottoman Empire enjoyed. Instead, they were forced to use increasingly extreme methods. Terrorism, particularly the use of nitroglycerin explosives in public places, was practiced by anti-government forces by the end of the 1800s. As the twentieth century opened, the Russian political landscape was marked by sharp divisions among the loyalist elites of the aristocracy, the bureaucracy, and the church on the one hand, and their radical opponents among students, middle-ranking military officers, and advocates for rural advancement on the other.

Despite its unstable internal political situation, Russia was feared by the European powers for its expansionist successes. Russian rule had been extended through Siberia to the northern Pacific coast, the Aleutian Islands, and eventually Alaska (which was declared a Russian colony in 1800 and sold to the United States in 1867), despite steady resistance from the Qing Empire based in China. During the nineteenth century, Britain and France had worked together to limit Russian influence in Central Europe, the Balkans, and the Caucasus. By the late 1800s, as the Qing Empire weakened, the focus of Russian expansion returned to Manchuria and the northern Pacific coast. Manchuria could potentially supply the Russian Empire with coal and iron to fuel its new industries and shipyards in the new city of Vladivostok.

In the late 1800s, the international standing of Russia was ambiguous. In the British view, kindly Russian monarchs had learned that the people were not ready for liberal institutions, and that reforms only embolden anarchistic agitators. The old ways would be best for them, so long as Russia did not return to its expansionist enthusiasms of the early 1800s. The American opinion of Russia was very different. A telegraph cable was laid across Siberia by American engineers and laborers, enabling the United States to have more rapid communication with the Middle East and Europe. Siberians—residents of Russian descent who had been exiled to Siberia for political or petty crimes and had been put to work in the mines, forests, and fisheries—had begun a movement for independence. Many were prolific writers and quickly gained some influence among the American travelers. The frontier experience, the wish to free themselves from an old-fashioned monarchy, and the independence and entrepreneurialism of the Siberians found immediate sympathy among Americans. Alexis de Tocqueville had written decades before that Russia and the United States were destined to dominate the world, and now Americans saw the point of his observation.

The Qing Empire

The deepening tensions between Russia and Japan in Manchuria were in many ways a result of the weakening of the Qing Empire. In name, the Qing Empire owned Manchuria, but it was too weak to defend it. This excited the ambitions of both Russia and Japan. Like the Ottoman Empire and Russia, in the 1800s the Qing Empire had experienced a rift between those who argued for reforms inspired by European models and those who struggled forcefully to maintain the traditional system. But the experience of the Qing Empire was different from that of the Ottomans and the Russians.

First, although China had been in continuous contact with Europe for centuries, it did not experience the volume of contacts or the rapidity of exchange that came from being nearer Europe. For instance, Qing leaders had inadequate information regarding Britain's commercial goals or its military abilities. The result was a disastrous Qing defeat by Britain in the first Opium War (1839–1842). This was followed by a series of treaties that, by 1900, allowed virtually all European nations and the United States, Russia, and Japan to import their products to China with little or no tariff, to have their nationals live in China under their own laws, to travel and promote Christianity without interference from Chinese officials, and to station their own military forces in China.

The presence of privileged, aggressive foreigners within Qing boundaries contributed to both the outbreak and the suppression of the Taiping Rebellion (1853–1864). This devastating civil war was the greatest armed conflict before the twentieth century. It cost more than thirty million lives, threatened to topple the Qing government, and left the empire economically as well as politically dysfunctional. Britain and France joined the Qing side in defeating the Taiping rebels, after which the Europeans proceeded to assume critical influence over the empire's management. China as a whole was never colonized, but portions of China were dominated by European powers, and the island of Hong Kong was given to Britain permanently.

In the late nineteenth century, Qing leaders and their foreign advisers cooperated in an attempt to equip China to resist military and naval challenges from Russia and Japan. A navy was regarded as essential, but that would require new mining ventures, new industrial complexes, and the creation of universities to educate chemists and engineers. The test of these programs came in war against France in 1884, and against Japan in 1894–95. Both wars were debacles for the Qing, and they demonstrated that no amount of military industrialization could compensate for a lack of preparation on the part of Qing military officers and engineers or for the corruption of Qing officials.

Between 1864 and 1900, Europeans and Americans arrived in China in increasing numbers. Chinese bureaucrats, journalists, and teachers hoped to learn foreign

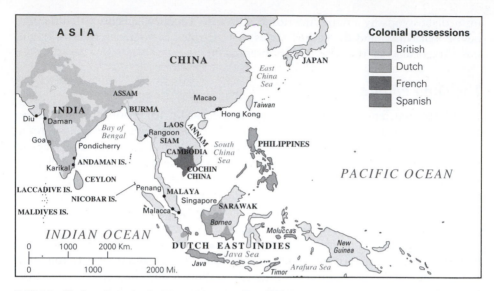

MAP 2.2   Western Expansion in Asia and Australasia to 1900.
The year 1900 marked almost 300 years of European expansion into Eastern Eurasia. Before the Sino-Japanese War of 1894–5, all imperialists had agreed that in continental China there would be no establishment of colonies. Instead, the powers recognized mutual zones of interest. The Treaty of Shimonoseki, which resolved the Sino-Japanese War of 1894–5, challenged this consensus and opened the way to international competition for more direct land and industrial rights in China.

methods. Many younger, educated Chinese came to the conclusion that the Qing Empire itself was China's greatest problem. Nationalism, much of it inspired by European and secondarily by Japanese ideas, led many to wish to foment revolution. Others felt that the Europeans and Americans, with their weapons, their economic ambitions, and their tendency to spread Christianity wherever they went were more dangerous enemies than the Qing Empire. These sentiments helped to incite the Boxer Uprising of 1900, in which contingents of martial arts enthusiasts banded together with spontaneous mobs to attack foreigners in the Qing capital, Beijing, and surrounding areas. An alliance of eight nations, including Japan, Russia, and the United States, sent troops to Beijing to protect their citizens and to put the rebellion down. When the dust settled in 1901, the foreign allies were in temporary control of Beijing.

Traditional Wealth and Modern Trade

In view of the weakness of the Ottoman and Qing empires by the late 1800s, one might ask how these large, unindustrialized, militarily weak empires managed to survive into the twentieth century. Their old mutual rival, Russia, did not have the power to annihilate them, but Britain and France together could have made a serious attempt to end either empire and seize its territories. However, these old land-based empires should be considered in the overall context of the global economy. Naval might and industrialization were important pillars of power and influence in 1900, but the ability to provide markets was also critical.

The land-based empires all drew most of their wealth from agriculture. They had experienced their greatest expansion in the 1700s, both in terms of the absolute increase in the amount of land they controlled and in terms of improvements in agricultural techniques that made the land more productive. The empires were large enough and encompassed a great enough variety of agricultural zones that they could achieve a high degree of specialization while retaining self-sufficiency. For instance, Ottoman and Qing farmers could devote their lands to highly profitable crops such as cotton, knowing they could turn their crops into cash in a nearby market and buy food and supplies for themselves. Wealth circulated easily within these empires, and they were not forced to seek external markets or external goods for survival. In the nineteenth-century, economic and social reformers acknowledged that agriculture continued to be of primary importance, and tended to protect the traditional patterns of landowning and social power that had produced their great wealth in the early modern period.

Early Trade Imbalances Between Europe and the Land-based Empires

The land-based empires magnified their wealth in the 1700s and early 1800s by selling products in Europe. Russian suppliers to the fur and timber markets made great profits. China's exports of tea to Europe created a huge trade deficit for Britain in the late 1700s and stimulated secondary exports of porcelain, silk, and lacquer-ware. Cotton, hemp, and coffee from the Ottoman territories also found markets in Europe, alerting Europeans to the fact that the Ottoman cities were reservoirs of profits from both internal and external commerce.

The market systems developed in these land-based empires must also be seen in relation to the empires' population structures. The Ottoman Empire, for instance, had a total population of about twenty million people in 1900. But the Ottoman territories were very far-flung, and the imperial system concentrated trade at Istanbul, Cairo, Beirut, and other large cities, bringing together goods and consumers from a territory stretching from Belgrade to Baghdad. Colonization of Ottoman territory by European powers would have detached the colonized region from the centralized and valuable trading system in which it was embedded. Control of the terms of trade at Istanbul through treaty provisions imposed by European imperialists—under threat of invasion—was a far simpler undertaking.

In the case of China, the arguments against colonization were even stronger. The Qing Empire's population in 1900 was about four hundred million—a quarter of the entire population of the earth and twenty times as large as the Ottoman population. Qing trade networks brought together goods and consumers from Siberia to Southeast Asia, and from Central Asia to the borders of Korea. Again, control of the terms of trade at the great ports of Canton (Guangzhou) and

Shanghai was more effective than detaching and colonizing large segments of Qing territory. The European practice, in the middle and late nineteenth century, of imposing predatory treaties upon these empires by using the threat of invasion or bombardment from the sea was called *gunboat diplomacy*, and in many cases it was more advantageous to European imperialists than the colonization of foreign lands would have been.

Imperialism and Market Exploitation

Prior to 1800, Europe produced very little that would bring it profits from the great wealth pools of the Middle East and Asia. Imperialism, however, played its role in reorganizing the global economy in such a way that the flow of wealth could be redirected. Britain used its treaty power to force the Qing Empire to abandon the laws forbidding the import of opium and to radically cut import fees on all British goods. Thereafter, Britain supplied opium to geometrically increasing numbers of Chinese, and it reaped high profits from this trade through the middle of the nineteenth century, after which Chinese opium growers and distributed enjoyed the greater profits. There were, however, more sophisticated ways of tapping the wealth of the land-based empires. Military reform and industrialization in the Ottoman and Qing empires (as in Russia) meant new sales for European manufacturers specializing in everything from gigantic shipbuilding tools to tiny sewing needles. In the middle nineteenth century, British military technology—most famously the "Maxim gun"—was desired by the governments of Russia, the Ottoman Empire, and the Qing Empire, not only to attempt to defend themselves against foreign aggression but also to suppress uprisings among distressed farmers, unpaid soldiers, and angry students.

Though both the Qing and Ottoman empires had reservoirs of great wealth, neither empire had reformed its tax system so that it could exploit this wealth for purposes of industrialization or military modernization. For that, both empires went heavily into debt to Britain, France, Belgium, Prussia, and other European powers. To protect their interests, the Europeans sided with these traditional governments against rebels or nationalists who would not repay the loans. When the governments themselves could not repay, the debts were sometimes forgiven in exchange for greater trade privileges awarded to the European creditors. Ultimately, the greatest European export to these empires was money, on which the Europeans earned a high profit in the form of interest rates. Once the Ottoman and Qing empires were debtors of the European powers, they were also their clients.

European manufactured goods such as cigarettes, matches, sewing machines, and weapons could now be imported at prices set by the Europeans themselves, making the goods cheap and popular. British and French nationals lived in the Ottoman and Qing empires under the protection of "extraterritoriality," which exempted them from prosecution under local laws. Where they owned property, British or French law applied. There were larger concessions too. At the conclusion of the Crimean War in 1856, Britain acquired from the Ottoman Empire the right to build and control the Suez Canal, giving it an invaluable direct sea route from the Mediterranean to the Indian Ocean. In China, Britain also controlled a part of the mainland north of Hong Kong island and a large portion of the city of Shanghai.

By 1900, the sea-based empires of Europe had achieved a restructuring of power and influence in very widely separated parts of the world. The Ottoman and Qing empires, after all, had for centuries dominated millions of square miles of territory, hundreds of millions of people, and the overwhelming portion of the world's wealth. Many more people had considered Istanbul or Beijing to be a center of culture and power than had ever looked at London or Paris that way. But in the nineteenth century these things had changed. Military power based on the sea was now a fundamental factor. With battleships, great guns, and adequate supplies of coal and steel, Britain, France, and Germany had begun to define Europe generally and themselves specifically as the new centers. Wealthy and educated people all over the world began to study the technologies, political and economic systems of Europe.

In the later 1800s, relationships between the Ottoman and Qing empires on one hand and the European powers on the other were still symbiotic, or mutually supportive. The European powers, who were now the most productive in the world and in need of both raw materials and markets, depended on the survival of these empires in order to keep tapping into their partly depleted, but still considerable, concentrations of wealth. The new patterns of empire, which would change these practices dramatically, originated in the Pacific with the emergence of two new imperial competitors.

Pacific Imperialists

The Ottoman and Qing empires were dominated and to a certain extent restructured by newly dominant European powers, but Russia was treated differently. The primary strategy of Britain and France in the nineteenth century was to impede Russia's expansion and its acquisition of strategically or commercially advantageous ports in the Black Sea. But by 1900 the focus of European concern over Russian expansion had shifted to the northern Pacific. The combination of commercial income from the development of Vladivostok and access to raw goods such as timber, iron, and coal promised that Russia could become an industrial power on the basis of its Northeast Asian holdings.

Russia's development of its "Maritime Province" in Asia was limited, however, by a weakening of the central government, growing indebtedness to European creditors, and a sparse population in the Siberia. Mining was labor-intensive, and miners were always in short supply. Railroads, which were used elsewhere by the late nineteenth century to move equipment, raw goods, and troops to develop mining and heavy industry, were late in being developed in Siberia and the Maritime Province. The ultimate result was that Russia, despite its long history in the region, was slow in building up its military and industrial strength there. As a consequence, by the first years of the twentieth century, Japan had emerged as the foremost challenger to Russian dreams of dominating the North Pacific.

Japan Arrives

Besides threatening Russia's ambitions in the Pacific, Japan was also a rival to Britain and France for exploitation of the remaining wealth of the Qing Empire. Japan's sudden emergence not only as an independent and industrializing nation but also as a new imperial power took many in both Asia and Europe by surprise. In the middle 1800s, it had appeared that Japan might be subordinated through an unequal treaty system, as China had been. This time the rival sea power was new—the United States of America. In 1853, the United States demanded that Japan agree to open its ports (which were closed by law to foreign trade). The result was a long political crisis in Japan, which by 1868 had risen to the level of civil war. In the traditional system, the emperor was head of state and the shogun was head of government. The government of the shogun was overthrown, and a group of young leaders from the provinces worked together to create a centralized, industrializing government that they hoped would spare Japan the humiliation and impoverishment to which China was being subjected. To command popular unity and support, they made the Meiji emperor the figurehead of the revolution and called the event the Meiji Restoration.

This group of young leaders had carefully studied European and American methods of government, education, military development, financing, medicine, culture, and fashion. They knew the importance of railroads and shipyards, and despite the high cost of industrialization, they were able to finance heavy industries in a very short period of time through innovative methods of deficit financing. At the same time, they used traditional loyalty to the emperor to motivate the Japanese people to throw themselves into projects for modernizing communications and education while creating very advanced industries. Within a generation, critical portions of the Japanese economy had been transformed, and the society as a whole was undergoing deep change.

The Japanese leaders, some of whom remained in power until the First World War, argued to protect Japan from encroachment by the imperialist forces that were at work in nearby China, the Japanese navy should become imperialist itself. Japan, like Britain, is an island with comparatively sparse mineral resources and little timber. A very small portion of the land (less than 20 percent) is suitable for farming or for the support of a growing population. In the later 1800s, Japan found much of the timber, minerals, and human labor needed for its industrialization in Korea. When the Qing Empire challenged Japan's growing power in Korea in 1894, the Japanese rapidly defeated the reputedly formidable new Chinese navy. After its victory, Japan wished to gain the same expansive economic and legal privileges as the other imperialists who had signed unequal treaties with the Qing.

The Japanese victory rang alarm bells for Britain and France. It also stunned and concerned the United States, which was in the process of establishing itself as a new power in China. These countries joined with others to keep Japan from demanding too many concessions from the defeated Qing Empire. In a treaty of 1896, Japan was permitted to take the island of Taiwan—as Britain had taken the island of Hong Kong—but was otherwise expected to be content with the treaty provisions that the other powers enjoyed. To underscore the point, the Americans and the Europeans developed the so-called Open Door policy in China, a restatement of the principle that no one country should try to seize control of large amounts of Chinese territory and exclude the others. The written agreements supporting the Open Door policy were being completed when the Boxer Uprising broke out in 1900.

In suppressing the Boxers, Japan joined the European imperialists, Russia, and the United States in occupying the Qing capital and deciding how to punish Qing leaders for permitting (or encouraging) the uprising. But when the Boxer Uprising was quelled in 1901, the Japanese found that they still were neither trusted nor fully respected by their fellow imperialists. Britain signed an alliance with Japan in 1902, but the United States refused to change immigration laws that discriminated against Japanese and other Asians, and Russia refused to back off from the portions of Manchuria it had seized before Japan could move to do the same.

The rivalry between Russia and Japan finally led to the Russo-Japanese War of 1904–1905. Russia was by far the most successfully expansive power in Asia, and had been engaged in a very sophisticated program of military industrialization for more than ten years. The port at Vladivostok seemed to offer a strategic advantage for any Russian military maneuvers in the North Pacific. But, once again, the Japanese were the surprise victors.

Ideological and Strategic Challenge of the Pacific Empires

The international ramifications of the Russian defeat were immediate. One of the strongest reactions was among American journalists and other opinion makers who had previously championed the cause of "progressive" imperialism. The height of their enthusiasm for the concept had come during the American acquisition of the Philippines in 1898. After defeating Spain—which had been demonized in the American press as one of the most despotic and obscurantist of the European imperial powers—the United States had forced the older empire to sell the Philippines for $20 million. The American navy steamed to Luzon, and American soldiers and marines—many of them former "Indian fighters" from the American West—established an overt military government on the islands.

Before Spain had sold the Philippines to the United States, a Filipino independence movement was already in progress. In summer and fall of 1898, the movement formed a government, created a university, drafted a constitution, and confirmed Emilio Aguinaldo y Famy as president. In June of 1899, the Philippine Republic declared a war of independence against the United States. Despite the fact that the American forces disarmed the population, resistance fighters continued their struggle with sticks, rocks, bows and arrows, and occasionally stolen

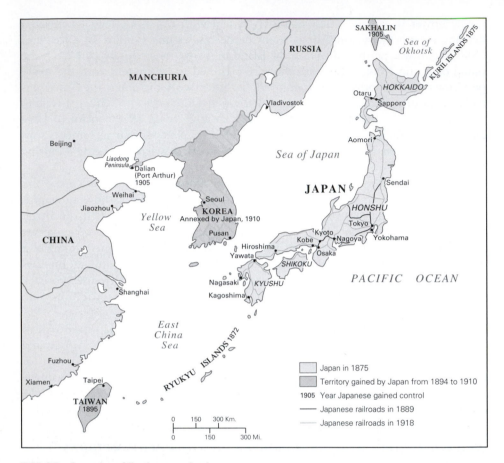

MAP 2.3 Expansion of the Japanese Empire.
As a result of treaties with the Qing Empire resulting from war or threat of war, by 1900 the Japanese empire included the Ryukyu Islands and Taiwan, and was a dominant military and industrial presence in Korea. Following the Russo-Japanese War of 1904–5, Japan made Korea a "protectorate" and assumed control of southern Sakhalin Island. Korea became a formal colony of Japan in 1910.

guns. In 1901, Aguinaldo was captured by the American authorities and forced to retire from public life. President Theodore Roosevelt ordered that the U.S. colonial government in the Philippines be transformed from military to civil. The army officers there protested that the military struggle had not been concluded—that, on the contrary, the widespread resistance of the whole population seemed as strong as ever. The Philippine Republic continued in name under the leadership of Macario Sakay y de Léon, until he was captured and hanged by U.S. authorities in 1907.

Robert Taft, who had been appointed the new civil governor of the Philippines, claimed publicly that no Filipino had ever spoken out against the occupation.

In fact, U.S. martial law in the Philippines made it a felony to criticize the United States or to call for an end to the occupation. It was left to a Filipino resident of the United States, Sixto Lopez, to point out that not only did the population of the Philippines reject the "blessings" of U.S. rule, but that Americans, of all people, should know exactly why it did so: "The Filipinos, like the Americans, prefer to be men, even in poverty, rather than subjects in luxury…. Surely the manly American must have temporarily forgotten all this when he speaks of 'giving' the Filipinos 'prosperity under American rule!' "[1]

Lopez was challenging the assumption, made famous at the time by Theodore Roosevelt and a host of writers, that there was a hierarchy of races. These ideas were a hodgepodge of Spencerian and Huxleyan notions, combined with a new "environmentalism," meaning that a people's mental, physical, and cultural traits are formed from their earliest environmental conditions and cannot be changed. The popular notion was that peoples who originated in temperate climatic zones suitable for agriculture, like the so-called "Anglo-Saxons," had the capacity to create orderly, prosperous societies in which individuals have maximum freedom. Other peoples who came from places where it is extremely hot or extremely cold were assumed to have deficiencies caused by their adaptation to harsh conditions. Such peoples, according to this ideology, must be taught how to do it by the more "progressive" races. Though the inferior peoples would never assume a leadership role, they could learn to be reliable servants and sidekicks, and they could enjoy

Bettmann/CORBIS

Emilio Aguinaldo led the armed resistance against Spanish imperialism in the Philippines. When the United States declared war on Spain in 1898, Aguinaldo was leading a Philippines independence movement, and in 1899 he was appointed president by a constitutional convention. When the United States refused to recognize the independence of the Philippines, Aguinaldo declared war on the United States.

---

[1]Sixto Lopez, "Do Filipinos Desire American Rule?" *Gunton's Magazine,* 22 (June 1902).

the benefits of orderly societies run by more advanced peoples. A decade before the American movement into the Pacific, this idea had been called the "white man's burden" by its advocates, claiming self-sacrifice on behalf of less fortunate, inferior people.

These claims were frequently met with opposition and derision by American writers. Mark Twain, Edgar Lee Masters, and William Dean Howells were prominent writers who denounced the new imperialism. Anti-imperial sentiment was also strong in women's publications, and the social activist Jane Addams— who argued that militarism and democracy were not compatible in the long run—was only one of the prominent women opposing U.S. imperialism in Cuba, Hawaii, and the Philippines. But they were an insignificant minority in comparison to the policymakers who advised and encouraged the McKinley, Roosevelt, and Taft governments. Theodore Roosevelt spoke for the majority of his generation when he proclaimed that the coming of American imperialism to the Pacific would mean the breaking of the shackles of the old despotic empires of Spain, Portugal, and the Netherlands, and the spreading of new forces for prosperity and liberation.

At about the same time that Roosevelt was proselytizing for American imperialism, a generation of Japanese educators and writers was producing a new amendment to the overall theory. Japan, they noted, was also in the temperate zone, and since 1868 the Japanese had proved efficient at adapting all the features of "progressive" culture to their own islands: capitalism, industrialization, imperialism, constitutional government, and even Christianity. This would seem, they pointed out, to give the Japanese a place among the band of progressive, liberal imperialists. Many of writers were too polite to point out that this seemed to poke a large hole in the theory of the superiority of the Anglo-Saxon race that was often advertised at the time. More radical Japanese writers with less international exposure did make such statements, however.

The international argument for Japan's inclusion among the imperialists was made. And although the leaders of Britain and the United States had no intention of allowing Japan to acquire enough territory to become a rival of their countries, they could certainly agree that Japanese influence over certain Asian nations— particularly China and Korea—would be beneficial. Japan would invigorate them and get them started on the path to prosperity and liberty. In Japan, academics, journalists, and young army officers began to discuss the idea of a "Greater East Asian Co-Prosperity Sphere," in which millions would advance and enrich themselves under Japanese leadership and instruction. Although Roosevelt and his peers might have approved of Japan's new role as a progressive, instructive, reforming imperialist in Taiwan and Korea, the Japanese historian Asakawa Kan'ichi—a 1909 graduate of Dartmouth College and an observer of the Portsmouth negotiations in 1906—was disturbed by the ambiguities of Japan's claims:

"In its economic aspects, does reform mean the creation of circumstances favorable to the quick exploitation of Korea's resources by the Japanese? This is certainly one interpretation. Another and very different interpretation is that reform means not the exploitation but the development of the resources; not exploitation for the sole interest of the Japanese but development for the large and increasingly large common interests of the Koreans and the Japanese. Which of these two economic interpretations forms the motive of Japan's reform of Korea?"[2]

Japan's characterization of itself as a progressive imperialist power was not a serious challenge to the United States until the Japanese defeat of Russia in 1905. People who were considered European and superior had been bested in battle after battle by this upstart Asian power. After the defeat of the Qing Empire by Japan in 1895, the Europeans had banded together to prevent Japan from maximizing its advantages. With Japan's defeat of Russia, the European powers and the United States intended to do this again. The Russians came to Portsmouth believing that the United States would lessen the blow of their defeat, and they were right. When the treaty talks concluded in 1906, Japan was given no territorial rights on the Asian mainland other than recognition of its interests in Manchuria and Korea and outright control of half of Sakhalin. Japan basically made no immediate material advances as a result of its victory at a time when victory in war was normally accompanied by substantial awards of money, territory, and privileges.

In Japan, reaction to the treaty focused less on Russia and more on the United States, which was seen as having designed the terms of the treaty. The rivalry between Japan and the United States in the Pacific was already keen. Japanese military strategists had targeted Hawaii in the early 1890s and were bitterly disappointed when the United States overthrew the Hawaiian monarchy and seized control of the islands in 1898. In the same year the United States gained the Philippines—another Japanese target. And in Japanese eyes the United States added insult to injury when it extended its ban on Asian immigration to both these newly acquired Pacific territories.

For Britain, the tolerance of Japanese expansion into Korea, Manchuria, and elsewhere in eastern Asia was now combined with a wariness regarding the development of Japan as a Pacific sea power. This was evident not only in the series of naval treaties restricting the growth of the Japanese fleet after 1905 but also in a newly cooperative position toward Russia. In 1907, Britain and Russia concluded a nonaggression pact that essentially ended a long-standing and wide-ranging British willingness to use military force to prevent Russian expansion. Britain and Russia even collaborated in dividing Iran into spheres of interest, each hoping for rights to the oil that was known to be somewhere under the Iranian soil.

But Japan's development of sea power remained an important issue. This was the most zealously guarded and regulated area of international military armament. The great sea powers—Britain, the United States, France, Germany, and Italy— attempted to draft new international laws that would stipulate ratios for the building of armored ships by the various powers. In these drafts, the United States and Britain were in the top rank, with the highest quotas. Germany was next, and

---

[2]Asakawa Kan'ichi, "Comment on The Treaty of Portsmouth," 1906.

France and Italy were in the lowest rank. These recommendations were among many drafts of new international laws, and a plan for an international court, that were written but not ratified by any of the proposed participants before World War I. After 1906, Japan was included in the ranks of international sea powers, but the intention was to keep Japanese production of military ships on a level with that of Italy or France. Though these ratios were not ratified or enforced, the basic concept persisted and eventually provided the foundation for multinational treaties after World War I.

Japanese Imperialism in Continental Asia

Seeking opportunities for expansion in Asia that would not provoke a head-on collision with the United States, Japanese military strategists looked once again to the Qing Empire. Meiji-era Japanese military strategists had stressed the need to control Korea, which could otherwise become a launching point for a Chinese or Russian invasion of Japan. In 1905, Japan was also able to force a treaty upon Korea, declaring the latter a "protectorate" (a concept borrowed from the U.S. control of certain Pacific islands) of Japan, putting it effectively under Japanese control.

The larger plan of Japanese strategic planners was to use northern Korea as a staging point for moving toward Manchuria, which was even richer in mineral deposits and agricultural productivity. Korea and Manchuria together supplied Japan with iron, coal, timber, wheat, and labor, while Taiwan supplied labor and some rice. Japanese manufactured goods began to dominate the markets of all East Asia. But the effects of Japanese imperialism on Korea, in particular, were harsh. Koreans were forced into labor camps in the north of their country and in Manchuria, while those remaining in their homes were required to provide shelter, food, and in many instances sex to occupying Japanese troops. Korean outrage was so intense that a Korean laborer assassinated Japanese Prime Minister Ito Hirobumi in 1909 in the Manchurian city of Harbin. Japan's reaction was to make Korea a formal colony in 1910.

By that year it was clear that the Qing Empire was on the verge of collapse, and Japan was poised to seize whatever gains were possible. Hopes that Qing reforms and industrialization would allow China to become at least marginally self-sufficient were gone by the beginning of the twentieth century. But among the provincial governors who became national leaders in the Qing Empire during the late nineteenth century were several who were actually successful on a regional basis. These men, most well-known among them Li Hongzhang, were able to make advances in reforming the regional military, establishing industry, restructuring education, and even getting international recognition. The result, however, was not a stronger empire but a more severely decentralized one. Some progressive areas, particularly in northern and coastal China, prospered as their governors became more powerful. Other areas, particularly in central China, became more lawless and impoverished and could not obtain support from the central government as they had a hundred years before.

Many of the regional leaders could see the end of the empire coming. This was particularly true in Manchuria, where after 1905 Japanese industrialists began to build a railroad system for the purpose of moving food, heavy goods, and people between Korea and Manchuria. The local Qing leaders were helpless to prevent this Japanese encroachment, and instead they began to enter into a kind of partnership with the Japanese military leaders sent to protect the new railways and mines. In exchange, the Japanese militarists did not assassinate or remove these leaders, and in many cases shared a small portion of the profits with them. The local leaders were also expected to share with the Japanese military any information they had about the imminent fall of the Qing Empire.

Given these circumstances, it may seem ironic that Japan became a leading inspiration for Chinese nationalists. Young Chinese students and professors who were convinced that the Qing Empire had to be replaced by a national republic had been looking to Japan for ideas and financial support ever since Japan had so unexpectedly defeated the Qing navy in 1895. To these young nationalists, Japan demonstrated that Asians could industrialize as quickly and effectively as Europeans. Indeed, Asian nations that followed Japan's example might become international powers in their own right. Japanese leaders had also publicly protested the American prohibition on Asian immigration, not only to the United States but to its new territories in Hawaii and the Philippines. This was particularly inspiring to young urban Chinese, who also protested the prohibition as part of their nationalist movement, organizing demonstrations and boycotts of U.S. goods but getting no support from either their own imperial government or from local governors. Nationalists from all over Asia—including India, Vietnam, and eastern Russia—flocked to Japan to find encouragement, funds, and freedom from the restrictive speech laws that pertained in their own countries.

Dr. Sun Yat-sen, a native of Canton who had been educated in Hong Kong and Hawaii, became the leader of the Chinese Patriotic Alliance (Tongmeng hui), which sought to overthrow the Qing and establish a nationalist republic in China. His headquarters in 1905 was in Tokyo, and many of his new concepts, such as nationalism and national sovereignty, came into the Chinese language through borrowings from Japanese. Sun was always working from a position of weakness and had to accept monetary contributions wherever he could find them. Many such contributions came from the Japanese government, which hoped that if Sun were successful he would consider Japan a sponsor and a friend. Japan was poised to gain great influence, and perhaps outright control, of large portions of China once the Qing Empire finally collapsed.

Abandonment of the Land-Based Empires

The collapse of the land-based empires continued into the second decade of the twentieth century. It is important to note two features of these individual declines. First, groups within the imperial borders noted and exploited the weakness of these

GLOBAL Technologies

Global Communications

Once the basic elements of electric current were understood in the eighteenth century, inventors quickly devised methods to transmit signals over wires. This permitted rapid, long-distance transmission of messages of syncopated electrical bursts, the basis of the telegraph. But to make this communication global, it was necessary to extend cables beneath the seas. The British Empire was the leader in these developments. The acquisition of gutta-percha (a flexible substance from the latex of certain trees) from Malaya allowed undersea cables to be insulated but remain relatively flexible. The first

trans-Atlantic cable was completed in 1858, and Latin America added to the network soon after. But the huge Pacific remained a daunting challenge. In 1902, Britain succeeded in laying a cable between Canada and Australia, with links to New Zealand. East Asia did not have a direct connection to the United States until the completion of the San Francisco-Honolulu-Yokohama cable of 1909.

As transoceanic cables were being laid, experimenters such as the American Elisha Gray and Alexander Graham Bell (a Scot working in the United States) were attempting to learn how to transmit speech via long-distance electrical impulses. Bell studied the behavior of the membrane in a corpse's ear to understand the analysis and replication of sound waves, or "harmonic telegraphy." Gray and Bell's patent applications for the telephone were filed the same day in Boston in 1876, and many of the technical aspects were similar, but Bell was awarded the patent. Many other

---

old imperial regimes as early as, or earlier than, foreign imperialists. The results were dispiriting and sometimes disabling internal troubles, ranging from rebellion to civil war. In all the land-based empires, secessionist movements like that of the Armenians in the Ottoman Empire—advocating the use of the local vernacular for newspapers and theater, self-government, and some political protections—appeared. In the Russian Empire, Ukrainian nationalism emerged, as well as movements for independence in the Caucasus and among the Tartars of Central Asia. Before the fall of the Qing Empire, Mongolia and Tibet established their independence.

But the situation in the Ottoman Empire was the most complex in many ways. By the 1880s, peoples under the control of the Ottoman Empire, such as the Arabs, Turks, Kurds, and Croats, had perceived that the empire was dissolving. To varying degrees, they succeeded in forming groups that advocated independent national governments for themselves. The Armenian group was formed in the 1870s and was very active in both Ottoman and Russian territories. By the 1880s, it was a definite threat, and beginning in 1896 Ottoman rulers licensed Turkish and Kurdish soldiers and mercenaries to slaughter Armenians of all ages and occupations. After they assumed power in 1908, the nationalist Young Turks

inventors, including Thomas Edison, worked on the problems of amplification and number dialing that made working telephones possible. In the United States, the telephone companies were always private corporations, of which the most dominant was American Telephone and Telegraph, which directly or through its subsidiaries controlled telephone use in the United States, Canada, the Caribbean and—after World War II—Japan. In 1984, AT&T was forced by the United States government to fragment into smaller companies. In Britain, local private telephone companies were permitted, but the post office controlled the long-distance, or trunk, cables and over time bought out many of the smaller local companies. In 1981, British Telecom became a public corporation separate from the post office.

Alexander Graham Bell had argued that it should be possible to send many separate signals simultaneously through a single cable, and this insight is at the heart both of the early telephone systems and of the modern Internet system. The wide application of computers in industrial and in military affairs in the very early 1960s led scientists to speculate on how information could be structured for transmission so that computers could talk to each other over the telephone lines. Computers that could perform the functions of handling and forwarding "packets" of information were the basis of the earliest internet, which was funded by the United States Department of Defense. All the elements familiar to modern Internet users—e-mail, bulletin boards, hypertext, encryption, and even the graphical user interface—were present in some form from the inception of the Internet. Since the 1970s, telephony and the Internet have advanced together, leading to the near universality of voice-over-internet-protocol communications today.

continued to authorize the slaughter of Armenians. Between 1896 and the end of the Ottoman Empire, it is estimated that well over a million Armenians were murdered in these openly genocidal campaigns. Whatever the Turkish motives behind these massacres were, the beginning of the story was Armenian attempts to establish an independent nation as the Ottoman Empire collapsed.

In the Middle East the disintegration of the Ottoman Empire produced more anxieties, because Egypt was already under British control and it was clear that either Britain or France would seize the territories of Syria, Lebanon, Palestine, and Jordan. In the Arabian peninsula there was fear that a new wave of European imperialism would threaten the independence of the loosely allied groups in the region. Sharif Hussein bin Ali, the ruler of Mecca, became the leading strategist in the movement for Arab independence. Though his plans for a single Arab state were not realized, he later aided the British campaigns against remnant Ottoman forces that concluded the First World War in the Middle East (see Chapter 3). Britain and France had entered into a secret agreement in 1916 to divide the Arab lands of the vanishing Ottoman Empire between themselves. France took Syria and Lebanon, and Britain took Palestine and Jordan. Britain's deal with Russia to split dominance over Iran had paid off, and oil had been discovered within the British sphere in 1908. By the time Britain acquired Palestine and Jordan, the Anglo-Persian Oil Company (later British Petroleum Company) had been formed, with the British government owning the majority of the shares. This gave Britain a dominant position in the Middle East for decades to come.

In East Asia, there was no real rival to the expanding Japanese Empire. As much as Europe or the United States fretted about the growing Japanese industrial and military presence in Korea, Manchuria, northern China, and the western Pacific, they were unwilling or unable to make a substantial intervention except through diplomacy. Japanese ambitions were not limited to coastal East Asia, but also extended to Siberia and Mongolia. By 1905, Mongols were looking forward to the end of the Qing Empire, and many were feeling nationalistic; they did not want Dr. Sun or other nationalist Chinese to control Mongolia. Japanese strategists attempted to create partnerships with Mongol nationalists, but they encountered strong competition from their old Russian rivals. Mongolia declared its independence from the Qing in 1910 and made a Buddhist religious leader head of state. However, Japan and Russia continued to compete with each other for influence with the new Mongol government.

Russia also attempted to gain power in the Qing province of Xinjiang, which had formerly been Eastern Turkestan. This largely Muslim, Turkic-speaking region had been conquered by the Qing in the 1700s after a series of very bloody campaigns, and in the 1800s it had been the site of many large, violent uprisings in which local military leaders attempted to achieve independence from the Qing Empire. Though none of these rebellions was really successful, each created hopes of success in the future, and each invited the attention of foreign powers hoping to gain influence with local leaders. Since control of Turkestan would be a strategic advantage in either protecting or invading Afghanistan, Iran, India, Tibet, or China, Russia was greatly interested in the area, as was Britain. They competed through the 1800s in the "Great Game," but by the 1905–1910 period it was still unclear who had the upper hand.

In Tibet, another Qing territory, Britain was the primary foreign interventionist. In the late 1800s, British scouts from India were investigating whether Britain should make an attempt to wrest Tibet away from the Qing. Instead, Britain opted to encourage Tibetan nationalists to declare independence from the Qing—exactly the strategy that Japan was following in Korea at this time. In 1910, Tibetan nationalists did indeed declare independence, and Britain supplied advisers and rifles to aid the Tibetan cause.

This left China in a very precarious position in 1910. The Qing Empire had all but evaporated, yet a Qing emperor—the infant Puyi—was still on the throne. China itself had not declared its independence, but Mongolia and Tibet had done so, and Manchuria was clearly not controlled by China any longer. When the Chinese nationalist revolution broke out in 1911, it was relatively limited in geographical scope and only months in duration. In early 1912, Puyi's guardians arranged for him to abdicate but to continue to reside in the Forbidden City in Beijing. However, the decentralization that had characterized China in the late

1800s continued to dominate the politics of the Republic of China in the 1910s. Powerful local leaders—now called "warlords" by foreign observers—forced the new republic to bargain with them for control, and in 1915 one of them attempted to have himself installed as emperor. The plot failed, but for the next ten years China was divided between a government headed by Sun Yat-sen in the south and a coalition of warlords based at Beijing. When Sun died in 1925, his dream of a unified Chinese republic with a civil government and liberal laws for the protection of the common people seemed to have no hope of being realized.

A weak and disunited China was unable to solve the problem of Japanese military expansionism in Asia. The old Qing Empire had been protected by the imperialist alliance from outright colonization by any single power, but the republic's situation was different. Though the republic promised to respect the conditions of the unequal treaties and continue foreign privileges in the colonies and treaty ports, it did not assume the debt of the extinct Qing Empire. As a result, foreign powers felt that protecting the republic against internal or external challenges was less urgent. Moreover, after 1912, Europe was distracted by its own tensions and could not maintain the unity of interest and action that had enabled it to protect China from colonization by Japan.

By 1915, the disintegration of the land-based empires and the momentum behind the new empires based on advanced sea technologies combined to create unusual possibilities and great dangers in many parts of the world. In the vast and diverse territories that had once been the Qing Empire, independent border states attempted to stabilize themselves, Chinese nationalists struggled unsuccessfully to centralize and control an enormous population, and local governors bargained with foreign powers to achieve some modest degree of economic security. In the lands of the weakening Ottoman Empire, Turkish nationalists were carving out the new Turkish Republic, which would attempt to centralize and control a modest population, while the more far-flung parts of the Ottoman Empire were left to declare their independence and fight against encroachment by the new imperial powers, particularly Britain and France. In Russia, the decline of imperial prestige and the economic exhaustion of the ambitious industrialization programs had stimulated many dissident and revolutionary movements. Army officers, university students, and farmers were all reservoirs of revolutionary sentiment and action, and were slowly working toward coordinating and focusing their efforts. In 1917, Russia underwent two revolutions. The first, in February, was an attempt to establish a liberal, nationalist democracy on the ruins of the old empire. The second, in October, was a tightly organized, radical, authoritarian revolution led by Vladimir Ilyich Lenin that within a few years created the Soviet Union.

CONCLUSION

The decline and dissolution of the land-based empires was a long process, during which profound changes in global political relationships, economic fortunes, and living conditions took place. The sea-based empires of Britain, France, Germany,

Belgium, and Italy at first did not colonize the old empires or destroy their traditional economies or market centers. On the contrary, once these old regimes had become debtors of the European empires and had lost the ability to regulate commerce across their own borders, the European powers actively worked to suppress domestic movements for major reform or national governance. But the arrival of the United States and Japan as new powers competing for control of Pacific resources and trade routes changed the outlook of the European empires. They attempted to support Russia, instead of frustrating it at every turn as they had done earlier. They incorporated the United States and Japan into the unequal treaty system in China, and the United States became a signatory of unequal treaties with the Ottoman Empire. And they found the United States a willing partner in their attempts to restrain Japan's prodigious industrial and naval development.

By the second decade of the twentieth century, however, it was clear that the late-nineteenth-century system was no longer viable. Attempts to codify the old values of respecting other powers' territorial interests and naval status failed. Japan had established a new pattern of colonization in Taiwan and Korea. Instead of concentrating on acquiring raw materials at low cost, Japan made its colonial possessions centers of industrialization. It built railroads, shipyards, extensive telegraph systems, trolleys, and factories that were the equal of those in Japan, and it also built schools to educate locals in the scientific and engineering knowledge that was necessary for industrialization. In this way, Japan transferred its industrial base to its possessions, keeping down the cost of its manufactured goods and by acquiring raw materials cheaply and employing low-paid workers. One of Japan's major conceptual conflicts with the European powers and the United States after its defeat of China in 1895. It claimed that it should be allowed to colonize parts of China and control its own industries there in order to make them efficient in ways that the weak and traditional Qing government would never be able to do. This was an argument that would prove very influential with Japan's imperialist rivals in China.

In its conflicts with the other sea-based powers over colonization, trade rights, and heavy ship ratios, Japan was the harbinger of a new era. Its colonization of Taiwan and Korea demonstrated that the old system of propping up traditional agriculturally based empires and their huge urban markets could not survive. The old land-based regimes collapsed within a decade of each other—the Qing in 1912, Russia in 1917, and the Ottoman in 1922. The European powers followed the Japanese example, scooping up the weaker border territories and bringing them under direct control, and eventually making them centers of outlying industry as well as agriculture, lumbering, and mining. Nationalists in the affected areas became more sure of their cause and more convinced that imperialism and exploitation went together. Theodore Roosevelt's ideal of imperialism as an elevating and progressive force was overshadowed by a new attitude—on the part of both proponents and opponents—that imperialism was as the Russian revolutionary leader Lenin described it: exploitative, unmerciful, and unjust.

For Further Reading

Frederick F. Anscombe, *The Ottoman Gulf: The Creation of Kuwait, Saudi Arabia and Qatar* (New York: Columbia University Press, 1997). A new study using Ottoman documents rather than British documents to analyze the disintegration of the empire in the Arabian peninsula.

Richard H. Collin, *Theodore Roosevelt, Culture, Diplomacy and Expansion: A New View of American Imperialism* (Baton Rouge: Louisiana State University, 1985). A specific discussion of Roosevelt's ideas on imperialism.

Joseph Esherick, *Origins of the Boxer Uprising* (Berkeley: University of California Press, 1990). One of the best scholarly works on this subject.

Suraiya Faroqhi, *The Ottoman Empire and the World Around It* (London: I. B. Tauris, 2005). A new, comprehensive, authoritative reference work.

Daniel Headrick, *The Tentacles of Progress: Technology Transfer in the Age of Imperialism, 1850–1940* (New York: Oxford University Press, 1988). An accessible and economical narrative of technological history.

John F. Hutchinson, *Late Imperial Russia 1890–1917* (London: Longman, 1999). An excellent narrative of Russia in this period.

Akira Iriye, *Across the Pacific: An Inner History of American-East Asian Relations* (New York: Harcourt, Brace, 1967). A classic study giving the background to Pacific competition in this era.

Marius Jansen, *The Emergence of Meiji Japan* (Cambridge and New York: Cambridge University Press, 2006). Very accessible reference text, composed of a chapter extracted from *The Cambridge History of Japan,* Volume 5.

George Kennan, *Tent Life in Siberia* (1871; reprint, with an introduction by Larry McMurtry; Layton, Utah: Smith, Gibbs, 1986). The development of American opinion regarding Russia, as it was made at the time.

Donald Keene, *Emperor of Japan: Meiji and his World, 1852–1912* (New York: Columbia University Press, 2005). The master study of the period, and of the milieu of imperial Japan's leaders, by an eminent American scholar of Japanese culture.

John Philip Langellier, *Uncle Sam's Little Wars: The Spanish-American War, Philippine Insurrection, and Boxer Rebellion, 1898–1902* (Boston: Stackpole Books, 1999). A good combined narrative of the U.S. military actions in Cuba, the Philippines, and China.

Stuart Creighton Miller, *Benevolent Assimilation: The American Conquest of the Philippines, 1899–1903* (New Haven, Conn.: Yale University Press, 1990). The classic study of American imperialism in the Philippines.

Diana Preston, *The Boxer Rebellion: The Dramatic Story of China's War on Foreigners That Shook the World in the Summer of 1900* (London: Berkley Publishing Group, 2001). A lively narrative based on English-language accounts.

Eugene L. Rogan, *Frontiers of the State in the Late Ottoman Empire: Transjordan, 1850–1921* (Cambridge: Cambridge University Press, 1999). An important study of life in the outlying provinces in the last decades of the Ottoman Empire.

Andre Schmid, *Korea Between Empires, 1895–1919* (New York: Columbia University Press, 2002). A revisionist study of the emergence of Korean nationalism.

Peter W. Stanley, ed., *Reappraising an Empire: New Perspectives on Philippine-American History* (Cambridge, Mass.: Harvard University Press, 1984). An interesting perspective on American imperialism in the Philippines.

Theodore von Laue, *Sergei Witte and the Industrialization of Russia* (New York: Columbia University Press, 1963). Still perhaps the best-known biography of Count Sergei Witte.

Leon Wolff, *Little Brown Brother: How the United States Purchased and Pacified the Philippine Islands at the Century's Turn* (New York: Doubleday, 1961). An interesting perspective on American imperialism in the Philippines.

Sin Kiong Kiong Wong, *China's Anti-American Boycott Movement in 1905: A Study in Urban Protest* (New York: Peter Lang Publishing, 2002). An important recent addition to understanding this period.

Related Websites

Alexander Palace: Everyday Life in a Romanov Palace
http://www.alexanderpalace.org/palace/mainpage.html
A superb website of interactive materials and original documents, constructed by Russian scholars.

Documents Relating to American Foreign Policy, 1898–1914
http://www.mtholyoke.edu/acad/intrel/to1914.htm
An extremely useful teaching tool.

The Empire That Was Russia: The Prokudin-Gorskii Photographic Record Re-created
http://www.loc.gov/exhibits/empire/ethnic.html
A superb website of interactive materials and original documents constructed by Russian scholars.

Asakawa Kan'ichi's private comment on the Treaty of Portsmouth
http://www.russojapanesewar.com/asakawa.html

La Belle Epoche Versus the Age of Progress
http://www.historyteacher.net/APEuroCourse/WebLinks/WebLinks-LaBelleEpoche.htm
An excellent resource for early twentieth-century history.

The Modern Middle East Source Book
http://www.umd.umich.edu/middleeastsourcebook/tablecontents.html

Text of the Treaty of Portsmouth
http://www.lib.byu.edu/~rdh/wwi/1914m/portsmouth.html

The Young Turks: Proclamation for the Ottoman Empire, 1908
http://www.fordham.edu/halsall/mod/1908youngturk.html
Materials on the return of the Young Turks and a few more contemporary documents.

CHAPTER 3

Great War, Little Peace, 1914–1919

"**W**ords fail to give any conception of the desolation. No convulsion of Nature could have done what man and man's machines have done. We bumped our way along a partly repaired road … passing craters from those 10 to those 30 feet across, and some almost as deep; passing rows and rows of old wire entanglements, communications trenches, line upon line of fighting trenches, all more or less obliterated. Finally past the German first line, barely recognizable except for the fact that the entrances to the dugouts now faced east instead of west.

"It was an upheaval of sandbags, accoutrements, broken rifles not worth salvaging, entrenching tools, cartridge clips and machine-gun ribbons, food tins, water bottles, helmets, trench mortars, unexploded shells of every size, hand grenades, to which we give a wide berth, a human tibia exhumed from somewhere, bits of clothing—and often smells, though two months have given ample time for burials. What may be in the bottom of the pits, however, one can only guess … the whole western side of the slope was seething with people making new roads and engaging in the ant-like activity of man when he too burrows and builds and carries up food and takes away grains of sand."[1]"

Here American neurosurgeon Harvey Cushing describes his first impressions of Flanders, where British troops had just captured a few miles of mud from the Germans facing them. The scarred earth, the odors, and futile labors dumbfounded

---

[1]Harvey Cushing, *From a Surgeon's Journal, 1915–1918* (Boston: Little, Brown, 1936), p. 136.

Cushing. The profligacy of the war astonished others as well, from those who took the bird's-eye view and totted up the billions spent to the humble soldiers who fired machine guns to heat water for tea. The sense of waste spread over time, infecting not just the participants but also a generation of writers, artists, and thinkers, for whom World War I became a symbol of great effort squandered on meager ends.

World War I, until 1939 known simply as "the Great War," was a struggle for power that degenerated into a struggle for survival. Paradoxically, many of the achievements that were celebrated as evidence of progress at the start of the twentieth century increased the risk and viciousness of war. Growing literacy and the wide circulation of inexpensive newspapers helped to broaden nationalist feelings and exacerbate international tensions. Railroads permitted the rapid mobilization of huge armies. The wealth generated by industry supplied capital for battleships and armories. And modern bureaucracies could manage the distribution of soldiers and munitions as easily as the distribution of social services or consumer goods.

Most observers understood that states had unprecedented war-making capacities, and many expected that violence would continue to be, as it had long been, part of statecraft. Few, however, anticipated the severity and scope of the war of 1914–1918 or the magnitude of its effects. It brought death to millions and hardship to many millions more. It was fatal to four empires that had long been integral to European politics—the Ottoman, Russian, Hohenzollern, and Hapsburg empires, and it sapped the vitality of the victorious European powers. By shifting capital to other parts of the world, especially North America and Japan, it stimulated the growth of new rivals to European hegemony.

The war also coarsened life among the peoples of all the belligerents and altered thinking about the possibility of moral progress, the rationality of human conduct, and the superiority of Western institutions. It generated global tensions that were to lead to a breakdown in international trade, the rise of extremist politics on both the right and the left, and a second, even more destructive global struggle just twenty years later. Rather than a war to end all wars, it was a catalyst for future conflict.

Origins of the War

The scope of the conflict, the haste with which governments chose sides, the enthusiasm with which ordinary citizens enlisted in the armed forces, and the persistence with which statesmen and soldiers continued the fight all suggest that the war had deep roots. European leaders were unprepared for the catastrophe, but several long-term trends and underlying conflicts make the Great War seem comprehensible, if not inevitable (Map 3.1).

German Expansion

The war began in the Balkans, but war in the Balkans was nothing new, nor was the nationalism that drove the Serbs to seek to expand their territory at the expense of neighboring multiethnic empires. In 1912, Serbia and other Balkan

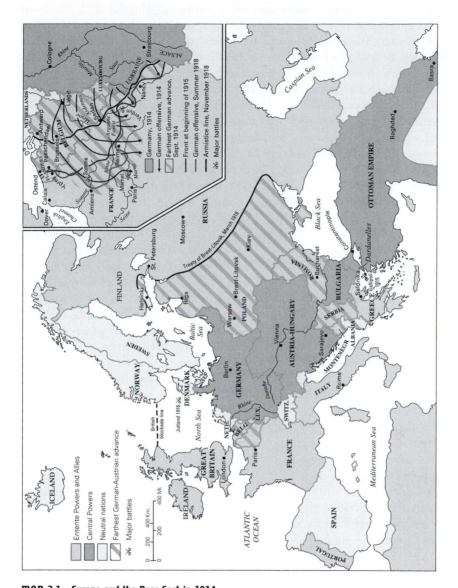

MAP 3.1 Europe and the Near East in 1914.

At the start of the war in 1914, the Central Powers (darkly shaded areas) faced adversaries with greater land area, population, and resources. But they enjoyed the advantage of interior lines and an excellent rail network and hence could shuttle forces from one front to another more rapidly than their enemies. Germany rapidly shifted troops to the east to exploit Russia's weakness after its opening offensive in the west (see inset) bogged down. When Russia sued for peace in 1917, Germany quickly refocused their attention on the west, although the effort was too little and too late to achieve victory.

states had driven Ottoman troops out of Macedonia, Albania, and much of Thrace in a quick but violent campaign. Only a year later, Serbia had defeated its former partner, Bulgaria, in a squabble over the spoils of that war. What made the crisis of 1914 different from earlier ones was the involvement of Germany. Germany's encouragement of Austria-Hungary; its truculence toward Russia and France; its naked ambitions for empire; and its meticulous plans for war all helped to turn a local crisis into a general melee.

Imperial ambitions accompanied Germany's spectacular expansion in the late nineteenth century. By 1900, Germany was the most populous nation in Europe outside Russia. Its industrial production had surpassed that of any other European nation save Britain, and in many areas it was challenging British leadership (see Table 3.1). German products were displacing British goods in many markets, and German ships were enlarging their share of international commerce. German universities turned out more engineers and scientists than those of any other nation; German was the international language of scientific communication. German-speaking peoples could be found in large numbers in many parts of eastern and southeastern Europe, and German-speaking immigrants were numerous in the Americas. Late in establishing colonies, Germany was striving to make up for lost time, taking parts of Africa, islands in the Pacific, and naval bases in China. The empire had little economic value to Germany but testified to the ambitions of the Kaiser and many of his subjects. Germany aspired to the global power that Britain and France already possessed.

Efforts to expand its modest empire drew Germany into a series of disputes in the two decades prior to the war. In Asia, German seizure of islands in the South Pacific provoked anxiety among the Dutch, who saw a threat to their control of the Indonesian archipelago, and the British, who were bound to defend their sparsely settled dominion, Australia. In Africa, Germany took claim to territories that held little economic promise but considerable strategic potential. Its colony in East Africa, now part of Tanzania, frustrated British dreams of a Cape to Cairo railroad; its colony in southwest Africa was uncomfortably close to the gold and diamond fields of British South Africa. To the north, Germany was cultivating closer ties with the Ottoman Empire and seeking to enlarge its influence in North Africa. These gambits menaced France's colony in Algeria, Britain's control of the Suez Canal, and Russia's avenue from the Black Sea to the Mediterranean.

Germany's growing power had pushed France and Russia into a military alliance in 1893. Britain, in keeping with its long-standing policy of supporting a balance of continental forces, began to tilt toward France and Russia in the years after 1904, despite its differences with France over imperial borders and its concerns about Russian expansion toward the Dardanelles and British India. The basic reason for this tilt was that in 1898 the German Reichstag, at the urging of the Kaiser, had begun to underwrite construction of a "High Seas Fleet" that might eventually challenge British control of the seas. Britain was prepared to compete with Germany for international markets and to bargain with Germany over territories in Africa or islands in the Pacific, but Britain could not rest easy with a naval threat. There could be no greater danger to an island nation that depended on a global empire for food, raw materials, and markets.

The British and German fleets were built around vessels such as this British battleship, the HMS *Royal Oak*. Fast and heavily armored, it could fire shells weighing a ton nearly twenty miles. At the focus of the prewar arms race, such behemoths proved vulnerable to mines and submarines and spent most of the war at anchor.

The Anglo-German Naval Race

Germany wanted a powerful fleet to support its imperial ambitions, safeguard its growing commerce, and deter Britain from entering any future continental conflict. Naval power had long made Britain invulnerable to attack and allowed it to intervene in continental affairs at points and times of its own choosing, thereby giving it a decisive role in Europe's balance of power. So long as Britain maintained undisputed control of the seas, Germany could never rest assured that its empire was secure or that it could act freely against European adversaries.

British policymakers viewed German naval construction as a provocation and responded by quickening its own building program. Nor was the response simply to build more vessels; the British also sought qualitative superiority by building warships that were bigger, faster, and more lethal than any that had hitherto been launched. The new battleships embodied national power and ambition like no other machines. Monarchs presided over fleet exercises, construction plans provoked national debates, and tens of thousands of civilians enrolled in Navy Leagues to promote larger appropriations.

Nor was the fever for larger fleets confined to Britain and Germany. Between 1905 and 1914, all of the major powers, and some would-be powers, either built dreadnoughts or bought them from shipyards in Britain and America. The United States wanted a strong navy to protect its growing overseas interests after its 1898 war with Spain. Japan was eager to maintain the naval superiority that it had achieved in the western Pacific through its war with Russia in 1905, and

Russia was bent on rebuilding the fleets that Japan had destroyed. France, Italy, and Austria-Hungary competed in the Mediterranean, where Britain also had a vital interest because of the importance of the Suez Canal to its commerce. A naval race even began in South America as Chile, Brazil, and Argentina competed for regional advantage.

These naval construction programs, especially Germany's, made it all but impossible for Britain to maintain its traditional margin of safety in naval power. Hence, while investing huge sums in new construction, the British also resorted to diplomacy to shore up their position. A mutual defense treaty with Japan, signed in 1902, freed Britain from the necessity of maintaining large squadrons in the waters around China. At the same time, English and French admirals drew up joint contingency plans in the event of a war with Germany.

The Ambitions and Insecurities of Other Powers

Germany was not the only rising power of the early twentieth century. The United States had overtaken Britain by most measures of industrial production and was extending its influence in Latin America and the Pacific. Japan, which had grafted Western technology and industrial practices onto its own institutions, controlled Korea and was tightening its grasp on resource-rich Manchuria. Its productive capacity, although still modest, was growing rapidly, and its warships could outgun the Pacific squadrons of any European nation. And Russia, although humiliated by Japan in the war of 1904–1905, was enjoying an economic expansion that promised to restore its status as a great power.

As the United States, Japan, and Russia expanded, other powers were in decay, most conspicuously the Ottoman Empire. Ottoman lands were both diverse and vulnerable. Russia had long coveted control of the narrow waters linking the Black Sea to the Aegean: the Bosporus and the Dardanelles. Britain had seized Cyprus, established dominance in Egypt and the Sudan, which were ostensibly under Ottoman rule, and was extending its influence westward from British India into Persia. France had established a protectorate over Morocco and had designs on the Syrian coast. And the Ottoman Empire's foothold in Europe involved it in the complex and volatile politics of the Balkans, where its territories had been shrinking since Greece had won its war of independence in 1832.

Ethnic Turks controlled the Ottoman Empire, but they constituted less than half of its population and had to manage tensions among its many Greeks, Armenians, Kurds, Slavs, Albanians, Arabs, Persians, and Jews. Lacking modern industry, the empire depended on Europe for finished goods, weapons, loans, and even bankers and administrators to run its finances. When a band of "Young Turks" (see Chapter 2) in the Ottoman army seized control of the government in 1908, there was much talk of importing European liberalism as well, although the new regime quickly evolved into a military oligarchy. Neighbors took advantage of the empire's instability. Austria-Hungary annexed the province of Bosnia; Bulgaria declared its independence; the largely Greek-speaking island of Crete left the empire and became part of Greece; Italy seized the Ottoman province of

Tripolitania (modern-day Libya); and in 1912 a coalition of Balkan states attacked the empire, further reducing its European territories.

The empire endured in part because its rulers had traditionally evaded trouble by canny combinations of concessions, bribes, and force, and in part because Britain and France found it a convenient barrier between Russia and Mediterranean waters. However, neither domestic tranquility nor foreign support was assured. The Young Turks were disposed to modernize, and this meant not only more European technology, such as warships and telegraph lines, but also more ethnic politics.

The government's efforts to "Turkify" institutions and territories inflamed tensions between Turks and other ethnic groups and stimulated nationalist sentiment among such minority groups as Armenians and Arabs. Linkages between discontented groups within the empire and foreign powers amplified Ottoman anxieties. Armenians in the Russian Caucasus provided cross-border encouragement to their fellow Christians in eastern Anatolia, and the British propped up Arab sheiks in Kuwait and along the coast of the Persian Gulf. As seen from Istanbul, Russian and British policies seemed designed to promote divisions within the empire, a technique of imperial domination that the Ottomans themselves had frequently used. The formal alliance between France and Russia and growing signs that Britain was lining up with these powers intensified Ottoman concerns. Harmony among these three powers might render the empire superfluous and lead to its partition. If the Ottoman Empire could no longer get reliable support from Britain and France, it had little choice but to look for assistance to Austria-Hungary, which shared Ottoman anxiety about Slavic nationalism and Russian expansion, and to Germany, which was eager to expand its influence to the southeast.

Another multiethnic empire sprawled across Central Europe, where Germans, Hungarians, Italians, and speakers of several Slavic languages formed the complex mosaic of Austria-Hungary. Governed by the Hapsburg dynasty, Austria-Hungary had evolved a complicated system of power sharing under which advantages accrued to Germans and Hungarians. Once a rival of Prussia, Austria-Hungary had gradually become the satellite of Prussian-dominated Germany. The economies of the two empires complemented each other. Austria-Hungary supplied Germany's expanding industry and population with food, horses, metals, glass, and other essential goods; Germany supplied Austria-Hungary with credit, textiles, steel, and finished products. German speakers constituted about a quarter of the empire's population and dominated its economic and cultural institutions. Above all, the two states were united by shared anxieties about Slavs in general and Russia in particular. Russia's size and resources made it appear formidable despite its humiliation by Japan and its internal problems. As long as it could maintain domestic tranquility, Russia seemed certain to become stronger in the future. Should it ever become the focus of the growing nationalistic sentiments of the Slavs of Eastern Europe, the balance of power in Eastern Europe would shift markedly.

Thus Germany, Austria-Hungary, and the Ottoman Empire shared the common goal of containing Russia. Russia, for its part, had no desire to be contained, but neither did it have any immediate ambition for territorial expansion. After the disastrous war with Japan, Russia was preoccupied with internal challenges: the construction of railroads and steel plants; land and tax reform; the Russification of provinces in which ethnic Russians were a minority, such as Latvia, Finland, and Georgia; and the reconstruction of its army and navy. But industrial expansion and rearmament required foreign loans, and the need for capital helped drive Russia into the arms of France.

France, for its part, was acutely conscious of erosion in its position as a global and a European power. The French Empire was huge, embracing Indochina, most of West Africa, and many islands in the Caribbean and Pacific, but its exotic territories were not nearly as rich as Britain's colonies and dominions. At sea, the French could not hope to challenge the British. On land, they faced a formidable German army to the east. France's population was static; it had to draft nearly all of its young men to maintain an army as large as Germany's, even though the latter typically called only two-thirds of each cohort to the colors. French industry, science, and technology were capable, but leadership generally resided elsewhere. French firms were often smaller than their rivals in Germany, England, or the United States, making it more difficult for them to achieve economies of scale or to find the capital for innovation.

France still possessed great advantages—a rich agricultural sector and diversified economy, a large, well-educated middle class with specialized skills, and abundant capital for investment at home or overseas. Nor did France have the nationality problems of the empires of Eastern Europe. Bretons in the north, Basques in the Pyrenees, and other minorities sometimes resented dictates from Paris, but the leadership of these communities was focused more on the preservation of their languages and cultural traditions than on political autonomy. The main political divisions in France involved the comparatively more tractable issues of left versus right rather than ethnic group versus ethnic group.

Despite these advantages, the French paid more attention to their shortcomings than to their strengths. A low birth rate, the eclipse of French leadership in science and industry, the lost opportunities for empire abroad, and, perhaps above all, the loss to Prussia in the war of 1870 created a sense of insecurity in France that infected both ordinary citizens and statesmen. Alliances with other powers offered some compensation, and the persistent theme in French diplomacy from the turn of the century until the start of World War I was to cooperate with Russia and Britain to contain the greatest threat to French interests, Germany.

The Alliance System

By 1914 all of the major powers of Europe had undertaken treaty obligations to other powers, some open and some secret. Germany, Austria-Hungary, and Italy were bound together since 1882 in what was known from its inception as the Triple Alliance. France and Russia had been allies since 1893. Even Britain, which traditionally avoided formal commitments, had signed a defensive alliance with Japan and obligated itself to defend Belgian neutrality. Although Britain had

TABLE 3.1 The Major Powers Circa 1914					
	Population (in millions)	Army (fully mobilized strength, in millions)	Dreadnoughts (including battle cruisers)	Merchant shipping (in millions of tons)	Steel production (in millions of metric tons)
Germany	67	4.5	18	3.4	17.6
Austria-Hungary	47	3.0	3	0.5	2.6
Ottoman Empire (excluding Egypt)	26	0.3	1		
UK	42	0.7	31	12.4	8.0
France	40	3.8	2	1.6	4.7
Russia	175	4.5	0	1.0	4.9
Italy	36	1.3	3	1.3	0.9
Japan	50	3.0	3	1.7	0.01
United States	92	0.2	10	5.4	23.4

Sources: The Encyclopaedia Britannica, 12th ed. (New York: Encyclopaedia Britannica, 1922) and B. R. Mitchell, International Historical Statistics, Europe 1750–1988, 3rd ed. (New York: Stockton Press, 1992).

no treaty obligations to France or Russia, it had understandings or *ententes* with those powers that created expectations of mutual assistance in the event of war.

Historians have sometimes attributed the war to the alliance system, although that system is probably better understood as a symptom rather than a cause of conflict. The interlocking alliances gave expression to the fears and insecurities of the great powers. Beneath the generally placid appearance of European civilization, diplomats and soldiers perceived a relentless testing of nations and races, much as Darwinian biologists saw an incessant struggle for resources in seemingly tranquil gardens and fields. In fact, political writers sometimes invoked Charles Darwin to justify the ruthless search for national advantage. Competition, it was said, is a universal law of nature, and those who were too delicate to jostle for space would fail like seed stunted by shadow. Darwin, who died in 1882, had made confusing and contradictory remarks about the implications of natural selection for human societies. But his musings, simplified and vulgarized, provided both a rationale and a vocabulary for power politics. The world would belong to the fit, no matter that fitness was a slippery concept and biology an imperfect analog for human social relations.

Fortified by this biological analogy, practitioners of power politics acted in accordance with their expectations about the behavior of their counterparts. Alliances reflected these expectations—some realistic, as in the case of Ottoman concerns about partition, and others less probable, as in the case of German anxieties about Slavic hordes pillaging East Prussia or English fantasies about German invasion. A popular press, eager to sell newspapers, magazines, and books, capitalized on latent fears, as did politicians currying public favor. Sober readers might see the gap between apparition and reality, but the barrage of words about struggle and conflict gradually made the unlikely seem plausible.

Treaty obligations provided several nations with a formal cause of war in August 1914, but when convenient major powers could ignore such commitments. Although a member of the Triple Alliance, Italy held back as its partners, Germany and Austria-Hungary, went to war. Dependent on coal and other raw materials that came by sea, it could ill afford a trade blockade by the Entente's superior navies. With little to gain and much to lose, Italy bided its time until 1915, when it was coaxed into the war by the Allies with promises of Hapsburg and Ottoman territories. For Italy, national interest trumped alliances, and it could have done so for other powers as well. But it was in Austria's interest to suppress the Serbs, and in Russia's to defend them; it was in Germany's interest to lay Russia low, and in France's to check Germany. It was in Britain's interest to deny continental hegemony to Germany, and in Germany's to seek such hegemony, even if by doing so it risked war with England.

The Assassination

The immediate trigger of the war was an act of political terrorism, one of many that litter the late nineteenth and early twentieth centuries. The victims were the heir to the crown of Austria-Hungary, the Archduke Franz Ferdinand, and his wife, Sophie. The date was June 28, 1914. The place was a narrow street in Sarajevo, Bosnia—formerly part of the Ottoman Empire but occupied by Austria-Hungary in 1878. The assassin was captured immediately and proved to be a young nationalist associated with a movement among Bosnia's ethnic Serbs to achieve union with neighboring Serbia. The murder made headlines around the world, but there was little immediate hint that this assassination would lead to a war. During the weeks after the event, however, Austrian leaders resolved to use the incident as an opportunity to assert primacy in the Balkans.

With the explicit approval of its German ally, Austria-Hungary sent an ultimatum to the Serbian government on July 23, demanding humiliating concessions. Serbia accepted all the provisions except for one that appeared to infringe on Serbian sovereignty: a demand that Austria-Hungary participate in Serbia's own inquiry into the assassination plot. Austria-Hungary, again with German encouragement, pronounced the response unacceptable and declared war on July 28. Both Germany and Austria-Hungary appear to have hoped that their quick action would leave Serbia isolated from the support of its principal ally, Russia, although elements in the German government were convinced that a war with Russia, should one occur, might provide Germany with a golden opportunity to strike down an adversary likely to grow more formidable in the future. When Tsar Nicholas II of Russia expressed firm support for Serbia, the German government plunged ahead and on August 1 declared war on Russia. That same day, France, which was committed to Russia's defense, ordered immediate preparations for war (see Map 3.1). Germany, confronting enemies on two fronts, put in motion a war plan developed precisely for such a contingency. The plan, devised in 1905 by the chief of the German general staff, Count Alfred von Schlieffen, called for the bulk of the German forces to move quickly through Belgium, into northern France, and southward toward Paris before Russia could fully mobilize along Germany's eastern frontiers. With or without Belgian permission, German divisions could cross the small nation in a few days and be in northern France before the French could react effectively. This sweeping movement, the Germans hoped, would envelop France's main armies, which would be concentrated along the Franco-German border to the south of the German breakthrough. Cut off from their supplies, those armies would be forced to surrender, and France, stripped of its sword and shield, would have to sue for peace. The victorious German armies could then be transferred by rail to the eastern front, where overwhelming force would be brought to bear against Russia.

Whatever its merits as military strategy, the Schlieffen plan risked a wider war. It could work only if German troops traversed Belgium, but Belgium's neutrality was guaranteed by international treaty, with Britain among the signatories. On August 2, Germany demanded rights of passage from Belgium's government; in response, Britain threatened war if Belgian borders were violated. The following day, Germany tested the English by launching its troops into Belgium; Britain's leadership saw no alternative but to declare war. During the following weeks and months, the war expanded further. Japan, Britain's treaty partner in Asia, joined the Allied cause by the end of August; in October, the Ottoman Empire joined the Central Powers, Germany and Austria-Hungary. If the imperial possessions and dominions of the belligerents are included, over half the land mass of the globe was embroiled in the war by autumn. A continental crisis had become global.

Military History of the Conflict, 1914–1917

In war, as in other complex human undertakings, foresight rarely extends very far. The war plans of all the major powers anticipated lightning-fast campaigns such as in the wars fought by Prussia against Denmark in 1864, Austria in 1866, and France in 1870, each won by decisive battle within weeks. Military doctrine held that, as in chess, the achievement of a superior position by daring and cleverness could place an adversary in checkmate before its forces could be brought to bear. Hence, the war plans of all the major powers emphasized speedy mobilization and rapid offensive action. All sought to execute such plans during the opening weeks of the war, but in every case unanticipated events frustrated their aims. France threw its main forces across the frontier opposite the provinces of Alsace and Lorraine, which had been lost to Germany in 1870. The German command had left this border undermanned in the interests of concentrating its forces in Belgium, but even so the French were stopped and thrown back within days, as much to the surprise of the German general staff as to the French. The casualties were astonishing: One out of every three French soldiers was killed or wounded during the first five months of fighting.

In the north, the main German armies met delays as they moved into and across Belgium. The Belgian army, although pushed back toward the French border, continued to resist, tearing up railroad tracks and blocking roads, which soon became choked with mule-drawn wagons. Then, three weeks after entering Belgium, the advancing German forces collided with a British army near the Belgian city of Mons. The encounter was a shock to both sides. The Germans had not expected the British to move across the Channel so quickly. The British had no clear sense of the size of the German force facing them. The British inflicted heavy losses on their adversaries, but nonetheless had to retreat in the face of overwhelming numbers and the retirement of French forces to the south. Over the next two weeks, the Allied armies fell back at the rate of about twenty miles a day. Within a month German columns had reached the banks of the Marne River, a day's march from Paris. Here, the French commander Joseph Joffre insisted on a counterattack.

The stakes were high. German victory would mean the isolation or loss of Paris. It would also expose the French armies to the east, still reeling from their defeat along the German frontier, to encirclement. Germany's Schlieffen plan, of course, intended exactly that—to bag the French in a pocket east of Paris where they would be cut off from resupply and forced to surrender. But the German position was nearly as precarious as the French. The German forces pouring across Belgium and northern France had moved in several discrete armies to take advantage of the road system. While this had made rapid movement possible, it had also created openings between the German columns into which Allied troops could move. By advancing into these gaps, the French and British could mount counterattacks on the flanks of the German armies and threaten their rear. Meanwhile, along the edge of the German advance, reinforcements arriving from western France threatened the Germans with an enveloping movement of their own.

Joffre's timing proved impeccable. His counterattack exposed the weaknesses in the German position and led the Germans to retreat to a more defensible position just north of the River Aisne, where German troops dug in along high ground. Almost simultaneously, the Germans and the Allies realized that the war of movement in central France was drawing to a temporary halt. Stocks of ammunition had dwindled, and a month of marches and losses had exhausted both sides.

To the north of the main fighting were large expanses of territory that were only lightly held by either party. Once the battle lines in central France stabilized, the thoughts of commanders on both sides turned to this region and especially the French ports along the English Channel. The Allies realized how important they were to the movement of supplies from Britain to France; the Germans recognized that their seizure might cripple Allied activity to the south and afford the opportunity for another grand flanking maneuver. In a race for position, the opposing armies seized what advantage they could, ending up in a jagged and almost continuous line of trenches from the scene of the fighting along the Aisne, through northern France and Belgium, and ending at the North Sea near the eastern mouth of the Channel.

Hulton-Deutsch Collection/Corbis

These French troops were recovering from an artillery barrage during action on the western front. Photos of the dead were deemed dangerous to morale and seldom appeared in newspapers.

Trench Warfare

The line separating the combatants in northern France and Belgium gives us many of the most durable terms and images of World War I. We can readily call to mind images of doughboys with fixed bayonets "going over the top" on dashes through a desolate "no man's land" on their way to seize enemy positions or, more often, to die vainly in the attempt. But for every day of such action, scores were spent building and reinforcing the trenches and defensive positions that housed and protected soldiers over the years of stalemate. Engineers laid down tons of barbed wire, built pillboxes for machine guns, poured concrete for blockhouses and bunkers, and built systems to drain soggy fields and marshes. Where feasible, they dug communication trenches between the front lines and rear areas for the movement of runners, stretcher bearers, and relief forces. Where the soil was too marshy for trenches, miles of duckboard were laid. Artillery placements were dug into hillsides opposite the enemy lines two or three miles from the front, from which shells could be fired without exposing the gunners to observation and counterfire. Roads were built to transfer supplies from railheads to forward sites and to expedite the deployment of reserves. Thousands of laborers maintained these roads, which needed constant attention because of heavy traffic and shelling. England and France recruited battalions of Chinese, Indian, and African workers to perform this dangerous work; the Germans dragooned laborers from the occupied territories in Belgium and northern France. Railways were extended to facilitate the movement of troops and supplies. Just beyond artillery range of the enemy, where the rail lines ended, sprawling tent cities sheltered headquarters units, field hospitals, ammunition dumps, and thousands of tons of provisions for troops and horses.

Trenches were as old as siege warfare, but never before had field armies settled into such elaborate positions for such an extended period of time. As season passed into season, troops "improved" their quarters—they dug deeper, created underground bunkers, and outfitted them with furniture from abandoned villages and farms. Soldiers might plant flowers in spring for a bit of color; some kept dogs and cats for companionship and to suppress the rats. But many positions were hard to improve. Where fighting was active, burial details could not keep up with the supply of human and equine corpses, and these became the meals of rodents and maggots. Lice, which were carriers of typhus, found ideal conditions among troops who could not bathe for weeks on end. In low-lying areas, such as much of Flanders, waste-contaminated water stagnated in trenches, causing trench foot and, in cold weather, frostbite. Shell holes could fill with water and become deathtraps for heavily laden soldiers seeking cover. Even in quiet sectors, long weeks of routine and boredom were punctuated by sudden death from sporadic shellfire or sniper bullets.

The frontlines of October 1914 remained essentially stable for the next three years, despite repeated efforts by both sides to break through. Conditions favored defense. The continuity of the trench systems from the Channel to the Swiss border made it impossible to maneuver around the enemy, as the Germans had sought to do at the outset of the war. Frontal attacks across the no man's land entailed huge losses. Machine guns, spewing hundreds of bullets a minute, swept the battlefield from protected positions. Barbed wire, ditches, shell holes, and mud slowed assaults, as did the heavy packs the soldiers had to carry. Shrapnel-firing artillery could cut down dozens of men with a single shot, and both sides deployed thousands of such guns along the front—on average, about one every thirty yards. Attackers who, through extraordinary luck or valor, succeeded in taking enemy trenches often found it impossible to hold them. Whereas attackers had to rely on human and animal to move ammunition and heavy guns across the torn-up battlefield, defenders could rely on well-prepared systems of rail and road for resupply and reinforcements.

Commanders explored several methods for breaking the stalemate. They saturated battlefields with ferocious shellfire before ordering infantry forward. A British and French offensive along the Somme in July 1916, for example, commenced with a seven-day artillery barrage that dropped a ton of steel on every square yard of the opposing German lines. But such barrages had little effect against deeply dug trenches and gave the defenders ample notice of the impending assault. British troops suffered sixty thousand casualties the day they went over the top at the Somme, and the Allied dead and wounded totaled more than six hundred twenty thousand in subsequent attacks during that six-month-long offensive, all for insignificant gains in territory. Later in the war, attackers adopted the tactic of unleashing a "hurricane" barrage to tear holes in barbed wire during the hours prior to the attack and then laying down a moving curtain of artillery fire just a hundred yards or so ahead of the advancing infantry to suppress small-arms and machine-gun fire. Despite occasional successes, such "moving barrages" were hard to coordinate with infantry. Once troops went over the top, they lost contact with their rear, and artillery spotters could rarely make sense of what was happening on the battlefield through the dust and smoke of battle. A moving barrage that advanced too quickly gave the defenders time to emerge from their bunkers and fire on attackers; a barrage that moved too slowly could retard advancing troops.

Poisonous gases, which were first used by the Germans in 1915 and were quickly adopted by the French and British, added extra terror to the fighting without much altering the stalemate. Gas clouds dissipated rapidly. Shifting winds could turn them into indiscriminate killers, as dangerous for attackers as for defenders. And both sides quickly equipped their troops with masks that chemically neutralized noxious agents. Another new technology, the tank, at first proved little more effective than gases. First used in significant numbers by the British in 1916, tanks had some local successes but were imperfect weapons. Only toward the end of the war did the generals learn how to overcome strongly prepared defenses. For the Germans, the key was meticulous preparation. Gunners painstakingly registered their artillery on targets before the opening barrage, and "shock" troops, carefully rehearsed on replicas of the battlefield, led the assault. For the Allies, the solution was a combination of technology and tactics. Tanks, they discovered, could be breakthrough weapons if they were massed in large numbers and sent forward in company with infantry units. The tanks could shield the advancing infantry from small-arms fire, while the infantry could protect the tanks from close-range attack by concealed antitank guns. By the end of the war, the Allies had begun to use ground-strafing aircraft in these coordinated assaults. Unlike heavy guns, which moved forward ponderously, ground-attack aircraft could keep up with a shifting battlefront, thus affording the advancing troops support even as they advanced beyond the range of fixed artillery. These innovations in tactics and technology were to inform military thinking over the coming decades and make the Second World War a war of movement. But until the final months of the First World War, troops in defensive positions generally had insurmountable advantages over those on the attack, as was demonstrated again and again in graveyard-filling battles in northern France and Flanders.

Stasis at Sea

The war at sea proved as frustrating as the campaigns along the western front. During the opening months of the war, the Allies hunted down and destroyed most of the German warships that were on patrol in open waters. These were not numerous. Germany had concentrated its warships in the North Sea and the Baltic before the war, where they were practically invulnerable behind the shield of submarines and mine-fields. Germany's strategy was to husband its

GLOBAL Technologies

The Tank

The tanks of World War I were ungainly but recognizable ancestors of the machines still in use today. They borrowed caterpillar drives from tractors for climbing power and the ability to cross trenches. They wore a sheath of steel plate to protect occupants and carried machine guns and cannons for use against blockhouses and breastworks. Unlike modern tanks, however, they were conceived as siege weapons—akin to the "turtles" and other mobile structures used to protect soldiers advancing against fortifications in antiquity and the middle ages. Indeed, the tanks first deployed by the British in 1916 could barely keep up with infantry. Powered by one hundred horsepower engines, the twenty-eight-ton behemoths crawled across battlefields, easy targets for artillery fire. Needing fuel every twenty-five miles, their task was merely to help the infantry seize opposing trenches so that horse cavalry might break through to the enemy's rear. At first they were not even competent in that modest role because many broke down or were swallowed by muddy shell craters before reaching their goal. By 1918, however, stronger engines, sturdier designs, and improved tactics had turned these white elephants into a key element in the Allied offensive that ended the war. Used in mass and supported by aircraft and mobile artillery, tanks punched holes in the strongest German defenses. The lesson was not lost on observers. During the 1920s, military strategists, especially in Russia and Germany, reworked the original notion of the tank as siege engine into the modern concept of tank as armored cavalry— a role that would make it a dominant force in key battles of World War II, the Arab-Israeli wars, and the wars in Iraq.

battle fleet until such time as it might, through cunning or a British error, achieve local superiority. The British sought to keep the German fleet bottled up in the North Sea and to engage it with superior forces should it emerge. Above all, the British sought to protect their substantial advantage in naval strength. One cabinet minister described John Jellicoe, the commander of the British fleet, as the only person "who could lose the war in an afternoon."[2]

Jellicoe could lose the war, but he could not win it. Germany depended on its army rather than its navy for survival. The loss of its dreadnoughts might be a great blow to German morale, but it would not alter the strategic balance much. Britain, by contrast, depended on its navy to survive. A power that could

[2]Richard Hough, *The Great War at Sea, 1914–1918* (New York: Oxford University Press, 1983), p. 290.

Bettmann/Corbis

Tanks played an important role during the final battles of World War I after generals learned their strengths and limitations. Here a British tank lumbers through a French village in the summer of 1918. Note the fallen horse beside the road. Was the photo composed to suggest that tanks would be the cavalry of the future?

control the seas around Britain would be able to starve the British people and strangle Britain's industries in months. These considerations dictated cautious naval tactics. Jellicoe kept most of his dreadnoughts at anchor in protected home waters, making sorties only to deflect occasional German raids. The Germans, too, had to be cautious. If concentrated, the British fleet was decidedly superior to the German. The best the Germans could hope for was to erode the British advantage by engaging the British piecemeal. In the meantime, the very existence of a powerful threat in the North Sea would tie down the bulk of the British navy, including destroyers and cruisers needed to protect commerce in the North Atlantic and Mediterranean. The German fleet likewise posed a constant threat to Russia in the Baltic, where German superiority not only halted Russian shipping but created the possibility of an amphibious assault behind the Russian lines.

These conservative strategies resulted in a maritime equivalent of trench warfare. Opposing battle fleets rusted in fortified harbors while mines and submarines took a toll on patrols in the no man's waters of the North Sea. The dreadnaughts, upon which so much money had been lavished, saw limited action. In January 1915, British and German battle cruisers met at the Dogger Bank, a fishing area near the center of the North Sea. Poor communication between British vessels gave the outgunned German squadron time to escape with the loss of only one vessel, although ships on both sides suffered serious damage.

In the spring of 1917, a far larger battle occurred, involving most of the British and German warships in the North Sea—about two hundred and fifty in all. The Germans sallied out of their ports in hopes of luring a part of the British fleet into a trap just northeast of the Jutland Peninsula. The British, who had deciphered the German naval codes, knew that something was afoot without understanding the magnitude of the German operation. They dispatched their two principal squadrons to intercept what they thought was a modest force. Over the course of an afternoon and evening, the opposing fleets met in a confusing melee that ended when the German fleet slipped away after giving somewhat worse than it got. Although the battle proved the excellence of the German ships, sailors, and guns, the German command understood that it had narrowly evaded a catastrophic defeat and kept its large warships in or near port for the remainder of the war.

The War in the South and East

The stalemates in northern France and the North Sea led the Allies to try to out-flank their enemies in the south, thinking that Ottoman Turkey might prove a soft target. In 1915, the Allies attempted to seize control of the Dardanelles by landings on the Gallipoli Peninsula. The idea was to knock the Ottoman Empire out of the war, link up with Russian forces in the Black Sea, and use the Danube River to conduct naval operations against Austria-Hungary. The campaign failed when minefields and submarines disrupted Allied naval operations, and Turkish troops held the invaders to narrow beachheads beneath Gallipoli's rugged mountains. After suffering a quarter of a million casualties, Allied troops took to the sea. Many were redeployed in an equally frustrating adventure at Salonika, a Greek port that appeared to offer the Allies a lane for resupplying their isolated ally, Serbia. Instead, the Allied force found itself bottled up by Bulgarian units holding the mountains north of the city, and Salonika became, in the words of German journalists, the world's largest internment camp.

Later in the war, the British tried another way of putting pressure on the Ottoman Empire—by exploiting the discontent of its Arab population. From 1916 to 1918, modest British forces cooperated with Arabs who were seeking to remove Palestine and Trans-jordan from Ottoman control. The effort won lasting fame for the British officer who advised the Arabs, T. E. Lawrence, but created a long-term dilemma for Britain because Britain made contradictory promises to the regions' Arabs and Jews.

The largest and most costly effort to outflank the Central Powers commenced in 1915, after the Allies persuaded Italy to enter the war through promises of postwar concessions in the Tyrol, the Balkans, Africa, and Anatolia. A vigorous Italian attack quickly stuttered along Italy's rugged border with Austria, and for the next two years Austrian and Italian troops fought a war as vicious and frustrating as that in northern France. The seesaw fighting yielded little advantage to either side until the final months of the war, when the Austrian army began to disintegrate.

While troops in Western Europe, Italy, and Gallipoli fought intense battles that yielded only yards of territory, armies in Eastern Europe moved to and fro over hundreds of miles of field, forest, and mountain. In part this reflected differences in equipment. The divisions of the Russian and Austrian armies were numerous, but poorly armed. Geography was even more important. The borders separating the belligerents in Eastern Europe were too long for continuous fortification, and so it was always possible to find locations where light defenses offered the opportunity for an advance. Extended thrusts into enemy territory could expose units in adjacent regions to flank attack or envelopment and expose the advancing armies to counterattack along their supply lines. Consequently, maneuvers proved more important than static defenses or overall numbers.

Agility required alert leadership, training, and a capacity to shuttle troops quickly along railways and roads. This became clear in the first months of the war. The German general staff had concentrated forces on the western front in accordance with the Schlieffen plan, leaving its border with Russian Poland lightly defended. In August 1914, two Russian armies crossed this border and advanced into Germany's easternmost province, East Prussia. Despite their great advantage in numbers, the Russian armies were defeated piecemeal by their more mobile opponent, with the southernmost Russian army being almost entirely destroyed in the Battle of Tannenberg. Later that year, a clumsy Austrian advance into Russian Poland resulted in an equally resounding defeat, this one handed out by the Russians.

Advance, overextension, and counterattack became the pattern on the eastern front. In the north, German armies had the advantage and established control over Russia's northwestern provinces. In the Balkans, a joint German-Austrian army occupied Serbia in 1915. Bulgaria, seeing an opportunity for territorial gains, cast its lot with the Central Powers. Along the border between Austria and Russia, Russian armies had the advantage and, in an offensive during the summer of 1916, seemed poised to knock Austria out of the war. So, at least, thought the leaders of Romania, who chose this opportunity to join the Allies. But the advancing Russian armies soon outran their supplies, and German units stiffened Austrian resistance. In the fall of 1916 a German-Austrian force swept through Romania, seizing its oil fields and grain supplies.

By the beginning of 1917, after two and a half years of devastating battles, neither side could feel confident about its prospects for victory. The Central Powers had won many tactical successes. In the west, their armies still occupied most of Belgium and much of northern France. In the east, they had achieved control over vast territories and had managed to connect Berlin and Istanbul by rail. Serbia was occupied; Romania was defeated. But the cost to the Central Powers in lives and material had been enormous, and the grinding losses were undermining their ability and will to fight.

Home Fronts

The war had become a contest of endurance that tested not simply the qualities of soldiers and strategists, but the resources of entire societies. This made World War I different from earlier conflicts. The war could neither be left to mercenaries nor paid for with quickly arranged loans. Rather, it called for single-minded effort and an unprecedented coordination of resources, production, and finance. The pressure to achieve greater efficiency led all the belligerents to centralize power in government. It imposed heavy burdens on civilians, many of whom saw their families torn apart, their way of life disrupted, and their liberties pared away. World War I was, in the phrase of Germany's chief of staff, Erich Ludendorff, a "total war."

Total War

The Allies enjoyed advantages in the factors that were critical to such a marathon: human and animal resources, raw materials, agriculture, industrial production, and money. The Allied armies suffered heavier casualties than the armies of the Central Powers, but the Allies had a larger population from which to recruit. To its foes, Russia's human reserves seemed limitless, although by 1917 even Russia was finding it hard to meet calls for new troops and began to train women for combat duty. Alone among the major belligerents, Britain was able to put off conscription and rely on volunteers, in part because of a skillful wartime recruiting campaign that reached into Britain's dominions. Canada, Australia, and New Zealand contributed significant numbers of volunteers, and India supplied willing mercenaries, especially Sikhs and Gurkhas. France found it harder to fill out its battalions, but like Britain it could draw on its overseas departments and colonies for help, especially Algeria and Senegal. Nearly thirty thousand Senegalese soldiers served in France during the war. Some volunteered, but most were pressured to enlist by village chiefs, who faced imprisonment if they failed to meet French quotas.

All of the European belligerents faced labor shortages as millions of workers, many with essential skills, went off to war. The Allies could draw on much of the globe for labor. Blockaded from the oceans, the Central Powers had to look closer to home. Children, the aged, and the wounded undertook light work in fields and factories. Belgians found jobs in German war plants after Belgium's ports fell inactive; Russian prisoners of war won parole by working in Austrian fields and German factories. Women became crucial to production across Europe. By the end of the war, women held 55 percent of all industrial jobs in Germany (compared to 35 percent in 1914) and about 36 percent of industrial jobs in Britain and France (compared with about 28 percent in 1914). Despite intensive efforts to maintain production, however, shortages of labor crippled the economies of the belligerents. By 1918 British factories were producing only 87 percent of their prewar quantity of goods; German output fell more dramatically—to 69 percent of prewar levels.

Castelnau/George Eastman House/Getty Images

France and Britain both drew heavily on their colonies for labor and soldiers during the war. These infantrymen, resting behind the lines, were among tens of thousands of Senegalese soldiers recruited, and sometimes coerced, to serve in France's army.

Food was another critical problem for the Central Powers. Although they controlled enough agricultural land to make self-sufficiency plausible, they lacked the labor and fertilizer needed to make the land productive. Prisoners, women, children, and old men might replace young men in the fields, but they could not replace farm horses. Austria-Hungary alone lost 650,000 of these animals in the fighting. Nor could the Central Powers maintain the fertility of their fields. Nitric acid was essential to the production of both explosives and fertilizers, and the demand for explosives left little for agricultural use. Consequently, the yield of crops per acre fell. England, France, and Italy faced some of the same problems, but these countries had access to meat and grain from overseas. Food prices rose in Britain, for example, but pronounced shortages did not occur until the final year of the war—two years after they had become severe in Germany. Russia alone among the Allies experienced food shortages comparable to those of Central Europe, but this was more because of shortcomings in distribution than because of lost production. Malnutrition became common in the cities of Central and Eastern Europe, as did diseases such as tuberculosis and dysentery, which flourish among undernourished populations.

Food was not the only essential material in short supply. Before the war, the economies of the European nations were highly interdependent. England, for example, was Germany's largest trading partner, and Germany was Russia's. Europe as a whole depended on trade to obtain such critical materials as rubber and cotton. All the belligerents suffered economic dislocations as trade patterns altered. The Allies found it difficult to replace the technologically sophisticated products of Germany: high-quality glass for binoculars and range finders, synthetic dyes, pharmaceuticals, and some specialized machine tools. But the Central Powers faced far more disabling shortages of basic materials: copper, nitrates, rubber, and cotton. Shortages disrupted production and compelled Germany to use imperfect substitutes. Clothing was made from paper; wood and iron wheels replaced rubber tires. Inadequate transportation could be as crippling as shortages. Field armies had first claim on locomotives and boxcars, and the steel necessary to make rails was being diverted to guns, and so railroads deteriorated. By 1917, the Austrian and Russian rail systems were nearing collapse, leaving factories idle, cities without coal and grain, and armies without munitions.

Money was also essential for war. Troops had to be paid; factories had to be built; planes, guns, and raw materials had to be bought. The British government, for example, spent more during the war than it had spent during the two centuries prior to 1914. It increased income and estate taxes and imposed a stiff tax on business profits arising from war orders, but even so, the public debt rose by a factor of ten during the war. And Britain was comparatively fortunate. Its large foreign investments and accumulated wealth gave it a cushion that other countries lacked. France borrowed heavily in England and the United States to finance its armies. The other powers, lacking comparable wealth or credit, printed additional money, with the predictable effect of stimulating inflation. Such policies proved corrosive to the social order. Skilled workers could sometimes keep up with inflation by parlaying their expertise into wage increases, but most workers and government clerks lacked such leverage. Well-to-do citizens who had made war loans to the state discovered that they would be repaid, if at all, in devalued marks or rubles. Those with nest eggs were penalized for their thrift as the purchasing power of savings wasted away.

Civilian Morale and the Control of Internal Dissent

The endless casualty lists, rationing, taxes, and inflation eroded public confidence in governments and their policies. Enthusiasm for war, which had been widespread in 1914, gave way to disenchantment and then to cynicism. Those in the trenches felt that they were sacrificing their lives for shirkers and profiteers. Wage earners felt that greedy employers were depriving them of the necessities of life. The middle classes saw their savings and their plans for the future destroyed. Businessmen found it impossible to plan ahead because of shortages, uncertain market conditions, and growing radicalism among their employees. City dwellers resented farmers, who had food to eat and to sell on black markets. Farmers resented officials, who confiscated their crops, horses, and sons. Governments promised that victory would resolve all problems, as the defeated could be compelled to pay for the war. But as the seasons passed and the stalemate continued, these promises lost credibility.

Multinational states were especially vulnerable to internal division. In Austria-Hungary, minority groups such as the Czechs and the Croats saw an opportunity for greater autonomy, while German and Magyar elites competed for power and resources. Many of Russia's Poles and Balts welcomed the German armies as liberators, and Polish nationalists such as Józef Pilsudski sought concessions about Poland's future from both sides as the price of cooperation. In the Ottoman Empire, Arabs rebelled against their Turkish rulers, while in eastern Anatolia, Turkish troops massacred at least half a million Armenian civilians suspected of harboring sympathies for their fellow Armenians in Russia. In Ireland, nationalists rose up against British rule in the Easter Rebellion of 1916; in Quebec, French speakers rioted against a Canadian government dominated by English speakers. Divisions along ethnic lines were not confined to belligerent states. Irish and German communities in the United States often sympathized openly with the Central Powers, and Woodrow Wilson's government harbored anxieties about internal disorder should its policy tilt too far toward the Allies.

Governments responded to economic and political instability by centralizing power and repressing dissent. Radical political parties were outlawed, labor unions were stripped of the right to strike, churches were enlisted in the war effort, newspapers were censored, and propaganda offices were created to mold public opinion. Public dissent or disorder provoked draconian responses. France, Austria, and Russia summarily executed mutinous soldiers; Germany and Russia drafted striking workers and sent them to the front.

Tensions between civilian and military authorities arose in all parts of Europe. Regions of France near the front were brought under martial law, and French generals, who were fundamentally suspicious of politicians, denied civilian officials even basic information about their plans. Under German law, the Kaiser was the nation's supreme warlord, but authority soon passed from him to the general staff, and later to the two generals who had won public acclaim for repelling the Russians at Tannenberg, Paul von Hindenburg and Erich Ludendorff. In Austria, power also shifted from the monarch to the generals, although they, in turn, found themselves increasingly dependent on their German counterparts, who controlled the flow of war loans and munitions.

Total war also meant unprecedented government involvement in economic life, even in a society such as Britain, where small government was an article of faith. Government spending ballooned. The necessity of maintaining millions of men under arms shifted investment from consumer goods to war materials. State borrowing squeezed credit markets, and the military's need for ships and boxcars led to greater government control of transportation systems. Government orders force-fed the growth of some industries, such as the production of chemicals, aircraft, and trucks, while shortages of labor, raw materials, and shipping pinched others, such as textiles. High government expenditures and shortages created inflation and ultimately led to rationing and controls on wages and prices.

State management of the economy proved relatively successful in Britain and France, but much less so in Germany, Austria, and Russia. The challenge facing the Western powers was smaller because they enjoyed wealth, credit, and overseas links that the Eastern powers lacked. English and French political leaders also gave a high priority to maintaining workers' living standards at close to their prewar levels. Other European states failed to do so, with disastrous consequences for morale and productivity. Food rations in Austria and Russia failed to meet subsistence standards. Starving civilians turned to crime and the black market to survive; soldiers turned to brigandage and plunder. By 1917, Austria and Russia had to use frontline troops to protect granaries from their own hungry citizens.

Influenza

As in many previous conflicts, disease proved a more efficient killer than weapons. Neither soldiers in the field nor refugees could protect themselves from the lice that carried typhus; epidemics of the often-deadly virus swept across Eastern Europe where living conditions were especially bad. Rates of venereal diseases soared around army camps. Malnutrition and the breakdowns in sanitation opened the door to many other diseases, both water-borne (dysentery, typhoid, cholera) and air-borne (tuberculosis).

Far and away the greatest killer, though, was influenza. Long a common winter illness, it ordinarily killed the infirm but rarely the young and healthy. In March 1918, however, a new and far more vicious strain broke out among troops living in overcrowded tents and barracks. Although sometimes called the "Spanish flu," the disease appears to have originated in Kansas, perhaps when a virus among birds mutated into a form that could infect and be transmitted by humans. Whatever its source, the infection spread rapidly along the routes of trains and ships that carried soldiers from camp to camp. By the beginning of summer, it had made a first sweep through the armies of the belligerents; a second wave broke on civilian populations across the world during the fall of 1918. Rather than giving victims a week of aches and pains, as influenza typically does, it could take the unlucky from work to wake in days. No one knows for sure how many died of influenza during this great pandemic, but by the end of 1919, when the worst was over, deaths in the United States numbered 675,000. In most of the world, statistical records were not kept. Estimates based on extrapolation from scattered sources place the global toll between twenty million and one hundred million. Even the lowest estimates are double the loss of life among soldiers during the entire war.

Was the pandemic traceable to the war? The mutation of a virus is a biological accident, and influenza pandemics come and go in war and peace. An uncomplicated "yes" to the question is impossible, but at the very least the war was an enabler of the pandemic. It created ideal conditions for a respiratory virus to catch hold and spread: overcrowded army camps and transport vessels, rapid movements of large numbers of potential carriers from one part of the world to another, and widespread displacements of civilians. At the same time, war crippled the power of public health agencies to respond to the threat through coordinated international efforts.

Looking at the other side of the coin, did the influenza pandemic alter the course of the war? Of course, it inflicted incalculable human suffering and substantial economic costs. But the indiscriminate cruelty that made the disease so awful for millions of individuals rendered it less powerful as an agent of political or social change. During the final months of the war, it sapped the energies of all belligerents by decimating troops and production workers. It contributed to a

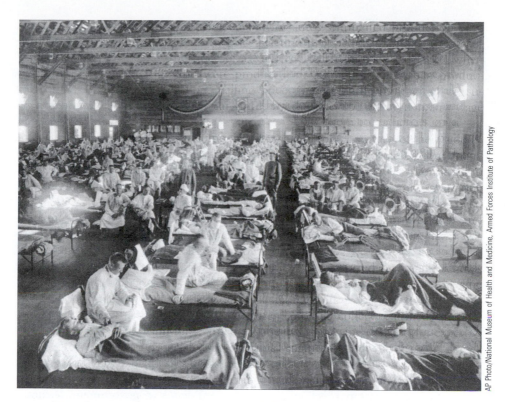

Some of the first reports of a new and vicious influenza came from Camp Funston, Kansas, where this photo was taken in 1918. Crowded army camps created ideal conditions both for the rapid transmission of influenza and for the propagation of secondary infections, such as pneumonia.

general sense of exhaustion, and in the peace that followed, burdened victors and vanquished alike. If the Central Powers were more vulnerable to demoralization, it was not because influenza struck them harder but because their citizens already suffered greater privations than those of the West.

Global Economic Repercussions

In parts of the world, war meant prosperity, as exports from Britain and Germany dropped precipitously. Industries in other parts of the world expanded to fill orders to fill the gap. Japan and India saw booms in the steel, shipbuilding, and textile industries. In South Africa, Brazil, and Argentina, light industry expanded to replace goods that could no longer be imported from Britain. The war also raised the prices of raw materials and foods bringing windfall profits to Argentinean ranchers and the farmers of Canada's wheat belt, to the nitrate mines of Chile and the tin mines of Malaya, to Brazilian harvesters of rubber and Indian exporters of jute.

Nowhere were the profits greater than in the United States, where farms and mines produced a broad range of essential commodities. With an already huge industrial capacity, a well-developed transportation network, a large and relatively well-educated workforce, and capital for expansion, the U.S. economy was able to accommodate rapid growth. Most notably the war created a significant role for U.S. firms in high-tech industries. The United States had previously relied on Germany for many sophisticated products—organic chemicals used in dyes and fine glasses used in binoculars, for example—but it now had to make these products itself. Private firms rushed to build the research laboratories necessary to develop these lucrative products, and the government promoted the effort by seizing German-owned patents and making them available to domestic firms.

The war also altered the financial situation of the United States. In 1914, the United States had been an industrial giant with enormous overseas debts, especially to England. Foreign loans had financed much of the industrial development of the nineteenth century. The war turned the tables. The European powers liquidated many of their investments in the United States to meet the costs of the war. They paid inflated prices for U.S. products and borrowed money from U.S. banks when domestic sources of credit were exhausted. By the end of the war, New York rivaled London as a financial center, and the United States had become the world's great creditor nation. Europe's catastrophe meant opportunity for much of the rest of the world.

The duration of the war testifies to the strength of European institutions and the weakness of those who controlled them. Each of the belligerents could draw upon deep reserves of national feeling and public confidence in government, accumulated over years of economic and social progress. That goodwill eroded at different rates in the different states. England, France, and Germany had the means to meet the basic needs of their civilians and soldiers through years of fighting, whereas Austria, Russia, and Italy quickly exhausted their modest resources.

The sustained conduct of the war was, by almost any measure, irrational. The human and material costs were so great that no realistic calculation of reparations or territorial gains could promise adequate compensation. Yet the war continued. The very magnitude of the losses suffered in the initial stages of the conflict made it politically and psychologically difficult for either side to accept anything less than total victory Each year promised new possibilities for triumph; each year's losses raised the price of defeat. And so neither side took seriously peace proposals offered by third parties. A war that began as an exercise in the quick and efficient use of force to secure limited ends had become a war of survival.

Stalemates Broken, 1917–1918

The stalemate of 1915–1916 prompted desperate measures. On the western front, the Allies, frustrated by their failures in Mesopotamia, Gallipoli, and Italy, planned great new offensives in hopes of using shellfire and numbers to break through the German defenses. The Germans, in contrast, resolved to concentrate their efforts in 1917 on a submarine war against shipping, which was vital to the British war effort.

The Offensives of 1917

The Allied offensives were abysmal failures. The French attacks broke against expertly designed German defenses. In Flanders, the English fought not just Germans but also nature. Heavy rains rendered troops, horses, and tanks practically immobile in mud. As usual, the attackers suffered higher casualties than the defenders, and in the end the Allied armies emerged weaker for their efforts. Mutinies among French troops became widespread during the spring, with entire units refusing orders to advance. Only by suspending offensive activity could the French command restore discipline.

The German strategy for 1917 ultimately proved even more self-destructive. Submarines had been used by both sides since the beginning of the war, but the submarines of 1914 were slow, small, and of limited range. Tethered to their bases by the need for frequent refueling, they operated mostly in coastal waters, where they could position themselves along the approaches to harbors. Their use was further handicapped by prewar agreements under which raiders were obliged to warn merchant vessels before attacking. These rules deprived submarines of their main advantages, concealment and surprise.

In 1915 Germany, citing Britain's violations of international agreements in its blockade, had declared the waters around Britain a zone of unrestricted submarine warfare in which all vessels would be subject to attack without warning. However, Germany's submarine force was too small to halt British commerce, and the diplomatic cost was high. Following the sinking of the passenger liners *Lusitania* in May and *Arabic* in August, American protests about the loss of civilian life became so intense that Germany curtailed submarine operations in the North Atlantic.

By 1917, however, Germany had expanded and improved its fleet of U-boats and was willing to assume greater diplomatic risk. German admirals believed they could compel Britain to seek peace and dismissed possible U.S. intervention as irrelevant if the Atlantic could be made unsafe for troopships and supplies. In February 1917, Germany again unleashed its U-boats, with dramatic effect. During the first three months of the new campaign, German submarines sank more than two million tons of ships, about 5 percent of the world's ocean-going cargo tonnage.

Had losses continued at the same rate, England might well have been forced to seek peace within a year because new construction could not possibly keep pace. A solution was found in June, however, when, at the insistence of British Prime Minister David Lloyd George, a reluctant Admiralty instituted a convoy system for ferrying supplies to England. Allied naval authorities considered convoys, which had been used since antiquity to protect merchant ships from raiders, to be unwieldy and vulnerable. They were slow, required painstaking coordination, and tied up warships in escort duty. But they also exposed submariners to counterattack as soon as their presence became known. The results were impressive. Whereas one in every four vessels that entered or left British harbors was sunk in April 1917, by autumn the monthly rate were cut to about one in a hundred.

The United States: From "Too Proud to Fight" to "Over There"

Not only did the German U-boat offensive fail to stop British trade, but it also brought the United States into the war. From 1914 to 1917, the United States had pursued a policy of neutrality. President Woodrow Wilson declared that his country was "too proud to fight." Although his policy was framed in moral terms, it reflected political, economic, and military realities. The sympathies of American voters were divided between the Central and Allied Powers, and up until 1917 most Americans believed neutrality to be the wisest course. Not only did the United States lack the will to fight, it also lacked the means. Its navy, although large, was untested and defended two long coastlines. Its army was minuscule— smaller than that of Bulgaria or Romania. Germany's occupation of Belgium in 1914 and its submarine attacks on passenger liners and neutral ships during 1915 had stimulated modest American efforts to prepare for war, but the presidential election of 1916 had given Wilson a mandate for continued neutrality.

Germany changed the political equation by renewing unrestricted submarine warfare in February 1917. Once again, as in 1915, U-boats were claiming American lives and property on a regular basis. A colossal blunder by the German foreign office heightened tensions just weeks before the submarine campaign began. The German foreign secretary, Arthur Zimmerman, offered Mexico the states of Texas, New Mexico, and Arizona in exchange for Mexican participation in a war against the United States. The offer, which made its way into the press, provided one more reason for Americans to think that they had a stake in the outcome of Europe's war. In mid-February, the United States broke diplomatic relations with Germany; on April 6, Congress passed a war resolution.

It would be months before American troops actually entered the fighting and a year before they reached France in significant numbers. Even then, the U.S. troops were of uneven quality and depended on Britain and France for gas masks, artillery, and planes. Nevertheless, the United States provided the Allies with tremendous new industrial capacity, large new supplies of food, much-needed merchant and escort ships, and plentiful credit. It promised eventually to field an army the size of those of the main combatants. The effect on Allied morale was immediate.

Russia's Revolutions

Allied morale was much in need of shoring up in the spring of 1917, and not just because of casualties on the western front and losses of merchant shipping. The war in the east was going badly. German armies had occupied Russia's western-most provinces and, by the end of 1916, had killed, wounded, or captured over five million Russian soldiers. Although the Russian economy had carried the burden of war more successfully than had Austria-Hungary's, it was beginning to face some of the same crippling problems: inflation, strikes, shortages of rolling stock, and breakdowns in the distribution of goods. And unlike Austria, Russia did not share a border with a richer and more powerful ally.

Of all the major powers, Russia's political system was the most fragile. The country had undergone a political upheaval during its war with Japan when large elements of its middle class had joined workers in the streets and successfully demanded political reforms from Tsar Nicholas II. Those reforms had created some of the trappings of constitutional monarchy, including an elected assembly, or Duma, but little of the reality. Many professionals and business leaders remained unsatisfied with the new arrangements because the tsar retained sovereignty, and they advocated more thorough liberal reforms along the lines of the British system.

Meanwhile, advocates of more radical change had enlarged their following. Socialist political parties, among them the Mensheviks and Bolsheviks, had made inroads among factory workers between 1905 and 1914, especially in the capital city of St. Petersburg, where about a quarter of Russian factory production was centered. Another socialist party, the Socialist Revolutionaries, found support among Russia's peasants, many of whom were discontented because land reforms promised in 1861 by Alexander II had never been carried out.

Nationalist movements among Finns, Balts, Poles, Georgians, and other minorities who were seeking greater autonomy further divided the empire. An economic expansion after the Russo-Japanese War had helped keep a lid on dissent, and in Russia as elsewhere in Europe most political groups had suspended their calls for domestic reform during the first year or two of the war. But disappointments in the field and growing economic problems exacerbated social divisions and undermined confidence in the tsar and his government.

Tensions reached a flash point early in 1917 when a walkout by women textile workers in St. Petersburg grew into a wave of strikes and public demonstrations for bread and peace. Order in the city dissolved when troops opened fire to disperse demonstrators. Some soldiers mutinied, mobs of workers took what food they could find in markets, and two groups put forward claims to authority: a council, or *soviet*, of St. Petersburg workers, led by Mensheviks and Bolsheviks, and a group of liberal Duma deputies, who claimed authority as a "provisional committee of the Duma." A week after the first demonstrations began, these two groups agreed on the formation of a "provisional government," composed almost entirely of liberals, to run the empire until such time as a constituent assembly might be elected to write a new constitution. At the same time, Nicholas II, informed by his generals that the troops could no longer be relied upon to obey his orders, abdicated. This effectively ended tsardom.

During the ensuing months, the provisional government and the St. Petersburg soviet jockeyed for power while public services and the military situation deteriorated. Although the nation could produce ample food to meet the needs of its people, peasants had little incentive to sell grain for inflated currency, and railroads failed to deliver what was sold. In April 1917, the provisional government introduced food rationing, even though it lacked the authority to make the system work.

Continuing food shortages led to renewed demonstrations and forced a reshuffling of the provisional government that brought an eloquent socialist, A. F. Kerensky, to power. Kerensky's government, however, subordinated domestic reforms to the war effort. Intent on preserving Russia's territories and meeting Russia's commitments to its allies, Kerensky ordered an offensive in July. It collapsed after a day or two of heavy losses. Counterattacking Germans discovered that entire units had lost the will to fight and surrendered readily, sometimes after killing their own officers. German troops advanced as quickly as their supply lines permitted. Many retreating Russian soldiers simply deserted—over a million by the end of the summer.

The chief beneficiary of this disorder, and an instigator of some of it, was the Bolshevik party under the leadership of Vladimir Ilyich Lenin. Lenin, a committed Marxist, saw the provisional government as a tool of businessmen, landowners, and professionals. He and his party portrayed themselves as the vanguard of the Russian working class. Building on a base of workers in the factories of St. Petersburg, Bolshevik organizers used the spring and summer of 1917 to widen their support, promising bread to hungry city dwellers, land reform to peasants, a relaxation of discipline to soldiers, and autonomy to ethnic minorities. Alone among the major political parties, the Bolsheviks insisted that Russia should make peace, whatever the price. This program, expressed in the slogan "Peace, Bread, Land," positioned the Bolsheviks as the alternative to liberals and moderate socialists, who had all compromised themselves by participating in the hapless provisional government.

As Russia's infrastructure and defenses collapsed, the authority of the provisional government melted away. A republican and a socialist, Kerensky engendered no enthusiasm among Russia's landowners and officer corps. A proponent of continued war, he found little support among conscripts. A leader who could deliver neither food nor coal to markets, he alienated urban workers and consumers. In October 1917, the Bolsheviks seized power in St. Petersburg, using the workers' soviet and friendly military units as their tools.

The revolution, which sent Kerensky into flight, was nearly bloodless but hardly complete. Few observers expected the Bolsheviks to extend their power much beyond St. Petersburg, or even hold it in the capital for long. The party had only about a quarter of a million active members. Its leaders were derided as unrealistic revolutionaries by liberals and as troublemakers by fellow socialists. They had achieved power by making promises that even they considered irredeemable. But although their critics were divided and demoralized, the Bolsheviks were united behind the charismatic Lenin and committed to the idea that all means were justified by their goal of building a dictatorship of the proletariat. Bolshevik leaders, especially Lenin, saw their victory as the first step toward an international revolution that would usher in an age of socialist government throughout the Western world. That victory would be to the twentieth century what the French Revolution had been to the nineteenth—a turning point in world history.

The Bolsheviks acted quickly to consolidate their hold on Russia's major cities. They shifted control of factories to soviets of workers, purged the police and the bureaucracy of critics, stripped political opponents of authority, closed down newspapers that preached counterrevolution, and granted political commissars far-reaching authority over professional soldiers. The new government issued orders for the seizure of great estates and the distribution of their land among peasants, although in many districts the peasants had already taken matters into their own hands. Lenin also issued a call for peace without annexations or reparations and then opened bilateral negotiations with the Central Powers.

Bolshevik hopes for lenient terms were quickly dashed. Although Germany had covertly funded the Bolsheviks' efforts to destabilize the Russian government, it had no interest in helping the Bolsheviks consolidate power. German negotiators demanded extensive territorial concessions. When Bolshevik negotiators walked out of the conference, German armies advanced along a broad front, seizing much of White Russia and Ukraine and even advancing into the Crimean Peninsula. Russian resistance was negligible. Neither officers nor troops could be relied on to continue a war that the Bolshevik leadership had declared to be over. The chastened Bolshevik negotiators returned to the table in the German-occupied city of Brest-Litovsk and signed an agreement in March 1918 that all but eliminated Russia from Europe.

The peace that Germany imposed cost Russia lands that held 30 percent of its population and 50 percent of its industry. Where the tsar had once ruled, there would now be many weak states dominated by Germany: Finland, Estonia, Livonia, Poland, and a Ukrainian Republic. Nevertheless, Lenin deemed the treaty a tactical retreat, unfortunate but necessary in order for his party to consolidate its power in Russia and prepare for the revolutions that it expected in other parts of Europe. Germany, by contrast, saw the treaty as a first installment of the long-promised fruits of war. It gave Germany access to much-needed grain and oil and seemed to leave Lenin and his Bolsheviks the transient governors of a dissolving empire.

The Allies saw the treaty as a calamity—not so much because the shaky new government in Russia would prove a direct threat, but rather because its policy of peace at any price left Germany free to concentrate its forces on the western front. In hopes of restoring a government that would fight the Germans, the Allies mounted modest efforts to assist anti-Bolshevik forces. These interventions helped to prolong a civil war in Russia between a "red" army that was loyal to the Bolshevik government and several "white" armies that were committed to a hodgepodge of often contradictory causes—the restoration of tsardom, the autonomy of minority groups, or the authority of more or less charismatic military leaders. Not until 1921 did the Bolshevik government fully consolidate its power. By then, approximately ten million Russians, mostly civilians, had lost their lives to war, famine, and disease—a toll that was roughly twice the Russian Empire's losses to Germany and its allies between 1914 and 1917.

End Game

The Central Powers very nearly eliminated another of their adversaries in 1917—Italy. The war along Italy's mountainous border with Austria-Hungary had dragged on for two years with little net change in the frontlines. The winter cold and heavy snows, the spring melt and mud, the difficulty of moving artillery and supplies in regions with few roads, the narrow passes and rocky crags—all these gave defenders important advantages over attackers. The Italians deployed larger armies but were handicapped by poor leadership, inadequate equipment, and shaky morale among the illiterate peasants who constituted the bulk of their troops. The Austrians, who were also fighting the Russians in the east, could bring only a fraction of their army to bear. Nevertheless, in 1917, with help from German alpine divisions, the Austrians shattered the Italian lines around the town of Caporetto and advanced to the foothills above the north Italian plain where they halted as much for lack of supplies as because of resistance. The quick rout testified to the low morale of the Italian troops and the fragility of the Allied position.

As winter commenced, both the Allies and the Central Powers took stock of their positions and made plans for the coming year. The collapse of Russia, the precarious situation of Italy, and heavy losses in France led Allied officials to believe that the war would continue for two or more years—until large American armies could be trained, equipped, and transported to Europe. The Central Powers, meanwhile, took heart from their victories of 1917 but faced growing shortages of soldiers, food, and raw materials. They were losing the war of attrition, so they resolved to deliver a knockout punch in the west before U.S. troops could affect the balance of power.

The German offensive began in March 1918 with an attack by specially trained shock troops that broke through the British lines along a broad front and swept forward, forming a large salient in northern France. Blocked from the Channel ports by renewed British resistance, the Germans turned south toward Paris. As in 1914, the cost of the advance proved higher than the German army could afford. Stopped in July, once again on the Marne, the Germans soon gave back the territory they had occupied as an Allied counterattack evolved into a full-scale counteroffensive. Tanks spearheaded British and French assaults, and ground-strafing aircraft harried retreating columns of German troops, who, for the first time in the war, surrendered in large numbers. About a quarter of a million enthusiastic but inexperienced American troops joined the attack. By October, all the territory lost in the German offensive had been retaken.

Allied successes elsewhere reinforced the sense that the tide had shifted. A British-Arab offensive broke Ottoman defenses in northern Palestine in September. In Mesopotamia, British and Indian troops advanced up the Tigris-Euphrates Valley past Baghdad. In Italy a desperate Austrian offensive in June stalled and gave way to an Italian counteroffensive in October that quickly won ground against hungry and dispirited Austrian troops. Even in the Balkans movement occurred as Bulgarian resistance collapsed and the Allied army, long idle in Salonika, moved northward into Serbia.

By the end of September, the Ottoman Empire and Bulgaria were both seeking an armistice, and even Ludendorff, the chief of the German general staff, recognized the situation to be hopeless. Unwilling to publicly acknowledge defeat,

Ludendorff and the German High Command delegated negotiations to a civilian government, which promptly made overtures to Woodrow Wilson for a truce on the basis of peace proposals that Wilson had made in January. An intricate dance ensued, in which the Germans sought to get all they could and the U.S. president sought terms that would be acceptable to both Germany and his own allies.

It was a short jig. Although Germany fought on, its Austrian ally could not. At the end of October, with its armies melting away and nationalist groups in various parts of the empire declaring their independence, the Austrian government capitulated. Under an armistice that took effect on November 4, Austrian troops laid down their weapons, agreed to evacuate occupied lands, and gave Allied forces the use of Austrian railroads. Meanwhile, in Germany sailors mutinied when ordered to put to sea for a final battle with the Anglo-American fleet, seizing control not only of their vessels but of their home ports as well. As revolts spread, the German Reichstag voted to deprive Kaiser Wilhelm II of his powers of command and to redouble efforts to achieve an armistice. The Kaiser, told that his army could no longer resist the Allies or even be depended upon to suppress rebellions at home, departed for exile in Holland. The Reichstag proclaimed Germany a republic; its new chancellor, the socialist Friedrich Ebert, quickly accepted Allied terms. Fighting ended on November 11.

Finding a New Equilibrium

It is harder to make peace than to declare war. Hatreds aroused by combat and propaganda must be controlled. Governments must find ways to satisfy those who sacrificed for victory and to reintegrate soldiers into civilian life. Industry must shift from the production of materials for war to the production of civilian goods. Controls on wages, prices, movement, and political expression that seem justified during the struggle become unbearable when the fighting ends. The victors must contend with one another as they divide the spoils; the defeated must accept their losses and such penalties as their former enemies choose to impose. And all parties must accommodate themselves to new political, social, and economic realities.

Strategic Outcomes

The scope, intensity, and duration of the Great War here made these challenges of peacemaking especially formidable. The war had been more destructive than any previous conflict. Between 8.5 and 10 million soldiers died: over 3 million in the service of Germany and Austria-Hungary and over 4 million under the colors of France, Russia, and Britain. And for every death there were two or three men who were wounded, including a future prime minister of England, Harold Macmillan; a future president of France, Charles de Gaulle; and a future chancellor of Germany, Adolf Hitler.

The war and its sequelae consumed wealth as well as lives. The direct costs were about $200 billion in prewar U.S. dollars, approximately four times the value of all the world's railroads in 1914. But the war also had indirect costs. Disabled veterans and the families of dead soldiers had to be cared for; in 1918, there were half a million war widows and a million fatherless children in Germany alone. Interest payments on public debt had to be met. And what a debt there was! By the end of the war, the annual interest payments facing Britain, France, and Germany exceeded their prewar annual tax revenues. The war had ravaged some of the richest districts of France and Belgium, rendering farms, mines, and factories unproductive. It had deprived Europe of many of its largest export markets and reduced the overall volume of world trade. A precise accounting of these and other costs is impossible, although they probably exceed the direct expenses of the conflict.

Power relations in Europe changed as a consequence of the war, although not all the changes were enduring. France became, for a few years at least, the greatest land power on the continent, and Britain had undisputed mastery of the seas around it. Germany was stripped of the means to defend itself; civil war consumed a Russia much shrunken from its prewar borders; Austria-Hungary and the Ottoman Empire had dissolved. Italy, although among the victors, had needed help to defend its own borders during the fighting and now needed more help to resuscitate a flagging economy.

British and French dominance was transitory. The war had not altered the demographic relationships between the various parts of Europe, nor had it permanently altered the comparative economic advantages. Both Germany and Soviet Russia retained the potential to be continental or even world powers. The German population remained significantly larger than the population of France or Britain. Germany's factories, rail lines, and mines were intact; its land was still productive. It remained astride the trade routes by which the raw materials of Central and Eastern Europe moved west. Just as important, Germany's workers, engineers, chemists, and businessmen retained their formidable skills. Russia, despite its loss of territory and lives, remained a vast land with tremendous agricultural and industrial promise. Allied military superiority was a dwindling asset, impossible to sustain indefinitely.

Versailles

The British and French leaders understood these realities and sought ways to bolster their positions at postwar peace conferences. The most famous of these conferences, the one that drafted a treaty for Germany, convened at Versailles in the early months of 1919. It attracted talent as bright as the palace's famous lights and mirrors. The delegations of the major powers were studded with expert economists and geographers, jurists and politicians, experts on public health and agriculture. Leaders of the new nations that were emerging from the former empires of Eastern Europe prowled the hallways seeking favor, as did representatives of Britain's dominions and France's colonies. While hundreds of journalists competed for scoops, humanitarians, businessmen, and labor leaders lobbied for terms that would benefit their causes. The treaty itself was the result of intense arguments among the leaders of the major powers: Woodrow Wilson of the United States, David Lloyd George of England, and Georges Clemenceau of France, sometimes joined by Vittorio Orlando of Italy. Diplomacy had never attracted more attention or generated higher expectations. Germany was allowed to send a delegation to observe public sessions but was not allowed to participate.

Wilson dominated the headlines as the conference opened. A scholar turned statesman, he seemed to personify what was best about the Unites States of America: a deep commitment to democracy, an optimistic confidence in human progress, and a conviction that better international laws and institutions could prevent war, promote trade, and improve living conditions. Wilson had sketched out a basis for peace in his famous Fourteen Points message of January 1918, and this became the basis of his negotiating position at Versailles. The victors in the war, Wilson maintained, should repudiate secret deals and make a generous peace, demanding neither large territorial gains nor huge reparations from the defeated. To minimize future conflicts, they should acknowledge the power of nationalism by aligning international borders with lines of ethnic division and by giving the inhabitants of disputed territories an opportunity to choose their own futures. Most important, they should create a League of Nations that would promote human welfare, adjudicate international disputes, and, if necessary, coerce respect for international law through the collective action of its member states. Backed by the great wealth of the United States and its productive farms and factories, Wilson appeared to have power as well as ideas. Europe needed U.S. dollars and grain.

Wilson's message of reconciliation raised hopes both in Europe and around the world. Its idealism reassured citizens of the Allied nations that their sacrifices had been made for a just cause. Its magnanimity won the confidence of the defeated. Its endorsement of democracy, the rule of law, and the rights of ethnic minorities to determine their political futures made Wilson a hero—not just in Eastern Europe, where former Hapsburg subjects were seeking to build new nations, but also among Arabs, Indians, Armenians, Chinese, and other peoples who aspired to political independence. Wilson appeared, in Winston Churchill's words, "like a messenger from another planet sent to the rescue of freedom and justice here below."[3]

Crowds of unprecedented size cheered Wilson in London, Rome, and Paris on the eve of the conference. His partners were less enthusiastic, seeing Wilson's moral passion as priggish self-righteousness and his idealism as naiveté or hypocrisy. God, Clemenceau sniffed, made do with just ten commandments. Lloyd George and Clemenceau were as determined to protect the interests of their nations as Wilson was to advance his program for peace. For the French, a secure peace could only mean structures that would keep Germany weak indefinitely. For the British, it meant the security of its trade and empire. The victors haggled for four months, trying to find a formula that would appear to satisfy Wilson's agenda while obtaining for the victors sufficient rewards to make the war seem worthwhile.

---

[3]Winston S. Churchill, *The Aftermath*, vol. 4 of *The World Crisis, 1918–1928* (New York: Charles Scribner's Sons, 1929), p. 98.

These efforts took place against a backdrop of ongoing death and disorder. Street fighting raged across Central Europe as new states took form. The Romanian army crushed a communist revolution in Hungary, and Austrian socialists put down another communist uprising in Vienna. In Germany, an elected national assembly had convened in Weimar in February 1919, written a new, democratic constitution, and formed a government of moderate socialists and centrists. But the new government called on a paramilitary veterans group, the Freikorps, to establish control over Bavaria, where radicals had declared themselves governors of an independent soviet-style state. These political conflicts took hundreds of lives; meanwhile, the influenza pandemic continued to sicken and kill millions.

As fighting continued in Eastern Europe and influenza skipped borders and oceans, a treaty emerged from the bruising negotiations at Versailles. Signed on June 28, 1919, it gave lukewarm approval to Wilson's cherished League of Nations and the principle of national self-determination. But the settlement satisfied Clemenceau and Lloyd George far more than it did Wilson's admirers. France regained the provinces of Alsace and Lorraine, which it had lost to Germany in 1871, along with the largest share of unspecified war reparations to be extracted from Germany and the promise of security guarantees from Britain and the United States. Stringent limits were placed on the size of the German military, and German troops were prohibited from entering the Rhineland, the German lands bordering France. Parts of Germany were assigned to the new states of Poland and Czechoslovakia, which Clemenceau viewed as natural allies in any future conflict. German-speaking Austria was prohibited from entering into a political union with Germany, whatever the wishes of its citizens. The Allies further reserved the right to march into Germany should it attempt to rebuild its military forces or fail to meet reparation payments.

The issues discussed at the postwar conferences generate nearly as much controversy among historians today as they did among the participants. Did Germany bear special responsibility for the war? Were the penalties imposed on Germany unreasonable, or should the Allies have done more to prevent a resurgence of German power in the future? Was the Treaty of Versailles a better document because of Wilson's idealism, or did the American president simply generate unnecessary friction among the victors and create unrealistic expectations among the vanquished? What did the principle of national self-determination mean? What constitutes a nation, and what happens when two or more groups claim nationhood in a single state? Is the principle a prescription for enduring peace, or for endless border disputes and civil wars? And how could such a principle coexist with colonialism? Was the League of Nations a step forward toward the rule of international law, a device for preserving the hegemony of the victorious powers, or simply a castle in the air?

There is no consensus today on these issues, but it is clear that Versailles, and the other peace conferences, generated more turmoil than tranquility. The defeated powers resented the extravagant reparations and territorial penalties imposed by the Allies. The war had ended before Allied armies entered Germany, and many Germans found it hard to understand why territories that had remained unconquered in war should be surrendered in peace. Their bitterness was all the greater because many had trusted Wilson to protect their interests. The settlement seemed to contradict his principle of national self-determination; areas that were German by language, culture, and history were granted to Poland and Czechoslovakia. Even his proposal for a League of Nations to help keep the peace rang false because the league excluded Germany and its former allies. Most galling to the German government and people, the treaty included an article that assigned to Germany the moral responsibility for the war. Germany's leadership, however, had little bargaining leverage. Germany had already surrendered its heavy weapons under the terms of the armistice, and the Allied blockade remained in force. The terms forced on Germany discredited the new German government in the eyes of many of its citizens and created a reservoir of rancor that right-wing political parties would draw on over the next two decades.

In Eastern Europe and the Balkans, the principle of self-determination had both successes and failures. Peoples who had long chafed under rulers who sought to suppress their languages and cultures found new freedom. But no adjustment of borders could capture the region's complex patchwork of nationalities, and new states such as Yugoslavia and Czechoslovakia incorporated nearly as many ethnic divisions as the empire they replaced. Nor did the redrawn borders reflect economic realities. The economies of Austria and Hungary had complemented each other before the war, but it was not clear that either could prosper on its own.

Even as treaties were being negotiated, ethnic tensions provoked bloodshed. In Poland, Poles murdered Jews and Ukrainians, and in Romania, riots occurred between Romanians and Hungarians. Poland's eastern border took shape only in 1920, after Polish forces defeated a Bolshevik army seeking to regain lands that Russia had lost in the peace of Brest-Litovsk. The creation of new states, such as Czechoslovakia, and the revival of old ones, such as Poland, could not satisfy all members of all ethnic groups or resolve conflicts that had developed over centuries and had sometimes been intensified by the recent war.

The postwar settlement created tensions among the victors as well as among the vanquished. Britain, France, and Italy suspiciously eyed one another's activities in the Mediterranean and Near East and bickered over the division of reparation payments, trade concessions, and territory. France resented the heavy payments it had to make on its loans from England, and both France and England resented the debt payments they owed the United States. Workers in all of the former belligerent states sought wage increases to compensate for inflation, and strikes paralyzed industries that were struggling to convert from wartime to peacetime production.

In the United States, Republicans castigated Wilson for neglecting U.S. national interests in the pursuit of unrealistic international goals, and Wilson's former supporters on the left decried his concessions to British and French interests. Despite efforts so strenuous that they destroyed his health, Wilson failed to obtain Senate ratification of the Versailles Treaty. The United States, therefore, did not take a seat in the League of Nations that Wilson had fathered. Nor did the Senate approve the security guarantees that Wilson had issued to Clemenceau at Versailles. Britain, which had never been enthusiastic about a postwar commitment on the Continent, took the opportunity to withdraw its own assurances to France, leaving the French government all the more anxious about the long-term security of its borders with Germany. In short, the peacemakers failed to satisfy the hopes of early 1919: They did not craft a league that included all nations, bring order to Eastern Europe, or quench the enmity between France and Germany.

Peace Treaties and the Larger World

The peacemakers focused on Europe, but their negotiations had consequences for much of the globe. The inhabitants of Germany's colonies, for example, found themselves subject to new rulers. Germany's island possessions in the Pacific were divided among Japan, Britain, Australia, and New Zealand. France took German colonies in West Africa; Britain took those to the east; those in the south were divided between Belgium and South Africa.

To minimize the all-too-apparent conflict between these dispositions and the Wilsonian rhetoric of national self-determination, the Allies invented a new legal form. Rather than being possessions, the colonies became League of Nation mandates. The new league would delegate control of the lands in question to trustees, who would work toward bringing their wards to statehood. The League would retain the authority to transfer mandates from one power to another, but the system provided neither timetables for independence nor clear criteria for assessing progress toward that goal.

Having invented this convenient device, the Allies applied it to Germany's ally, the Ottoman Empire, as well. Under the terms of a draconian peace treaty signed at Sèvres in 1920, the Allies carved up Ottoman lands like a goose at a holiday table. France assumed a mandate over Syria and Lebanon, and Britain assumed one over Palestine, Persia, and Iraq. The treaty also recognized Britain's control of Egypt and the Sudan and Italy's control of Libya, which had already been established before the war. Even Turkish Anatolia was slated for division into Greek, Italian, French, and Armenian districts.

The Allied terms gave little consideration to the wishes of the peoples of the German and Ottoman empires. But they showed no more consideration to the peoples of their own colonies. The Allies had drawn heavily on their empires for troops, labor, and materials during the war, sometimes dangling assurances of greater autonomy to ensure cooperation. Britain, for instance, promised both Ireland and India prompt movement toward home rule following the war's end. Even where such promises were absent, the war had stirred hopes that wartime sacrifices would be compensated—hopes that Allied rhetoric about the virtues of democracy could not help but raise. When the war ended, these promises came due, and nationalists were ill disposed to tolerate foot-dragging. But colonial reform was not high on the list of priorities at Versailles. Even as the peace treaties were being drawn up, violence erupted in Ireland, Egypt, and India when colonial subjects sought to seize the right of self-determination that had long been denied them.

The war and the subsequent peacemaking stimulated nationalist movements, not just in Europe's colonies but also in Turkey and China. Here, modernizing elements were already reshaping political institutions when the war broke out, sometimes drawing on European models and sometimes reacting against them. Turkey had cast its lot with the Central Powers and China with the Allies; Turkey had suffered heavy losses in combat, while China's contributions to the war were limited to labor battalions. Nevertheless, the war and, perhaps even more, the peace settlement catalyzed nationalism in both societies.

In China, the Treaty of Versailles delivered a sharp blow to the pride and the hopes of a generation of students and reformers, who saw it as yet another in a long series of insults stretching back to the Opium War with Britain in the early nineteenth century. Despite China's cooperation, the victors had ignored Chinese interests. In particular, the treaty awarded the privileges that Germany had enjoyed in China to Japan including a naval base and the rights to police a large part of the Shantung Peninsula, on which that base was sited. The Allied decision demonstrated that the great powers would continue to treat China as something less than an independent state. Worst of all, from the point of view of many Chinese nationalists, China's own officials were prepared to acquiesce in the decision, in part because Japan had sweetened the distasteful deal by promising the Chinese government a loan.

News of the Treaty sent Chinese students to the streets in Beijing and other cities. Their protests swelled into a broad nationalist movement, called the May Fourth Movement after the date of the first demonstrations in 1919. Boycotts of Japanese goods ensued, as did more street protests. Undeterred by mass arrests and strengthened by the participation of labor unions, businessmen, and, for the first time in China's political history, large numbers of women, the movement ultimately forced the Chinese government to reject the Versailles Treaty. More important, the movement engaged large numbers of young Chinese in politics, bringing new strength both to Sun Yat-sen's Chinese Nationalist Party, the Kuomintang, and to socialist groups from which the Chinese Communist Party would emerge in 1921.

As in Europe, nationalism had both constructive and destructive consequences. Both were on full display in postwar Turkey, whose very name, formally adopted in 1921, announced the identity of nation and ethnic group. Turks, descended from the tribes of northwestern Asia Minor that had created the Ottoman Empire, had long dominated the Ottoman army, although they constituted only about half of the empire's population. Nevertheless, the Ottoman sultans were willing to accept service from loyal subjects regardless of their ethnicity, and Greeks, Armenians, and Jews dominated the empire's commercial life. To be sure, reform-minded army officers had already yoked their ambitions to the promotion of Turkish nationalism before the war, but their message found only modest support outside the army.

The war changed all this. Thousands of Turks, both well-born officers and peasant conscripts, discovered a national identity as they suffered common hardships and sometimes bested Allied forces on battlefields such as Gallipoli. Equally important, the war stimulated the growth of nationalist feeling among minorities within the empire, often with the encouragement of the Allies, and this in turn evoked a new and stronger Turkish consciousness. The revolt against Ottoman rule in the south, led by the ruler of Mecca and supported by the British, set Muslim Arab against Muslim Turk. The hundreds of thousands of Greeks living in Anatolia found themselves subjects of an empire at war with the Greek state, awakening ambitions for a greater Greece among some of these Ottoman subjects and fears of Greek subversion among Turks. And the million or more Armenians living in eastern Anatolia came under suspicion both because of their Christian religion and because of their links with Armenians living in, and fighting for, Russia. Tensions and suspicions led to violence and atrocities: riots between Greek and Turkish populations in western cities, the destruction of Turkish villages in Armenian districts along the Russian frontier, and—worst of all—the murder of hundreds of thousands of Armenians in eastern Anatolia.

The Allies sought both to resolve these tensions and to benefit from them through the Treaty of Sèvres, which declared league mandates over Arab districts, accorded the Greeks and Armenians autonomy, and established Italian and French zones of control within Turkish Anatolia. The Allied plan found support among Turkey's Greeks and Armenians, but it fanned nationalism among Turks, who formed a majority in most parts of Anatolia.

Mustafa Kemal, a charismatic Turkish officer who had gained fame for his heroic defense of Gallipoli in 1916, drew on this popular nationalism, first to eject Allied forces from Anatolia through a combination of statecraft and force, and then to secure new and more favorable terms from the Allies. Having established Turkish control over Anatolia, he undertook sweeping reforms of Turkey's government and social institutions. Eclectic in his methods, Kemal borrowed political concepts from France to craft a new republican constitution and ideas about party organization from the Bolsheviks to ensure his personal domination of the state. He overlaid both with heady rhetoric about the history and destiny of the Turkish nation. Above all, he was interested in education. He created secular schools, simplified the written form of the Turkish language to promote literacy, and extended political rights and economic opportunities to Turkey's peasants and women. Adopting the surname Atatürk, or "father of the Turks," Kemal encouraged an intense nationalism among his people that promoted development but also resulted in large-scale population transfers and the suppression of ethnic minorities.

CONCLUSION

The Great War was a consequence of the political rivalries of European powers. It did not end those rivalries, although it weakened or destroyed all of the European states that had participated. The real winners of the war were not the great powers of Europe but the United States and Japan, which gained wealth and influence at a modest cost in lives and material.

States with democratic institutions at the start of the conflict preserved those structures, but the war hardly made the world safe for democracy[4] as Wilson had hoped. Britain and France continued to repress democratic movements in their enlarged empires. Germany's postwar democracy was born under duress and faced challenges from extremists on both the right and the left from its outset. Other states adopted some of the forms of democratic governance but fell under the sway of strongmen such as Atatürk and Lenin. Throughout Europe there were veterans, workers, and members of the middle class who felt betrayed by their government and were ready to follow prophets of radical reform.

Although optimists could point to widespread disenchantment with war as a means of solving international conflicts and to the creation of the League of Nations as hopeful signs for the future, the years of fighting and peacemaking left old problems unresolved and created new fissures in world politics. Neither Germany nor Russia was content with its borders or its position in world affairs. Unsatisfied, too, were some Japanese nationalists, who, despite Japan's territorial and economic gains, found their ambitions for dominance over China frustrated. The United States, pleased with the outcome of the war, showed only sporadic interest in using its power to rebuild international institutions and, like Germany and Russia, was absent from the League. Britain and France, much reduced in economic power, showed little understanding of how to satisfy the emerging nationalist aspirations within their colonies. Even the most determined optimist would have been hard-pressed to find greater security in the postwar than in the prewar world.

For Further Reading

Manfred F. Boemeke, Gerald D. Feldman, and Elisabeth Glaser, *The Treaty of Versailles: A Reassessment After 75 Years* (Washington, DC: German Historical Institute and Cambridge University Press, 1998). The best single volume on the peacemaking after World War I.

John M. Barry, *The Great Influenza: The Epic Story of the Deadliest Plague in History* (New York: Viking, 2004). Illuminates both the social and medical history of the influenza pandemic.

Niall Ferguson, *The Pity of War* (New York: Basic Books, 1999). An iconoclastic account of the beginnings of the war.

Holger H. Herwig, *The First World War: Germany and Austria-Hungary, 1914–1918* (London: Arnold, 1997). Supplements Keegan by focusing on the Central Powers.

James Joll, *The Origins of the First World War* (London and New York: Longman, 1984). Concise and judicious analysis of European power politics.

Joe Lunn, *Memoirs of the Maelstrom: A Senegalese Oral History of the First World War* (Portsmouth, N.H.: Heinemann, 1999). The war from an African perspective.

Hew Strachan, *The First World War* (New York: Viking: 2004). An expert history of the military conflict.

---

[4]Woodrow Wilson, address to joint session of Congress, April 2, 1917. http://historymatters.gmu.edu/d/4943

Richard Wall and Jay Winter, eds., *The Upheaval of War: Family, Work and Welfare in Europe, 1914–1918* (Cambridge: Cambridge University Press, 1988). Examines the domestic policies and experiences of the European belligerents.

J. M. Winter, *The Experience of World War I* (New York: Oxford University Press, 1989). Notable for superb illustrations, maps, and quantitative data.

Related Websites

The World War I Document Archive
   http://wwi.lib.byu.edu/
   Includes many significant documents, such as the texts of the Zimmerman Note,
Wilson's Fourteen Points, the Treaty of Brest-Litovsk, and the Treaty of Versailles.
FirstWorldWar.Com
   http://www.firstworldwar.com/
   A large and well-designed collection of documents, photos, sound clips, and articles.
The Medical Front WWI
   http://www.vlib.us/medical/
   Diverse primary source materials pertaining to medical practice and the experience
of patients during the war.

PART II

Struggles for Supremacy, 1919–1945

CHAPTER 4

Internationalism, Empire, and Autarchy, 1919–1929

O n March 1, 1919, Koreans gathered on the streets of Seoul, both to pay their final respects to the last Korean king, Kojong, who had been forced to abdicate by the Japanese in 1907, and to remind the world leaders meeting in Versailles of Korea's claims to nationhood. The draft Treaty of Versailles left Korea under the control of Japan, which had annexed the peninsula in 1910. There was little prospect that this provision would be altered. Japan had won control over Korea through its wars with China (1895) and Russia (1904–1905) and was bringing it administrative reforms that were widely admired in the West. When leaders of the demonstrators publicly signed a Korean declaration of independence, Japanese troops cracked down. Hundreds of Koreans were killed and thousands imprisoned during the weeks following the March 1 demonstration. Korea would remain a Japanese colony until 1945.

The massacres in Korea exemplify some of the key tensions of the postwar years. The crowds in the streets of Seoul were marking the end of a dynasty that had presided over a "hermit kingdom"—an inward-looking state that sought to maintain independence through self-sufficiency. Some lamented the passing of that kingdom and may have hoped for its return. However, the leaders of the protests, many of them young and foreign-educated, were committed to a new Korea that would enjoy the benefits of modern commerce and take a place in the League of Nations. They looked to Woodrow Wilson, the Allied powers, and international public opinion for help in attaining independence and security. The country's Japanese occupiers also wanted to bring Korea into the twentieth century, but under Japanese management, with Korea supplying raw materials to Japan's growing economy and Japan supplying Korea with capital, manufactured goods, and political guidance.

Three visions of the future intersected here: one of autarchy, or independence through isolation; a second of national development through integration into a global community; and a third of development through empire.

Different as these visions were, they all expressed aspects of nationalism. The Japanese considered themselves agents of an enlightened empire that was redeeming an ancient province from a history of misrule. The mourners for Kojong were turning a corrupt and incompetent king into a symbol of centuries of independent cultural development. The signers of the declaration of independence were splicing together a sense of ethnic identity with Western ideas about popular sovereignty and universal human rights to fashion a program for independence, political reform, and economic regeneration.

Nationalism was swelling in the early twentieth century, not just among Koreans and Japanese but among other peoples who had been mute in earlier times. Mass movements that made the nation a primary reference point were taking shape in Mexico, Egypt, Turkey, India, China, and elsewhere. These movements differed greatly but all reflected trends that had begun in the late nineteenth century: the spread of literacy, the extension of railroads and modern forms of communication, and the integration of larger and larger regions into the global economy.

Most of these movements also benefited from the war. Wartime propaganda had relentlessly celebrated the nation as the hub of human loyalty and hopes. That message, confirmed by the spectacle of collective self-sacrifice, reached audiences around the world, including peoples whose nations had not as yet been formed. Not only had the war glorified nationhood, it had loosened the grip of the European powers on their colonies and informal empires. The war had consumed Europe's wealth, demoralized its citizens, and vacated its claims to superior civilization.

Tensions between national and supranational commitments, between the ambitions of empires and imperial colonies, and, within nations, between isolationism and outward-looking programs of development run through the history of the twentieth century. But tensions were especially pronounced in the wake of a war that left Europe so weakened. The new balance hardly stripped Europe of all its advantages, but it opened the way to hopes for new forms of international integration, as well as to dreams of vigorous national development largely independent of external constraint.

Internationalism

Woodrow Wilson's program for lasting peace rested on two ideas that he saw as complementary: self-determination and international law. All peoples, he maintained, have a right to govern themselves. And nations have common interests, such as preventing aggression, maintaining peace, and fostering conditions of prosperity, which are best protected by lawful authority. Wilson's principles owed much to the American experience of federal union, in which a national government coordinated and checked the behavior of states that had their own institutions and interests. The U.S. system protected minorities through the application of laws. It guaranteed rights to every state under a universal charter or constitution, but it also gave the nation as a whole the means to preserve itself, by force if necessary, under that same charter. It was a way to integrate local and regional ambitions into a commonwealth, and Wilson hoped it would be a model for the world.

The treaties ending World War I were stamped with an imperfect imprint of Wilson's vision. Redrawn borders could neither segregate the scrambled peoples of Eastern Europe one from another nor ignore promises made to regional allies like Serbia and Italy. The settlement thus created a host of "minority" problems, similar to those of the old Austrian and Ottoman empires. Outside Europe, self-interest consistently trumped self-determination. The victors refused to consider the wishes of minorities—whether in the shattered Ottoman Empire, of Chinese under Japanese control in coastal China, or of subjects in Germany's former colonies—for fear of losing their own empires. The principle of self-determination itself could not withstand scrutiny in the absence of commonly accepted criteria for nationhood. Wilson had urged the satisfaction of "all well-defined national aspirations" consistent with the preservation of peace. The vagueness of his phrase gave the victors wide latitude to play favorites as they redrew international borders and gave nationalists ample cause for disappointment.

The League of Nations

The peace negotiations resulted in a League of Nations that embodied some of Wilson's cherished ideas about international law and collective security. The charter or covenant of the League, which was approved at Versailles and eventually signed by sixty nations, established a permanent body with the trappings of government: a General Assembly of all member states; an executive Council of five permanent members (the United States, Britain, France, Italy, and Japan) and four rotating members chosen in the General Assembly; a Secretary-General commanding an international civil service; and an International Court of Justice. Members committed themselves to the peaceful resolution of conflicts and renounced secret alliances. They also agreed to take economic and military action against states that went to war in violation of the covenant. The League thereby gave a voice to states without large armies or rich treasuries and established precedents that were to shape diplomacy throughout the rest of the century.

Despite appearances, however, the League of Nations was not an international government. Governments both make and police laws, but the League lacked the unambiguous power to coerce. Its covenant provided for action against aggressors but neither defined aggression nor mechanisms to gather and apply force. The League had no standing army, no command over the soldiers of member states, and no staff to plan a war. The gap between rhetoric and reality reflected the ambivalence of the League's authors. They were caught between the desire to give the League some teeth and the need to write a charter that was acceptable to member states protective of their sovereignty. The solution was an organization with some moral authority but little command over other instruments of power.

Not only did the League lack the clout of a true government, it also failed to represent large parts of the globe. Roughly half of its members were European nations, and the twenty republics of Latin America constituted another third. The only votes from sub-Saharan Africa belonged to Ethiopia and South Africa, the latter a British dominion governed by a white minority. Only six Asian states ever held membership, two of which—India and Iraq—were largely controlled by the British. Nor did the League enroll all the powers of Europe and the Americas. The United States never took a seat, in part because of a long-standing reluctance to become embroiled in European quarrels and in part because of fears about League interference in the Western Hemisphere. Germany was excluded from membership by intention and secured membership only in 1926; by then many Germans had come to see the League as a thinly veiled anti-German alliance. Soviet Russia, despite occasional overtures, refused to join the League until 1934. Its avowed goal of overthrowing other governments and its repudiation of its huge debts to Western lenders made it a pariah among nations. Its ruling Communist Party had embraced this role, finding it convenient for domestic purposes to depict the League as a capitalist conspiracy aimed at strangling Soviet communism.

German and Russian critics had a point when they charged that the League was a tool of Britain and France. As holders of permanent seats on the Council, Britain and France enjoyed veto power over most crucial decisions; as victors in the recent war, they had leverage over other states in the General Assembly. Their trade and empires gave them security interests that were as global as the peace-keeping mandate of the League. Whenever a threat to world peace emerged, their calculations of self-interest would inevitably affect judgments about where and when the League should act.

Even so, the League was hardly a veiled tool of an Anglo-French condominium. For one thing, French and British aims often diverged. Britain's interest in rebuilding trade with Germany, for example, undercut France's interest in keeping Germany weak. Furthermore, even when France and Britain could agree, the structure of the League often frustrated action. Neither great power wished to handle delicate matters in the open deliberations of the General Assembly. The Council gave greater latitude for secrecy, but each of its nine members held veto power over important decisions. In any case, the absence of the United States, Russia, and Germany from the League often made diplomacy at the highest levels impossible. As a result, Britain, France, and the other great powers resorted to smaller, more secretive gatherings for their serious business, much as they had before the war.

The Washington Naval Conference and Treaty of Locarno

Most of the noteworthy international agreements of the postwar era took shape at ad hoc conferences rather than under League auspices. In late 1921, for example, the United States hosted a meeting of the former Entente partners in Washington to discuss the balance of power in the Pacific and limits on naval forces. Britain

GLOBAL Technologies

Radio

Citizens of Buenos Aires, London, or New York could keep informed about events such as the Washington and Locarno conferences by means of a technology that some thought might change the world: radio.

Radio communication by encoded signals such as Morse code was, of course, nothing new. Within a decade of Heinrich Hertz's 1885 discovery that electrical energy could be transmitted across distance without wires, entrepreneurial engineers such as Guglielmo Marconi were selling radio apparatus to shipping companies and governments. By the first years of the twentieth century, hobbyists in many parts of the world were tinkering with batteries, spark generators, and

crystal receivers—the basic equipment necessary to send and receive radio signals.

Radio spawned possibilities and problems—many similar to those that would accompany the emergence of the Internet toward century's end. Enthusiasts imagined that it would decentralize power by weakening the monopoly of states and publishers on news, improve life by linking rural farmhouses with medical doctors and schoolteachers, and build international understanding by establishing direct contacts between private citizens across borders. Some of this indeed happened as ham operators developed their own community and chatted with other operators in Morse code. But chatting was not always so easy amidst the unregulated babble of signals that soon filled the radio bandwidth. By World War I, the chaotic conditions were prompting governments to claim jurisdiction over the air waves by licensing operators and regulating the strength and frequencies of transmitters.

---

and the United States, the world's largest naval powers, were eager to avert an expensive naval race with Japan and to restrain growing Japanese influence in China, which threatened their access to Chinese markets. Japan, for its part, wanted assurances that it would continue to enjoy naval supremacy in East Asia and effective control over resource-rich Manchuria, where it had extensive rail, mining, and agricultural enterprises.

A bargain was struck that accomplished these aims. Britain, the United States, and Japan agreed to limits on tonnage of large naval vessels in the ratio of 5:5:3, with France and Italy signing on to even lower limits. In return, Britain and the United States agreed to refrain from fortifying new bases in the Pacific and signed a mutual security agreement guaranteeing the status quo. In addition, Japan agreed to grant China control of the Shantung Peninsula, which Japan had seized from Germany in World War I, and the United States and Britain tacitly acknowledged Japan's special interests in Manchuria. The Washington Conference thus achieved arms control, but only by carving the Pacific up into spheres of influence,

The electromagnetic spectrum was on the way to becoming property.

As ham radio boomed, engineers and inventors improved radio technology. Continuous wave transmitters that sent out signals on a single frequency replaced the spark transmitters whose noise spilled across many. New ideas in circuitry extended transmission into higher parts of the radio spectrum and improved control over tuning and filtering signals. And vacuum tubes were introduced that could serve as emitters, receivers, and amplifiers of signals. Together these improvements made it possible to transmit voice or music as well as code and to transmit clear signals at modest cost over hundreds of miles.

Beginning about 1920, broadcasting stations began to appear, first in the United States, Argentina, England, and Germany, and then in many other countries as well. Launched by amateurs, educators, and companies seeking to build a market for radio equipment, the stations played music, broadcast speeches, and relayed weather reports and news. The response exceeded all expectations. As sales of "radio music boxes" boomed, businessmen realized that airtime itself was something that could be sold. Companies began to sponsor regularly scheduled programs and to advertise their products with commercials. Nor did it take long for governments to recognize a powerful new means of communicating with, and influencing, listeners.

By the mid-1930s, radio had evolved into forms that remain familiar today: a hobby for the technically proficient, a tool of education and emergency communication, and powerful medium to reach the masses. Where dominated by commercial programming, as in the United States and much of Latin America, radio shaped popular culture and consumer tastes. Where state-run broadcasting agencies dominated, as in the Soviet Union and Nazi Germany, it sometimes became a tool to mold political opinion and rally listeners behind the leaders of state and party.

---

with Britain supreme in the southern waters around Singapore and Australia, Japan near its home islands and along the north coast of China, and the United States in the seas from California to the Philippines.

In 1925, a meeting among representatives of the European powers at Locarno, Switzerland, led to similarly sweeping agreements regarding Europe. Here the problem was finding a way to restore Germany to the community of European powers without reversing the outcome of World War I. The reintegration of Germany was a problem largely because the Allies had made it one. By excluding Germany from the League of Nations and from normal diplomatic relations, they had pushed it into closer relations with the other international pariah, Soviet Russia, thereby raising the specter of an alliance that would shift the center of power in Europe eastward.

The solution reached at Locarno was a framework of alliances and guarantees that elicited German commitment to the territorial status quo in exchange for a restoration of its position in world diplomacy. In a treaty with France and

Belgium, Germany agreed to accept the western borders imposed at Versailles as permanent, with Britain and Italy agreeing to act should any signatory violate those borders. Germany further agreed to maintain the Rhineland as a demilitarized zone and to renounce force as a tool for altering its borders with Poland and Czechoslovakia. In return, Germany gained admittance to the League of Nations, a permanent seat on the League Council, and informal assurances that Allied troops would evacuate the occupied Rhineland according to the schedule outlined in the Treaty of Versailles. France, in turn, promised Poland and Czechoslovakia assistance should Germany violate its promise.

The Washington and Locarno conferences stabilized international relations, but in neither did the League of Nations play a direct role. Nor did the entry of Germany strengthen the League, as some internationalists had hoped. Germany's addition to the Council enlarged the number of states that enjoyed a veto over Council actions. More important, Germany negotiated a revision in the League charter as the price of its entry. Reluctant to become embroiled in any future war because of treaty obligations, Germany insisted that members be freed of the obligation to participate in sanctions against aggressors. In short, the Locarno Conference further undermined the League's already weak peacekeeping authority.

The League at Work

National interests prevailed over internationalism throughout the history of the League. Even so, the organization managed to fulfill some of its promise, largely by acting in disputes where the interests of the major powers converged. In Eastern Europe, for example, the League adjudicated numerous border conflicts between the new states that had been carved out of the empires of Austria-Hungary and tsarist Russia (Map 4.1). It also oversaw the negotiations that resolved a potentially explosive dispute between Poland and Germany over the control of the rich mines and industries of Upper Silesia. Here and throughout Eastern Europe, the Western powers were eager to muffle conflict and restore order. A stable and prosperous Eastern Europe would check the expansion of Soviet communism from the east and German militarism from the west.

The League also undertook a range of social and humanitarian activities that restored some of the international cooperation that had existed before the war. Working with the International Health Office, which had been set up in Paris in 1908, the League's Health Organization intervened to check the spread of epidemic diseases. Its Refugee Organization helped arrange for the resettlement of nearly two million Russians fleeing the Soviet Union and nearly a million Greeks and Armenians expelled from Turkey. Its Communications and Transport Organization established conventions governing the operations of ports, the transmission of electricity across state borders, and the administration of passports and visas.

These achievements testified to both the usefulness of the League and the tragedy of the war. The war had generated the conditions that made epidemic disease and refugees such urgent problems and had ushered in an era of state-imposed restrictions on immigration that made passports and visas necessary for international travel. The League was not so much reforming the world as undertaking damage control and restoration.

Other Internationalisms: Comintern and Pacifism

The enormous suffering and waste of the war stimulated expressions of internationalism other than the League of Nations, most notably pacifist organizations and political movements such as international communism. Pacifist groups, which were especially popular in Britain and the United States, tended to view weapons themselves as a spur to militarism. They labeled arms manufacturers "merchants of death" who prospered by promoting conflict among nations and maintained that politicians engaged in provocative behavior because they had the means to wage war. For pacifists, disarmament was the key to ending war, and public pressure was the way to bring governments behind this goal. Communist groups, organized into a Russian-sponsored Communist International, or Comintern, in 1919, expressed many of the same ideas, although they saw little hope of disarmament in a world dominated by capitalism. Communists thought that states organized around capitalist systems of production would inevitably fall into conflict with one another over resources and markets. An end to war, in their view, would await a social revolution that struck down both arms makers and all privately held industry.

Both pacifists and communists echoed the wartime propaganda campaigns that had decried German militarism and the real and imagined power of large German arms makers such as Krupp. Neither group was able to translate the widespread revulsion against the war into a firm repudiation of defense spending, but the pacifist organizations helped keep disarmament on the agenda of postwar governments in both Britain and the United States. Hopeful observers saw this as a sign that pacifism could make some headway in the rough and tumble of politics. Skeptics pointed out that neither Britain nor the United States had land borders with hostile powers or need of large armies.

The war stimulated the growth of several forms of internationalism, but loyalties to nation ran deep and had been intensified by years of combat and propaganda. When push came to shove, the interests of nation prevailed over those of international cooperation, which became abundantly clear in the 1930s when governments brushed aside pacifist objections to escalating arms spending and Soviet Russia purged the Comintern of dissenters from the Soviet party line. The failures of the League of Nations were particularly conspicuous. Incapable of preventing Japanese expansion in China or the Italian conquest of Ethiopia, the League became irrelevant to the diplomacy of the major powers. Some historians, focusing on the spectacular failures of the League in the 1930s, have gone so far as to implicate it in the creation of a dangerous illusion of peace. By fostering false confidence in collective security, this argument runs, the League led governments that sought a lasting peace to lower their guard and thereby invited more

MAP 4.1 Europe and the Middle East after World War I.

The peace treaties ending World War I dissolved the great land empires of central Europe and the Middle East. Few of the European successor states had the size, economic power, and stability to survive without powerful allies. They had to look to Britain and France for support or seek to play Germany and Soviet Russia off against one another. The League of Nations granted Britain and France mandates over former Ottoman provinces such as Palestine and Syria.

aggressive regimes to seize opportunities for expansion. A new world war thus was a result of the idealism of the covenant.

This view may attribute both too much and too little to the League and its sponsors. Confidence in the League was neither deep nor broad in the 1920s. Far from enjoying too much influence, the League possessed too little. Nor does this view acknowledge the roles that the League was able to play despite its limited means. Unable to make a perfect world, it nevertheless made a modestly better one, as millions of refugees and victims of disease could have testified. And, through both its successes and its failures, it established precedents that would continue to have influence long after the League itself dissolved in the tragedy of a new world war.

Old Empires and New Nationalisms

As diplomats integrated the new League of Nations into older patterns of state-craft and struggled to define spheres of influence among the shards of broken empires, other contests were under way in regions distant from the palaces of Versailles and the halls of Geneva. In growing numbers, people who were under colonial rule or dependent on imperial powers were asserting their own right to national self-determination.

The War and Independence Movements

The great powers repeatedly compromised the principles of democracy and self-determination in arranging the postwar borders of Eastern Europe. The gap between their rhetoric and behavior was even greater in their colonial policies. Phrases about the sacred rights of peoples to govern themselves through institutions of their own choosing clashed directly with imperial and trade interests. The contradiction was not lost on critics of empire, who gleefully turned these phrases, which had originally been aimed at adversaries in war, into tools for exposing the hypocrisy of imperialism.

But the war exposed the hypocrisy of empire in more than just words. The colonial troops that were dispatched to Europe saw firsthand a side of European civilization that had long been veiled from its colonial subjects. The imperial states were not lands of enormous wealth and enlightenment but rather places with poverty, injustice, and violence. European troops were capable of panic and cowardice, especially when facing adversaries with up-to-date arms and equipment. The imperial powers drew heavily on their colonies in the war, and many subjects believed that those powers had an obligation to make good on their debts after the war was over.

World War I stimulated independence movements in other ways as well. In the colonies, the war exacerbated social tensions between the agents of empire and their subjects. The expansion of industry and the high demand for commodities fed inflation, which in turn generated labor militancy. Businessmen, whose factories had expanded to satisfy demands that could no longer be met from abroad, sought to protect their enterprises from imports after the war was over. Their interest in nurturing colonial industries threw them into conflict with imperial administrators and importers, who were eager to restore the prewar order. Taxes rose, putting new pressures on many members of colonial societies, but especially on the peasants, who paid the land taxes upon which most colonial governments subsisted. And the departure of European administrators, called away for service at home or in the field, threw open the doors of the civil service to natives and gave them a taste for authority. The net effect was the growth of coalitions united by a common interest in winning control over tax, tariff, land, and labor policies.

Britain and its colonies proved especially vulnerable to these tensions. Its empire was larger than any other, and its investments abroad, although shrunken by the war, remained deep and extensive. Some of its colonies, most notably Egypt and India, had the resources to sustain independence, and elites in those colonies had already been eyeing such a goal before the war. Britain's investments in colonial infrastructure, which tended to be more intensive than those of other imperial powers, inadvertently fostered such ambitions. Railroads built to transport goods and soldiers could also carry political organizers from one district to another. Laws and courts, established to preserve order and symbolize British power, also afforded some protection to journalists and political activists. Schools established to train clerks, surveyors, and lawyers exposed colonial subjects to ideas that were subversive of imperial authority. History books, for example, glowingly described the growth of individual liberties in England, America, and France, and the rights of individuals and nations to rise up against oppression. British notions of democratic government, fair play, and the rule of law, often deployed for propaganda purposes, could also become rallying cries for reformers who were conscious of the gap between their rulers' words and their actions.

By the time Britain went to war in 1914, independence or home rule movements not only were crystallizing in the colonies but had also found support in Britain itself. Idealists recognized the hypocrisy in denying liberties abroad that were deemed natural rights at home. Pragmatists saw little profit in retaining colonies by force against determined opposition, especially when that opposition was well organized and carried modern weapons. The war against the Boers of South Africa, concluded in 1902 after three years of intense fighting, had illustrated both the moral and the material hazards of imperialism. British armies had subdued the Boers, the descendants of Dutch settlers who had arrived in South Africa in the seventeenth century, but only after forcing tens of thousands of civilians into concentration camps and expending more wealth and lives than in any other colonial war in British history, with the possible exception of the American War of Independence. Despite the military victory, Britain ended up negotiating away much of its authority in the agreement of 1910 that established the Union of South Africa. That agreement, while preserving Britain's control of South Africa's ports and foreign policy, granted white South Africans control of South Africa's internal affairs. Ultimately this gave the Boers, who outnumbered the English settlers, political authority over a larger region than they had defended against Britain.

Britain had won the Boer War, but it wanted no more such costly and ambiguous victories. Consequently, the settlement of 1910 rather than the campaigns of 1899–1902 became the more common model for dealing with obstreperous colonials. Faced with powerful opposition, Britain would try to trade home rule, meaning control of internal administration, for continued management of a colony's defense and foreign policies. Before moving toward negotiations, however, the British government and public indeed had to be convinced that preservation of full imperial control in a colony would be more trouble than it was worth. Typically, the peoples of British possessions had to demand their independence, insistently and forcefully—often by resorting to violence.

And so, much the same cycle occurred in a number of British colonies after World War I: Coalitions of local interests demanded greater autonomy; opposition to imperial rule found expression in strikes, boycotts of British goods, and street protests; British efforts to suppress the disorder provoked bloodshed, which, in turn, intensified opposition in the colony and polarized public opinion at home; negotiations brought concessions, including home rule or the promise of such in the not-too-distant future. This was the pattern in Ireland, Egypt, and India, and in some of the Ottoman provinces that fell under a British mandate after the war, such as Iraq and Palestine.

It is easy to imagine masses of exploited peasants and workers rising up against imperial rule under a vanguard of enlightened patriots, but the reality was more complex. Ambitions for greater control over government could divide a society as easily as they could unite it. Religious, economic, and social fissures ran through colonial societies just as they did through European states. The prospect of home rule or independence immediately raised questions about the redistribution of power—questions that seldom had obvious answers. The history of Egypt illustrates some of these complexities.

Egypt

In Egypt the divisions were social and political. Occupied by Britain in 1882, Egypt had previously been a province of the Ottoman Empire under the control of a khedive, who acknowledged Ottoman sovereignty but otherwise behaved like a monarch. The British had found it convenient to preserve this fiction until 1914, when it declared Egypt a British protectorate, deposed the Ottoman khedive, and installed his uncle as sultan.

After the armistice, a three-way tug-of-war quickly developed between the British, intent on protecting the Suez Canal; the sultan, eager to enlarge his political authority; and a small group of independence-minded activists drawn primarily from Cairo and Alexandria, Egypt's major cities. The latter group had sought to seize the moment in 1919 by sending a delegation, or *Wafd*, to Versailles to lobby for Egyptian independence. Denied visas by the British, members of the would-be delegation called their supporters into the streets. The riots that ensued demonstrated the power of the *Wafd*, which now became the name of a political party, and rattled the British, who had little desire to maintain control of Egypt at the point of bayonets. Yet while the *Wafd* could tap into broadly shared yearnings for independence, it was not a party of the people. Led by absentee landlords, civil servants, and businessmen, the *Wafd* was more interested in winning control over tariff policy and patronage than in advancing a program of land reform, public education, and representative democracy. The question in Egypt, then, was not so much one of self-determination by an entire people as one of which elite would end up in control of the state.

Despite the differences between Egypt and other scenes of revolt against British rule, such as Ireland and Iraq, the dilemma facing the British was the same. Continued British rule entailed a commitment of troops and wealth; neither was in abundant supply after the war, and neither could guarantee order. However, capitulation to independence movements had large political and strategic costs. Not surprisingly, the British sought to find a middle path that would relieve them of the need to garrison hostile colonies but that would protect vital interests. As in South Africa earlier in the century, this meant striking a bargain with those local forces that were best able to guarantee order.

In Egypt, this took the form of a power-sharing solution imposed unilaterally. In 1922, Britain declared the nation independent while reserving to itself control of the Suez Canal and Egypt's foreign policy. At British insistence, the sultan approved a constitutional monarchy and a bicameral parliament with a democratically elected lower house. Nevertheless, power resided elsewhere—with the landed notables, who controlled the upper house, and with the sultan-king, who had the authority to convene and dissolve the parliament, veto legislation, and appoint ministers. This outcome fell short of the complete independence sought by the *Wafd*, but it restored order, satisfied many members of Egypt's elites, and afforded Britain continued control of the empire's lifeline. It did little, however, for the peasants and agricultural laborers who constituted 90 percent of Egypt's population. They had had little land or power before the British arrived, and they remained destitute and largely voiceless after the British effected their partial disengagement.

In Egypt and elsewhere, peasants and workers were often pawns of better-educated elites in the struggle for political power. This is not to say, however, that the humble people who constituted the great majority in Egypt and other colonial societies lacked grievances against imperial rule or aspirations for an independent future. The *Wafd* drew support from rural villages, and the throngs who shouted anti-British slogans in Egypt's city streets were composed largely of workingmen, many just a few years removed from the fields. A continent away, about half of the Koreans arrested during the 1919 independence demonstrations against Japan were farmers, many of them desperately poor.

The leaders of the *Wafd* and the authors of the Korean declaration of independence were cosmopolitan by comparison with the masses they sought to lead. Egypt's elites were largely schooled in France; many of the Korean leaders were members of Christian congregations, and some had studied in Shanghai or Tokyo. These activists read newspapers and books, kept up with current events, and knew of documents such as the American Declaration of Independence and the French Declaration of the Rights of Man. It is hard to know what independence may have meant to the people who took to the streets, few of whom could read and most of whom had only sporadic contact outside their village or neighborhood. The promise of lower taxes or of better prices for their crops or their labor? The hope for a school for their children, a few acres of land, or a medical clinic? Redress for slights or a visceral hatred of the alien? Or the restoration of some happier and perhaps mythical time when life was easier and justice prevailed? Neither slogans nor manifestoes tell us much about their motives, but the upheavals of the postwar era testify to the capacity of the masses to play a role in colonial politics.

Raj and Swaraj: The Struggle for Indian Independence

Of all the independence movements under way in the early twentieth century, India's was especially notable for the magnitude of its task, the innovativeness of its tactics, and its influence on liberation movements in other parts of the world. It exemplifies, on a grand scale, the recurring problems of decolonization. Those seeking independence must find ways not only to end a colonial regime but also to preserve order and the integrity of a state as imperial authority erodes.

British India and the Origins of the Indian National Congress

India was easily Great Britain's largest and richest imperial possession. In population and area it was equivalent to Europe west of the borders of tsarist Russia. Through much of the century prior to World War I, India had supplied Britain with raw materials and markets, secure ports for its ships, and mercenaries for its colonial armies. Its products—cotton and jute, tea, sugar, and grain—fed British mills and stomachs. Its purchases—coal and steel, steam engines and cloth—kept Britain's factories and mines busy, its workers employed, and its trade accounts in the black. Not only was India a huge and rich prize, it was also a showplace for British imperial rule—for its laws, technology, and administrative efficiency.

Geography—mountains, deserts, and jungles—isolated India from the rest of Asia, but it also divided India internally, giving it a rich variety of climates and habitats. Its peoples were even more varied. The subcontinent held speakers of over two hundred languages. Many of these groups found common ground in Hindu religious beliefs, but more than 15 percent of the subcontinent's three hundred million people were Muslims. Smaller, but still significant, religious groups included the Sikhs, Christians, and Buddhists.

Social and political differences further divided the peoples of India. In predominantly Hindu areas, a caste system divided people into more than two thousand hereditary groups based on occupation and status. Beneath this elaborate caste structure were tens of millions of so-called Untouchables, people deemed so impure by virtue of the lowly occupations of their ancestors as to be without any status whatsoever. Rigid prohibitions on contact across these groups, especially between the highest and the lowest, remained powerful in the early twentieth century.

Politically, India was fragmented between the two-thirds of the subcontinent under direct British supervision and a remaining third under the nominal control of hereditary princes or maharajahs. These princes, remnants of the aristocracy that had dominated India in the eighteenth century, acknowledged British authority over foreign affairs and British supervision of their budgets, armies, and borders in exchange for annual subventions and the retention of the trappings of power.

Britain maintained dominion, or *raj*, over this huge empire with a small commitment of its own troops and administrators—fewer than one hundred thousand on the eve of World War I. Three circumstances explain the striking disparity between British numbers and power. First, India's internal divisions made it possible for British administrators to play off one group against another. Britain had made alliances with some princes against others to expand its authority during the eighteenth and nineteenth centuries. Later, it found loyal and able recruits for the colonial army among minority groups such as the Muslims, the Sikhs, and the Gurkha tribesmen living in the foothills of the Himalayas. Second, technology afforded the British advantages. Their weapons were superior to those available to the maharajas; their telegraph lines could carry early warnings of trouble; their railroads could concentrate troops quickly where needed; their engineers built visible symbols of British power across the subcontinent in the form of canals, dams, bridges, and rail lines. Third, and perhaps most important, the British won considerable respect from India's indigenous elites, despite the pervasive racism of imperial rule. British policing reduced fratricidal warfare and banditry; British capital financed both railroads and vast irrigation projects; British schools enlarged access to education; British courts, magistrates, and officials supervised a stiff but generally honest civil service. Imperial rule served the mother country first and foremost, but it had the acquiescence of many Indians and the active support of some.

The history of India's independence movement testifies to the British success in co-opting Indian elites. Although British rule had inspired sporadic rebellions and conspiracies, the first political party to speak for all of India emerged only in the mid-1880s with the organization of the Indian National Congress. Its goals were initially modest: the achievement of a larger voice for Indians in the British-run civil service and gradual movement toward home rule and dominion status within the empire. Isolated from the majority of Indians by caste, education, and privileges, members of the Congress feared social disorder as much as they wanted self-governance.

Broader opposition to British authority began to appear in the early twentieth century. Famines, an uncontrolled epidemic of bubonic plague, and falling prices for Indian-made cloth, grain, and indigo called into question the benefits of British rule. Terrorist bombings, inspired by reports of Russian anarchist attacks, and a boycott of British cloth escalated tensions. Britain responded to the turmoil with stick and carrot, clamping down on militant opposition while giving moderates a larger, although still advisory, role in administration. This policy had some success. While many Indians distrusted Britain, others retained a basic faith in British institutions and good intentions. The Congress Party exemplified this divide. By 1908, it had split into two wings. One sought self-rule by encouraging demonstrations, boycotts, and other forms of civil disobedience; the other, larger wing continued to work for gradual reform within the framework of British laws.

World War I, however, helped to heal that divide, principally by undermining the gradualists' confidence in British competence and intentions. Britain's conduct of the war illustrated both the importance of India and British indifference to Indian interests. More than eight hundred thousand Indians served in British uniform, and another five hundred thousand worked in labor battalions; over fifty thousand Indian troops died in the service of the empire. Indian mines and mills supplied Britain with essential war materials; by the end of the war, India enjoyed a surplus in trade with Britain for the first time since accounts had been kept. Yet many Indian lives had been needlessly sacrificed in the trenches of France and the deserts of Mesopotamia, India's magnificent rail system had fallen into disrepair, and antisedition laws had abridged Indians' rights to free speech. Not for the first time, Indian interests had been sacrificed for the good of the mother country.

The Congress Party recognized that the peace settlement would bring an opportunity for India to achieve greater autonomy. By 1915, the party had begun to enlarge its support in the thousands of small villages in which most Indians lived. Allied propaganda about the virtues of national self-determination nurtured Indians' hopes for home rule, as did a British promise of eventual self-governance made in 1917. But confidence in British promises eroded quickly after the war. The British government, intent on restoring the prewar order and stifling sentiment for independence, extended wartime antisedition laws instead of repealing them, thereby giving colonial authorities broad authority to arrest and imprison political activists without the traditional right to a jury trial.

Arrests made under the new laws provoked protests in several Indian cities, and by the spring of 1919 incidents of anti-European violence and rumors of a nationwide uprising were common. The most serious violence occurred in April 1919 in Amritsar, a city of about a hundred and fifty thousand in India's northwest. The arrest of two Indian nationalists provoked riots; these led to assaults on Europeans, including the murder of three bankers and the beating of a female British physician. The commander of the city's garrison ordered Indians passing the site of the assault to crawl on their hands and knees. When a huge crowd gathered to protest this and other indignities, the brigadier ordered his troops, mostly Gurkhas and Sikhs, to open fire. Nearly four hundred civilians died, and more than a thousand were wounded.

The British government quickly relieved the officer of command, but irreparable damage had been done to the British cause. The massacre undid the effect of decades of homilies about Christian charity and the rule of law and brought hundreds of thousands of Indians over to the cause of independence. The violence also tipped the balance of opinion in India's Congress Party away from patient negotiation and toward a policy of mass mobilization and public confrontation with imperial authorities. The architect of the new policies was a middle-aged lawyer, Mohandas Gandhi.

Gandhi, Congress, and the Dilemma of Finding a Formula for Home Rule

In many respects, Gandhi was a child of the British Empire. Born to a well-connected family in one of India's princedoms, he had studied law in England before moving to an eastern province of South Africa, Natal, in 1893. There he practiced in a thriving Indian community that included many servants brought to Africa under indenture. During the next two decades, Gandhi saw the gap between British principles and practice firsthand and became a leader in efforts to secure greater political rights for his fellow Indians. An eclectic thinker, Gandhi drew upon both Western and Indian traditions in working out a program of reform. From the West, he took Christian precepts about the brotherhood of humankind and the virtues of nonviolent action. He grafted these onto a belief that social change was linked with the spiritual development of the individual—a conviction rooted in the Hindu tradition. Superimposed on both was a loyalty to his people and a fierce desire to improve their condition—spiritually, politically, and economically.

Gandhi evolved a synthetic philosophy of life and political action during his years in South Africa. Indians, he maintained, must mobilize the force of truth, *satyagraha*, to overcome injustice. Truth would strengthen the resolve of reformers and set change in motion within the hearts and minds of oppressors. Reform, in other words, would depend in part on the innate goodness of those in authority—a goodness that could be called forth by the display of virtue among the dispossessed. Violence, whether employed by oppressors or the oppressed, would ultimately be self-defeating. When wielded by those in authority, violence revealed the illegitimacy of their power; when directed against authority, it only hardened hearts and elicited more oppression. It was far better for reformers to meet injustice with reverence for life and nonviolence. This could take the form of peaceful demonstrations and noncooperation with authorities. The ultimate goal would be the attainment of greater *swaraj*, or self-rule, a term that embraced both the mastery of private passions and political self-governance. Gandhi's philosophy combined personal holiness and political savvy.

Shortly after the beginning of World War I, Gandhi returned to India, where he lived and traveled among the rural poor, deepened his acquaintance with Hindu thought, and promoted the construction of village schools and clinics. Eager to substitute domestic products for imports but suspicious of large-scale industry, Gandhi advocated small-scale craft enterprises as a way to enrich both the family and the nation. More than this, he prescribed manual labor for all Indians as a way of breaking down the barriers between thinkers and doers that the caste system had long encouraged. The spinning wheel, a symbol of his movement, could teach humility to the privileged, thrift to the poor, and self-reliance to the community as a whole.

Gandhi had endorsed the British cause in the war and hoped that the British would fulfill their promises of home rule expeditiously when the war ended. Nevertheless, like many others, he came to realize that British withdrawal would come about only as a result of determined pressure. By the time the armistice was signed, Gandhi had extended the scope of his activities from the local to the national level and had achieved a unique position in Indian politics. Many leaders of the Congress Party knew the world of the upper-caste Indian; some knew the world of the British; very few knew much about the world of the humble villager. Gandhi knew all three. Some members of Congress had strong constituencies in particular provinces or among particular religious communities. Gandhi was known nation-wide and—almost alone in Indian politics—found admirers across religious lines. While many members of the Congress Party were preoccupied with the control of patronage jobs and the preservation of caste privileges, Gandhi was focused on achieving an India that was not just independent of Britain but unified, democratic, and just. His blend of politics and spirituality was an enigma to the British. His countrymen saw in him a great spirit or *mahatma*, a teacher and master who expressed the best in Indian traditions by personal example and public acts.

British efforts to suppress dissent before and after the Amritsar massacre led to a struggle for the control of India that would continue for thirty years, waxing and waning through several major cycles. A nationwide satyagraha campaign

Margaret Bourke-White/Time Life Pictures/Getty Images

Gandhi, seen here with a spinning wheel, promoted household manufactures as a way to relieve rural poverty and to avoid the evils of industrial capitalism. In this he differed with other leaders of the Congress Party who believed that India needed heavy industries to gain economic independence and long-term prosperity.

launched by Gandhi and the Congress in 1920–1922 secured concessions giving propertied Indians greater influence in provincial government, the army, and the civil service. A second campaign, begun in 1930, had the immediate aim of ending the government's tax on salt—the production and sale of which was a state monopoly—and the broader goal of demonstrating the illegitimacy of British authority. The campaign's centerpiece was a trek across southern India that ended at the sea, where Gandhi publicly violated the law by gathering and consuming salt deposited by ocean waters. Police arrested Gandhi and more than sixty thousand of his supporters, and the government secured his agreement to end the campaign by offering modest concessions. Imperial officials thought they had dealt Gandhi a defeat, but instead it proved to be a huge political victory for the independence movement. Not only had Gandhi demonstrated, for a second time, his ability to tie India up in knots, he also had won sympathy around the world.

Gandhi and the Congress Party together made a winning combination. Gandhi's rectitude, shrewd understanding of international opinion, and affinities with the Indian masses complemented the Congress Party's political organization and access to the resources of Indian entrepreneurs and professionals. Under Gandhi's prodding, the Congress had enlarged its membership, opening its doors to the humble as well as the rich, enrolling students in a Young India League, and enlisting thousands of Indian women in an All India Women's Conference. Gandhi also understood the importance of maintaining solidarity within the independence movement. Exercising leadership as Congress president in the early 1920s and informally thereafter, Gandhi steered the party away from violent measures, which were advocated by some of its radical members, and away from Hindu particularism—a temptation that became stronger in the 1920s and 1930s as more and more Muslims gravitated toward their own political organizations, such as the Muslim League. Faced with a broad, popular movement, a succession of British governments saw little option but to withdraw from India at the lowest possible cost to Britain's international position and economic interests. As in Egypt, however, the problem was, "What comes next?"

The Congress and Gandhi were committed to a united, democratic India with a strong central government. This solution aroused anxiety among minorities, especially Muslims. The Congress Party was open to Muslims, and many Muslims respected Gandhi. Nevertheless, the Congress Party was dominated by Hindus. Any democratically elected central government would be dominated by Hindus as well, and this meant that they would command the civil service, the police, the courts, and the award of government contracts.

Muslim politicians, among whom an English-educated barrister, Mohammed Ali Jinnah, was rising to prominence, insisted that any formula for independence guarantee the political rights of Muslims. At the very least, they wanted a federal system under which predominantly Muslim provinces would enjoy considerable autonomy and a share of seats in the Indian parliament that exceeded their representation in the general population. From the perspective of the Congress, such a federation was a recipe for partition. Muslim and Hindu provinces would go their separate ways, and other minorities would demand equivalent autonomy, returning

India to the weak and divided condition it had been in when the British arrived. Extremists on each side suspected the other side of plotting forcible conversions, organized theft, or even massacres. These suspicions and fears intensified as it became clear that independence was approaching.

No one could find a formula for independence that was acceptable to all major groups. The British lurched from one short-term expedient to another, at times offering concessions and at other times clamping down on outspoken advocates of change. Through it all, the Indian economy suffered. Uncertainty about the future, strikes, and boycotts discouraged British investment. World agricultural prices were weak through the 1920s and disastrously so in the early 1930s, driving millions of peasants off the land. Indian industry could not absorb the surplus labor. As a global depression began to settle in, millions fell into lives of desperate poverty in cities that could offer neither relief nor basic services. As in Egypt and elsewhere, the urban destitute amplified political tensions by serving as an ever-visible sign of social dysfunction and an ever-ready source of disciples for political and religious extremists.

After failing at repression and negotiation, in 1935 the British resorted to a unilateral solution—a Government of India Act that declared India to be a confederation of largely autonomous provinces. The scheme offered every group part of what it wanted but satisfied none. The franchise was broadened, but only to include about 20 percent of adults. Minorities were guaranteed seats in provincial assemblies by a system of separate electorates. The assemblies exercised broad powers of government, but British governors retained crucial reserve powers. An elected federal legislature appointed members of a federal Executive Council, but the British viceroy continued to hold the power to veto legislation and to rule under emergency decrees. Hereditary princes retained seats in the upper house of the federal parliament but lost some of their customary privileges.

The act was never fully implemented and failed to resolve the issues that were vexing India. Minorities continued to feel exposed to abuse by majorities. The Congress Party objected to the wide powers granted to provincial governments, the role of hereditary princes in the federal legislature, and the powers reserved to the British governors and the viceroy. Many British officials saw the act as a surrender; those who sought disengagement saw in it a commitment of indefinite duration and expense. The act did lead to nationwide elections in which the Congress Party won a mandate in all but the predominantly Muslim parts of India. Whatever India's future, the Congress Party would be a crucial part of it.

The Quiescent Colonies

The independence movements in Egypt and India were the most vigorous challenges to Britain's empire in the aftermath of the war, but there were others. In Iraq, Britain defended its League mandate by waging war against Kurdish tribesmen who were seeking their own nation. In Palestine, another League mandate, Jews pressed Britain to fulfill its wartime promise to create a Jewish homeland, while Arabs assailed the British for permitting thousands of European Jews to settle on their land. Headlines about skirmishes in the mountains of Iraq and the alleys of Jerusalem competed for space in London's newspapers with stories about bombings in Ireland, riots in Cairo, and demonstrations in India. Taken together with reports about anti-imperialist movements in China, the outspoken nationalism of Kemal Atatürk in Turkey, and the anti-imperialist tirades of Russia's Bolsheviks, readers could easily imagine that the entire globe was rising.

But this was not so. The independence movements that flourished in India and Egypt after the war found few analogues elsewhere among Europe's colonies. Sub-Saharan Africa, despite the economic dislocations caused by the war, remained generally quiescent. So, too, did the extensive Dutch and French colonies in Southeast Asia, despite sporadic outbursts of nationalist rhetoric from students and urban professionals. The Philippine Islands, an American possession since the Spanish-American War, saw no recurrence of the guerrilla warfare of the early years of the century. And the United States continued to intervene frequently in the affairs of its neighbors in the Caribbean and Central America, much as it had done before the war.

The contrast between the colonial areas that caught the fire of nationalism and those that did not underlines the importance of certain internal factors in the formation of popular anti-imperialism. A history of exploitation and abuse of authority was not, in itself, sufficient to generate mass movements. Independence movements such as those that appeared in Egypt, India, and Korea required leadership, an audience receptive to a nationalist message, and means by which leaders and followers could make connections with each other.

In many colonies, one or more of these conditions were absent. Consider the case of sub-Saharan Africa, a region in which Britain, France, Belgium, and Portugal all administered huge empires during the 1920s. Exploitation there certainly was; in many areas it was egregious. During the war, France had impressed hundreds of thousands of West Africans into service as soldiers and laborers. Village chiefs were threatened with jail if they did not produce a certain number of "volunteers," and African recruiters, working for the French, roamed the countryside seizing young men, much as slave raiders had done a century earlier. The French gave scant attention to the hardships this caused until faced with insurrections in the countryside and plunging food production. Britain also drafted tens of thousands of Africans into its service during a long campaign against an army of German colonials in East Africa. The British typically relied on cash rather than coercion to find recruits, but the conditions of service were severe, and villages in the prime recruiting grounds of Kenya and South Africa suffered the prolonged absence or loss of their young men, three hundred fifty thousand of whom were engaged as bearers, laborers, and soldiers.

Such abuses were not a wartime aberration. Both before and after the war, colonial officials sacrificed the interests of Africans to those of the state, European-owned business firms, and European settlers. Colonial administrators built railroads and telegraph lines by mandating a certain number of days of obligatory labor and pressured villagers to work in Western-owned mines or on Western-controlled plantations by imposing hut or head taxes payable in scarce European currency. Village lands were declared vacant and transferred to the control of European entrepreneurs who grew peanuts, rapeseed, rubber, sugar, bananas, and coffee for export. Legislation passed in 1913 stripped Africans of the right to own land in more than 90 percent of South Africa. In 1936 a government run by about thirty-five thousand white settlers reserved half of all land in Rhodesia for white ownership. In Kenya, British authorities granted a few thousand white settlers control of four-and-a-half million acres of prime agricultural land. France gave a few dozen investment companies thirty-year concessions over huge tracts in Gabon and Chad in return for rent and a modest share of the profit (little of which was realized).

Regulations governing the working and housing conditions of African laborers, where they existed at all, were slanted to promote the interests of white management. African workers were segregated into overcrowded and filthy barracks or shantytown sections of cities. While the British made sporadic efforts to improve the health, education, and living conditions of their subjects, Portugal squeezed as much as it could from its colonies in Angola and Mozambique at the minimum possible cost. Perhaps worst of all was the Belgian administration of the vast area in central Africa drained by the Congo River. It had been run as a personal fiefdom by Belgium's King Leopold II from 1884 to 1908. The abuses of his regime, which ranged from pillage to the mutilation of Africans accused of petty theft, had shocked even apologists for imperial rule and had prompted the Belgian government to assume management of the colony. The Congo's new administrators curbed some of the violence, but they made the Congo the scene of a development project as cruel as it was grand. The colony's Katanga province, rich in copper, gold, and other metals, became the site of huge investments in mines, railroads, and metal-processing plants during the 1920s. By 1925 this mini-Manchester in the jungle, complete with European-style public buildings and prisonlike barracks for native labor, was the world's third largest producer of copper, after the United States and Chile, and was well on its way to becoming a source for much of the world's uranium and radium. The Congolese saw little of this bounty, except as they loaded it onto railcars for shipment overseas. The Belgians called it progress.

Where workers concentrated—on docks, in mines, and on plantations—there was resistance, although it was rarely coordinated. Angry laborers might steal, loaf, strike, or even riot, but conditions did not lend themselves to political organization. Workers in large mines or on big plantations were often recruited from different tribal or language groups. They worked seasonally or for specified terms and then returned to their villages. Unions were discouraged or prohibited.

The colonial powers, with the exception of Britain, gave little attention to promoting literacy in their African colonies, and in some there was no indigenous tradition of book learning. Consequently, very few workers were literate. The ability to read and write was not, of course, essential to politics, but it is difficult to convert aspirations into a political movement or party without a literate leadership.

Except in South Africa, modern forms of communication and transportation had not penetrated far into the interior. Telegraph lines were sparse and primarily served the colonial bureaucracy; railroads and paved roads hardly existed outside a few locales of extensive exploitation, such as the Belgian Congo's Katanga province. Rivers provided the only access to the interior of Africa, as had been true for centuries. Huge tracts of forest, savannah, and desert were barriers to transit and obstructed political organization at levels beyond the village.

Even where shipping, heavy industry, or plantation agriculture was taking root, there were few signs of popular nationalism. The histories and unique cultures of Korea and Egypt had undergirded the nationalist aspirations of their twentieth-century leaders. India, despite its internal divisiveness, had been a single political entity at times in the past and was administered as such by the British, who, over generations of rule, had knit the subcontinent together with an extensive rail network and powerful civil service. By contrast, borders in sub-Saharan Africa were recent and often ignored cultural and linguistic filiations. Consequently, while exploited Africans might feel aggrieved and resentful, they seldom channeled these feelings into anything resembling nationalism. Grassroots yearnings for change typically focused on strengthening tribal or kinship groupings or on redressing local labor grievances, if they found expression at all.

The imperial exploitation of Africa was brutal and large-scale, but not unique. Similar abuses occurred in the Dutch East Indies, British Malaya, French Indochina, and Japanese Formosa, Korea, and Manchuria. Although apologists for imperialism had argued that colonies would eventually benefit from foreign control, the exploitation grew more intense and widespread after the war than it had been before. Technological change had much to do with this trend. Agricultural research led to new strains of tropical crops that were well suited to commercial cultivation. Medical research led to better preventives for malaria and sleeping sickness, thereby making tropical climates safer for European settlers. Larger and faster merchant ships propelled by reliable and fuel-efficient diesel engines could carry bulk cargoes at lower costs than the steamships of 1900. These changes created opportunities for profit in regions that hitherto had been deemed too poor, too dangerous, or too remote to merit attention.

Over time imperial rule tended to create the conditions necessary for the formation of organized resistance, as it had done in India. The construction of railroads or the improvement of ports turned villages into towns and towns into cities and set in motion economic changes that had far-reaching social effects. Agile members of local elites might adapt to the changes by cooperating with the new authorities, taking advantage of commercial opportunities, and placing their sons in missionary schools to acquire skills that were of use to business and the state. The Indian independence movement emerged from such elites, and similar movements were under way in Africa, the Dutch East Indies, Malaya, and Indochina by the 1920s. But they were small and weak by comparison with India's, finding support mainly where commercial development was intense: in Dakar, the port city of Senegal; in Elisabethville, the industrial hub of Katanga; and in Jakarta, the great trading port of the Dutch East Indies.

In most of these regions, larger-scale movements toward independence would emerge only after economic development advanced further and a second world war disrupted the empires that had survived the first.

Dependency and Development

World War I led to the creation of a host of new states in Eastern Europe and accelerated independence movements in colonies where local conditions were ripe for change. What about those large parts of the world that were nominally self-governing but were dependent on Europe for capital and markets? This was the condition of the great majority of the non-European members of the League of Nations: a group that included China, Australia, New Zealand, and the republics of Latin America. The histories of these societies were quite diverse, reflecting their distinct cultural traditions, geographies, and resources. Nevertheless, they confronted some common dilemmas. To one degree or another, all had become integrated into the global economy on unequal terms. Although they were often rich in agricultural and mineral resources, they were deficient in the capital necessary to make those resources productive. Most lacked internal markets that were sufficiently large and wealthy to sustain diversified industrial economies. Some, like the British dominions and the larger states of Latin America, were well along in building the infrastructures necessary for participation in global trade: railroads and ports, legal and administrative systems, banks and corporations. Others, including most of the nations of Central America, were at early stages in this process. But all developing nations wrestled with the social and political effects of economic development: urbanization, the circulation of new ideas about governance, the growth of new economic groups, and conflicts over the control of land. Development meant clashes between old and new ways of life.

Export Economies, Boom-Bust Cycles, and Political Instability

With few exceptions, these nations were debtors. They borrowed abroad to finance development at home and met payments on their loans by exporting commodities. The strategy had both benefits and risks. Foreign capital not only financed railroads, port facilities, mines, and plants for processing raw materials but also underwrote electrical, telegraph and telephone networks. The export of commodities provided the income to purchase imports, upon which tax revenues were typically based. Higher government income sometimes meant improved social services, especially in the urban districts—more schools, more housing, and better provision for public health. By 1900 Buenos Aires had become *la reina del Plata*, the queen of the River Plate, or, as the French claimed, the Paris of South America. Carriages with rubber tires, automobiles, and electric-powered trolleys rode the newly asphalted streets and the wide avenues connecting the city's landmarks. In Brazil, new prosperity brought about by a boom in coffee and rubber prices began the transformation of São Paulo into the leading industrial center of Latin America. Even Manaus, in the middle of the Amazon, boasted the amenities of European cities, including electric street lighting and an imposing theater. In Canada, Australia, New Zealand, and Argentina, prosperity extended beyond the major cities and into large parts of the countryside, where grain, cattle, and sheep afforded growers and their suppliers a comfortable lifestyle.

Nevertheless, all of these states, to a greater or lesser degree, had an exaggerated sensitivity to the business cycle: When Europe or America sneezed, much of Latin America got pneumonia. One reason for this sensitivity was an unevenness in investment that tied prosperity to the performance of one or two industries. A nation that derives income from a broad array of industries will generally be able to absorb economic downturns more easily than one that is dependent on a few sources of income because economic recessions rarely affect all sectors of an economy simultaneously. In times of rapid growth, diversified economies will tend to grow at a moderate pace for much the same reason: Prosperity moves through an economy like a wave, raising some boats before others. By contrast, the economy of a nation whose resources are heavily concentrated in a single industry often careens from highs to lows. Such a nation can grow at a dizzying rate if its special strength is in a sector that enjoys high demand but faces catastrophic failure if that demand dries up. The damage done by downturns is obvious: unemployment, shortages of credit, and falling tax receipts. But rapid growth can also carry penalties. A boom will often encourage investors to increase their wagers on the winning industries, thus producing an even greater concentration of resources in a few sectors.

Commodity prices remained stable during the late nineteenth and early twentieth centuries. Economic growth in Europe and the United States proceeded apace with the expansion of the supply of raw materials; Europe provided a reliable source of credit, and an international gold standard made it easy to transfer funds from one currency to another. But the era of stable prices ended with World War I. Britain and other major trading nations suspended convertibility of their currencies into gold, redirected capital from foreign to domestic investments, and shifted production and shipping from civilian to military needs.

These sudden changes in long-established patterns caused global dislocations. The war proved a boon to exporting nations that produced materials of strategic importance. Bolivian tin, Peruvian copper, Chilean nitrates, and Venezuelan oil were in high demand, as were the grains of Canada, the beef of Argentina, and the wool of New Zealand and Australia. After the war, however, commodity prices oscillated rapidly and unpredictably. Producers of grains, sugar, cotton, and meat, who had expanded their operations during the war, now found themselves in a cutthroat competition that depressed prices. Exporters of materials essential to war, such as the nitrates that were an ingredient in explosives, faced wholesale cancellations of contracts. The economic news was not all somber. The rapid growth of the U.S. automobile industry and the worldwide expansion of electrical utilities sustained strong markets for rubber, oil, copper, tin, and lead. Demand grew, as well, for coffee and bananas, products that millions of middle-class consumers in Europe and the United States put on their breakfast tables after the war. Nevertheless, the abrupt shifts in trade created challenges for both winners and losers.

Latin America was both the main beneficiary and the chief victim of these oscillations. Between 1913 and 1928 it doubled its share of the world market in petroleum, copper, lead, and wheat, and significantly increased its share in such other important commodities as tin, silver, beef, sugar, and maize. Yet its income did not consistently track the growth in the volume of trade. While South America continued to produce large quantities of coffee and rubber, for example, plantations in Africa and Asia became potent competitors, ending Latin America's monopolies and bringing prices down to levels at which profits were hard to realize.

Price instability afflicted industrial nations as well. U.S. agriculture, for example, after enjoying unprecedented prosperity during the 1910s, entered a prolonged slump after the war. The hard times extended, almost without interruption, into the global depression of the 1930s. But the plight of American farmers had only a modest impact on the U.S. economy as a whole during the 1920s because the manufacturing and construction sectors were expanding vigorously. The situation was quite different in a nation such as Argentina, which derived a much larger share of its national income from the sale of farm goods than did the United States.

Most vulnerable of all were states in which only one or two commodities dominated exports. Strong international prices for the key export would trigger a frenzied boom in employment, construction, and public spending, and the flood of money would drive up the prices of foodstuffs and imported goods. Weak prices for the key export would bring unemployment, defaults on debt, government deficits, shortages of cash and credit, and, sometimes, price deflation. Whereas inflation eroded the value of savings and impoverished those workers whose incomes lagged behind prices, deflation was devastating to borrowers because the real value of payments on loans rose as the purchasing power of currency decreased.

Economies would thus lurch from one crisis to another in response to changing world demand (Map 4.2). In Cuba, the key commodity was sugar; in Bolivia, it was tin; in Colombia, coffee; in Peru, copper; in Guatemala and Honduras, bananas. In most cases, national governments could do little to temper the oscillations because commodity prices were beyond their control. Prices for sugar depended not only on the size of Cuba's crop but also on such factors as production by sugar cane plantations in the Philippines and Africa and tariff policies in the United States and Europe. Large-scale cultivation of a single crop also exposed growers to biological risks. Plant diseases, for example, sharply curtailed the export of bananas from Costa Rica and destroyed the cacao industry in Ecuador during the 1920s.

Reliance on the export of a few commodities to Europe and North America has been a recurring pattern in Latin American history, going back to the gold and silver mining of the colonial era. Some historians have viewed this pattern in trade to be the basic reason for many of the differences between North and

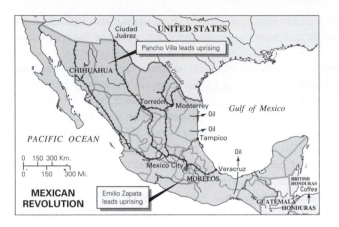

MAP 4.2 Latin America, 1929.
Latin America, like Africa and much of Asia, depended on the export of commodities for the foreign exchange to purchase industrial goods. This dependence created boom and bust economic cycles and sharpened tensions between economic classes in nations such as Mexico.

South America. Dependence on the production and sale of commodities for export, so the argument runs, magnifies inequalities in wealth and status, serves to keep political power concentrated in the hands of a landed elite, and leaves nations vulnerable to domination from abroad. Critics of this "dependency theory" have pointed out that exports rarely constituted more than a modest fraction of the economic activity in South American nations and noted that many factors contributed to the dominance of landed elites in Latin America. Nevertheless, even critics acknowledge that economies drawing a large fraction of their foreign exchange from the sale of a handful of commodities expose themselves to boom-bust cycles that exacerbate social conflict.

As in India, Africa, or any large and complex region, the conflicts were many and varied. Latin America was a kaleidoscope of societies that differed from each other in ethnic and racial makeup, wealth, social structure, and attitudes toward Europe and the United States. In some, such as Bolivia, enduring divisions between those of predominantly Indian or Spanish origin remained politically potent; in others, such as Chile, Indian populations were modest by comparison with more recent immigrant groups from Germany or Italy. Skin color was less central to identity than in the United States, but it nevertheless was often a marker of status and wealth in Brazil, Cuba, and other societies where African slaves had once worked fields of sugar cane. Whereas Argentina had sufficient wealth to provide near-universal schooling to its children, illiteracy was the rule in large parts of the Andes and the back-country of Central America, where wealth and its privileges were tightly held by a tiny land-owning elite. Yankee imperialism reverberated more powerfully in Colombia, which had lost its Panamanian province through U.S. intervention, than in Argentina, where foreign investors more often spoke with a British than an American accent. Greatly as these fracture lines differed, they all could become deep fissures under the wedge of economic boom and bust.

Tensions were most acute in those Latin American republics making the most rapid economic progress. In growing cities such as Rio de Janiero, Buenos Aires, and Mexico City, ideas about political reform began to circulate among professionals, civil servants, and businessmen. These well-educated groups tended to see liberal political institutions, designed along the lines of those of Britain, France, and the United States, as the surest road to sustained economic development, and to see economic development as a precondition for broad improvements in standards of living. Many of these reformers sought to open government to persons of their own social background and to shift some of the tax burden from import duties to land taxes. This agenda placed them in direct conflict with older elites—a landholding oligarchy and the Catholic Church—that saw much to lose and little to gain from change. Growing cities were also nurseries for labor unions. Although most unions began with narrow aims (better wages and working conditions), some evolved into organizations with broad political goals that sometimes coincided with and sometimes conflicted with those of the educated elites.

The population of industrial workers and urban professionals in the cities of Latin America was growing rapidly during the decades around the turn of the century, but these groups remained small in comparison with the peasantry. In most regions, peasants remained too isolated to be a factor in politics, but where railroads went, they, too, could become a force for change. As elsewhere in the world, modern means of communication and transportation brought large, previously isolated regions into contact with the institutions of the state and with capitalism.

As ways of life changed and local elites came to be nested within the elites of nation or empire, social conflict and political disorder often ensued. Economic development served the interests of those who were plugged into the network of international exchange but engendered resentment among others who were still attached to older forms of social life and production. The result could be fierce rivalries that pitted established landowners against newly arrived speculators, and traditional authorities such as the clergy against secular authorities representing the state, capital, or science. Contests for local power could easily enlist villagers and peasants, who often had grievances against both parties. Sometimes peasants also found the opportunity to press their own interests: rights to land, higher wages, education, and influence over courts, tax collectors, and magistrates.

The conflicts generated by economic development in the early twentieth century varied from society to society, although general patterns are visible in the history of many nations. Mexico's history exemplifies many of the tensions generated by rapid economic change, and it is especially interesting because of the way the country responded to them. Mexico underwent a revolution that nearly dismembered the state, but that ultimately led to the broadening of economic opportunity and political participation. The events in Mexico inspired other revolutionaries later in the century, among them Cuba's Fidel Castro. They also provide an object lesson in the risks of rapid economic and social change.

Mexico's Revolution

Mexico did not participate in World War I, but it underwent a trauma that was no less severe—an extended civil war that profoundly altered its political and social structure. The Mexican Revolution began in 1910 after nearly thirty-five years in which Mexican politics had been dominated by Porfirio Díaz, a wily general-turned-politician who promoted economic development while maintaining firm control over Mexico's political system.

Grow, Mexico did, under Díaz. Workers, some of them from as far away as China, laid down some fifteen thousand miles of railroad tracks. Telegraph lines followed the railroads, and submarine cables linked Mexican ports to the United States and Europe. Mines and smelters prospered, as production of copper, zinc, silver, and gold all grew, and a new industry appeared when large reserves of oil were tapped near the Gulf ports of Tampico and Veracruz. Manufacturing, too, expanded. By the turn of the century, Mexico was producing significant quantities of cloth, carpets, cement, and beer. This industrialization, however, did not spur the development of a Mexican entrepreneurial class. Foreign investors financed the construction of railroads, telegraphs, and urban streetcar systems; foreign firms underwrote mining and oil drilling. Dividends on these investments went to those who provided the capital, and many of the best jobs went to British and American managers and engineers.

Although the Díaz regime was successful in attracting foreign investment, in the end it became a victim of the economic and social changes it had stimulated. Railroads, mines, and other large business enterprises brought rural districts into contact with the global economy, encouraged land speculation, and gave rise to new forms of commercial agriculture. The large farms and ranches, or haciendas, which had once been the nuclei of self-sufficient communities, turned to commercial crops such as sugar and tightened their control over land and water to which villagers had traditional but not legal rights. Indians, such as the Yaqui of Sonora, were pushed aside. Those who resisted were sent to work on plantations in the Yucatan; others retreated to a hardscrabble life in the mountains. By the turn of the century, the vast majority of the rural population was landless.

But even landowners could feel threatened by the economics of the Díaz era. The banks that financed capital improvements and the railroads that moved produce acquired new influence in rural districts, diluting the authority of local grandees. So, too, did agents of the state, who interested themselves in regions with cash crops and rising land values. Workers in the railroad towns nursed grievances against the Chinese laborers who had been imported to help build the rail lines and against Spanish shopkeepers, who were the most visible representatives of outside exploitation. At the same time, new elites associated with mobile capital and commercial development were becoming dissatisfied with older institutions that preserved the power of old landed oligarchs and a small ruling clique. Urban doctors and lawyers yearned for honest elections and honest administration, businessmen for legal and administrative reforms, and commercial farmers and ranchers for more influence over provincial governments.

The revolution began when one of these wealthy outsiders, Francisco Madero, contested a loss to Díaz in the presidential election of 1910. His call to arms, "Effective Suffrage and No Reelection," enlisted well-to-do reformers and disaffected politicians, workers, and peasants. The rebels quickly overwhelmed Díaz's poorly trained and demoralized troops. In May 1911, the aged Díaz resigned and left for Europe.

The events of 1910–1911 were the prelude to an extended civil war that sometimes resembled a free-for-all. Madero could neither quiet the turmoil in the countryside that his campaign had unleashed nor satisfy the exaggerated expectations of his supporters. Provincial revolts and disloyal lieutenants soon rose up against his government. Madero fixed his attention on controlling agrarian revolutionaries, such as the charismatic Emiliano Zapata, who demanded land for their peasant followers. But the federal army was more dangerous to Madero's shaky rule. In early 1913, the leader of that army, Victoriano Huerta, overturned

Madero's government with the connivance of the U.S. ambassador, who despaired of Madero's prospects for restoring order. Madero and his vice president were killed in February 1913.

Huerta proved no more successful than Madero at consolidating power. Huerta sought to impose authority with brutality, but ended up only strengthening the opposition. Within months of his coup, he faced three rebel armies: A guerrilla band under Zapata had all but seized control of the countryside south of Mexico City, and two more conventional armies were working their way toward the capital from Mexico's northernmost provinces. One, under the command of Alvaro Obregón, moved along the Pacific Coast; the other, under the bandit-rebel Francisco (Pancho) Villa, followed the rail line that ran through Mexico's central plateau. All three acknowledged the nominal authority of a fourth opposition leader, Venustiano Carranza, former governor of the northern state of Coahuila. In a series of battles, Villa and Obregón defeated the federal armies facing them, and in August 1914—just as war was beginning in Europe—Carranza entered Mexico City.

Culver Pictures

Three leaders of the Mexican Revolution, Emiliano Zapata, Venustiano Carranza, and Pancho Villa, are seen here during a moment of comity in 1914. Having toppled the government of their common adversary, Victoriano Huerta, the alliance disintegrated after Carranza assumed Mexico's presidency.

Once again, a coup led to a new cycle of violence. The years of disorder had left provincial strongmen in command of many parts of Mexico; the most powerful among them was Villa, who neither trusted nor feared Carranza. Carranza, however, displayed more skill in consolidating power than had his predecessors. Combining tact, force, and propaganda, he slowly extended his control over Mexico. To Zapata's peasant army, he promised land reforms and influence over administration and courts in the districts in which they held power. To urban professionals, he promised a new, more democratic constitution and stringent controls on the Catholic Church, which liberals saw as having too much wealth and political influence. To labor, he promised free unions and socialist policies on the control of capital. To many strongmen in the provinces, he promised autonomy in the management of local affairs. And to Villa, he turned the sword. A reformed federal army under the command of Obregón ultimately defeated and dispersed Villa's forces in 1915. During the next five years, Carranza turned against weaker opponents: provincial strongmen (including Zapata, who was killed while fighting federal forces), anarchist and socialist unions, and bandits.

The new regime delivered on some promises—enough to retain public support while reassembling Mexico under a strong central government. A new constitution, ratified in 1917, provided Mexicans with a list of legal rights, although neither Carranza nor his successors respected those rights when their own interests were at stake. Carranza dissolved many estates and confiscated church property, distributing some land to peasants but using much of it for payoffs to political supporters. He enforced rigid controls on the church, provoking atrocities against clerics and rural insurrections among the faithful. The regime opened opportunities to many Mexicans, rich and poor, who had been shut out of polite society and government in earlier times, but less out of deep conviction than out of pragmatic self-interest. It claimed national ownership of mineral resources, including the oil that was beginning to flow in large quantities from fields developed by American firms, but it did little to enforce the claim. It decried the graft of the Díaz era but turned a blind eye to its own corruption.

Carranza was assassinated in 1920, but his successor, Alvaro Obregón, continued his pragmatic style of administration. To his predecessor's cautious land reforms, Obregón added a campaign to wipe out illiteracy. He gave labor unions influence in government so long as they did not challenge his power. And he encouraged intellectuals and artists to create a Mexican/Revolutionary culture rooted in Mexico's Indian past, a task undertaken by painters Diego Rivera, José Clemente Orozco, and David Alfaro Siqueiros, among others.

Through a mixture of genuine (if incomplete) reforms, political responsiveness (alloyed with corruption), coercion, and nationalistic propaganda, Obregón found a recipe for consolidating power centrally. His successor, Plutarco Elías Calles, perfected it, founding in 1929 the Partido Nacional Revolucionario, later renamed the Partido Revolucionario Institucional, or PRI. It was to retain power in Mexico through the rest of the century, giving Mexico neither complete democracy nor naked tyranny. Mexico avoided the brutal dictatorships of left and right that afflicted many other parts of the world. It recovered from the disastrous decade of civil war, inflation, famine, and disease. By the end of the 1920s, per capita income was up, food prices were down, the government had taken partially effective measures against epidemic disease and illiteracy, and foreign investment had grown, if not as quickly as during the long Díaz administration. Mexico's revolution subdued the forces of class and region that had threatened to dismember the state and succeeded in giving millions of Mexicans some stake in the nation.

CONCLUSION

Mexico's revolution illustrates the dilemma facing nations that were on the periphery of the industrial West during the early twentieth century: Economic development along European lines demanded foreign capital, but such investment triggered social changes that no one could control. By enlarging the literate middle class, development created a group that was receptive to European and U.S. ideas about politics and was eager to achieve influence commensurate with its growing knowledge and wealth. By building large-scale enterprises, such as mines and railroads, it created concentrations of landless laborers who were vulnerable to unemployment and open to mobilization for political ends. By creating a standing army, it enlarged the role of the officer corps in public affairs. By granting foreigners influence on economic life, it provoked resentments that could easily turn into violent xenophobia. And by creating winners and losers in the countryside, both among landowners and among the lower classes, it upset old patterns of deference and stimulated local feuds—small fires that could spread into conflagrations as leaders of local factions aligned themselves with regional strongmen and enrolled peasants, disaffected minorities, bandits, or mercenaries in their cause.

Much the same general patterns are visible in the other republics of Latin America during the early twentieth century. In some, especially those in which economic development was less far-reaching than in Mexico, established landowners and the church remained dominant. In others, old oligarchies worked with businessmen and professionals to maintain order despite sporadic challenges. In most, however, economic development provoked chronic political discord as old and new elites, unions and peasant-based popular movements, increasingly radical intellectuals and conservative military officers all competed, legally and extra-legally, for control of the state. The growing dependence of many South American economies on commodity exports during the 1920s intensified instability, both by extending the influence of capitalist development from coastal ports into the hinterlands and by amplifying the effects of boom-bust cycles.

The global economy was hard to resist but dangerous to enter. In states where land and wealth were distributed broadly and political institutions were open to gradual reform, such as Canada, Australia, and New Zealand, the conflicts elicited by integration into the global economy remained essentially peaceful. In states where wealth was concentrated in the hands of a few and political institutions were closed to the expression of new interests, rapid economic change led to violence.

Upheavals during the early twentieth century occurred not just in Mexico but also, as we saw in Chapter 3, in Russia and Ottoman Turkey. As we shall soon see, China, too, underwent a revolution that stretched from the collapse of the Qing dynasty in 1912 to the consolidation of Mao Zedong's control of mainland China in 1949. Humiliating defeats in war and foreign intrusions played much larger roles in the Russian, Turkish, and Chinese revolutions than in the Mexican Revolution. Although all four revolutions led to one-party states, the victors in Russia and China combined nationalism with a universalistic Marxist ideology. The victors in Turkey and Mexico, by contrast, were more eclectic in their ideas and less expansionist in their ambitions.

Despite differences, these upheavals shared the common denominator of conflict between old political and social institutions and Western-style economic development. As in Mexico, urban intellectuals in imperial Russia, Ottoman Turkey, and Qing China were eager to modernize their nations by adopting the technology and institutions of the industrial West. Russian liberals and socialists, the Young Turks, and the Chinese leaders of the May Fourth Movement shared an interest in land reform, democracy, and education with liberal reformers in Mexico, such as Francisco Madero. As in Mexico, the social conflicts associated with development soon eclipsed the narrower political conflicts between liberal and conservative elites. In all four societies, the growth of rail lines and ports had given rise to new commercial undertakings that threatened old interests, altered patterns of land use and tenure, created pockets of industry, undermined traditions of deference, and created pools of mobile labor that were vulnerable to fluctuations in global economic conditions. In Russia and China, revolutions evolved along class lines as revolutionary parties under the leadership of Lenin and Mao enrolled disaffected workers and peasants in their campaigns to sweep aside old elites and their institutions. In Mexico and Turkey, revolutionary leaders such as Carranza and Atatürk achieved the same result by grafting programs of land and social reform onto more xenophobic forms of nationalism.

Whether they emphasized the overriding importance of class or nation, the leaders of the revolutions in Mexico, Russia, Turkey, and China were discovering a lesson that was dawning as well on the leaders of independence movements in India and Egypt: Peasants and workers, when organized and led, could be powerful agents of social and political change.

For Further Reading

Victor Bulmer-Thomas, *The Economic History of Latin America Since Independence* (Cambridge: Cambridge University Press, 1994). Up to date and reliable.
Basil Davidson, *Africa in Modern History: The Search for a New Society* (London: Allen Lane, 1978). An introduction to the complex history of sub-Saharan Africa.

Susan J. Douglas, *Inventing American Broadcasting, 1899–1922* (Baltimore: Johns Hopkins University Press, 1987). Situates radio in the U.S. social context.

Daniel R. Headrick, *The Tentacles of Progress: Technology Transfer in the Age of Imperialism, 1850–1940* (New York: Oxford University Press, 1988). Discusses relations between European powers and their colonies in the 1920s and 1930s; unique in its broad scope and originality.

Lawrence James, *Raj: The Making and Unmaking of British India* (New York: St. Martin's Press, 1998). Engaging but Anglocentric.

Marius B. Jansen, *The Making of Modern Japan* (Cambridge: Belknap Press of Harvard University Press, 2002). A good source for readers seeking to learn more about Japan in the early twentieth century.

Alan Knight, *The Mexican Revolution*, 2 vols. (Cambridge and New York: Cambridge University Press, 1986). Balances rich detail on Mexico's social history and penetrating analysis of the politics of the revolutionary era.

Sally Marks, *The Illusion of Peace: International Relations in Europe 1918–1933* (New York: St. Martin's Press, 1976). A critical appraisal of postwar diplomacy.

Jonathan D. Spence, *The Gate of Heavenly Peace: The Chinese and Their Revolution, 1895–1980* (New York: Penguin, 1982). An exquisite study of social change, political thought, and action in modern China.

Stanley Wolpert, *A New History of India*, Eighth Edition (New York: Oxford University Press, 2008). A broad survey of India's political and social history.

M. E. Yapp, *The Near East Since the First World War: A History to 1995*, Second Edition (London: Longman, 1996). Sensitive to the social and political differences within a complex region.

Related Websites

World War I Document Archive
http://wwi.lib.byu.edu/index.php/Main_Page
Includes texts of peace treaties ending World War I and documents on the League of Nations.

League of Nations Photo Archive
http://www.indiana.edu/~league/photos.htm
A well-organized collection of historical photos of individuals and conferences.

The Mexican Revolution
http://www.latinamericanstudies.org/mex-revolution.htm
Photographs and documents pertaining to the Mexican revolution and links to other sites.

CHAPTER 5

Knowing and Doing: Science and Technology, 1919–1939

"The sound struck her like a blow. She crouched together against the masonry and looked up…. There was nothing else in the world but a crimson-purple glare and sound, deafening, all-embracing, continuing sound…. She had an impression of a great ball of crimson-purple fire like a maddened living thing."[1]

This scene is all too familiar to modern readers, who may simply ask whether the city being described is Hiroshima or Nagasaki. Yet the passage does not describe the atomic bombings that ended World War II but rather the destruction of Paris by a fictional atomic bomb. It appears in *The World Set Free*, a novel published in 1914—decades before such a weapon existed. The author, H. G. Wells, invented a future in which a means is found to release the abundant energy that holds atomic nuclei together. He predicted that nuclear energy would be harnessed both to produce both electricity and bombs. The latter, he wrote, would be used in a cataclysmic world war during the 1940s. Dropped from planes, the bombs would destroy world capitals, force a peace, and lead to the formation of a new international government.

Wells was not alone in expecting science to produce startling discoveries about nature nor in anticipating that they would have practical consequences. Like all futurists, Wells was projecting ahead from trends that were already visible. Since the seventeenth century, science had demonstrated a capacity to constantly renew itself; since the mid-nineteenth century, it had demonstrated a growing power not only to explain but to control the physical world. Wells's readers around the globe were adjusting to machines, materials, and technological systems that relied on

---

[1]H. G. Wells, *The World Set Free in the Works of H. G. Wells*, Vol. 21 (New York: Charles Scribner's Sons, 1926), pp. 78–79.

science. Dynamo-lit cities, gasoline-powered automobiles and aircraft, electrically transmitted voices, and synthetic dyes and food preservatives had all appeared within the previous fifty years, as had the armor, high explosives, and range finders of modern battleships. Science-based inventions were creating new industries, integrating distant parts of the world into global networks of exchange, and altering patterns of life from great capitals to distant hinterlands. Wells saw a world in which knowledge was coming to be the source of power and foresaw a future in which it would become even more potent.

Still, Wells's crystal ball yielded some misapprehensions. His nuclear power plants were small enough to power automobiles. Pilots dropped his atomic bombs by hand from biplanes. His new world government was run by scientists, to whom politicians gladly yielded power. Wells credited the discovery of both nuclear fission and the first nuclear reactor to a lone scientist working in a dusty academic laboratory. Here, as elsewhere, Wells imagined a future based on his present. For Wells, as for most of his contemporaries, scientific discovery and invention were the creative acts of individual genius. Although he understood that a transformation was under way in the relation between knowing and doing, he failed to appreciate the broad social foundations upon which the revolution depended. Wells could conjure up an atomic bomb, but not a Manhattan Project.

World War I and the postwar decades illustrate both what Wells understood aright and what he was, understandably, less conscious of. It was an era of continuing revolution in science and technology and of broadening interaction between ways of knowing and doing, much as Wells anticipated. But it was also an era when societies committed unprecedented resources to institutions, old and new, that sustained science: universities and schools, industrial research laboratories, and state agencies engaged in the creation and application of knowledge. These investments had consequences for production, agriculture, and commerce, for public health and medicine, and for the prediction and control of human behavior. They also altered the way in which human beings understood the world and themselves. The consequences were felt most intensely in the industrial West, which had the infrastructure, the traditions, and the capital to prosecute research aggressively. But they were felt in other parts of the globe as well, where both agents of the West and indigenous peoples looked to science and technology as a source of profit and power.

The Convergence of Science and Technology

Many societies have valued science, but few have cultivated it as intensively as Western Europe. As early as the seventeenth century, Western states were building astronomical observatories and sponsoring expeditions to measure and inventory the globe. Enthusiasts for science, such as England's Francis Bacon, predicted that patient observation and experiment would eventually give humankind dominion over nature. His optimistic predictions were amplified by scores of successors, including the Marquis de Condorcet, a French mathematician who sketched out a grand future in which advancing science would extend life, ease labor, and generate material plenty even as he was being hunted by agents of the Terror during the French Revolution. By the end of the nineteenth century, millions shared Condorcet's confidence.

European investments in science paid rewards. Cartography, physics, chemistry, and the study of agriculture, mining, and medicine all helped Europe achieve global power. But the value of formal scientific knowledge should not be exaggerated. Many of the crucial technical advantages of the West resulted from centuries of patient craftsmanship rather than from scientific breakthroughs. The ironmaster, watchmaker, or shipbuilder might know a little science, but he usually relied on experience to make and improve his products. Scientists typically had little acquaintance with mills or foundries; their knowledge was of limited practical use. While a physicist of 1850 could describe the forces on a girder, for example, he could not predict the strength of steels very well, as they varied greatly in composition and quality. And while a chemist would know that steel is composed of iron and carbon, he knew little about how small quantities of other elements, such as phosphorus, could affect its properties or how common foundry techniques, such as the quenching of a hot metal in water, influenced its hardness and tensile strength.

Until the end of the nineteenth century, connections between science and technology were sporadic and serendipitous, even in Europe. Scientists found intriguing puzzles in technology—for example, finding ways to describe the translation of heat into motive force in a steam engine. Their inquiries sometimes generated new technologies as a byproduct, as when Michael Faraday sketched out the principle of the electrical dynamo during his studies of electricity. But scientists' claims for the utility of knowledge rested less on concrete examples than on a general faith that, as Bacon suggested, "knowledge and power meet in one."

Scientists had only a modest role in Europe's Industrial Revolution and remained peripheral to many forms of technology even into the twentieth century. But gradually, and in an ever-larger number of fields, science came to have sufficient precision and complexity to predict real-world behavior, replicate natural processes, and shape the material environment. In 1850 chemists were only beginning to synthesize the simplest organic compounds; fifty years later they could reproduce some of nature's most complex molecules. Physicists were just beginning to explore the electromagnetic spectrum in 1850; by 1920 they had developed principles sufficient to manipulate not only light and electric currents but also forms of radiation that were unknown to their predecessors: X-rays and radio waves.

Perhaps most important, new kinds of experts appeared who could mediate between the world of formal knowledge and the world of know-how. By 1930 "applied psychologists" were designing industrial workplaces and economists were shaping government policies. Electrical engineers were using the equations of physics to design electrical grids, chemical engineers were using thermodynamics to plan petroleum refineries, and aeronautical engineers were using hydrodynamics to improve wings and cowlings. In these and many other fields, engineers and applied scientists improved the flow of ideas between universities and industries and developed new forms of expert knowledge that were appropriate to practical needs.

Government, Industry, and Science

The integration of science and technology was an expensive process. Research required money for equipment and salaries; it also required human capital. Scientists and engineers received a long and costly education. Attrition was high, and dozens of schoolteachers, lab instructors, and technicians contributed to the preparation of each PhD in chemistry or electrical engineering. For every scientist who gained notoriety, there were scores who labored more anonymously. The translation of ideas into products often involved many other kinds of experts as well: surveyors and engineers to design factories and lay out railroads, tradespeople able to comply with blueprints, metalworkers to fabricate complex machine tools and factory hands able to use them, technicians to assay the purity of materials, clerks to route boxcars and maintain shipping records, bookkeepers to pay employees and suppliers, and lawyers to prepare contracts and patent applications. Scientists and engineers were part of a large network engaged in the production and transmission of knowledge and skills.

Systems of schooling were essential to the construction of such networks. The industrial nations of Europe, the United States, and Japan had come to recognize the value of a literate and numerate citizenry during the late nineteenth century and had invested heavily in education. By 1914 all of these societies mandated schooling for children to the age of fourteen, or sixteen in some cases, offered vocational schooling in trades such as metalworking and carpentry, and supported universities that combined education in the traditional professions with advanced training in engineering and the sciences. One consequence was that by 1930 about 90 percent of Europeans, North Americans, and Japanese could read, compared with roughly 50 percent in 1850. Even so, opportunities for higher education were restricted to very small fractions of the population in Europe and Japan, with most seats in universities going to males of the upper middle class. In Germany, for example, only about one in every hundred students went on to a university education in 1900.

By 1930, however, barriers to higher education were falling, especially in North America, where state governments built systems of public high schools and universities. The U.S. population doubled between 1890 and 1930, and the number of students in colleges and universities increased ninefold. Scientific and technical fields were among the most popular courses of study, and booming industries hired as many chemists and engineers as the colleges could produce. Even though Europe retained intellectual leadership in many branches of science, by 1914 the United States was home to more scientists and engineers than any other nation. This reservoir of talent gave U.S. industries significant advantages over foreign rivals in the postwar era and eventually led to substantial improvements in the quality of the scientific research done in America, as illustrated, for example, by patterns in the award of Nobel Prizes in the sciences (Figure 5.1).

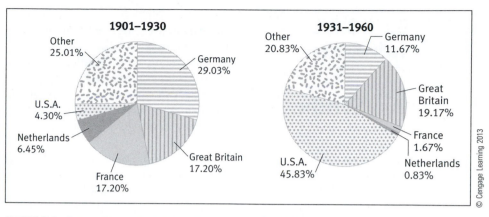

FIGURE 5.1   Nationalities of Nobel Prize winners in the natural sciences.
Since first awarded in 1901, prizes funded by a bequest of the Swedish industrialist Alfred Nobel have been the most coveted honor for creative work in the natural sciences. Distribution of these awards affords one illustration of the central role of Europeans in these fields during the early twentieth century and the growing importance of the United States in the decades after 1930.

Other institutional changes also promoted the integration of science and technology in the early twentieth century. Following the lead of Germany, for example, the industrial powers built national laboratories for systematic research on materials and standards. These institutions, which included the National Bureau of Standards in the United States (founded in 1901) and the Institute of Physical and Chemical Research in Japan (founded in 1917), performed costly research on problems that were important to a broad range of industries, such as determining the values of basic units of measurement.

Tax monies supported scientific research in agriculture as well as in manufacturing. Germany and the United States, for example, built networks of agricultural experiment stations to study animal and plant nutrition, the properties of soils, the control of pests, and methods of breeding better crops and animals. Scientists at these institutions played key roles in identifying the vitamins essential to human and animal health, in developing crops resistant to drought and fungal infection, and in discovering ways to check the spread of diseases of livestock. In the United States, extension agents—technicians associated with the stations—carried knowledge from the laboratories to the fields by offering farmers advice on fertilizers, soils, and seeds.

The governments of industrialized nations thus promoted the application of science to practical needs. But in Europe and the United States, private enterprise was equally important. Improvements in transportation and communication had helped some small firms grow into goliaths during the late nineteenth century. Railroads and steamships made it possible to ship raw materials and finished goods cheaply over long distances; telegraphs made it possible to wire orders and payments from one part of the world to another almost instantaneously. By

GLOBAL Technologies

Ammonia Synthesis

The synthesis of ammonia (NH_3) was the most important outcome of Germany's intensive R&D in the early twentieth century. Ammonia is familiar to most of us as the pungent gas emitted by household cleaners. Chemists know it as the starting point for the production of many important substances, including nitric acid, nitrogen-rich fertilizers, and the nitrogen-containing chemicals used in high explosives, such as trinitrotoluene (TNT).

By 1900, demand for both fertilizers and explosives was growing rapidly, yet the supply was limited. Ammonia and other nitrogen-rich substances were derived primarily from manures and from deposits of sodium nitrate in Chile. Some scientists saw a crisis looming. Shortages of nitrogen fertilizers would make it impossible for agriculture to meet the demands of a growing population.

The solution to this impending crisis was obvious to many chemists. Nitrogen gas constitutes almost 80 percent of the atmosphere—a supply vastly larger than industry could ever use. The difficulty, however, was that the gaseous form of nitrogen (N_2) is almost inert. Nitrogen became useful in fertilizers and in explosives only when it combined with other elements to form more reactive molecules, such as ammonia and nitric acid. A few types of bacteria were able to fix atmospheric nitrogen into such compounds, but these bacteria flourished only on the roots of legumes such as clover and alfalfa. It was these

the 1920s, firms such as Britain's Imperial Chemical Industries, Germany's Krupp Steel, and America's General Electric Company had come to dominate their national markets and to find customers in distant parts of the world. In so doing, they acquired the financial resources and motives to undertake systematic research.

Research and Development

Inventors with modest scientific learning devised most of the basic technological innovations of the nineteenth century: the telegraph and telephone; the first electric lighting systems; the steam engines, brakes, and rails that made railroads possible; and the internal combustion engines that began to appear in horseless buggies near the century's end. They created scores of ingenious tools for town and mill; bicycles, sewing machines, and typewriters; phonographs and cameras; not to mention such simple inventions as barbed wire and paper clips. The act of invention sometimes involved the use of off-the-shelf science. Samuel F. B. Morse, for example, drew on a textbook knowledge of physics in devising the

microbes that renewed nitrogen in the soil and were the ultimate source of the nitrogen-containing compounds in all living matter. But their methods for fixing atmospheric nitrogen could not be replicated by industry.

Early in the twentieth century, chemists developed several solutions to the dilemma. The most important was a process that made ammonia directly from atmospheric nitrogen and hydrogen gas using very high pressures and catalysts. First demonstrated in 1912 by the German chemist, Fritz Haber, this process helped Germany meet its needs for high explosives during World War I. After the war, plants using the Haber process went up around the globe to produce the fertilizers to sustain a growing world population. By 1931 these plants were synthesizing enough ammonia to meet half the world's need for nitrogenous compounds.

By the end of the century, they supplied nearly 100 percent.

The growth of the industry was a great misfortune to Chile, which lost lucrative markets for its nitrates. But it was a boon to agriculture. As the supply of nitrogen fertilizers grew, their use spread, first in Europe and North America and then, after World War II, in regions with lower incomes and faster-growing populations. By 2000, farmers were applying 125 times more nitrogen fertilizers to the average acre of cropland than they had in 1900. These applications came at a cost to the environment: Run-off of nitrogen-enriched waters disturbed the balance of microbes in rivers and plankton in the sea and damaged fishing industries. Yet nitrogen fertilizers were a key factor in boosting crop yields. By one estimate, 40 percent of the globe's population in 2000 owes its existence to the nitrogen produced in Haber-process plants.[2]

telegraph. Inventors might also call on scientists for advice during the commercial development of a product. But technological innovation rarely entailed cutting-edge research.[2]

Nor did invention have much support from large organizations, private or public. Typically, the inventor absorbed the costs of developing a new product or secured backing from friends and family. Corporations might purchase the rights to manufacture and market an invention, but few made innovation integral to their operations. Managers of large firms saw invention as an unpredictable activity, as did most government officials. Even armies and navies bought much of their technology on the open market rather than developing it themselves. At the start of World War I, for instance, British and German submarines alike were based on the designs of an Irish-American school teacher, John P. Holland, and their machine guns were derived from the design of Hiram Maxim, a British

---

[2]Vaclav Smil, *Enriching the Earth: Fritz Haber, Carl Bosch, and the Transformation of World Food Production* (Cambridge, MA: MIT Press, 2001), p. 204.

immigrant to the United States. Invention was generally seen as too risky to justify elaborate in-house research.

Only toward the end of the nineteenth century did industry and government start to support systematic R&D, and then only in a few nations and industries. Germany was the pioneer. Its universities had achieved leadership in most branches of science by 1870. Gradually some of its businessmen came to recognize that science might play a role in industry. Patent legislation, enacted in 1877, gave firms extra incentive to invest in research by providing innovators with state-sanctioned monopolies on new processes. By 1900, several German producers of chemicals, responding to a worldwide demand for novel colors in textiles, had built extensive laboratories for the synthesis and testing of new dyes. The work entailed research on the frontiers of organic chemistry because most dyes are complex carbon-based compounds. The synthesis of these compounds from cheap raw materials, such as coal, was an art in which university-trained scientists proved far more adept than traditional dye masters.

Thereafter, industrial research expanded quickly in the chemical and electrical industries. A single German company, Bayer, employed nearly three hundred chemists by 1914, compared to only eleven in 1880. These chemists, organized in teams and provided with the finest assistance and equipment, synthesized thousands of new substances (3,500 in 1906 alone) seeking the handful (less than 1 percent) that might prove suitable for marketing. Additional scientists and engineers were necessary to adapt methods of production from the laboratory to the plant, maintain quality control, and teach salespeople about new products. The scope and complexity of this work far exceeded the capacities of any independent inventor.

Having invested so heavily in research, firms like Bayer soon seized opportunities to diversify. Much the same knowledge and techniques that went into producing a dye could be applied to synthesize pesticides, photographic dyes, and drugs. By the beginning of World War I, for example, the same firms that were producing dyes were also making such compounds as aspirin and barbiturates. R&D was expensive, but patent laws shielded manufacturers from competition long enough to earn high profits on successful products. The diversified chemical firms that emerged from this process proved as valuable to Germany in war as in peace by producing such essentials as artificial rubber, explosives, and fertilizers.

Large-scale corporate R&D commenced in the United States not long after it had in Germany. As in Germany, scientific expertise was available. U.S. universities had expanded rapidly in the late nineteenth century. Although not as close to the forefront of research as the universities of Europe, they turned out chemists, physicists, and engineers in abundance. As in Germany, U.S. patent law afforded innovators legal monopolies. And, as in Germany, decades of industrial growth had spawned banks with the capital to finance risky forays into new industries and new methods. By 1900, scores of companies had organized research programs, although intensive efforts along the German pattern began only after the turn of the century at firms such as General Electric and AT&T. World War I quickened this trend. Denied German imports by the Allied blockade, U.S. firms scrambled to copy or develop substitutes for the numerous high-technology products that Germany had supplied, including dyes and other organic chemicals, high-quality optical glass, special-purpose paints and resins, and sedatives, analgesics, and other drugs. By the 1920s, such U.S. firms as DuPont and Corning Glass rivaled German corporations in these and other areas. Each nation, however, had its own special areas of strength.

Germany, with its deep ranks of organic chemists, continued to lead in the synthesis of useful chemicals and drugs from coal. Many coal-derived dyes readily stained living tissues. Some were selectively absorbed by certain types of bacteria and other parasites. And some were toxic or could be made so. Compounds with such properties held promise for therapeutic medicine. The research was tedious, involving trial-and-error testing of thousands of substances for antimicrobial activity and safety. But by the mid-1930s, these painstaking efforts had led to effective new drugs for treating syphilis, sleeping sickness, and malaria. The work also led to the identification of an entire class of sulfur-containing molecules with powerful therapeutic properties. These compounds, which came to be known as the sulfa drugs, were the first effective treatment for the common and dangerous diseases caused by streptococcal infections, such as childbed fever, and also provided new tools to treat bacterial pneumonia and meningitis. The prosaic search for new dyes thus evolved into broad-scale research that transformed therapeutic medicine.

The United States, with its large petroleum reserves and a booming automobile industry, took leadership in research related to oil. Oil companies put geologists and physicists to work on new methods of locating petroleum, such as using shock waves to infer underground structures. Refiners' chemists studied ways to crack the large and relatively inert compounds of crude oil into the smaller and more volatile molecules found in gasoline. And automakers, eager to satisfy consumer demand for powerful, high-compression engines, developed chemical additives that boosted the octane ratings of the gasoline coming from refineries. At the same time, U.S. producers of chemicals, such as Union Carbide, invested heavily in research aimed at using petroleum as a raw material for other products ranging from antifreezes for engines to varnishes, plastics, and synthetic fibers.

Industrial research brought profits to business but also a multitude of new products and services to consumers. By 1930, middle-class Americans took for granted scores of materials, devices, and elixirs that were either unknown to or prohibitively expensive for their parents, from inexpensive automobiles and radios to artificial silk (rayon) and milk fortified with vitamin D.

Hundreds of inconspicuous innovations made these products possible. The mechanical guts of a 1930 Chevy would have been comprehensible to a backyard mechanic in 1905. But inspection would have revealed components and substances that were unknown at the beginning of the century: the electric self-starter, safety glass, lacquer paint, and alloys used for gears, among others. More important, in just a little over two decades, enormous wealth and ingenuity had been invested in systems to produce and support automobiles: Steel mills gulped in ore and coal and rolled out sheet metal, glassworks mass-produced windshields, and chemical plants made thousands of gallons of paint a day. The oil companies developed new oil fields, pipelines, and refineries, and the government laid down thousands of miles of new roads. Maps, signs, and traffic lights evolved with them to make transportation easier and safer. Finally, networks of garages, fueling stations, and dealerships opened to sell and maintain cars, while collection agencies repossessed them when loans went unpaid.

Resources for Innovation

Science and engineering were two of many factors enabling the construction of these systems, into which millions of Americans were almost unconsciously integrated in the early twentieth century. Broadly distributed wealth was also essential. The streets of U.S. cities were not paved with gold, and large numbers of Americans lived in poverty, but wage rates and farmers' incomes were high in comparison to those in other countries. Even as big business grew, opportunities expanded for small businesses that supplied goods and services and for professionals who sold expertise. Farmers and salespeople, insurance agents and medical doctors had sufficient income to purchase automobiles and reason to value the

Brown Brothers

Moving assembly lines, such as the one in this Ford plant of the 1930s, greatly reduced the hours of labor needed to make an automobile. Reductions in assembly time and the bulk purchase of materials created economies of scale and brought the price of an automobile within the reach of millions of middle-class Americans.

mobility that they afforded. Their demand for autos stimulated production, and as the scale of production grew, the price per unit dropped as manufacturers realized efficiencies of scale. The price of a Model T fell from $600 in 1912, when one hundred seventy thousand were produced, to $290 in 1924, when production stood at nearly two million. Falling prices increased the number of consumers who were able to afford a car until, by the late 1920s, even many wage earners could drive to work.

Families with disposable income could spend it on a variety of new goods, such as automobiles, vacuum cleaners, washing machines, and radios. But many chose to invest. Ownership of stocks and bonds, which had been confined to institutions and the wealthy before World War I, became common among middle-class households in the 1920s. Home ownership, which had always been the rule in rural America, became more common among urban workers, and modest wood frame houses sprouted on the outskirts of cities where land was cheap and new roads were being laid down.

Education was another form of investment. Tax-supported secondary schools spread from the urban East and Midwest into rural districts and the South. The high school diploma, once a mark of social status, came to be an expectation for the children of the middle class, and attendance at college climbed quickly. Collegiate study was a sound investment, as there was growing demand for expertise of all sorts. Corporations needed accountants, engineers, and chemists. Insurance companies needed actuaries. Schools needed teachers. All large organizations, public and private, needed managers who could manipulate words and numbers and keep up with the technological change.

Other industrialized nations moved along the same trajectory as Germany and the United States, developing research capacity, novel products, and new connections between science and technology. After World War I, for example, Britain and Japan offered private industry tax credits and other incentives to invest in research. Both expanded their systems of higher education and built national laboratories for research on such essential products as textiles and fuels. And in both, private industry built research facilities on the model of those of German and U.S. companies.

These investments had some significant successes during the interwar years. British laboratories stayed near the forefront in the physical and biological sciences, and British firms attained leadership in such technically demanding fields as the production of synthetic fibers. Japanese scientists showed excellence in bacteriology and, by the end of the 1930s, in some branches of physics. Japan's production of such knowledge-intensive products as chemicals and drugs increased rapidly. But neither Britain nor Japan had the battalions of scientists and engineers that were available in Germany and the United States, and neither had a domestic market as large and affluent as America's. Consequently, whereas Britain and Japan developed strengths in particular areas, Germany and the United States demonstrated excellence across a broad range of sciences and industrial technologies.

In most industrialized nations, science and technology advanced through a combination of public and private support. Tax monies typically supported schools and research institutes that were useful to a broad range of industries (such as the bureaus of standards). Business paid for research on new products and processes that might earn a profit. In the United States large philanthropic foundations, endowed by tycoons such as Andrew D. Carnegie and John D. Rockefeller, also supplied significant sums for basic research. Supported by this multitude of public and private organizations, science and technology grew without central guidance or control. Even in Japan, where government often influenced the direction of private investment, many institutions played a role in shaping science policy.

Soviet Russia followed a different path. Like other productive forces (such as labor and capital), science came under the control of the Communist Party and was turned to the needs of the Soviet state. Under a Five-Year Plan announced by Stalin in 1928, the Soviet government built an elaborate bureaucracy, staffed with reliable party members, to oversee education and research as well as manufacturing and agriculture. Central planners focused resources on heavy industries because their products, such as steel and electricity, were basic to the production of other goods. New mills, hydroelectric plants, and power grids needed engineers, and so the state expanded universities and engineering schools. Between 1927 and 1932, enrollments in technical subjects quadrupled and expenditures on research and development grew sixfold.

World War I and the ensuing civil war had caused economic havoc in the Soviet Union, and resources were scarce. The Bolshevik government could hardly expect generous loans from overseas after confiscating foreign property and repudiating tsarist-era debts. The only way to finance rapid industrial growth was to ruthlessly limit consumption, especially of food and consumer goods. Peasants were offered a pittance for grain and livestock; those who refused to sell at prices determined by the state were imprisoned or executed. Intent on squeezing as much wealth as possible from the countryside, officials forced millions of peasants off their plots and onto giant collective farms where land and equipment were communally held. The productivity of most of these collectives proved disappointing, but collectivization gave party officials a tighter grip on the countryside and new means to control hoarding. In mines and factories workers were pushed to work longer and harder; by 1938 they needed official permission to quit or change jobs. Central planners allocated little money to the production of luxury items, such as automobiles, or even to the production of such amenities as safety razors. By keeping the shelves bare of consumer products, planners could reserve resources for steel mills, dams, and tank factories.

The human cost of Soviet ambitions was unprecedented. Worst hit were peasants, especially those who owned their own land. Some resisted state seizures by hoarding grain and slaughtering their livestock—crimes made punishable by death. Many others, numbering in the hundreds of thousands, were torn from their communities and transported to agricultural labor camps on the semi-arid steppes of Central Asia, often without means to make the vast lands fertile. The forced transports, executions, confiscations of grain, and breakdowns in the supply of seed created famine across wide areas of the Soviet countryside, including areas that had long been productive. Observers described villages bereft of animals and fields naked of grain, men and women who were gaunt as shadows, and children starving in their cradles. Upwards of two million peasants died in 1932–1933, and the total loss of life during the decade beginning in 1929 probably exceeded ten million.

Stalin's labor camps swallowed up millions of others: intellectuals who were deemed unreliable, managers who failed to meet quotas, members of minority groups suspected of having nationalist ambitions, Bolsheviks harboring doubts about the party line, and petty criminals—some convicted of no more than gleaning leftover grain from the fields of collective farms. Some prisoners were deployed in huge labor battalions to build roads, dig canals, and perform heavy labor on public works projects such as the Moscow subway. Most were shipped to distant camps in the frigid north and Siberia to lay rail, cut wood, and haul coal out of mines. Housed in drafty wooden barracks and fed a subsistence diet of bread and potatoes, these victims were lost to the world. For many, there was no return.

Economists today doubt whether the vast labor camps contributed much to Soviet economic growth. But the Soviet leadership in the 1930s was adept at

David King Collection

Stalin's plans for the economic development of the Soviet Union emphasized grand infrastructure projects, including canals, railroads, and hydroelectric power plants. Prisoners, including millions arrested for political offenses, provided much of the labor. Some are here seen breaking rocks on the one-hundred-forty-mile canal linking the White Sea and the Baltic Sea, circa 1932.

advertising its successes and concealing its failings, in part because it controlled information tightly, in part because many intellectuals abroad were eager to believe the best about a Marxist state, and in part because it did have some achievements to point to. Soviet output of coal, metals, concrete, and machine tools soared and continued to grow even during the 1930s, when Europe and the United States were mired in a deep depression. The state's new schools produced more engineers, agronomists, and technicians than those of any other nation in the world except the United States. And in the handful of technologies most favored by the Kremlin, Soviet engineers achieved remarkable results. Soviet designers, for example, turned out aircraft that set records for distance, altitude, and speed in the 1930s. And they built hydropower plants on a scale equaled only in the United States. Many foreign observers concluded that the Soviet system was indeed more efficient than its capitalist counterparts in harnessing knowledge for economic growth.

The shortcomings of the Soviet's top-down system of development were less visible. Communist Party officials, who were in full control of the press and radio, concealed the forced labor camps, the starvation in the countryside, and the harshness of working conditions. They wrapped much of Soviet science in secrecy by denying most Soviet scientists contact with foreigners. The secrecy and centralized management stifled innovation. Institutes of engineering research were isolated from production facilities, making it hard for new ideas to travel. Managers feared to take the risks, in part because they faced harsh penalties if such experimentation interfered with their meeting quotas. To make matters worse, Communist Party officials, including Stalin, often made policy decisions on the basis of incomplete or misleading information. During the 1930s, for example, an erratic agronomist, T. D. Lysenko, won Stalin's confidence and assumed the direction of Soviet investments in agricultural research. Over the next three decades, Lysenko used his power to promote fruitless schemes and to purge his critics, including the most accomplished Soviet plant geneticist of the era, Nikolai Vavilov. As in all parts of Soviet life, dissent carried heavy penalties. Vavilov died of malnutrition while serving out his prison term.

The highly centralized Soviet system mobilized resources for grand engineering projects, but it also stifled the competition of ideas that was so important to Western science and technology. It achieved the goal of rapid industrialization by ignoring the wants and human rights of its citizens. It pushed some fields of science and engineering forward while letting others atrophy. The result was an uneven pattern of development. It could design superb tanks but could not make ordinary consumer products competitive on world markets. While its aircraft set records, its peasants still plowed fields behind horses and moved produce to market in carts.

Environmental Consequences

The engineers, scientists, and managers who designed roads and factories, dams and power grids, and refineries and pipelines generally did so with little thought for environmental consequences. In both the capitalist United States of America and the communist Union of Soviet Socialist Republics (USSR), engineers and scientists tended to view nature as either a resource to be exploited or an enemy to be conquered. This attitude, deeply embedded in Western thought, was reinforced by pressures for profits among Western corporations, by governments' eagerness to satisfy the material needs of their citizens, and, in the Soviet case, by a Marxist ideology that identified nature as humankind's common adversary. Already in the nineteenth century, industrial wastes, smoke, rail lines, canals, and roads had transformed the landscape of districts such as the Ruhr in Germany and the Midlands of England. Nature was reworked on a new scale in the twentieth century. The U.S. government dammed remote rivers in the West and sometimes rerouted them to bring water and power to farms and cities. It also reengineered the river systems of the Midwest and South to make additional miles navigable, to control floods, and to generate electricity. Corporations began to lease forests to produce pulp and paper and mountain ranges to produce iron and coal. Deserts were brought under cultivation through irrigation.

Some of the grand engineering projects of the interwar years proved to be durable successes: the Golden Gate Bridge, for example, married graceful form to useful function. Many projects led to economic growth and improved standards of living. The federally financed Tennessee Valley Authority brought electricity and jobs to a desperately poor region, the arid interior valleys of California became rich farmlands with waters diverted from surrounding lakes and rivers, and agriculture and trade flourished in the central and eastern parts of Washington State as dams went up on the unruly Columbia River and its tributaries.

But many projects had unintended consequences for both humans and nature. The drainage of lakes and wetlands destroyed the habitats of birds and fish, and dams stopped salmon from reaching their spawning grounds. The cutting of forests and the straightening of rivers promoted erosion. Large tracts of land were scarred by open-pit methods of mining, and wastes from oil fields and mines poisoned rivers and groundwater. Heavy construction, mining, and forestry were labor-intensive and dangerous undertakings. And while these projects often stimulated the growth of industries, they could also destroy traditional ways of life. Disruption of salmon runs, for example, hurt commercial fishing and deprived Native American tribes in the Pacific Northwest of a creature sacred to their mythology. Engineers could predict the amount of electric energy that a new dam could generate, but they could not anticipate all the effects of rearranging nature and human communities.

Soviet officials, eager to prove the efficiency of state-owned industry and central economic planning, were at least as ambitious as their capitalist counterparts. Dams spanned great rivers, such as the Dnieper, bringing electricity to large parts of the Soviet Union and irrigation waters to semi-arid lands. New canals improved the movement of goods, and new cities grew in Soviet Russia's Ural Mountains and its vast Asian reaches. Some of these grand undertakings were built using the blueprints of American and European projects. The new steel city of Magnitogorsk, for example, bore an uncanny resemblance to Gary,

Indiana. Other projects were plainly designed to one-up the capitalist West. A new building to house the Soviet government was begun in Moscow in 1939 that was to use six times as much steel and tower one hundred feet higher than the recently completed Empire State Building in New York. A statue of Lenin, twice the size of the Statue of Liberty, would crown the structure. Like many Soviet projects, the building was never finished; after World War II its excavation site became a public swimming pool, which Soviet authorities described as the "largest in the world."

The Soviet system placed the full resources of the state at the disposal of central planners and offered few avenues for dissent. Local and environmental interests rarely counted for much in decision making, and leaders seldom acknowledged their mistakes, which could be as grand as any of their successes. Among the most striking examples was the effort to integrate the semi-arid lands of the Aral Sea basin into the industrializing Soviet economy. Under Stalin, the small plots and pasturelands of this district were combined into large collective farms and turned from the production of livestock and grain for local consumption to the production of cotton for Soviet textile mills. Cotton fields demanded intensive irrigation, and the water was taken from the rivers feeding the Aral Sea. Deprived of fresh water, the sea began to shrink and to become more saline. Cotton production soared in the short term, but the fisheries of the Aral Sea were ruined and millions of hectares of land eventually were rendered sterile by the nutrient-hungry cotton and the effects of saline waters. Uzbekistan, Turkmenistan, and the other republics of Central Asia inherited these problems after the breakup of the USSR in 1991.

Large-scale engineering projects transformed local and regional environments, but the global movements of goods and people had more far-reaching effects. The proliferation of coal-fired industrial plants and automobiles increased concentrations of carbon dioxide in the atmosphere and may have initiated a global warming trend that became manifest later in the century. Increases in the pace and volume of long distance commerce had more immediate ecological consequences. Species that had long flourished on isolated islands found themselves challenged by new competitors that were imported, accidentally or intentionally, by merchants, investors, and colonial officials. At the end of the nineteenth century, for example, planters in Jamaica and the Virgin Islands imported the mongoose from India to control rats in the sugar cane fields; it did its job, but it also made short work of many native lizards, toads, and birds. American muskrats released near Prague in 1905 spread across Europe and became so destructive by the 1930s as to prompt costly campaigns of eradication. Rodents and snakes that hitched rides on cargo ships played havoc with the ecology of many Pacific islands, including the Hawaiian chain, where they drove some species of birds into extinction. But islands were not uniquely vulnerable to ecological disruption. A 1929 survey of the insects that were most destructive to crops in the United States revealed that nearly half were of foreign origin.

Microbes were the most mobile and harmful travelers. Among the victims were two of the most common species of trees in North America: the chestnut and the elm. The chestnut blight appeared in New York in 1904 following the importation of infested trees from Japan. By 1930 nearly every stand of chestnuts in the United States was infected with the disease, which was fatal to almost all mature trees. Dutch elm disease, another fungal infection, probably crossed the Atlantic on contaminated shipping boxes. First identified in Ohio in 1930, it spread relentlessly across the continent, denuding countless Elm Streets of their trees.

Improvements in transportation have always had environmental consequences. Dogs and grains spread across the world with human settlers, as did rats and dandelions. The European conquest of the Americas initiated global movements of plants (such as the sweet potato) and microbes (such as those causing smallpox). These movements surely extinguished some species, although such ecological effects generally went unrecorded. In the twentieth century, however, humankind became increasingly aware of its unique capacity to alter the biosphere. Conservation and preservation movements appeared in the United States and Europe, where the effects of development were easiest to see, and small groups of scientists started to focus on the study of problems in ecology. From these modest beginnings, a broad international environmental movement would emerge later in the century.

Prediction and Control

Novel products such as radio sets testified to the growing importance of science in the twentieth century, but science was also shaping life in less obvious ways. Predicting the weather, for example, had been the preserve of almanac writers in the nineteenth century. Their annual forecasts relied on little more than statistical averages and hunches. Complete reliability in forecasting remained an impossible dream in the twentieth century, but predictions improved significantly as physicists developed more sophisticated models of atmospheric behavior and governments invested greater resources in the collection of the data those models required.

Nineteenth-century economists had little more prognostic power than meteorologists. The "iron law" of supply and demand offered a rough guide to the movement of prices and wages. Some thinkers, like Marx, ventured long-term predictions based on a reading of history. But economists had neither the data nor the theories to frame specific and reliable advice for business or government. Economic policy was set largely on the basis of old bromides about the importance of balanced budgets and the sanctity of the gold standard; business decisions were made on the basis of cunning and accounting. When governments confronted the task of organizing wartime production, however, precedent and sharp pencils proved inadequate. Tasks such as allocating scarce raw materials, controlling wages and prices, and routing boxcars and ships led the belligerents to seek advice from economists. Economists' involvement in the organization of production, in turn, stimulated their efforts to build models of how economies work.

They achieved modest success. As in weather forecasting, the number of variables and the complexity of their relationships exceeded the capacity of the theory builders. Nevertheless, the process of trying to identify and measure these variables, from business inventories to housing starts and unemployment, created more understanding of how national economies work and new ambitions for their control. Such ambitions found extreme expression in the Soviet Union, where central planners sought to correct the boom-bust cycles of capitalist economies through state ownership of industry and state control of wages and prices—with mixed results.

Whereas Soviet planners used brute force to promote economic growth, Western governments tended to nudge their economies through the more traditional methods of tax and monetary policy. They used tariffs, for example, to protect domestic industries from foreign competition and the interest rates charged by central banks on loans to accelerate or retard economic growth. As in the past, government officials, bankers, and businessmen set these policies, but they consulted more frequently with experts who had schooling in economics. In the United States, for example, Herbert Hoover oversaw an expansion of the federal gathering of economic data as secretary of commerce between 1921 and 1928. An engineer by training, Hoover believed that such data would facilitate wiser investment decisions by businesses with minimal central planning.

While meteorologists were developing new models of the atmosphere and economists were working to understand and shape economies, other professionals—psychologists, pollsters, and propagandists—were seeking more systematic knowledge of human behavior. The study of behavior was hardly new. Psychology took shape as a science during the late nineteenth century when academics in Europe and the United States took up the study of such questions as how the mind makes associations between ideas and how to measure intellectual acuity. Empirical studies of behavior had also commenced in industry, most notably among the followers of an American engineer, Frederick Winslow Taylor, who called his approach "scientific management." Long on management and short on science, Taylor's methods emphasized meticulous "time and motion" studies in which Taylor and his experts measured workers' motions with stopwatches and tape measures to eliminate wasted effort and slack time. Their prescriptions ran the gamut from directions about how to hold a shovel to advice about the arrangement of machines and materials on the factory floor. Workers often found Taylor's techniques intrusive and demeaning, and what scientific management achieved in productivity gains was often offset by labor unrest. Even so, the movement spread from the United States to Europe and Europe's colonies—testimony not so much to its efficacy as to the tendency to equate quantitative measurement with progress.

World War I catalyzed the combination of academic knowledge and industrial practice in psychology, as in meteorology and economics. By the beginning of World War I, psychologists had devised a number of tests that purported to measure human intelligence on a standard, age-adjusted scale. First used in Parisian schools by Alfred Binet, these tests were revised by the American psychologists Lewis Terman and Robert M. Yerkes, who persuaded army officials to use their tests to determine the aptitudes of hundreds of thousands of recruits as the

United States mobilized for war. The prospect of having a quick, inexpensive, and quantitative index of mental dexterity proved irresistible to school administrators and many business executives after the war was over. Other forms of testing soon appeared to assist employers in gauging the personality characteristics and reaction times of employees. By the end of the 1920s, universities in the United States and parts of Europe were offering degrees in industrial psychology, a field that was concerned with both testing and designing workplaces to maximize productivity.

It is arguable whether experts in any of these fields—meteorology, economics, or psychology—were dramatically more effective than their predecessors. But the authority of science was great, even in the absence of clear-cut benefits. Great, too, is the human desire to learn more about the future. Even marginal improvement in predictive capacity will find buyers when profit and power are at stake.

High Science in a Mass Culture

Western science affects most of us through technology. Along with capital, mechanical ingenuity, and demand, it is one of the factors that generated rapid technological change in the twentieth century. But science is not just about fabricating new products, tools, and industrial processes. It also informs many of us about who we are, where we came from, and our place in the natural world. It shapes worldviews and can provide humans in disparate cultures with a common vocabulary and shared frames of reference. In 1900, science played such a role primarily in those parts of the world where Europeans dominated social institutions and, within those areas, primarily among literate and urban peoples. The Irish potato farmer, the Chinese or Russian peasant, the Mexican silver miner, and the cattle herder in British East Africa had little if any contact with Western science; their beliefs about the natural world were rooted in religion and local cultural traditions. Their children and grandchildren continued to cultivate old religious and cultural traditions during the twentieth century, but more and more often with an overlay of ideas derived from the West, taught in schools and universities that themselves were based in part on Western models. The diffusion of Western science to colonial regions, often begun as part of the "civilizing mission" of the Western imperial powers, became part of the modernization program that most former colonies undertook as they achieved independence. Whether they sought to emulate the West or to build on indigenous cultures, few of their leaders saw any alternative but to cultivate the scientific institutions and ideas that seemed so important to the West's power.

The parts of science that were affecting worldviews most profoundly in the first half of the twentieth century were typically not the same as those that were shaping technology and everyday life. Few laypeople entertained themselves by reading about progress in organic chemistry, for example, despite its importance to industry. And while millions of radio listeners in the 1920s tinkered with crystal receivers, not many took an interest in the equations of James Clerk Maxwell that describe radio and all other forms of electromagnetic radiation. But newspaper readers around the world knew Albert Einstein's face, marveled at the discovery of new subatomic particles, puzzled over the unexpected magnitude of the universe, chuckled over Freudian slips, and grew excited by research on the history of life and the origins of humankind. The very small, the very large, the very old, and human beings themselves—ideas about these subjects touched imaginations in ways that merely useful knowledge could not. Thoughtful persons hunger to know about the extremes, those areas where scientific inquiry seems to touch questions of origins and essential nature, the ancient questions of myth and religion.

The opening third of the twentieth century supplied rich scientific fare for active imaginations. In physics, not one but two revolutions occurred. One of them, often described by the single word *relativity,* flowed from Albert Einstein's extraordinary imagination, although it was extended and enlarged by many others. A second, the quantum revolution, was the product of decades of work by scores of physicists. The theory of relativity attracted more publicity, in part because of Einstein's charisma; quantum theory had the broader impact on science. By the late 1920s, it had led most physicists to surrender long-held theories of electromagnetic radiation and matter. Some went further and revised bedrock assumptions about causality and the continuity between the world of ordinary objects and the world of the minuscule particles of which those objects are composed.

Relativity

Relativity is an unusual theory because it arose largely in isolation from the other theoretical work of its time. It carried implications for quantum theory and nuclear physics, but it can stand independent of these other parts of physics. When Einstein began to work on his theory, he himself was in an unusual position. Educated at the Zurich Polytechnic Institute, Einstein found his first job not in a university but as an examiner in the Swiss patent office. Despite this humble position, Einstein published four papers of startling originality in 1905. The most famous of the quartet described a theory of special relativity—special in the sense that it pertained solely to bodies moving with uniform velocity relative to one another.

Einstein's paper caused a sensation, first among physicists and later in wider circles. Others had already discussed the relativity of motion. In the seventeenth century, Galileo noted the equivalence of uniform motion and rest as part of his argument for the diurnal rotation of the earth on its axis. We cannot distinguish between being at rest or moving with a constant velocity unless we have reference to a fixed point. This insight was subsequently incorporated into the physics of Isaac Newton, who believed that space was the reference frame for absolute motion. Describing it as "God's sensorium," Newton imagined that the geometrical grid of uniform space formed a backdrop to the motions of bodies as a cosmic clock ticked uniformly throughout. In this universe, Galilean relativity applied only because human observers have an incomplete grasp of the local environment, as when passengers on a ship that is moving gently over a smooth sea may wake in their cabins and imagine that the ship is at rest. A more knowledgeable observer, looking down from above, would know better. Over the following two centuries, physicists had subtracted God from this worldview but added an all-pervading ether to perform much the same function. Space might appear empty, but in fact it was filled with an extremely subtle substance in which motions occurred and in which forms of radiation, such as light, moved like waves in a sea.

This picture of the universe proved consistent with experimental evidence until the end of the nineteenth century when developments in a number of areas began to raise troubling questions. Most disturbing to Einstein was a contradiction between the equations that Maxwell had developed in 1859 to describe electromagnetism and assumptions about the velocity of light. Maxwell's well-verified equations led to the conclusion that light travels through space with a constant velocity regardless of the velocity of the source from which it is emitted or of the observer who is measuring it. This contradicted classical notions about the behavior of waves in a medium. If light is a wave propagated in an ether, then it should be influenced by the properties of that medium. An observer at rest relative to the ether should report the intrinsic speed of light, but an observer in motion relative to the ether should measure a different speed, one that was greater if the observer was moving in a direction opposite to that of the light and lesser if the observer was moving with the light. The discrepancy suggested flaws either in Maxwell's equations or in classical assumptions about the motion of light and its measurement.

Einstein was not the only physicist to detect this contradiction, but he offered a daring explanation. He opted to trust Maxwell's equations, even though this had devastating consequences for many of the fundamental concepts of physics. If the velocity of light was constant, as Maxwell's work indicated, then the ether was a substance that had no observable effect on either matter or radiation. As Einstein realized, this was equivalent to rejecting the ether altogether, for there was no reason to grant the existence of a substance without measurable effects on other bodies. If there was no ether, there was no fixed frame of reference for plotting the absolute locations or velocities of objects. And if the speed of light was constant regardless of the motion of its source or its observer, then there was no possibility of establishing the absolute simultaneity of events in different parts of the universe. The fissure between Maxwell's equations and the Newtonian worldview turned out to be a chasm.

Einstein drew out these and other implications in his 1905 paper, putting forward a radically new version of many of the basic concepts of physics in a few pages of equations. Time did not pass uniformly throughout the universe, as Newton believed, but varied along with the velocity of an observer's platform, slowing down as velocity increased. Likewise, at speeds approaching that of light, bodies contract in the direction of motion and gain mass. Energy and mass, which had been considered categorically distinct by earlier physicists, were manifestations of a single reality, as summed up in the most famous equation of modern physics: $E = mc^2$.

Equally difficult and unexpected ideas followed when Einstein, in 1916, published a much larger and more complex paper on general relativity; that is, a theory that was sufficiently general to handle bodies undergoing changes in velocity relative to one another. Here Einstein completed his revision of classical physics, tackling such problems as acceleration and the centerpiece of Newtonian science, universal gravitation. Understood by Newton to be a force emanating from matter and acting over distance, gravitation became, in Einstein's theory, a consequence of the curving of four-dimensional space-time in the vicinity of matter. Objects accelerate toward massive bodies, such as the sun, not because they are pulled toward these bodies but because they are falling into the equivalent of depressions in the fabric of space and time. The distortions caused in space-time by matter also affect light, which will appear to be deflected as it passes near massive bodies.

Einstein's results seemed absurd on first hearing, but careful study persuaded many physicists that his ideas were not only plausible but true. While overturning the basic assumptions of classical physics, his theory preserved many of its results. Newtonian laws of motion, for example, offered results closely approximating Einstein's at the speeds of ordinary human experience. Where the two theories diverged, subsequent tests verified Einstein's predictions. For example, careful measurements of the path of stellar light passing near the sun during the solar eclipse of 1919 revealed the slight deviation that Einstein's theory demanded.

Quantum Theory

Relativity theory challenged what had long been considered common sense. Quantum theory went further by challenging basic assumptions not only about the structure of the world but about causation itself. As in the case of Einstein's work, quantum theory grew out of efforts to explain a seemingly esoteric anomaly in classical physics. Nineteenth-century physical theory predicted that bodies that emit a continuous spectrum of radiation should emit energy equally over the entire spectrum, yet experiments revealed maxima and minima at certain wavelengths that changed with temperature. Max Planck, a physicist at the University of Berlin, proposed a solution to the problem in 1900: Such bodies were emitting radiation in discrete packets, or quanta, the energy of which was proportional to the frequency of the radiation. His solution accounted for the phenomenon, but it undercut a fundamental assumption of physics—that radiation is a continuous process.

A cautious thinker, Planck did not follow up on his own idea very aggressively, but Einstein did. In one of his four papers of 1905, Einstein extrapolated from Planck's work to frame a broader hypothesis: The vibrational energy in matter that is excited by heat can be converted into radiant energy only in whole multiples of basic quantum units. Radiation, including light, is particulate, much like matter. When it impinges on matter, it conveys energy in discrete packets. Einstein illustrated his idea by reference to the photoelectric effect. When ultraviolet light falls on metals, it dislodges electrons from their surfaces. If energy were absorbed by electrons continuously, their velocities should also increase continuously with the intensity of the incident radiation and with the duration of the exposure. In fact, experimental evidence suggested otherwise. The velocity of ejected electrons was proportional to the frequency but not the intensity of the incident light, and electron emission commenced when a metal surface was struck by light above a certain threshold frequency, no matter how dim the light source. These results were inexplicable under the classical assumption that energy is transferred continuously, but they made sense if light energy is quantized. Some incoming packets of light energy would strike electrons, no matter how weak the light source. Once struck, those electrons would receive only as much energy as the incoming particles of light (later called photons) themselves possessed. That energy was dependent on the frequency of the light. Above a certain threshold frequency, photons would impart sufficient energy to tear electrons from the metal, and the velocity of the ejected electrons would depend solely on the energy or frequency of the incoming photons, not their density or intensity.

Einstein's elegant solution to this puzzle earned him the Nobel Prize. More important, it provided a powerful argument for the particulate nature of light and energy and for discontinuity in the interaction between radiation and matter. During the next twenty years, more and more physicists began to make use of the quantum theory, extending it and applying it to new issues. A young Dane, Niels Bohr, took the lead here by attacking such difficult problems as the electronic structure of the atom, the nature of chemical bonds, and the interpretation of the spectra that atoms produce when emitting energy. With each extension, however, contradictions between quantum theory and classical physics became more apparent.

In fact, the quantum theory had revived one of the oldest controversies in physics: Does light consist of a stream of particles, or is it a wave motion? The wave theory had won the field in the nineteenth century by providing elegant solutions to such vexing puzzles as the refraction of beams of light, colors, and the interference effects produced when light passes through the narrow slits of grating spectrometers. It also seemed consistent with many of the basic facts of vision. An observer viewing a beam of light sees no effect when a second beam is directed across the path of the first. If light is particulate, should not collisions weaken the beam? Treating light as a stream of particles had undeniable advantages in the treatment of such problems as the photoelectric effect, but the older wave theory of light had resolved many other difficulties in physics, and it was impossible to overlook its long record of success.

The contradictions between quantum and classical physics came to seem irresolvable in the mid-1920s, and the outcome was more radical than either Planck or Einstein envisioned. The basic issue, Bohr and others began to argue, was not to decide between the competing models of light or the competing visualizations of microscopic behavior, but rather to acknowledge that matter and radiation defied description by models drawn from everyday experience. To describe light as either a wave or a particle was to distort a reality that was stranger than either analogy suggested. When probing the fundamental constitution of matter and

Albert Einstein gave a face to physics for millions of newspaper readers and newsreel watchers. He stands on the right in this photo, taken in Berlin in 1929. On the left is Max Planck. Although Planck did not have Einstein's public following, he played a pivotal role in the transition from the classical physics of Newton to quantum physics.

Bettmann/CORBIS

energy, analogies and mechanical models failed. Only mathematics could begin to describe the world as it truly is.

Such a mathematical description emerged in the mid-1920s in the work of Werner Heisenberg, Max Born, Paul Dirac, and a host of others. Avoiding visual models and mechanical analogies, these scientists framed a new quantum mechanics that reworked earlier quantum theories into a more rigorous and comprehensive form. Fully accessible only to the mathematically sophisticated, the new mechanics generated conclusions that both startled and befuddled many scientists. Light and other forms of electromagnetic radiation have the properties of both waves and particles simultaneously. Matter, too, exhibits dual wavelike and particulate properties that become manifest at the level of atoms and their components. There are inflexible limits to our ability to specify the location and velocity of very small particles such as electrons, and these limits may arise not simply because of the physical impossibility of studying such objects without altering their motions, but because the objects may not have precise values at all times.

Ideas about the continuity of the physical reality that we experience, in which trucks and planets occupy definite locations and move with specific velocities, may not extend down into the microstructure of matter, where such entities as electrons exist in the form of smears or probability distributions. Even our intuitions about cause and effect may fail because the mathematics of the quantum suggests such bizarre possibilities as the instantaneous influence of events in one part of the universe upon those in another.

Not surprisingly, many physicists, most notably Einstein, strenuously opposed the most radical implications of quantum mechanics, even while conceding the power of the theory to provide verifiable predictions about atomic structure, radiation, and the interaction of energy and matter. "God does not play dice with the universe," Einstein retorted in response to attacks on causality and determinism. But by 1930 most quantum physicists were not so sure.

Relativity theory and quantum mechanics were revolutionary in the sense that they turned many of the assumptions that had guided physicists since the early modern era upside down, making what was familiar and secure seem suddenly strange and uncertain. But these two lines of inquiry represented just a small part of the effort and imagination invested in physical science during the early twentieth century. The discovery of radioactivity in the 1890s had led over the next few decades to theories of atomic structure. By the 1930s, experimental techniques had advanced sufficiently to detect the existence of several kinds of subatomic particles, ranging from the now-familiar neutron to the more esoteric antiproton and meson. Other physicists used a new generation of reflecting telescopes, such as those built atop Mt. Wilson in California, to gather starlight for spectrographic analysis. They framed new theories of stellar evolution and energy with their results and extended the dimensions of the universe to include galaxies other than the Milky Way. Still others used new seismic tools to look into the earth, inferring structures from patterns in the transmission of shock waves.

Improved tools and methods of measurement were vital to all these lines of inquiry; the relationship between science and technology was a two-way street. Vital, too, were the decades of social investment in education and research that had been made by institutions ranging from profit-seeking corporations to philanthropic foundations and state-supported universities. A curiosity about nature could be found in all parts of the world, but it found the most favorable opportunities for expression where such institutions were densest, in the wealthy nations of the industrial West.

Life Sciences

The vigor of the physical sciences was very nearly matched by that of the life sciences in the first half of the twentieth century. Once the concern of amateur naturalists, by 1900 biology had become a broad and variegated subject, with professional scientists pursuing topics ranging from ornithology to biochemistry and from comparative anatomy to cytology. Some biologists worked in museums and others in the open air; a growing number performed experimental work under controlled laboratory conditions. Biologists as yet had only modest connections with the world of advancing industrial technology, but they had much to offer in the way of deeper understanding of human life and history.

Nowhere were the questions more exciting than in the study of heredity and evolution, fields that had been largely independent of each other until late in the nineteenth century. The mechanism of heredity had long puzzled naturalists. How are resemblances transmitted across generations? And why do differences between parents and offspring sometimes appear, despite the strong tendency of heredity to preserve parental form? These questions assumed new importance following the publication of Darwin's theory of evolution in 1859. His central principle of evolutionary change, natural selection, depended on the appearance of occasional novelties in organisms, for example, wolves with slightly longer legs. These variations, which arose spontaneously in populations, could become more common over generations if they afforded their possessors even modest advantages in the struggle to survive and reproduce. Over many generations, such variations could accumulate by incremental steps to the point where a new variety might appear. Since characteristics that were advantageous in one environment could be detrimental in another (wings may serve beetles on a prairie but endanger them on a windswept island), species found in diverse habitats could diverge into two or more distinct forms, each suited to the particular conditions of life in its own region. Darwin assumed that heredity could produce novelties of structure and instinct, if only quite minor, despite a general tendency to conserve the form of the species. But he could not supply a mechanism that was adequate to explain how this took place. In search of such a mechanism, scientists concentrated more intensively on experiments in the breeding of plants and animals and on cell structures that might offer clues to the transmission of hereditary traits.

These studies generated a new science of genetics that could answer many of the questions left unresolved by Darwin and was as rich and powerful as any of the new theories being simultaneously advanced by physicists. Systematic experiments in breeding yielded the first major breakthrough. In 1900, the year of Planck's initial paper on quantum physics, biologists from different parts of Europe independently converged on a set of ideas about heredity that an Austrian monk, Gregor Mendel, had anticipated a generation earlier. Many of the observable traits of organisms—the color of pea seeds, for instance—are determined by the transmission of hereditary factors, later called genes, that exist in egg and sperm cells and are passed on from parents to offspring unaffected by mixing. When parents possess different forms, or alleles, of the same gene, offspring receive both. But they often "express," or show, the visible characteristic associated with only one of these forms, called the dominant allele. In pea plants, for example, Mendel found that the offspring of plants with yellow seeds and plants with green seeds will always yield plants that produce yellow seeds. These offspring, although resembling only one parent in this visible characteristic, nevertheless continue to harbor the recessive allele for green seeds, and they can pass it on, unchanged, to their progeny. This becomes apparent when plants that possess both the dominant and the recessive alleles are crossed. The recessive characteristic (green seed color) will again appear among their offspring, even though it was visible in neither parent.

These patterns of inheritance are common but hard to discern. Some characteristics (human eye color, for example) are determined by several genes, while others (human height, for example) reflect both genes and nutrition. Even the simplest patterns of inheritance, such as those Mendel described in pea plants, become clear only when large numbers of organisms are observed over several generations. Mendel's conclusions, for example, rested on experiments with nearly thirty thousand plants over a decade.

The principles of heredity that Mendel described in the 1860s went almost unnoticed by his contemporaries, who hardly expected to learn a theory of heredity from a central European monk. In 1900, however, Mendel's ideas received a far more enthusiastic hearing. A generation of labor on evolution had sharpened curiosity about heredity, and the scientists who retrieved Mendel's papers from obscurity had themselves already retraced many of the steps in his thinking. In short, scientists were much better prepared in 1900 than in 1860 to understand Mendel's questions and answers.

Even so, it took biologists the better part of the next two decades to realize how fully Mendel's principles complemented Darwinian evolution. The existence of multiple forms of many genes in a population provided abundant diversity in structure—a necessity for evolutionary change since selection requires individual differences. The idea that genes could pass unchanged from generation to generation helped explain how useful traits could spread through populations even as their possessors mated with others who lacked them. Between 1910 and 1940 the fit became even better as biologists discovered that mutations in genes could occur spontaneously in populations, thereby introducing occasional novelties in form or behavior, and as statistically sophisticated studies demonstrated how Mendelian patterns of inheritance could yield evolutionary changes in populations.

Mendelian genetics was further strengthened and deepened as biologists developed evidence linking genes to specific structures in the living cell. Mendel and later advocates of his ideas assumed that hereditary information was carried by material particles or structures; their suppositions were confirmed when cytologists discovered that the inheritance of specific traits, most notably gender, could be correlated with the transmission of particular chromosomes, minute bodies that were observable in the nuclei of cells.

The linkage of Mendelian genetics and cytology opened the door to subsequent efforts to find the specific molecules in chromosomes that held genetic information—a pursuit that by 1940 was beginning to draw attention to one type of molecule in particular, DNA (deoxyribonucleic acid). The determination of the structure of that molecule by James Watson and Francis Crick in 1953, and the subsequent deciphering of the code of life that it contained, completed one of the most impressive achievements of the twentieth century. Scientists could move by continuous steps from the chemical properties of molecules, to the cellular structures holding those molecules, to the genes encoding the forms that organisms can potentially assume, and to the evolutionary forces that, over time, mold species.

Small wonder that some biologists and many amateur enthusiasts grew hopeful about the potential of genetics for solving human problems. By the 1920s,

Mendelian genetics was useful in understanding hereditary diseases and in breeding crops and livestock. These efforts led to some remarkable successes, especially in the second half of the century, when geneticists helped breeders double and redouble the yields of grains. Indeed, the development of new varieties of corn, wheat, and other cereals ranks alongside the synthesis of ammonia among the most important achievements of twentieth-century science because the growth of the global population could not have been sustained without these advances.

But enthusiasm had its dangers. The rapid progress in genetics in the early twentieth century also stimulated overconfidence about the depth of human understanding and efforts to use genetic knowledge to sort and mold human populations. The boom years of classical genetics also saw the growth of an international movement to improve humankind through better breeding that went under the banner "eugenics."

Eugenics, defined by its proponents as the science of better breeding of human beings, had its beginnings in the nineteenth century when some scientists and laypeople warned that welfare and charity were protecting society's weak from the sieve of natural selection; as a consequence, individuals who could not survive to reproduce under "natural" conditions were not only leaving behind progeny but out-reproducing the biologically fit. Civilization, in other words, was undermining the competition that had honed human intelligence and vigor in the first place. The solution, according to advocates of eugenics, was intervention by the state or some other agency, guided by expert advice.

The motives of eugenicists varied, as did their prescriptions. Some advocated a program of sterilization for individuals or groups that were deemed biologically inferior. Candidates here included the infirm, paupers, the insane, the feeble-minded, and criminals—all of whom were deemed, naively, to be suffering from some genetic deficiency. Several thousand individuals were sterilized under state-sponsored programs in some parts of the United States and Sweden during the interwar years; in Germany, legislation passed shortly after Hitler came to power in 1933 led to the sterilization of between two hundred thousand and four hundred thousand citizens for reasons ranging from epilepsy to alcoholism.

Most eugenicists, however, were less enthusiastic about such coercive measures than about encouraging higher reproductive rates among society's fittest, although there was no consensus about who exactly these might be. English academics tended to believe that the world needed more English dons, whereas Americans tended to place as much emphasis on moral virtue as on intellect. Eugenicists in the USSR wanted "new Soviet men and women" who would be loyal to their comrades and selfless in building a socialist state, whereas Nazis wanted Siegfrieds with Teutonic looks and swagger. And while many Europeans identified fitness with racial purity, eugenicists in Brazil, Mexico, and the Dominican Republic, with their large mixed-race populations, sometimes identified the mulatto as naturally superior.

Despite their different ideals, eugenicists shared a misplaced confidence in the simplicity of human genetics. Ironically, even before the eugenics movement peaked in the 1920s, many geneticists, including some who had once favored eugenic measures, were coming to question the easy attribution of complex human traits and behaviors to simple Mendelian genes. Although some human characteristics followed Mendelian patterns of inheritance, most did not—sometimes because they resulted from the interaction of several genes, sometimes because environmental conditions influenced the expression of genetic potential, but usually for reasons that were entirely unknown. Scientific scruples about oversimplification did not take all the wind out of the eugenicists' sails, but the excesses of some of the proponents of eugenics did. The racial laws of Nazi Germany, premised in part on the outdated biology of eugenics, stripped eugenics of its remaining claims to respectability.

Big Science

Prior to 1900, most scientific research was inexpensive in comparison with the cost of luxury goods or the expenditures of large firms and government agencies. The American banker J. P. Morgan spent more than $100,000 a year to run his ocean-going yacht in the 1890s, far more than the operating expenses of any laboratory or astronomical observatory in the United States. The largest investments in science

Courtesy of the Archives, California Institute of Technology

The telescope atop Mount Palomar in southern California was the largest and most powerful instrument of its era. Its mirror, two hundred inches in diameter, gave astronomers a view of galaxies near the edge of the universe.

generally went for the education and salaries of scientists and for the construction of buildings for their work. Physical laboratories, for example, were often the most expensive structures on college campuses because they required special utilities and protection from vibration and temperature change. Even so, many experimenters fabricated their own instruments, and theoreticians often required only chalk.

The cost of research escalated dramatically in the twentieth century as scientists pushed the limits of technology in their inquiries into the very small and very large parts of nature. Telescopes, already the most expensive of instruments, grew in scale and complexity until their construction taxed the resources of the richest philanthropic organizations. The Rockefeller Foundation spent $6 million on the Mount Palomar observatory, completed in 1948 after thirty years of planning and construction; it was almost enough to pay for a battleship.

Terrestrial physics was cheaper, but the cost was still no trifle. The American physicist Robert Millikan measured the charge on the electron with apparatus that cost the University of Chicago about $10,000. This experiment, which won Millikan a Nobel Prize, was considered extraordinarily expensive in 1910, although the outlay was roughly equivalent to the annual income of a good lawyer or surgeon. By the end of the 1930s, however, another American experimentalist, Ernst Orlando Lawrence, spent more than $1 million to build a cyclotron for his experiments in nuclear physics.

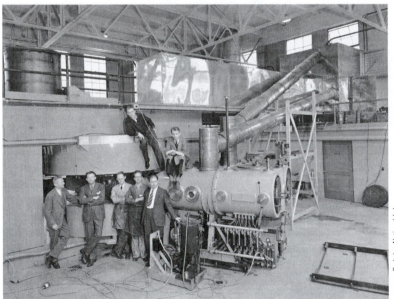

Lawrence Berkeley National Lab

Although astronomy was the first science to become truly capital intensive, experimental physics was not far behind. Here Ernst O. Lawrence (standing second from left) poses with some of his coworkers in front of (and atop) the most powerful atom smasher of its day, a cyclotron of Lawrence's design at the University of California, Berkeley, circa 1939.

The development of such large instruments changed the practice of science. Teams of specialists developed around the big machines, fundraising became an essential skill for the project leader, and time on the machine became a jealously guarded commodity. After World War II, only governments, and rich governments at that, could supply the capital necessary for cutting-edge research in fields such as nuclear physics. This meant that scientists often had to become lobbyists as well as managers. It also meant that scientists from societies with modest resources often had to go to Europe or the United States to find the best tools. Even as nations such as India and South Korea were building the universities and laboratories to sustain active scientific communities, the price of a ticket to the inner circle of research was going up, often to levels beyond their means.

Science, Technology, and Economic Development

It was comparatively easy to transport scientific ideas from one part of the world to another. The leading European and American scientific journals circulated wherever there were universities and libraries. Scientists traveled the world, lecturing to colleagues and taking visiting professorial appointments. Machines, drugs, and other products of modern technology also moved quickly. By 1900, electric power and telephone exchanges could be found in large cities around the world. Ford sold its tractors to Soviet Russia, and Germany sent its dyes to textile factories in Brazil and China. The people of Brazil were as enthusiastic about radio as those of the United States.

It was much harder to transplant the institutions that created new science and technology. This often had nothing to do with resistance to Western ideas. Once peoples in other parts of the world were acquainted with Western medicine, science, and technology, they generally were eager to integrate them into their own cultures. But the process proved difficult. The complexity of science and technology, their dependence on social and material support, and their integration into habits of life made quick and simple grafts impossible. In the turn-of-the-century United States, the great majority of children attended schools where instruction in science accompanied lessons in reading, writing, and arithmetic. Most lived in homes where they were surrounded by machines. Many entertained themselves by playing with chemistry sets or, later, by building simple radio receivers or tinkering with model railroads. They learned to use tools by helping their parents troubleshoot Model Ts and sewing machines and by fixing their own bicycles, and they often had ready access to books and magazines about science and invention. The result was a population with a high level of mechanical skill, broadly diffused scientific knowledge, and a disposition to seek more of both. Decades of investment in higher education afforded many the opportunity to satisfy such ambitions, and the ever-growing demand for persons with technical skills made a degree in science or engineering a sure path to a rewarding career.

Most of the world's peoples did not enjoy such opportunities. In their absence, relations between the industrial nations of the West and other parts of the globe were as unequal in science and technology as they were in wealth and military power. During the first half of the twentieth century, some of the preconditions for Western-style scientific research appeared where Europeans had settled in large numbers. New Zealand, Australia, and the richer nations of Latin America, for example, mandated universal schooling and invested resources in universities. Yet these states generally lacked the diversified industrial economies to generate a large and sustained demand for scientific and technical expertise. Their most promising scientists might find a career in teaching, but few could find the resources and stimulation to satisfy their research ambitions at home. Many of the best young scientists from these nations ended up migrating to Europe or the United States; for instance, the young Ernst Rutherford, a native of New Zealand, did Nobel Prize–winning work on nuclear structure in England.

Opportunities to participate in science hardly existed in most of Europe's colonies. Schooling was rudimentary at best in large parts of colonial Africa. Even where the imperial powers made an effort to promote literacy, only a handful of students had access to secondary education, never mind collegiate study. Colonial administrators saw little reason to promote scientific education, both because of prejudices about the aptitudes of "the natives" and because of general satisfaction with a status quo that left technical and scientific skills in the hands of Europeans. The few Africans with access to Western-style education generally preferred to seek surer paths to influence and wealth than science. There were few positions for African engineers or scientists at home or abroad; degrees in law could more readily translate into jobs.

India, the largest and richest European colony, presented a more complex picture. It had an ancient tradition of mathematical and scientific inquiry. Its middle class, although a small fraction of the total population, was nevertheless large in absolute numbers. Hundreds of thousands of Indian families could afford to invest in a child's education. India also needed engineers and certain types of scientists. By 1900, the colony had an extensive rail system, a small but expanding industrial sector, and a large civil service that managed activities ranging from the construction of dams and irrigation works to the preparation of maps and mineral surveys. Even ambivalent British administrators could not ignore the pressures for scientific and educational development because meeting all of India's needs for expertise with imported talent would be too expensive. Consequently, the British cooperated with the Indian elites in creating Western-style schools, technical colleges, and opportunities for advanced study in Britain. As in other colonies, ambitious students often preferred legal to scientific training. Nevertheless, by the beginning of World War II, India's schools, while still enrolling only a small minority of Indians, were turning out as many scientists and engineers as some Western nations. Some Indian scientists achieved international reputations for their contributions. One of these, Chandrasekhara V. Raman, won the Nobel Prize in physics in 1930 for his work on spectroscopy. But the advantages of the West were so great that even when exceptional talents found opportunities to develop, it was in Europe and the United States that they generally made their marks.

The one exception to this pattern was Japan. Although it was not among the leaders in technological innovation or scientific discovery, by 1930 Japan had become largely self-sufficient in the engineering talent necessary for diversified industrial production. Japanese scientists, both at home and abroad, were beginning to participate in cutting-edge research in both the physical and biological sciences. These developments reflected the policies pursued by Japanese governments since 1868, when power shifted from regional shoguns to the imperial court. Intent on achieving military and economic security, imperial bureaucrats had created many elements of the infrastructure essential for science and engineering. By 1900, the state had mandated universal primary schooling and created national universities. Although these focused on educating civil servants and managers, they also replicated some of the scientific research institutes so important in Germany and the United States.

Japanese governments also pumped money into industries that they deemed vital to national defense, including many in the engineering-intensive communications, transport, electric power, and chemical sectors. Japan imported engineers and scientists when necessary but encouraged private industry to train their own wherever possible. Perhaps equally important to the growth of Japanese industry was a large pool of labor with mechanical skills. Cottage industries such as the production of textiles and ceramics had long thrived in Japan, and these pursuits, which were common in numerous homes and small workshops, provided Japanese workers with many of the basic mechanical skills that were common in the West.

The Japanese case demonstrated that the science and technology of the West could take root in other cultures. But the exceptional nature of the Japanese achievement prior to World War II also demonstrates the difficulty of such transmission. Scientific and technological innovation flourish best in diversified industrial economies, but such economies themselves depend, to some degree, on scientific and technical resources. This was one of the cruel dilemmas of development in the twentieth century. To build modern industries, societies needed many forms of expert knowledge, but that expertise was unlikely to exist unless it was called into being by such industries and the systems that surround them. Japan found a way to jump-start the process, in part because of determined government intervention, in part because of the mechanical and entrepreneurial skills of its people, and, perhaps just as important, because so many of the empire's subjects tolerated low standards of living while government invested resources in plants, education, and infrastructure. Few other societies had Japan's combination of good fortune and discipline.

CONCLUSION

The drive to understand and control the natural world was not unique to the twentieth century. But never before had the tasks of knowing and doing, science and technology, come into such close harmony. Even physical theories that at first seemed utterly irrelevant to practical needs had by mid-century begun to yield useful knowledge. Indeed, one of the most powerful technologies of the second half of the twentieth century, the engineering of semiconductors such as transistors, silicon chips, and integrated circuits, depended on the esoteric physics of the quantum.

The convergence of knowing and doing satisfied the hopes of prophets like Bacon and Condorcet. It also carried dangers and costs, few of which were anticipated. Improved seeds encouraged monoculture agriculture, which, in turn, laid crops open to devastating attacks by insects and disease. The insecticides and fungicides devised to control such outbreaks themselves poisoned wildlife and, sometimes, human beings. The plants producing those chemicals created jobs and wealth but also generated toxic wastes that spoiled water and air. Oil pumped from the huge reserves discovered in the twentieth century was a raw material for those plants and for others making thousands of products for home and industry, but its consumption contributed to urban smog and even, as some meteorologists were beginning to suspect, global climate change. The chemistry that yielded new dyes also generated poison gases, and the physics that revealed unsuspected complexity in the atom also suggested the atomic bomb. Science, for all, its power, cannot arrive at an exact balance between the costs and benefits of such intensive technological change.

For Further Reading

James R. Bartholomew, *The Formation of Science in Japan* (New Haven, CT: Yale University Press, 1989). A broad survey of the adoption of Western science in Japan.

Ronald Clark, *Einstein: The Life and Times* (New York: World Publishing, 1971). A place to start on Einstein.

Daniel R. Headrick, *The Tentacles of Progress* (New York: Oxford University Press, 1988). Technology transfer within Europe's empires.

Thomas Parke Hughes, *American Genesis* (New York: Viking, 1989). Focuses on the history of invention and industrial research.

Daniel Kevles, *In the Name of Science* (New York: Knopf, 1985). A vivid history of eugenics in England and the United States.

———, *The Physicists* (New York: Knopf, 1977). A superb history of the physics discipline in the modern United States of America.

Helge Kragh, *Quantum Generations: A History of Physics in the Twentieth Century* (Princeton, N.J.: Princeton University Press, 1999). An in-depth account of twentieth-century physics.

Melvin Kranzberg and Carroll W. Pursell Jr., *Technology in Western Civilization*, 2 vols. (New York: Oxford University Press, 1967). Numerous short articles by specialists on the history of technology.

David S. Landes, *The Wealth and Poverty of Nations* (New York: W. W. Norton, 1998). A witty and learned work giving the long perspective on science, technology, and economic development.

Vaclav Smil, *Enriching the Earth: Fritz Haber, Carl Bosch, and the Transformation of World Food Production* (Cambridge, MA: MIT Press, 2001). A broad-gauge treatment of the history of ammonia synthesis.

Kozo Yamamura, ed., *The Economic Emergence of Modern Japan* (Cambridge: Cambridge University Press, 1997). A useful guide to Japanese economic history.

Related Websites

The Center for the History of Physics of the American Institute of Physics
www.aip.org/history
The home page of the Center for the History of Physics of the American Institute
of Physics. Includes exhibits on Einstein, Heisenberg, and the cyclotron.
Nobel e-Museum
www.nobel.se
Biographical information on Nobel laureates.
Chemical Heritage Foundation—Chemistry in History
http://www.chemheritage.org/discover/chemistry-in-history/index.aspx
Although the site covers all of chemical history, the sections on "People" and
"Themes" include much information on twentieth-century science and chemical
industries.

CHAPTER 6

The Economic Consequences of War and Peace, 1919–1938

I n 1919, the economist John Maynard Keynes warned of chaos in Europe if the victors of World War I did not revise the Treaty of Versailles and aid Germany as part of the rebuilding of the European economy. If they did not, he predicted, "famine, cold, disease, war, murder, and anarchy" would spread across the continent, dooming all hopes for a lasting peace. Although his fears were of revolution and social conflict, his analysis stressed economic problems. Keynes argued that political stability had to be built on economic prosperity and productivity, both of which had been undermined in Europe by World War I. His aim was to reestablish a "perpetual circle of production and exchange in foreign trade."[1] This interlocking circle had been shattered and could not easily be rebuilt. New countries, new products, and new patterns of production had to be integrated into the circle, but banks and other financial institutions, as Keynes had feared, were too weak and unimaginative for the task. Although Keynes's message was largely disregarded during the 1920s, it was later accepted and used to guide the post–World War II program of reconstruction.

Understanding why the peace of 1919 was so fragile requires a look at the world economy, which entered a new phase in the period between the wars. The economic troubles of the 1920s and early 1930s changed the relationships among countries and between countries and their colonies, while undermining citizens'

---

[1]John Maynard Keynes, *The Economic Consequences of the Peace* (New York: Harcourt, Brace, and Howe, 1920), pp. 235, 255.

faith in their rulers. Government controls replaced relatively free trade as states attempted to build protective walls against foreign threats and competition. Many of the problems of the interwar economy can be summed up under the headings "markets" and "money." The market side of the economy involved trading goods and services produced by independent firms around the globe, and money referred to the international movements of financial capital. Countries around the world, whatever their stage of economic development, found that the markets for their goods had shrunk and that their ability to finance trade had been compromised. Depression soon followed, bringing with it a host of social and political problems. Ordinary people struggled to cope with the economic legacy of World War I, which, as Keynes feared, helped to produce World War II.

Markets and Money

Before World War I, the international economy resembled the ideal world of classical liberals: Taxes were low and budgets balanced. Although governments spent little on their citizens, they also required little of them in return. Low tariffs (taxes on imports and exports) and stable currency exchange rates encouraged the expansion of trade and economic growth in Europe, Asia, and the Americas. Selling goods abroad was made easy through general acceptance by banks in most countries of "the gold standard," which obligated participating nations to make their currencies convertible into gold at a fixed rate of exchange.

In different ways, Britain and Germany served as motors for this worldwide system. Not only did British bankers manage the gold standard, which enabled the trading nations of the world to arrange multilateral payments easily, but Britain's capital exports financed much of the development of Latin America, Russia, the Middle East, and East Asia. Countries that had difficulty paying their international debts borrowed from British bankers. In addition, the demand by British consumers and industrialists for food and raw materials from around the world stimulated global trade. Meanwhile, Germany acted as the economic locomotive of Europe, exporting capital and manufactured products to neighboring countries and importing their goods. These two economies had sufficient power and energy to draw many other societies into trading relations. Investors in Europe bought stocks and bonds in the Americas and Asia, while their merchants sent goods to the bazaars of the Middle East and India. Plantation managers in the Caribbean and Africa and Southeast Asia sent their products to the United States and Europe, while buying food from farms elsewhere. A circle of exchange, guaranteed in gold, stretched around the globe.

Disruption and Change in the 1920s

During World War I, all major countries abandoned the gold standard. Governments decided not to risk a loss of gold and thus stopped exchanging their currency for that metal. They also began to control exports and imports, blocking the sale of certain goods and forbidding the importation of others. International

GLOBAL Technologies

The Oil Industry

World War I sent a clear message to states around the globe: "oil is power." Tanks, airplanes, and automobiles needed gasoline and fuel oil; engines and machinery used petroleum-based lubricants. The world's major navies shifted to the use of oil because it permitted faster speeds, took less space, and labor power to supply than did coal. Oil fed the emerging twentieth-century military machine, and those states with a secure supply were in the best position to benefit.

The modern commercial industry began in the United States in Pennsylvania, when a prospector struck oil in 1859 after drilling deep into the earth and rock. Later discoveries in California, Texas, and Oklahoma made the United States the world's largest supplier of crude oil, but by the late 1930s, international companies had developed oil fields in Russia, Persia, Mexico, Venezuela, Sumatra, Iraq, and Saudi Arabia, making the industry both global and highly competitive. Pipelines and tankers moved oil from distant fields to refiners and urban consumers.

Petroleum, or crude oil, is a fossil fuel, composed of complex hydrocarbon molecules of different sizes and properties. When heated to very high temperatures, the crude oil can be "fractioned" or separated into many different products, such as kerosene, fuel oil, lubricants, and gasoline, but the supply of each depends upon the specific composition of the petroleum. To free themselves of this constraint, refiners and petroleum chemists explored ways to alter the composition of petroleum stocks. In 1913, the Standard Oil Company of Indiana began to use high pressures and temperatures to "crack" petroleum—that is, to break down its heavy hydrocarbon molecules into the smaller ones that are the main constituents of light petroleum products, such as kerosene and gasoline. During the 1930s, a French chemist, Eugene Houdry, devised a process that achieved the same purpose more efficiently by using catalysts to promote the breakdown of viscous oils. Improved by American firms, catalytic cracking doubled the amount of gasoline that could be extracted from a barrel of crude oil, thereby greatly enhancing the value of the oil reserves and, more immediately, supplying high octane fuels necessary for auto and piston aircraft engines.

Industrial economies today depend on oil, not only for fuel but as a necessary material in tires, plastics, and a long list of consumer goods. World economic development and population growth has increased the demand for oil, and wars been fought over access to its supply. Abundant oil comes, however, at a cost. While it permits relatively cheap travel by car and plane, it also contributes to global warming by increasing the carbon dioxide in the air. Alternative technologies for energy for wind and solar power cannot yet compete with oil in terms of price and availability. We remain in the Age of Oil in our quest for increasing, renewable, and clean energy supplies.

trade declined sharply as states tried to control their economies and attempted to solve their economic problems by restricting contact with their neighbors.

Few countries had the natural resources to permit a retreat from international trade without lowering their citizens' standards of living. Increasingly, consumers had to make do with what was produced locally, which meant making do with less. Moreover, the British central bank no longer had sufficient funds to manage the world's finances, yet the U.S. banking system had not yet replaced it. During the 1920s and 1930s, the shift from one pattern of political economy to another brought about hard times, confusion, and ill will.

The breakdown in the international economy intensified the difficulties caused by increasing competition among countries. By the 1920s, many states were producing finished goods in significant amounts, as Map 6.1 shows. Industrialization had advanced in regions far distant from Europe and North America. Not only had Japan and the Soviet Union joined the ranks of rapidly industrializing societies, but India, Mexico, the Union of South Africa, and China also had growing industrial regions. More than 50 percent of the working population in Australia, New Zealand, Canada, Brazil, Argentina, Uruguay, and Chile no longer worked in agriculture. On the back streets of Singapore, Shanghai, Rio de Janeiro, and Durban, small factories produced consumer goods and processed food and raw materials. Even in undeveloped economies, such as the Belgian Congo or Rhodesia, factories processing locally grown food and raw materials operated successfully under the protection of colonial governments and internationally controlled joint stock companies. The international economy had already become multicentered and competitive.

When the countries that fought in World War I shifted production from exports to war needs, other countries substituted their own products for many European imports. As a result, factories in Latin America, the Middle East, and East Asia produced growing amounts of cloth, processed food, and household goods. After 1919 the British found it increasingly difficult to compete against low-cost manufacturers in Syria, India, and Colombia. Technological changes had led many consumers to shift to oil, diminishing the worldwide demand for coal. At the same time, new national boundaries and regulations—in Eastern Europe, for example—cut long-term trading relations, forcing businesses to find new sources of supply for their raw materials and new outlets for their goods. Worldwide shifts in production had to be incorporated into trading patterns, but adjustments took time and exacted a human cost. Meanwhile, every firm that failed meant that workers lost jobs.

By the mid-1920s, however, the most difficult readjustments had been completed, and economic growth had been reestablished in most regions. Latin American countries expanded rapidly, as did Japan, the United States, and most of western and northern Europe. New products—automobiles, radios, and films— transformed transportation and leisure time as they boosted gross national products. More than just the wealthy benefited; rising incomes meant that ordinary people could afford these new consumption goods too. Families purchased radios and bicycles. In the United States, Henry Ford's Model T became affordable by the middle classes. In cities around the world, attractive ready-made clothes and makeup gave working women a chance to copy the fashionable. As long as no one looked too closely, the illusion of prosperity held.

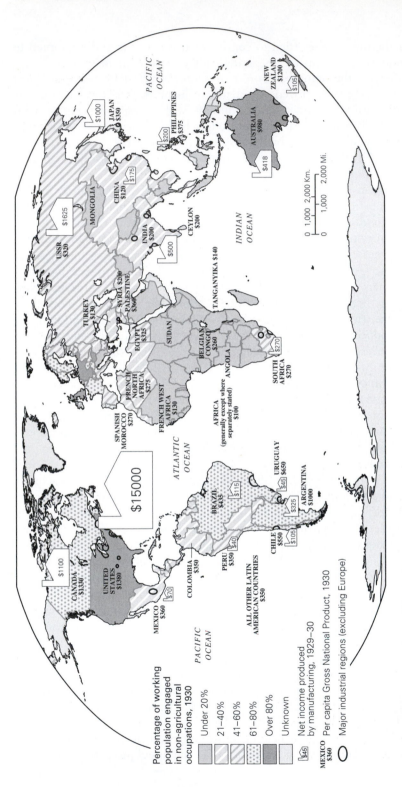

MAP 6.1 Industrial production around the globe, circa 1929.
Manufacturing accounted for a rising share of national incomes in many states, but the relative size of that economic sector varied greatly.
Notice the regional differences in the relative share of populations still employed in agriculture.

Inflation and Deflation

Economists think of economic activity as cyclical: Periods of expansion, in which sales, prices, and employment rise, alternate with periods of contraction, in which prices, sales, and employment decline. The two decades after World War I were years of sharp business cycles, particularly when looked at in terms of changing prices. Markets and employment were unstable.

In places where defeat and revolution had disrupted political life, price changes were dramatic and destructive. In Germany, Austria, Hungary, Poland, and Russia, where weak governments kept printing money to pay their expenses, runaway inflation (rising prices produced by an expanding money supply) destroyed the value of currency, and along with it the savings of the middle classes and the workers. In the Weimar Republic, the social and political impact of hyperinflation was disastrous. The liberal democratic government used increasingly worthless paper money to pay social benefits, reparations, and war loans, trying but failing to buy support from the population. Wages and prices spiraled upward. In 1923 prices in Germany reached an index level more than fifteen trillion times that of 1914. Any money received had to be spent immediately before it lost its value. Creditors and people living on fixed capital or fixed incomes lost heavily, while

In 1923, this German woman burned paper currency, instead of firewood, because it burned longer than the logs that could be purchased with it.

Bettmann/CORBIS

big industrial firms that could export German goods and sell them for foreign exchange earned great profits. Resentment against the republican government grew intense, and its enemies began to win elections. In 1924, the right-wing Nationalist party won almost 25 percent of the seats, promising vengeance against those who had destroyed the nation's currency.

In such chaotic times, bankers and politicians began to look back on the prewar world with nostalgia. When they looked for ways to reestablish their control of markets, they settled on a return to the gold standard. They hoped to make it easier for traders to buy and sell goods abroad and to ease international transfers of capital. Great Britain, France, Italy, and Japan returned to the gold standard between 1925 and 1930. But economic conditions had changed so dramatically since 1900 that these efforts to recapture stability through fixed exchange rates were bound to fail. In Britain, reestablishment of the gold standard triggered a depression, which increased unemployment and produced a general strike in 1926.

Other countries managed to achieve economic stability along with significant economic growth. France experienced an industrial boom from the early 1920s to 1929 as the country rebuilt war-torn regions. Productivity grew at a rapid clip in Japan. The U.S. economy, whose per capita growth rates were also impressive, prospered until 1929. These numbers signaled important changes in the way ordinary citizens lived. With the spread of electrification, people in many regions could buy refrigerators or electric fans. Telephones ended the isolation of farming families. For industrial workers in countries where there had been neither revolution nor hyperinflation, the 1920s were a time of improvement. People ate better because of lower food prices and increased supplies; they had easier access to consumer goods as industrialization spread. These gains depended on international trade and capital flows, which in turn depended on international financial arrangements.

International Capital in Motion

The health of the interwar international economy depended on large movements of capital among industrialized nations, both for rebuilding after the conflict and to finance trade. Politics as well as economics drove these transactions because the issue of war loans and debts had to be settled. The United States insisted that the money it had loaned to Great Britain and the other allied governments be repaid. The British government, which had lent large sums to France, Italy, and Belgium to help them continue fighting, made the same request in order to pay the United States. This chain of demands rested not only on bankers' ideas of sound finance but also on the U.S. government's need to balance its budget. Without debt repayment from its creditors, Congress would have to raise taxes, then as now a politically suicidal action for elected officials. Self-preservation as well as fiscal conservatism pushed U.S. politicians to take a hard line with their European allies.

The second imperative that pushed international financial arrangements in the 1920s came from the Versailles settlement and other treaties, which had set the initial ground rules for debts and credit. Immediately after the end of the war, politicians in Britain helped convince voters that Germany should be forced to cover the British and Allied war losses. Sir Eric Campbell Geddes, a British government minister, boasted, "The Germans … are going to pay every penny; they are going to be squeezed as a lemon is squeezed—until the pips squeak. My only doubt is not whether we can squeeze hard enough, but whether there is enough juice."[2]

In specific terms, this meant that the new German state had to agree to send 132 billion gold marks, or $31.4 billion, to the victors. France, in particular, wanted to exact punitive damages from its former enemy, and politicians found it easy to ride into office on the notion that the costs of rebuilding their country could be passed along to their former enemy. But where could the Germans get the money to rebuild the countries of their former enemies if their industries lacked capital for reconstruction and if the protectionist United States would not import German goods? During the early 1920s, the issue of reparations for war damages destabilized Germany and hampered the ability of other Allied governments to rebuild their economies.

Acceptance in 1924 of the Dawes Plan, a U.S.-financed scheme to ensure that international war debts were paid, reestablished financial stability until late in the decade. In the new agreement, the U.S. government agreed to link the repayment of sums owed by the Allies to the United States to the payment of reparations by Germany. American bankers helped to set up a circular system that satisfied all parties for a time. As U.S. banks loaned money to Germany, Germany could pay reparations to Western European governments, who then could pay the interest on their war debts to the United States. In the end, not only did the United States get its money back, but German cities and industries were rebuilt and international trade was financed. Economic revival encouraged other lenders too, with the result that investments moved from Britain, France, and other Western European countries into Eastern Europe, Latin America, and the European empires.

Unfortunately, this circle of capital movements worked only as long as the United States, Britain, and France kept on lending. Moreover, German industries and cities took on large debts, which could be called in quickly. Although much of this international investment was in the form of short-term loans, large amounts of it went into long-term projects. In retrospect, these arrangements look more like a house of cards than like a solid foundation for expansion. By the end of the decade, the lending circle broke as economic pressures on both creditors and debtors mounted.

Depression Around the Globe

The world economy disintegrated between 1929 and 1932, throwing millions of people out of work and onto the streets or back into the fields. Although economic cycles of growth and decline occur regularly, the Great Depression hit

---

[2]Speech at Cambridge University, December 10, 1918, quoted in *Oxford Dictionary of Quotations* (Oxford: Oxford University Press, 1999), p. 332.

harder and wider. It was the greatest crisis of the world economy in modern times. Spreading from the United States to Europe to the rest of the world, it brought financial ruin to firms, hunger to the unemployed, and disgrace to politicians.

In retrospect, the weaknesses of the international economy during the 1920s can be identified. The United States had become the world's largest economy and its major creditor, as well as the largest exporting nation and the second largest importer. American economic problems were contagious, and they soon spread around the world. Once the international economy had begun to contract, American insistence on the repayment of war debts, high U.S. tariffs, and deflationary monetary policies (shrinking money supplies leading to declining prices) made a bad situation worse.

The Domino Effect

The Great Depression started in the United States. In 1928, money poured into the New York Stock Exchange as investors competed to purchase stock at ever-rising prices. This economic boom had shaky foundations, however, because the U.S. market was not large enough to absorb the goods being produced by the country's factories. The mass of the U.S. population had too little income to buy all the cars and refrigerators that firms needed to sell. Only with higher wages could workers purchase enough goods to support a shift to a consumer economy.

Major industries, such as oil, agriculture, and textiles, were also in trouble. Their profits rested more on paper transactions, on stock values and manipulations of balance sheets, than on increasing sales. Instead of buying hard assets and increasing the size of their companies, businessmen turned to stocks and bonds to make their fortunes. Bankers joined in the frenzied buying of property, whose value was bid up by rumor and wild hopes. Each new purchase, only partially paid for, served as collateral, or security, for the next deal. Holding companies acquired holding companies, which acquired other holding companies, supported by little cash or entrepreneurial energy.

After stock prices went up and up, they came tumbling down. In October of 1929 the market crashed, and thousands of people lost their investments. In an effort to stop the wild selling of stocks, the acting president of the New York Stock Exchange, Richard Whitney, walked onto the exchange floor and began buying stocks in $20 million lots to restore confidence. His efforts produced a brief rally in prices, but on the next trading day, stock values tumbled down even faster. The Federal Reserve Board stood aside and did not intervene effectively.

Unfortunately, the contraction of the U.S. economy after the stock market crash in 1929 reduced both the U.S. demand for imports and its willingness to lend. When the United States raised tariffs in 1930, world trade contracted, with devastating results. The rest of the world lost not only a major market but also its supply of credit. Countries in debt to the United States had to pay in gold when they could not sell enough goods abroad to cover their loans. As prices, profits, and incomes declined, their economies moved into depression.

In 1930 and 1931, European and Latin American banks began to fail, causing Bolivia and other Latin American countries to default on their foreign debts. The German government ended its payment of reparations, stopping the flow of funds into Western Europe. Soon the financial crisis in Central and Eastern Europe spread to London, forcing Parliament to abandon the gold standard. Within a few months, more than thirty countries stopped exchanging their paper money for gold at a fixed rate.

These financial crises pushed industry and agriculture into a deep depression. When manufacturers could no longer get credit and falling prices eliminated profits, firms failed. Indebted farmers lost their land. The international economy entered a downward spiral as bankruptcies multiplied and trade contracted around the globe. Countries that depended on the export of food or raw materials saw their markets disappear and their access to credit end.

The New York stock market crash and the financial problems of the industrialized countries had repercussions even for villagers in Southeast Asia and Africa. People who had gone into debt, perhaps to finance a daughter's marriage or to buy additional land, found themselves hit hard by the declines in prices and market demand. They had to pay back loans at interest rates they had agreed to when prices were much higher and they could sell more goods in the marketplace. Credit arrangements chained the fortunes of New York's bankers to those of moneylenders and their clients at the opposite ends of the earth.

The severity and scope of the crisis can be seen through a comparison of changes in world production and prices between 1929 and 1932 (see Table 6.1). Within three years, the value of world trade had decreased by two-thirds. Factories throughout the world had cut back their output of manufactured goods, firing workers or cutting their hours. Manufacturers in North America were the hardest hit, but the declines in Argentina, Brazil, Germany, Britain, and Italy were also severe. The trading of raw materials—ores, coal, and oil—declined almost as sharply as demand from the factories contracted. Moreover, deep price declines intensified the problems of that sector. Food producers also had to cope with declining prices, although they maintained their output and partly protected their incomes. Although the depression hit economic sectors and world regions with varying intensity, all suffered.

Alternative Explanations

How can the apparent collapse of the capitalist, liberal economy be explained? Economists offer two sorts of theories, one stressing markets and the other stressing money. The former group links levels of supply and demand to economic production and to wages. During and just before the depression, the effective demand for goods did not keep up with the supply. This lack of demand posed a problem for the world economy. Ordinary people could not easily turn their wants into purchases in the market because they lacked cash. Not only in Europe

TABLE 6.1 World Production and Prices, 1929–1932 (index numbers; 1929=100)	1929	1930	1931	1932
1. Industrial production				
a. World[a]	100	87	75	64
b. Europe[a]	100	92	81	72
c. North America	100	81	68	54
2. Primary production-food				
a. World	100	102	100	100
b. Europe[a]	100	99	102	104
c. North America	100	102	103	100
3. Primary production-raw materials				
a. World	100	94	85	75
b. Europe[a]	100	90	82	73
c. North America	100	90	80	64
4. World prices				
a. Food	100	84	66	52
b. Raw materials	100	82	59	44
c. Manufactures	100	94	78	64

[a]*Excluding USSR.*
Sources: Blocks 1–3: League of Nations (1939b: 423–4); block 4: League of Nations (1939a: 61).

and North America, but also in Latin America, Southeast Asia, and the Middle East, millions of people bought their food and clothing, but collectively they did not have sufficient income to purchase the quantity of goods produced by the market. Despite the growth of the world population, there was not enough effective demand to sustain production.

A second group of theorists focuses on financial policies, arguing that money and credit shape the working of the "real economy," or the production of goods and services. For an economy to continue on an even course, the monetarists maintain, the money supply (the amount of money in circulation) should be kept steady. Central banks can manipulate the money supply through the buying and selling of government bonds and Treasury bills; they can also raise or lower the amounts of money that banks have to hold as reserve funds. When the United States, the major economic power in the world, did not act to stabilize the money supply in 1929 and withdrew from the international economy, monetarists argue, the result was a major slump in the global economy. This explanation appears to make the United States the culprit in triggering world depression. Troubles in the U.S. economy had an impact around the globe, but the world's financial problems and instabilities in the 1920s came from many sources.

Monetarists also suggest that the gold standard produced sharply declining prices in the early years of the depression, before countries ended the convertibility of their currencies into gold. Through the 1920s and the early 1930s, the international monetary system magnified the problems of overproduction and demand. Once governments freed themselves from the shackles of the gold standard, they were able to use monetary policy to counteract, rather than intensify, the depression.

Depression in the Third World

Although the depression began in the industrialized countries, it quickly spread to less-developed states in Asia, Africa, and Latin America, which were linked to the world market through the sale of food and raw materials. The world market for agricultural products contracted along with the demand for industrial goods. Whereas, in theory, farmers can feed themselves and thus are insulated from market trends, during the 1930s this was possible for relatively few. Many in the countryside were either landless or held a tiny plot that was already at full production. In many parts of the world, rural economies depended on wages from agricultural employment, as well as on the sale of produce in a market. Rural smallholders were hit by both declining wages and sinking prices. Making matters worse, unemployed relatives returned from the cities to their home villages demanding to be fed. Rural populations suffered too.

During the 1930s, agricultural prices for wheat, rice, and coffee plummeted, along with prices for a wide variety of products used in industry, such as rubber, palm oil, and cotton. The larger farmers responded actively to this catastrophe. Because people still needed to eat, the demand for food remained high. Under these conditions, farmers had one recourse that was not open to industrial workers, and those with enough land used it effectively. By increasing their output, these farmers could sell more in the market, making up at least part of their lost income. During the depression, world agricultural production was steady or even increased. More aware than governments of ways to protect themselves, farmers ignored official orders to grow less. The depression revealed the limited ability of democratic governments to control output and markets.

By the 1930s, much of the world had been divided into competing blocs, shielded by tariff walls and drawn together by monetary linkages. Great Britain, its empire and dominions, and Scandinavia had joined together, working out preferential trading arrangements. Japan deepened its control over Korea and Manchuria and extended its influence in China. France, the Netherlands, and Belgium worked aggressively to control their imperial markets and sources of supply. Nazi Germany built a trading bloc in eastern and southeastern Europe. Only the largest countries, the United States and the Soviet Union, kept their distance from these regional arrangements. For capitalists as well as communists, the strategy of autarchy (economic independence) had replaced that of free trade and equal access. The ideal of international economic cooperation died during the depression.

Unemployment

One of the aims of the new trading blocs was to export unemployment. If a tariff could shift home buying power from an import to a domestic good, then more citizens could find work. This "beggar-thy-neighbor" strategy ceased to be effective, of course, if everyone followed it. In any case, any marginal advantages were small when compared to the overall decline of trade and production.

The human cost of the depression is best seen in the unemployment rates of the time. In 1932–1933, when the depression was most severe, 44 percent of German, 31 percent of Norwegian, 29 percent of Austrian, 27 percent of U.S., and 22 percent of British workers were unemployed. Moreover, in Britain and Scandinavia, rates of industrial unemployment had reached double digits in the early 1920s and then worsened during the 1930s. Young workers and the elderly found it hardest to get a job. Once fired or furloughed, it proved virtually impossible for men in their fifties to find another position.

These statistics signaled hardship of many sorts. Idleness proved to be socially corrosive as well as individually difficult. In Austria, the depression increased the isolation of rural villages, whose citizens could not afford to travel into town or to read newspapers. Suspicions of neighbors mounted. Families fell apart as adults became too depressed to look for work or to cope with their kin. Women, who had homes to maintain and food to cook, coped better than their husbands, who lost their self-respect along with their jobs and public status.

People lived on carbohydrates—bread and potatoes—along with a few homegrown vegetables. In rural Canada, hungry families hunted gophers and wolves to make stews; in the cities, the unemployed made ketchup soup, and mothers fed their children on oatmeal and beans. Shantytowns of evicted farmers grew up around major cities in the West. In Britain, the young unemployed used cheap thrills, such as movies, dancing, and chocolate candy, to compensate for poor diets and empty hours. Many families were forced to evict elderly relatives, moving them into rooming houses, in order to keep government welfare payments. In the United States thousands of bored, unemployed men hopped onto passing trains, riding the rails into an isolated world of migratory labor. Others drifted onto urban skid rows, where they stole to stay alive. Poverty spurred many to superhuman efforts to make money and keep their families together, but others dropped out of the struggle for respectability.

The depression was embarrassing and confusing. People's assumptions about self-help and stability suddenly fell apart. Many people blamed themselves rather than business cycles. Others, however, got angry and became active in local or national politics. Championed by trade unions and socialist parties, workers went on hunger marches in the United States and Britain to dramatize their needs. Homeless families squatted in vacant houses, daring authorities to evict them. In India, thousands of people followed Gandhi's lead and refused to pay a salt tax. In 1930, peasants joined anticolonial rebellions in both Burma and Vietnam.

Socialism and communism attracted those who saw the deepening inequality of rich and poor and thought that a different set of governing ideas could lift the weight of human misery. The spectacle of starvation seemed to require political

On December 11, 1933, unemployed men and women marched to Paris to confront the French government and to demand help. Their signs, several of which identify their town of origin, ask for work and bread.

Bettmann/CORBIS

action. A wealthy Alabama woman linked her social activism to what she saw during the depression:

> I had been a conformist, a southern snob.... What I learned during the Depression changed all that. I saw a blinding light like Saul on the road to Damascus. It was the first time I had seen the other side of the tracks. The rickets, the pellagra—it shook me up. I saw the world as it really was.[3]

The political right was also energized by the depression. In Berlin, Nazi gangs fought communists, and in London, Oswald Mosley organized his neo-fascist party out of frustration with socialist inefficiency. The depression had put the world's economic system on trial, and it failed its first set of tests.

National Solutions

Between the wars, governments battled against recession and unemployment with varying degrees of success. Since international organizations were relatively weak and few in number at this time, nations dominated global economic relationships.

---

[3]Studs Terkel, *Hard Times* (New York: Avon, 1970), p. 461.

But nation-states, then and now, differ markedly in terms of their political frame-works, social institutions, laws, and culture. As a result, their economic systems are distinctive. An American political scientist, Chalmers Johnson, distinguishes three different types of economies that can describe major nations in the interwar period. Most of Western Europe, Latin America, and the United States can be seen as regulatory states, where national governments set the conditions within which individual companies operated but left the decisions about investment, production, and distribution to them. Although politicians set financial policies and worked to regulate trade, they left the direction of industry in private hands. Japan, in contrast, can be called a developmental state because of its active industrial policy, which targeted certain sectors of the economy for preferential development. Japan not only set the rules for economic activity but encouraged industrialization through state investment and unequal treatment of different sec-tors and firms. The Soviet Union represented a third sort of political economy, the planned communist state. Not only did the Soviet government own most of the property and firms within the country, but the state also controlled invest-ment and the allocation of resources. Bureaucrats, rather than the market, set prices and production targets. Policies were driven by ideology. Regulatory, devel-opmental, and planned communist states responded to the Great Depression in different ways, illustrating how political systems shape economic life.

Regulatory States: The United States and Latin America

During the first years of the depression, the U.S. government held fast to the notion that government should not actively intervene in the economy. Conservatives argued that depressions would naturally change to recovery when the time was right, and that in any case they improved human character by forcing people to work harder. The government encouraged voluntary agencies to provide the relief that elected officials hesitated to supply. Herbert Hoover, a mining engineer and interna-tional administrator who became the thirty-first president of the United States, has come to personify a weak, voluntary approach to economic crises. Hoping to rally popular confidence and morale, he announced in the spring of 1930 that the depres-sion was over. Unfortunately, he was wrong. Voters in 1932 rejected this hands-off approach and elected Franklin D. Roosevelt as president, a man who promised bold attempts to combat hard times. Roosevelt, a wealthy Democrat who had been the governor of New York, began to reform the nation's institutions and to bring relief to the unemployed. He brought a group of professors (his "brain trust") to Washington and encouraged them to think creatively and act quickly.

The U.S. response to the depression was Roosevelt's New Deal, a series of domes-tic programs that coupled progressive ideas with planning techniques learned during World War I. Proclaiming that "the only thing we have to fear is fear itself,"[4]

---

[4]Franklin Delano Roosevelt, First Inaugural Address, March 4, 1933, quoted in *The Public Papers and Addresses of Franklin D. Roosevelt*, Vol. 2, *The Year of Crisis, 1933* (New York: Random House, 1938), p. 11.

Roosevelt promised action to rebuild the U.S. economy. During the first few months of his presidency, the government tried to reestablish confidence in the banks, raise farm incomes, and put people back to work. The government went into the electric power business through the Tennessee Valley Authority, a program designed to revitalize a poor farming region through the construction of dams and regional planning. Congress passed legislation to reduce agricultural production, moving government into the business of setting limits on crops. Other laws pushed industrialists to combine forces to regulate production, prices, and working conditions.

A series of programs offered the unemployed temporary jobs working on conservation and public works projects. The Civilian Conservation Corps and the Works Progress Administration employed millions of Americans. Artists painted murals, archaeologists excavated mounds, and opera singers toured rural areas, all at public expense. Markets, whether for goods or for people, had become units to be manipulated rather than independent forces to be respected.

Political opposition eventually led to the cancellation of parts of the New Deal, and in practice these initiatives usually did less than had been anticipated. Nevertheless, they launched the U.S. government into the practice of active economic intervention, which lasted through most of the twentieth century. Although criticized as a radical by the political right, Roosevelt was a liberal who preserved the capitalist economy by reforming it.

Intervention at home was coupled with disengagement abroad. Much of U.S. policy and rhetoric had an isolationist tone, ignoring impacts on the global economy. High U.S. tariffs kept out foreign imports, undermining the ability of other nations to revive their economies. "America first" characterized U.S. policy.

When Roosevelt returned to a strategy of balancing the U.S. budget and raising taxes, he helped to trigger a renewal of the depression around the world in 1937–1938, just at the moment when Adolf Hitler was threatening war over Czechoslovakia and Austria. Economic pressures mounted at the same time as political ones, pushing European governments to agree to Hitler's demands and shifting the course of world history.

States in Latin America had far fewer resources with which to combat the depression than did the United States. As producers of primary goods—food, minerals, and raw materials—their exports depended on the demand from industrialized countries. The collapse of the world capital markets in 1929–1930 and then of trade hit their economies hard. As industrial production contracted and prices fell, both the amount and the value of their exports declined sharply.

How to pay for imports posed a major problem. The wealthy families who controlled many Latin American governments were intent on raising their incomes and protecting their dominant positions. Where trade and big businesses were largely controlled by foreigners—in Cuba and Honduras, for example— national economic options were limited because governments did not have the power to design independent economic policies. In contrast, the larger Latin American countries, particularly Brazil, Colombia, Peru, and Mexico, developed economic strategies that stressed import substitution. States financed new

industries to compete with foreign producers. When these programs were successful, domestic manufactures replaced traded goods under the protective cover of
high tariffs and import quotas.

Financial policies offered another line of defense. Most of Latin America went
off the gold standard between 1929 and 1932, and at the same time these countries
defaulted on much of their foreign debt, increased the money supply, and levied
exchange controls. Rather than letting international obligations and free trade
push them into bankruptcy, policymakers in these countries attempted to build
walls around their national economies. The Brazilian government was the most
adept at this game, trading coffee to Germany in return for machines in a bilateral
arrangement of controlled prices and quantities. The beneficiaries of most of the
regulatory policies were the large producers and importers rather than the peasants.
Little was spent on welfare measures, and the unemployed drifted away from the
cities back to their villages to find family help. Yet if Latin American regulatory
states paid little direct attention to the poor, by 1938 they had succeeded in
rebuilding domestic production. In fact, rates of economic growth in Latin America
between the wars exceeded those of Asia, Europe, and North America. The strategy
of looking inward benefited Latin Americans of all income levels.

The Developmental State: Japan

The Japanese state adopted even more aggressive strategies of economic control
during the 1930s than did Latin American countries. Coping with declining
amounts of international trade was a central problem in Japan too. The first
Asian state to industrialize, it had exported silk in exchange for coal and Western
machinery to launch the transformation of its economy. The Japanese state had
played a central role in this transformation by not only financing but also operating many mines, factories, and shipyards. Its Ministry of Commerce and Industry
set economic policies with specific goals for industrial development.

In partnership with the state were a number of giant-sized, family-led industrial conglomerates called *zaibatsu*, which combined ownership of banks, shipping
companies, trading firms, mines, and other manufacturing industries. In addition
to their size and their government contacts, their many functionally linked firms
gave the *zaibatsu* immense power in Asian markets. By the 1920s, Japan had
become an economic powerhouse; its ships, banks, and merchants competed
aggressively against European rivals throughout Asia. In the interwar period,
Japan became China's top investor as well as its chief trading partner. Throughout the 1920s, despite a major earthquake and periods of inflation, the Japanese
economy continued to grow at a rapid clip.

The depression hit Japanese industry hard, in part because firms still relied on
export earnings to pay for the raw materials and fuel they imported. Moreover,
demand for silk dropped sharply as incomes fell around the world and as cheaper
synthetic fabrics, such as nylon, became popular. As trade declined, unemployment rose sharply. Even those who retained their jobs found their real incomes
declining as wages dropped faster than prices.

The response to the economic crisis in Japan took two forms, each of which was directed by the state. The first line of defense was financial, which proved a failure. The government tried orthodox economics and returned to the gold standard. The timing of this decision, undertaken in 1930 after the U.S. stock market crash, could not have been worse. Foreign investors converted their yen into gold, pulling capital out of the country as Japanese prices fell sharply and the impact of the depression intensified. Within a few months, not only had the government fallen and abandoned the gold standard, but terrorists with strong links to the army had begun a campaign to assassinate public officials whom they held responsible for the growing poverty. As the depression gained strength, so did the political influence of Japanese fascists, who blamed parliamentary government and liberal economic policies for the country's hard times.

By the mid-1930s, the Japanese government had begun using state actions to help solve economic problems. First, it spent increasing amounts of money on rearmament, adding jobs in heavy industry. Second, Japan exploited the territories it controlled in Korea and Manchuria, extracting raw materials and using cheap labor. Third, it developed new industries at home that substituted for foreign imports. Finally, it permitted the *zaibatsu* to subcontract work and depress wages to lower production costs. The term *hunger export* captures both the impact and the aim of these Japanese policies. By keeping the prices of manufactured goods low, Japanese industrialists were able to increase their exports during the depression. Citizens had to eat less and work more under the watchful eye of the state. Funds earned via exports helped to finance rearmament and the growth of heavy industry. Self-sufficiency within an East Asian Empire became the goal of the Japanese developmental state in the 1930s.

The Planned Communist State: The Soviet Union

The Soviet Union, itself a multinational empire, was more inward-looking than Japan in its strategy for coping with economic crisis. The combination of international war, civil war, drought, and epidemic had brought the country to the brink of collapse by the early 1920s, but the Soviet Union could expect no aid from its capitalist neighbors to the west, who were hostile to its revolutionary government and economic programs. The slogan "Socialism in One Country" captures the Soviet policy of self-reliance.

The Communist Party was determined to force the country toward socialism via industrialization, and for this purpose it had taken over the commanding heights of the economy (banking, transportation, and heavy industry). But the collapse of agricultural production and industrial output during the civil war in 1921 forced the Soviet government to compromise its communist principles and to permit a private sector to grow.

But, by 1928, the Soviet Union's innovative type of market socialism was replaced by tight government direction of the economy through the first Five-Year Plan. Bureaucrats set production targets, built new plants, and reorganized the labor force, shifting resources into heavy industry. Instead of the market allocating resources and investments, state planners would do so. Rapid industrialization of the economy was their main objective. The town of Magnitogorsk in the Ural Mountains was the showpiece of the new socialist construction. Over a quarter of a million people were lured or forcibly taken to the construction site, where temperatures dropped to −50 degrees Fahrenheit in winter. Peasants, nomads, street kids, and prisoners moved into tents and earth huts that became a city almost overnight. Workers built blast furnaces and foundries on the steppe, but lacking adequate tools and clothes, many of them died in the process.

Initially the result was disastrous: The Soviet national income decreased an estimated 20 percent under the first Five-Year Plan. Nevertheless, as Western democracies struggled with unemployment, the Soviet Union simply ordered the population to work. Millions of peasants left the countryside for cities and industrial towns. Human rights were ignored and political opposition eliminated, but the increase in production was spectacular. Despite enormous waste and inefficiency, the output of metals and machinery in the Soviet Union rose by a factor of fourteen during the 1930s. The government succeeded in lifting the country by its own bootstraps to a position of rivalry with the United States and Germany. Political isolation and communist ideology distanced the Soviet Union from both the economic troubles and the solutions of Western democracies, giving its rulers a free hand to try an extreme version of economic planning.

Another important area of economic change was agriculture, where the party decided to move from private to collective ownership of farms. By the late 1930s, Communist efforts to reorganize rural areas had born bitter fruit. The collectivization of agriculture had moved millions of people onto communal farms, resettling many of them far from their original homes. When the kulaks, or traditional farmers, resisted, they were condemned as enemies of the state and slaughtered. Historians estimate that as many as ten million people died in the process of resettlement alone, and that as many as seven million more died as a result of declines in agricultural production and the famine of 1933. Collective agriculture had a horrific human cost.

Joseph Stalin was a driving force behind the turn toward forced industrialization and the growth of authoritarian rule in the Soviet Union during the interwar period. During the 1920s, he rose through the ranks of the Communist Party to become the most powerful member of its Central Committee. A short man with a withered left arm and a bristling, nicotine-stained moustache, he soon established himself as a semidivine ruler, hailed during his lifetime in Soviet propaganda as "the hero, Joseph-Our-Light Vissarionovich."[5]

Stalin took a bureaucratic position, general secretary of the Communist Party, and transformed it into a vehicle for personal dictatorship and autocratic rule over millions of people. After Lenin's death, Stalin was the only Bolshevik with representation in all of the important party institutions, and he placed loyalists in key

---

[5]Sheila Fitzpatrick, *Ordinary Stalinism. Ordinary Life in Extraordinary Times: Soviet Russia in the 1930s* (Oxford: Oxford University Press, 1999), pp. 15, 72.

positions. He eliminated his rivals through assassination and purges. As state organizations were made subordinate to the party, Stalin's control of the party put
him in sole charge of the state.

Although industrialization had great support within the Soviet government,
collectivized agriculture and its associated disasters elicited much less enthusiasm.
Nevertheless, criticism became a ticket to destruction. In the purges of the later
1930s, the older generation of revolutionaries, the victors of the struggle against
the tsars and the civil war, were arrested and tortured into confessing invented
crimes against the state. After widely publicized trials, they were executed.

Ordinary people also suffered at the hands of the state. Millions were arrested
and imprisoned for no discernable reason. The party used the fear of arrest to
enforce obedience and conformity. Meanwhile, a huge expansion of the state
bureaucracy gave more and more adults a stake in the Soviet state and its
survival.

Liberal capitalism died in the 1930s, as both democratic and autocratic states
took control of their economies to curb unemployment and revive industry.
A strategy of beggaring one's neighbor took precedence over devotion to free
trade and international exchange. By going off the gold standard and allowing
exchange rates to fluctuate, most countries could insulate their monetary systems
and act domestically without worrying about international effects. Recovery from
the depression came slowly as each country increased the amounts of money in
circulation, controlled production, and provided aid to the unemployed.

Domestic Life in Hard Times

To understand the history of the 1920s and 1930s, one must change focus from
the national to the local. Family events—births, marriages, and deaths—shaped
the ways in which people experienced the hardships of the 1930s.

Demography in East and West

Although the twentieth century seemed modern, in the interwar period much of
the world's population lived under demographic conditions very different from
those today. In parts of China, India, and sub-Saharan Africa in 1920, life expectancy at birth was only twenty to thirty-five years, not much different from that
in agricultural societies several hundred years ago. Under those conditions, over
half of all children died before their twentieth birthday, and few lived past
age fifty. The deaths of young fathers and mothers shattered families in the
same way that divorce does today. Although parents might live to see the birth
of one or two grandchildren, they would not survive to watch those children
become adults. High death rates were matched by high birth rates, so that populations remained roughly stable or grew slowly. Women gave birth on average to
between five and seven children, but then had to watch as their offspring died.

Periodically, "dismal peaks" of high mortality from famines or epidemics swept through communities, carrying off the elderly and the very young.

But industrialization, birth control, modern medicine, and sanitation had changed demographic relationships in several regions of the world by the early twentieth century. Margaret Sanger, a public health nurse born in the United States, led an international campaign during the 1920s and 1930s to popularize birth control, which became legalized in many countries. By the 1930s most European countries had experienced a demographic transition much lower death rates combined with declining birth rates slowed population increase.

Under these new conditions, family life changed dramatically. Life expectancy reached about sixty years of age. Three out of every four infants not only lived to school age but also survived to see their grandchildren marry. As a result, communities had fewer children and rising proportions of the elderly. By the interwar period, child rearing had contracted from a lifelong occupation for adults to a phase in the life cycle. Europeans and migrants to "neo-Europes" (e.g., North America, Australia, and New Zealand, areas settled by European migrants) all lived under this demographic regime.

Women and Power

Families function as communities whose members have both duties and rights, and age and gender often determine an individual's position within them. Women, particularly younger ones, were frequently perceived as inferior and had fewer rights and opportunities than their male relatives. In many cultures, women's position was undermined by customs whereby males inherited land and continued a family lineage. Demographers who have examined gender ratios among infants in China, India, and Africa have found evidence of selective infanticide and neglect of female infants. Where resources were limited, male children got more of them. Men ate before women and got larger shares of the available food. Although this practice had little impact in normal times, during famines and depressions it could raise female death rates.

Nevertheless, women's work could give them bargaining power. Where women owned property or contributed to family income or food production, they had resources with which to bargain. In Africa and Latin America, women's activities as traders and farmers made them essential contributors to family income and brought them a measure of independence. Still, limited access to education and to employment outside the home or off family land made it difficult for women in most societies to support themselves outside the context of their family. For most women, families remained indispensable structures of support.

Although the assumption that adults should control children and that men should control women was shared around the globe, important differences among cultures can be seen in the position of women. Under Muslim law, a woman could divorce a husband who violated the terms of a marriage contract or did not provide support. Her male relatives could bring her and her children to live with them or select another husband for her. Non-Muslim women in Africa and Asia did not have this right.

In European and neo-European societies, new laws in response to feminist demands brought important changes in women's position in the later nineteenth and early twentieth centuries. In the United States, the USSR, and those European countries that were predominantly Protestant, women could sue for divorce and gain custody of their children. Married women gained the right to own and to inherit property, and they could enter into contracts. In the Soviet Union, the state tried to legislate gender equality during the 1920s, giving women easy divorces and abortions, along with political rights. By 1940, the state had taught most women to read and forced their entry into the industrial labor force. Gender relations after the Bolshevik revolution were to be modern and secular. In Turkey, the revolutionaries who established a secular republic in 1923 worked to increase women's rights. Wearing veils was discouraged, and women's education increased. In 1934, women gained the right to vote and to sit in the state assembly.

In the larger cities, changes in women's dress, education, and public behavior signaled a transformation in social standards. Dances became more sexually suggestive as skirts became shorter. The figure of the "New Woman" with bobbed hair and a cigarette represented both new hopes and new fears. Sex could be discussed openly in some circles, and the spread of birth control information suggested that behavior might be changing too. During the Jazz Age of the 1920s, young people challenged their parents' morality at the same time as they rejected older styles of music and gender relations.

Village Life

In the 1920s, the vast majority of the world's population still lived in rural areas. In many parts of Africa, Asia, and Latin America, most people lived in little communities where everyone knew everyone else and lived within sight of their neighbors. Villages ought not to be idealized as places of social harmony and peace. Family could feud against family, and the young rebel against elders. Those who challenged custom often suffered. But in the 1920s and 1930s, villages found themselves under continuous pressure for change. Even in remote places, battles over types of medical care, appropriate standards of education, new production technologies, and women's rights erupted. The return of a migrant or the arrival of a medical officer introduced information on alternative choices.

The experience of American medical missionaries in the village of Karimpur in northwestern India highlights the pressures for change coming from international contacts. In the 1920s the village sheltered about seven hundred fifty people, who, along with their animals, lived in family compounds behind mud walls. The houses lacked electricity and running water; fields served as toilets. The village had sections for people of different statuses—one for the Brahmin landlords and priests, a second for the carpenters and other artisans, a third for farmers, and a fourth for shepherds. Untouchable castes, who worked at jobs that were considered impure and therefore polluting (e.g., midwives, collectors of refuse and sewage, laundrymen, or leather workers), also lived separately.

Center for American History, University of Texas/Austin, DI Number 00208, Prints and Photographs Collection

Female athletes at the University of Texas, 1920s. The women's short hair and skirts represent an enormous change from two decades earlier. The basketball player wore bloomers, a costume developed for female bicycle riders in the late nineteenth century, but it too had been made shorter and tighter.

The village lacked an official administration and modern services. Its public spaces and institutions consisted of a primary school, several wells, and a shrine to a Muslim leader whom local people considered the protector of the village. For marketing, secondary education, medical care, legal help, police protection, and taxpaying, the citizens of Karimpur went on foot or by cart to the district capital. Trips to town, however, were mainly a male activity. Because respectable women were not supposed to be seen by men other than their kin, most women remained in their family courtyards. In 1925, neither girls nor children of the untouchable castes attended the village school.

When U.S. medical missionaries arrived by car one day and settled in for five years, they brought more than motor transportation. Quietly, they began to offer medical care to anyone who wanted it, and discussions of diet and sanitation soon followed. Although their efforts to widen opportunities for the poorest children failed, they forced discussion of education for boys from the untouchable castes. During the later 1920s, the male children of the Brahmin elders went to schools and offices in the market town. They took exams and earned qualifications that enabled them to take on government jobs after independence. During the twentieth century, the isolation of rural areas around the world slowly decreased.

Migration and Urbanization

Migration is a normal fact of social life. In all societies, people sometimes move to escape hardship or to improve their positions. Secondary schools and universities are usually located in cities, and the desire for education draws young people out of villages and smaller towns. Men travel when they join the army or work in a migratory occupation, and in many societies, young women are permitted to take jobs away from their families of origin to make money for their families. Migration can thus involve short distances only, from one village to another or from the countryside into a nearby town, or long-distance moves, perhaps across the Atlantic or from India to another British colony.

People migrate more often in hard times or after a political revolution, both of which sometimes trigger massive migrations. The 1920s and 1930s were decades of continued movement. At the end of World War I, several million Germans, Russians, and Poles fled into Central Europe from regimes in turmoil further to the east. Hundreds of thousands of Greeks and Armenians were expelled from Turkey. Nazi race laws intimidated Jews, leading them to flee Germany in large numbers during the 1930s. During decades of political instability in China, millions of people traveled south into Vietnam, Thailand, Malaya, and Indonesia. Well over a million unskilled laborers left India between the two world wars to take jobs in other British colonies in Asia and in Africa. During the interwar period, favored destinations were North and South America, Southeast Asia, and the more prosperous British colonies of eastern and southern Africa. Yet the depression forced many of these new settlers to return home. Plantation owners repatriated their contract workers or fired them. Unemployed Mexicans walked south across the Rio Grande. When hard times hit, families seemed a more secure source of support than a foreign government or an indifferent boss.

Long-distance migrants often move to cities. During the 1920s and 1930s, the foreign-born population of New York, Chicago, Paris, and Buenos Aires rose sharply. All over the world, the largest cities increased in size, fed by movement from other urban areas and from the countryside. In the USSR, the urban share of the population doubled during the years between the revolution and the Second World War. Levels of urbanization in Europe, North America, and Japan also rose during the 1920s. In economically developed regions, about 40 percent of the population lived in towns and cities. Migrants bridged rural and urban worlds, bringing the customs and ideas of the old realm into the new.

CONCLUSION

The economic woes of the interwar period were felt globally. Restoring international trade and financial systems after 1919 proved difficult, cutting the incomes of countries on every continent. The return of prosperity depended heavily on U.S. willingness to loan money to its European debtors. When that source of financial capital dried up as a result of the U.S. stock market crash, economic collapse spread around the globe. On the national level, politicians schemed and negotiated to shield their countries from depression, while individuals followed more personal strategies for survival. States of all political types developed nationalist economic programs. The tremendous pressure to reemploy the masses transcended political ideologies.

Despite the miseries caused by the world war and the business crash that followed, some benefits flowed to ordinary people. Those who had jobs and steady incomes could buy more because prices fell; improvements in medical care raised life expectancy. Airplanes speeded travel, and radio brought the wider world into villages and small towns around the world. On every continent, distances shrank under the impact of the media and motorcars. As international politics became more threatening during the 1930s, individuals in cities around the globe could follow late-breaking developments.

The powerful economic currents of the 1920s produced large political waves. Poverty and depression generated pressures for political change in states around the globe. As confidence in the ability of liberal democracies to solve their citizens' economic problems declined, the willingness to try other political arrangements increased. The appeal of communism, of fascism, and of Zionism mounted. Colonial populations pushed more strongly for control of their own governments. The story of interwar economic arrangements has to be considered alongside that of interwar politics, the subject of Chapter 7.

For Further Reading

Leslie Bethell, *Latin America: Economy and Society, 1870–1930* (Cambridge: Cambridge University Press, 1989). Topically organized analysis of Latin American history in the early twentieth century.

André Burgière et al., eds., *The Impact of Modernity*, Vol. 2, *A History of the Family* (Cambridge, Mass.: Harvard University Press, 1996). A collection of articles tracing the impact of industrialization, birth control, and women's employment on families around the world.

Chalmers A. Johnson, *MITI and the Japanese Miracle: The Growth of Industrial Policy, 1925–1975* (Stanford: Stanford University Press, 1982). A discussion of the Japanese developmental state and its impact on the Japanese economy.

John Maynard Keynes, *The Economic Consequences of the Peace* (New York: Harcourt, Brace, and Howe, 1920). An angry, contemporary response to the Versailles treaty by one of the greatest economists of the twentieth century.

George Orwell, *The Road to Wigan Pier* (London: Victor Gollancz, 1937). Orwell links poverty and unemployment to the politics of class as he urges the English to fight fascism.

Dietmar Rothermund, *The Global Impact of the Great Depression, 1929–1939* (London: Routledge, 1996). A global survey of problems caused by and responses to the depression of the 1930s.

Studs Terkel, *Hard Times: An Oral History of the Great Depression* (New York: Avon, 1971). Americans reflect on the Great Depression and describe how it changed their lives.

William H. Wiser and Charlotte Viall Wiser, *Behind Mud Walls, 1930–1960*, Rev. ed. (Berkeley, Calif.: University of California Press, 1969). An American missionary family describes their life in a northern Indian village during the 1930s.

Related Websites

The depression
  http://www.fordham.edu/halsall/mod/modsbook41.html
The New Deal
  http://newdeal.feri.org/
The Oil Industry in North America
  http://www.priweb.org/ed/pgws/history/history_home.html
The Soviet Union in the 1930s
  http://memory.loc.gov/frd/cs/rutoc.html

CHAPTER 7

The Murderous Politics of the 1930s

I n 1935, when Benito Mussolini, the Fascist dictator of Italy, proudly announced his country's unprovoked attack on Ethiopia, millions of Italians poured into town squares to listen to his radio speech. Crowds chanted their approval of his call for Italy to take its place in the sun as an imperial power. To show support for the Italian army, the Fascists organized a "Day of Faith" in which Roman Catholic priests blessed those who would donate money for the Catholic colonizers of Africa. Queen Elena of Italy led a parade of women up to a fiery bronze urn in central Rome near the Tomb of the Unknown Soldier. After tossing her own and the king's wedding rings into the fire and giving a Fascist salute, the queen exclaimed, "Young sons of Italy, who are defending her sacred rights and are opening new paths for the brilliant march of the Fatherland, we wish that you may bring about the triumph of Roman civilization in the Africa which you have redeemed."[1] More than a quarter of a million women, many dressed in tattered clothes, lined up to throw their jewelry into the urn. For a moment at least, war was the shining path to a glorious future.

Political appeals on behalf of the nation gained a wide audience in the 1930s. The nationalist leaders with the greatest mass appeal were not, however, the ordinary elected politicians of earlier decades. New movements and new men marched into power in the wake of war and revolution. They used ideology effectively to bolster their position and to gain support. The national conflicts that led to

---

[1]Quoted in Piers Brendon, *The Dark Valley* (New York: Knopf, 2000), p. 323.

World War II arose from the ideologies and social movements that reshaped societies in the 1930s.

Alternative Designs for the Future

It is easy to dismiss the 1930s as a time of disillusionment. The British poet W. H. Auden called that period "a low, dishonest decade,"[2] and many agreed with that statement because of their disappointment with their elected political leaders. The liberal democracies of Europe and North America seemed unable to cope with the political and economic problems of the interwar years. Politicians' weak defenses of the status quo had little appeal for the unemployed and the dispossessed. Some stronger medicine seemed necessary for the ills of the time.

Alternative prescriptions for the healing of the body politic therefore held great appeal. The Russian Revolution triggered utopian hopes of revitalization via communism, and Mussolini offered fascism as a cure for Italian weakness. Adolf Hitler called on Germans to save themselves and their country through National Socialism. Zionists presented their commitment to a Jewish homeland as the answer to the problems of a persecuted people. Between the two world wars, national loyalties fused with new ideologies of redemption to create aggressive political movements whose destructive potential was largely ignored or even welcomed.

The Challenge of Communism

Communism is an ideology that holds that property should be owned by the community and that wealth should be shared equally by citizens. Political theorists in many places and times have designed ideal communist communities that would eliminate economic inequality; in fact, several such groups existed briefly in the United States, France, and Britain during the early nineteenth century. Most of these societies were small in size and rural in location.

In *The Communist Manifesto,* written in 1848, however, Karl Marx and Friedrich Engels linked the future of communism to the growth of industrial societies. In their view, historical change progressed as a result of the struggle of class against class for power. In the modern period workers, or the proletariat, would fight back against their exploitation in factories and in industrial cities, taking power away from the middle classes, or bourgeoisie. They believed that industrialization would lead inevitably to rule by the workers, who would establish a "dictatorship of the proletariat," removing property from private hands and shifting wealth into communal ownership. Eventually, the state would disappear and the people would rule directly. Marx and Engels called on the workers of the world to unite for a Communist revolution.

---

[2]"September 1, 1939," *The Collected Poetry of W. H. Auden* (New York: Knopf, 1945), p. 57.

By 1917 communism had been again reinterpreted through the ideas and actions of Vladimir Ilyich Lenin. Lenin argued for the importance of intellectuals in awakening the masses to the need for revolution. In a society that had not yet industrialized, there was no strong proletariat to lead the way to a stateless society. The movement toward communism in Russia would also require a disciplined party of professional revolutionaries. Lenin's contributions to communist theory pointed the way to a bureaucratically run state, in which the Communist Party attempted to control all aspects of Russian life.

In 1917, Lenin showed that, under wartime conditions, a small, determined group of revolutionaries could take over a state. Once in power, the Bolsheviks proclaimed the virtues of communism: an economy owned and run by the producers, the indignities of capitalism ended, the triumph of international brotherhood, the defeat of racism and colonialism. Communist ideology took human longings for equality and universal brotherhood and tied them to the future of the Soviet state, where leaders of the Communist Party ruled in the name of the proletariat.

Fascism in Europe

Communism was echoed in a number of respects by Fascism, a nationalist ideology that was highly popular in southern, Central, and Eastern Europe between 1919 and 1945. Both opposed parliamentary democracy, individualism, and an unregulated economy, and both used violence to attain political power. Their economic ideas and plans for social organization were different, however. Fascists worked within capitalist economies, accepting private property, inequality, and existing class differences. They feared, not celebrated, workers' power and independence. Moreover, Fascists supported national traditions, which they thought were threatened by Communist internationalism. For most of the interwar period, Fascists and Communists were political opponents, with each group identifying the other as its principal enemy.

Benito Mussolini, the dictator who founded the Fascist Party in Italy, spent the early years of World War I defending a communist society as his long-term goal. But he abandoned Marxism for Italian patriotism when he saw how effectively conventional states could mobilize citizens and hold their loyalty. Using as his emblem the *fasces*—a bundle of birch rods concealing an axe—which was an ancient Roman symbol of authority, he organized his followers into the Fascist Party, which attacked the Italian government. The group staged a march on Rome in 1922 to demand political power. The Italian king gave in to their threats of violence and appointed Mussolini prime minister, giving him the opportunity to seize control of the government.

Fascists were political opportunists, not political philosophers. Mussolini admitted that Fascist theory was invented after the party came to power to give the state a sense of direction. Mussolini promised to substitute strong leadership for elected weaklings, and many citizens thought that the change would be an improvement. He promised cultural regeneration of the state through his stress on military virtues—strength, discipline, obedience, and hierarchy. Through violence, the legacy of liberal-democratic weakness could be eliminated and a new social order constructed. The center of his appeal was an extreme nationalism that called on citizens to make the Italian state the primary object of their loyalties. The Fascists worked to create an authoritarian state ruled by the Fascist Party. Social classes were to be organized into corporate groups representing different parts of Italian society—industry, labor, women, young people, and the press. Groups, not individuals, had political representation. Italy was mobilized in the service of the state.

Fascism was a theatrical style as well as a political program: Black shirts and torchlight parades, flags, and salutes had dramatic appeal. The party celebrated a masculine youth culture of sport, which was reinforced in the schools and in urban neighborhoods. Its violent, bullying tactics made opponents back down and increased its power.

By the later 1930s, organized Fascist parties had appeared in most European countries: National Socialists in Germany, Arrow Cross in Hungary, the Legion of the Archangel Michael in Romania, the Faisceau and the Francistes in France, the Falange in Spain, and the British Union of Fascists. Although these parties differed from one another, they all opposed democracy and liberal values. They defended their nation-states aggressively and attacked groups of people whom they identified as enemies—socialists, immigrants, ethnic minorities, and Jews. They celebrated violence both in theory and in practice, using paramilitary gangs to terrorize their opponents and to enforce their will. Extreme racism characterized the Nazis in Germany and the Eastern European Fascist parties.

SZ Photo/Scherl/DIZ Muenchen GmbH, Sueddeutsche Zeitung Photo/Alamy

Mussolini's and Hitler's cooperation began before the outbreak of World War II. This handshake took place on September 30, 1938, after both men had signed the Munich Agreement, which gave Germany the right to occupy the Sudentenland, as well as de facto control of Czechoslovakia.

Zionism in the Middle East

Jewish nationalism became a force in the Middle East as a result of Zionist activists. Seeing other ethnic groups win their own states, a persuasive group of Jewish intellectuals reasoned that Jews were also a nation with the right to rule themselves. They argued that Jews should leave the countries in which they were currently settled and move to the land of Zion, their biblical homeland. Resettlement in and around Jerusalem in Palestine would end the scattering of the Jews and transform them into a strong and independent people. A romantic vision of a new life based on farming drew thousands of Jews into the Zionist movement as anti-Semitic threats mounted in Europe.

By the 1930s, tens of thousands of Zionists had migrated to Palestine. They purchased land from local Arab landlords and built houses, constructing settlements that were designed to be independent and self-supporting. They saw themselves as pioneers of a new moral and social order. The socialists among them established communes in which members ate together and reared their children collectively. In the words of David Ben-Gurion, the future prime minister of Israel, Zionism meant transformation: "It means taking masses of uprooted, impoverished, sterile Jewish masses…, [and] implanting them on the land, integrating them into primary production in agriculture, in industry, and in handicraft."[3] Zionist socialists worked to create a Jewish working class in Palestine, whose members, they hoped, would be warriors in the crusade for a Jewish nation-state.

The major difficulty with Zionist designs was the hostility of the Arab populations, who claimed the same lands and who made nationalist claims for their own states in the areas of Palestine and Transjordan. While the Zionist leadership supported compromise solutions and made the gaining of a Jewish state a long-term goal, more radical Zionists in the 1930s called for the immediate establishment of a Jewish state and a Jewish armed force to defend it. As conflict in the area grew, so did calls to arms. When Arabs rose in rebellion in 1936 against the British colonial government and Jewish settlers, the Jewish defense forces, the Haganah, smuggled new settlers into Palestine and carried out attacks on Arab populations. During the 1930s, Jewish and Arab nationalists each claimed Palestine, and they fought to enforce their opposing visions.

Nationalism in East Asia

Nationalism has been one of the most powerful ideologies of the modern period. It exalts loyalty to one's home country, placing national interests above the interests of the individual or the group. Nationalists see nations as the primary source of individual identity and of citizens' allegiance. These ideas spread throughout Europe and Latin America during the nineteenth century and became powerful in Asia during the early twentieth century.

---

[3]S. Avineri, *The Making of Modern Zionism* (New York: Basic Books, 1981), p. 200.

In China in the 1930s, the vision of a strong nation-state had many supporters, and far too many leaders and parties wishing to rule such a state. Artists, writers, and scholars of many sorts debated the ends and means to be used to drive the colonial powers out of China and to create a modern nation-state. The republican leader, Sun Yat-sen, defined Three Principles of the People—nationalism, democracy, and the people's livelihood—which guided the Nationalist Party in its attempts to gain power. He wanted China to be free of foreign influence, to be ruled in some fashion by the masses, and to modernize in order to raise standards of living. Citizens owed loyalty to the Chinese state. However, the republic that resulted from revolution in China would not resemble Western democracies. To overcome social turmoil, foreign threats, and poverty, a strong government would be necessary. Instead of guaranteeing rights to individuals, it would provide freedom and equality to corporate groups. Rather than the people shaping politics, political structures were to reshape the people into worthy citizens.

In 1934 the Nationalist government under Chiang Kai-shek, hoping to discipline rural Chinese society and resist the challenge of communism, initiated the "New Life Movement." This movement, with its concentration on cleanliness, self-restraint, obedience to superiors, and devotion to national dignity, was designed partly to emulate the Fascist movements of Europe, which Chiang and

Zionist poster from the 1930s inviting Jews to join a kibbutz in Palestine. Jewish nationalism was to be built through agricultural communities, which would help to create a new social order and would prepare the way for a Jewish state in the Middle East.

his followers saw as leading the poor and disordered masses from weakness and division to strength and unity. Campaigns to awaken China came from both the Nationalist government and the Communist guerillas, as well as from many liberal groups during the 1920s and 1930s, but trust in the state remained a consistent theme. Revolutionaries and reformers of every stripe wanted to capture a strong state, not to divide or weaken it.

Several Forms of Authoritarianism

The 1930s were years of expansion for Fascist states and of increased power for central governments generally. Totalitarian rule in the Soviet Union emerged during the 1930s as a result of three factors: Communist Party control of the state, Josef Stalin's consolidation of power through terror, and the creation of the centrally planned economy. Each of these developments curbed Soviet citizens' rights, greatly accelerating the authoritarian tendencies that had developed under Lenin's period of rule after the revolution.

Germany under Hitler

Democratic government in Germany lost popular support during the depression when its leaders proved unable to get people back to work. Many blamed the politicians for Germany's defeat in World War I and what seemed to them to be an unfair, unduly harsh peace treaty. Adolf Hitler capitalized on this dissatisfaction, attacking Jews and Marxists as the source of Germany's problems. In 1923, he and a few followers, who called themselves the National Socialist German Workers' Party, attempted to overthrow Bavaria's republican government, but they failed and landed in jail. Hitler used his time in prison to write a book, *Mein Kampf* ("my struggle"), which outlined his case against the Jews and his plan for world domination.

When the depression intensified Germany's economic problems, the National Socialists, or Nazis, attracted a mass following. Their torchlight parades and their rhetoric of hatred convinced many people that they could save Germany. In his powerful speeches, Hitler offered a disillusioned population targets for their fears and insecurities. The Nazis gained more and more votes. They remained a minority party in the parliament, or Reichstag, but with one-third of the seats they were much stronger than any of their competitors in the fall of 1932.

The inability of conventional politicians to govern effectively led the German president, Paul von Hindenburg, to appoint Adolf Hitler chancellor in January of 1933. Once in power, Hitler used his position to solidify his position. He suppressed opponents on the political left and unleashed anti-Jewish boycotts. When an arsonist burned the Reichstag building in early 1934, Hitler blamed the communists and pushed through an emergency decree suspending civil liberties in Germany, which was not revoked until after World War II.

Beginning in 1934, citizens no longer enjoyed the rights of free speech and assembly, the right to form associations, or the right to maintain control of private property. The German democracy had become a police state. After eliminating sources of organized opposition, the Nazis could reorganize the state as they wished.

The new Germany worked through both repression and persuasion. Hitler pledged to purge schools, films, newspapers, and radio to make them serve party and state. "Blood and race will once more become the source of artistic intuition,"[4] he said. Joseph Goebbels, a tiny man with a clubfoot and a huge, seductive voice, became minister of public enlightenment and propaganda. One of his first acts was to mastermind public burnings in German cities of works by major German authors such as Heinrich Heine and Thomas Mann. After Nazi students raided public and private libraries and seized books that they claimed would poison the German nation, they flung the books into bonfires, yelling "Heil Hitler!" Only people licensed by Goebbels's ministry could write, publish, or produce art.

Courses on "race science" entered school curricula as part of a nazification program that removed people who were not racially "Aryan" or ethnically German from faculty and staff. All organizations for young people became part of the Hitler Youth, where members absorbed Nazi racial ideas. Nationalist propaganda was staple fare in the newspapers, books, and schools of the Third Reich.

The repression of citizens became organized under the authority of the SS (*Schutzstaffeln,* or security units), who were originally Hitler's personal bodyguards. These black-shirted paramilitary groups policed the party, carried out purges, and ran concentration camps for Marxists and other targets of state repression during the 1930s. Along with the Gestapo, or secret police, the SS enforced Nazi racial policy and worked to rid the state of "non-Aryans" and resisters.

Despite all this, the Nazi state was popular with most Germans because it reduced unemployment. The government began to put men to work in 1933 constructing interstate highways and making munitions. By actively pursuing rearmament, Hitler brought Germany to full employment by 1936. Social policies and foreign policies were, in fact, closely connected: Hitler was determined to get the German economy ready for war quickly. Effective production generally meant working with private industry. Only when existing firms could not or would not supply enough for the army did the state become actively involved in manufacturing. The state bought raw materials as needed or seized them from neighboring countries. Totalitarian rule was more intrusive in some areas of German life than in others. Although ruthless and vigilant in the political arena, the government's control over economic life was less complete and less effective.

---

[4]Brendon, *The Dark Valley,* p. 286.

Japan

During the 1930s, the Japanese state formally remained a parliamentary democracy under its mid-nineteenth-century constitution. With universal male suffrage, multiple political parties, a legislature, and cabinet government, the political system of Japan resembled those of Western European countries. But a closer look shows that power resided not with the electorate and a House of Representatives but with the army, the House of Peers, and the cabinet, who ruled in the name of the emperor, not the people. Elections were mere formalities; political parties were weak.

Political structures that had permitted a degree of liberal rule in the 1920s changed radically in their functions during the 1930s when repeated military coups intimidated elected officials. High-ranking army and navy officers held government positions, and only generals and other high-ranking officers on active duty could serve as minister of war. In debates over policy, military leaders won. Prince Kanoye and his military advisers advocated a "New Asian Order," in which Japan would dominate her neighbors and work with them for mutual advantage.

When agricultural depression combined with a collapse of trade and finance in 1930, the parliamentary system in Japan faced an insuperable challenge. Intense misery in the countryside inspired new radical movements in the Japanese army. Army factions were soon demanding that Japan take advantage of its colony in Korea to expand military control to China and other parts of Asia to create new markets for Japanese agricultural products and to find new resources for Japanese industry.

The Japanese government initially resisted these demands for expansion, but between 1932 and 1936 the radical militarists expanded into Manchuria and China on their own (see Map 7.1). They also conducted terror campaigns in Tokyo that included the assassination of government and industrial leaders. In 1937, the government submitted to the pressures of the militarists, and parliamentary government was, in effect, disbanded. Prince Konoye became prime minister and head of the "Greater East Asia Co-Prosperity Sphere," which was to link Japan to the rest of Asia by economic and political ties. He gave government approval to an ideology that asserted the equality of Asians in relation to Europeans and advocated resistance to further expansion by the United States. In fact, Prince Konoye had become the leader of a national policy of imperialism in East Asia, Southeast Asia, and the Pacific. When the League of Nations condemned Japanese aggression in Manchuria and China and the new Japanese-directed puppet state named Manchukuo, the Japanese government walked out of the League. Japanese participation in the international treaty structures of East Asia and the Pacific ended, and Japan became, in effect, a rogue state.

In the later 1930s, the Japanese state was increasingly driven by the needs of the military and its demands for resources in order to continue its seizures of Chinese land. The government increasingly diverted food and material goods from civilian to military uses, suspending the operation of a free market.

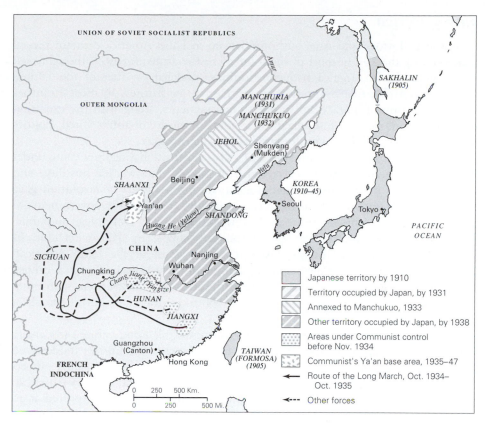

MAP 7.1   China and Japan in the 1930s.
Japanese control had expanded from Manchuria to south of the Yangtze River.
Communist-held territories, which were small, lay inland and to the south.

Bureaucrats built up a new economic order based on heavy industry and state, rather than private, profits. The government even employed economic police to hunt down those who defied official economic policies.

The army, which wanted support for military adventures in China, worked together with politicians who wanted to transform Japan into a centrally controlled state based on heavy industry. Each group benefited from the activities of the other. Opposition in the country was muted and ineffectual, protected neither by the constitution nor by mass support.

Scholars debate whether to label the Japanese political regime of the 1930s Fascist. Certainly no mass party mobilized citizens behind the state and its military adventures. Unlike European Fascist leaders, Emperor Hirohito considered himself a constitutional monarch who left the formulation of policy to others. Nevertheless Prince Konoye and the chief Japanese military officers shared with Fascists an enthusiasm for a nationalist, authoritarian, corporate state, as well as the willingness to go to war for an empire.

Latin America

Like that in Europe and Asia, authoritarianism in Latin America came in several forms during the 1930s, most of them linked to the armed forces. Although most countries in Latin America had constitutions modeled on that of the United States, authorizing rule by presidents and elected legislatures, in most countries the combination of literacy and property requirements, along with the exclusion of women from the franchise, meant that only a minority of adults voted. Politics remained the province of wealthy families and the military.

During the economic collapse of the 1930s, constitutional regimes came under increasing pressures. Mass protests signaled student and worker hostility, and street muggings by paramilitary gangs alarmed citizens. Fears of revolution gave the military the opportunity to intervene in politics. In 1930 the governments of six very different Latin American states—Argentina, Brazil, Dominican Republic, Bolivia, Peru, and Guatemala—fell to military coups; by 1932, Ecuador, El Salvador, and Chile had followed suit. By 1945 most of the Latin American republics had military regimes, and the army had great power in several others. Whether they worked with existing state institutions or replaced them with other systems, military dictatorships became a common form of Latin American government.

Why did the military become so active and powerful? Long before most males became voters, they were soldiers. When Latin American countries modernized their armies, they had made military service compulsory and given career officers professional training in elite academies. Chile has been called a Latin American Prussia because it adopted a German military model and then exported it to many of its neighbors. A French military mission remained in Brazil for years, training its army and its officers, who moved into the Ministry of War.

These armies spread an ethic of national service, turning soldiers into professional patriots who felt entitled to demand changes in the state. Young officers who flirted with socialism or communism attacked corruption in Brazil and Chile. Officers demanding welfare legislation and "equality for all" carried out a coup in Ecuador that established a reformist regime. In a period of depression, few citizens rushed to defend the conservative landowners and wealthy families who represented the old ways, which seemed increasingly inadequate. A nationalist military seemed the best antidote to economic crisis and social chaos.

The consolidation of power in Brazil by Getulio Vargas illustrates clearly the interconnections among demands for reform, the military, and authoritarian rule. In 1930, dissatisfaction with what was probably a rigged election and the assassination of an opposition leader led to a successful military coup that ousted the president. The military junta resigned power quickly, however, turning it over to Vargas, the head of the political opposition. Vargas, a lawyer from a wealthy ranching family in the south, wanted to overhaul the political system. His coalition of coffee growers, military men, and liberals was willing to abandon republican institutions for something new. Politics quickly became radicalized, with active Communist and Fascist groups springing to life and alarming the middle classes. After Vargas was elected president under a new constitution, he led his own coup, promising to eliminate extremists. Political parties and the Congress were among the first to go. Vargas offered citizens a strong government of peace, justice, and work.

For the next fifteen years, Vargas ruled what he called the "Estado Novo," or new state. He cultivated the image of being a great nationalist leader standing above politics, while at the same time aggressively widening the powers of the state. Labor unions lost their independence and were forced, along with employers, into industrywide *sindicatos,* or corporations. Moreover, Vargas made the state an active economic actor, supervising the production and marketing of coffee and other products. Federal ownership of railways and shipping in conjunction with mixed public/private corporations gave the government widened influence over the domestic economy. Meanwhile, the state encouraged industrialization and the substitution of home industries for imports. New Ministries of Labor, Industry, and Commerce swelled both the functions and the size of the central bureaucracy. Although Vargas never built a mass party and avoided the street theater of the European Fascists, he too ran an authoritarian state based on the military power of the army and police. He was a dictatorial modernizer who ruled without the consent of the country's citizens.

The Media Send Strong Messages

By the 1930s, information flowed easily between city and countryside. Newspapers, radios, photographs, and films reached rural populations as well as city dwellers. The media and the arts took on great political importance as they were used to defend ideas or parties. Politically engaged artists and journalists, as well as government censors, worked to mold public opinion.

Radio in Service of the State

Radio served states and empires. The French built stations throughout their West African colonies and in the South Pacific and Indochina. The British Broadcasting Corporation, a government monopoly on wireless transmission, started the Empire Service in 1932 with a Christmas message from the British king beamed to Australia. Radio had indeed gone global. Within a few years, the BBC was sending regular programs in Arabic to the Middle East and in Spanish and Portuguese to Latin America. BBC announcers speaking in German, French, and Italian sent their version of diplomatic events to a wide European audience.

The British government used the BBC to unify the empire. Home news, music, and sports, as well as regular doses of royal rituals and messages, brought British subjects closer to the culture and politics of the capital. In Sierra Leone, an elaborate radio system began in the capital city in 1934. The governor, a radio enthusiast, bought a good receiver and lots of loudspeakers, which he had erected in public squares, hotels, restaurants, and the homes of subscribers. Residents could hear political speeches from London along with world news. Local sporting events and music were part of the package too, and African subscribers reported that people walked into town from the surrounding areas to listen.

During the 1920s, most Latin American countries set up national radio companies and built multiple stations, using U.S. and European technology. Radio offered nations an easy way to influence public opinion. In countries that had military or other forms of dictatorial rule in the 1930s, particularly Brazil, Argentina, and Peru, governments censored political news and limited the licensing of stations.

The Japanese state seized the opportunity offered by radio to reach into the homes of citizens. The government merged existing stations into a national network in 1926, and then pushed forward with plans for stations that could cover the entire country. When the Japanese army began its expansion into Manchuria, news broadcasts of the fighting, along with favorable interpretations of the attacks, could be heard several times a day. Musicians played the national anthem each morning and encouraged citizens to bow in the direction of the Imperial Palace to show respect for the throne.

In the United States, radio was privately owned, although national networks were in place by the 1930s and were in control of much programming. National radio drew people into a new public sphere. Simply by turning a knob, housewives in Seattle, farm boys in Iowa, and factory workers in Detroit could tune in to the same radio dramas. Franklin and Eleanor Roosevelt both used the medium to build support for the New Deal. "Fireside chats" brought families in Florida and Oregon close to the president.

But U.S. radio in the 1930s was as notable for what it did not say as for what it preached. African Americans had little access to the airwaves and even less control over the images of their culture that were carried. Crude racial stereotyping dominated radio programming until the late 1930s, when the U.S. government produced a few programs that praised the contributions of African Americans, Jews, and other minorities to U.S. society. African American voices gained greater access to radio as the United States moved closer to involvement in the Second World War and as demands for equal civil rights mounted. The National Urban League and the National Association for the Advancement of Colored People used radio broadcasts to discuss their political views and to argue for racial equality. As soon as informal forms of censorship began to weaken, the structure of radio in the United States permitted multiple voices and points of view to be heard.

Movies as Political Tools

Film also proved to be a successful political tool during the 1920s and 1930s. Not only in Hollywood, but in studios throughout Europe and Asia, seductive

GLOBAL Technologies

Motion Pictures

The technology of motion pictures brings together those of photography, film, camera projection, and sound. The earliest motion pictures were still photographs taken by separate cameras, which human eyes perceived as moving if flashed in a series faster than fifteen images per second. During the 1880s, the photography of moving objects became possible with the development of rolled, slotted celluloid film by George Eastman and the design of a camera that used slotted gears to advance, stop, and then advance the film again rapidly in coordination with the movement of the lens shutter. Gaining a patent in 1892, the Thomas Edison Studio pioneered commercial motion picture technology and shot short action films (one of the first showed a sneeze), but the equipment was too bulky to leave the studio.

After Auguste and Louis Lumière developed in 1895 a relatively light, handheld camera and projector, the Cinématographe, filmmakers could shoot scenes virtually anywhere and then show them to audiences on a screen. The first commercial movie theater opened in Paris in 1897. The Electric Theater opened in Los Angeles in 1902, in time to show *The Great Train Robbery,* the world's first Western movie, which ran for ten minutes. Soon, screens around the world filled with comedies, melodramas, and newsreels. By the mid-1920s, big-budget films, such as *Phantom of the Opera* (1923–1925), included color sequences. The addition of sound to motion pictures also took place in the 1920s, initially through the addition of synchronized disc recordings, and later directly on film. In 1928 Walt Disney introduced Mickey Mouse to the world via animated cartoon and soundtrack. The industry had a global reach long before the Second World War. Today, major films, which open simultaneously in cities around the world, are produced by multinational production teams and companies.

images swayed audiences. The film industry in Japan, which produced several hundred movies each year, came under the direct control of the army and the Ministry of Home Affairs in 1937. As the country moved toward war, love stories and melodramas were replaced with battle scenes and portrayals of heroic warriors. Nationalist messages spread across India via the movies, despite the efforts of British censors to block unfriendly treatments of the empire. During the 1920s, newsreel films included Gandhi's tours and speeches on Indian home rule. The Soviet film industry worked for the state, turning out a centrally determined list of films every year, whose content was carefully specified. Enthusiastic Communist directors took on the task of portraying heroes and heroines of the revolution.

In the right hands, propaganda films could be works of genius. In Germany, the filmmaker Leni Riefenstahl produced *Triumph of the Will,* a 1935 documentary of a Nazi rally in Nuremberg. Its imagery linked the defense of a traditional Germany to the technologies of modernism. Hitler swooped down from the sky to the cheers of an adoring public; light, sound, and movement combined to glorify the Nazi leader. Hitler understood the importance of film, and after gaining power, he quickly moved to take over the film industry, going beyond censorship to overt control; it was placed under the Ministry of Propaganda. Many famous Jewish directors quickly left the country because they could no longer get work as filmmakers.

Even without state control, films could carry heavy messages. In the United States, the prevailing tone was optimistic. Charlie Chaplin's *Little Tramp* made audiences laugh at hard times. In general, films agreed with Herbert Hoover that prosperity was definitely just around the corner, and that clever Americans could beat the odds. The most popular film of the late 1930s—and the biggest moneymaker—was *Gone With the Wind,* a tale of happy plantations whose attractive slave owners unfortunately had their comfortable lives ruined by the Civil War. Most U.S. movies in the 1930s took place in a mythical land of economic security where virtue was rewarded and problems were easily solved. Hollywood's politics were patriotic even without censorship or state ownership.

Art in the Service of the State

Art in the service of the state took a number of forms during the 1930s. In the United States, the New Deal employed artists through schemes like the Federal Art Project, in which men and women were paid by the government to produce sculptures, murals, photographs, and paintings for public places or public collections. Arguing that artists were not only workers but guardians of democracy as well, the government decided that a strong U.S. economy and culture needed the beauty and symbolism of the fine arts. Exhibits, demonstrations, and local classes brought art to people across the United States.

Similarly, after 1920 the Mexican state began to commission murals for public buildings to bolster political support. Public art would spread the history and the values of a new Mexico to the country's citizens, many of whom could neither read nor write. During the 1920s and 1930s, Diego Rivera and other painters decorated major public buildings throughout Mexico with compelling images. They fused the heritage of an Indian past with a revolutionary present to glorify the Mexican people and their revolution. Diego Rivera and other Mexican artists also worked in the United States during the early and mid-1930s, decorating public buildings in several states.

Whatever the political backdrop, state-sponsored art in Europe and the Americas turned away from modernism to embrace realism. Abstraction disappeared, and artists used simple compositions and clear perspectives to picture a world under control. In terms of technique, this was a conservative art that turned its back on the changes of the first three decades of the century. Hitler's opinion—that those who

Mural of the Aztec city of Tenochtitlán painted by Diego Rivera in 1945 in the National Palace in Mexico City. The mural identified the Mexican state with idealized images of pre-Columbian Indian cultures.

would paint skies green and fields blue had either defective eyesight or bad motives—appear to have been widely shared. Closeness to real life was a sign of achievement.

At the same time, the definition of real life was narrowed to exclude quite a lot. Stalin had decreed that good art should be "national in form and socialist in content." Socialist realism, in practice, concentrated on a small list of subjects: the revolution, its leaders, and its workers. On canvas, the state was peopled by strong, healthy bodies working enthusiastically for the party. Official art told one political story with a small cast of characters. Even if realism was its technique, political mythmaking was the result. Virtuous communists defeated evil capitalists and corrupt tsars to produce a new world of happiness and prosperity.

Architecture and the Impulse to Control

Social engineering through architecture was an aim of many regimes in the twentieth century. The illusion that human character can be changed by redesigning the physical environment was powerful during the 1930s. The Swiss architect Le Corbusier proposed to make modern cities efficient by leveling much of what existed and substituting a mathematically regular plan of skyscrapers and straight streets joined at right angles. During the 1930s, Le Corbusier produced designs for a rebuilt Paris, Algiers, Rio de Janeiro, and Moscow. Le Corbusier's ambitions far outran his political influence, however, and his modernist designs did not interest those who were renewing cities during the 1930s.

Both Hitler and Stalin saw themselves as great builders and planned to reconstruct their capitals as fitting symbols of their regimes. In Berlin an enormous plaza and avenue intended to "stupefy travelers with the power of the Reich" would lead to the gigantic House of the People, whose dome would rise three hundred feet in the air. Albert Speer's designs brought together all the major institutions of government and industry along one new, monumental Berlin street, which was never built.

In 1935, Stalin signed a plan for a reconstructed Moscow, which would double the city's area. Long, straight streets and a modern subway system would permit easy movement around the metropolis. High-rise apartments would house the growing population, and parks would add green space. Architects designed the new Palace of the Soviets to be taller than the Empire State Building and to have more than six thousand rooms. The plan proved too ambitious, and the war stopped the reconstruction of the city.

Official architecture, whether Communist, capitalist, or National Socialist in origin, followed classical models blown up to super sizes. In a conscious attempt to identify themselves with the Roman Empire, bureaucrats borrowed its forms—columns with bases and capitals, symmetrical designs, flat roofs with heavy cornices, and a rigid geometry of squares and straight lines. Only the decorations—the added swastikas, eagles, or sheaves of corn—announced political differences. The nationalisms of the 1930s coexisted with many international flows of ideas and designs.

Citizenship, Gender, and Ethnicity

In an era in which travel required passports and the United States had slammed almost shut its formerly open door to immigrants, the issue of who belonged within each nation-state was politically sensitive. Moreover, what did "belonging" mean? Being born in a country did not automatically mean being a citizen. Which residents had full political and social rights? Both rights and duties were tied to gender, to ethnicity, and sometimes to skin color or religion. Since strong states, whether they were authoritarian or democratic, kept track of residents through demographic records, registers of addresses, and social security numbers, it was not difficult to discriminate.

Women and the State

As states found themselves facing mounting political and economic pressures in the 1930s, they called on women to contribute more aggressively. Women became a national resource, asked to work and to reproduce for the health of the larger community. The question of what work they were to do and what they would be paid for that work was hotly debated, however, and women got mixed, as well as changing, messages.

The expansion of mechanized textile production and service industries around the globe meant that factories and offices in Japan, China, Latin America, North America, and Europe hired increasing numbers of young women. Their cheap labor powered continued industrialization. Nevertheless, the onset of the depression intensified the competition for jobs. Should women workers be treated differently from their male counterparts? At the same time, fears of a demographic crisis, which hit many of the countries that had fought World War I, meant that having more children became a national priority. But how could states encourage both larger families and greater female participation in the labor force? Answers to this question differed.

During the later 1920s and 1930s, many governments codified family law, passed legislation governing women's employment, and worked to define national meanings of femininity and motherhood. Since propaganda campaigns during World War I had popularized images of militant, strong women mobilized for national victory, what women could do and still be considered feminine expanded. But softer, more traditional images continued to identify women with home and family. Germany's National Socialists argued that women's place was in the home raising a family, but they also cleverly identified home and family with the entire German community. Women could do state and family service in the factory as well as in the kitchen at times when the state wished them to do so.

During the 1930s, social policies toward women swung in a more conservative direction in many countries. The depression led to restrictions on the hiring of women in order to provide more jobs for men. In the United States in 1932, Congress prohibited spouses from being employed in the civil service at the same time. The law soon triggered a host of local and state laws restricting married women's employment. By the late 1930s, school boards, insurance companies, and banks commonly refused to hire or to retain married women. Fascist Italy also moved to restrict women's employment. Not only were women barred from higher-level teaching jobs, the military, and higher-ranking civil service and court posts, but in 1938 a decree set a 10 percent quota on women's labor in public and private firms.

This conservative swing in policy concerning women was most striking in the Soviet Union, where immediately after the 1917 revolution the Bolsheviks had legislated their vision of women's liberation. Mutual consent divorce, common-law marriage, collective child rearing, and unrestricted abortion gave Russian women more control over reproduction and their marital status than women in most other countries. Sex roles were to be redefined in the interest of equality and greater participation of women in politics and the new state.

By the 1930s, however, social problems produced by these legal changes inspired a backlash against them. After Soviet birthrates plummeted and family instability alarmed conservatives, the Soviet government outlawed abortion and prostitution and made divorce harder to get. The media began to praise motherhood and curbed criticism of conventional families. Soviet women gained a broad set of educational, political, and social rights, but they now shouldered a double burden. To the female responsibilities of childbirth and child rearing were added the expectation that wives would take on paid work. Women became servants of the state in the realms of both production and reproduction.

Jews and Gypsies in Germany

Although states empowered and organized some of their citizens, they also worked aggressively to exclude others. In many parts of the world, being of a religion, ethnicity, or race that was different from that of the dominant group signaled second-class status or worse. Some differences were deeply threatening. The Nazis went the farthest in this direction, turning anti-Semitic propaganda into policy as soon as they seized power. In 1935, the Nuremberg Laws took away citizens' rights from Jews and prohibited marriages between "Aryans" and Jews. Gypsies and blacks were also identified as "alien types" who were not allowed to intermarry with "true" Germans. Nazi propaganda called for the elimination of all who were not "of German blood and Nordic race: four-square in body and soul."

For Jews, the first stages of removal meant exclusion from many occupations, from higher education, and from cultural events. By the late 1930s, mobs were burning Jewish stores and homes and beating Jews on the streets. What had begun as discrimination would soon grow into a monstrous campaign to purge the nation of its Jewish citizens. The lucky ones managed to emigrate. By 1939 around three hundred thousand German Jews had left their homeland for other parts of Europe, North America, Palestine, and Asia.

Efforts to rid Germany of social undesirables targeted other groups as well. Those who were thought to be asocial, such as gypsies, homosexuals, prostitutes, and beggars, were isolated to keep them from "contaminating" others. Nazi racial biology demonized gypsies in particular, identifying them with criminality and vice and calling for their suppression. The rights due to citizens dissolved under the pressure of a pseudo-scientific racial and social biology that judged character on the basis of a bizarre mixture of religion, ethnicity, sexual behavior, and body type.

The German government carried the demonizing of difference to its logical extreme, but discrimination and popular hostility to minorities flourished in many countries during the interwar period. Jews in Poland, Koreans in Japan, Armenians in Turkey, and South Asians in South Africa are only a few of the groups whose human rights were severely compromised during the 1920s and 1930s.

Marginalized Groups: Indians and Blacks

The belief in racial differences and in the superiority of European culture led to restrictions on the civil and political rights of many groups. Inuit in Canada, aborigines in Australia, Indians on much of the American continent, blacks in the Union of South Africa, and Hawaiians and African Americans in the United States found themselves excluded from many institutions and deprived of political power.

The project of nation building in the young states of the Americas made Native Americans seem a threat to the unity of the new body politic. As states became nations, their inhabitants were supposed to change into citizens, speaking a common language and accepting a common identity. Amerindian populations (see Map 7.2)

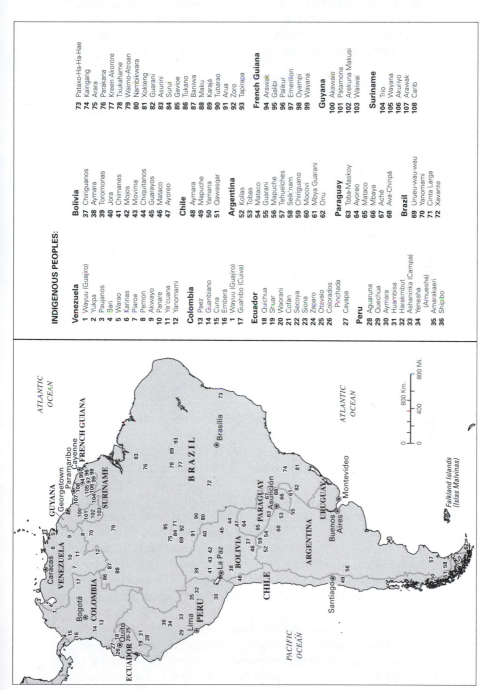

INDIGENOUS PEOPLES:

Venezuela
1 Wayuu (Guajiro)
2 Yukpa
3 Paujanos
4 Bari
5 Warao
6 Karinas
7 Piaroa
8 Akwayo
9 Panare
10 Panare
11 Ye'cuana
12 Yanomami

Colombia
13 Paez
14 Guanbiano
15 Cuna
16 Emberá
1 Wayuu (Guajiro)
17 Guahibo (Cuiva)

Ecuador
18 Quichua
19 Shuar
20 Waorani
21 Cofán
22 Secoya
23 Siona
24 Zaparo
25 Otavalo
26 Colorados
  Pinchada
27 Cayapa

Peru
28 Aguaruna
29 Quechua
30 Aymara
31 Huambisa
32 Harakmbut
33 Ashanínka (Campa)
34 Yenesha
  (Amuesha)
35 Amarakaeri
36 Shipbo

Bolivia
37 Chiriguanos
38 Aymara
39 Toromonas
40 Jora
41 Chimanes
42 Mojos
43 Movima
44 Chiquitanos
45 Guarayos
46 Mataco
47 Ayoreo

Chile
48 Aymara
49 Mapuche
50 Yamana
51 Qawasqar

Argentina
52 Kollas
53 Tobas
54 Mataco
55 Guarani
56 Mapuche
57 Tehuelches
58 Sek'nam
59 Chiriguano
60 Mocovi
61 Mbya Guarani
62 Onu

Paraguay
63 Toba-Maskoy
64 Ayoreo
65 Mataco
66 Mbaya
67 Aché
68 Ava-Chiripá

Brazil
69 Urueu-wau-wau
70 Yanomami
71 Cinta Larga
72 Xavante

73 Pataxo-Ha-Ha-Hae
74 Kaingang
75 Arara
76 Parakana
77 Kreen Akorore
78 Txukahame
79 Waimo-Atroan
80 Nambikwara
81 Xokleng
82 Guarani
83 Asurini
84 Surui
85 Gavioe
86 Tukano
87 Baniwa
88 Maku
89 Karajá
90 Tubarao
91 Arua
92 Zoro
93 Tapirapa

French Guiana
94 Arawak
95 Galibi
96 Palikur
97 Emerillon
98 Oyampi
99 Wayana

Guyana
100 Akawaio
101 Patamona
102 Arekuna Makusi
103 Waiwai

Suriname
104 Trio
105 Wayana
106 Akuriyo
107 Arawak
108 Carib

MAP 7.2 Amerindians of South America.
The map depicts some of the larger Amerindian groups, which are especially numerous in Brazil, Bolivia, and Ecuador.

did not, and usually did not want to, conform to this ideal of homogenization. Different in language, cultural practices, and self-identity, they remained outside the growing national communities in the Americas. Although in theory they were citizens with equal rights, they were discriminated against in practice.

Some Latin American states, particularly Chile and Argentina, used their armies to assert control over Indian populations, breaking up their communities and seizing their land. In other cases, states declared themselves the protectors of indigenous peoples but used education and legal restrictions to "civilize" them and to integrate them into the wider society. The Panamanian government campaigned from 1915 to 1925 to force the Kuna people to speak Spanish and to change their modes of dress and dancing. The government also forbade the Kuna to wear nose rings or to hold puberty ceremonies. The state's introduction of ballroom dancing and jazz music to the group produced a rebellion, which led the central government to end its campaign.

Indigenista policies and ideology, designed to identify the Mexican state with its indigenous or native populations, were developed in the 1920s and 1930s to help that government build a strong state and to emphasize Mexico's differences from Spain. In 1939, President Lazaro Cardenas invited representatives of Indian groups throughout the Americas to meet to discuss plans for their future and to encourage more positive attitudes toward them. After the meeting, Indian groups began to organize to defend their rights in Chile, Argentina, and Bolivia, and these groups were able to operate freely.

Indian populations in Latin America had an advantage that was not shared by many minorities in Europe, who were often seen as unwelcome intruders. Indians symbolized not only preconquest cultures but also resistance to outside rule by Europeans. Indians in Latin America represented their states' traditions of independence and anticolonialism. As a result, "Indianness" could be valued by a government, even when Indians themselves were not. It has proved easier in Latin America to incorporate forms of Indian culture than it has to integrate Indians themselves.

When the Union of South Africa was formed in 1910, the constitution and early governments designed a segregated state in which white male citizens shared political power. (Only a small number of Africans who could pass tests of "civilization" could vote in the Cape Colony.) Laws limited African land ownership to areas the government identified as "native reserves", and official policy tried to restrict African employment in industry and in the towns. Government policies attempted to separate peoples by race for the protection of white economic and political interests.

Geographical segregation broke down, however, because the economy depended heavily on African labor. Nevertheless, during the depression of the 1930s, the South African government combated the unemployment of white workers by moving them into jobs formerly held by blacks. The government also tightened segregation rules and took educated Africans off voter lists in the Cape Colony. Thereafter, Africans could elect a small number of white representatives to the Union's parliament and select the members of a Native Council.

The main African voice against government policy came from the African National Congress, which was formed in 1912 by a small group of Western-oriented elites. It brought together the chiefs of various tribal groups, African Christians, and professionals. Its program called for equal rights for all South Africans, but its conservative leadership had to battle for public support. By the 1930s, a multiracial Communist Party, industrial unions, and black separatist groups had organized, presenting black citizens with an array of political choices. At that time, most black leaders worked within the existing political structures, encouraging people to elect representatives to the Native Council. While they protested their exclusion from power, few recommended militant actions.

In the United States, African Americans continued to be second-class citizens. Excluded from voting in most areas and shunted into separate schools and residential areas, the majority of them lived segregated lives. Growing migration from the South to the North meant competition for jobs and housing in industrial cities. The Ku Klux Klan, a group that worked to defend the privileges of white people, spearheaded a wave of terror against African Americans during the 1920s. Proclaiming that the United States was "white man's country", this racist group incited and justified floggings, brandings, and hangings in the name of racial supremacy.

African American leaders searched for effective strategies for protesting violence and widespread discrimination. The National Association for the Advancement of Colored People used the courts, the U.S. Congress, and the media to fight for equal rights. Although they mobilized a large number of elite blacks, they did not enlist the support of black workers. Their efforts to force the passage of a federal anti-lynching law failed when Southern senators successfully blocked the bill.

During the 1920s and 1930s, African American voices became more eloquent and more explicit in presenting their views of U.S. society. Novelists such as Richard Wright and Langston Hughes wrote hard-hitting descriptions of racial inequality and injustice. These men and other New York–based African American writers of the Harlem Renaissance group gained national recognition for their work. Actors in African American theater, independent black filmmakers, and painters and graphic artists reached a widening audience. Their portrayals of African American life became part of the cultural scene of the United States.

Overall, however, the political power of African Americans remained limited. The single African American elected to the U.S. Congress in 1928 had to speak for a nationwide constituency. President Roosevelt appointed several African Americans to advisory and administrative posts in New Deal agencies, and his wife, Eleanor, demonstrated a commitment to racial equality in her political visits and loyalties. Government service became a way in which African American leaders could influence U.S. policy. But for the mass of African Americans, the 1930s were a time of deepening unemployment, poverty, and continued racial discrimination.

Welfare Programs: A Response to Domestic Problems

The word *crisis* has often been applied to the 1930s. Economic depression, political instability, and ideological intolerance combined to create hostility and fear. People found it easier to hate and to lash back when their stomachs were empty and their perceived enemies were in power. Street fights, hunger marches, riots, and political murders signaled rising dissatisfaction. It did not matter whether their societies were industrialized or underdeveloped, democratic or authoritarian; angry people sometimes ignored the law when expressing their grievances. Political leaders feared for the stability of society. Not just their continued legitimacy in the eyes of citizens but also their survival seemed to require strong action by the state to combat poverty and defuse conflict.

Possible responses came in many forms, but a common and a quite effective one was the adoption of social welfare measures to raise citizens' incomes. To be sure, some governments had more resources than others, and not all had political parties that were willing to vote for and to fund social insurance and benefits. By the 1930s, however, awareness of social welfare measures had become international.

By the 1920s, the idea that the state should protect its citizens from economic insecurity was widely accepted in wealthier countries. The modern "welfare state"

National Portrait Gallery, Smithsonian Institution/Art Resource, NY

Langston Hughes, poet, playwright, and novelist, as painted in 1925 by Winold Reiss. He is portrayed against an abstract background evoking cities and jazz music, which emphasizes the cultural modernism of the Harlem Renaissance.

developed in Europe and Scandinavia during the later nineteenth century, moving beyond poor relief to the provision of services and insurance against social risks. By the early 1930s, over half of government expenditures in Germany, Britain, and Sweden went for social insurance and assistance, health, education, and housing.

After World War I, what had begun as programs for industrial workers widened to include the mass of the population. Even if no country had yet moved to universal coverage, the idea that citizenship brought with it social rights had been accepted in most of western and northern Europe, as well as in Australia and New Zealand. Socialist parties and trade unions had mobilized to demand greater protection against loss of income, and they commanded enough votes to force democratic, parliamentary regimes to pay attention to their claims. Social welfare plans also appealed to authoritarian governments as proof that they could protect their citizens without granting them political rights. These entitlement programs cost a great deal, and they relied on effective bureaucracies and tax collection. As a result, they spread only in strong states with mobilized political parties and unions—in industrialized or industrializing nations.

Fascist states introduced their own versions of welfare during the interwar period. In Germany, the Nazis tried to improve the health of racially pure citizens. Strong antismoking campaigns signaled an early awareness of the dangers of tobacco. The Nazis built maternity hospitals and country camps, but the physically or mentally handicapped received different treatment. Nazi racial theory demanded that the "unfit" not reproduce. Murder by injection or sterilization became the fate of those who were deemed unworthy of membership in the German nation.

Among industrialized nations, the United States lagged in its provision of social welfare until the reforms of the New Deal. Then, in 1935, Congress passed the Social Security Act, which provided pensions to the elderly and payments to the unemployed. With the help of federal funds, states provided support for the handicapped and for dependent children. Although many rural workers and disproportionate numbers of African Americans were not covered immediately, the Social Security Act remains the foundation of the U.S. welfare system.

In other areas of the world, state welfare systems were limited or nonexistent. In Brazil, Vargas introduced a few benefits for industrial workers during the 1930s: They had the right to a minimum wage, an eight-hour work day, and paid holidays, but they were not entitled to protection from unemployment or old age. Some firms provided limited welfare services for their employees, such as health care and housing, but these were individual benefits that ceased with the job. Churches, charities, and families remained the chief sources of support in times of need.

Welfare measures in the imperial colonies offer an interesting contrast to the programs of the European nations. Imperial rulers had to demonstrate the benefits of European control, and what better way to do so than by improving public health among their charges? Particular populations were targeted because of race or ethnicity. The Belgian government financed a program of rural medical clinics and midwives for the population of the Belgian Congo. British administrators in India demanded that South Asian workers who staffed plantations in other parts of the empire be paid minimum wages and be given medical care, clean water, and adequate housing. Official standards of care and hygiene remained well below those expected by the European population, and only a small part of the subject population benefited.

Although the political effectiveness of welfare policies in colonial settings seems doubtful, these policies were, and have remained, very popular in the industrialized countries, and they expanded greatly after World War II. The political calculation that welfare benefits would increase loyalty to the state paid off, and in the short run welfare gave families added resources in the depression years.

CONCLUSION

The economic troubles of the 1930s intensified a series of bitter conflicts over ideas, land, and power. Communists and capitalists, nationalists and imperialists worked to legitimize their views of the world. Fascists tried to reorganize states in their own image, while democratic governments struggled to keep popular support in hard times. Due to perceived lack of manpower, many states mobilized women as workers and as mothers to increase their resources. Governments everywhere used the media for a relatively soft sell of their regimes, but authoritarian states also used hardline tactics to silence their opponents. Purge trials and concentration camps signaled a new era of rising intolerance. Particularly in Central Europe and Japan, strident nationalism pushed minorities to the edges, or even outside, of communities.

Nationalism mobilized citizens to defend their states against those identified as their enemies. These could be external, as well as internal. The lesson that nations could try to solve their problems through war was taught by Hitler's successful attacks on Germany's neighbors and by the Japanese expansion into Manchuria. As the 1930s drew to a close, levels of conflict increased, as did attacks by one state on another. The stage was set for a much wider conflict that would pit the major powers of Europe, Asia, and the Americas against one another.

For Further Reading

W. G. Beasley, *Japanese Imperialism, 1894–1945* (Oxford: Clarendon Press, 1987).
    A discussion of an Asian empire and its impact on that region.
Leslie Bethell, ed., *Latin American Politics and Society Since 1930* (Cambridge: Cambridge University Press, 1998). Thematic analyses of recent Latin American history by specialists.
Piers Brendon, *The Dark Valley: A Panorama of the 1930s* (New York: Knopf, 2000).
    A lively narrative of major political events in Europe, the United States, and Japan.
Victoria de Grazia, *How Fascism Ruled Women: Italy, 1922–1945* (Berkeley, Calif.: University of California, 1992). Material on women's lives during the 1930s.

Lloyd E. Eastman et al., *The Nationalist Era in China, 1927–1949* (Cambridge: Cambridge University Press, 1991). A discussion of politics in East Asia.

Ann Farnsworth-Alvear, *Dulcinea in the Factory: Myths, Morals, Men and Women in Colombia's Industrial Experiment, 1905–1960* (Chapel Hill, NC: Duke University Press, 2000). Oral histories of women in Colombian textile factories.

Sheila Fitzpatrick, *Everyday Stalinism: Ordinary Life in Extraordinary Times: Soviet Russia in the 1930s* (Oxford: Oxford University Press, 1999). A fine study of the impact of totalitarian politics on daily life.

Igor Golomstock, *Totalitarian Art in the Soviet Union, the Third Reich, Fascist Italy, and the People's Republic of China* (London: Collins Harvill, 1990). A good comparative discussion of art and culture in the 1930s.

Marion A. Kaplan, *Between Dignity and Despair: Jewish Life in Nazi Germany* (New York: Oxford University Press, 1998). Pays particular attention to the roles of women.

Barbara Dianne Savage, *Broadcasting Freedom: Radio, War, and the Politics of Race, 1938–1948* (Chapel Hill, NC: University of North Carolina Press, 1999). An excellent study of radio in the 1930s.

Colin Shindler, *Hollywood in Crisis: Cinema and American Society, 1929–1939* (London: Routledge, 1996). A detailed look at the links between film and politics.

Françoise Thébaud, ed., *Toward a Cultural Identity in the Twentieth Century*, Vol. 5, *A History of Women in the West* (Cambridge, MA: Belknap Press, 1994). Discussions of feminism and family life in several countries.

Related Websites

Benito Mussolini
   http://www.spartacus.schoolnet.co.uk/2WWmussolini.htm
Harlem Renaissance
   http://www.jcu.edu/harlem/index.htm
Nazism in Germany
   http://www.fordham.edu/Halsall/mod/modsbook43.asp
World Directory of Minorities
   http://www.minorityrights.org/directory

CHAPTER 8

From Regional Wars to Global Conflict, 1936–1946

In the historic Chinese city of Nanjing in 1937, the German businessman John Rabe witnessed what he considered to be indescribable and inexplicable atrocities committed by Japanese soldiers against the civilian population and against Chinese prisoners of war. By dozens and often by hundreds, helpless people were lined up before trenches, shot, dumped, and buried, whether alive or dead. Men were lined up with their hands tied behind their backs and slaughtered. Women were raped by marauding Japanese soldiers, then bayoneted. Babies were torn from their mothers' arms and tossed into the air to be impaled on swords or bayonets. Japanese officers hunted down Chinese men on the streets and beheaded them for sport.

Rabe was sickened by the violence and hoped to intervene. He imagined that he would be in an influential position because his nation, Nazi Germany, was an ally of Japan. But Rabe found that his reports were ignored. He appealed to U.S. missionaries for help in getting out the word about the atrocities in Nanjing. At every step his actions were frustrated, but he continued his attempts to restrain the Japanese soldiers and help the Chinese victims.

Unknown to Rabe, in Hungary the Japanese ambassador, Sugihara Chiune, was attempting his own efforts to relocate Lithuanian Jews. Sugihara had heard rumors of a planned systematic elimination of Jews and Slavs by the expanding Nazi regime, and he arranged passports that allowed nearly five thousand of the Hungarians who were most likely to become victims of the Nazis to escape to Shanghai. It was ironic that Shanghai was available as a haven for Sugihara's protégés only because Japan had occupied the city in 1937 after a series of brutal invasions of Chinese cities by Japanese troops and prolonged urban warfare against Chinese defenders.

During The First World War I Sugihara and Rabe were among those who risked their comfort and at times their lives to intervene in what they saw as a widening and increasingly irrational network of degradation, enslavement, and death. They were not as well known in their time as the American Varian Fry, who helped scientists, artists, and writers escape from occupied France. Nor did they gain the international reputation of the Swedish diplomat Raoul Wallenberg, who actually went behind Nazi lines to escort prospective victims to freedom, and who died in Soviet detention after the war had ended. The many Europeans who protested the stigmatizing of Jews and who sheltered Jews in their homes were not known by name. Some German businessmen and even civilian officials throughout Europe helped to rescue Jews by passing on information to the resistance networks. Other remarkable incidents in Hungary, the Netherlands, Denmark, Bulgaria, Italy, and Finland demonstrated the general truth that individuals could act humanely in the midst of very dangerous and apparently unstoppable madness.

One of the most important instances of German civil resistance occurred in 1943, in the Rosenstrasse district of Berlin. Nearly two thousand men who had been identified as Jews who were married to women identified as "Aryan" were detained and marked for deportation to concentration camps. Their wives, families, neighbors, and sympathizers began to gather outside the building where the men were being detained, and the women began a sit-down demonstration that eventually attracted as many as six thousand protesters. Orders from the police to disperse were ignored, as were threats of arrest and gunfire directed over the heads of the women. In the end the local official, Josef Goebbels, agreed to release the prisoners. The released men were never rearrested, and nearly all of them survived the war.

The numbers of lives saved in actions such as these, nevertheless, do not compare with the horrific slaughter that proceeded in areas where civilians did not bother to protest. Though nearly all Danish Jews survived the Nazi occupation of their homeland, their total numbers were less than eight thousand. In Bulgaria, nearly fifty thousand Jews were rescued. These numbers have to be compared to the millions of Jews—perhaps as many as six million—who are known to have been executed or died of hardship under Hitler. And, as we will see below, the murder or removal of the Jewish population of Europe was only a part of the many mechanisms by which the Second World War produced a death toll of 70 to 100 million people.

The Wars of the Northern Hemisphere

When the Second World War came to a conclusion in 1945, large parts of Europe and Asia were in ruins, and the whole world was on the verge of political transformation. The causes of the two regional wars were vaguely connected by the effects of the First World War and the global economic difficulties of the 1930s. But they became linked into a world war because of the participation of two countries that, in their geographical and political spans, united the Atlantic and the Pacific: the Soviet Union and the United States of America (see Map 8.1).

Although the roles and ambitions of the United States and the USSR in the later years of the war were similar, their experiences in the war contrasted starkly. One great difference was in the sheer numbers of people lost. Deaths in the Soviet Union are thought to have been roughly twenty million, somewhere between twenty-percent and forty-percent of the total losses in the war. Half of these were soldiers, but half were noncombatants who died of starvation, illness, exhaustion, and cold. Russians not only fought in Europe and in Asia but also experienced the horrors of having the war brought to their own cities and villages. The number of deaths among citizens of the Soviet Union was higher by far than the number for any other country—the next highest number of casualties, in China, may have been only half as great as the Russian losses. Germany's total deaths, in turn, were probably about half of China's, and Japan's about half of Germany's. American fatalities, in comparison, were probably around four hundred thousand—about one-fiftieth of the Russian cost (see Figure 8.1). Despite the enormous contrast between the USSR and the USA, these two nations in many ways defined the Second World War: They shaped not only the end stage of the war, but the political contours of the entire world for decades afterward.

The First War: Japanese Invasion of China

When militarists in Japan finally achieved total control of the country in 1937 and created a government headed by Prince Konoye and General Hideki Tojo, they felt that the time had come to mount a massive invasion of China. Some Chinese military leaders understood the urgency of forming a united front—a temporary alliance—between the Nationalists and the Communists. But during the middle 1930s, China's leader Chiang Kai-shek had the fixed idea that the Communists would have to be eliminated before effective resistance could be mounted against Japan, which had already seized the resource-rich and industrialized region of Manchuria and converted it into the puppet state of Manchukuo. A Chinese warlord who had been a supporter of Chiang Kai-shek was so overcome with disgust at the ineffectiveness of the Chinese war effort that, in 1936, he kidnapped Chiang from a rural command base and flew him to forced negotiations with the Communists. Chiang promised to cooperate with the Communists against the Japanese. But in fact it was not until the gruesome events of the Nanjing Massacre that the Chinese side was galvanized into focusing on the war against Japan.

Chinese cities and the countryside were open to Japanese assault from the air and with heavy artillery, and the Japanese had effective troop transport by rail and by motor vehicle. China's best hope was intervention by a force capable of containing or reversing the momentum of the Japanese conquest. The nearest real prospect was the Soviet Union, which had been friendly to both

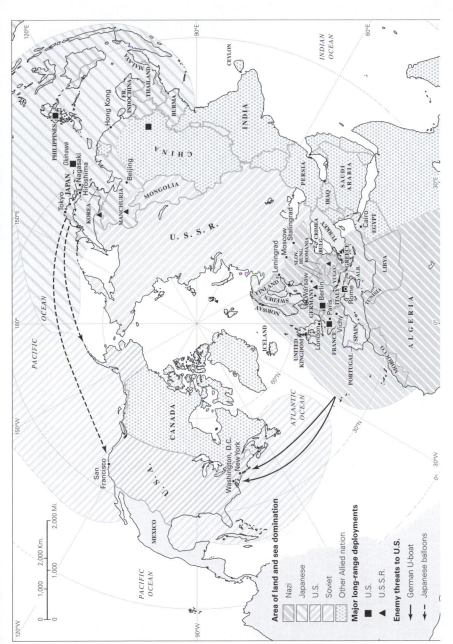

MAP 8.1 The War of the Northern Hemisphere.

Prior to 1941, the two regional wars in East Asia and in Europe were distinct. Beginning in 1941, the involvement of both the USSR and the United States as combatant nations meant that the entire Northern Hemisphere was at war. As this map suggests, the USSR mostly fought a defensive war, keeping its forces within its own borders. The United States was most involved in sustained, long-range deployment of troops and weapons and least vulnerable to attack from enemy forces.

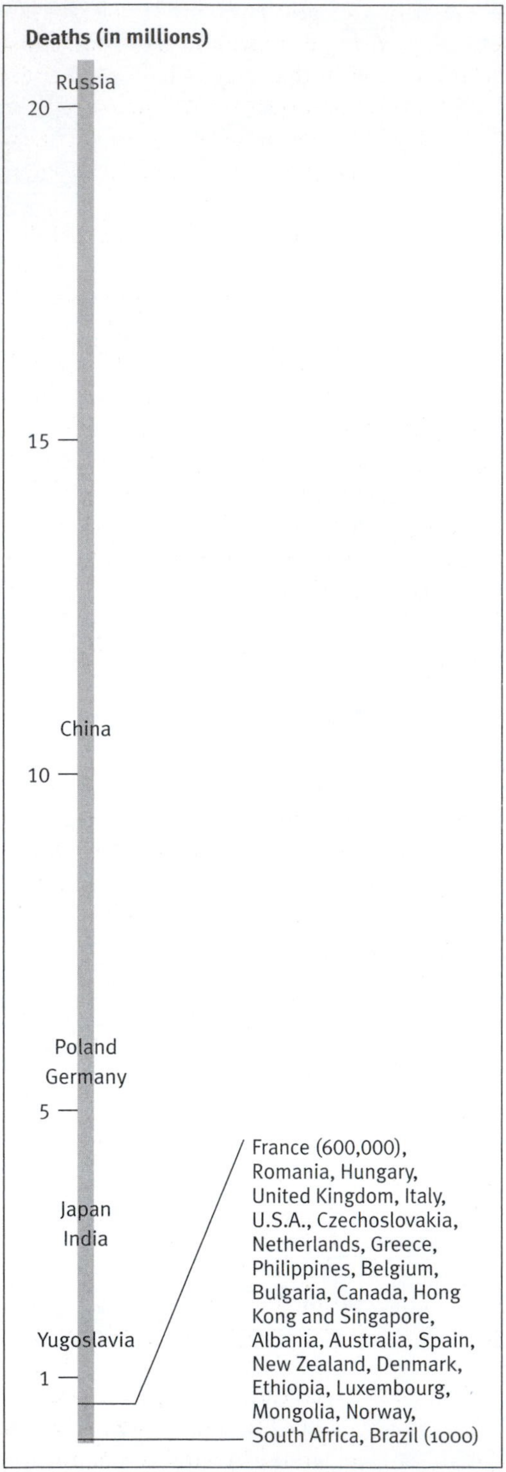

Deaths (in millions)

Russia
20 —

15 —

China
10 —

Poland
Germany
5 —

France (600,000),
Romania, Hungary,
United Kingdom, Italy,
Japan   U.S.A., Czechoslovakia,
India   Netherlands, Greece,
               Philippines, Belgium,
               Bulgaria, Canada, Hong
               Kong and Singapore,
Yugoslavia   Albania, Australia, Spain,
               New Zealand, Denmark,
1 —   Ethiopia, Luxembourg,
               Mongolia, Norway,
               South Africa, Brazil (1000)

© Cengage Learning 2013

FIGURE 8.1

Comparative death rates during World War II (numbers on the left represent deaths in millions). These are very general numbers; the conditions under which people died during the war make the exact numbers a continual source of disagreement among historians.

the Chinese Communist Party and the Nationalist government. In 1936 Germany and Japan signed a pact of alliance against the international communist movement—the Comintern—which in practice meant that they were both enemies of the Soviet Union. In 1939, Japan and the Soviet Union engaged in several battles in Mongolia, where both were rivals for dominance. The Japanese were decisively defeated there, and afterward they focused their attention on China even more intensely.

Not only were Chinese hopes in 1939 for intervention by the Soviet Union realistic, but the signs were very encouraging. The Soviet Union was a leader in the development of tank technology and had shown a willingness to deploy its tanks abroad during the Spanish Civil War. Unfortunately for the Chinese, Stalin unexpectedly concluded a nonaggression pact with Germany in 1939, and this seemed to eliminate finally any hope of Soviet intervention on behalf of China against Germany's ally, Japan. As a result, the United States was China's only real hope. While U.S. opinion gravitated toward support of China, the Nationalist Party, and Chiang Kai-shek, the U.S. government resisted providing direct support. One reason was the series of Neutrality Acts drafted and passed by the U.S. Congress between 1935 and 1939. Japan continued to expand its control from Shanghai and Nanjing westward along the Yangtze River, and from Manchuria westward toward Beijing.

Germany's Expansion in Europe

Chapter 7 described how the economic pressures of the 1920s and very early 1930s fostered authoritarian political movements in Europe. In Spain, a government attempt to ease economic difficulties through socialist land reform policies incited a rightist backlash that culminated in a coup d'état by General Francisco Franco in 1936. Franco intended to smash the socialist movement by imposing a military dictatorship and reinstating the power of the Catholic Church. As civil war between the Spanish Republicans and Franco's Falangists split the country, other nations in Europe chose sides. The pattern of alliances foreshadowed the pattern of the Second World War: Italy and Germany supported the Falangists, and German air forces bombed the Basque town of Guernica, whose sufferings were immortalized in the painting of the same name by Pablo Picasso. The USSR supported the Republicans, and Britain and France were neutral. In 1939, Franco forced an agreement on the Republicans and became leader of the country for the rest of his life.

Italy and Germany were surprised and encouraged by the lack of reaction from Britain and France to the Spanish conflict. By the 1930s Mussolini was attempting to resolve some of Italy's persisting problems by advocating—and, when possible, practicing—aggressive military expansion. In 1935, Italy invaded Ethiopia. Mussolini was careful not to step on the toes of Britain (which dominated Egypt) or France (which had colonized Algeria), and so those countries shrugged off the invasion of Ethiopia. The lesson was not lost on Hitler, who realized that a large war in Europe would inevitably encompass

Guernica by Pablo Picasso. In late April of 1937, Fascist forces in the Spanish Civil War destroyed the Basque town of Guernica (in northern Spain) by aerial bombardment. In Paris, the Spanish painter Pablo Picasso was inspired to paint this mural, full of images of chaos, wanton death, and victimization, on the walls of the Spanish Pavilion at the Paris Exhibition. Completed only three months later, the painting was popularly received as a protest against both the brutality of the attack and the Fascist overthrow of the elected Spanish government.

North Africa too, including the Suez Canal in Egypt. In March 1936 Germany confronted its neighbors with a more direct action than Italy's: It occupied the Rhineland, which it had been explicitly prohibited from doing by the provisions ending the First World War. There was no protest from other governments; as a result, Hitler was convinced that he had implicit permission from his European rivals to continue to arm and expand. On July 19, 1936, he formalized an alliance—the Axis—with Italy.

In March 1938, Hitler's forces occupied Austria—also prohibited under the provisions ending the First World War. Hitler then demanded permission in advance to conquer Czechoslovakia, and British Prime Minister Neville Chamberlain agreed, ratifying the occupation at the Munich conference. Hitler then turned his sights toward Poland. The most important acquiescence now came from the Soviet Union, which proceeded to sign the mutual nonaggression pact with Germany in August, 1939. In return, Germany approved of the Soviet Union's invasion and occupation of Finland. But this time, Britain and France did not agree so easily. They opposed the invasion of Poland by declaring war on Germany, although it was nearly a year before either Britain or France took any military action at all.

Memories of the horrors of the First World War, combined with the economic constraints of the worldwide depression, evidently caused leaders in Britain and France particularly to seek to avoid another war at all costs. In addition, there was a certain ambivalence about fascism. As we saw in Chapter 7, the economic crises of the early 1930s had been met in a variety of ways by assertive, highly centralized governments, many of which used authoritarian policies to suppress political reactions to social and economic distress. Most of the European democracies, and the United States as well, had some sort of Fascist movement, even if it was marginal or short-lived. Although Hitler's Fascism added a strain of racism (a political combination that was first practiced in Romania in the 1920s), which had not been very important in Spanish or Italian Fascism, it was nevertheless regarded by many foreign observers as a tolerable response to Germany's social and economic ills.

Britain's attitude toward Hitler was in many ways reinforced by that of France, which was much closer to Germany and obviously would have been more easily threatened by German aggression. France had suffered profound material destruction during the First World War, resulting in agricultural underproduction and endemic housing shortages through the 1930s. Nevertheless, it was France that mounted the most expensive and most sophisticated technical military project of the time, one that seemed to make aggression from the direction of Germany almost impossible: the Maginot Line, completed in 1938. This phenomenal project involved a series of underground fortifications, superbly armed, encased in impenetrable concrete, and designed for long-term secure habitation, even being air-conditioned for comfort. These underground cities were connected by huge tunnels, essentially underground highways, that also included full-scale railway lines.

The amazing scope and technical innovations of the Maginot Line seemed to ensure that Germany could never again advance westward from the Rhineland into France or beyond to Britain. This fantasy of complete safety provided by the Maginot Line was punctured in 1939 when Germany rapidly destroyed Poland's formidable military resources, then rolled through and occupied Denmark, Norway, and the Netherlands. Finally, in April, Germany conquered Belgium and exposed the greatest fallacy of the Maginot Line: They had simply cut through the great Ardennes forest in Belgium and gone around the huge but immobile defense system.

With enormous numbers of infantry troops, with tanks that maneuvered very rapidly, and with innovative air power provided by the Stuka dive bombers, a German force of nearly five million combatants was now poised for a full invasion of France in June of 1940. British troops stationed in France and Belgium recognized the futility of engaging the German forces and beat a retreat to the port of Dunkirk, where German forces intended to apprehend them. But the British admiralty cobbled together an expedition of naval ships, fishing boats, and private craft that crossed the English Channel and rescued nearly two hundred fifty thousand British, French, and Belgian fighters before the Germans closed in.

French leaders surrendered two-thirds of the country to direct control of Germany and created an occupation government at Vichy to administer the remaining third of France and all of Algeria under the direct authority of Hitler. Marshall Philippe Pétain, one of the towering French national heroes of the First World War, signed the agreement that gave France to Germany in the same

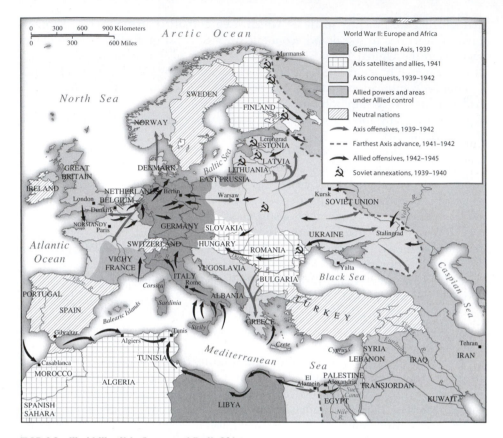

MAP 8.2 World War II in Europe and North Africa.
Before the United States entered the European theater of the war in 1942, virtually all of Europe and North Africa was either under the control of the Axis powers Germany and Italy or had claimed neutrality. Britain was the only unoccupied country actively opposing the advance of the Axis. The arrows here show the major campaigns of 1942–1945, with the Allies north and west from the French coast and from the Mediterranean, while the Soviet Union came in from the east.

railway car in which German representatives had signed the armistice that had marked their surrender in The First World War. Those French leaders, including Charles de Gaulle, who opposed the surrender and were able to escape the country set up a French government-in-exile in Britain.

Clearly, Britain was Hitler's next target. Greece joined the British side by fighting Germany's ally, Italy, and by providing information and support to British forces whenever possible. But by early 1941, Greece was overwhelmed by the two-pronged German sweep through the Balkans and North Africa. Now Britain stood alone as the only nation in Europe opposing the Axis forces. The British government, led by the new prime minister, Winston Churchill, turned to the United States for support.

First Steps to a World War: The Soviet Union

The Soviet Union was the link between the European/North African war to its west and the Japanese/Chinese war to its east. Like the nations flanking it, the Soviet Union was in social crisis and in economic disarray in 1939. Hitler was aware that the Soviet Union was militarily formidable, and that it would not be reluctant to mobilize its forces in Eastern Europe. Hitler also knew that his virulent persecution of communists had made the Soviet Union leadership wary of him. Indeed, in 1935 Stalin had signed mutual assistance pacts with both France and Czechoslovakia to prevent Nazi expansion. To further his conquests now, Hitler had to not only avoid a conflict with the Soviet Union in the east but also prevent the Soviet Union from intervening in German campaigns in Western Europe.

To Stalin, accommodation of Hitler was as important as it had been to Chamberlain. Stalin was continuing to suppress opposition at home and force industrialization, but his control was tenuous. He knew that his society could not be mobilized to face devastation on the scale it had experienced in the First World War. Thus a solution to both sides' problems appeared to be found when they signed their nonaggression pact in 1939. The public provisions of this pact stated that neither country would attack the other, which meant that Hitler was free to concentrate his forces on his western front. Its secret provisions were that when Hitler conquered Poland, the Soviet Union would move to occupy eastern Poland, Lithuania, Latvia, Estonia, and part of Romania. All these things followed in early 1940. Finland, which bordered the Baltic republics, soon found Stalin's tanks at its borders; it briefly resisted the Soviet invasion before being conquered in 1941.

The Western European leaders and both Mao and Chiang in China were outraged at the Soviet actions. Hitler and the Japanese militarists were allies. Therefore, in the view of Chinese leaders, the Soviet Union should have refused to sign a pact with Nazi Germany. But Stalin replied that the British refusal to block Hitler's invasion of Czechoslovakia had left the Soviet Union no choice. It could not single-handedly contain Germany, and it could certainly do little except defend itself against Japan in Siberia and the Maritime Province.

Stalin knew that he had only bought time with Hitler because it was absolutely necessary for Hitler to gain oil for his armies and airplanes. And while Germany had no direct source to major oil deposits, the Soviet Union did: the supremely productive oil fields of the Caucasus region, particularly the city of Baku on the Caspian Sea. About 90 percent of all Russia's oil came from this region. Stalin knew that Hitler coveted the Baku resources, and that if the USSR refused him the oil, he would abandon the partnership. In Britain and the United States, too, analysts were alarmed at the possibility that through his connection to the USSR, Hitler might now have access to unlimited oil supplies.

When, in June 1941, Hitler indeed invaded the Soviet Union, his plans for moving toward Baku were already in place. In 1942 German troops seized the less productive portions of the oil wells of the Caucasus, and Hitler ecstatically celebrated what he thought was his coming oil supremacy. But in fact Hitler had made a tactical error in dividing his armies between the Caucasus expedition and the simultaneous invasion of northern Russia. Nearly four million German and Axis troops under Hitler's command swept into the Ukraine, a portion of them ultimately heading for Stalingrad. The Soviet forces drew back, taking with them all the supplies, weapons, and building materials they could carry. They burned everything they left behind, giving the Germans nothing that they could not bring with them. By the winter of 1942, the Axis forces had been surrounded outside Stalingrad and defeated. But the Soviet Union could hardly claim victory. They had killed about one hundred fifty thousand Axis troops and captured more than ninety thousand, but it is estimated that as many as half a million Soviet soldiers died. After huge losses on both sides, the German forces were stopped at Stalingrad, and in the Caucasus they could not go the last few miles to take Baku. In the meantime Stalin moved the Soviet munitions industries thousands of miles to the east, into Central Asia and Siberia. It was one of the most daring of his many long-distance transfers, preserving the Soviet Union's remarkable core of military technology and offering a hope of effective struggle against Germany.

Realization of World War: The United States

Historians generally agree that President Franklin Roosevelt and his government advisers favored stronger action in both China and in Europe than American popular opinion would support. With respect to Britain, Roosevelt had the advantage of dealing with the new prime minister, Winston Churchill. Before 1940, Churchill had had a flamboyant but not very successful career as one of the champions of the British Empire, colonialism, imperialism, suppression of labor organizing, and constant warfare against nonwhite populations. But when elected prime minister in 1940, Churchill emerged as a magnificent orator, able to articulate tremendous sentiments of hopeful, courageous defiance of Hitler. The British public, which had been taken unawares by the speed and magnitude of Hitler's conquests, hung on Churchill's words. Roosevelt was also impressed with Churchill, but he was perhaps even more impressed with the critical position in which Britain now stood. Since the English Channel was only about thirty miles across at its narrowest point, the chances of Britain's surviving a combined Axis onslaught were slim. Roosevelt was eager to offer material assistance, but the American law of the time severely restricted his ability to do so.

Roosevelt imposed an embargo on the sale of scrap metal and of all weapons to Japan. When Japan took advantage of the fall of France to seize French territories in Vietnam, Roosevelt imposed an oil embargo as well, insisting that it would hold until the Japanese withdrew from China. American public opinion supported these actions, which in spirit were consistent with the

Neutrality Acts but which nevertheless appeared to be a strong brake on Japanese aggression. Certainly the Japanese government took them that way, protesting that the United States was interfering in Japan's pursuit of its national security.

American opinion had also changed somewhat on the question of aid to Britain, the USSR, and China. Congress appropriated very large sums for enlargement of the navy and for new army weaponry. Roosevelt managed to give Churchill fifty battered warships in exchange for ninety-nine-year leases on British territories in the Caribbean and in Latin America. And he took a further economic step. By law, noncombatant foreign nations (which Britain certainly was at this time) could buy U.S. weapons only by paying cash (the so-called Cash-and-Carry policy). During 1939 and early 1940, Britain paid out nearly all its cash for U.S. munitions. Roosevelt arranged for Britain to have credit through the innovative Lend Lease Act. In return for Congress's cooperation, Roosevelt had to promise that no U.S. ships would enter battle zones.

Britain had surprising success in resisting the German attacks, which commenced in July 1940 with German airplanes attacking British ships in the English Channel. Historians now believe that two factors were primarily responsible for Britain's effective defense. The first was Britain's use of radar. The new device allowed British forces to track the oncoming aircraft and shoot them down at a very efficient rate (two German planes were downed for every British plane lost). While this helped pare down Germany's material advantage, it hardly was enough in itself to change the course of the Battle of Britain, given Germany's superiority in weaponry.

An even more determinative factor may have been a strategic error on Hitler's part. His air war advisers decided to change their focus from the British military installations on the coast to London itself. Their evident plan was to demoralize the London population, perhaps even causing the fall of Churchill's government. This idea of "terror bombings" (the contemporary phrase for attacking civilian targets in the hope of destroying political support for the enemy government) was a novel tactic of the war, and it would later be used by Britain and the United States against German and Japanese cities.

But the effect was the opposite of what was intended. Churchill's popularity deepened, and the bond between leader and people was only further consolidated. Britons worked continually to provide their own defenses by organizing warning patrols to spot enemy planes, staffing hospital aid stations, and even training themselves to shoot pistols in case of ground attacks by German paratroopers. When the government's resources ran too low to keep the little Spitfire planes (which at the time cost about $25,000 each, or about $392,000 in today's dollars) in good repair and fueled, private citizens or groups of citizens banded together to sponsor individual planes with their own funds. Kennel clubs, cricket teams, women's organizations, red-haired men, and families of prisoners of war named and sponsored their own planes. Queen Wilhelmina of the Netherlands sponsored an entire British squadron.

In the meantime, the shaky alliance between Hitler and Stalin had broken down, and Hitler's financial losses in the failed attacks against the Ukraine and the Caucasus were considerable. The result was a marked reduction in what could be done against Britain. Roosevelt signed up China and the USSR for Lend Lease and began to send supplies across Iran to Stalin's base areas. Churchill realized that he now had the military strength and endurance of the Soviet Union on his side, which forced Hitler to divert his thoughts and resources to a new front.

But what Churchill most wished for was the active involvement of the United States, and by the time the Nazis were mired in Ukraine, the United States was indeed part of the war, although the participants were careful to observe the letter of the Neutrality Acts. American pilots were serving in their own volunteer "Eagle Squadrons" in the British Royal Air Force. American naval convoys had been accompanying British supply ships carrying weapons across the Atlantic, turning back before entering contested waters. But this task was not as safe as Congress may have imagined. The Roosevelt government knew that technological change had eaten away at America's famous geographical invulnerability. German submarines (U-boats) roamed the Atlantic as far as the east coast of the United States. Many nations, including Japan, were capable of mounting explosive devices on high-altitude balloons that could penetrate at least some portion of U.S. airspace. It was only a matter of time before American ships or planes suffered the direct effects of the military conflicts in Europe and in Asia.

As it happened, the event that brought American involvement came in the Pacific. For decades the United States had intervened to limit or pre-empt Japanese expansion in the Pacific, and in recent months Roosevelt had actively worked to undercut Japan's material resources. Japanese army commanders were eager to take action against the United States if possible. Naval leaders in Japan were cautious and advised against any direct confrontation with the United States. But the army leaders argued that the oil issue would force a showdown between Japan and the United States. Since this conflict was inevitable, and since Japan was the weaker party, Japan must strike before its resources were further depleted. It would be best, they suggested, to make a surprise attack. Their research confirmed a surprising thing: American naval and air forces were concentrated at the Pearl Harbor base in Hawaii, and defenses there were lax. A Japanese air strike launched from aircraft carriers in the north Pacific, they argued, could immobilize the entire American Pacific force. The naval leaders reviewed the plan and considered it possible, though risky. They described the United States as a sleeping tiger: You can kill it only when it is asleep.

The first Japanese naval pilot to drop his bombs on Pearl Harbor on December 7, 1941, radioed back the taunt, "Tiger! Tiger! Tiger!"

The Pearl Harbor attack did indeed deliver a massive and temporarily crippling blow to American forces in the Pacific. Five battleships were sunk and three made inoperable; a dozen other major sea vessels were severely damaged; one hundred eighty aircraft (parked wing to wing on the open tarmac) were destroyed; nearly twenty-five hundred men were killed and half that number wounded. While the United States was immobilized that same day, Japan bombed Clark Field in the Philippines, destroying half of the remaining American air power in the Pacific. The Japanese forces then proceeded to conquer the Philippines, swept quickly into Indonesia (where only Australian troops were present to represent the Allied side), and then moved into the British colonies of Hong Kong and Malaya.

The active involvement of first the USSR and now the United States quickly changed the major trends in the conflicts that had raged since the late 1930s. Although the damage to existing U.S. ships and planes in the Japanese strikes of December 1941 was severe, the two aircraft carriers based at Pearl Harbor were away on maneuvers at the time of the attack. American technicians managed to get several damaged battleships seaworthy almost immediately, providing capabilities that Japan did not expect. More important, U.S. factories had been working at full capacity building ships, tanks, planes, military transport, guns, and ammunition since the beginning of 1941 when the Lend Lease Acts had been passed and a large demand for U.S. armaments was expected. U.S. ships in the Pacific were replaced with surprising speed, and in short order U.S. weapons were being pumped to allies in both Europe and Asia.

In 1942 a second supply route to the USSR across the northern Pacific supplemented the one that had already been opened through Iran. American oil production jumped to 184 million metric tons in 1942, compared to 7.7 million tons for Germany and 236,000 tons for Japan (down from 301,000 tons the previous year). American warplane production shot upward continuously until the end of the war, so that by 1944 the United States had produced nearly 300,000 planes—a third again as many as Britain had produced in nearly eight years. Within a year of the Pearl Harbor attack, the United States had more than six million men enrolled in the armed forces and ready for combat; by the end of the war, more than sixteen million Americans would have served. At full strength, the United States fielded as many troops as the USSR. In weapons, materiel, and fresh forces, the United States provided the key to defeating the Axis powers.

Japanese forces had alleviated some of their energy crisis with the seizure of most of Indonesia, and they quickly extended the air war to Sri Lanka (then Ceylon) and the northern coast of Australia. But the speed of the U.S. rearmament and restoration of the Pacific force stunned the Japanese planners. By the middle of 1942, American forces deflected Japan from Australia, while massive landings of American combat infantry began to challenge the Japanese forces in the Pacific islands and in the Philippines. Japan was forced for the first time to pour massive resources of men and weapons into the conquest of Southeast Asia, which in time took a toll on its efforts to extend its conquests in China. Overall, the Japanese military efforts in the Pacific and Southeast Asia had been underfunded. In total, Japan would spend the equivalent of about $56 billion on the war, approximately one-sixth of the total American expenditure. Japanese resources were stretched to the limit before Pearl Harbor, and thereafter the Japanese forces functioned with only a fraction of the energy resources and weaponry available to the United States.

The resulting hardships not only wore down the soldiers but also sapped the welfare of the Japanese civilian population. Japanese sacrificed more and more in economic terms to support the war, and also supplied increasing numbers of young males—some of them now teenagers or less than physically fit for service—to the imperial forces. The thin economic foundation of the Japanese military machine also took its toll on the thousands of Asian, American, and European prisoners of war. Germany took slightly less than 100,000 prisoners during the war, of whom about one percent died in captivity. Japan took perhaps 35,000, of whom nearly a fourth died of starvation, exposure, or exhaustion from being used as slave labor.

In China, Chiang Kai-shek's army had withdrawn from northern and coastal regions in the east to the remote city of Chongqing (Chunking), on the upper reaches of the Yangtze River. By 1942 the base of Chinese resistance there was losing its ability to acquire food and supplies as the Japanese extended their control of the ports and main communications channels. The U.S. commanders organized a group of pilots—called volunteers but actually all selected from the Army Air Corps—to fly from the British colony of Burma (now Myanmar) over the Himalayan Mountains. These "Flying Tigers" kept the Nationalist forces in supplies, and also in communication with American military planners. By late 1942, American advisers had been flown in, and the Chinese Nationalist government was in effect allied with the United States and Britain against Japan and Germany (the USSR still had not declared war on Japan). The Chinese Communists, in the meantime, were supplying additional resistance against the Japanese in North China, without benefit of American aid. And in its colony of Korea, Japan faced a new challenge. Nationalist rebels, encouraged and supported by the Soviet Union, were sabotaging railways and organizing resistance against the occupiers.

The fight to contain and beat back the Japanese conquest was very bloody throughout Southeast Asia and the Pacific. Until 1945, the anti-Japanese force consisted primarily of American infantry and American planes, aircraft carriers, and battleships at sea, supported when possible by troops from Australia and in all venues by local guerrillas fighting to destroy Japanese imperialism. This was particularly true in the Philippines, where U.S. land forces and Filipino freedom fighters formed a close partnership. The Japanese forces on land were tenacious, and both sides were afflicted by the diseases and discomforts of the tropics. Progress was agonizing, and the Allies were discouraged by the discovery that American prisoners captured in the Philippines and British prisoners captured in Southeast Asia at the time of the Japanese conquest had been abused, tortured, or murdered. But by the end of 1943, Japanese power in the Philippines had been broken, thanks in large part to the Filipino guerrilla fighters.

The turning point at sea also came in June 1942, at Midway Island in the central Pacific, where U.S. aircraft destroyed four Japanese aircraft carriers. Thereafter, the Japanese navy and its air forces dwindled quickly, leaving Japan with worsening scarcity of ships, weapons, and fuel. By 1944 the Japanese navy resorted to the desperate *kamikaze* ("divine wind") air tactics. These were suicide flights in which very young pilots who had been psychologically conditioned to sacrifice their lives flew very small, very light, very rudimentarily constructed air-

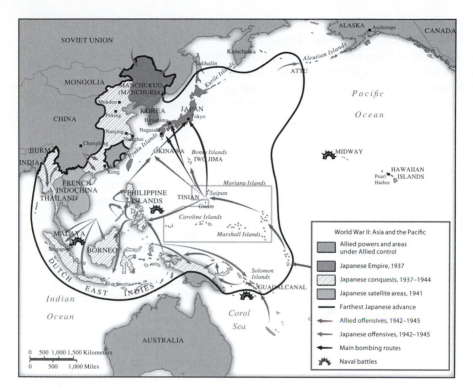

MAP 8.3   World War II in Asia and the Pacific.
Before problems with oil supplies and the entry of the United States into the war in 1942 stalled their expansion, Japanese forces controlled most of northern, central and south China, all of continental Southeast Asia, and most of island Southeast Asia. They were driven back from Midway Island in 1943 and thereafter Allied forces and local resistance movements weakened and fragmented Japanese occupiers.

planes directly into the decks of aircraft carriers or battleships. In many instances the dives missed or the expected explosions did not occur. Nevertheless, the Japanese navy continued to use the *kamikaze* flights because they did not require the fuel for a return flight.

Outside the Battlefields

In nearly all the societies involved in the war, unprecedented opportunities for women arose in industry and in some areas of the military, as the war drew men away from skilled, high-paying jobs in manufacturing. Women served as military pilots for the first time. In the U.S. and British forces, women flew only to deliver planes from one location to another, behind the lines. But in the Soviet Air Force there was an entire regiment of women combat fliers, who shot down thirty-eight German planes. Opportunities that were first offered to women in the military or the armaments industries created skills and expectations that carried over into civilian life. Although women after the war could not retain the status or the wages they had enjoyed during the war, the independence and responsibility they experienced clearly changed life for them and their children.

Despite the new opportunities enjoyed by some, the general story of life for noncombatants in the Northern Hemisphere was one of anxiety, loss, and no small amount of outright suffering. But in the First World War, only about five percent of all casualties were civilian. In the Second World War, nearly 70 percent of all casualties were civilian—fourteen times the proportion of noncombatant deaths in the earlier war. These figures omit the million or more people killed in the conflicts leading up to the Second World War—for example, the approximately three hundred thousand killed during the Japanese conquest of Manchuria, the five hundred thousand killed in the Spanish Civil War, and the two hundred thousand killed in the Italian invasion of Ethiopia. Nor do the totals normally include deaths from famine in areas that were affected by the war but are not usually considered part of the war, such as Bengal province of India, where more than a million people died of starvation in 1943, and Vietnam, where more than a million died in 1945.

The extent of the human loss is not directly related to geographical proximity to the conflict. For instance, France, which was a contested region and was located squarely in the middle of the European war theater, had many fewer than a million deaths. This was partly due to the fact that France capitulated to Germany early, and for more than three years was not an area in which the Allies chose to fight the Germans. But it is also related to the fact that France's agriculture remained intact, food and information could be supplied from nearby countries when necessary, and the French climate is mild enough that the relatively small number of displaced persons had a strong chance of surviving.

The opposite was true of the Soviet Union: A huge swath of its western territories was invaded by Germany, the USSR fought the Germans longest and most consistently of any of the Allies, and the Russian climate was such that its agricultural infrastructure could be easily damaged, with shattering results for the population. Soviet territories such as Ukraine and Belarus were savage battlefields, and the Battle of Stalingrad, which destroyed the city and its inhabitants, raged from July 1942 to February 1943. Ukraine is also an example of what can happen when areas change hands in the course of war. Under German occupation in 1941, masses of Jews, suspected or proved resistance fighters, and perceived weaklings who could not contribute to the war effort were exterminated. When the Russians returned to control in 1943, suspected collaborators and economic opportunists were executed by the thousands.

Death from Above

The starkest difference between North Americans and others in the Second World War was that North Americans did not live with the fear of being bombed by planes raiding from overhead. Japan tried to bomb North America, sending many hundreds of helium balloons with explosives attached drifting across the

Pacific. A few hundred actually landed, but only a handful of people were killed by them. In contrast, well over 50,000 people in Britain were killed and well over 60,000 wounded by bombings from planes and rockets. Although German bombs over Britain were deadly, Britain and the United States together dropped twenty times as many tons of explosive on German cities, killing approximately six hundred thousand people.

The Allies raised the killing of noncombatants to a new level by deliberately producing firestorms—carpet bombing so intense that the fires fed upon themselves, producing flames and heat too powerful to be contained. The first German city to be made an example of in this way was Hamburg, which was set ablaze in the summer of 1943. In the center of the fire, temperatures reached as high as 1400 degrees Fahrenheit (about 800 degrees Celsius), causing a plume of flame to rise three miles above the city and winds from the surrounding countryside to rush toward the fire at 150 miles an hour. Escape was impossible, and death from suffocation, decompression, or combustion was instantaneous. In a few days of bombing, 30,000 people were killed. Soon afterward, Dresden was subjected to the same treatment. But firebombing became even more efficient after the introduction of napalm as an accelerant in 1944. On a single night in March 1945, nearly 300 American planes flew over Tokyo, dropping 19,000 bombs. Eighty thousand Tokyo residents died in this single incident, and by the end of the war about as many Japanese as Germans had died in firebombing.

In addition to the loss of life and cultural treasures in these bombings, there was terrible ecological devastation. The tree-lined avenues and great urban parks for which Europe was renowned were destroyed, assaulted first by fire and then by desperate urban residents eager to build and outfit makeshift dwellings or to gain fuel for warmth. Very little that was made of wood managed to survive in any of the attacked zones. Houses that were not destroyed became uninhabitable, with perforated windows, ruined plumbing, and unsafe stairways. City sanitation systems could be inoperative for weeks at a time. Power was frequently not available, or was strictly rationed. City dwellers who survived bombings were forced to double up with friends or relatives, flee into the countryside, or just sleep amid the rubble.

Cities subjected to this treatment were usually totally destroyed, and the casualties—by definition overwhelmingly civilian, with no distinction being made between adults and children, and many people dying of malnutrition or disease long after the attack itself—were spectacular. The idea behind these bombings was, as in Hitler's bombing of London, that the populations would be demoralized and the government would fall. The outcome, however, was different. These firebombings only unified the population and renewed their defiance at a time when they might otherwise have considered withdrawing real support from their leaders. They adjusted their habits and had to help their neighbors in order to survive. During the London Blitz in 1940, at least 250,000 people were homeless. In London, working people who were afraid to sleep in multistory apartment houses slept in the underground (subway) stations, imagining that they would be safe. Several of these stations took direct hits, killing dozens or even a hundred people at a time. Unexploded bombs lay exposed in ruined houses, parks, gardens, and fields—on a single day in November 1940, three thousand huge bombs were waiting in various areas of London for the disposal teams to get around to them.

Many people fled such dangers. Others were relocated forcibly, perhaps for political reasons, perhaps for strategic reasons. Some moved toward conditions of greater safety, but huge numbers were forced toward greater privation, danger, and death. Destruction from the air or from the ground fighting left millions of people homeless, often as refugees in distant lands with no knowledge of the fate of their families and friends. In the late stages of the war, as brutalized victims turned on their aggressors, the levels of violence spiraled upward and outward. By the end of the war, there was hardly a resident of Europe, Asia, or the USSR who was not scarred by its direct or indirect effects.

Hunger

Everywhere, the war put great pressure on agriculture, and failures in food production and distribution had devastating results. In the United States these effects were felt only mildly, mostly in the form of rationed gasoline and price controls on agricultural produce. In Western Europe, the countryside often came to be filled with urban refugees who needed to be fed but could not be profitably employed. In Eastern Europe, the western Soviet Union, and eastern and southern China, conflict left the fields scorched by design, or simply by the effects of battle. The source of food had itself been obliterated. In other parts of Asia, the destruction of roads made the movement of grain to where it was needed impossible, and shortages of oil meant that vehicles could not move over the roads even if they were open. Irrigation systems were destroyed, cattle needed for plowing were killed, and what little food could be produced was often violently appropriated by the occupying army.

The greatest danger to populations in war is exposure to nature without the benefits of food, clothing, shelter, and medicine. Half of China, for example, was engulfed in the war against Japan at one time or another. The Japanese invaders slaughtered Chinese men and boys in huge numbers as a matter of policy, and the homeless, drifting populations were unable to feed or shelter themselves. Survivors by the hundreds of thousands were herded into concentration camps and left to starve. Refugees flooded the unconquered cities, set out to sea in boats, or fled to the rugged mountains, where they did not have the skills to survive. During the war, regular maintenance of waterworks was neglected. Floods turned dangerous situations into crises and resulted in millions starving —or expiring of common illnesses because their health was so poor—without a shot being fired. In 1943 about 3,000,000 people died of the effects of drought, flood, and famine in central China alone. Such tragedies were repeated throughout Asia, but were also shared by Europeans. The harsh winter of 1944–1945 resulted in the starvation of about 18,000 men, women, and children in the Netherlands. Perhaps 50,000 more died as a result of secondary effects of malnutrition and exposure.

Relocation

During the war years, relocation could be caused by a variety of circumstances, but in all cases the results were that victims who did not lose their lives or their health certainly lost their property and their community. Many of the relocated were refugees, who had fled of their own volition from areas of fighting or from areas that were so devastated by fighting that they could not support normal life. Many tens of millions of people were on the move as refugees throughout Europe and Asia.

The earliest to migrate were Jews, who fled from Germany after Hitler's seizure of power in 1933. The flight of Jews to safety became more urgent after the *Kristallnacht* ("Crystal Night") attacks of 1938, in which Jewish homes, businesses, and synagogues were destroyed and Jews were personally threatened or attacked by roving gangs. Many Jews were successful in moving to Palestine, France, Britain, or the United States. However, their fate was not always in their own hands. Nearly a thousand Jewish emigrants chartered the German ocean liner *St. Louis* to take them to Cuba, thinking they would find a new home there. They were turned away, and then they were also turned away from Miami by U.S. authorities. Eventually the governments of Britain, France, the Netherlands, and Belgium agreed to take separate portions of the group. But a majority of those who were taken by France, the Netherlands, and Belgium ended up in Nazi death camps anyway after those countries fell.

Nearly all the countries involved in the war practiced some form of internment—the imprisonment of civilians in camps or walled compounds. The most obvious reason to intern civilians was suspicion that they would collaborate with the enemy by spying or sabotage. Hitler's regime was showing such distrust when it incarcerated 300,000 of its own "Aryan" citizens in 1939, and throughout the war Germany imprisoned a million people solely because of distrust due to their political or religious beliefs.

In Britain, its former colonies (the Commonwealth), and the United States, the idea arose early that people who came from one of the Axis countries, or whose parents might have come from one of these countries, would harbor loyalties to their ancestral land. Immediately after the declaration of war against Germany, the British government moved to identify "enemy aliens"—individuals who had come from Germany or Italy, or who were thought to be German or Italian. Of the nearly 80,000 who were identified, about 10,000 were put under curfew, forbidden to travel, and required to report regularly to the police. Some of the Germans swept up by the authorities were actually German or Austrian Jews who had immigrated to Britain to escape the Nazis.

At first, the British practice was to deport these aliens to Canada, Australia, or New Zealand for internment. However, Churchill's government was embarrassed when a boat loaded with 569 deportees headed for Canada was sunk by a German U-boat and all aboard were killed. The policy was changed to keep internees in Britain. That included Northern Ireland and the Isle of Man. The Republic of Ireland had declared itself neutral and denied Britain the use of its ports as military bases. Irish whose loyalty to Britain was suspect were liable to be interned until the war was over. After 1941, about a thousand Finns were added. They were joined there by prominent British Fascists such as Oswald Mosley and his wife, Diana Mitford. Altogether, Britain interned about 27,000 civilians during the war.

Australia's internment camps not only served as termination points for British deportees but also received a good number of home-grown aliens. Like the North Americans, Australians were concerned by Asian as well as European enemies. At the time, Australia had an inflexible whites-only immigration policy, although temporary Asian laborers were admitted. Such Japanese as were present in Australia in 1940–1941 were rounded up, as were Germans, Austrians, and Italians. The Australian government determined that fully half of its non-British population was worthy of internment, and it incarcerated them in much higher numbers than did Britain. They were put to work enlarging the camps to receive Axis prisoners from Europe, although internal detainees outnumbered prisoners of war through the entire period.

In the United States, an order of January 1, 1942, required all Japanese, German, and Italian resident aliens to observe a curfew; to surrender all handguns, cameras, flashlights, and short-wave radios; and not to change their place of residence without permission from the police. In February 1942, Roosevelt issued an executive order for the internment of Americans of Japanese descent who lived within two hundred miles of the Pacific coast. Pursuant to this order, 120,000 Japanese-Americans or Japanese residents of the United States were forcibly relocated to camps in seven western states. About 11,000 Germans, German-Americans, and Eastern Europeans were interned in separate camps. The number of Italians and Italian-Americans interned has been estimated at over 50,000. In Canada, an order for internment of Japanese-Canadians was instituted at the same time as the American plan. About 23,000 people were moved to camps in British Columbia.

Internees of European descent tended to be kept in the eastern part of the United States, usually in existing buildings (as at Ellis Island). For internees of Japanese descent who were relocated to the harsh mountain climates of the Rockies or the southwestern deserts, living conditions in the internment camps of North America were a rough approximation of refugee life in Europe. Tarpaper huts with plywood siding were quickly slapped together as shelter for the prisoners. There was no plumbing or electric heat. On good days, there might be coal for a fire. Food rations were minimal, and all meals were taken in a mess hall with hundreds of other people. Inmates had no independence, no privacy, and no status, and everything they had worked to build for themselves on the outside was lost. In 1944, Roosevelt ordered the internments discontinued (though some internees of European descent were kept in custody until 1948).

Among the dangers for prisoners of the Allied countries was forced repatriation after the war. The most impressive number of returnees were Russian. More than two million Russian farmers and workers attempting to cross into Poland and deserting army officers were returned by the Allies, as were scholars and businessmen who had taken up residence in Western Europe. Most of them protested being returned; some committed suicide. Army officers were frequently shot as traitors when they were back in Soviet custody. Others were sent to labor camps in Central Asia or Siberia. A certain number of German-Americans were handed to Nazi authorities in exchange for non-German American civilian captives.

Relocation was also the fate of individuals from the conquered countries who were sent to work as slave labor in Germany. Hundreds of thousands of people from Poland and the Netherlands were put into slavery, most of the women as household servants, and the fate of such individuals is obscure, although it is believed that many tens of thousands never made it back to their homes after the war. Another form of relocation was the abduction of children for adoption into German families. In Poland, Ukraine, and Russia, children with blond hair and blue eyes—Aryan" looking, according to the Nazis—were taken from their parents and sent to Germany. In Poland, at least 200,000 children disappeared this way, and perhaps 50,000 were taken from Eastern Europe and Russia. It is estimated that only 20 percent of these children discovered during or after the war that they had been stolen from their families and were able to discover the whereabouts of their birthparents after the war.

Institutionalized Death

The most dramatic form of relocation was incarceration in the Nazi concentration and death camps, to which prisoners who were not executed outright were transported. As we saw in Chapter 7, conditions in Germany in the 1930s produced persecution of Jews, Romany (Gypsies), Poles and other Slavic peoples, homosexuals, leftists, communists, labor leaders, Christian dissidents, and other political opponents. Almost a third of those died at one single camp: Auschwitz, in Poland. Nearly 90 percent of all Jews living in Poland perished between 1940 and 1945. Nearly 250,000 Romany died along with Jews at Dachau and Auschwitz. Approximately 2 to 3 million Soviet prisoners of war also died in German camps. And as with other aspects of the Second World War, children suffered disproportionately. It is estimated that about a third of the Jewish population of Europe survived the war, but only about 11 percent of Jewish children.

The camps had been designed to work the inmate population to death, although they occasionally supplied experimental subjects to sadistic Nazi "scientists" investigating the particulars of every sort of death. Those who arrived weak were exterminated rather than having food and shelter spent on them. Carbon monoxide and simple smothering, which were the methods used in the camps at the beginning, were replaced at many installations by the lethal gas Zyklon B. Officials of many conquered nations, but particularly those of occupied France, Poland, and Hungary, aided the Nazis in the identification, incarceration, and murder of Jews and Romany.

After 1942, when war authorities in Britain and the United States learned the facts connected to the death camps, more and more people were murdered by the camps' Nazi managers, partly to hide the evidence and eradicate the testimony of the suffering. As awareness of the death camps grew, so did the degree of resistance offered by those expecting to be sent to the camps, particularly in Eastern Europe, where both the camps and their potential victims were centered. At Warsaw, Poland, in April 1943, 60,000 Jews armed themselves to resist Nazi detention and slaughter. The Nazi campaigns against the Jews, however, were not slowed. The Warsaw Jewish community was obliterated; in all, somewhere between seven and eight million Europeans —of whom five to six million were Jews—were sent to their deaths in the camps.

Churchill, Roosevelt and Stalin at Yalta, 1945 At the time of the February 1945 conference of the Allies at Yalta on the Black Sea, the Soviet Union had helped defeat Germany, but had not yet declared war on Japan. In order to convince Stalin to help in Asia and the Pacific, Roosevelt made concessions to Soviet interests in Europe and in China, and agreed to recognize the independence of the Mongolian People's Republic. Churchill attempted to be a voice for human rights in Europe, but the global role of his nation was fading, as Roosevelt and Stalin were designing the post-war world.

The war planners in Britain and the United States considered whether anything, short of outright and total obliteration of the camps and all their inhabitants, could be done to slow down the progress of this "Final Solution"—Hitler's plan to eliminate Jews from Europe. They did not find a method that they thought could save the death camp victims, and there also was no consensus among international advisers on whether the most extreme and deadly methods should be employed. Though air reconnaissance and some human intelligence alerted the Allies to the existence and purpose of the death camps, they were still not prepared for the shock of seeing the real places and the few survivors who could be liberated as Allied forces captured Poland. Ironically, the American liberators of Dachau were the "Fighting 442nd" composed of about 1,200 enlisted men from the Japanese internment camps in the United States. Many could not hold back their tears as they tenderly helped the starving victims out of the filthy cells and holding pens.

Endgame

Hitler's expansion in Europe was contained by the end of 1942, and the challenge then was to take back territory from his occupation forces. Stalin insisted to Britain and the United States that direct engagement of the German forces, on land, was the only way to end the war. Up to that time, Stalin's own soldiers had been doing virtually all the real fighting with the Germans in Europe, and he did not see how he could fight the Germans as long as there was only one front. Churchill proposed that instead of confronting the Germans in Western Europe, the Allies attack from the south, destroying Nazi power in North Africa. His suggestion that North Africa become a pivot in the war strategy was the product of Britain's successful campaigns against the Italian forces in Ethiopia (which concluded in 1941) and against the brilliant German commander Erwin Rommel, who in a two-year game of tag had nearly driven the British out of Egypt before being defeated in 1942. The Allies had retained control of the Suez Canal and a great expanse of North Africa as well, and now Churchill recommended that it be exploited.

Things did not go as easily as Churchill had predicted, but the Allied landing on Sicily in 1943 shocked the Italian public and Italian leaders. Mussolini was dismissed from power and imprisoned, but German storm troopers rescued him and established him as head of a puppet government in north Italy in late 1943. This forced the Allies to conquer the whole of Italy, finally reaching and destroying Mussolini's base in 1945. Mussolini was executed by anti-Fascist Italian resistance fighters (with the permission of the Allies), and Italy changed sides in the war.

Europe/North Africa

At the first meeting of the new allies in Tehran, Iran, in 1943, Stalin had demanded that his allies set a date for sending an expedition into Europe. At this point, Roosevelt demanded that in return for the Allies' directly engaging the Nazis in Western Europe, Stalin would declare war against Japan and agree to an international peacekeeping organization of some kind after the war. According to remarks made by Roosevelt at the time, he saw the Tehran meeting as an eye-to-eye negotiation between the two decisive powers of the future, and he regarded Churchill as a valiant but dated defender of the days of European imperialism. The Allies agreed that they would mount their invasion of Western Europe in the summer of 1944.

The expedition of June 6, 1944 (D-Day), was as much a technological as an outright military feat. Portable wharves and breakwaters were towed across the English Channel to provide suitable landing points, and pipelines were laid across the seabed to assure an adequate supply of the critical ingredient, oil. A shrewd campaign of disinformation suggested that the invasion would take place at the most likely spot, Belgium, when in fact the Allied planners were secretly preparing to land in Normandy in France, a farther and less hospitable spot. The fighting, when it began, was terrible, and casualties among the landing force of Americans, Canadians, and Britons were high. But Paris was taken by August, and France was now an active participant on the Allied side.

The tide quickly turned against the Nazis. Hitler's war managers were forced to send boys and sick and unfit men into battle, where they quickly died or surrendered. In another desperate attempt to retake the initiative, German engineers built V-2 rockets to resume the bombing of Britain. The early V rockets were robot planes loaded with explosives that would fly the approximate distance to London or another major British city, then plummet to earth. The advanced V-2s flew faster (and even more expensively) toward London, but apart from raising the fear level did little to help the German war effort in its last eighteen months.

In the meantime, the forces of the Soviet Union were closing in on Hitler from the east. Ahead of them came a reputation for extreme brutality. In Eastern Europe, hundreds of thousands of civilians were rounded up and trucked into the Soviet Union to work as slaves in Soviet industries until the late 1940s. Hitler's own fortress in Bavaria was stormed by the Soviets on April 30, 1945, before the Allies arrived. Hitler shot himself and his mistress rather than face this enemy, and a week later Germany surrendered.

The reversal of the directions of attack and defense unleashed profound chaos in the cities and countryside. As the occupying Nazi troops withdrew, enraged mobs in Poland, Czechoslovakia, and Ukraine set upon neighbors who were of German descent or who spoke German, many of them people who had been born in the localities. Many thousands of women were raped and murdered; men and children were tortured, mutilated, and killed. Retreating soldiers were set upon and lynched, often being burned alive or mutilated before being shot. It is estimated that over two million Germans or people of German descent were killed in Eastern Europe by civilian mobs at the end of the war.

In Germany itself, hundreds of thousands of civilians who heard of the approach of the Soviet troops fled westward into liberated Denmark. There they were put into concentration camps. Though they were not intentionally harmed, they were at the bottom of the distribution list for scarce food and clothing. Tens of thousands died of malnutrition, dehydration, or disease—dysentery, malaria, measles, or pneumonia. Still, their fate was better than that of Germans who were arrested in Eastern Europe but not permitted to cross borders into Austria or Czechoslovakia. They were herded by the thousands into open fields and left to die of cold.

Japan and the Pacific

When Hitler died, the world was in the grip of a barrage of stunning and disorienting news, including the death of Franklin Roosevelt on April 12, 1945, after which Harry S. Truman became president. With Germany defeated, the Allies were eager to get out of the war business, but Britain, the USSR, and other Allies had also signed on as enemies of Japan, and Japan still had not surrendered. A British force drawn from the colonies, consisting of Nigerians, South Africans, and Indians, took up the fight to drive the Japanese out of Malaya and Indochina. Meanwhile, the United States concentrated on the battle in China, and on pursuing the Japanese fleets and dwindling air forces toward Okinawa and, if necessary, to Japan itself.

By the summer of 1945, Japan had not surrendered, although it had in effect been defeated throughout Asia and the Pacific, both by the forces of the Allies and by the forces of nationalist guerrillas in the territories they had occupied. The United States and its allies were impatient for the war to end. The Japanese, like everybody else in the Northern Hemisphere, had suffered in the war, and in the final stages had suffered terribly. Their economy was destroyed, the young men had been ground down by the brutal and now pointless war, and civilians had suffered horrific bombings. Still, American military leaders found little concrete evidence that there was much sentiment for surrender in Japan and found no evidence of an opposition movement that might topple the government or assassinate its leaders. General Douglas MacArthur estimated that a land invasion of Japan would result in tens of thousands of American casualties, with Japanese civilian casualties incalculable. And time was also a factor. While Japan delayed, the USSR could elect to take unilateral action in eastern Asia, perhaps seizing Sakhalin Island and mounting its own invasion of Japan from the north. Communist-inspired insurgents in Japan's occupied lands could claim their own victories, and seize control.

The United States had been working on the development of a devastating weapon for most of the war, and especially since 1943. There were rumors that the Germans were working on a similar weapon, but their progress evidently did not match that of the secret American project at Los Alamos, New Mexico. President Truman had been in office less than two weeks when, to his surprise, he was given a handwritten message from the war officials stating that within four months the United States would have at its disposal "the most terrible weapon ever known in human history."[1] It was the atomic bomb—a weapon that generated previously unimaginable power through the forced disintegration of atomic nuclei and the conversion of atomic-level matter into energy. The destruction would be accompanied by radiation of such a magnitude that it would itself be intensely and protractedly destructive of all living beings in the vicinity.

The development of the bomb was an unprecedented technical achievement, but there were many difficulties involved in deploying it, particularly the weight of the bomb. The report to Truman indicated that all the practical problems had been solved, or nearly so. Truman and his advisers wondered if this was the answer to the problem of getting Japan to surrender. The United States could use the new weapon to shock Japan into capitulation before the USSR could invade and claim credit for ending the war. At the same time, a demonstration of America's new power could inspire the USSR to be more constructive in its postwar dealings with the United States and American interests throughout the world.

On one ground or another—historians debate the exact reasons for the decision—Truman ordered the bombing in rapid succession of two Japanese provincial cities, Hiroshima and Nagasaki. The bombings took place on August 6 and 9, 1945, respectively. About 50,000 people in Hiroshima died instantly; in Nagasaki, about 30,000. Many were vaporized; others were destroyed in the resulting wind and fire disasters. And unlike previous weapons, this one kept on killing. By the end of the

---

[1]This widely quoted phrase is from Stimson's memo of April 25, 1945, and can be found in, among other sources, Stimson's diary, now at Yale University.

GLOBAL Technologies

Digital Communications

The Second World War not only marked the transition to a new structure of global power, but also a new structure of information processing and transmission. Concepts relating to information management from the 1930s were combined with innovations in mechanized calculation, rapidly producing not only the first computers but the first systems for programming the computers themselves.

From ancient philosophers in China, India and Greece in the eighteenth century, philosophers had realized that most arithmetic or physical conditions could be represented as a binary yes or no—by hand gestures, written symbols, flags up or down, or intermittent broadcast of sounds or smoke. In the eighteenth century Gottfried Leibniz suggested a standard scheme for representing numbers as binary strings of 0 and 1, which is essentially the system used for digitized communications today. Binary representation of letters was based upon a reading system for the blind which also had very ancient roots but was refined by Louis Braille in the nineteenth century. It was also influenced by the Morse code system of using combinations of binary signals to transmit letters over cable systems. And since binary tags can be used to describe virtually any physical state, the foundation for digital reproduction of music, art, film, and abstract design was laid in the early twentieth century.

Digital expressions all depend upon distinct markers of initiation and conclusion, so secret messages could easily be nested within longer messages appearing to have a different meaning. This was only one of many tactics used in the Second World War to pass coded messages by radio and by cable. Both sides in the war also made use of complex geared machines to transpose one letter or number into another; the recipient of the message would use the same gears to reverse the code and interpret it on their own machines. German diplomats and businessmen were the first to use such a machine, called Enigma, in the 1930s. Japanese diplomats were using a cypher that was similar in concept, called Purple.

After Britain declared war on Germany, Britain appropriated the earlier work of Polish researchers and

---

year, a total of 140,000 had died in Hiroshima, and 70,000 in Nagasaki had died of the long-term effects of burning and radiation poisoning. By August 15, the emperor had instructed the Japanese war leaders and the Japanese people to surrender.

Between the destructions of Hiroshima and Nagasaki, the USSR finally declared war on Japan and began its sweep into Manchuria. Anti-Japanese fighters from the Mongolian People's Republic (a Soviet client state since its founding in 1921) and from some units of the Chinese Communist armies coordinated with

set up a deciphering center at Bletchley Park, a large community of 12,000 whose existence was a total secret for thirty years after the war. Their work was impressive, but it was the capture of a German code book that allowed Bletchley Park to make its first break-through in deciphering Enigma. In North Africa, in the Atlantic, and most decisively in the D-Day Allied invasion of Normandy, intelligence gleaned by the Bletchley Park staff was indispens-able to the Allied victories. American researchers never captured a Purple machine from the Japanese and were able only to decode diplomatic messages. But in 1943, Americans achieved a mathe-matical breaking of the code, a factor in the rapid turn in war fortunes for Japan in that year. On the other hand, the American secret messages, supplied by Navajo speakers using coded language to translate reports and commands, were never broken by the other side.

Both the mathematical work and the mechanical innovations of Bletchley Park became influential in the develop-ment of post-war digitization. Wartime advances in informational abbreviation by Claude Shannon and Norbert Weiner were essential, but the develop-ment of programmable machines capa-ble of very rapid calculations was also needed. The ancestor of modern hardware was developed by the German Konrad Zuse in the late 1930s. Using binary numbers and instructions punched on strips of celluloid, Zuse's electronic rapid calculator, once adapted and deployed by both sides in the war, helped in the calculations necessary for the aiming of artillery and long-distance missiles, and maintaining supplies of fuel, food and medicine.

The final element in the creation of modern digitization was the creation of a method of instructing, or programming, computers. Alan Turing (a Bletchley alumnus) and the American mathema-tician John von Neumann were able to build on the insights of earlier logicians such as George Boole to give computers complex, editable instructions based on if-then or either-or statements, essen-tially allowing rapid computational machines to cross into the arena of independent, extended logical operation. To allow humans to avoid the cumber-some task of using binary code to instruct computers, mathematicians and computer engineers such as John Backus, Grace Hopper, John Kemeny and William Gates, among many others, worked on the design and execution of languages and mechanical compilers that have made digitized human intentions and perceptions interpretable by and through machines.

Soviet troops to surround the substantial Japanese forces. When the Japanese surrendered, the standard Soviet practice of transporting tens of thousands of pris-oners to work camps in Siberia and Central Asia followed. Japanese officers and the Manchukuo "emperor" Puyi were taken away to the Soviet Union for impris-onment and eventual trial for war crimes.

The Manchurian conquest by this amalgamated force also opened a chapter of global history that continues to challenge our understanding of this era and its relationship to our times. At Pingfan in Manchuria (headquarters of what is now notorious as Unit 731), records and material evidence were discovered that gave a detailed narrative of Japanese experimentation on prisoners of war, including Chinese, Okinawans, Koreans, Russians, Americans, Australians, and some Europeans. The horrors visited on the victims were inconceivable. They were frozen alive, vivisected, infected with fatal bacteria, and allowed to be fed upon by parasites while Japanese researchers coolly recorded the statistics. The results of the research were confiscated by the Allies and are known to have played a role in the development of many postwar health measures, including mass vaccination programs. But with very few exceptions, the perpetrators of scientific atrocities at Pingfan and related sites in Manchuria were never tried for war crimes as their military counterparts were. Indeed, the highest-ranking officers at the experimental complexes were given privileges, employment, and status after the war, and most of them lived comfortably until their natural deaths in the 1950s and 1960s.

As we will see, after the conclusion of the war, the victorious powers created various institutions to investigate and punish the atrocities perpetrated by the German and Japanese forces. The extent of these violations of humanity was not known until the end of the war, when the experimentation facilities in Manchuria, Poland, and Germany fell into Allied hands. It took some years for the leaders of the postwar era to comprehend the extent and the implications of the monstrous science of the Nazis and the Japanese militarists. Even in the late stages of the war, the daily horrors of displacement, starvation, mob violence, and exposure were enough to occupy the exhausted populations of Europe and Asia.

CONCLUSION

Although it is common to see the conclusion of the Second World War as the threshold for the bipolar global pattern of the following decades, it is more useful to see the bipolar world as beginning with the entry of the USSR and the United States into the wars against Germany and Japan. Their involvement in these wars was not the result of haphazard events that ensnared them in the fates of faraway places. Rather, it was the predictable outcome of their placement between the two centers—Europe/North Africa and East Asia. These two giants were drawn into the struggle with powers that, as of 1939–1940, had far fewer natural resources and far more brittle social and economic structures, and whose leaders had far less insight into the global dynamics that would follow the end of imperialism.

The USSR and the United States determined the outcome of the regional wars, escalated them to a new level of global war, and introduced the new technologies that would change both war and peace in the future. They emerged from the war acutely aware of the importance of oil and accustomed to long-range planning based on the location and the quantity of known oil reserves. They knew that the war—from the British resistance to German bombing, to the landing at Normandy, to the destructions of Hiroshima and Nagasaki—had been a war of science, and that those who were pushing science toward new horizons would control the condition of much of humanity.

They also decided the questions remaining from the end of the conflicts. Nations throughout the world, but especially those in Africa and Asia who were emerging from the final stage of imperialism and from the direct control of Germany or Japan, were to have their independence either ratified or undermined by these two powers. Certain nations, such as Germany, Vietnam, and Korea, were partitioned between the two great powers. Other countries, such as China, ended the war in a state of civil war of their own, and the United States and the USSR would attempt to manipulate those situations for their separate advantage. The standards of guilt and the methods of punishment to be imposed on newly identified "war criminals" in Europe and in Asia were to be negotiated and imposed by the United States and the USSR. And those countries would take great care to monopolize the technologies of communication, construction, production, and death that would keep them at the pinnacle of global power and make them the arbiters of new questions of national and international scale for decades.

For Further Reading

Paul Addison and Angus Calder, eds., *A Time to Kill: The Soldier's Experience of War in the West* (London: Pimlico, 1997). At present the single most comprehensive collection of personal narratives, encompassing both men and women soldiers of many national origins (limited to Europe, Russia, and North Africa).

John Bierman, *Righteous Gentile: The Story of Raoul Wallenberg, Missing Hero of the Holocaust* (New York: Penguin USA, revised edition 1996). Story of the Swedish diplomat who worked to rescue Jews and other Nazi victims and then disappeared into Soviet custody after the war.

Miriam Chaikin, *A Nightmare in History: The Holocaust 1933–1945* (New York: Clarion Books, 1987). A popular single volume that recounts the experiences of European Jews.

Iris Chang, *The Rape of Nanking: The Forgotten Holocaust of World War II* (New York: Basic Books, 1997). On the atrocities in Nanjing and elsewhere in central China.

Haruko Taya Cook and Theodore F. Cook, *Japan at War: An Oral History* (New York: The New Press, 1992). Based on interviews and oral reminiscences of Japanese soldiers and some civilians.

John W. Dower, *War Without Mercy: Race and Power in the Pacific War* (New York: Pantheon, 1986). The most revered history in English of the Second World War in the Pacific.

John Ellis, *World War II: A Statistical Survey* (New York: Facts on File, 1993). An invaluable reference that includes and compares varying estimates on casualties.

Hillel Levine, *In Search of Sugihara: The Elusive Japanese Diplomat Who Risked His Life to Rescue 10,000 Jews from the Holocaust* (New York: Free Press, 1996). The only study of the Japanese diplomat who worked to rescue intended Nazi victims in Hungary.

Andy Marino, *American Pimpernel* (London: Arrow, 2000). The story of Varian Fry, an American private citizen working to rescue Jewish writers and artists from Nazi-occupied territories.

The Oxford Companion to the Second World War (Oxford and New York: Oxford University Press, 2000). A very comprehensive illustrated reference source.

The Oxford Illustrated History of Modern War (Oxford and New York: Oxford University Press, 1998). Helps with understanding larger changes and comparing periods and places.

John Rabe [John E. Woods, trans.], *The Good Man of Shanghai: The Diaries of John Rabe* (New York: Alfred A. Knopf, 1998). The story of a German businessman attempting to stop Japanese atrocities in China, based on his diaries.

Ronald Takaki, *Double Victory: A Multicultural History of America in World War II* (New York: Little, Brown and Company, 2000). Covers complex experiences of African American and Asian American soldiers, including the dramatic stories of Japanese American intelligence officers in the Pacific War.

Peter Williams and David Wallace, *Unit 731: Japan's Secret Biological Warfare in The First World War I* (London: Hodder and Stoughton, 1989). Studies of war atrocities by Japanese troops and scientists in Manchuria.

Yoshimi Yoshiaki, [Suzanne O'Brien, trans.], *Comfort Women: Sexual Slavery in the Japanese Military During World War II* (New York: Columbia University Press, 2002). The plight of Asian women from many nations enslaved to Japan's army as "comfort women."

Related Websites

BBC: Hitler's Invasion of Russia in World War Two
http://www.bbc.co.uk/history/worldwars/wwtwo/hitler_russia_invasion_01.shtml
China – World War 2 on History
http://www.history.co.uk/explore-history/ww2/china.html
China Defensive 1942–1945
http://www.history.army.mil/brochures/72-38/72-38.htm
Jone Johnson Lewis, "Women and World War II"
http://womenshistory.about.com/od/warwwii/a/overview.htm
The Legacy Project: Echoes of Guernica
http://www.legacy-project.org/index.php?page=exhibitions
U.S. Holocaust Memorial Museum
http://www.ushmm.org/education/foreducators
Virtual Tour of the Maginot Line
http://www.maginot-line.com/
WGBH American Experience: Victory in the Pacific
http://www.pbs.org/wgbh/americanexperience/films/pacific/
The First World War I in the Pacific
http://www.ushmm.org/wlc/en/article.php?ModuleId=10005155
The First World War I Maps
http://www.lib.utexas.edu/maps/historical/history_ww2.html

PART III

Rise and Fall of the Bipolar Order, 1946–1981

CHAPTER 9

From the United Nations to a Bipolar World, 1945–1953

Photographs of the Japanese surrender on September 2, 1945, seemed to say it all. The scene was the deck of the U.S.S. *Missouri,* at anchor in Tokyo Bay. In one picture, a small band of formally clad Japanese diplomats and soldiers stand ready to wield their pens in the shadow of the battleship's enormous 16-inch guns. Others show them surrounded by hundreds of U.S. sailors and the assembled representatives of the United States and its allies. The Japanese, dazed and forlorn, are a striking contrast to the casual attire and easy command of Douglas MacArthur, the American general designated to receive the surrender. Still other photos focus on gaunt spectators in khaki, Allied officers just freed from Japanese prison camps. Off camera, an armada of hundreds of Allied ships surrounded the *Missouri;* overhead droned a thousand B-29 bombers and five hundred fighter aircraft. Tokyo Bay overflowed with U.S. power.

Three months earlier, the USSR, partner of the United States, had celebrated the victory over Germany in Moscow's Red Square. Tens of thousands of troops paraded past two million spectators who had come out despite a cold, pouring rain. The troops carried the captured banners of more than two hundred German units, including the personal banner of Adolf Hitler. Atop Lenin's Mausoleum stood Josef Stalin and the Soviet Committee of Defense. As the troops marched past, they threw the German banners in a great pile before the socialist heroes, the living Stalin and the long-dead Lenin.

The images of the two events traveled far and wide, by still photo and newsreel. They announced victories, but they also said something more. Here were two colossal states—one the master of much of Eurasia, the other with dominion over the seas—that had the power to finish what others had started. In 1835, the

Hulton Archive/Getty Images

General Douglas MacArthur (foreground, left) observes a Japanese general signing the surrender document aboard the USS *Missouri* in Tokyo Bay, September 2, 1945. The surrender provided for the disarmament of Japanese forces and the occupation of Japan's home islands by U.S. troops, an occupation that would continue until 1952.

French historian Alexis de Tocqueville had predicted that the United States and Russia would someday dominate the globe. That day, it seemed, had arrived.

World War II created enormous human suffering and need, but it also created great opportunities. The United States possessed industrial leadership, unprecedented wealth, and command of the seas and the air. The Soviet Union, much poorer and facing a far greater task of rebuilding, nevertheless had powerful armies and influence among Communist parties throughout the world. Partners in war, the two states had sharply contrasting political and economic systems and different visions of the future. But they also had important common interests—a desire for greater international stability, a commitment to preventing either Germany or Japan from again becoming a military threat, and a common distaste for European imperialism. In 1945, neither American nor Soviet leaders wished for confrontation. Although wary of one another, they nevertheless hoped that their wartime alliance might extend into the peace. If the United States and the USSR could cooperate, they had the power to shape a more open and peaceful world.

Such a world did not emerge. Instead, with stunning swiftness, a new bipolar political system took shape. All but complete by 1950, much of the globe was divided into hostile camps by economic and political contradictions that seemed immutable: capitalism versus communism, and pluralistic democracy versus totalitarian rule. This chapter examines how the relations between these one-time allies deteriorated, how the two great powers sought to remake those parts of the world that were under their influence, and how their ambitions intersected with those of other peoples who were charting their own futures.

The World in Motion

The war had set millions of people in motion, and peace did not bring rest. Some moved voluntarily, in search of better jobs; in the United States, for example, defense spending had stimulated rapid growth along the west coast and in parts of the south. More often, however, the movements were involuntary. In Asia, more than four million Japanese soldiers and civilians were repatriated to Japan from Korea, Formosa, and other parts of Japan's former empire. Some had served short stints in occupying armies and were glad to return home. Others were giving up jobs and homes they had occupied for years or, in the case of Korea, even for decades. Many Japanese soldiers and civilians in China were less fortunate still. Tens of thousands simply disappeared into prison camps in Soviet-occupied Manchuria or died at the hands of Chinese lynch mobs.

In Europe, Germans suffered similar fates. Approximately seventeen million fled or were ejected from Poland, Czechoslovakia, and Hungary. Most migrated westward to join the hungry and homeless in Germany's bombed-out cities where survival often depended on the charity of the Allied occupiers. Meanwhile, further to the east, Soviet authorities ruthlessly uprooted entire villages and towns in regions that had been Russian before World War I but had been independent or German-occupied since. Suspicious that the sympathies of the inhabitants of these areas might reside elsewhere, the Soviet government concluded that forced repatriation would both ease the process of reintegrating these lands into Soviet Russia and provide much-needed labor for new farms and industries in the Urals and Siberia. At the same time, Russian nationals thought to be more reliable were encouraged to move west to occupy farms and apartments in the Ukraine, eastern Poland, and the Baltic states. Within a year of the end of the fighting, the ethnic map of Eastern Europe was transformed.

These massive relocations were just part of a more general turmoil. Prisoners of war were being repatriated to all the former belligerents. Hundreds of thousands of laborers were making their way home: French and Belgians who had been forced to work in German factories; Koreans who had been impressed into service in Japan as laborers and prostitutes; and Chinese who had been dragooned into labor in the industries of Japanese-occupied Manchuria. Families took to the road to find more plentiful food. In Germany and Poland, Japan and China, parents searched for lost children and children for missing parents. Minority groups were vulnerable in all of the countries of Eastern Europe and sought protection by crossing borders to be among others like themselves.

The surviving Jews of Europe had no European homeland. Released from concentration camps and hiding places, they found their villages occupied by strangers, their possessions looted, and their families destroyed. Perhaps a million found passage to Palestine, still under British mandate, where Zionists sought to build a Jewish state in the face of British obstruction.

The turmoil led to famine. Ration cards distributed by the Allies in Germany during the winter of 1945–1946 entitled adults to less than a thousand calories a day, well below subsistence levels, while in Japan only last-minute shipments of grain from the United States averted mass starvation. Famine, in turn, was an open invitation to diseases. Rickets and other diseases of nutritional deficiency, long common in China, became widespread in Japan and Europe. Death rates from tuberculosis went up across Eurasia. Smallpox, seldom seen in Western Europe for a century, made a brief return, prompting emergency vaccination efforts. Wherever armies traveled, gonorrhea and syphilis followed.

Abysmal sanitary conditions were as dangerous to public health as starvation diets. Bombing had destroyed municipal sewer and water systems along with

Brown Brothers

A Berlin street scene, 1945. Bombing raids devastated many of the cities of Europe and Japan during World War II, leaving massive challenges of reconstruction. Food, water, and public health were atop the agenda; housing would be a problem for years to come.

GLOBAL Technologies

Antibiotics

The discovery of penicillin is a classic illustration of the maxim that chance favors the prepared mind. In the summer of 1928, Alexander Fleming, a Scottish bacteriologist working at St. Mary's Hospital in London, noticed an oddity while studying staph bacteria. A mold had accidentally contaminated one of the nutrient-rich agar plates upon which he was growing bacteria, and all around the mold the bacteria had died, as if by the action of a powerful antiseptic. Antiseptics were Fleming's main interest; he had already attained some notoriety for discovering that bodily secretions such as saliva and mucus contain an antibacterial substance, lysozyme. So Fleming took note of what others might have dismissed as a fluke. He quickly cultured more of the mold (*Penicillium notatum*) and demonstrated that it produced small quantities of a substance, which he called penicillin, that was lethal to many types of bacteria. Neither Fleming nor others followed up on the discovery, however, perhaps because Fleming had conceived of penicillin as a local antiseptic rather than as an agent that might treat systemic infections.

A decade later, in 1939, scientists at Oxford picked up where Fleming had left off. The group, led by an Australian, Howard Florey, and a Jewish refugee from Hitler's Germany, Ernst Chain, isolated a sufficient quantity of penicillin to conduct clinical tests. In 1941, they issued their report: penicillin had powerful effects on patients suffering from deadly staph infections and

---

hundreds of thousands of homes. Governments that had dissolved or were insolvent could hardly organize prompt repairs. Occupation armies, intent on protecting their own troops as well as maintaining public order, could provide some help, but hardly enough to prevent recurrent outbreaks of the diseases of filth such as typhus and dysentery.

The breakdown of systems built up over generations left health experts fearful that new epidemics might sweep the globe, as influenza had in 1918–1919. Public health, therefore, became one of the first priorities of international organizations, from the new United Nations to the ancient Catholic Church. New drugs and insecticides played a role in controlling infections and the insects that transmitted disease. Allied occupation forces and public health agencies dusted millions of soldiers and civilians with DDT, a powerful insecticide that had been discovered in Switzerland before the war. Effective against both the lice that carried typhus and mosquitoes that spread malaria, DDT was inexpensive and had few discernible effects on human health. Even more exciting was a new drug that was capable of rescuing patients on the verge of death from raging bacterial infections: penicillin. Still in short supply after the Allied victory, it joined nylon

promised to cure other diseases as well. Research on how to produce large quantities of the new drug then shifted to the United States, where resources were plentiful and laboratories had experience in culturing molds on an industrial scale. Introduced for use among troops in 1942, penicillin quickly eclipsed earlier remedies in treating a broad range of bacterial infections.

Even as clinicians were learning the powerful effects of penicillin, a Russian-born bacteriologist, Selman Waksman, working at Rutgers University was finding other microbes that produced antibacterial substances in the soil. Among these was a species that produced a substance, "streptomycin," that proved effective against some bacteria immune to penicillin, including the bacteria responsible for tuberculosis. During the next decade dozens of additional antibiotics were identified and produced, many from soil microbes and

others from laboratory synthesis. The nearly miraculous power of antibiotics, and their falling prices, prompted their wide use for preventive as well as therapeutic purposes. By the mid-1950s, antibiotics were being added to animal feed and given routinely to millions of patients suffering from nothing more than common colds.

Indiscriminate use had unintended consequences. Many bacteria had the capacity to evolve resistance to these miracle drugs after repeated exposure. And so, instead of savoring a decisive triumph, medicine found itself in an arms race with microbes, with scientists constantly seeking new antibiotics to supplement those that were losing their edge. Ironically, the evolutionary forces that had endowed some microbes with the power to produce antibiotics came to undermine the therapeutic revolution that had begun with penicillin and streptomycin.

---

stockings, cigarettes, and whiskey as a favorite of smugglers and black marketeers in Europe's desolated cities.

Valuable as the new substances were in controlling disease, the most important remedies were more basic: vaccination, the reconstruction of water and sewage systems, and the distribution of food to the hungry and coal to the cold. The work was carried out by private and public agencies, armies of occupation and local governments, physicians and laborers. Their collaborative efforts not only checked disease in many parts of Europe and in Japan but also helped overcome distrust between the victors and the vanquished. Healing had begun.

Even as millions struggled for existence, birth rates began to rise, first in the United States, which saw a 20 percent increase between 1945 and 1946, and then in Europe and Japan. This baby boom, an expression of the private yearnings of millions for the intimacy and satisfactions of family life, had far-reaching social consequences. Small children require care, and many women who had entered the labor force during the war gave up their jobs to tend their families. Bumper crops of babies led millions to seek roomier homes and apartments, thus stimulating housing construction in areas where money was available, such as North

America, and making housing a critical political issue where it was scant, including most of Europe.

Later, as toddlers reached school age, teacher training and classroom construction became high priorities. An insatiable demand for toys, clothing, and other products for children fed the economic revival of Japan, where home workshops and factories catered to the tastes of Western consumers. Still later, as the baby boomers reached young adulthood, universities expanded to meet the swelling demand for higher education; industries discovered huge new markets for jeans and records, stereo systems and sports cars; and governments struggled to contain the explosive idealism of youth. Like a great tide, the demographic bulge could lift many boats, but it also tested their moorings.

In 1945, however, few observers anticipated a baby boom, and fewer still were anticipating its consequences. Reconstruction, not reproduction, dominated the headlines. The task was not simply to rebuild cities and rail lines but to reconstruct the economic and political systems that had failed so badly. World War I, the Great Depression, and World War II were catastrophes that showed how inadequate those systems were to control the passions, wants, and tools of modern times.

Memories of Versailles and Plans for a Postwar World

When confronted with large and complex tasks, human beings look to the past for ideas and lessons. We draw on experience when we build bridges, plan business enterprises, write laws, make wars, and negotiate peace. As World War II moved toward an end, the leaders of the Allies naturally looked for precedents to guide the reconstruction of international politics and trade.

The Political Settlement

The precedent that was nearest at hand was Versailles and the other treaties ending World War I. Allied leaders viewed this settlement as a model of the errors to be avoided. The peacemakers of 1919 had not sufficiently impressed Germany with the fact of its defeat, nor had they rooted out the militaristic tendencies in German society. They had created a League of Nations to promote world peace, but without giving it the authority to accomplish that goal. They had excluded an important power, the Soviet Union, from the settlement and quarreled among themselves. And the economic lynchpin of the Allied coalition, the United States, had turned its back on the peace treaty that it had helped to shape. Nor had the victors in World War I given serious attention to rebuilding international trade. Focusing on reparations and debts, they had failed to devise new mechanisms to manage such critical issues as tariffs and the interconvertibility of world currencies. The leaders of the Grand Alliance agreed that these mistakes had inadvertently created instability that had led to a depression, the growth of fascism and militarism, and renewed global warfare.

Each of the leaders of the Grand Alliance appears to have been committed to building a durable peace. Britain and the Soviet Union had suffered tremendous losses in the war and faced formidable problems of recovery. The loss of life in Britain had been smaller than that in World War I but was large by any other measure: a quarter-million dead soldiers. The Germans had punished British cities with bombs and torpedoed hundreds of British merchant ships. The British people had been rationed and taxed to the point where, as soon as Germany was defeated, they voted Churchill's Conservative Party out of control of government. Two wars and a depression had turned Britain into a debtor nation. Workers were desperate for better food, more coal, better housing and medical care, and higher wages; they vented their dissatisfaction through widespread strikes. Many wealthy Britons had seen their estates broken up to pay taxes. British industries were falling behind their American rivals in technology; the British Empire was in disarray.

Soviet losses had been even greater. German armies had devastated European Russia, destroying cities, factories, mines, railroads, and farms. At least twenty million Soviet citizens had lost their lives; millions more were disabled. Soviet citizens lacked the opportunity to express their dissatisfaction publicly but yearned for more food, better housing, and an end to long working hours and shortages of basic consumer products. Stalin's grip on power was secure; so too was his understanding of Soviet Russia's need for a breather to recover from its extraordinary exertions.

The United States alone emerged from the war stronger than at the beginning. Its casualties had been smaller than Britain's, and they had been spread over a population three times as large. Its cities had been untouched by the fighting. War orders had meant jobs for the unemployed and growth for industry. Output of goods and services had doubled between 1939 and 1945. The state had taken on a massive amount of debt, but mostly in the form of war bonds sold to its own citizens. As in England, there was dissatisfaction with rationing and a demand for new housing, consumer goods, and higher wages. But the United States had far greater resources with which to satisfy those desires.

Whereas Britain and the Soviet Union wanted peace to rebuild, the United States wanted peace to enjoy. Its citizens were eager to welcome home the men and women who had gone overseas, rid themselves of ration coupons, and once again have the freedom to satisfy deferred wants. U.S. firms wanted to get back to business, building cars instead of tanks and selling products overseas as well as at home. The country's political leaders wanted to find a way to avoid another depression or another war. Most agreed that this would demand engagement in global politics rather than isolation.

As the armies fought, the Allies held a series of conferences at which they outlined the contours of a postwar settlement. They shared a common concern with the control of their main adversaries, Germany and Japan, and a common desire to prevent future wars. But each Allied nation also had national interests to protect. The challenge was to weave a peace that would satisfy those interests while creating lasting stability.

There was reason for optimism. Churchill, Roosevelt, and Stalin had worked together effectively during the war, despite strong differences in ideology, values, and personalities. More important, before World War II, Britain, the United States, and the Soviet Union had focused their main geopolitical ambitions on different parts of the world. Britain had given first priority to its empire and to Western Europe. Soviet Russia had concerned itself primarily with the security of its borders, especially in volatile Eastern Europe. The United States had traditionally held itself aloof from European affairs and concentrated on the Western Hemisphere and the oceans that flanked it. While the Big Three understood that the collapse of Germany and Japan would create new and overlapping security interests, especially in Europe and China, they also had reason to believe that their differences could be managed through compromise.

The most famous of these wartime conferences, held in the Crimean city of Yalta in February 1945, reinforced this confidence. There the Big Three approved a framework for administering occupied territories, pending a more comprehensive settlement, and completed plans for the first meeting of a new United Nations Organization, to be held later that year in San Francisco. Their agreements recognized the realities that were emerging on the ground. Anglo-American forces would hold much of Europe west of Germany's Elbe River; Soviet armies would occupy most to the east. Each of the Allies would assume primary responsibility for order and the restoration of civilian governments in the regions under its control. Germany itself would be divided into occupation zones, with each of the victors administering a slice; a council of the Allies would make decisions affecting the entire nation. Berlin, which was deep in the Soviet sector, would also be partitioned into zones but would be governed jointly. Further decisions about Germany's future would await a denazification of the nation. The Allied governments were divided, among themselves and internally, over whether Germany should ever again be reunited, but they all harbored deep concerns about Germany's proven capacity for war making. They believed it was essential to purge those responsible for the war from authority, not only in government but in other institutions as well. International courts would try those suspected of the most egregious conduct.

These agreements were generally satisfactory to each of the wartime partners. Stalin achieved recognition of what his armies were already winning: control of Eastern Europe. The Soviet frontier would be moved westward, roughly to the line that had been Russia's border before World War I. The Baltic states of Lithuania, Latvia, and Estonia would lose their independence, a large slice of prewar Poland would become Soviet territory, and other states along the Soviet border would lose smaller areas to Moscow. Nations that had been victims of Germany would be compensated for these territorial losses. Thus, while Poland would lose its easternmost province to the USSR, it would acquire neighboring districts of Germany, including much of East Prussia, Pomerania, and Silesia.

Churchill and Roosevelt were also satisfied with the outcome of these meetings. The North Sea and Suez Canal would again be secure for Britain. Britain and the United States together would supervise Italy, and England would assume primary responsibility for maintaining order in Greece, Crete, and the Middle East. Roosevelt and Churchill won assurances from Stalin that the new governments of Eastern Europe, organized under Soviet auspices, would incorporate non-Communist groups that had established governments in exile in London during the war and would hold free elections at the earliest practicable date.

At least as important, they secured from Stalin a promise to enter the war against Japan within three months of the cessation of fighting in Europe. This was especially welcome to the United States, which was carrying the main burden in the Pacific. A Russian attack on Manchuria would tie down a large Japanese army that could otherwise complicate American plans for an invasion of Japan's home islands. In return for Soviet entry into the war, Stalin was promised a restoration of imperial Russia's former rights in Manchuria and control of Japan's northernmost islands, the Kuriles and Sakhalin (half of which was already Soviet territory). But the Allies also agreed that a postwar settlement in the Pacific would be largely a matter for the Americans and British to arrange, with the Americans assuming responsibility for the occupation of Japan and the British for accepting surrenders from Japanese forces in Southeast Asia.

The collegial relations among the Allies were reflected in the plans they made for a United Nations Organization. At the very least, the UN would be a vehicle for extending the Grand Alliance into the postwar era. Roosevelt, who nursed some of the idealism of his predecessor, Woodrow Wilson, hoped for more—that it would be a means of promoting international law and a first step toward the formation of a true world government. Like most governments, it would have legislative, executive, and judicial branches. The legislative part consisted of a General Assembly, in which all member states would have a vote. A smaller Security Council, with five permanent members (China, France, Britain, the United States, and the USSR) and several temporary members elected by the General Assembly, would respond to immediate threats to world peace and oversee the operations of an executive, the secretary general, who was charged with administering a civil service and a peacekeeping force. An International Court of Justice would adjudicate disputes between member states. The United Nations would also inherit many of the functions of the old League of Nations, including the distribution of trusteeships over the territories that had been League mandates, such as Palestine, and the coordination of international efforts to improve public health, education, and economic and cultural development.

Unlike the old League of Nations, the new UN would have the authority to undertake military action in the defense of peace, although only with the unanimous consent of the victorious powers. At Soviet insistence, the UN's charter granted the permanent members of the Security Council veto power over any of its resolutions, and peacekeeping required such a resolution. In practice, this meant that the UN could be a powerful agency for the control of international disputes only so long as China, France, Britain, the United States, and the Soviet Union agreed to make it so.

The Economic Settlement

While Churchill, Roosevelt, and Stalin concentrated on politics, treasury officials and economists attended to the more technical but nonetheless crucial issue of postwar economic planning. Here the United States took the lead, with policies that flowed from U.S. assumptions about the war's causes. American officials, by and large, believed that Europe had suffered a second great war because the victors in World War I had shortsightedly imposed an unbearable burden of reparations on Germany and had failed to make realistic plans regarding the huge debts that Britain and France owed the United States. The burden of debt had disrupted international trade and banking and had triggered the Great Depression. That economic disaster, in turn, created the conditions under which Japanese militarists and German Nazis could seize power.

This analysis, which owed much to the writings of the British economist John Maynard Keynes, suggested that a more durable political settlement would have to rest on sound economic planning. Consequently, one of the first international conferences devoted to planning for peace was a meeting among treasury officials and economists. It convened in Bretton Woods, New Hampshire, just after the Normandy landings in 1944. The meeting, dominated by U.S. officials, produced a new framework for international trade that was to prevail for decades. Participants, including forty-four Allied nations, agreed to make the U.S. dollar the medium for settling international accounts. Other nations agreed to fix the value of their currencies to the dollar, meaning that they would buy dollars if their currencies were losing purchasing value and sell them if their currencies were gaining value. The effect would be to impose discipline on central banks by making it more difficult to finance trade deficits by deflating the value of their currencies, as had often been done during the depression. In turn, the United States agreed to maintain the value of the dollar by agreeing to purchase dollars with gold on demand at a fixed rate of one ounce for $35. The architects of the system hoped that these fixed exchange rates would foster confidence among traders and investors and thereby encourage commerce. Not incidentally, they would also pry open new foreign markets to American business, especially in regions where the British pound sterling had reigned supreme. To further promote stability, the Bretton Woods agreements created an International Monetary Fund (IMF) and an International Bank for Reconstruction and Development. The former would lend dollars to member nations that faced deficits in their balance of payments. The latter, which became the nucleus of the World Bank, would promote economic growth by financing roads, docks, power plants, and other infrastructure projects. Both would be governed by those countries that contributed funds to them, with contributors enjoying influence proportional to their investment—an arrangement that gave the United States effective control of both institutions. In

1947, under U.S. prodding, another element was added to this framework, the General Agreement on Tariffs and Trade (GATT), which provided a venue in which barriers to international trade could be removed through collective effort. In 1995, this organization's ungainly name was simplified to the World Trade Organization.

American officials hoped that these new institutions would not only promote postwar reconstruction but also inoculate the world against the economic ills of the interwar years: trade wars, currency crises, high tariffs, and breakdowns in international commerce. The outcome could be beneficial to all, but perhaps most especially to the United States. American firms, with their efficiencies of scale, would thrive in a world without trade barriers. U.S. banks could find safe and lucrative investment opportunities abroad. Perhaps most important, free trade would foster peace and prosperity. Trade would breed interdependence, economic growth would expand the middle class, wealth would foster investment in education and social welfare, and prosperity would ultimately strengthen democratic political institutions. The outcome would be a world with little appetite for war or revolution.

From Allies to Adversaries

Despite the optimism of 1945, the Grand Alliance did not survive the war. Historians differ as to why. Some emphasize the clash of ideologies, seeing a breakdown of relations as inevitable when Western capitalism and Soviet communism came into contact. Others stress the clash of national interests: The victors quite predictably came into conflict as they filled the power voids left by the defeat of Germany and Japan. In both groups, there are schools of thought that highlight the aggressiveness of one side or the other: A capitalism that was hostile to communism sought to surround, contain, and choke the Soviet Union; or a communism that was hostile to capitalism expanded relentlessly to achieve the victory predicted by Marx and Lenin. Alternatively, Britain and the United States threatened Soviet security by pushing too hard for influence in Eastern Europe. Or the Soviets precipitated the Cold War by building an empire in Eastern Europe and threatening to extend it westward. These interpretations appeared in the late 1940s and 1950s and became part of the fabric of Cold War debate.

The collapse of the Soviet Union in 1989 did not end this contention, but it opened new sources of information to historical inquiry and sapped much of the political fervor of earlier times. Today historians generally agree that political factors generated the Cold War, while recognizing that ideological commitments often intensified the conflicts and eventually came to dominate public understanding of events. Stalin was a Marxist, but the interests of the state and the party often coincided. When they did not, Stalin consistently adopted policies that served the nation rather than ideology. Western leaders such as Churchill,

FDR, and Truman, while appalled by the Soviet Union's Communist system and alarmed at the prospect that Stalin might exploit Communist parties around the world to advance Soviet interests, were much more concerned with limiting the advance of Soviet power than in leading a crusade to eradicate Marxist ideas and politics. Only gradually did Western leaders, especially those in the United States, become convinced that all Communists were tools of the Soviet Union and implacable enemies of the free world. Ironically, this confusion of Soviet and Communist interests grew more common in the West just as the Communist movement itself began to show signs of deep division. The conflation of Soviet expansion and Marxist-inspired politics led to some of the worst excesses of the Cold War.

Increasingly, historians have come to view the Cold War as avoidable rather than inevitable. And they have also come to appreciate how often Soviet and American policy became captive to the interests of allies and client states. Despite their formidable resources, neither superpower could fully control its confederates, and both more than once found themselves drawn into a local conflict that escalated into an international crisis, not because they desired confrontation but because their clients did.

The Grand Alliance: Wartime Doubts and Postwar Insecurities

As the war in Europe ended, the United States, Britain, and the Soviet Union could draw some hope for the future from their cooperation in the recent past. In 1943 Stalin, in a concession to his allies, had disbanded the Comintern, the international organization promoting world revolution. The United States had supplied Soviet armies with billions of dollars worth of weapons and supplies. Britain had sacrificed lives and ships in delivering those supplies to Russian ports. And the leaders of the three allies had earned one another's respect through their wartime dealings.

Yet the past also provided grounds for suspicion. The Soviets recalled Western support for White Russian armies during the civil war of 1917–1920 and resented Western efforts to isolate the Soviet Union during the interwar years. Repeated postponements of the Anglo-American invasion of France had led Stalin to suspect that his allies wished to see Germany and Russia bleed each other dry. Western leaders were well aware of Soviet efforts to promote revolution in Europe following World War I and of the Marxist ideologues' announced aim of overthrowing capitalism around the world. They recalled the 1939 nonaggression pact between Moscow and Berlin with bitterness and found their ally's obsession with secrecy disquieting.

The victors put aside many of their suspicions during the heady days of 1945, but new tensions soon arose as the agreements reached at wartime conferences were put into effect. To the West, it seemed that Stalin was not only securing Soviet frontiers but also seeking every opportunity to increase Soviet influence. In Poland, Stalin maintained that it was impossible to satisfy both the Soviet desire for a secure border and the British and American insistence that the country have a government that was representative of its people's wishes. To the south, the Soviet Union issued a clumsy ultimatum to Turkey in 1946, threatening severe consequences should the Turks not share control of the Dardanelles with Moscow. Stalin backed down when faced with Anglo-American opposition, but the attempt invited the British and Americans to interpret a Communist revolt against a British-backed government in Greece as another Soviet effort to reach the Mediterranean. Further east, a Soviet army that had occupied northern Iran during the war delayed its departure past a date agreed upon by the Allies, provoking a sharp exchange of words at the UN. These conflicts—squabbles, really—provoked anxiety about Soviet intentions.

The Soviets, for their part, were disappointed by U.S. reluctance to discuss reconstruction loans and angered by what they saw as Anglo-American efforts to renew the diplomatic isolation of the Soviet Union. In the background, but never forgotten, was the atomic bomb. Britain and the United States had collaborated closely in developing the weapon, but revealed nothing about the project to the Soviets until July 1945, weeks before the atomic bombing of Japan. Spies had given Stalin what diplomats did not: regular reports on his allies' progress. When the power of the weapon was demonstrated at Hiroshima, the Soviets were ready to launch a crash program to build their own atomic weapons. Even so, the Soviets did not test a bomb until 1949. In the meantime, U.S. leaders held an ace that the Soviets did not have, and this asymmetry only intensified Soviet suspicions of the West.

The Problem of Germany

Above all, Germany was a point of contention between the Soviets and the West. Germany's importance was obvious. Unified and rearmed, it could pose a mortal threat to the Soviet Union, and it was the only state on the European continent that could possibly do so. Should it ally itself with the USSR, it would be no less dangerous to Anglo-American interests because such an alliance would dominate Eurasia. In 1945, it was unclear whether a reunited and independent Germany would look east or west. The idea of dividing Germany pleased the French, who, as one journalist quipped, loved Germany so much that they wanted two of them. Other Allied governments made reunification their official policy, but none had a formula to achieve the goal. Many Germans wondered if their occupiers truly wished to do so.

Meanwhile, the Allies governed Germany through the awkward medium of zones and a Council of the Allies. Where the four occupiers could agree, action was swift. It was in the interest of all of the victors to make public examples of the leaders of the Third Reich, for example. Hence, they cooperated in trying high-ranking Nazis for crimes against humanity, most famously at Nuremberg in 1945 and early 1946. But cooperation soon broke down over economic and political issues. The Soviet Union, citing a wartime promise of reparations, stripped eastern Germany of industrial equipment, livestock, and civilian goods. At the same time, the Soviets encouraged millions of homeless Germans, displaced from Poland,

Czechoslovakia, and eastern Germany itself, to migrate west, thereby exacerbating the shortages of food, housing, and fuel in the Western zones.

The Western powers, faced with the task of feeding the swelling population of their sectors, came to believe that the economic recovery of Germany would, in the long run, better serve both German and Allied interests. From their perspective, the Soviets were seeking to satisfy their demands for reparations unilaterally and to extort political concessions by promoting instability in western Germany. From the Soviet perspective, the Western powers were seeking to rebuild a former enemy before aiding a partner.

Toward Cold War

Tensions over these and other issues grew as it became clear that the Soviets had no intention of allowing free elections in Poland or moderating their demands for German reparations, and as the United States and Britain took firmer measures to limit what they were coming to see as Soviet expansionism. In Germany, the United States and Britain canceled reparations payments to the Soviets and amalgamated their zones of control into a single economic entity, "Bizonia." To the south, they increased their support for Turkey and funneled assistance to the government of Greece, embroiled in a war with Communist guerrillas. At the same time, the United States began to aid centrist political parties in France and Italy, where Communists were making alarming gains at the ballot box. In 1947 George Kennan, the influential American diplomat, found a word to describe the new policy: *containment*. The West, he argued, faced a determined adversary in Moscow that was intent on extending its power; it would have to respond vigorously to Soviet probes whenever they threatened vital interests.

It is conceivable that even as late as the beginning of 1947, solutions to many of the issues separating the United States and the Soviet Union could have been found. But confrontation was often easier than compromise. Soviet leaders had routinely portrayed the Soviet Union as a victim of encirclement. Stalin and his aides expected capitalist intrigue and used it, real and imagined, as a ready explanation both for the economic shortcomings of the Soviet system and the rigid discipline that the Communist Party imposed on political life.

Western leaders understood that Stalin sometimes used international tension to buttress his hold on power, but Moscow's rapaciousness in Eastern Europe, its clumsy diplomacy, and its renewed promotion of international Communism made it easy to suspect more: that by fusing Russian imperialistic ambitions to the universalistic doctrine of Marxism, the Soviets had developed ambitions that were comprehensive and global, not limited and local.

Recently opened Soviet archives make it clear that Stalin's strategy was far more cautious. He was focused on regaining the territories and spheres of influence that had been lost by Russia at Brest-Litovsk and on ensuring that Germany would not again strike eastward. World revolution would have to wait until the Soviet Union was much stronger and the West much weaker than in 1945. But to Western observers in the months after World War II, the Kremlin was inscrutable, "a mystery wrapped in an enigma," in Churchill's phrase.[1] And the experience of the past decade seemed to teach that ruthless leaders of powerful nations had best be treated firmly.

Stalin was not Hitler, but the American leader who was best prepared to appreciate the differences was no longer in the White House. Franklin D. Roosevelt had felt confident of his ability to work with Stalin and may well have had the agility and authority to do so. His successor, Harry S. Truman, lacked both. Truman came to the presidency in April 1945 with meager experience in foreign affairs and a tendency to think in terms of black and white rather than shades of gray. The Soviets, Truman soon came to believe, were bullies that needed to be stood up to. Otherwise, Stalin might, like Hitler, consume his neighbors, bite by bite.

The American intention of standing up to the Soviets became unmistakable in 1947. Great Britain, burdened by debt and a balance of payments crisis, was withdrawing as fast as it could from regions where it had expensive commitments. The eastern Mediterranean was one such area. Traditionally, Britain had made exclusion of Russia from the Mediterranean a lynchpin of British policy because it was on Britain's line of supply to India and Asia. But by 1947 Britain's Asian empire was fast dissolving, as were British military and economic capacities. The Big Three of World War II had become a Big Two. In recognition of its reduced circumstances, Britain invited the United States to assume its role in the Aegean—a role that Truman accepted eagerly. In March, Truman asked Congress to support the Greek and Turkish governments and announced that the United States would assist "free peoples who are resisting attempted subjugation by armed minorities or outside pressure."[2] This broad policy, soon dubbed the Truman Doctrine, gave public expression to what had become private conviction: An expansionist Soviet empire would have to be contained by vigorous American efforts.

The Truman Doctrine embodied several ironies. Neither the Turkish nor the Greek government was a product of free elections, and the Greek military was only slightly less brutal in its methods than were the rebels it sought to defeat. Those rebels themselves, we now know, owed far less to Stalin than to Tito, the Communist partisan who had assumed control of Yugoslavia after World War II. Indeed, Tito's support of the Greek Communists violated Stalin's own more cautious policy and was one source of the friction that would ultimately lead to a public break between the two Communist leaders. To American eyes, however, Tito was little more than a front man for the Soviets. In a final irony, by publicly associating the Soviets and the Greek Communist Party, Truman had

---

[1]Winston S. Churchill, "The First Month of War," Broadcast, London, October 1, 1939, in Robert Rhodes James, ed., *Winston S. Churchill: His Complete Speeches, 1897–1963*, vol. 6 (New York and London: Chelsea House, 1974), p. 6161.

[2]Harry S. Truman, "Address Before a Joint Session of the Senate and the House of Representatives," March 12, 1947, in Dennis Merrill, ed., *Documentary History of the Truman Presidency*, vol. 8 (Bethesda, MD: University Publications of America, 1996), p. 102.

inadvertently raised the stakes in the Greek civil war and given Moscow a reason to support the rebels. To have done less would have undermined Soviet claims to leadership of international communism and Stalin's title as personal leader of the movement. With Soviet help, Communist partisans prolonged the bloody fighting until 1949.

The blunt Truman Doctrine was followed, in June 1947, by the announcement of a more ambitious and subtle proposal for the revival of Europe: the Marshall Plan. Named after George C. Marshall, then U.S. secretary of state, the plan sought to jump-start the economies of America's trade partners. Both in Britain and on the continent industrial production remained far below prewar levels, currencies were weak, and food and coal remained in short supply. It seemed that Europe was falling into deeper economic trouble rather than recovering, and an impoverished Europe could never absorb the goods that U.S. industry was churning out. This raised the specter of a renewed global depression that would be disastrous for Europeans and Americans alike. Rather than impose solutions from Washington, however, Marshall urged European governments to negotiate priorities among themselves. The United States would then support the European agenda to the extent of its capacities.

Political goals were implicit in this economic program. In the two years since Germany's surrender, a wave of strikes had crippled European production, Communist parties had grown to the point where they threatened to win control in Italy and France, and many Europeans had resorted to smuggling, crime, and prostitution. Neither democracy nor peace, it seemed, could take root and flourish under such conditions. The plan also gave European governments a strong incentive to coordinate their planning and integrate their economies. This, too, was an American goal. Nations that were economically interdependent would be less likely to make war in the future and might even someday integrate to form a single superstate. Several influential European statesmen were already hatching such plans, most notably Jean Monnet, a French businessman and the architect of France's postwar economic policies. As seen from Washington, a unified, democratic, and prosperous Europe would share American interests and resist both Russian expansionism and domestic radicalism.

Marshall Plan loans and grants began to flow to Europe in 1948 and helped ignite two decades of robust economic growth. As U.S. officials had hoped, cooperation on economic planning also generated greater economic and political integration. In 1952, shortly after Marshall Plan aid ended, France and West Germany took the lead in forming a European Coal and Steel Community. The initiative eliminated barriers to the free movement of the two most basic industrial materials across the borders of participating states, which also included Italy, Belgium, the Netherlands, and Luxembourg. In 1957 these same states reached agreement on the formation of a broader European Economic Community (EEC), or Common Market, that had the aim of lowering tariffs between participating nations on a broader range of products.

Through these and other measures, the nations of Western Europe were creating a single market for goods that was about the size of the market in the United

States, albeit not as rich. The benefits were clear: Areas with distinctive resources or human skills could specialize and achieve economies of scale by producing goods for the entire EEC rather than for a single nation. By the early 1950s, Dutchmen were riding French-made bicycles, Italians were listening to German radios, the French were buying Italian shoes, and Europeans were again beginning to sell products in the United States.

Absent from the Marshall Plan and the Common Market were the nations of Eastern Europe. The United States had invited most European nations, including the Soviet Union, to participate in the Marshall Plan, although few in the West thought that the Soviets would take up the offer, and even fewer wanted them to. After some hesitation, the Soviets denounced the plan as an American plot to control European economies. Poland and Czechoslovakia initially announced that they would seek American assistance, but almost immediately reversed course under Soviet pressure. In the end, Europe divided along the Elbe on this issue, as it already had on others, and the plan that brought Western Europe together simultaneously distanced West from East.

Any residual hopes for cooperation between the United States and the USSR soon thereafter evaporated. In a breathtaking flurry of moves and countermoves, accompanied by increasingly vituperative rhetoric, the two great powers sought to solidify their positions in Europe. The Soviets drove non-Communists from the governments of Eastern Europe and purged Communist parties around the world to ensure their subservience to Moscow. In the West, the French and Italian governments excluded Communists from cabinet positions, and the United States adopted domestic security measures to exclude Communists not only from government but also from responsible positions in industry and education.

Britain, France, Belgium, Luxembourg, and the Netherlands formed a mutual defense pact, and the foreign ministers of France, Britain, and the United States began to take steps to unify their zones of Germany both economically and politically. The Soviets, alarmed by that prospect and determined to demonstrate their power, shut down roads and railways leading from the western zones of Germany to Berlin, intending to force the West to acknowledge Soviet control of Germany's capital. Rather than try to force entry by land—a hopeless task if superior Soviet ground forces resisted—the Western powers undertook to supply Berlin by air. The result surprised even many of their own experts: The airlift managed to supply the city's essential needs for over a year, until the Soviets lifted their blockade in September 1949.

The blockade did irreparable damage to the Soviet public image in the West and created a sense of crisis in many Western capitals. The Soviet army occupying East Germany greatly outnumbered the British, French, and American forces in the western sectors. The Soviets had demonstrated a willingness to use their power on the ground, not just to blockade Berlin but also to control the states of Eastern Europe. There they were imposing their will with a chilling ruthlessness— murdering uncooperative political leaders, imprisoning clerics, censoring the press, and attacking all institutions that could challenge the authority of their puppet governments.

Lacking certain knowledge of Soviet intentions but suspecting the worst, the governments of Western Europe lobbied Washington intensively for ironclad assurances that the United States would defend them against Soviet expansion. The best such assurance would be the continuing presence of American troops on the ground. At the same time, American officials came to see a sustained military presence in Europe as essential not only to check Moscow but also to ensure the stability of its Western partners. Should the governments of Western Europe be uncertain of American support, they might, it was feared, seek an accommodation with the Soviets along the pattern of Finland, where a peaceful border had been purchased at the price of a Soviet veto over Finnish foreign policy.

The governments of Western Europe and the United States converged on a solution that few had imagined in 1945: the formation of an alliance, the North Atlantic Treaty Organization (NATO). Aimed squarely at Moscow, the NATO pact bound member nations to contribute troops and materials to a unified military command, led by American officers, that would defend both the borders of Western Europe and the sea lanes connecting Europe and North America. Formed in 1949, NATO ensured that an U.S. army would remain in Europe into the indefinite future, thus giving rattled Europeans tangible evidence of the U.S. commitment to their defense and anxious Americans a new tool to contain Soviet expansion.

Fear of the Soviets also had a second effect: It eclipsed Western concerns about a renewal of German militarism. Almost as soon as the new Federal Republic of Germany took form in 1949, Western officials began to urge its government to contribute to the collective security of Western Europe. In a sharp reversal of its earlier policies, France acceded to a full role for West Germany in the Western alliance, a position that reflected both France's deep concerns about the Soviet Union and its ambition to counterbalance British and American influence in Western Europe. By 1954 West Germany, led by a chancellor with impeccable credentials as an anti-Nazi and anti-Communist, Konrad Adenauer, had gained entry to NATO. The Soviet Union responded: In 1949 Moscow declared its own sector of Germany a state, the German Democratic Republic. Then, in 1955, the Soviets enrolled both East Germany and their other Eastern European satellites into their own military alliance, the Warsaw Pact.

Eastern and Western Europe thus came to be, in some respects, mirror images of each other—each had its own superpower patron, its own trade and currency community, and its own defensive alliance—but with important differences (see Map 9.1). The Western economies galloped ahead during the late 1940s and 1950s, while growth in Eastern Europe was modest. In Western Europe, the benefits of prosperity were diffused widely, through both improved wages and the expansion of government pensions, health insurance plans, and welfare benefits. In the East, the interests of workers and consumers were more often subordinated to those of the state; savings were invested in heavy industry and collectivized agriculture. While the United States pumped $13 billion in Marshall Plan aid into the West, the Soviet Union extracted roughly the same amount from its neighbors through unequal trade contracts and war reparations.

In the West, democracy flourished, even if occasionally marred by the intervention of the United States in election campaigns; in the East, the Soviets exercised rigid control over political life, extinguishing democratic institutions where they had appeared after the war, as in Czechoslovakia and Hungary, and repressing dissent among workers, among the clergy, and even within the Communist Party itself. East and West shared responsibility for the Cold War, but their systems did not have equal claim to economic efficiency, humanity, or political freedom.

Asia in the Aftermath of World War II: Occupations and Nationalisms

The Cold War began in Europe but soon spread to Asia. As in Europe, conflict arose over territories that had been fought over during World War II. Following the Japanese surrender, the United States, the Soviet Union, and their allies all occupied parts of Japan's empire. The Soviets, whose armies had rushed into northern China during the final week of the war, occupied Manchuria and the northern half of the Korean peninsula. U.S. forces occupied Japan, the southern half of Korea, and parts of the Chinese mainland opposite Japan. British and Indian troops reclaimed the former British colonies of Burma, Malaya, Singapore, and Hong Kong and helped to reestablish the French in Indochina and the Dutch in Indonesia.

From Enemies to Partners: Japan and the United States

The Allies encountered some common challenges in each of these areas. Japanese armies had to be disarmed, new arrangements had to be improvised to maintain order and permit the movement of food and other essentials, occupiers had to find local leaders to assist in administration, and Japanese who were suspected of wartime atrocities had to be dealt with. The justice was often very rough. Military courts tried and ordered the execution of several hundred Japanese officers and officials in the Philippines, Indonesia, and Southeast Asia. In Manchuria, the Russians executed even larger numbers and put many of their Japanese prisoners into labor camps. Spontaneous attacks on Japanese occurred in China, Korea, and elsewhere, and even in Japan itself former war leaders were reviled for the suffering they had brought on their people.

An international tribunal that convened in 1946 under American auspices eventually handed down death sentences for a small number of Japan's top leaders. Its methods were far from perfect. American prosecutors assiduously protected Emperor Hirohito from indictment, selected targets for prosecution in arbitrary ways, and tried defendants on charges that many jurists considered weak, such as conspiring to mount a war of aggression. By the time of their end in 1948, even American authorities had lost confidence in the proceedings.

MAP 9.1 Postwar Europe.

Churchill, Roosevelt, and Stalin sketched out the main contours of Europe's postwar map at wartime conferences. Territorial changes in Eastern Europe reflected Stalin's aim to regain regions lost in World War I. The long-term division of Germany and its former capital, Berlin, into East and West was an unplanned outcome of the postwar occupation. As tensions grew between the Soviet Union and its former allies, enduring division came to seem preferable to a unified Germany that might tip the balance of power in Europe to one side or the other.

Politics made strange bedfellows in many parts of postwar Asia. In Japan, Hirohito needed MacArthur's consent to retain his throne, and MacArthur needed a cooperative emperor to establish his own authority to govern. Therefore, MacArthur established a cordial working relationship with the emperor who had given at least tacit approval to the war and had been a focal point of American hatred. In Indochina and parts of Indonesia, Allied officers armed their Japanese prisoners to help control Nationalist movements, while in South Korea Americans, utterly ignorant of local conditions, kept Japanese officials in administrative offices out of frustration with the politically fractious Koreans.

Much to the surprise and relief of Allied planners, MacArthur found it relatively easy to establish control of the Japanese main islands. He did not have to share power with the other Allies, and most Japanese accepted the occupation as a natural outcome of defeat. Many were disillusioned with their wartime leaders and exhausted by years of short rations and hard labor. Japan's cities had suffered even more damage than Germany's, its railroad system was in a shambles, and the nation was desperately short of food and fuel.

The U.S. occupation army brought essential supplies, currency, and far-reaching changes to Japan's political institutions. A team of American lawyers wrote a new constitution, which was adopted with modest changes by the Japanese Diet in 1946. It declared Japan a parliamentary democracy, limited the emperor to a largely ceremonial position, established universal suffrage and the equality of men and women under law, and renounced war as an instrument of national policy. Freedom of the press was guaranteed, although censors vetted newspapers and books for anti-American criticism until the occupation ended in 1952. Additional legislation gave hundreds of thousands of peasants title to their farms, strengthened the rights of labor unions, broke up some of the large, family-controlled trading companies, and broadened access to education. Here, as in Europe, the aim was to promote the development of a stable middle class as an anchor for the democratic political system.

The occupation-era reforms did not utterly change Japan. Many large firms associated with the wartime regime flourished under the occupation, as did the government's powerful bureaucracy. Officials in these large organizations exercised great influence on policy behind the scenes, both during the occupation and in subsequent years. Nevertheless, the changes that Japan underwent during the postwar occupation were dramatic even if not total, and on the whole they made Japan a far freer, more democratic, and more egalitarian society than ever before.

The War and Asian Nationalism

Neither peace nor democracy came so easily to other parts of Asia. Japan had launched the Pacific war on the pretext of liberating Asians from their European masters. It had quickly turned many European colonies into Japanese colonies, exploiting their peoples with a ruthlessness that often surpassed that of the Europeans. Nevertheless, the Japanese had worked with Nationalists in some areas, such as Burma, and had stimulated the development of nationalism in others through anti-Western propaganda. An unintended consequence of Japanese occupation was at least as important: In many regions, Japanese rule evoked resistance, and those who had fought Japanese imperialism were little disposed to accept renewed European imperialism. Above all, the Japanese had demonstrated that European rule need not be a fact of life; Asians could defeat Westerners if they were properly armed and organized.

The Allies were divided over how to respond to nationalism and what to do about European colonies that had been occupied by Japan during the war. The old powers of Europe were reluctant to surrender their Asian territories. This was especially true of France, which was determined to reassert its control over Indochina, and the Netherlands, which quickly sought to reclaim oil-rich Indonesia. Both saw their colonies as dividend-paying assets that might help finance reconstruction at home. Imperial possessions also gave these much-diminished powers some claim to a role in global politics, a consideration that was especially important for the French, whose influence had declined dramatically in the twentieth century.

Britain, which had the most extensive empire of all, proved more flexible. While it was interested in retaining control of such strategic colonies as Hong Kong and Singapore, it had come to recognize the futility of trying to hold on to lands in which large and dogged Nationalist movements flourished. It had promised India its independence during the war, and when the Labour Party took control of the British government in 1945, negotiations quickly began on Burmese, Ceylonese, and Malaysian independence. Until the 1960s, British leaders hoped that their former colonies would assume positions in a British Commonwealth of Nations, a voluntary association offering members special trade privileges and a largely symbolic association with the mother country." But much more than the French or the Dutch, the British recognized that the handwriting was on the wall for old-style European imperialism.

The Soviet Union simultaneously preached an aggressive anticolonial line while diligently working to rebuild and extend the old tsarist empire. Soviet ideology was clear: Lenin had denounced imperialism as a form of capitalist exploitation, and Soviet policy was to defend the rights of colonized peoples. But despite the anti-imperialist rhetoric, Stalin generally showed little interest in Asian nationalism. As in the west, he was concerned primarily with ensuring that the regions bordering the USSR were favorably disposed toward the Soviet state. This meant restoring the influence that imperial Russia had enjoyed in Manchuria and preventing Japan from again extending its power onto the Asian mainland.

American interests were more diffuse. The United States opposed closed trading systems, whether they were dominated by Europe's imperial powers, the Soviet Union, or Japan. It sought a stable Asia in which no power could again threaten U.S. control of the sea-lanes, as Japan had done. It also voiced support for Nationalist movements on the old Wilsonian principle that peoples should have a right to choose their own forms of government. These goals led the United States to grant the Philippines its independence in 1946 and to urge its allies to follow suit in their own empires. They also led Roosevelt to insist that China should have a permanent seat on the UN Security Council. An independent China would be open to American trade and investment; it might also serve as a counterweight to the Soviets and the Japanese in the years to come. But America's European interests remained more important than its Asian interests, and neither Roosevelt nor Truman was willing to alienate Europe's imperial powers by pushing decolonization vigorously. Consequently, Nationalists in Asia had to struggle for their independence (see Map 9.2).

Wars of Independence: Vietnam and Indonesia

For some, the struggle began during the war. Ho Chi Minh, a widely traveled Vietnamese Marxist, launched a League for the Independence of Vietnam, or Viet Minh, shortly after Japanese troops entered Indochina in 1940. Working from a base in southern China, he and his associates ran a clandestine resistance in Vietnam's northern provinces. As soon as the war ended, they took possession of Hanoi and Saigon, Vietnam's two largest cities. On September 2, 1945, Ho issued a formal declaration of Vietnam's independence, quoting liberally from both the U.S. Declaration of Independence and the French Declaration of the Rights of Man.

The declaration, however, did little to impress the Western Allies. Within weeks British and Indian troops, working with Japanese prisoners of war, had ejected Ho's followers from Saigon. French forces, mostly mercenaries enrolled in the French Foreign Legion, soon arrived. Assuming control of the south, the French offered Ho a deal that would have given limited autonomy to North Vietnam. Unwilling to accept either a divided nation or incomplete independence, Ho returned to Hanoi and reasserted his government's claim to represent all of Vietnam.

In November 1946, the truce between the French and the Viet Minh failed. France, having enlarged its forces in Indochina, seized Hanoi and other northern cities and threw the outnumbered Viet Minh on the defensive. Ho responded to the reverses by adopting guerrilla tactics and cultivating support in rural districts with his program of land reform and independence. Bolstered by supplies and recruits from Vietnam's many small villages, the strength of the Viet Minh swelled until, in the early 1950s, it was ready to engage large units of the French army. This the Viet Minh did brilliantly. It capped its campaign in the spring of 1954 by compelling a French army to surrender after a grueling battle over the town of Dien Bien Phu, a strong point in northwest Vietnam.

The Viet Minh victory came on the eve of an international conference in Geneva that had been convened by Britain, France, the United States, and the Soviet Union to broker a cease-fire in Indochina. The French, exhausted by the long war and demoralized by their recent defeat, agreed to the creation of three nations in Indochina: Cambodia, Laos, and Vietnam. Under the terms of a cease-fire agreement, Vietnam was temporarily divided at the seventeenth parallel of latitude, pending nationwide elections. Ho's Viet Minh government assumed

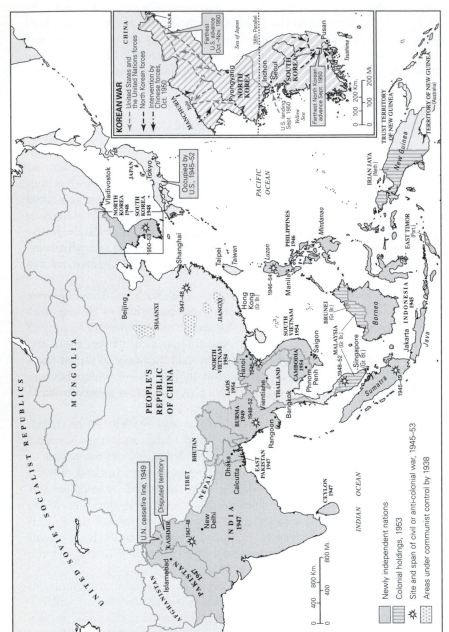

MAP 9.2 South and East Asia, 1945–1953.

Nationalists across Asia were quick to seek independence following the collapse of Japan's empire in 1945, leading to guerrilla wars against European imperial forces that were trying to reestablish authority in their prewar colonies. Independence sometimes introduced a new round of bloodshed as rival Nationalist parties, sometimes backed by outside sponsors, contended for power. The Korean peninsula, where a seesaw war was fought between North and South between 1950 and 1954, saw the bloodiest of these conflicts.

control of the north and an anti-Communist Nationalist, Ngo Dinh Diem, took power in the south. Elections, however, were not held. Instead, the United States incorporated South Vietnam into an alliance of anti-Communist states, the South-East Asia Treaty Organization (SEATO), and began subsidizing the Diem regime with money, military equipment, and advisers. Ho Chi Minh, who was securely in control of North Vietnam, had achieved a partial victory. It would take another two decades to accomplish his full goal: the unification of Vietnam under a Viet Minh regime.

While Ho Chi Minh contended with the French, another Asian National-ist, Sukarno, led a campaign against the Dutch for the independence of Indonesia. Unlike Vietnam, Indonesia lacked a precolonial history as an inde-pendent state. An archipelago stretching more than three thousand miles from end to end, Indonesia was largely a creation of Dutch colonial rule. Its popu-lation included Malays, Chinese, Polynesians, and Papuans with diverse lan-guages and cultural traditions. During World War II, Japanese occupiers had treated these subjects with contempt and brutality, impressing hundreds of thousands into forced labor in mines, oil fields, and rice paddies and causing approximately a million deaths. But the Japanese had also demonstrated the fragility of Dutch colonial rule and had sponsored the creation of an Indone-sian militia.

Within days of Japan's surrender Sukarno and Mohammed Hatta, a pair of Indonesian Nationalists who had played a double game of collaborating with both the Japanese and the anti-Japanese resistance, seized the moment and declared Indonesia an independent republic. The Netherlands was in no position to respond forcefully, but Britain was. Alarmed that Nationalists in its own empire might follow the Indonesians' lead, Britain landed troops on Java, the most populous island of the archipelago, and, together with rearmed Japanese prisoners, established control of the island's major cities.

By late 1945, however, fighting on a large scale had begun between British forces and elements of the militia that Japan had armed. Neither the British nor the Dutch forces that replaced them could reestablish full control. Passive resistance in the cities, continuing violence in the countryside, and heavy pres-sure from the United States, the Soviet Union, and Australia eventually con-vinced the Dutch that they were in a conflict they could not win. In December 1949, after four years of fighting, the Netherlands recognized Indonesia's inde-pendence, and a new government, under the presidency of Sukarno, assumed power.

Ethnicity, Religion, and Asian Decolonization: *Burma and India*

The nations of Indonesia and Vietnam were born of protracted wars, but anti-colonial movements could also take a more peaceful form. Following the Labour Party's victory in Britain's 1945 general elections, British policy shifted from the determined imperialism of Churchill's government to a more prag-matic stance. The Labour Party was eager to deliver on campaign promises of

French ambitions to regain control of Indochina collided with Ho Chi Minh's independence movement after World War II. The struggle culminated in a long siege of the French base at Dien Bien Phu, where ten thousand French prisoners, some pictured here, were taken prisoner in 1954. The defeat forced France to withdraw from Indochina later that year.

more plentiful food and housing, national health care, and the modernization of aging industries. It could not hope to accomplish such ambitious goals and simultaneously garrison unruly colonies from one end of the world to the other. The solution appeared inevitable: Britain would have to grant independence to those colonies that appeared to be ready, especially those that promised to be costly to hold. A series of agreements on the independence of India, Ceylon, and Burma followed in rapid succession.

In none of these states was there protracted fighting between colonizer and colonized, but in two of them, Burma and India, independence nevertheless brought bloodshed. The reason is not far to seek. Asian politics during the postwar years cannot be understood simply in terms of a conflict between Nationalists and imperial powers. The peoples under colonial rule were themselves often divided, and these divisions could make political change a contest involving three or more parties.

In some colonies, ethnicity was a critical issue. Such was the case in Burma, where tense relations existed between the Burmese of the lowlands, who constituted a majority of the population, and inland hill peoples, the Karens and Kachins, who had long depended on the British for protection. The Nationalist

Party that assumed power in 1948, when Burma obtained its independence, represented the interests of the lowlands; its control of government quickly sparked a rebellion among the Karens. The situation quickly grew yet more complex as Communist guerrillas, Chinese Nationalist troops, and other groups launched their own separatist movements. Under the pressure of these rebellions and political infighting among the Burmese Nationalists themselves, Burma's government evolved from a parliamentary democracy to rule by a military junta.

In India, the issue was religion. By 1946 the British were eager to withdraw. But to whom should power be transferred? Internal divisions, which had been convenient for the British when they ruled India, now created a dilemma as they tried to leave. About one in five of India's four hundred eighty million inhabitants was Muslim, with the great majority of the others being Hindu. Although concentrated in the northwest and northeast, Muslim communities were scattered across the subcontinent. While the Congress Party advocated the formation of a unified India offering equal rights to all citizens, its leaders, including Gandhi and Jawaharlal Nehru, were Hindu. A Moslem League, led by Mohammed Ali Jinnah, had come to speak for many of India's Muslims. It advocated the partition of colonial India into separate Hindu and Muslim states. Britain could not satisfy one of these independence movements without denying the other.

In the end, religious divisions proved more powerful than the ideal of unity. In an agreement brokered by the British, the Congress Party and the Moslem League agreed to the creation of two successor states, a predominantly Hindu India and a largely Muslim Pakistan. All parties hoped for a peaceful division, but rioting commenced even before British rule officially ended. The bloodshed intensified when power was transferred in August 1947. Between a quarter and a half million Muslims died, some in their homes and many others as they fled India for Pakistan along refugee-filled roads and rail lines. Within weeks of independence, ten million Muslims had crossed the borders. Smaller numbers of Hindus moved in the opposite direction, and they, too, suffered appalling losses as the anti-Muslim riots in India sparked anti-Hindu violence in Pakistan. These convulsions generated hatreds among millions of citizens of both new nations. The enmity was only intensified as soldiers of India and Pakistan, once part of a common British-led army, fell to fighting over Kashmir, a district that straddled the northwestern frontier of the two new states. The combat found a temporary end in January 1949 through a UN-sponsored truce.

Religious and ethnic conflicts were not peculiar to India, Pakistan, and Burma. In Malaya, ethnic Chinese and Malays, nearly balanced in numbers, resented each other at least as much as they did their British rulers. Independence in Indonesia brought fighting between competing groups of Muslims on Java, some of whom were more influenced by indigenous religious traditions than others. Meanwhile, in the Philippines, Muslims, who were concentrated in the southern island of Mindanao, nursed grievances against Catholics to the north who controlled the economy and the government. In Vietnam, there was tension between minority Catholics and Buddhists and fighting between tribal hill peoples, who were allied with the French, and Viet Minh lowlanders. As in Europe after World War I, ethnic and religious loyalties could inspire both the construction and the destruction of states.

Asian Communism

Ideological divisions also rent many of the new nations of Asia. Communist parties, most of them led by intellectuals, had enjoyed modest success in Asia during the 1920s and 1930s by appealing to the interests of workers in such commercial centers as Shanghai and Manila. These methods were consistent with both Soviet experience and Marxist-Leninist theory, and they reflected the broad authority that Moscow enjoyed among Communists. The Bolsheviks had made a revolution and were running a state; other revolutionaries quite naturally looked to them for legitimacy and guidance.

Nevertheless, the urban proletariat in Asia was small, and Communist parties flourished only after indigenous leaders adapted Marxism to local conditions. This often meant emphasizing issues that concerned peasants: land reform, tax reform, the control of official corruption, medical care, and education. Not only were peasants far more numerous than urban workers, but rural districts were safer for revolutionaries than urban ones. When they were concentrated in a few cities, Communists could be watched and controlled by imperial authorities, whether European or Japanese. In the countryside, imperial control was generally weak, and revolutionaries could more easily blend into the background—so long, that is, as they enjoyed good relations with their hosts.

Several peasant-based Communist movements appeared in the 1940s, often as much out of necessity as of choice. While Communists had been harassed and sometimes imprisoned by European colonial governments in the 1930s, the Japanese imperial government had treated them as enemies of the state, often killing those they could catch and driving the survivors underground. Thus rural Communist movements took form in the agricultural districts of northern Vietnam; on the plantations of Luzon, the largest Philippine island; and among impoverished Chinese squatters in Malaya's jungles.

Red Star over China: China's Communist Revolution

The first and most influential of these movements had developed in China during the 1920s and 1930s. Its chief strategist, Mao Zedong, had long believed that peasants would be the surest base for a revolution in China. During the early 1930s, he had organized a stronghold in the villages and market towns of Jiangxi province, a couple of hundred miles west of the Taiwan Straits, by redistributing the land of uncooperative gentry and protecting peasants from the depredations of warlords and Guomindang tax collectors.

In 1934, after Chiang Kai-shek's Guomindang government cracked down on Communists throughout China, Mao and his small army were forced to take flight, undertaking what would later become known as "the Long March." Moving first to the west and then to the north, pursued much of the way by Guomindang troops, they finally settled in 1935 in a remote part of north central China near the Mongolian border. There, Mao and his band regrouped and gathered fresh support among the local peasantry, who found the honesty, discipline, and land reforms of the Communists appealing. As China's war with Japan intensified, Chiang was compelled to strike a truce with Mao. Thus relieved, Mao slowly enlarged his army and its range of operations, extending his control westward and undertaking more ambitious operations against the Japanese.

Throughout the long war with Japan, both the Soviet Union and the United States had recognized Chiang's Guomindang government as representing China, and the great bulk of American aid went to the Guomindang armies, which operated primarily in southern and central China. But the élan and aggressiveness of the Communist army contrasted sharply with the passivity of the Guomindang forces, and by the end of the war both Soviet and American observers began to consider Mao a significant threat to the Guomindang's authority. Although some American diplomats thought that a more even-handed policy might serve American interests, after the war the U.S. government opted to throw its full support to Chiang. The Soviets, meanwhile, began assisting Mao's army with captured Japanese weapons and war materiel.

The truce between the Guomindang and the Communists broke down in 1946, when Soviet occupation troops in Manchuria began to withdraw and both Mao and Chiang rushed to fill the vacuum. General warfare soon erupted. The Guomindang, with far larger armies, achieved a string of early successes and established control over almost all of China's major cities. Nevertheless, it was unable either to inflict a decisive defeat on the Communist. In 1949, after years of hit-and-run tactics, the Communists took the initiative and never again lost it. Moving from north to south, they isolated Chiang's forces and defeated them piecemeal. Within months a swelling Communist army secured control of most of the rest of China and drove Chiang and his half a million remaining troops to the island of Taiwan, where his government continued to claim it represented all of China. Mao, for his part, swiftly consolidated control of the Chinese mainland, replacing Guomindang officials with his own, driving foreign missionaries into flight, and executing many landowners and merchants. Stalin, who had long neglected the independent Mao, quickly acted to repair the damage by offering him diplomatic support, military aid, and advice on how to go about building a socialist economy.

Repercussions in Washington

Reports of Mao's victories arrived in Washington while relief flights were still flying into blockaded Berlin. In August, just months after Chiang fled to Taiwan, American reconnaissance aircraft detected evidence that the Soviet

Union had tested an atomic bomb, thus ending the U.S. monopoly on nuclear weapons. The American public reacted to these rapid-fire developments with shock and alarm. Not only had the Grand Alliance dissolved, but it now appeared to many Americans that Soviet Russia was leading an international conspiracy against U.S. interests.

And Soviet Russia seemed to have the initiative. Newspapers and magazines illustrated their coverage of these events with maps showing a red tide sweeping across Europe and Asia. Scientists planned radar systems to provide early warning of Soviet air attack. Missionaries returning from China recounted the horrors inflicted by the "godless" Communists, as did Catholic priests in speaking of the trials of the church in Eastern Europe. The Truman administration had watched the disintegration of Chiang's forces with dismay, at first pumping weapons and money into the cause, and finally deciding that such assistance was largely wasted on the corrupt and hapless Guomindang. Now, with Mao firmly in control of the mainland, critics of the Truman administration began to ask, "Who lost China?"

Many Republicans thought they knew. The Truman administration, they claimed, had underestimated the Soviet threat and had failed to stop the advance of communism in China. Worse, it had neglected the danger that international communism posed at home. Pointing to evidence of Soviet espionage, of which there was a great deal, and of Communist influence among American intellectuals, the Republican Party honed its attacks on the Truman administration in the 1948 congressional elections. Successes in those elections produced the first Republican Congress since 1928 and led to even more aggressive use of the issue. When, in 1950, Senator Joe McCarthy of Wisconsin recklessly charged that the U.S. State Department was itself riddled with traitors, a majority of Americans were prepared to believe him.

The Globalization of the Cold War

By 1950 the Cold War had come to the United States. It had also reached Asia. The defeat of the Guomindang altered both Soviet and American views on the balance of power in the Far East. Stalin, who had consistently underestimated Mao and overestimated Chiang, now had to scramble to justify his claims to leadership of international communism. This entailed a renunciation of privileges in Manchuria that had been granted to the Soviet Union at the end of the war and increased support for other Asian Communist parties, which the Soviets had long treated with benign neglect. More aggressive support of Mao and other Asian revolutionaries also served larger Soviet interests. It aligned the USSR more clearly with nationalist aspirations; sapped the power of America's allies and client states such as France, Britain, and the Philippines, which all were fighting wars against Communist guerrillas; and forced the United States to divide its attention and its resources between Europe and Asia.

Containment and Korea

U.S. policy in the wake of World War II had taken account of Soviet threats in Asia but was flexible in dealing with the complex politics of decolonization. The United States had backed Indonesian independence, even though significant elements of the Indonesian Nationalist movement identified themselves as Marxists. The United States had armed and trained Ho Chi Minh's Viet Minh while it was fighting the Japanese, and, after the war, it refused to sell the French military equipment for use in Indochina. In China, the United States sought a power-sharing deal between Chiang and Mao until events made that possibility utterly unrealistic. Even then, some U.S. diplomats, sensing a fissure between Mao and Stalin, believed that a good working relationship with Mao might someday be possible. But Mao's triumph was not seen as an isolated event; it was all too easily woven into a larger narrative that attributed all the disappointments of the postwar years to a masterful conspiracy hatched in Moscow.

After 1949 U.S. containment doctrine, which was already being applied in Europe, was extended to the Pacific. The U.S. government began to assist anti-Communist forces wherever they called for help against Communist challenges. Aid began to flow to the French in Indochina, where the Viet Minh was intensifying its war with Chinese help; to the newly independent Philippine government, which was combating a Communist insurrection on the island of Luzon; and to the British, who had become enmeshed in a war against Communist guerrillas in the jungles of Malaya. Each of these conflicts could have been understood in terms of local conditions. In the Philippines, it was a conflict between landless peasants and the estate-owning elites who dominated Philippine politics both before and after independence. In Indochina, it was a war of independence. In Malaya, it was at once an anticolonial war and a war of secession by a radical segment of Malaya's ethnic Chinese. But the lenses of Cold War anticommunism rendered these complexities invisible to the American public and, increasingly, to policymakers in Washington.

Mao's victory in China broadened and deepened the involvement of the superpowers in Asia, focusing their attention on regions that had been of secondary importance only a few years earlier and encouraging them to increase their stakes in local conflicts. One of those local conflicts was in Korea.

Neither the United States nor the Soviet Union had given much thought to the Korean Peninsula at the end of World War II. Soviet forces had occupied the better developed northern half of the Japanese colony in 1945, and American troops had occupied the more populous, poorer, and agricultural south. The thirty-eighth parallel, which bisected the peninsula, served as the line of demarcation. Korea's partition, like Germany's, was intended to be temporary but soon became fixed. Talks aimed at reunification repeatedly broke down, with the Americans first agreeing to and then rejecting a joint Allied trusteeship over the entire peninsula and the Soviets rejecting UN-sponsored general elections. In 1948, UN-supervised elections to a general assembly in the south led to the formation of a Republic of Korea under the presidency of a prominent Nationalist, Syngman Rhee. A few months later, the Soviets organized a separate state in the north, the Democratic Peoples Republic of Korea, under the control of Kim Il Sung, a long-time Communist who had chaired a provisional government under Soviet auspices since 1946. Kim Il Sung employed the full range of Stalin's methods to impose an iron rule on his people, rooting out opposition, and committing North Korea to the expansion of heavy industry, collectivized agriculture, and military strength. Rhee, a fiery Nationalist but a poor democrat, developed his own brand of author-itarianism, albeit less efficient than Kim Il Sung's. By mid-1949, both American and Soviet occupation forces had withdrawn from the peninsula.

Few American observers gave the inefficient South Korean government a strong chance of survival, and fewer still believed that the peninsula was impor-tant enough to merit determined support. Both in public and in private, Ameri-can diplomats carefully excluded South Korea from those regions where vital American interests were in play.

American diffidence toward Korea had an unintended consequence: It encour-aged both Kim Il Sung and Stalin to believe that North Korea might achieve control of the entire peninsula by a swift military strike. In the spring of 1950, Kim secured Stalin's permission to attack the South, with the understanding that Soviet support would be indirect. The destruction of a nearby state that was allied, even if only loosely, with the United States would serve Soviet interests so long as Soviet troops could remain uninvolved. And here, as elsewhere, Stalin was to some degree a captive of his claims to leadership of an international strug-gle against capitalism. Mao, who was just consolidating his power in China, was less enthusiastic about Kim Il Sung's plans than Stalin, but he acceded to the wishes of his neighbors and allies.

In June 1950, the North Korean army launched a sudden and massive attack across the thirty-eighth parallel. The Soviet-trained North Koreans, some of who had fought for Mao in the Chinese civil war, possessed superior numbers and equipment and brushed aside the weak and ill-organized South Koreans. Within three days they had captured Seoul, the seat of the South's government; within a week South Korean resistance was on the verge of collapse.

The invasion stunned Washington and the West, not so much because of what it said about Stalin's intentions but because it indicated a recklessness that he had seldom shown before. With one eye on Europeans who were anxious about U.S. commitment and the other on domestic politics, Truman quickly ordered U.S. forces to assist the South Koreans and asked the UN Security Council to act against the aggressor. A Soviet veto would have blocked UN action, but the Soviet Union had absented itself from the Security Council some months previ-ously in protest against the UN's failure to recognize Mao as China's legitimate ruler. In the absence of a Soviet representative, the Security Council swiftly con-demned the North's action and called upon member nations to go to the defense of the South.

As the South Koreans retreated, a UN command was organized under Douglas MacArthur, and U.S. occupation troops in Japan were hurriedly ferried to Korea.

Ill prepared to fight and introduced piecemeal, they could at first do little to check the North Korean advance. But as additional troops arrived, including British and Australian units, and as U.S. air and naval forces were brought to bear, the North Koreans were halted just short of winning complete control of the peninsula. In September, MacArthur made surprise amphibious landings at Inchon, almost two hundred miles behind the lines of the North Korean army. The strike immediately reversed the tide. With their lines of supply cut, Kim Il Sung's armies began a headlong retreat. Within two weeks, UN forces, now including troops from fifteen nations, had retaken Seoul and ejected the North Koreans from most of the South.

MacArthur, convinced that he held a winning hand, secured permission from Truman to continue his drive northward, with the aim of not only repulsing the North Koreans but also reuniting the peninsula. By December, UN forces had all but achieved this goal. But once again, the tables were turned. Mao and Stalin, alarmed by the prospect of an American army on their borders, came to the aid of the North Koreans. With assurances of supplies and air support from Stalin, Mao ordered a quarter of a million Chinese troops to cross the Yalu River into North Korea. There, in December 1950, they surprised advancing UN columns, turning what had seemed a certain UN victory into a stunning defeat. Within weeks, the Allied troops were pushed south of the thirty-eighth parallel. The bloodshed was enormous as the Chinese units struggled to overcome the UN superiority in weapons with numbers. Eventually, though, firepower and UN reinforcements stopped and reversed the tide.

By the summer of 1951, UN forces had again pushed northward to the vicinity of the thirty-eighth parallel. Once again MacArthur urged a sustained advance, this time publicly expressing the desire to attack Chinese bases in Manchuria and to make use of Chiang's Guomindang troops. But neither Truman nor his UN allies wished to renew the Chinese civil war. MacArthur was relieved of his command, and after two more years of inconclusive fighting the war ended in a truce that left the Korean Peninsula divided in two. The United States and its allies, chastened by the Chinese intervention and heavy casualties, had become convinced that any further advance to the north would only evoke yet stronger Chinese and Soviet countermeasures. The Chinese, stunned by the intensity of the combat and the magnitude of their losses, decided that North Korea would afford an adequate buffer to protect their interests.

Korea became an Asian counterpart to Germany: a nation divided between Communist and capitalist spheres, a continuing source of friction, and the scene of bizarre maneuvers that ran the gamut from old-fashioned cross-border espionage to sabotage, assassination, and tunnel digging beneath the demilitarized zone separating North and South. American armies were to remain in Germany and Korea for decades to come as shields and tripwires. Large-scale fighting did not recur in either locale, but in both places the United States and the USSR sought to construct replicas of themselves—states that would exemplify the advantages of their competing economic and political systems.

CONCLUSION

It wasn't just Germany and Korea that were divided. By the mid-1950s, so was most of the rest of the globe. On one side, the Soviet Union had built a network of alliances that incorporated its satellites in Eastern Europe, China, and North Korea. On the other, the United States, which had never before committed itself to peacetime alliances, constructed a web of bilateral and multilateral agreements that included most of the nations of Western Europe, Greece, Turkey, and all the nations of Latin America, along with Japan, South Korea, the Philippines, Australia, New Zealand, and Pakistan.

Intensive preparations for war accompanied the binge of treaty signings. The United States and its European allies reinstituted conscription, opened new defense plants, built airfields and naval bases all around the perimeter of the Communist world, and freely distributed surplus equipment from World War II to allied states. Believing that superior technology might serve as a counterweight to Soviet and Chinese numbers, the West accelerated research on new weapons: fission bombs with higher yields, miniaturized nuclear weapons for use in artillery and mines, intercontinental bombers, nuclear-powered submarines, long-distance radar systems, digital computers to improve the command and control of forces, and, most potent of all, a new and radically more powerful nuclear weapon, the hydrogen bomb. The Soviets, for their part, poured scarce resources into the weapons that had brought them victory over Germany—tanks, artillery, and fighter aircraft—and embarked on their own ambitious program of research and development, with the focus on nuclear weapons, jet engines, and rockets.

The remilitarization of international relations so soon after World War II affected economies and cultures throughout the world. The burden of defense spending crippled economic development in the Soviet Union, where upwards of 15 percent of gross domestic product was dedicated to preparations for war at the expense of investment in its backward agricultural sector and consumer products industries. The United States, with a much larger economy, absorbed the costs of the Cold War with less strain, but only by holding down spending on social services.

Some of its allies were not so fortunate. Britain, which tried to preserve its global military reach and at the same time provide its citizens with cradle-to-grave social services, lurched from one economic crisis to the next, unable to keep pace with the economic growth of its partner across the Atlantic, or even with some of its allies on the continent that were less ambitious in their postwar goals. Ironically, Japan, which was forbidden from rebuilding its military under an American-imposed constitution, found economic opportunity in this increasingly militarized world, investing resources in education and infrastructure that might otherwise have gone to defense.

Until the 1960s, the Cold War dominated culture as well as politics and economics. A stultifying Marxist-Leninist orthodoxy spread from Soviet

Russia, where it had already prevailed in the 1930s, into Eastern Europe. Artists, writers, and scientists who tested the limits of official censorship risked imprisonment. In China, Mao's regime periodically purged the ranks of intellectuals in the name of ideological purity. And while greater liberty prevailed in the West, new forms of censorship and self-censorship appeared, especially in the United States, where by the end of the 1940s anticommunism had become an article of faith. McCarthyism singed universities, movie studios, newspapers, and other institutions. As public and private organizations imposed loyalty oaths and conducted security investigations of their employees, the spectrum of respectable political opinion contracted to a narrow band.

The Cold War was to be the cardinal fact of international politics for two decades. It was a matrix for the emergence of new states from European colonies, for political debate, and for economic and technological development. But important as it was, the Cold War was not the only fact of international life. Diversity of opinion and ambition existed within each of the competing blocs, and outside of both were nations and peoples seeking their own paths to the future.

For Further Reading

Judith M. Brown, *Modern India*, 2nd ed. (Oxford: Oxford University Press, 1994). Sets the 1947 partition into a broader history of democracy in India.

Robert Bud, *Penicillin: Triumph and Tragedy* (Oxford: Oxford University Press, 2007). A broad-scale history of antibiotics in modern culture.

John W. Dower, *Embracing Defeat: Japan in the Wake of World War II* (New York: Norton, 1999). A masterful work on Japan during the U.S. occupation.

David W. Ellwood, *Rebuilding Europe: Western Europe, America and Postwar Reconstruction* (London: Longman, 1992). Strong on the intersection of politics and economics during the era of the Marshall Plan.

John Lewis Gaddis, *We Now Know: Rethinking Cold War History* (Oxford: Clarendon Press, 1997). Makes excellent use of archives opened in the 1990s.

Robin Jeffrey, ed., *Asia: The Winning of Independence* (London: Macmillan, 1981). Fine essays on decolonization in Southeast Asia.

Tony Judt, *Postwar: A History of Europe Since 1945* (New York: Penguin, 2005). Unsurpassed on how Europe moved from world war to Cold War and beyond.

Jonathan D. Spence, *The Search for Modern China*, 2nd ed. (New York: W. W. Norton, 1999). China in the postwar years.

William Stueck, *The Korean War: An International History* (Princeton, N.J.: Princeton University Press, 1995). Reliable and thorough.

Daniel Yergin, *Shattered Peace: The Origins of the Cold War and the National Security State* (Boston: Houghton Mifflin, 1978). A good book on the history of the Cold War, notable for its balanced judgments and fluid style.

Vladislav Zubok and Constantine Pleshakov, *Inside the Kremlin's Cold War: From Stalin to Khrushchev* (Cambridge, Mass.: Harvard University Press, 1996). A penetrating analysis of Soviet policy.

Related Websites

Documents on American foreign policy, the NATO Treaty, the Bretton Woods Agreements, and the UN Charter
  www.yale.edu/lawweb/avalon/20th.htm
Links to many excellent websites on the Cold War and U.S. foreign policy
  www.mtholyoke.edu/acad/intrel/coldwar.htm

CHAPTER 10

Two Poles and Perpetual Crisis, 1950–1964

In October 1962, U.S. president John F. Kennedy was presented with evidence that the ongoing struggle of words and wills between the United States and the USSR for international domination had taken a terrifying turn. U.S. military intelligence services had proved that missile silos suitable for launching nuclear warheads had been constructed in Cuba, ninety miles from the coast of the USA. The silos had been built by the USSR, which might be in the process of loading them. The president and his advisers soberly discussed the chances that the Soviet Union would actually use nuclear weapons if the United States should demand that the silos be destroyed and prevent more Soviet ships from reaching Cuba. Nobody knew the answer.

The president called former president Dwight D. Eisenhower to ask his advice. The older man calmly assessed the possibilities, then said that Soviet intentions were unfathomable. But at bottom he thought that no man would actually be able to bring himself to launch the missiles and initiate a nuclear war. Kennedy chuckled grimly, "Yeah. Well, we'll hang on tight." Eisenhower also chuckled, and said, "Yes, sir!" Turning to his advisers and officials, Kennedy announced that the United States would demand destruction of the silos and would hope that what was regarded as improbable was actually impossible.[1]

---

[1]Ernest R. May and Philip D. Zelikow, eds., *The Kennedy Tapes: Inside the White House During the Cuban Missile Crisis* (New York: W. W. Norton, 2001), p. 146.

Presidents Eisenhower and Kennedy represented two phases in the management of the postwar world. When Eisenhower was the American president from 1953 to 1961, the emphasis in both the United States and the USSR was on building up nuclear weapons capabilities and intelligence technology so that a direct confrontation between the superpowers became unthinkable. The absolute destructive power of nuclear weapons, combined with rapid advances in technological surveillance, meant that neither of the two great rivals could attack the other without being destroyed itself. The arms race severely taxed the economies and the cultures of both societies, but by the end of the 1950s it had rendered the possibility of nuclear war abstract. Thereafter, the superpowers engage in "Cold War" rivalry, competing for allies and resources without directly fighting each other.

The Cuban missile crisis, however, demonstrated that new leaders of the United States and the Soviet Union could still see the use of nuclear weapons as possible. The crisis was an example of the dangers of the constant brinksmanship between the superpowers—each trying to see how far it could push the other before the threat of nuclear war caused one side or the other to back down. Each side knew that one day there could be a miscalculation, and the other side might refuse to back down even if it meant a nuclear conflict. Moreover, within only a few years of the crisis in Cuba, the proliferation of nuclear weapons around the world began, bringing with it new dangers that "limited nuclear war," very hot wars, could become a reality.

Crisis and Compromise in the Management of the Postwar World

After the Second World War, the emergence of new nations in Asia, Africa and Latin America represented many sorts of challenges to the two world powers. Stalin had made it clear to the American and British leaders that he intended to spread communism to as many nations as possible. U.S. leaders and their foreign allies considered every part of the world lost to capitalism to be a diminution of their own access to natural resources and markets. In theory, the leaders of the capitalist world agreed with Stalin: Capitalism and communism were fatally opposed, and they could not coexist. But that was in theory. In practice, they would have to coexist for some indefinite period. Indeed, when Stalin died in 1953, his successor Khrushchev announced that his own foreign policy would be based on "peaceful coexistence" with the United States and its allies.

The New Supremacy of "Security"

An ultimate conflict between the superpowers would be pointless unless one side or the other gained a decisive advantage in self-protection. In both the United States and the Soviet Union, organizations that collected information about the opposition, prevented the opposition from collecting its own information, and detected ways in which the opposition might be encouraging domestic troubles were all reorganized and enlarged. The development of surveillance technologies became a high priority. Strategies for finding the best placement of listening posts and analytical centers became part of the global calculation behind new alliances and the protection of emerging states.

In the Soviet Union, organizations for state security were already well prepared for their duties in the era of the Cold War. Through the Second World War, intelligence organizations were an important part of the Soviet defense efforts. These organizations were separate from, but worked together with, the Comintern. While the Comintern sponsored the Communist education and political advancement of activists from Europe, Asia, and Africa, the secret police organizations picked certain foreign activists for training as intelligence officers. After Stalin's death in 1953, the new Soviet leader Nikita Khrushchev created the KGB (from the Russian words for "Committee of State Security") from the older organizations. The feared Stalin intelligence chief Lavrentyi Beria was arrested on Khrushchev's orders and his intelligence organizations dismantled and replaced by the KGB.

In the postwar era, and particularly after 1950, the entire political pattern of the globe was determined by the fact that the Soviet Union and the United States were the only nuclear powers, and that they were challenged by no other nations. As we saw in Chapter 9, the Soviet Union, as Germany's enemy after 1940, felt pressured to make headway in atomic research, but it did not have the resources to complete its projects. It had to depend on espionage. The final bit of information enabling the creation of a Soviet bomb was provided after the war, probably by a spy network that included several Los Alamos scientists. Soviet scientists, led by I. V. Kurchatov, quickly interpreted and applied the information. To prevent infiltration by American spies, Soviet scientists were removed to special compounds (*sharashka*), where they lived comfortably but without contact with the outside world while they worked secretly on projects relating to weapons and aviation. There was no official acknowledgment that the *sharashkas* existed, and they had military-style security that permitted trespassers to be shot.

Before the Second World War, the United States did not have well-developed organizations for gathering intelligence, whether military or scientific. Spying and surveillance tended to be focused on an individual's actions, not on his or her thoughts or opinions. During World War II, the American government created several military intelligence organizations. These were reorganized during 1946 and 1947 under American president Harry S. Truman as the Central Intelligence Agency. By law the CIA was supposed to mount operations only outside the United States, and to leave all domestic intelligence work to the FBI. Beginning in the 1950s, the FBI—still under its founder, J. Edgar Hoover—began to investigate unions and universities where it thought communist sympathizers might be residing. Files were opened on most major American intellectuals; these included copies of their publications and, in fewer cases, data from direct surveillance of their personal lives. These methods were used to indict and convict Julius and Ethel Rosenberg, who were executed for espionage in 1953. This division of labor between the CIA and the FBI was usually observed through the 1950s,

GLOBAL Technologies

Long-Distance Weapons

As any boxer knows, superior "reach" is an important advantage in a fight. Since antiquity soldiers have looked for ways to land punches on adversaries while standing beyond their range. In the First World War, admirals valued dreadnoughts for their capacity to deliver shells to targets twenty miles distant. In the Second World War they used aircraft carriers capable of striking targets two and three hundred miles away. The race for greater range also drove competition on land, first in artillery and later in aircraft. The infamous German siege gun of the First World War, Big Bertha, could lob shells sixty-five miles; by the end of the Second World War, American B-29 bombers flew fifteen hundred miles to incinerate Japanese cities. The U.S., dealing with the vast expanses of the Pacific, explored ways to build bombers with even greater range than the B-29. Germany, after developing the V-2 rocket that could fly a one ton warhead from Holland to London, planned a successor that might span the Atlantic to strike cities in North America. The Soviet Union built replicas of the American B-29 and undertook its own research on long-range rockets.

During the 1950s and 1960s both the USSR and the US drew upon captured German rockets and rocket scientists to build intercontinental strike forces.

although incidents such as the communist spying at Los Alamos created gray areas in which the CIA could operate inside the United States.

Though the CIA did not open its own research departments until 1962, from its creation the agency concentrated on certain areas of scientific research that had special importance—drugs that would be useful for the interrogation of spies ("truth serums"); photography and mapmaking; high-altitude aircraft; radio, radar, and sonar surveillance; missiles; and nuclear weapons. Like the KGB, the CIA was especially concerned with keeping track of new candidates for the "nuclear club," and during the 1950s both organizations were especially observant of the progress made by France.

The New Reach toward Space and Sea

Both the Soviet Union and the United States realized that surveillance satellites would provide a powerful intersection of new technologies in jet propulsion, radio navigation, and precision photography. The CIA knew that Russian ICMBs (see Tech Box) could be used not only as weapons but also to launch satellites. The United States planned to launch a similar device in 1958, but in October 1957 the Soviet Union leaped ahead of schedule, using its R-7 rocket to launch its first satellite, *Sputnik*. The CIA knew that the USSR planned to launch as many as thirteen more. These would be primarily surveillance platforms, permitting

Bombers such as the American B-36 and B-52 and the Soviet TU-95 (Bear) achieved sufficient range to carry nuclear bombs across polar routes. Missile research produced projectiles with ever longer ranges, greater payloads, and faster launch times. The Soviets built and tested the first ICBM (intercontinental ballistic missile), the R-7, in 1957. Spurious reports of large-scale deployment of these missiles sparked fears in the US about a 'missile gap,' although by 1959 the US was beginning production of its own Atlas and Titan ICBMs. These first-generation missiles were unreliable. Fueled with volatile liquids, they took hours to prepare for launch; once in the air, their mechanical guidance systems offered little more accuracy than those the V-2s and so were suitable for use only against targets as large as cities. These limitations dissolved in the 1960s as engineers and scientists on both sides developed even-burning solid fuels and on-board electronic digital computers for guidance.

By the 1970s, the missile and bomber forces of the US and USSR were so large as to ensure mutual destruction in the event of war, and both parties were seeking to reduce extravagant spending on new strategic weapons. Strategic Arms Limitation Talks (SALT) between the US and Soviet Union led to agreements that essentially froze the size and technical capacities of the superpowers' long-range weapons. Later, in the early 1990s, Strategic Arms Reduction Talks (START) resulted in the partial dismantlement of the massive Cold War arsenals of the United States and the USSR. But other nations, such as China, India, North Korea and Pakstan, continued development of their long-range capabilities.

high-resolution photographing of American military installations around the world, as well as of all of the United States itself.

Sputnik represented a scientific achievement that both stunned and delighted many around the world. Americans felt the humiliation and many criticized President Eisenhower for being indifferent to the scientific competition with the Soviet Union. Many people misunderstood *Sputnik*'s capabilities, thinking that it could fire death rays at Americans or drop nuclear bombs from space. It did not help that in the same week in which *Sputnik* was launched, Soviet premier Khrushchev had banged his shoe on a table at the United Nations and threatened to "bury" the United States.

More than any other single event of the 1950s, the *Sputnik* launch created a cultural and political revolution in the United States. The political witch-hunts of the McCarthy era, which had banished or imprisoned many American scientists, were never to return. Government funding for science education rose very sharply, and for the first time women were recruited eagerly into graduate programs of science and technology. Military and commercial development of missile and satellite technology was streamlined, coordinated, and when necessary bolstered by new government grants. Abroad, American diplomats worked to recoup some of the losses. The strategic partnership with Britain, which had weakened somewhat since the end of the war, was revived. U.S. participation in NATO became more consistent. Equally dramatic, U.S. government leaders who had previously dismissed outer space as of no strategic importance publicly realigned themselves with the new policy of an all-out drive to develop propulsion science and satellite technology.

In fact, an American program to launch a satellite similar to *Sputnik* was already well under way. But there were public relations complications because the most promising candidate for a rocket to carry America's first satellite into space was designed by Wernher von Braun, a German scientist who had designed Hitler's V-2 rocket, and then been protected from war crimes prosecution by the American government. An alternative project to launch America's first satellite burned on the launch pad in December 1957, deepening the government's embarrassment and the American public's anxiety. Eisenhower gave von Braun the signal to proceed, and on January 31, 1958, the United States evened the new "space race" with the Soviet Union by launching *Explorer I*.

At the same time, the United States was pursuing a remarkable program to position revolutionary cameras in space, and this was secretly achieved in August of 1960 with the launch of the CORONA satellite. By means of the new observation device—the existence of which was not declassified or known publicly until 1995—the United States not only closely monitored the size and placement of Soviet nuclear devices throughout the world but also created a method for recovering film from space that would be important in learning to safely return human astronauts to earth in the 1960s.

Observation from satellites was only one part of the new systems of security and surveillance. In the late 1940s, the U.S. Navy had begun to develop extremely sensitive underwater listening devices that could detect submarines at five hundred miles. In 1954 the United States launched the first nuclear-powered submarine, the *Nautilus*. This was the culmination of eight years of collaboration between Navy engineers and nuclear researchers at Oak Ridge, Tennessee. The new submarine was so fast that it could outrun conventional torpedoes. More important, its nuclear power plant allowed it to stay submerged and nearly undetectable for unprecedented periods of time.

The U.S. Navy immediately began experimenting with launching von Braun's V-2 rockets from submarines, and by late 1965 had developed a long-distance sea-launchable missile, *Polaris*, with a range of twelve hundred miles. Feeling intensely pressured by the U.S. deployment of nuclear naval technologies, the Soviet Union rushed ahead to implement stolen but not completely understood American designs. By 1958 the Soviet navy had two-dozen nuclear submarines patrolling the seas. It is thought, however, that the hurry to get them into action resulted in many Soviet sailors and technicians dying of radiation poisoning.

The Road to Confrontation

Because the United States and the Soviet Union were each able to destroy the other with nuclear weapons, they competed for power through client states in regional wars. Many of these new participants in the international chess game were former colonies of Britain, France, Belgium, and Portugal. The official U.S. policy was to encourage European countries to surrender their last colonies. Many in the U.S. government considered colonialism to be historically obsolete, and all agreed that the persistence of European colonialism only disposed aspiring nationalists throughout the developing world to sympathize with the Soviet Union's "anti-imperialist" stance. Along with decolonization, the United States also advocated that the Allied occupation of Germany be ended (as the United States was ending its own occupation of Japan in 1954). The end of the Allied occupation of Germany, of course, would mean reunification of the country and an end to the agreement under which the Soviet Union had gained control of East Germany.

The Soviet Union was uneasy with the American position on Germany. Soviet dominance in Eastern Europe appeared tenuous for a time in the spring of 1956 when the Hungarians attempted to throw off Soviet control. The United States had encouraged the Hungarians to revolt, but did not intervene on their side when the Soviet Union violently suppressed the uprising. Tensions between the United States and the Soviet Union mounted over the fate of the former German capital, Berlin. Though it was located in East Germany, the western part of Berlin was maintained as an American and British zone and was heavily fortified.

Soviet intelligence networks constantly warned that the West German government (then based in Bonn) was attempting to subvert East Germany by smuggling in Western European goods (and political influence) and inviting out East German workers—over two million of whom had escaped, attracted by the wages of the West. The only real hope of retaining East Germany was to insist that it be completely cut off from contact with West Germany. In November 1958, Khrushchev demanded that the United States and Britain give up their control of West Berlin, and that all of Berlin eventually be governed by East Germany. For a time there was consternation in the governments of the United States, Britain, and France. As 1960 approached, Khrushchev decided to wait out both the chancellor of West Germany (who was coming up for reelection) and U.S. President Eisenhower (who would have to end his term in office in January 1961).

Kennedy and Castro

In the 1960 election, John Fitzgerald Kennedy defeated Eisenhower's former vice president, Richard Milhous Nixon. Kennedy had campaigned on an aggressive platform criticizing the Eisenhower administration for dithering over a solution to the Berlin problem. Kennedy belabored the notion of a "missile gap" between the Soviet Union and the United States, claiming the Soviet Union had the advantage (the facts were the opposite). He also claimed that Eisenhower had neglected to prevent the rise to power of Fidel Castro in Cuba.

For half a century before this, Cuba had been under U.S. domination. Part of it was (and still is) a U.S. military base at Guantánamo Bay. The Cuban dictator Fulgencio Batista y Zaldivar had done little for the local population during his various periods in power since 1933, but he was an effective guardian of American economic interests in Cuba, most of which were connected to sugar and gambling. Batista was frequently opposed by peasant leaders and guerrilla fighters, among them Fidel Castro. With his allies from both the intellectuals and the peasants, Castro attempted several uprisings against Batista. He finally succeeded in 1959 and forced the dictator to flee to the Dominican Republic. At first, officials of the Eisenhower administration thought that Castro would come under the influence of the United States. They knew that the Cuban economy depended on U.S. tourism and on selling agricultural goods in U.S. markets. The head of the CIA advised that Cuba should be pressured with tariffs on its sugar sales in the United States until it would agree to become a U.S. ally.

Within months of his accession to power, Castro declared himself a Communist and began to court economic aid from the Soviet Union. The United States was startled to have a Communist republic so close to its own shores. It sought ways to warn the Soviet Union off the Western Hemisphere while continuing attempts to intimidate Castro or to work with right-wing anti-Castro Cubans to overthrow him. After his election in 1960, Kennedy was informed by the CIA that a plan to finance and organize an invasion of Cuba by anti-Castro Cuban exiles was already in progress. Kennedy said both privately and publicly that the campaign must have no direct American involvement. When the invasion of Cuba by the anti-Castro forces occurred at the Bay of Pigs in April 1961, the invaders were turned back (though the losses were greater on Castro's side than on theirs). Kennedy enacted the long-threatened trade embargo against Cuba, depriving it of income from the sugar sales to North America.

The Berlin–Cuba Crisis

In the last months of Eisenhower's administration, the Berlin crisis had worsened, as the Soviet Union had shot down an American spy plane over its territory and then had walked out of the ongoing negotiations over Berlin, claiming to be shocked and outraged by this brazen American act of espionage. This meant that Kennedy now faced a Berlin problem that had no prospect of solution, with the complications of an American intelligence pilot in Soviet custody and the simmering problems in Cuba coming to a boil.

For his part, Khrushchev also faced serious problems with his own government because he had not driven the Allies out of Berlin. Unlike Stalin before him, Khrushchev could not simply mark his rivals for elimination. If he lost the confidence of the Soviet Union's governing council, he could be deposed or imprisoned. The last time Khrushchev had been near to losing the support of the government, he had banged his shoe on the podium at the United Nations and publicly threatened the United States. Now he decided on something much more dramatic: He ordered that a barrier of barbed wire be built across Berlin on the night of August 12–13, 1961. East Germans trying to escape to West Germany would be apprehended or shot. Access to East German contacts by British and American spies would be eliminated. In the following weeks, the barrier was made more elaborate, becoming a high and thick brick wall surmounted by barbed wire and broken glass.

For the sake of public appearance, John Kennedy and Nikita Khrushchev concluded a stormy meeting in Vienna with a warm handshake. In fact their differences over the government of Berlin and the strategic situation in Cuba were not resolved, and shortly afterward led to a series of crises that deeply alarmed both the leaders and the publics of the United States and the USSR.

The population of Berlin was in panic. Families had been separated and stranded; travel lines were broken; food supplies were uncertain. In Berlin, the Allies, with their plans for a possible nuclear confrontation in Europe completed, drew their tanks into a zone on the western side of the wall that the Soviet Union had declared a no-trespassing area. The Soviet and Allied tanks, only a few feet from each other on either side of the wall, stood ready for a solid day to open fire. The next day, the Soviet tanks backed off. The Allied tanks did likewise. Both sides claimed victory.

Though nuclear weapons had not been used at Berlin, both sides had threatened more or less explicitly to do so, and both sides believed that actual use of nuclear weapons by the other side was a real possibility. By now Kennedy knew that apart from some temporary leads in missile technology, the Soviet Union was not equal in strength to the United States. Outside of Europe, the United States had stored nuclear bombs in Canada, Greenland, Morocco, Okinawa, the Philippines, Korea, Taiwan, and Puerto Rico. They were available if American submarines or airplanes should have to be armed or to replenish their supplies of nuclear warheads. U.S. missiles loaded with nuclear bombs had been in Italy since 1957, ready to be used if the Soviet Union should become aggressive in Europe.

Europe itself was becoming a nuclear arsenal. In all, the number of nuclear weapons in Western Europe had risen from about 3000 warheads in 1959 to about 4500 in 1961, of which 80 percent belonged to the United States. By the time of the construction of the Berlin Wall, the European countries keeping nuclear weapons for possible use against the Soviet Union included Britain, West Germany, Italy, France, the Netherlands, Greece, Belgium, and Spain. The total of U.S. weapons for all of Asia and the Pacific was about a third that of Europe (see Map 10.1). And these were only the weapons kept on land. The number of nuclear bombs that the United States kept at sea, whether on ships or on submarines, exceeded the total number kept on land, and may have peaked at over 30,000 in the 1960s. The number of bombs distributed by the Soviet Union is unknown, because, unlike the U.S. government, the Russian government has not declassified this information. But the numbers were certainly much, much lower than the American reserves, and their distribution was limited to Eastern Europe, the Balkans, Central Asia, and Northeast Asia (including North Korea).

The most provocative U.S. placement of weapons was in Turkey in February 1959. During the Second World War, Turkey had worked out an effective neutrality by signing nonaggression pacts with all the warring parties. However, in 1945 Turkey declared war on Germany just as the Soviet Union declared war on Japan. Turkey was awarded a place at the negotiations ending the war and became a founding member of the United Nations. During the Korean War, Turkey fought on the side of the United States and the United Nations, and in 1952 it became a permanent member of NATO. In its postwar role as a consistent ally of the United States, Turkey agreed in 1959 to host U.S. missiles aimed at the Soviet Union. These missiles were virtually on the Soviet border and were accompanied by U.S. listening posts in both Iran and Turkey, tracking the movement of Soviet planes and, of course, any missile launches from the Balkans or from Central Asia.

The discovery of the missiles in Turkey was yet another blow to Khrushchev's shaky standing with his colleagues on the Soviet governing council. He had failed to make the United States back down in Europe, and now he was allowing the Soviet Union to have missiles pointed at its heart. The pressure on Khrushchev to do something that would demonstrate the Soviet Union's strength and determination mounted. With his military advisers, he hit on the plan of placing missiles in Cuba—the closest strategic parallel to the placement of U.S. missiles in Turkey.

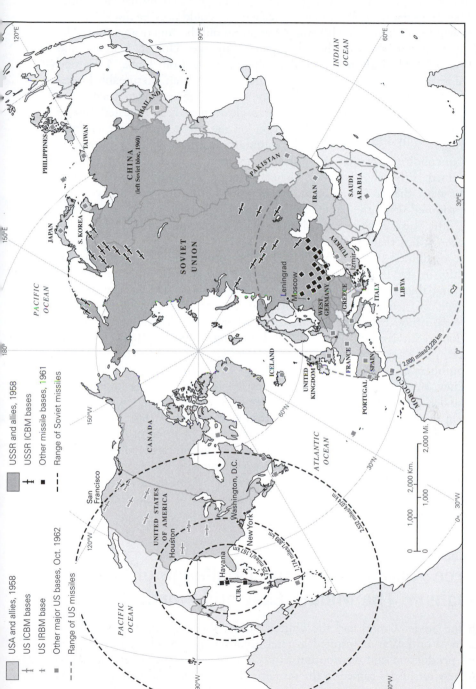

MAP 10.1 Mutual Missile Threats.

During the 1950s and the early 1960s, the United States and the Soviet Union competed to place nuclear missiles and weapons stocks at strategic points around the world. At the time, most of the long-range ICBMs were in fixed silos, aimed across the North Pole at the other superpower. The intermediate-range missiles placed in Turkey by the United States in 1957 were close enough to threaten the USSR and became a motivation for the Soviet attempt to place large numbers of armed missiles in Cuba.

In October 1962, U.S. surveillance planes flying over Cuba photographed the construction of silos for the launching of medium-range intercontinental ballistic missiles. The photographs revealed that the technology could only be Soviet. When the U.S. government found out what was going on, so did the American public. The Kennedy government showed the photographs to the United Nations and announced a naval blockade of any Soviet shipping to or from Cuba. Television news carried images of Soviet ships moving toward the Caribbean, presumably loaded with nuclear weapons mounted on missiles to be placed in the completed silos.

To both Kennedy and Khrushchev, it was clear that these repeated threats would themselves eventually force one power or the other into a corner from which it might well lash out with the ultimate weapon. Publicly, Kennedy demanded unconditionally that the Soviet ships turn around and the silos be decommissioned. Privately, Attorney General Robert Kennedy was dispatched to negotiate with the Soviet ambassador, Anatoly Dobrinin, and the younger Kennedy promised that the American missiles in Turkey would be secretly withdrawn. The Russian ships turned away from Cuba and headed home. The crisis was over in less than two weeks.

After the combined crises of Berlin and Cuba, both sides lost their taste for brinkmanship. In the 1950s the superpowers had pushed each other toward the limit, assuming that outright nuclear war was unthinkable. By the time of the Cuban missile crisis, nuclear war not only had become thinkable but had been planned several times. Each side was hatching schemes to allow some portion of its population to survive a nuclear strike and refining means of attempting "limited" nuclear war. They now realized that they had crossed into territory that had put huge numbers of people at immediate risk.

Khrushchev, the older of the two rivals, was left without political capital after the crisis, and resigned his position as premier in 1964. Kennedy enjoyed great popularity in the United States for his fortitude in the crisis, but to his close advisers he made it clear that he regretted the riskiness of some of his decisions and was resolved to focus on more local, militarily conventional, politically limited points of contention in the future. The president who had so relied on his youthful image to inspire the country toward greater optimism now saw himself returning to the more cautious, more compromising style of his predecessor. The next year, on November 22, 1963, Kennedy was assassinated.

Resource Anxieties and the Challenge of Secular Nationalism: The Middle East and North Africa

For both the Soviet Union and the United States, the lingering memory of oil shortages in World War II inspired a determination to control as much of the world's oil production and distribution as possible. Each of the superpowers was patrolling new territories gained in the settlement of the war, and each now had a set of allies to supply with new weapons. In addition, domestic recovery, particularly in the United States and Europe, was intimately connected to the automobile. President Dwight Eisenhower considered the construction of a national system of highways a major step toward both military effectiveness (since troops and weapons could be moved rapidly over the roads and evacuation plans could depend on them) and economic vitality. Highways also began to appear in Europe and in American-occupied Japan. Postwar development took the automobile and its associated phenomena as the centerpiece of all modernization. Fresh concepts of suburban living, with each family having its own yard, gardens, and garage, were dependent upon using the automobile to disperse human living spaces. But cities, too, were now thought of as hearts that depended on high-capacity traffic arteries. At the 1964 World's Fair in New York City, Robert Moses's sweeping plans for great flyovers intersecting the city and long entry and exit roads surrounded by scenic parks were as surprising and as popular as exhibits showing a future full of robots and computers.

Together with the rapid development of the plastics industries, highways and increased use of the automobile sharply increased the demand for petroleum derivatives. While the search for oil across the world increased in intensity, so did the search for energy alternatives. Nuclear power had showed its potential to contribute to energy supplies. Both Britain and the United States had made distinct strides by the middle 1950s. But in 1957 a reactor fire at a British nuclear plant polluted a great stretch of Western Europe and deeply unsettled a public that was still shocked by the images of human damage and long-term disease resulting from the American nuclear bombings in Japan. For at least a half century after the end of World War II, oil remained the most critical energy resource.

The cheapest oil sources were located in large quantities relatively close to the surface. Continental American supplies of such oil had been diminished long before the Second World War. The use of seismic equipment to test the structure of the rock strata deep beneath the soil had come into use before the war and had revealed deep but large deposits in California and in Texas. Soviet oil supplies were in the Caucasus, in Siberia, and along the Pacific coast. These deposits had been known and partly developed in the nineteenth century, but they were far from the population centers, making transportation very difficult. Both nations therefore had to look abroad for their oil supplies. The greatest concentrations of accessible crude oil were known to be in the Middle East, Central Asia (including the region of the Caspian Sea), and North Africa. These regions became areas of intense competition between the superpowers, and this translated into violent struggles in three hot spots: Israel, Iran, and Egypt.

Strategic Alignments in the Middle East

In 1948 the former British territory of the Mandate of Palestine was divided into the Kingdom of Transjordan (soon to be Jordan) and the State of Israel.

The connection of Israel to European history, culture, and political interests remained very strong. The history of the Holocaust convinced Jews all over the world, and many non-Jews too, that there must be a safe haven for those who might become the victims of new waves of anti-Semitism. European governments and the United States supported the creation of a strong, independent Israel not only because of the lessons of the Holocaust and the wishes of some of their Jewish citizens to return to Israel for religious reasons, but also because of the emerging strategic patterns in the Middle East. Israel would be a critical listening post for detecting Soviet attempts at expansion into Iran, the Middle East, and parts of Central Asia. It might also be an important client, should competition between the United States and the Soviet Union for oil and preeminence in the region turn hot.

But the creation of Israel meant the displacement of Arabs living in Palestine. This process had begun with the creation of the British mandate in 1917, and by the time of the creation of Israel perhaps as many as 750,000 Arabs had been driven out of the land. From having been the majority population of Palestine, Arabs were reduced to a minority. They were concentrated in the marginal territories of the Gaza Strip and the West Bank, while others migrated en masse, with no resources, to the holding camps that were created in Jordan, Lebanon, and Syria. Arabs who resisted the removal were subjected to terrible violence, sometimes by the new settlers and sometimes by the authorities managing the transition to the Israeli state. The most famous incidence of Palestinian deaths in the removal was that at Deir Yasin in 1948, in which members of the Israeli paramilitary group Irgun killed hundreds of villagers.

Jordan, Egypt, Syria, and Lebanon were outraged by the forced displacement of Arabs and the construction of the state of Israel. In 1948 Jordan attacked and occupied the West Bank, to which many residents of the former Palestine had fled. It also seized a portion of the city of Jerusalem. Israel won its survival in this skirmish, but the disputed city of Jerusalem was divided, with one part under Israel's control and the other under Jordan's (eventually to come under international jurisdiction).

For a decade afterward Israel remained locked in battle against its Arab neighbors, particularly in the Sinai Peninsula. Because the Arabs in Palestine had inhabited and worked the land under the traditional collective institution of the Islamic trust (*waqf*), the new Israeli legal authorities declared the land ownerless and appropriated it for redistribution to Israeli farmers or military installations. Until the later 1950s, Israel depended for its survival largely upon the zeal of its farming population, its crack intelligence service, and occasional military and financial support from Europe. In the later 1950s, the United States became interested in supporting Israel financially. This was done primarily through a "Food for Peace" program of the early 1950s. Military assistance did not begin until 1959, but it quickly blossomed to large proportions. This was inspired in part by two large shifts in the power balance, first in Iran and then in Egypt.

In 1948 Golda Mabovitz, later known as Golda Meir, signed the Israeli declaration of independence from British rule. Born in Russia, Meir had lived in Palestine since 1921 and been active in the movement for local rule by Jewish immigrants. After independence she would serve as foreign minister, and finally in 1969, as prime minister—the third woman prime minister of the twentieth century after Sirimavo Bandaranaike of Sri Lanka and Indira Gandhi of India, and the first to lead a nation aligned with the West.

Struggles for Self-Direction: Guatemala, Iran, Egypt, and Algeria

As we shall see, many nations made attempts to negotiate a middle path between the superpowers in the 1950s. They depended on ideas of nationalism, self-determination, and, when possible, self-reliance. One of the first episodes in the history of the aspiring nonaligned nations took place in Guatemala. In 1951 Jacobo Arbenz Guzman was elected president of Guatemala, and he promised land reform as the central program of his new government. Arbenz's policies were intended to bring stability to a country that had been governed by dictators for decades. Under the previous government system, the United Fruit Company, an American corporation once based on banana sales but now controlling many aspects of the Central American economy, had been permitted to dictate wage and landholding conditions in Guatemala. The result was a situation in which barely more than 2 percent of the population owned 70 percent of the land.

Most working men were agricultural laborers; many had been rounded up by Guatemalan army troops and sent to jungle or mountain regions to work as slaves. Guatemala circa 1952 has given us our phrase "banana republic."

When UFC saw that it could not continue its previous practices in Guatemala under the Arbenz government, it lobbied the Eisenhower administration in the United States to declare that Arbenz "tolerated communists." The U.S. government then pursued a multifaceted strategy that was to become a model for eliminating troublesome governments in the future. First, it worked to brand the Guatemalan government as being not "democratic" but "communist" and to isolate it in the region. Nicaragua, Honduras, Panama, and eventually Mexico all became helpers of the United States in the anti-Guatemala campaigns, some of them acting as staging grounds for the planned military invasion. Next, leaders of the Guatemalan army (and Arbenz himself) were offered rewards to change their loyalties. Arbenz refused, but many of his army officers accepted. In the meantime, the United States disrupted the shipment of agricultural goods out of Guatemala and oil supplies into the country. The economy crashed. Finally, the CIA oversaw continual aerial bombardments of Guatemala, attempting to destroy its fields and its cities. In June 1954, the Guatemalan army demanded Arbenz's resignation. He left the country to live in Mexico City. After his departure, a military dictatorship that was friendly to both the United Fruit Company and the United States was established.

This model of ideological stigmatization and regional isolation, economic destruction, and finally invasion by U.S.-trained troops was used elsewhere even while it was being deployed in Guatemala. One target had been Iran, and the purpose was to preserve U.S. access to oil. Iran, which was a monarchy under the control of the *shah* (king), Reza Pahlavi, had been contested by the United States and the Soviet Union before the end of World War II. In the agreements among Britain, the United States, and the Soviet Union that followed the conclusion of the war, Stalin withdrew from the parts of Iran that he had occupied. British companies, which had dominated Iran's oil industry before the war, regained control of their facilities. At the same time, the United States and Britain won a very important listening post for monitoring the movement of Soviet armaments and industries throughout the Caspian region and Central Asia.

Soon, however, the United States and its allies were shocked at the turn of local political events. Iran and its neighbor Iraq were undergoing many transformations in the years after the war and after the ending of European colonialism. Nationalist enthusiasms were high, and labor movements, particularly among oil workers and dockworkers, were becoming strong. Many of the unions were socialist in orientation, and the United States had feared for years that the Soviet Union would exploit labor unrest in order to preach communism. In 1951 Mohammad Mosadegh was elected prime minister. He declared Iran's oil resources and industries to be national assets and demanded the abdication of the *shah*. Mosadegh argued that Iran should be a nonaligned nation instead of a client state of Britain and the United States.

Though Mosadegh's ideas appeared very radical to the British and Americans, they were actually in the tradition of Kemal Atatürk (see Chapter 4), the founder of the Turkish republic, because they stressed not only nationalism but also secularism—the idea that Islamic law and culture should not control the society but that the more religious and less religious should live under a government that fostered individual rights and privacy. But Britain was unwilling to lose a lucrative industrial base and the United States found the prospect of losing control over Iran strategically intolerable. In 1953 the CIA led a plot to convince the Iranian public that Mosadegh intended to end the Iranian monarchy and seize dictatorial powers. They funded an opposition leader who forcibly deposed Mosadegh. British ownership over the oil companies was restored, and after the *shah* returned to power he was encouraged to rely less on democratic legitimacy and more on surveillance and force. This was the second time that foreign intervention had put the *shah*, Mohammad Reza Pahlavi, on the throne—the first was in 1941 when Nazi Germany had installed him as *shah* in place of his father. A secularist who advocated industrialization, modern education, women's voting, and close cooperation with the United States and Britain, Pahlavi tended over time to favor authoritarian symbols and repressive policies. His secret police, SAVAK, became renowned worldwide for terrorizing the population.

The sabotage of the Mosadegh government left the United States and Britain even more deeply invested in Middle Eastern affairs. By the middle 1950s, Egypt attracted American and British attention as a direct threat to their interests. Along with Morocco, Liberia, and Ethiopia, Egypt had emerged from colonial rule, and it sat close to the newly discovered oil deposits in North Africa. Gamal Abdel Nasser, a young military officer of very humble origins, was a key figure in a series of remarkable events in Egypt that, between 1952 and 1954, both ended the Egyptian monarchy and ended the British military presence in the country.

Like Atatürk and Mosadegh, Nasser was a nationalist first and a Muslim second; he thought that a civil regime should be able to accommodate many religious or even nonreligious attitudes. Nasser was also a bitter enemy of Israel, he traded arms with Czechoslovakia (a client state of the Soviet Union), and he recognized the government of the People's Republic of China, all actions that annoyed the United States. Nevertheless, he was bold enough to ask Britain to help finance his plans for a huge dam on the Nile, to supply water for city residents in Cairo as well as farmers in southern Egypt.

When Britain refused to help finance the project, Nasser seized the equipment and assets of the private British company that ran the Suez Canal, by which oil and other goods were shipped from the Persian Gulf to Europe. In October 1956 Israel invaded Egypt with the military support of Britain and France. The intention was clearly not only to regain control of the Suez Canal but to depose Nasser himself. As it happened, the invaders were stymied by the basic dynamics of bipolar brinksmanship. The United States and the leaders of the United Nations, fearful that the Soviet Union would enter the fight on the side of Nasser, refused to endorse the invasion. In 1957 the Israeli, British, and French forces all withdrew from Egypt, and Nasser enjoyed a reputation at home and abroad that put him in a category with Castro—a brash young nationalist who could stand up to the aging, corrupt colonial powers as well as the two imposing superpowers.

The echoes of Nasser's achievement were felt very strongly in Algeria, where France was attempting to perpetuate its colonial rule. Algeria, like other parts of North Africa and the Middle East, had a vigorous movement for secular nationalism developing among its younger generation. But there was also a large population of native-born descendants of the French colonial settlers, who were called *piéds-hoirs* ("black feet"). This group, like the descendants of British colonialists in Ireland and Rhodesia and of the Dutch settlers in South Africa, feared that any lessening of imperial power in the colony would leave them destitute, or perhaps even place their lives in danger. The *piéds-noir* were long-standing opponents of granting any powers to Muslim Algerians, and they threatened civil war if France should abandon colonialism in Algeria.

For its part, the French public seemed equally determined to hold Algeria. Vietnam had been surrendered in a political agreement with the United States in 1954, and this had been followed by France's humiliation by Nasser. To many in France, Algeria was the last symbol of French imperial greatness. When Algerian nationalists, who had been active since the late 1930s, rose in open rebellion in 1954, it was regarded as a national crisis in France. By 1958 suppression of the Algerian guerrillas had reached a high point of violence, incarceration, and torture of prisoners, but the independence movement had not been crushed. The political right wing in France called on Charles de Gaulle to come out of retirement and assume the presidency. France's Fourth Republic ended, and a new regime was founded. De Gaulle swore to the *piéds-noir* that he would end the Algerian uprising, and thereafter a savage campaign to strangle Algerian independence began. In 1962 de Gaulle and the National Liberation Front in Algeria reached an agreement to cease fire and hold a referendum on independence in Algeria. When the Algerians voted overwhelmingly for independence, France was forced to grant it in 1962.

As many in both France and Algeria feared, the withdrawal of the colonial government did not bring peace to Algeria. Violence between the *piéds-noir* and Algerian Muslims persisted for years. The triumvirate that assumed control of Algeria after the French withdrawal fell out among themselves, and Ahmed Ben Bella soon emerged as the most powerful. By this time Algeria was a shambles. Nearly a million people had died in the fighting first against the French and then among themselves, twice that many were homeless, and 70 percent of the normally working population was unemployed. Ben Bella attempted to institute a sort of "Algerian socialism," founded on land reform, universal health care, and centralized education. These hopes were not realized, mostly because of constant challenges to Ben Bella's authority that eventually descended into a new civil war.

Continuation of Cold War in Vietnam

When Japan had invaded and occupied Vietnam in 1943, the Communist activist Ho Chi Minh became a leader of the guerrilla resistance, supported by American advisors and supplies. But when Japan was defeated, the Vietnamese nationalists were not given control of the country. The United States, fearing Soviet expansion after the war, was chilled by Ho's history as a Communist. It supported a restoration of French rule in Vietnam, and in fact it paid the majority of the expenses of the French colonial regime in its efforts to reassert rule. Between 1946 and 1954, Vietnam was an early proxy theater in the Cold War, with France as the U.S. client and Ho Chi Minh as the Soviet client.

In 1954 France decided to withdraw from Vietnam after suffering heavy losses at the battle of Dien Bien Phu. An international conference at Geneva determined that Vietnam would be provisionally divided into north and south. The north was to come under the governance of Ho Chi Minh and his Viet Minh party, while the United States would stand in for France as the protector of southern Vietnam. The agreement provided for free elections in the south, but the United States decided to ignore this and to install Ngo Dinh Diem as president. When Kennedy inherited this situation in 1960, he realized that Diem could not make himself popularly accepted, but he saw no alternative to giving him military support.

In early November 1963, however, Diem's own officers assassinated him and established a new government. Kennedy was murdered only weeks later, and President Lyndon Johnson, who succeeded Kennedy, decided to aggressively prop up the government of South Vietnam. His advisers at the time, notably Robert McNamara and George Kennan, believed that containment of the Soviet Union and its "Communist bloc" required vigorous opposition to every Communist or socialist movement. If the local representative of anti-Communist interests was incompetent, he might be replaced. If he was unpopular, there must be a propaganda campaign to make him lovable. If his military resources were inadequate, they must be improved by supplying him with increasing quantities of deadlier weapons, including tanks, planes, assault rifles, grenades, and land mines. The Communist movement should be fought in "hearts and minds" (in the culture and the politics of the society) as well as on the battlefields, because in the view of these strategists, a single loss of territory to the Communists would strengthen all Communist movements in the world.

"Third" Forces and the Changing Structure of Power

Just as President Johnson was preparing to invest a massive American military presence and large amounts of foreign aid in his advisers' idea that the "Communist bloc" would expand and increase its power unless Communists everywhere were defeated, parts of the Communist bloc were falling apart. Signs of the fracture were evident in the later 1950s when Yugoslavia became quite independent under its leader, Josip Broz Tito, and the 1956 rebellion in Hungary had to be crushed by Soviet troops. The troubles in Eastern Europe and the Balkans had inspired the Albanian Communist leader Enver Hoxha to declare in 1956 that he felt much more closely allied to the People's Republic of China than to the Soviet Union. For its part, China was becoming more and more distant from

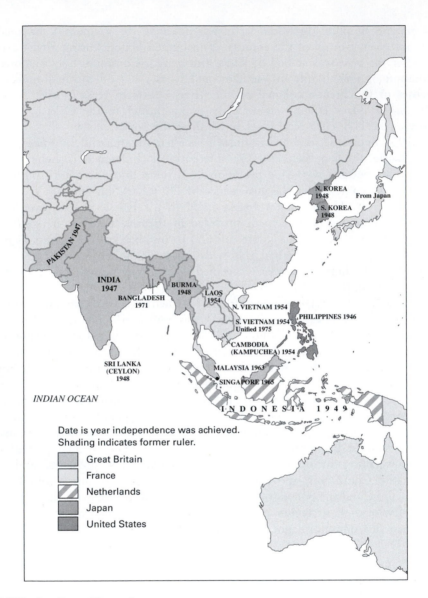

MAP 10.2 New Power Alignments.
Asia was one of many venues in which nations emerging from colonialism were pressured eitherd to become allies of the United States or the Soviet Union, or to become part of the "Third World," or non-aligned nations, who first gathered at Bandung, Indonesia in 1955. Of the nations seen here, North Korea and North Vietnam were allies of the Soviet Union while South Korea and South Vietnam were allies of the U.S.; Burma (Myanmar) was neutral for some years but eventually became an ally of the Soviet Union and the People's Republic of China; Cambodia and Laos attempted to remain neutral but were gradually overwhelmed by Communist insurgencies; Sri Lanka pursued an independent path; the Philippines remained closely connected to the U.S. after independence; India and Indonesia became leaders of the Third World.

the Soviet Union, and Mao was promoting himself internationally as a truer successor to Stalin than Khrushchev was.

The place of China in a "Communist bloc" had always been problematic. The Chinese Communist Party had been founded in 1921 with Soviet encouragement, and with the exception of Mao Zedong the CCP's early leaders had all been trained in Moscow and acknowledged by the Comintern, the Leninist organization for the international promotion of communism. Mao's theories of rural revolution (instead of Marxist revolution based on an urban proletariat) were regarded by the Comintern-educated Communist elites as ignorant, and Mao never had a position of real power in the party until the Soviet-controlled CCP leaders were driven out of the Chinese cities between 1927 and 1931. They had to drag themselves in humiliation to Mao's remote base in the countryside and join his "People's Liberation Army" in fighting both the Japanese and the Nationalist government of China. After Japan surrendered in 1945, the Communists and Nationalists turned against each other in a civil war that concluded with a Communist victory in 1949 (see Chapter 9).

After the establishment of the People's Republic of China, relations with the Soviet Union worsened almost immediately. Mao felt that the Soviet Union did not provide suitable support to China in its war against the United States in Korea between 1950 and 1953. At the end of the war, Mao denounced the accession of Khrushchev to leadership of the Soviet Union as a betrayal of Stalin's legacy. Through the middle 1950s, Mao constantly criticized Soviet actions in Eastern Europe and the Balkans. Nevertheless, from the point of view of the United States, a Communist victory in China in 1949 had necessarily meant an increase in the power and influence of the Soviet Union. There were fears of Chinese intervention in Vietnam, or threats to Taiwan, which some countries in the world still recognized as the home of the official Chinese government. The American intention was to isolate the PRC internationally, deprive it of foreign aid, and keep it under constant military pressure from South Korea and from Taiwan itself (where U.S. nuclear weapons were stockpiled).

Both Mao Zedong in China and Kim Il Sung in North Korea initiated radical programs of "self-reliance." Their idea was that a fundamental decenralization of agriculture and industry, along with suppression of foreign trade and forcing each individual to focus on work basic to survival, would insulate their societies from a nuclear conflict between the Soviet Union and the United States. In both countries, these extreme programs were accompanied by severe policies suppressing dissent and imprisoning large numbers of intellectuals, farmers, and industrial workers who might resist.

In 1957 Mao Zedong initiated an "anti-rightist movement" in China to flush out and silence critics of his radical decentralization plan—not coincidentally including those Soviet-connected party functionaries who had always annoyed him. With the "rightists" out of the way, Mao proceeded to reorganize agriculture, moving all farmers into massive "communes," where they were to run their own factories, hospitals, schools, storage facilities, and garages. In some areas there was resistance and violence, particularly in northwest China where Muslim nomads hoped to keep their pastures and religious buildings from being absorbed. In 1959 Tibet came under direct military occupation because of its resistance to agricultural reorganization and cultural suppression.

The immediate effects of the policies at the end of Mao's first radical transformation, the "Great Leap Forward" (1959–1961) were, we now know, disastrous. Perhaps as many as thirty million to forty-five million people died as a result of agricultural failures, inability to move food where it was needed, or violence as troops and villagers fought over the little food that was available. Mao was unimpressed by this human cost, considering it part of the process of socialist transformation. Criticism of Mao within the CCP was intense by 1959. But moderate party leaders failed to convince their colleagues to abandon Mao's course and replace him as party secretary. In 1960 relations with the Soviet Union broke down completely. After decades of rancor and mutual suspicion, the supposed "Communist bloc" had formally split.

Part of Mao's program for China was assumption of leadership in the global "Third World" movement for freedom from domination by the two superpowers. Mao had laid the groundwork for this in 1955 when his officials attended a conference of the leaders of twenty-nine developing nations at Bandung, Indonesia. These countries shared problems of agricultural development, public health, and industrialization, and they all feared becoming embroiled in the global competition between the United States and the Soviet Union; American novelist Richard Wright described them, sympathetically, as "the underdogs of the human race." As a group they represented the majority of the world population. The Chinese representatives portrayed themselves as the champions of these nations struggling for independence. India, itself ambitious to lead the Third World movement, was indignant. In 1957 China engaged in a brief border skirmish with India, and the Soviet Union took the Indian side.

When the full extent of the human disaster caused by the agricultural radicalization of 1958 to 1961 was realized by the CCP, Mao finally had to appear to share power with his moderate rivals. But by 1962 he was plotting to return to full power, with a stronger base than ever. His new push, when it came in 1966 as the "Cultural Revolution," would be both domestic and international. Domestically, it would be based on an appeal to youth, a demand that the national revolutionary spirit be renewed, and a call for China to make new efforts toward Mao's own ideal, self-reliance. Internationally, it would build on the Third World leadership that China had established at Bandung, but with an important new element: China became the world's fifth nuclear power (after the United States, the Soviet Union, Britain, and France) when it tested a device in 1964.

This breakthrough was not a complete surprise, but it was nevertheless an unlikely achievement in many ways. Mao's China had been in the midst of a radical move away from the centralized planning of agriculture, and also from all centralization and hierarchy in industry and education. Mao appeared to be going the opposite way from the superpowers, which were moving toward more centralization and more rationalization in the development of communications, education, and research. But Mao had been careful to protect the extremely secret centers for nuclear research and other military weapons research in the country. The research was led by the physicist Qian Xuesen (H.S. Tsien), who had been educated in the U.S. and had been serving in American rocketry development before being driven out of the country by false claims of being a communist and forced to return to China in 1955. Their research facility, on the nearly unpopulated frontier between Tibet and Qinghai province, was completely isolated, relatively safe from the prying eyes of Soviet and U.S. surveillance, and certainly out of the way of China's ideological enforcers.

The United States and the Soviet Union both realized that although the Chinese nuclear device was no direct threat to them, Mao was very likely to use it to intimidate his Asian neighbors, and that the bomb would become a symbol of Chinese preeminence in the Third World. They sought a local champion that could create a modest "balance of terror" in Asia. Their choice was India.

The parallels between China and India were remarkable, but the differences were also striking. India's population rivaled China's, and India—like China—could lay claim to the cultural prestige of thousands of years of civilization. It used land reform and Lenin-style "five-year plans" to develop the economy and redistribute wealth. Like China, India had determinedly steered a course between the superpowers. Again like China, India had been led through the turbulent period of the 1950s by a single leader: Jawaharlal Nehru, who became India's first prime minister after independence in 1948 and continued in that position until his death in 1964.

There were, however, very vivid differences between the two countries. Though many people criticized Nehru's patrician attitudes and authoritarian style, India was a democracy. Nehru had been educated as a lawyer and in his youth had been a follower of Gandhi. He was a prolific writer in English, and his publications helped to create international sympathy for India in the postwar world. Secure as he was in his communications with both the United States and the Soviet Union, Nehru was often frank with the two powers, demanding respect for India's neutrality.

Nehru's plan for India was extremely ambitious, going far beyond mere agricultural self-sufficiency to full-scale industrialization. The country had the advantages of high literacy rates and several outstanding educational institutions. There were certain formidable obstacles, however. Nehru did not reform India's rigid caste system, and so he did not create maximum opportunity for talented people to enter the educational stream. Agricultural reforms were successful in some areas, but in other areas the climate was too poor or natural disasters occurred.

Most devastating was the deepening divide between Hindus and Muslims. Nehru had wished to avoid the partition of South Asia between predominantly Hindu India and predominantly Muslim Pakistan. But the British had insisted on the partition, and Nehru—a native of Kashmir, which was beset by religious troubles from the time of independence—struggled to deal with the complex regional tensions in addition to continuing conflicts within India itself. In the middle and late 1960s, both the Soviet Union and the United States avoided China and grew closer to India. They lavished foreign aid and good press on the country, and they actively encouraged it to pursue a program of nuclear development. Though India did not develop a nuclear bomb immediately, it became an important potential partner to both the superpowers, and a political and educational model for many of the developing, nonaligned nations. The foundation was laid for another great power to emerge in Asia.

CONCLUSION

During the Cold War, the United States and the Soviet Union based their relationship with each other on their shared monopoly of nuclear weapons and the constant search for the point at which the other party would back down rather than risk unlimited destruction. Both parties realized in 1962 that they had gone too far, and had risked too much over the fates of Germany and Cuba. They tended thereafter to seek ways of containing their own rivalry within limited, conventional theaters of conflict, and they also attempted to limit their need to invest in further development and production, manufacture, and maintenance of nuclear weapons. Increasingly through the late 1950s and 1960s the superpowers transferred their rivalry to their client states, fighting each other through proxy wars.

By this time, however, the science of nuclear weaponry was no longer completely under the control of these two powers. Most significant of the new nuclear powers was China, which after 1960 was an unfriendly rival of both the Soviet Union and the United States. China now competed with the two superpowers for influence over the nations of Africa and Asia that were emerging from colonialism. It relied on the ideology of Third World hopes for agricultural success, accessible industrialization, military independence, and national dignity. The Cold War was not over, but by the mid-1960s it was no longer the primary determining factor in the distribution of world weapons and resources.

For Further Reading

Christopher Andrew and Vasili Mitrokhin, *The Sword and the Shield: The Mitrokhin Archive and the Secret History of the KGB* (New York: Basic Books, 1999). One of the few histories of the KGB, based on documents reported to have been supplied by a defector.

Ali M. Ansahri, *A History of Modern Iran Since 1921: The Pahlavis and After* (London: Longman, 2003). A focused history of modern Iran.

Tin Bui, *Following Ho Chi Minh: The Memoirs of a North Vietnamese Colonel*, Judy Stowe and Do Van, trans. (Honolulu: University of Hawaii Press, 1999). An inside look at the Communist campaigns to drive the United States out of Vietnam and reunite the country.

Iris Chang, *Thread of the Silkworm* (New York: Basic Books, 1995). A study of the origins of China's success in missile and nuclear technologies, focused on Qian Xueshen (H.S. Tsien).

Laurence Chang and Peter Kornbluh, eds., *The Cuban Missile Crisis*, 1962: *A National Security Archive Documents Reader* (New York: W. W. Norton, 1999). Based on the materials in the National Security Archive, supplemented by the materials provided during meetings of the participants in Havana in 1988; supplements from ongoing conferences and document releases are included.

Paul Dickson, *Sputnik: The Shock of the Century* (New York: Walker and Company, 2001). Insights into the technological world of the the late 1950s.

Frank Dikotter, *Mao's Great Famine: The History of China's Most Devastating Catastrophe, 1958–62* (London: Bloomsbury, 2010). New, definitive research on the devastation of the Great Leap Forward.

Robert A. Divine, *Eisenhower and the Cold War* (Oxford and New York: Oxford University Press, 1981). A classic study of the politics, strategic pressures, and technological issues of the 1950s.

Richard M. Fried, *Nightmare in Red: The McCarthy Era in Perspective* (Oxford and New York: Oxford University Press, 1991). A scholarly study of a period of extremism in American political life and its international effects.

Aleksandr Fursenko and Timothy J. Naftali, *Khrushchev's Cold War: The Inside Story of an American Adversary* (New York: W. W. Norton, 2006). Based on Soviet as well as American archives, presents a dramatic narrative of the Cold War rivalry in Cuba, Africa, Asia, and the Middle East.

Mark J. Gasiorowski, *U.S. Foreign Policy and the Shah: Building a Client State in Iran* (Ithaca: Cornell University Press, 1991). A scholarly study of the Mosadegh overthrow and return to power of the Shah of Iran in the 1950s.

Robert S. Norris, William M. Arkin, and William Burr, " Where They Were," *Bulletin of Atomic Scientists*, Vol. 55, No. 6, 1999, pp. 26–35. A brief scholarly study of the placement of nuclear weapons since the end of the Second World War.

James L. Schefter, *The Race: The Uncensored Story of How America Beat Russia to the Moon* (New York: Doubleday, 1999). Popular account of the political dynamics behind the "space race."

Stephen C. Schlesinger, Stephen Kinzer, John H. Coatsworth, and Richard A. Nuccio, *Bitter Fruit: The Story of the American Coup in Guatemala* (Cambridge, Mass.: Harvard University Press, 1999). A thorough, scholarly account of the destruction of the Arbenz government in the 1950s.

A. I. Solzhenitsyn *The First Circle*, Thomas P. Whitney, trans. (Evanston, Ill.: Northwestern University Press, 1997). A fictional account of life inside a *sharashka* based on the author's own experiences.

B. Tad Szulc, *Fidel: A Critical Portrait* (New York: Avon Books, 2000). A popular biography of Castro.

Related Websites

Brayton Harris, World Submarine History Timeline, 1580–2000
    http://www.submarine-history.com/NOVAfour.htm
The Cold War Science and Technology Studies Program
    http://www.cmu.edu/coldwar
The Cuban missile crisis, The National Security Archive, George Washington University
    http://www.gwu.edu/~nsarchiv/nsa/cuba_mis_cri/
Manhattan Project, Special Collections Research Center, Manhattan Project and Atomic Scientists Collections, University of Chicago
    http://www.lib.uchicago.edu/e/spcl/manhat.html

The National Security Archive, George Washington University
    http://www.gwu.edu/nsarchiv/nsa/cuba_mis_cri/
Paul Halsall, Internet Modern History Sourcebook: A Bipolar World
    http://www.fordham.edu/halsall/mod/modsbook46.html
Mohammad Mosaddeq and the 1953 Coup in Iran
    http://www.gwu.edu/~nsarchiv/NSAEBB/NSAEBB126/index.htm
The Red Files
    http://www.pbs.org/redfiles

CHAPTER 11

Border Crossings, 1946–1975

In 1959, an exhibition of U.S. machinery opened in Moscow to show Soviet citizens American science and technology. The exhibition hall featured a suburban-style ranch house, complete with built-in appliances and furniture from Macy's department store, not space satellites or airplanes. Visitors could watch dinner being produced from frozen foods and boxed mixes and admire the washing machine. When Vice President Richard Nixon toured the site with Soviet Premier Nikita Khrushchev, the two men stopped in a model kitchen and debated the relative power of civilian and military production. Conceding that the USSR might be ahead in rocket science, Nixon claimed victory in color television and predicted that a consumer revolution would eventually transform the USSR. He added, "We won't force it [the American way of life] upon you," but "your grandchildren will see it." Khrushchev rejected Nixon's appeal to shift Cold War competition to consumer goods, but the Soviet government could not block knowledge of a rising standard of living outside the USSR or its attraction.

The three decades after World War II were a heady time of innovation and cross-cultural borrowing. On every continent, local communities adapted to outside influences. Globalization is far more than an economic process of integrating markets. It forces the interaction of cultural, social, political, and economic systems, and, most important, it raises individuals' consciousness of a wider world. The appeal of Hollywood movies, American jazz, rock and roll, and sports teams exploded when supported by the media and artful advertising. The launching of satellite broadcasting in 1974 by NASA (National Aeronautics and Space

Administration) ushered in the era of international television, permitting house-holds around the globe to experience the same images and sounds.

But if crossing borders became normal, it could also be threatening. The pro-ducts and ideas that swing around the globe are difficult to stop or to censor, though governments have often tried: Think of the unsuccessful international efforts to curb the trade in heroin. Neither acid rain nor an oil spill is stopped for lack of a passport. In the thirty years after World War II, governments had to come to terms with their inability to close national borders and the need to inter-act with international organizations.

A New Order of Things

Consumption

If you opened the pages of an American women's magazine—*Good Housekeeping*, for example—in the 1950s, you found a familiar world of goods: refrigerators, washing machines, vacuum cleaners. Well-dressed women and their electrical appliances kept homes and children sparkling clean. This mass-produced afflu-ence, which had begun to transform daily life in the United States during the 1920s, accelerated in the postwar period as incomes rose rapidly. Each year thousands of families, blue- and white-collar alike, bought well-equipped houses complete with lawns and garages. The second car for the wife or teenager, chosen for its "sporty look," began to appear in some suburban driveways.

These spending patterns spread from the United States to Western and Central Europe as employment and productivity rose. The baby boom of the 1950s and 1960s increased the demand for goods and services, and a revived manufacturing sector and international trade supplied a tempting array of products. Phonographs and records, colorful china, telephones, refrigerators, and washing machines were soon found in ordinary homes. Access to this bounty spread beyond the cities as rural areas were wired for electricity. The combination of a steady income and consumer credit bought a motorbike, a car, or a television. With wheels, people traveled more and traveled farther. Single-family homes with modern kitchens and bathrooms lured people from their older neighborhoods into a suburban-style existence, not only in the United States but throughout Western and Northern Europe. Home improvements and shopping trips became forms of entertainment.

This new consumption changed ways of life and undermined social distinc-tions. When industrial workers could buy cars and clothes similar to those used by professionals and managers, how could differences be recognized and main-tained? In a world in which consumption signaled status, easier access to goods lessened social distances. Mass consumption was democratizing.

It also changed women's work. Although ads promised liberation from drudg-ery, the new appliances raised housekeeping standards and forced their owners to take the place of servants, who had vanished from European middle-class homes. Although working outside the home became a more attractive option, wives found that the demands of home and family continued, and that they had less help. Nevertheless, employment rates among married women began to rise in the United States and Western Europe during the later 1960s and 1970s. The new consumption transformed the organization of households as well as material culture.

Europeans thought the growing taste for fast cars and clean bodies was an indication of "Americanization." Indeed, the United States did launch much of the new because it could export freely while its major competitors were still recovering from World War II. U.S. factories churned out blue jeans and cars, while its media transmitted pictures of the good life in America. The seemingly effortless creation of excess both attracted and repelled Europeans, who saw it as threatening older standards of behavior and modes of living.

The export of U.S. culture was actively pushed after 1945 by the federal government as well as by U.S. corporations. Coca-Cola bottling plants came along with US troops after World War II. The arrival of the five-cent Coke triggered culture wars in France during the 1950s. While French students guzzled the new drink, farmers and winemakers attacked it as a menace to the nation's health and its agriculture. For traditionalists, the red bottle cap symbolized a distinctly unwelcome economic and cultural imperialism, but for the young it offered cheap and tasty modernity. The fight against Coke, as against many of the new products, soon ended in defeat and was forgotten.

Films became tools of U.S. economic and foreign policy. After the war, the U.S. government demanded "freedom of information" in Europe, which in practice meant that American aid and credit were linked to open access to European markets for U.S. media. In the longer run, Hollywood studios evaded import quotas by investing in European companies and shifting production to overseas locations. The net effect was the triumph of Hollywood films over their European rivals and the broadcasting of particular values championed by those films: individualism, competition, free markets, and the melting pot.

For millions of people, Hollywood became a gigantic U.S. information agency, creating film worlds that eclipsed reality. As Eric Johnston, president of the Motion Picture Association, explained to the U.S. Senate in 1953, "Pictures give an idea of America which is difficult to portray in any other way, and the reason, the main reason, we think, is because our pictures are not obvious propaganda."[1] The United States Information Agency, which operated two hundred film libraries around the world, and the Motion Picture Export Association teamed up for their mutual benefit. During the 1950s, Hollywood produced over half (and in some cases well over half) of the films screened in the countries of Africa, the Middle East, Central and South America, Western Europe, Australia, and New Zealand. Only the Communist states refused Hollywood products.

---

[1]Reinhold Wagenleitner, *Coca-Colonization and the Cold War: The Cultural Mission of the United States in Austria after the Second World War*, Diana M. Wolf, trans. (Chapel Hill: University of North Carolina Press, 1994), p. 229.

The idea of Americanization attracted the young, who were among the earliest to embrace postwar cultural changes, but over time the identification of the new consumption with the United States became less easy to sustain. In the longer run, the revival of the European and Japanese economies made these countries active producers and exporters of a similar basket of goods. The consumer revolution of the postwar period and the creation of an international mass culture were driven eventually by a number of industrial countries. Yet because of continuing differences between the rich and the poor, the end result was not homogeneity. Although international exchanges diminished the differences among cultures, they also intensified the gap between those who were part of a global economy and those who had few and weak links to it.

Exports from the cities to rural areas moved slowly and incompletely, but by the 1960s changes in consumption patterns were evident from the highlands of Chile to the rice-producing areas of Java. A stream of rubber boots, soft drinks, kerosene lamps, and cotton shirts flowed from cities to towns to local markets. A few such items reached the farming village of Karimpur in northern India (see Chapter 6). Some of the wealthier families bought bicycles and ready-made clothes. People could make trips to town to see films and buy newspapers. Regular bus service made urban visits easier. At the same time, imports of new technologies changed methods of production and daily labor. Hand pumps and electric motors made it possible to drill tube wells in the fields or inside house courtyards.

The dashing new Corvette (left) and the Bel Air Sport Coupe.

Chevy puts the <u>purr</u> in performance!

Getty Images

This advertisement from *Life Magazine* was selling not only cars but the American Dream of the early 1950s. Well-dressed parents, child, and pets enjoy their modern, suburban house, complete with palm tree and garden. Her Bel Air Sports Coupe complements his Corvette, the first Chevrolet sports car.

Even if people still lived behind mud walls, the outside world was beginning to reach them directly. By the 1960s, television sets could be found throughout Latin America, the Middle East, northern Africa, and Southeast Asia. This revolution in consumption continued to deepen and widen during the 1970s and 1980s as incomes rose.

It has proved impossible for governments to stop the international flow of goods that they wish to ban or to regulate. Drug trafficking illustrates the problems involved in attempting to block trade when profits are high and markets vast. Democratic governments do not have the power to close their borders. Although the international drug trade, particularly in heroin, had virtually collapsed by the end of World War II, it quickly revived after the war. The drug story joins regions around the globe.

It begins with the cultivation of opium poppies by thousands of small farmers in the mountains of Asia, from Turkey east through Pakistan and down into the upland regions of Burma, Thailand, and Laos. The opium poppy is a major cash crop in these regions, and growing it is the most profitable occupation in places where the soil is poor and demand for other crops that can be grown is low. The flowers' seedpods produce a milky sap, which a few simple operations turn into bricks of morphine.

"Lucky" Luciano, an American Mafia boss deported to Italy in 1946 and one of the great criminal talents of his generation, organized the international narcotics syndicate that smuggled morphine into refineries in Marseilles and Sicily, converted it to heroin, and then moved it into the United States via Canada and Cuba. His Turkey-Italy-America heroin route operated successfully during the 1950s and early 1960s, until it was disrupted by the deaths and arrests of key Italian figures, the Cuban revolution, and, most important, the Turkish government's crackdown on poppy production. Soon the traffic reorganized around Saigon and Hong Kong, with shipment into Miami via Latin America. U.S. soldiers had easy access to cheap drugs in Vietnam, and their habits as well as their suppliers followed them home. As the number of addicts in the United States rose, so did the potential profits and the lure of the trade. International law enforcement has been unable to do more than disrupt this smuggling temporarily.

Production

The consumer revolution rests, of course, on mass production and on the output of thousands of firms and factories. Advances in transportation and communication in the postwar decades significantly lowered national barriers and encouraged more and more firms to turn international in the 1960s and 1970s. In a world in which many countries could produce at least simple industrial goods, relative costs influenced factory locations.

Along with international marketing strategies came international divisions of labor. Because wages in the industrialized countries rose sharply, so did the potential savings for employers from moving some types of production or distribution into low-wage countries, particularly in Asia and Latin America. Even before World War II, U.S. employers produced goods in other countries in order to be close to foreign markets. But by the 1970s, the primary target was the U.S. market.

Companies built factories in Mexico, Haiti, and Colombia to assemble goods that were then re-exported to the United States. Employers sent textiles to Central America and the Caribbean to be cut and sewn into shirts, pants, and jackets, which then made their way back to America's suburban malls. Electronics firms, struggling to compete against Japanese rivals, decentralized the production of TV sets and other electronic goods. Plants in Mexico and Taiwan produced parts, which then went to Korea to be assembled before shipment to Los Angeles or New York The Japanese shifted much of their electronics manufacturing to China and Southeast Asia. Mass production went international.

The restructuring of manufacturing overturned earlier gender divisions of labor. In the early examples of industrialization, men dug the coal, worked the furnaces, and ran most of the machines. Only in textiles did women hold a significant share of industrial jobs. But in the new, postwar international division of labor, women took on a major share of industrial work in developing countries. Their need to earn money for their families made them an easily exploitable group, unorganized and cheap to employ. Since such jobs were relatively scarce and wages and conditions in the export factories were better than their other options, many women had little incentive to strike or complain. They moved into these jobs while in their twenties and then turned away from factory labor as they married and had children. In the early 1960s, women held over 30 percent of all wage and salary jobs in a wide variety of economies—not only in the core states of the industrial world, such as the Soviet Union, the German Federal Republic, and the United States, but also in peripheral economies, such as those of Jamaica, Haiti, Nepal, and the Philippines. Throughout Central America, Eastern Europe, and parts of the Middle East and East Asia, women made up a significant share of the paid labor force in the 1960s, taking on not only factory work but jobs in the service sector, commerce, agriculture, and unskilled labor.

Along with increases in women's labor outside the home came smaller families. Birthrates declined sharply in many parts of the developing world during the 1970s as women became better educated and set higher goals for themselves and for their children. Particularly in Latin America, Eastern Europe, and East Asia, access to contraception and other forms of fertility control meant that couples on average had fewer children. Working parents turned to birth control to lessen the pressures of jobs, crowded housing, and rising aspirations. Nevertheless, patterns of authority within families and communities changed very slowly. Despite women's increased participation in the world economy, lack of access to education and laws limiting their rights restricted women's public activity in much of the world.

The second consequence of the changing international divisions of labor was a slow but significant deindustrialization of the United States and Europe. By the late 1960s, all the industrialized countries were producing similar sets of products, which they traded among themselves. Soon several Asian countries joined this race, leading to excess capacity in one industry after another. Unfortunately for the United States and Europe, the rising industrial powers had newer machines and lower labor costs. Those who had industrialized first found themselves at a significant disadvantage.

Entrepreneurs moved toward two different strategies: They could either "go high-tech" or "zap labor." The first solution required much investment and highly skilled workers. That combination permitted companies to produce high-quality products that were not duplicated elsewhere. Using this approach, the Japanese took over the markets for fuel-efficient cars and consumer electronics. Germans and Swedes dominated the machine tool industry, and Italian firms mass-marketed high-style clothing.

Many U.S. employers took the second approach in the 1970s and 1980s. They cut labor costs by moving production and investment abroad. All over Europe and the United States, coal mines and shipyards closed because their markets had shrunk or had been captured by cheaper competitors. Mills shut down in the textile regions of Britain, France, and the United States. Steel mills in West Germany, Belgium, and the United States laid off workers as their markets were captured by Asian rivals. When more Americans began to buy Japanese and European cars, the decline in Detroit's fortunes accelerated. Older U.S. centers of production in the Midwest and East were supplanted first by plants in the South, where workers had not yet unionized and wages were lower, and then by factories abroad. Although 27 percent of employed Americans worked in manufacturing in 1970, only 19 percent did so by 1986, and this trend has continued.

The social cost for particular families, towns, and regions was enormous. Towns like Detroit, Glasgow, and Lille had to deal with mounting unemployment and a shrinking tax base. Areas that had been economic leaders in the late nineteenth century became poor relations, needing extra welfare funds and social services. Trade unions lost members as the middle-aged dropped out of the workforce and young people left for more progressive regions or countries. Boarded-up buildings lined city streets, and empty factories stood silent on the riverbanks. The slowdown in the international economy after the oil shock of 1973 pushed older areas of production in North America and Western Europe into recession and decline.

Agriculture and the Green Revolution

Production in factories required more production in the countryside to permit food and raw materials to flow from region to region. The challenges posed to agriculture by expanding populations and rising standards of living were enormous and worldwide. Not only did factory and plantation workers have to be fed but machines needed cotton, palm oil, and rubber to transform into cloth, soap, and tires. The combination of division of labor and large populations without land meant that even in mostly rural areas, workers needed to import their food.

GLOBAL Technologies

DDT

In his poem, *Choruses from the Rock*, T. S. Eliot suggested that post-war culture would be remembered for the asphalt road and a thousand lost golf balls. Equally long-lasting are many of the synthetic molecules of the era, including the polymer films that wrapped foods and the artificial fabrics that clothed bodies. These durable monuments of synthetic chemistry changed the tastes, textures, and colors of post-war societies and sometimes altered patterns of life. Some later became the target of jokes, as in the one word of career advice given to the young Dustin Hoffmann in the 1967 film *The Graduate*: "plastics".

One of these many and mostly anonymous molecules stands out as a symbol of power and hubris: dichlorodiphenyltrichloroethane or DDT for short. First synthesized in the

nineteenth century, the substance showed no signs of useful properties until 1939, when a Swiss chemist, Paul Herrmann Muller, discovered that it killed most insects quickly after contact. Subsequent testing suggested it might be the ideal insecticide. First, it was potent disrupter of nerve action in most insects, even in minute concentrations. Second, it was a very sturdy compound that did not decompose readily under exposure to sunlight and moisture; once applied to foliage or even marsh grasses it remained active for weeks or even months. And, most important, it had no discernable effects on human beings or farm animals, mainly because of differences between the chemistry of mammalian nerve cells and those of insects.

Put into production in the U.S. by 1942, DDT became famous as one of the miracle compounds of World War II. In Europe, medical officers herded troops and civilians through tents where fans maintained a blizzard of DDT powder. In the Pacific entire islands were bombed with DDT dust to make them safe for Allied troops. In both cases, the targets were insects that carried deadly diseases: typhus-carrying

For how long could the world continue to feed an expanding population? Arable land and water have been, and continue to be, scarce resources, distributed unequally. How could the interests of producers and potential consumers be reconciled? The issues of famine and food distribution posed not only technical problems to be solved but moral dilemmas to be debated. Countries that could not grow enough food to feed their citizens had to either export goods to pay for imports or beg for international charity. Moreover, people began to want to consume more. For individuals as well as for nations, having enough to eat requires both the production of food and the ability to buy that food. Revolutions in agriculture have technical, financial, and social consequences.

In the immediate postwar period, the revival of international markets and U.S. aid allowed enough food to be transferred to Europe from the Americas and

lice and mosquitoes that could transmit malaria, yellow fever, and dengue fever. After the war, public health officials at the World Health Organization hatched plans to eradicate malaria by destroying the mosquitoes that carried the parasite. Meanwhile, farmers began to apply the compound to their fields and homeowners to their lawns. Within a decade, aerial DDT sprays were being used in the United States to make parks more comfortable on summer evenings and to rid forests of invasive species like gypsy moths.

DDT had successes and failures. It was quite possibly critical in saving post-war Europe from the kind of typhus epidemic that had killed hundreds of thousands after World War I; it played a role in ridding warm-weather islands, such as Sardinia, of malaria; and it helped reduce the incidence of malaria in many parts of Africa, Asia, and Latin America where it was sprayed on the walls of homes and public buildings. Used indiscriminately, however, it rarely suppressed unwanted insects for more than a few months, and it did so only by destroying populations of species beneficial to human beings, such as honey bees.

By the late 1950s, nature lovers and ornithologists were beginning to notice another effect: bird counts were shrinking in areas bombarded with DDT. By the early 1960s, the evidence was clear: birds were consuming DDT when they ate insects and seeds, and this DDT was then causing female birds to lay eggs with lethally fragile shells.

Most readers learned the bad news about DDT and related compounds from *Silent Spring*, a book by an American naturalist and science writer, Rachel Carson. Published in 1962, Carson's best-selling book provoked stringent controls on insecticides in the U.S. and Europe. It also helped stimulate a widening public concerns with other environmental issues—concerns that found expression in clean water and air legislation, tougher regulations on hundreds of industrial chemicals, and a growing public interest in ecology and the environment. By the end of the century, the movement had grown from a modest number of activists, almost all American and European, to millions who were enrolled in Green Parties and hundreds of environmental organizations around the globe.

Australia to fill the deficit left by the destruction of Europe's fields. Luckily, the mechanization of farming in the United States and Canada allowed those countries to produce large surpluses, which could be sent elsewhere. Moreover, the U.S. government committed itself to giving grain or selling it at reduced prices to countries that were threatened with famine. The combination of high productivity and international financing eased the transfer of U.S. grain and other food abroad.

In the longer run, European farmers mechanized too, replacing human and animal energy with tractors. During the 1950s and 1960s, methods of mass production in agriculture spread rapidly in Europe, increasing yields there and helping farmers to raise their incomes while decreasing the amount of labor needed to produce crops. First in the United States and then in Europe, farming became more and more heavily capitalized and specialized as energy use in the form of electric-powered machines and fertilizers multiplied With these changed methods, farmers could more than double their yields while the amount of human labor used shrank to insignificance.

In contrast, mechanization made little progress in Latin America, Asia, or Africa, where labor was abundant and capital for investment limited. Electricity, gasoline, fertilizer, insecticides, and machinery cost more than local farmers could afford. Moreover, in terms of energy expended per unit of food produced, their hand methods were actually more efficient than mechanized agriculture.

Genetic research led to more easily exportable changes in technology. Plant breeders and botanists in the United States developed hybrid varieties of wheat and corn that not only resisted plant diseases but also bore more seeds. In the longer run, scientists perfected new types of rice, dwarf plants that matured rapidly and raised yields. To adapt these plants to conditions in the tropics, geneticists worked with research institutes in other countries to find the best varieties for particular climates and soils.

Some of the first of this international cooperation took place in Mexico, where the Rockefeller Foundation financed a joint scientific mission to introduce and adapt disease-resistant wheat to local conditions. By the later 1960s, fields planted with the new seeds grew more than three times as much as had been produced there during the 1930s. The Ford Foundation started a program of rural development in India in 1951 that helped introduce the so-called Green Revolution there. The introduction of new types of rice and wheat in northern India and Pakistan was a spectacular success, raising output dramatically. In many parts of Asia, not only could farmers grow more rice with every crop, but under proper conditions they could double- or triple-crop their land without resorting to highly mechanized methods. The miracle seeds have made it possible for farmers in many areas to increase their incomes by growing a much larger amount and exporting it. Genetic engineering of plants has vastly increased the chances that the world can continue to feed itself despite heavy population growth.

The Green Revolution changed more than outputs; it had major social and ecological consequences. To produce new crops, traditional ways of farming had to be abandoned, and many small farmers did not survive the shift. They sold out to large owners who had enough money and other resources to risk changing their way of life. Because the new seeds need large amounts of water, chemical fertilizers, and pesticides, the Green Revolution required big capital investments, either by governments or through borrowing from moneylenders. Chemical fertilizers, derived from oil, had to be purchased abroad or produced locally from imported materials. Irrigation systems had to be devised and maintained. Relatively isolated villagers had to work with agronomists, engineers, and merchants.

Commercial agriculture is an international agriculture, dependent on long distance flows of knowledge, seeds, fertilizers, and marketed crops. Even as this high-energy farming shielded producers from the impact of drought and plant disease, they became vulnerable to wider market pressures. When oil and fertilizer prices rose in 1973, farmers around the world saw their production costs rise sharply too, and many had to abandon the new crops. During the middle 1970s, the Green Revolution stalled because of its high price tag and its link to the availability of cheap oil. Ecological costs rose as well. Irrigation increased the salinity, or salt content, of fields and changed water table levels. Where dams and open irrigation systems were built, silt and herbicides washed off the land and clogged and polluted rivers. By increasing the demand for water, the Green Revolution intensified one more area of competition.

Despite the Green Revolution and the consequent increases in production, major famines that killed several hundred thousand people occurred between 1945 and 1975. In the 1970s, people starved in Ethiopia, in the Sahel of Africa, and in Bangladesh despite aid sent by the UN, the European Economic Community, and the United States. Economist Amartya Sen has shown that famine in the contemporary world is less a matter of scarcity than of entitlement: In many recent famines, enough food to feed the hungry has been available within the country, but those who died were too poor to buy it. Marginal groups, such as nomads, landless laborers, small holders, and transport workers, did not earn enough cash to purchase food in the market. Even if imported agricultural methods and crops have made it possible for the world to feed its growing population, the problem of uneven distribution results in mass starvation in certain regions. In the second half of the twentieth century, agricultural regimes around the globe became more tightly interconnected, both in feast and in famine.

People on the Move

At the end of World War II, as the victors rearranged political boundaries and the colonial powers retreated, millions of people found themselves in the wrong nation-state, vulnerable because of their ethnicity, their party affiliation, or their religion. For them, crossing borders seemed a necessity. Some moved voluntarily, and others fled invading armies or angry mobs. The category "displaced person" covered a wide variety of losses and humiliations. After the defeat of their country, Germans fled Poland, Czechoslovakia, and the USSR. Poles, Yugoslavs, and Hungarians moved out of areas of Soviet influence. Jews who survived the concentration camps left Europe for Palestine or North America, if they could.

For a few years after the war's end, Argentina, Australia, Canada, New Zealand, and the United States welcomed European refugees. Each of these former European colonies temporarily lowered barriers to international migration, allowing some people that it perceived as racially and culturally similar to its own citizens to enter the country and stay. Other war refugees found new homes in Western Europe or northern Africa. These migrations increased the cultural complexity of the neo-Europes around the globe, while diminishing the political and economic problems of those societies that had been torn apart by the world war.

Refugees and Migrants

These wartime rearrangements continued in the later 1940s as new countries formed. When the British left South Asia in 1947, millions of Muslims moved west into Pakistan, and millions of Hindus fled east into India. The lucky ones survived the trek and the accompanying massacres. The creation of Israel exiled several hundred thousand Palestinians into refugee camps in other areas of the Middle East. The Communist victory in China pushed Nationalist Chinese into Taiwan. The creation of Communist regimes in East Germany, Czechoslovakia, North Korea, Cuba, and Vietnam triggered massive emigrations into neighboring states, as did uprisings against Soviet control in Eastern Europe.

The uprooting of people and their movement across international boundaries continued well beyond the end of World War II. The Vietnam War sent hundreds of thousands of individuals from several Southeast Asian countries into refugee camps in Thailand, Malaysia, and Hong Kong for later resettlement in North America, Europe, and Australia. The Soviet invasion of Afghanistan pushed millions into Iran and Pakistan. To stay alive during civil wars in Guatemala, El Salvador, and Nicaragua, hundreds of thousands left their homes for more stable, prosperous societies. Ethnic conflict and political hostilities created more than seventy million refugees in Africa during the period from 1960 to the end of the century. Political turmoil in the modern age intensified migration and cultural mixing.

But for every person who was forced to emigrate by hostile armies or political parties, dozens more voluntarily walked or rode away in search of a different life. Few places are so isolated that rumors of jobs or tales of greener pastures do not penetrate. The uneven economic development of societies around the globe tempted the young and healthy to go where their labor was needed and better paid. Heavy movement out of the islands of the Caribbean into Britain and North America began in the 1950s when transportation costs declined and the economies of industrialized areas boomed. The long and relatively porous U.S. border permitted millions of Mexicans and other Latin Americans to move north across the Rio Grande. Workers from Uruguay, Chile, and Bolivia trekked into Argentina.

Although migrants can be found virtually everywhere in the world, a few places stand out as major exporters of labor between 1945 and 1980: the Philippines, India, Pakistan, Turkey, Greece, Mexico and Central America, the Caribbean, and northern Africa. For some small, overpopulated, poor countries, voluntary migration became a way of life, a necessity because farms were too small and families too large. The destinations of these migrants were generally North America and Europe, although Africa and urban areas of the Middle East have been secondary targets (see Map 11.1).

For the most part, it was adult males who made the trip, many on temporary job contracts. Wives and children initially stayed behind, deterred by the cost and by immigration regulations. But when fathers did not return, family members joined the exodus to the industrialized lands, producing large communities of immigrants in capitals and factory towns.

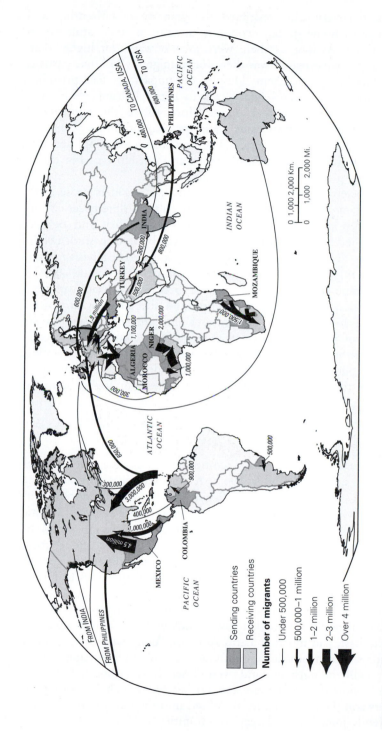

MAP 11.1 Global voluntary migrations, 1945–1980.
Millions of people moved within and among continents in the decades following World War II. Although North America and Europe attracted the most new settlers, Southern Africa, Nigeria, and the Middle East were also favored destinations.

Although European governments restricted the granting of citizenship and tried to send immigrants home during economic downturns, their attempts to repatriate migrants failed. As long as there were jobs at wages far higher than could be earned at home, what reason was there for immigrants to leave, particularly after their families had joined them? Despite the impact of racial prejudice and social discrimination, immigrants had access to better housing, education, and medical care than in their home societies. Moreover, as the numbers of immigrants mounted, the newcomers built their own communities, complete with mosques, temples, and ethnic societies. They reconstructed simplified versions of their home culture around key institutions and kinship ties. For them, cultural imports brought protection and self-esteem.

Within the host society, opposition to the arrival of outsiders arose. The need for labor did not mean automatic tolerance of cultural differences. Mobs in Indonesia periodically attacked Chinese residents. The French and Belgian governments banned the wearing of Islamic headscarves by female students. In some U.S. states, voters lobbied to end bilingual education. The divisive issues posed by international migration have continued to simmer in the multicultural societies of the contemporary world. The balance between inclusion and exclusion has been the basis of many bitter fights, and the answers have been provisional. As second and even third generations of immigrants have grown in size, the problems of integration have changed. Many countries have conferred automatic citizenship on the children of newcomers, giving them voting rights and increased political power. Others have not done so, continuing to define membership in the nation-state by ethnicity or religion rather than by birthplace.

Moving to the City

Encouraged by cheaper transportation and communications, the international mixing of populations speeded up after 1945. As incomes rose, people spent more on travel. In 1947 Pan Am began the first round-the-world service, a trip that had shrunk to sixty-nine hours in 1969 when jet airplanes came into commercial use. Getting to Athens from London required three days by train in 1950, but only four hours by plane in 1960. Business travelers and tourists could hop a plane and find themselves in a different culture within a few hours.

It is easy to exaggerate the isolation of places distant from the cities of North America and Europe. Although in 1950 more than 80 percent of Asians and Africans lived in villages or rural areas, as did a majority of Latin Americans, most places were within reach of a market town, and rural bus services operated in India, the Middle East, and much of Latin America. Along with the spread of electricity came radios, which broadcast international news and sporting events. Later, television brought the outside world even closer. Boys in South American and Indian villages followed World Cup and cricket test matches, rooting for their favorite players and their national team. Wired into the outside world, ordinary folk intermittently joined much larger communities.

Such mental connections encouraged movement into the cities. Rates of urbanization in Africa, Asia, and Latin America rose sharply during the postwar era. Although in 1930 only about 12 percent of people in the Third World lived in towns of more than five thousand, that percentage had leaped to 20 percent by 1960 and to 27 percent by 1980. Urban populations exploded in Mexico, India, and Egypt. West Africans moved into the towns of Nigeria and Ghana looking for work. In China, government policy tried and failed to force city dwellers into the countryside and to slow the rush into the older cities.

With each passing decade, the number of cities with more than a million inhabitants climbed. No longer were most of the world's largest cities in industrialized countries By 1980, about a third of the urban population in Third World nations lived in cities with more than one million inhabitants. When high population growth in the countryside forced people to move, the country's capital was a logical choice. The net result tended to be highly unbalanced urban networks— sleepy small towns and an exploding metropolis that was unable to provide work or decent shelter for its residents.

The big cities of new nations gained thousands of people each year, with disastrous results. Shantytowns built of recycled junk hugged the hillsides of São Paulo and the roadsides near Lagos. The price was right, even if the new address lacked running water, electricity, paved streets, and services. Called oil-drum cities (*bidonvilles*) in French, little villages (*kampongs*) in Indonesian, and canned food towns (*halabi abad*) in Farsi, their names mirrored their semi- urban, semi-accepted status. By the 1970s, the United Nations estimated that almost half the population in sixty-seven large Third World cities lived in such squatter settlements. Unplanned and unwanted by everyone except their inhabitants, shantytowns typify the new urbanism of the late twentieth century. These communities with few public services and less legal security have become the permanent homes of millions of new city dwellers.

The Pressure of Demography

The urban explosion was fueled by high levels of population growth in rural areas, distributed unequally around the globe. Birthrates in Europe and Russia declined to the point where fertility dropped below replacement levels, virtually ending population growth in those countries. In contrast, by the 1960s, annual rates of population increase in Latin America, South Asia, and Africa were approximately double those in North America and Europe.

At the same time, changes in sanitation, medicine, and nutrition led to declining death rates in most parts of the world. Since the difference in birthrates among regions was much greater than the difference in death rates, the net result was a large surplus of births and a much more rapid increase in population among the peoples of Asia, Africa, and Latin America than among those of North America and Europe. Moreover, high fertility produces young populations, whose death rates are relatively low and whose prospects for marriage and additional child-bearing are high. By 1980, virtually all of the world's population growth was taking place in Asia, Latin America, and Africa.

Skyscrapers in the financial district of Manila loom over this Philippine shantytown, where houses lack electricity, sewage connections, and, probably, piped water. Similar social inequalities can be found in many of the world's largest cities.

ROMEO GACAD/AFP/Getty Images

Demographers argue that by the 1970s, two different demographic regimes were operating around the world, one produced by low fertility and the other by high fertility. In the industrialized countries, low birth and death rates led to an aging population, with few children and more and more elderly. The chance of dying young dropped sharply, and women spent fewer years in childbearing and child rearing. But as new opportunities opened for women and for the middle-aged, other risks increased. The death or serious illness of an adult could bring disaster to a household that had too few kin to help. Moreover, aging populations need extra social services and medical care. Such societies need more young workers to pay the bills for the elderly. In short, they need migrants, who have to come from outside. This demographic deficit has fueled much of the importation of foreign labor, which flowed from east to west and from south to north in the postwar period.

In contrast, the less-industrialized countries moved into an extraordinary phase of growth in the postwar period. High birthrates combined with declining death rates to produce a population explosion. Around 1950, in twenty-five of the poorest, most heavily populated countries around the world, women commonly gave birth to between 6 and 7.5 children during their reproductive years; in comparison, their European sisters gave birth to 2 children. Women in much of Africa, the Middle East, and South Asia spent a large portion of their lives bearing and rearing children. Such a pattern of population growth, where land is scarce and industrial employment is unavailable, made migration necessary for survival. Demographic inequalities have pushed people across international boundaries into the more heavily industrialized regions of the world. One hallmark of the modern world is mass migration into cities, where ethnic categories are blurred and cultural choices challenged.

International Styles

Mass media and mass migration eroded national borders. If Korean Americans in Los Angeles watched James Bond movies, sang Beatles songs, and ate Tex-Mex food, what kind of cultural world did they inhabit? Not only identities but also cultural constructs came into question. The uniqueness of place dissolved under the pressure of imports. International styles of architecture, consumption, dress, and leisure made it increasingly difficult for travelers to distant cities to identify differences. With rising incomes came more choices, but those choices were drawn from a standardized pool of goods and styles.

Whether a person lived in Buenos Aires, Singapore, Tel Aviv, or Copenhagen, elements of similarity, of familiarity began to multiply throughout the 1960s and 1970s. The same sorts of angular, air-conditioned glass towers loomed above city streets in central financial districts, whatever the country. The business suit served as a male uniform on several continents. The look of the "modern," the growth of international businesses, youth culture, and international sports diminished cultural distances.

Modernism

New York City's Museum of Modern Art, whose aim was to spread appreciation of contemporary styles of painting, sculpture, film, and architecture, became an international arbiter of taste. Its collection of works by Picasso, Mondrian, and Brancusi ratified the value of the stark, geometric forms that had been pioneered by European artists and architects and condemned by the Nazis. With the Fascist defeat came the triumph of a modernist aesthetic. After 1952, the museum's international department regularly sent exhibitions around the world, spreading interest in modernism as it was defined in the United States and Europe. In 1958–1959, a traveling show of New York painters starring Jackson Pollock spread the gospel of abstract expressionism. Audiences in cities around the world flocked to see photographs, films, and objects that had been selected as representing the new taste.

Modernism meant different things in different fields, but in architecture and design in the first decades after the war, it translated into a triumph of the so-called international style—unadorned geometric shapes constructed from industrial materials. Le Corbusier's sweeping structures of poured concrete and Philip Johnson's one-story, rectangular glass house represent two influential varieties of modernism.

The most easily recognizable modernist structure in the postwar period was the skyscraper. Built of reinforced concrete with glass curtain walls, dependent on elevators and air conditioning, it testified to the mastery of and dependence on advanced technologies. Such buildings multiplied in the 1950s and 1960s on the streets of Caracas, São Paulo, and Tokyo, as well as in North America and Western Europe. New York architectural firms translated their Manhattan successes into commissions in foreign capitals, and younger Dutch, Italian, and Latin American architects gave the internationalist geometry a local flavor.

Architectural superstars worked all over the world, worrying little about linkage to local traditions. City planners, whatever their nationality, hopped from project to project and from continent to continent. Le Corbusier designed Chandigarh, the new capital of the Punjab; Brasilia was planned by Oscar Niemeyer and Luis Costa. Planners confidently proclaimed that there were universal principles of modernist design that would work in the tropics or the tundra. Rather than reflect cultural specificity, modernist architecture denied it (see pp. 213–214).

A reaction against modernism intensified during the 1970s, changing cityscapes. In 1976, the Aga Khan, head of the Ismaili Muslims, funded a prize to recognize architecture built to reflect the spirit of contemporary Islam. An international jury surveyed territory from Indonesia to Morocco, looking for architecture that successfully expressed Islamic culture and values. Inspired by the form of a Bedouin tent, one architect used stainless steel panels and poles to create a soaring hotel courtyard that was open to the sky. Most important, the process of selection publicized and validated the idea of an Islamic alternative to the international style. In the 1970s, there was increasing awareness that modernism came in several varieties.

Youth Culture

Long before their elders, young people in the 1950s and 1960s found it both appealing and possible to adopt U.S. cultural styles. Becoming "modern" required very little: Jeans and a T-shirt could do it. The media provided the models, and as soon as postwar scarcities eased, the market supplied the goods. The growing international communications industry found eager audiences everywhere. The sounds of *Blue Suede Shoes* brought teenagers onto dance floors in Berlin and Buenos Aires and New York, and the Elvis Presley film *Love Me Tender* became a hit worldwide. The Beatles and the Rolling Stones, based in Britain, quickly acquired a global following.

Access to images of these cultural styles was not difficult. By 1970, the USIA published one hundred forty magazines with a circulation of over thirty million copies. The International Communication Agency distributed U.S. materials in more than a hundred countries, and the U.S. government funded over a hundred radio stations, which then sent materials to several thousand others. The Voice of America and its equivalents were beamed south, east, and west. News, music, and entertainment crossed the Cold War divide as well as the world's oceans. Rock groups, such as Bill Haley and the Comets, went on world tours, and their local imitators packed city clubs. Even if access to American casual clothes was initially limited to the wealthy and well-connected, others could see, admire, and eventually take their cast-offs. Films brought together the new music and clothes, setting them in motion with a dash of romance.

After the release of *Rock Around the Clock*, Bill Haley and the Comets acquired an international audience, which could hear their songs on long-playing records. Skirt decorations and song titles proclaim the group's global appeal.

Youth culture signaled limited rebellion, which was popular and possible in many places. The soft-edged defiance of respectability communicated through styles of dress and choice of music disturbed adults, who were eager to preserve a unified, hierarchical society, whether of a communist or a capitalist variety. In both East and West Germany, the consumption of rock 'n' roll led to public defiance of elders' cultural conservatism.

Occasionally, teen rebellion crossed the line from symbolic representation to riot. During the mid-1950s in West Germany, street fights begun by teenagers at movie theaters or by those at concerts of American music infuriated German adults. Jazz, which was seen as African American, symbolized the racial dangers of U.S. culture. When East German youths marched the streets demanding rock 'n' roll and denouncing their country's leaders by name, the Communist government saw these rowdy adolescents as a challenge to state authority. West German officials blamed Marlon Brando and his film *The Wild Ones* for dozens of riots that broke out in 1956 about the time the film opened. The cultural choices of young people challenged gender, race, and class norms in ways that adults found politically threatening, whatever their politics.

In the longer run, however, economic development softened the impact of youth culture. When produced locally, jeans and T-shirts seemed less foreign, and they eventually became just ordinary dress. Ironically, the effect of greater consumer choice was a lessening of international differences and a homogenization of styles.

The Global World of Sports

Globalization can also be seen within the world of sports. By the 1950s, eighty countries, including several from Asia and Africa, belonged to the international federation of football associations, and this number had almost doubled by 1980. Teams from Japan, Europe, and the Americas battled one another annually in the world baseball championships. The numbers of fans and participants exploded as organized sports became the world's most popular form of entertainment.

Television created the modern sports industry. Network coverage of baseball in the United States boosted team revenues and players' salaries as it turned local stars into national heroes. Baseball's postwar popularity in Japan rose after the Tokyo-based Yomiuri Giant's games appeared on TV. Cable and satellite broadcasting of games in the late 1970s and 1980s turned national audiences international as media moguls, such as Ted Turner and Rupert Murdoch, bought sports teams and captured their coverage. The appeal of American professional basketball spread around the world after Michael Jordan joined the Chicago Bulls, and CNN showed fans his amazing jumps not only in games but in multiple Nike ads. Astute telemarketing sold shoes and sport at the same time. An estimated one billion people watched the 1976 Olympics, and more than two billion people, half of the world's total population, saw the 1978 World Cup matches on television.

Spectator sports fostered nationalism as well as international contacts. When athletes from the Soviet Union and the United States faced one another competitively, more was thought to be at stake than individual victory. Sportscasters translated gold medals into signs of national triumph. As a result, Olympic competitions became Cold War battlefields, with propaganda stakes far higher than the breaking of individual records. After 1947, the International Olympic Committee (IOC) spent years working out the rules under which Russians and East Europeans would join the games. Would a divided Germany have one or two teams? Whether the Communists or the Nationalists in Taiwan would have the right to represent China triggered disputes for twenty-five years.

Because of their large international audience, the Olympics became important symbolic territory for a range of political disputes. In 1956, the governments of Egypt, Lebanon, and Iraq refused to send athletes to the games as a protest against the British and Israeli attempt to seize the Suez Canal. Newly independent countries in Africa pushed the IOC to restrict South African participation as long as sports competitions in that country remained segregated. The IOC waffled repeatedly, but it suspended South Africa from participation in 1964, and finally expelled it from the games in 1970. The most dramatically politicized Olympics were the Munich games in 1972, when Palestinian terrorists raided the headquarters of the Israeli team and seized several hostages. After long negotiations, captors and captives left for the airport, where they intended to fly to an Arab country. But the German police opened fire on the tarmac; by the end of the shootout all the hostages and three of the terrorists had been killed.

Although the IOC insisted that the games were competitions between individuals, not nations, this argument had become culturally obsolete. No one believed it. When Sukarno of Indonesia barred Israeli and Nationalist Chinese teams from the 1963 Asian Games, he unleashed a furor of protests and name-calling by the IOC and by other governments. Sukarno's statement, "Let us declare frankly that sport has something to do with politics," recognized the obvious.[2] The Olympics permitted easy international exchanges, but they intensified the identification of athletes with their states, which in the case of Munich proved fatal.

International Organizations

Internationalism and nationalism coexisted in an uneasy balance in the postwar period. The need for global ties and commitments to counter the destructive energies of states was an article of faith after 1945. Yet even the United Nations operated through nation-states, which had strong ideas concerning their own self-interest. The five permanent members (United States, the USSR, China, France, and Britain) ran the Security Council, aided by an elected group of temporary representatives, and every state had a seat and one vote in the General Assembly. By the early 1970s, virtually every country in the world except Switzerland and a few microstates belonged, and the nations of the Third World had an easy majority. Either the USSR or the United States and its allies could veto action by the Security Council, yet each superpower could be outvoted and outmaneuvered in the General Assembly, where the smaller, poorer states clamored for better treatment. Although the UN acted to defend South Korea after its invasion by North Korea, either the USSR or the United States blocked most Cold War interventions. As a result, the UN acted most decisively in regional conflicts that were unrelated to the bipolar balance of power. UN peacekeepers went into Egypt in 1956 and into the Belgian Congo and Cyprus in the 1960s. In other conflicts, the UN found itself attempting to undo damage—for example, by dealing with refugees—rather than preventing it. Only where the United States and the USSR did not see their interests directly threatened was action possible. The United

---

[2]Allan Guttmann, *The Olympics: A History of the Modern Games* (Urbana: University of Illinois Press, 1992), p. 110.

Nations was not designed to challenge the system of independent states that composed it.

In a strongly bipolar world, international cooperation happened much more readily in cultural and economic areas than on political terrain. The United Nations operates a series of special agencies designed to further a vague set of commitments to social progress. To that end, large international groups—for example, the World Health Organization (WHO), the Food and Agricultural Organization (FAO), the United Nations Children's Emergency Fund (UNICEF), and the United Nations Educational, Scientific, and Cultural Organization (UNESCO)—were formed. The UN sponsored conferences on women's rights and on the environment. WHO helped to organize a successful campaign to eradicate smallpox. UNESCO has worked to increase literacy and to improve libraries and universities around the world. Its World Wildlife Fund (WWF) helps to manage and protect dozens of spectacular, threatened sites, among them the Serengeti National Park in Tanzania, the Manas Tiger Reserve in India, and Australia's Great Barrier Reef.

The United Nations and its agencies need the cooperation of national states, which benefit from international resources and ties. Not only did most countries join the United Nations as soon as they could, but their leaders pursued the World Bank and other agencies for loans. Governments courted international foundations and research groups and worked with charities like the Red Cross and Oxfam in the wake of natural disasters. Countries competed for the right to host the Olympic games and world's fairs, which attracted hundreds of thousands of visitors. To broadcast international sports competitions, they improved and expanded TV transmission, which then brought in U.S. programs like *Dallas* and *Sesame Street*. Moreover, national school systems commonly taught their advanced students the few worldwide languages. The pursuit of national interest is compatible with internationalism, which helps to explain the continued support of the United Nations and its many specialized agencies by the major industrialized countries.

Language and Globalization

One of the most effective forces for globalization in the postwar period was increased knowledge of the English language. Spread first by migration and political control, English was then adopted as an official or almost official language in several of the successor states of the British Empire.

After 1945, the political, economic, and technological predominance of the United States,, along with American linguistic ignorance, helped spread knowledge of English around the globe. Not only did English become the language of international aviation, but scholars in several scientific disciplines made it their language of choice. Many multinational corporations function primarily in English. The populations of Scandinavia and the Netherlands have adopted English as a second language, as have better educated Malaysians, Koreans, Mexicans, Israelis, and Indians.

Despite the efforts of purists to isolate and preserve linguistic independence, Franglish, Spanglish, Singlish, and other hybrid, slangy varieties of standard languages flourish internationally, spread by television and mass tourism. Since 1945, global linguistic diversity has been overlaid by the almost universal conversion to English as a second language. Although Russian filled that function within Communist societies during the Cold War period, the evaporation of the Soviet Union in 1991 led former satellite countries to cast their lot with the English-speakers.

English, through the accidents of history and international relations, provides a common ground for the exchange of ideas, but it does not and cannot produce common interpretations of those ideas. What produces laughter in one audience triggers disapproval in another. The conduct of international negotiations in English in no way guarantees agreement.

It is important to distinguish the forms and mechanisms of globalization from their content and impact. People act and react to global influences locally, in terms of their own perceptions and values. Language transmits and shapes, but it does not determine outcomes.

Earthly Concerns and Alternative Faiths

The benefits of modernism have become an article of faith in much of the contemporary world, where rising standards of living indicate progress. Yet criticism of secular modernism has also spread among many who reject at least part of that legacy. Since the 1960s, many churches have moved into an expansionist phase, working against what they see as the defects of modernism. This religious revival signals a conflict in value systems and dissatisfaction with some of the changes that have come along with rising incomes and greater freedom of choice. Fundamentalists, asserting the need for doctrinal purity or for rejecting social policies, such as abortion, have spread their messages widely.

During the nineteenth century, the idea of a secular state and secular societies grew in importance. The United States proclaimed the separation of church and state, and France ended Roman Catholic control of publicly funded education. In the early twentieth century, Communists replaced church with party membership and pushed Marxism in place of religious doctrine. By the mid-twentieth century, both liberal and Communist regimes had moved to delimit the status and influence of churches in order to create secular societies.

In the view of many, modern societies had no place for religion. In 1947, Nehru and the Congress Party established India as a secular state, both to assert its modernity and to de-emphasize internal religious divisions. Particularly where citizens came from different religious traditions, secularism seemed a safe sort of neutrality, the best design to avoid conflict. For example, Marxism usefully dampened, at least for a time, the murderous hatreds of Muslims, Catholics, and Orthodox Christians in Yugoslavia.

Through the 1960s, churches seemed to be on the defensive. The Labor Party, representing a secular, socialist Judaism, governed in Israel, and socialist regimes pushing a civic religion of party and nation came to power in much of sub-Saharan Africa. Religion seemed to be fading as a force shaping twentieth-century society.

Then, during the later 1960s and 1970s, religious groups moved aggressively into politics. In Latin America, Catholic missionaries preached liberation theology and drew thousands into renewed fights for political and economic justice. In Israel, conservative religious parties representing Orthodox Jews gained influence and numbers. In the United States, Jerry Falwell formed the Moral Majority, increasing the voice of fundamentalist Christians in U.S. politics. The Iranian revolution of 1979 produced an Islamic republic run according to Islamic law. In India newly organized groups worked to unite Hindus and to demand pro-Hindu reforms. But by the 1970s, this activity had led to major social changes in only a few places—in Iran, as a result of revolution and in Burma, where a new constitution enshrined Buddhist rights.

The number of theocratic states in the world are few, but many countries have important religious lobbies. The impact of religion on politics continued to grow during the 1980s in countries around the world. Orthodox Jewish parties sometimes held the balance of power in the Israeli legislature. In India, Hindu parties gained votes by calling for curbs on Muslims' rights. The drive to institute religious controls over states grew in intensity. Since the 1970s, churches and independent religious groups have become active voices in national politics and have expanded their international presence, crossing borders in search of support.

Islam in Politics

The Muslim world is vast; it stretches from Indonesia and the southern Philippines westward through Pakistan, Turkey, the Middle East, and northern Africa (see Map 11.2). Moreover, significant Muslim populations live in China, the states of the former USSR, and North America. The fastest-growing religion in the world today, Islam has spread via conversion, migration, and reproduction. Islam has a sacred text, the Koran, and a long legal tradition, the Sharia, which gives believers a guide for proper conduct. Each year, millions of people flock to Mecca on pilgrimage, repeating actions and prayers that have unified Muslims for centuries. Nevertheless, even with these pressures for uniformity, Islam means vastly different things in different countries. Not only are Muslims divided into different sects and schools of thought, but their political orientations vary from ultra-conservative to revolutionary. Islam has its modernizers and its traditionalists, those who preach respect for Islamic authority and those who express more personal visions of their faith. What has been called "fundamentalist Islam" is only one strand in a complex tradition, and it too takes multiple forms. Both ethnic divisions and national loyalties hinder any sort of common action despite regular calls for Muslim unity.

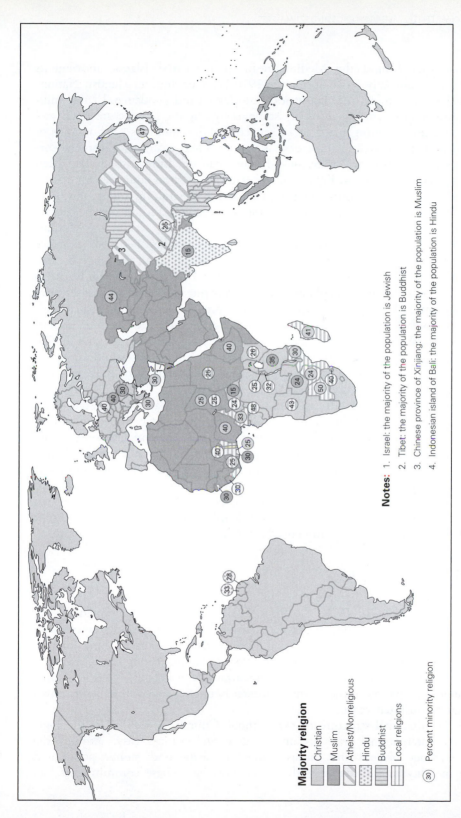

Majority religion

- Christian
- Muslim
- Atheist/Nonreligious
- Hindu
- Buddhist
- Local religions

㉚ Percent minority religion

Notes: 1. Israel: the majority of the population is Jewish

2. Tibet: the majority of the population is Buddhist

3. Chinese province of Xinjiang: the majority of the population is Muslim

4. Indonesian island of Bali: the majority of the population is Hindu

MAP 11.2 Distribution of world religions in the late twentieth century.
The map identifies countries with the religion of the majority of their citizens, although religious minorities exist everywhere. Where one predominant religious minority exists, it is tabulated in a small circle, as can be seen on the continent of Africa and in India.

In countries around the Mediterranean, reinvigorated Islamic movements became more politically active during the 1970s, challenging the Marxist, Nationalist parties that had led these countries' struggles for independence. Islamic militants gained respect among university students by offering free lecture notes and tutoring classes. They organized social services for the hundreds of thousands of poor migrants flocking into the cities. When measured against government corruption and incompetence, they looked good. Muslim brotherhoods had been important political actors in Egypt and other North African countries for several centuries, and their successors could draw on much recognition and goodwill.

But the relative importance of Muslim groups has varied with shifts in the balance of power in the Middle East. After Israel's victory in the 1967 war, young Muslims transferred their allegiance from older Nationalist heroes to the Palestinian resistance movement, and the idea of a revolutionary answer to the Israeli challenge became more attractive. When oil prices rose sharply in the 1970s, petrodollars began to flow from Saudi Arabia throughout Asia to propagate a Wahhabist conservative version of Islam. A coalition of Palestinians and progressive Muslims helped push Lebanon into civil war in the mid 1970s, challenging automatic Christian control of that country. But only in Iran did a revolutionary alliance—in this case linking frustrated students, conservative clergy, and poor migrants—successfully defeat an autocratic government and institute a theocracy. The influence of militant Islam has continued to grow, particularly in Algeria and Egypt.

In many parts of North Africa, Muslims worked within an existing state without challenging elected authorities over policy differences. At its independence in 1960, Senegal proclaimed itself a democratic, socialist, and secular state, using French models. New codes of family law drew on French, rather than Islamic, traditions. Although more than 90 percent of the Senegalese are Muslims, few objected. The government traded tax money and legal protection for votes, keeping Muslim brotherhoods and a majority of citizens loyal. They accepted the rules of the existing political game within Senegal. Muslim politics has to a great extent been national politics, deeply influenced by local circumstance and organization.

Christianity in Politics

Christian churches also became more militant in the postwar years. After John Paul II became pope in 1978, the Roman Catholic Church attempted to "re-Christianize" a secular world. In practice, this meant encouraging demonstrations to protect Catholic schools, opposing abortion and divorce, and calling for religious freedom in Communist states and for social justice in Latin America. Catholics built new churches and youth organizations in Poland, voted for Christian Democratic parties in the German Federal Republic, and worked with Indian communities in Guatemala.

The organizational structure of the Catholic Church, as well as its theology, made the international transmission of ideas and stances easy. Around the world, Catholic bishops and priests worked to shape both public policy and private morality in accordance with church doctrine. These commitments had strikingly different political implications, depending upon their setting. In Western Europe and North America, Catholic stances on marriage law, sexuality, and reproduction led to cooperation with social conservatives. These commitments led to similar social alliances in Latin America. At the same time, however, dislike of social and economic inequality pushed significant numbers of Latin American Catholic priests and lay members into partnerships with political radicals. Both in Guatemala and in El Salvador, priests influenced by liberation theology worked with groups that were attempting to oust military regimes and to empower the poor. Missionaries both from local churches and international denominations stoked the fires of religious radicalism.

Protestant Christianity also developed a large international presence. During the heyday of empire, European and American missionaries either preceded or followed national flags, building churches and using conversion to draw local people into new communities. Although the empires had vanished, the churches remained. No longer staffed by Europeans, they maintained links with similar denominations abroad.

Newer churches accelerated the pace of missionary activity in the postwar period. The Mormons, or Church of Jesus Christ of the Latter-Day Saints, require missionary service from young members, who travel to other countries to convert local people. Several American fundamentalist denominations have poured resources and people into sub-Saharan African countries and have established fast-growing congregations.

Where born-again Christians gained political power, they encouraged and aided this expansion. In Liberia, Togo, and Kenya during the 1980s, fundamentalist churches allied themselves with existing regimes to protect their freedom to preach and to convert. Moreover, their conservative social message found an eager audience in African countries where governments oppose abortion and the extension of equal rights to women and to homosexuals. The social activism that has come to characterize many groups of Protestant missionaries in Latin America has been largely missing in Africa.

Environmentalism

Faith comes in many forms. For some, saving nature has taken on the importance of saving souls. The celebration of Earth Day in 1970 announced a powerful international movement dedicated to changing the relationship of humans to the natural world. In the decades after World War II, awareness of the many costs of industrialization grew along with pollution.

Whether angered by oil spills or choked by urban smog, more and more people began to question the automatic equation of economic growth with progress. Particularly where sufficient wealth had accumulated to lift the standard of living, citizens could afford to worry about issues other than survival. In the longer run, industrialization encouraged anti-industrialism and an intensified commitment to preserving the natural environment. Nature ought to be conserved, not merely used for humans' benefit, many argued.

The science of ecology, or the relationship of organisms to their environment, spread after 1950 from a fringe academic subject to a popular field in conservation science. In the 1950s, the Sierra Club and the Wilderness Society blocked the building of a dam in Colorado parkland, successfully arguing that the goal of land protection outweighed development. Their lobbying encouraged Congress to pass the Wilderness Act in 1964, which prohibited commercial exploitation of national forests, wildlife refuges, and Indian reservations. In North America, the notion that nature had to be preserved became politically popular.

Similarly, the protection of other species became respectable. The International Whaling Commission, whose original purpose was to protect the price of whale oil, shifted somewhat ineffectively to preservation of whale stocks. But in the longer run, agitation by conservationists and growing scarcity drove most whaling fleets out of business. Groups like Greenpeace publicized violations of an international moratorium on whale hunting and worked to increase popular support for regulation.

During the 1960s, environmentalism spread from a hardy band of enthusiasts to a mass audience. The notion that concern for the environment must be weighed against efforts to industrialize has gained a large following. Many countries now have a Green Party that champions the cause of environmental protection. Although the successes of these parties have been mixed, their ability to elect representatives to legislatures testifies to the growing respectability of their message.

Conservationists have lost more battles than they have won, but they have changed the legal and political environment within which economic policies are made. Sweden's decision in 1967 to set up an environmental protection agency was only the first of many such actions that committed governments to conservation. During the 1970s, the U.S. Congress passed the Clean Air and Water Act, as well as legislation designed to protect endangered species. Even in poorer countries, grassroots groups of ordinary citizens and scientists have worked effectively. Women in Kenya organized tree planting for soil conservation, and Indian activists in Brazil worked to stop destruction of the Amazon rainforest. Support for conservation comes from more than an international elite.

Discussions of how to balance local, short-term needs for survival against the longer-term needs of the planet began. Rich countries lined up against poorer ones, and little was resolved. From the early 1970s, the United Nations worked to make international law and international policies that would recognize the need for environmental protection. Since the 1970s, a long series of issues, such as trade in elephant ivory, global warming, and acid rain, have been discussed internationally.

Conservation has received more support in theory than in practice. At an early meeting in Stockholm in 1972, developing countries insisted on their right to continue to pollute. Oil-producing nations resisted agreements restricting carbon emissions. In the early 1980s the U.S. government actively opposed existing levels of environmental regulation. Nevertheless, the limited successes of the environmental movement since the late 1960s have shown that citizens in many countries want ecological prudence. Environmentalism has crossed international borders and transformed local politics. Its appeal, particularly to younger voters, has drawn people into parliamentary politics in Europe. The idea of "biosphere earth" has had an international appeal, giving globalism a new focus.

CONCLUSION

The first wave of international exchanges after 1945 looked like Americanization, but countries soon created their own versions of a modernist youth culture. Jazz, rock 'n' roll, blue jeans, and U.S. movies spawned local imitations, which then circulated internationally. Borders proved to be porous, particularly in an era of rising incomes and technological change. Along with millions of migrants to the big cities and international television coverage came new ideas, new products, and new languages, all of which were particularly appealing to young people who wanted more exciting lives.

This globalization of consumption did not happen automatically or without conflict. Governments and corporations worked actively to promote it, and the advertising industry and the independent media built their fortunes on it. One consequence was globalized production, which added new factory jobs in developing countries and subtracted them in the older manufacturing regions. Because different people paid the costs and reaped the benefits of such production, the implications of global economic change were, and continue to be, controversial. What labor standards and wage rates should apply?

Since the early 1950s, international economic and cultural exchanges have triggered multiple conflicts between conservatives and liberals, old and young, men and women, who saw the imports with different eyes. These cultural clashes were part of much larger political battles that raged internationally during the 1960s and 1970s, raising issues of values. Fundamentalist religious groups joined the fray, working to move their societies closer to their vision of an ideal world. International organizations added another level of consultation to complex political debates.

The 1960s and 1970s were decades of intense political conflict, both within states and between them. Issues of civil rights that pitted individuals against state governments or group against group convulsed societies in the Americas, Africa, Europe, and Asia. Both Communist and capitalist nations had to reexamine their fundamental principles. Angry students, who questioned the actions and values of their elders, protested against laws and habits they found unjust. In the early postwar decades, political dissatisfactions could cross borders just as easily as films and music.

For Further Reading

Rachel Carson, *Silent Spring* (Boston: Houghton Mifflin, 1962). An attack on the use of pesticides in the United States, which became a bestseller and encouraged environmentalists to fight pollution.

Deborah Davis, ed., *The Consumer Revolution in Urban China* (Berkeley: University of California Press, 2000). Analyses of the growing availability of consumer goods in China and resulting changes for city dwellers.

Victoria De Grazia, *Irresistible Empire: America's Advance Through Twentieth-Century Europe* (Cambridge: Harvard University Press, 2005). A discussion of advertising and its relation to changes in consumption in Europe.

Allan Guttmann, *The Olympics: A History of the Modern Games* (Urbana: University of Illinois Press, 1992). A narrative treatment of the modern Olympic movement, its growth, and the political contests it has generated.

Dirk Hoerder, *Cultures in Contact: World Migrations in the Second Millennium* (Durham: Duke University Press, 2002). Discussion of the many streams of world migration and the conditions that have encouraged movement.

Walter LaFeber, *Michael Jordan and the New Global Capitalism* (New York: W. W. Norton, 1999). An exploration of the links between the NBA, Nike, and television coverage centering on the career of Michael Jordan.

J. R. McNeill, *Something New Under the Sun: An Environmental History of the Twentieth-Century World* (New York: W. W. Norton, 2000). An analysis of what humans have done to their air, water, and soil in a century of rapid urbanization and industrial growth.

Uta G. Poiger, *Jazz, Rock and Rebels: Cold War Politics and American Culture in a Divided Germany* (Berkeley: University of California Press, 2000). A comparison of the cultural and political impacts of rock 'n' roll in East and West Germany during the 1950s.

Michael T. Teitelbaum and Jay Winter, *A Question of Numbers: High Migration, Low Fertility, and the Politics of National Identity* (New York: Hill and Wang, 1998). Discussion of population problems in the twentieth century and their linkage to politics in North America, Europe, and the Middle East.

Kirk Varnedoe and Adam Gopnik, *High and Low: Modern Art and Popular Culture* (New York: The Museum of Modern Art, 1991). Commentary on the links between popular and elite art in recent decades.

Herman van der Wee, *Prosperity and Upheaval: The World Economy, 1945–1980* (Berkeley: University of California Press, 1986). A wide-ranging study of the changes in postwar shifts in economic fortunes around the globe.

Related Websites

The Green Revolution
http://www.ars.usda.gov/is/timeline/green.htm
History of Rock and Roll
http://rockhall.com/story-of-rock/
Religion since 1945
http://www.fordham.edu/halsall/mod/modsbook58.html
The United Nations
http://www.un.org/aboutun/milestones.htm

CHAPTER 12

The Many Dialects of Rebellion, 1960–1975

I n early April 1968, the civil rights leader Reverend Martin Luther King Jr. and his staff arrived in Memphis, Tennessee, to support a strike by garbage collectors. Like Gandhi (whom King admired), King stressed not only nonviolence but the importance of combining economic self-sufficiency and commercial influence with political assertiveness. He was concerned about the convergence of racial prejudice, labor oppression, economic dependency, and poverty. Injustice, he believed, was corrupting for both the victims and the perpetrators. Resistance to injustice was the greatest good.

By the time of his appearance in Memphis, King had attracted the enmity of racists, anti-labor forces, local governments, and even his own rivals for leadership in the civil rights movement, many of whom despised his nonviolent strategies. In Memphis he acknowledged that his life was at risk, but he asserted that he would have chosen no different time to live, and that if he must die, he would know that he had not died in vain:

> If I were standing at the beginning of time, with the possibility of a general and panoramic view of the whole human history up to now, and the Almighty said to me, "Martin Luther King, which age would you like to live in?" …I would turn to the Almighty, and say, "If you allow me to live just a few years in the second half of the twentieth century, I will be happy." Now that's a strange statement to make, because the world is all messed up. The nation is sick. Trouble is in the land. Confusion all around. That's a strange statement. But I know, somehow, that only when it is dark enough, can you see the stars. And I see God working in this period of the twentieth century in a way that men, in some strange way,

are responding—something is happening in our world. The masses of people are rising up. And wherever they are assembled today, whether they are in Johannesburg, South Africa; Nairobi, Kenya; Accra, Ghana; New York City; Atlanta, Georgia; Jackson, Mississippi; or Memphis, Tennessee—the cry is always the same—"We want to be free."[1]

King was murdered the next day, at the age of thirty-nine.

The troubled world to which King referred was obvious to everyone at the time. The United States was in social and political turmoil over its role in the Vietnam conflict, which together with problems of racial strife and economic dislocation created a series of urban crises. Labor issues combined with ethnic tensions in the campaigns of César Chavez for better working conditions for migrant workers in North America. Everywhere it seemed that liberal societies, authoritarian societies, and even some Communist countries were being swept up in massive dissidence. In some regions, farmers and workers were engaging in civil disobedience and violence. Guerrilla movements were gaining momentum and attracting greater followings.

Nevertheless, there was a structural logic to much of what was happening throughout the world. The bipolar system that had emerged from World War II, based on the monopoly of nuclear power by the United States and the Soviet Union, was weakening. After decades of tense sparring, the two superpowers had learned that the idea of using nuclear power was so horrible—and therefore so unthinkable—that the threat of doing so was meaningless. They concentrated on more conventional conflicts in more contained regions. In the process, they empowered many more countries as their partners, and in time they lost their monopoly on nuclear weapons. By 1964, five countries, including the People's Republic of China, had demonstrated that they could construct nuclear weapons, and by the middle 1970s Israel and India joined the group. The hostility between China and the Soviet Union also made international relations very complex, as China joined the competition to gain influence, military bases, and commercial advantages in Asia, Africa, and Latin America.

In this more fluid international environment, improving communications and the coalescing of a global popular culture permitted the growth of new connections that crossed national lines, as described in the previous chapter. Ironically, though nationalists such as Patrice Lumumba and Nelson Mandela were important icons of resistance and protest, their nationalist message was sublimated to a greater movement for international connection and the improvement of the lives

---

[1]Reprinted by arrangement with The Heirs to the Estate of Martin Luther King Jr., c/o Writers House as agent for the proprietor New York, NY. Copyright 1968 Dr. Martin Luther King Jr; copyright renewed 1996 Coretta Scott King.

of a majority of people on earth. Some of these connections created new political dynamics, particularly those that were related to the international "nongovernment organizations" (NGOs), foremost of which was the United Nations. Others stirred new cultural connections, promoting apparent solidarity across regions. Pan-Africanism, pan-Asianism, pan-Celticism, and pan-Arabism were now cultural as well as political themes. They permeated the popular media, but they also had very strong effects on academic curricula, international publishing, and tourism.

At important points, subnational and supranational concerns could mesh. Days before the 1968 Summer Olympics began in Mexico City, government troops had fired on student demonstrators, killing hundreds and wounding as many as a thousand. When the U.S. runners Tommie Smith and John Carlos won their events and stood for the playing of the American national anthem, they raised their right hands in black gloves, the "black power" salute—for which they were expelled from the competition. In the circumstances, it was not merely a gesture of support for their own movement but also a gesture of solidarity with Mexicans who were demanding land and labor rights. Incidents such as the Mexico City drama suggest the structural changes that were fundamental to a series of civil disorders around the world in 1968-1970 that marked the beginning of the end of the Cold War.

National Independence in the Weakening Bipolar System

In the 1960s, a pantheon of "Third World" (see Chapter 10) revolutionary heroes were celebrated around the globe. They included conventional nationalists such as Patrice Lumumba (who was killed in 1961), but also radical, revolutionary figures such as Mao Zedong, Ho Chi Minh, Fidel Castro, Che Guevara (killed in 1967), and the leaders of an emerging black revolutionary movement in the United States, the Black Panthers. Guevara himself had acknowledged that the greatest influence on him after Marx was the leader of the Chinese Communist revolution, Mao Zedong, who appeared to have been the most successful at translating resistance to the superpowers into a national identity of self-reliance and social equality.

New Patterns of Competition and Control in Africa

As of 1960, Africa was still experiencing the lingering hold of the old European colonialist powers. Only five African nations were regarded as independent in 1945, but in 1970 there were 42 African countries represented in the UN. The 1960s in particular had seen a dramatic rise in the number of newly independent nations. Ghana had recently become independent, the Congo gained its independence in June 1960, Nigeria and Sierra Leone became independent later in the same year, Kenya and Uganda became independent in 1963, Tanganyika (now Tanzania) in 1964, and Gambia in 1965. Some of these transitions, like that in Kenya, had followed years of bloody fighting between nationalist activists and colonial loyalists. Portugal attempted to retain its colonial influence, creating new complications in Angola, Portuguese Guinea, and Mozambique in the early 1960s.

The leading independence hero in Africa in 1960 was Patrice Lumumba. A Christian and former bureaucrat from the city of Leopoldville (now Kinshasa) in what was then Belgian Congo, Lumumba had had little interest in political activism before being imprisoned in 1958. He served a sentence of a year and emerged as an advocate for Congo's independence, as well as becoming active in the pan-African movements for political independence from either the United States or the Soviet Union, for economic development, and for greater access to education. Though Belgium had already agreed to eventually make Congo free, the movement in which Lumumba participated, and which sometimes involved violence, convinced Belgium to permit the creation of a national government in Congo in 1960, years ahead of the proposed schedule. The transition became confused, however, when elements in the Congo military attempted to seize control of one of the country's provinces, and the new civilian government requested outside help from Belgium, the United Nations, and the Soviet Union. Only Belgium and the Soviet Union responded, but the help was too little and too late. Lumumba was abducted and executed by the militarist (Joseph) Mobutu Sese Seko, who subsequently assumed and kept control of Congo.

The murder of Lumumba sent shock waves around the world. European leaders and the UN strongly denounced Mobutu's actions but left him in power. Many noted that Lumumba's campaign recalled that of Muhammad Mosadegh in Iran in 1953 and Jacobo Arbenz Guzman in Guatemala in 1954 (see Chapter 10). Like Mosadegh and Arbenz, Lumumba was elected on political promises of land reform, full or partial nationalization of natural resources, and political independence from the superpowers. In the aftermath of Lumumba's death, many aspiring nationalists in Africa and elsewhere abandoned hopes of perpetuating his ideologically nonaligned style. It appeared that radicalism and militancy were the only options, and many American activists considered the African-American and African movements to be one.

In southern Africa, particularly in South Africa and Rhodesia (now Zimbabwe), white minorities tenaciously clung to rule over the majority, using military force, secret police, and legal racial segregation (apartheid) to enforce their superiority. The new trend toward African nationalism and demands for local land rights produced increasing violence in many parts of Africa in the 1960s. Nigeria's civil war had claimed as many as five hundred thousand lives by the late 1960s. By the middle 1970s, the situation had become somewhat less violent. A new military junta that had come into power in Portugal in 1974 had no choice but to grant all the remaining colonies their independence. South Africa attempted to ameliorate its race problems and its international image by creating special zones of black

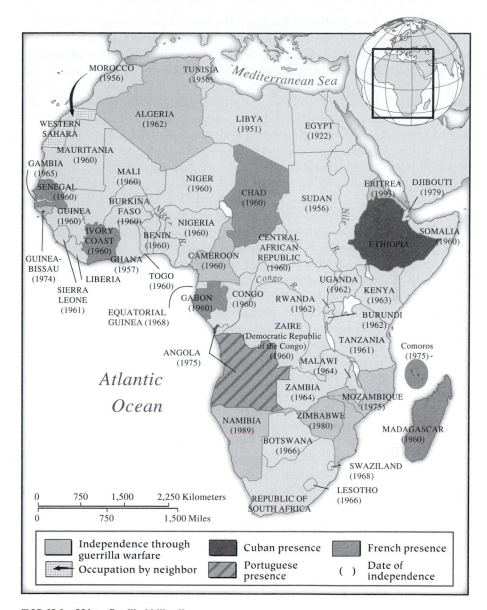

MAP 12.1   Africa after World War II.

Decolonization in Africa produced the emergence of many new nations and many regional reconstructions of power between 1950 and 1995. Dark and striped areas show the extent of Cuban intervention, most of it led by Che Guevara (see below), in the 1960s. In 2011, Sudan south of the Abyei Region became the Republic of South Sudan.

"home rule" (as in Nyasaland and Zambia). The limited political rights and miserable living conditions of these regions quickly exposed them as a sham.

In this period, Nelson Mandela became the international figure who symbolized the struggle for majority rule and national justice in Africa. Mandela had been born to a prominent family in South Africa, and in the early 1940s he had become interested in politics while studying law at Johannesburg. He joined the African National Conference, a movement advocating majority political participation. After becoming a lawyer, Mandela continued his political activism, always working within the context of the courts and of peaceful protest. Nevertheless, he was a critic of the older leaders of the ANC, who he thought prized lawfulness too highly and were too timid in challenging white rule in the country. He was a strong opponent of the "homelands" policies used in South Africa in the 1950s and 1960s to remove and isolate African majorities in undesirable territories.

In 1960, the ANC was outlawed. Mandela was arrested, but in 1961 his trial for treason was abandoned as South Africa began to revise its constitution from a British "dominion" to a republic. Mandela demanded that the black majority participate in the creation of the constitution. The government responded with military patrols to keep the majority quiet and peaceful while the minority completed the constitution. Mandela became a fugitive, and also changed his feelings on the practicality of nonviolence in the African situation: "At the beginning of June 1961, after long and anxious assessment of the South African situation, I and some colleagues came to the conclusion that as violence in this country was inevitable, it would be wrong and unrealistic for African leaders to continue preaching peace and nonviolence at a time when the government met our peaceful demands with force. It was only when all else had failed, when all channels of peaceful protest had been barred to us, that the decision was made to embark on violent forms of political struggle. ... The Government had left us no other choice."[2]

Mandela traveled to other parts of Africa, advocating a "Pan African Freedom Movement," but on his return to South Africa he was arrested for traveling abroad illegally and was sentenced to five years imprisonment. He was subsequently charged with sabotage and sentenced to life in prison at the notorious facility on Robben Island. Mandela became an international cause, with some regarding him as a principled hero of nationalism, justice, and democracy, and others regarding him as a dangerous subversive. Like Che Guevara, Mao Zedong, Ho Chi Minh, and Fidel Castro, he was a figure onto which people projected their understanding of the great trends and great issues of their time.

Africa was rich in some resources that were very important in the postwar world, particularly oil in Nigeria, diamonds in Sierra Leone, uranium and cobalt in Congo, and gold, silver, and copper in South Africa. These resources, combined with the number of new nations that could be won as supporters or clients, attracted the Soviet Union, the United States, China, and Cuba. Most of the new countries were in need of immediate financial aid to develop agriculture and

---

[2]Nelson R. Mandela, "Statement During the Rivonia Trial," April 20, 1964.

education. China contributed not only money, as the superpowers did, but also manpower, which it had in abundance. Chinese engineers and workers helped create major railroads and mining installations throughout Africa in the 1960s, and in the 1970s China reaped some political rewards as the new African nations all signed agreements recognizing the PRC as the government of China and either ignoring Taiwan or calling it merely a province of the PRC.

By the end of the 1970s, however, many African nations experienced a decline of foreign interest and support. Continuing political instability prevented the effective development of new industries and often disrupted supplies of oil. More immediately devastating, a drought in the middle 1970s enlarged the Sahara, driving refugee populations both into North Africa and southward into Ghana and Nigeria. The marginal agricultural development of many regions was incapable of supporting the influx. Hundreds of thousands died in refugee compounds, and in other regions new violence resulted from competition for land and water. By the late 1970s, Africa was generally regarded by the competing international powers as a lost cause. China maintained a substantial relationship with oil-rich Nigeria but otherwise followed the pattern of the other leading nations and stepped back from Africa.

Black Activism in the United States and the Pan-African Movement

In the United States, Martin Luther King was seen as a model for the struggle against the limitations imposed by race, class, or national circumstances. He led marches in which blacks and whites, northerners and southerners, elites and working people came together to protest racial segregation, attempts to prevent African Americans from exercising their voting rights, and local anti-labor policies. As King became more prominent, his public speeches tended more and more to stress the value of all individuals rising above racial distinctions and the necessity for the law to become colorblind.

This message had a strong impact on a large segment of the U.S. public, but it was troubling to some young black intellectuals and activists. Some of them criticized King for being interested in calming the anxieties of American whites and for promoting an unrealistic image of the United States as a society in which race had no significance. For this group, race was an indelible element of the identity of all Americans; equality of the races could not be gained through charm or uplifting spiritual messages, but only through struggle that would either win blacks respect through their actions or make white society pay a price; and blackness was not something to be transcended, but something to be celebrated, reinforced, and brought to its highest potential. A small number in this group saw the only hope for change as being violent confrontation between black forces and the U.S. government. Until his murder in 1965, Malcolm X (Malcolm Little, Malik el-Shabazz), a former convict who joined the Nation of Islam and became an uncompromising advocate of justice for African-Americans, was himself ambivalent about the degree to which violence should be part of the struggle. After his death, violence and radicalism became more prominent in some sectors of the "Black Liberation" movement.

An important transitional figure in black activism in the United States was Muhammad Ali, born Cassius Marcellus Clay Jr. in 1942 in Louisville, Kentucky. On the night he won the world boxing championship in 1962, he announced his conversion to Islam and his new name, Muhammad Ali. When he was drafted into the U.S. Army in 1967 to serve in Vietnam, Ali refused to serve. He was stripped of his world championship title, his license to continue boxing was revoked, he was tried for draft evasion and sentenced to five years in prison. In 1971, the U.S. Supreme Court ruled 5–4 that Ali had the right to conscientiously object to the war and also had the right to continue boxing (under his restored title of world champion). For Ali, the factors compelling poor blacks to do military service and kill in the service of white elites were similar in the United States and in Africa. On visits to Africa, he was hailed as a hero of the struggle for African dignity and independence. Ali combined civil disobedience, a rejection of violence, and Islamic religion in a new style of Pan African identity.

Che Guevara and Trans-National Revolution

An evolving international culture embraced athletes, musicians, actors, and writers as celebrities who had chosen to add heroic political activism to their primary achievements. But increasingly political activists were also being hailed as heroes who were also celebrities. The French philosopher Jean-Paul Sartre, himself an international celebrity and admirer of Muhammad Ali, said of one of these activists: "In his life and in his story one sees the complete man of this age." Sartre was referring to Che Guevara.

Born Ernesto Guevara de la Serna Lynch in 1928, Guevara came from an upper-class Argentinean family. He was educated as a physician but had strong interests in philosophy, reading Karl Marx at the socialist end of the spectrum and Sartre (his later admirer) at the existentialist end. After his graduation in 1952, Guevara rode a motorcycle throughout Latin America. From his diaries, we know that he was profoundly impressed by the poverty and misery of agricultural workers employed by international agricultural companies—mostly American and British—that sucked out great profits and left nothing behind but broken workers and damaged environments. He went to Central America to work among the very poor farmers there and soon became involved not only in political activism but also in guerrilla warfare. He was in Guatemala at the time of the overthrow of Arbenz (see Chapter 10). The lesson, he later wrote and taught, was that democracy in itself and civil political action would never be sufficient to overthrow what he saw as the undeniable collaboration of international corporations and the U.S. military.

In the late 1950s, Guevara went to Cuba to help overthrow the Batista regime, and he became a very high-ranking lieutenant of Fidel Castro. The combination of Guevara's influence on Castro and Castro's rejection by U.S. policymakers resulted both in Castro's public declaration in 1960 that he was a Communist and that Cuba was a socialist state. After the U.S. defeat at the Bay of Pigs in 1961 and the resolution of the Cuban missile crisis in 1962, Cuba began its own international revolutionary campaign, supporting guerrilla fighters in Guatemala, Mexico, and Bolivia. Castro also decided to support guerrillas in Congo, Guinea, Mozambique and other African colonies fighting the last remnants of European imperialism. In all these campaigns, Guevara was sent by Castro to be the main adviser, strategist, and ambassador.

Guevara was admired for his determination to aid countries that were not his own. But his actions were sometimes contradictory. With great tenderness he cared for enemy soldiers who had been taken prisoner. But when the Castro regime was newly victorious and was struggling to consolidate its hold over Cuba, he accepted personal responsibility for executing Batista military commanders without trial. He was a committed Marxist in the sense that he understood and was convinced by the ideas of Marx himself. Nevertheless, he did not approve

AP Photo/Jose Luis Magana

Alberto Diaz Gutierrez (professional name Korda) edited his casual photo of Che Guevara in 1960 into a portrait that captured the attention and imagination of the world. In various forms the image became one of the best known and most enduring in the world, used not only to promote social reform and revolutionary causes but also to serve commercial ends. Korda died in 2001 without ever having received any payment for the image— primarily be cause the laws of Cuba do not protect intellectual property.

of many so-called Communist governments in his own time, and he despised self-styled revolutionaries who mindlessly adhered to the dictates of foreign regimes. He was brave and ruthless in combat, but between 1961 and 1965 he served as a Cuban bureaucrat, and he hoped that in his retirement he would have time for writings on history and philosophy.

In Bolivia, Guevara hoped to organize peasants to resist new encroachments by American-based companies. However, the peasants failed to rally to his cause and let him fall into the hands of CIA-trained Bolivian forces. He was shot in October 1967. To prove that they had killed Guevara, the Bolivian soldiers photographed his corpse and removed his hands to take with them before burying the body. His grave was left unmarked to prevent it from becoming a site of pilgrimage (the bones were discovered and identified thirty years later).

Anti-colonialism and Self-reliance in Asia

After Guevara was killed in 1967, he was internationally celebrated as a martyr to Third World struggles against injustices perpetrated by the United States and Britain and their intelligence agencies. Guevara himself had acknowledged that the greatest influence on him after Marx was the leader of the Chinese Communist revolution, Mao Zedong, who had been the most successful at translating resistance to the superpowers into a national identity of self-reliance and social equality.

Mao Struggles Against Revolutionary Success

As we saw in Chapter 10, Mao's plan for decentralization of China was opposed by a faction within the Chinese Communist Party who had been partly educated in the Soviet Union and adhered to the Soviet model of professionalization and centralization in the military, in science, and in education. Particularly in the late 1950s, this group felt that China should be emphasizing centers of research and training, along with specialization in the military and in the medical and scientific professions. In Mao's eyes, his opponents were threatening to use the success of the revolution to create a new elite of cadres who would soon become as corrupt and self-centered as the old landlord classes had been. In 1962, following the stupendous disasters of the Great Leap Forward and the break with the Soviet Union (see Chapter 10), Mao was weakened at home but still commanded great prestige abroad, where the facts of his disasters were unknown. Those who had lost earlier debates about centralization, specialized advanced education, and military professionalization were expected to move into the top positions in the PRC government.

But in 1962 Mao began a new political campaign that would culminate in the "Cultural Revolution" (1966–1976). This began as a student movement (instigated by Mao) that was opposed to supposedly archaic methods of teaching. Mao believed that intellectuals should not have a distinct place in society but should be merged with the mass of workers, all of whom would be both highly educated and fit for hard manual labor. There should not be a choice between being a devoted Communist and being a highly trained professional—one should be "both red and expert." But Mao claimed that the "counterrevolutionary" mentality of teachers and other intellectuals was preventing this cultural transformation from occurring.

Mao encouraged students to identify counterrevolutionaries personally, beginning with their teachers and parents but spreading out to anyone who appeared to be an opponent of socialist transformation. In public demonstrations, identified enemies were paraded before crowds and humiliated, then taken to huge public meetings where they were expected to confess their sins and beg forgiveness, usually by requesting to be made manual laborers. These scenes frequently degenerated into violence. Supposed counterrevolutionaries were beaten, sometimes to death. They were tossed out of windows, strangled, or deprived of food and water until they expired. Gangs of students soon began to vie with one another for local power. The government suppressed this kind of disorder in 1969, and many of the students were subsequently condemned as counterrevolutionaries. But the political campaigns of the Cultural Revolution continued, and Chinese lived in terror of having a neighbor, a family member, or a rival report them for having said counterrevolutionary things. The economy degenerated as the urban centers were dismantled and their professional elites dispersed. A social and economic chill gripped China until Mao's death in 1976.

Mao's campaigns for socialist transformation were accompanied by a phenomenal international publicity campaign that overlapped in time with the internationalization of other revolutionary heroes and placed Mao in the company of Ho Chi Minh and Guevara. The PRC ran an enormous printing and communications enterprise in Shanghai. With the aid of many foreign translators, Mao's words were available in virtually every language. More important, the fantasy of vigorously productive farms, active and modern factories, and happy, healthy, educated workers was supported by the beautiful photographs (most of them heavily retouched) in magazines such as *China Reconstructs,* which was available in all languages and was supplied free or at little cost to every country. Very effective "documentary" films also showed China as a model of agricultural modernization, with beautiful, abundant crops springing from the rich soil.

To viewers in the developing countries, where agricultural production and water supplies were constant worries, China seemed a shining beacon of what could be accomplished through self-reliance. To viewers in the developed countries who were weary of Cold War rhetoric and fears of the "military-industrial complex," China was a refreshing hope for the possibilities of honest, humble government. The uniting of a dream of national self-reliance with one of economic abundance resonated strongly with the plight of Vietnam, which under U.S. bombardment enjoyed neither. The image of China in the 1960s was one of the best managed, most ubiquitous, and most appealing publicity campaigns of all time. In fact, the period of the Cultural Revolution produced no economic gains, and it left a death toll of perhaps five hundred thousand to a million, in addition to the losses of the Great Leap Forward. But it achieved its goals of reestablishing the aging Mao at the pinnacle of power and of providing the primary imagery for people's revolutionary, agrarian, communitarian, guerrilla movements during the late 1960s and the early 1970s.

Guerrilla Ethics in Post-War North Korea

In North Korea, the new president, Kim Il Sung, had a parallel career to Mao's in many ways. Kim had begun his political life as a resistance fighter against the Japanese colonial authorities. While he had been put in power in the north (that is, in the Democratic People's Republic of Korea) and was sustained there by his ally the Soviet Union after the war, Kim nevertheless claimed that South Korea was still under colonial occupation by the United States. A patriotic war of national reunification must, in his view, be prosecuted to end colonialism in Korea for good. Kim's tactics in that war (see Chapter 9) were basically those of a guerrilla fighter. The people had to forgo modern conveniences supplied them by the imperialists to wean themselves from the patronage of the colonizers. They must be self-sufficient in food production, in managing their health care, and in creating their own industries and weapons.

Kim wrote up his thoughts on self-reliance (in Korean, *ju che*) and demanded that they become the basis for student indoctrination. They were later translated into English and had wide distribution throughout Asia and Africa. *Ju che*, rather than outright military confrontation, was the first line of resistance and defense. After that, guerrilla tactics would maximize the strengths of the liberation forces and diminish the strengths of the forces of oppression. Success would go to those who had the greatest determination, the greatest courage, and the greatest capacity to survive without conveniences. The final stage of victory would be the creation of a socialist economic system, in which it would be impossible to revive the exploitative relationships between the elites and the majority that had been the hallmark of imperialism.

Though Kim's ideas were an authentic reflection of his years as a nationalist fighter against Japanese colonialism, they were not particularly original. The same complex of ideas had been important to Jacobo Arbenz Guzman and Patrice Lumumba (although they had been democratic nationalists and not guerrilla fighters), as well as to Sukarno in Indonesia (another resistance fighter against Japanese imperialism who assumed control of his country after the Second World War), Mao Zedong in China, and Ho Chi Minh in Vietnam. By the middle 1960s, it was Ho and Mao who represented these ideals in the global consciousness more vividly than any others. These two relatively old men (Ho was seventy-five in 1965 and Mao was seventy-two) came to be intensely admired by young people all over the world because of their exemplification of self-reliance and national independence.

"People's War" and New Models of Justice

When the United States assumed France's role in Vietnam in 1954, Ho Chi Minh immediately received more weapons and advisers from the Soviet Union

MAP 12.2   The War in Vietnam.
Since the division of Vietnam between the North and the South in 1954, North Vietnamese campaigns to reunify the country depended upon the so-called "Ho Chi Minh Trail," which actually ran through Laos. Attempts by U.S. forces to disrupt the North's lines of travel and transport eventually extended to bombing Laos and Cambodia, which provoked widespread popular protests in 1970 and pressured the American government to move to end the war. American and South Vietnamese positions were gradually overwhelmed in a roughly north-to-south progression, with Saigon falling in 1975.

(where he had spent some time as a student and had signed on as an activist for the international Communist revolution). But in general Ho realized that the struggle against the United States in southern Vietnam would require protracted guerrilla warfare. The society of the north must be organized both to put the largest possible workforce into the fields and to put the largest possible workforce into the military struggle. That meant rebuilding society to erase the distinctions between soldiers and farmers, as well as between male and female roles. To Ho, this was the "people's war," the only way that poorer countries could resist domination and exploitation by the richer and more heavily armed superpowers. To U.S. military planners, a "people's war" meant that every civilian was a potential guerrilla fighter and a potential spy. The distinction between combatants and noncombatants, which had been weakened but had survived the Second World War, began to crumble completely.

Ho and his generation of Vietnamese military leaders proved brilliant at maintaining the morale of their organizations and making the most of the nationalistic enthusiasm that years of French colonialism had instilled in the Vietnamese. Though they certainly could not have expected to win the war without help from the Soviet Union or China, the basic contribution came from the Vietnamese people and their leaders. Ho himself had a fellow champion of "people's war" in Mao Zedong of China. Both men made their nations symbols of the serious, protracted war of self-sufficient but less industrializing societies against the previously industrialized, predatory superpowers.

GLOBAL Technologies

Assault Rifles and the Global Arms Trade

In the Second World War, German armies first explored the design of medium-range rifles that could be switched between select and automatic firing, and were small enough and light enough to fit the needs of moving, and sometimes crowded, troops. To power the magazine supplying the continuous flow of bullets, the gun captured its own explosive gases produced by the firing of the bullets in the first place. Many machine guns worked by a similar method, and hand-held versions of automatic rifles were developed in several countries during and after the First World War. The infamous Thompson submachine gun, for example, is familiar to all viewers of 1930s gangster films. Expensive, inaccurate, and prone to mechanical failures, these weapons found little use in professional armies after the Second World War. Soviet armorers used the German idea or powering by recycled gases to develop the AK-47. Its name stood for its type (*Avtomat* or Automatic),

its principal designer (Mikhail Kalashnikov), and the year of its development (1947). The gun sacrificed accuracy and range for light weight, reliability and simplicity, making it easy for untrained shooters to use. It is the ancestor of what is now called an assault rifle.

The AK-47 became the weapon supplied by Soviet Union to its allies and clients in the Korean War, the Vietnam War, and many ongoing conflicts in Africa. No one knows exactly how many copies of the original rifle and its many derivatives and knock-offs came off production lines, but a hundred million is a plausible estimate--a number far exceeding the military needs of the USSR and its allies. By the 1970s, the guns were being traded for political influence or simply for hard cash; by the 1980s they had become ubiquitous wherever state authority was weak and political tensions were high. They were sufficiently rugged to be reliable in the dusty hill country of Lebanon or Afghanistan and the humid jungles of Columbia or Mindanao, sufficiently simple even for child soldiers to maintain, and sufficiently destructive to make poorly trained insurgents dangerous to well-trained soldiers. AK-47s (bought with U.S. and Saudi funds) became great equalizers in the war between Afghan tribesmen and Soviet troops during the 1980s and between Taliban fighters and NATO

"Vietnam" and the Peak of International Awareness

The central development in the global uprisings of 1968 and 1970 was U.S. involvement in the war in Vietnam, which is often referred to in shorthand as "Vietnam." After the accession to office of President Lyndon Johnson in 1963,

troops in the 2000s. Today, at least 26 countries, most with some connection to the former Soviet Union or to China, manufacture their own variants and upgrades of the AK-47, for their own use and for the international arms market.

For centuries, governments have often put weapons in the hands of potential allies, including groups engaged in irregular or civil warfare. China, for instance, was supplied with machine guns by Britain and the United States in the nineteenth century for suppression of internal rebellions; by the early twentieth century, China in the age of the warlords purchased perhaps as much as fifteen percent of the world's arms. German submarines landed handguns and ammunition in Ireland before the 1916 Easter Rebellion; in the 1930s, Italy, Germany, and Soviet Union supplied their allies with weapons during the Spanish Civil War. Nonetheless, the international arms trade of the late twentieth and early twenty-first centuries is unprecedented both in volume and destructiveness. Inexpensive, plentiful, and lethal weapons like the AK-47 shift power from police forces and standing armies to insurgents, militias, and even criminal gangs.

It is difficult to be precise about the quantity of manufactured and traded weapons, because a small portion of the parties involved work illegally and

make no reports. But globally the value of the trade is believed to have risen from about $45 billion in 1998 to $51 billion in 2007, accounting for about three percent of all global trade. The United States exports about 30% of all weapons, followed by Russia, Germany, France and the United Kingdom. The largest importer of weapons is believed to be India (at about nine percent) followed by China, South Korea, Pakistan, and Greece.

MAGNUM/Steve McCurry

the United States sharply increased the number of soldiers and the amount of expenditure it was putting into the campaign to defeat North Vietnamese guerrilla fighters. In early August 1964, operatives of the U.S. government claimed that Vietnamese boats had attacked a U.S. ship that was on a routine patrol in the Tonkin Gulf and that two days later, without provocation, Vietnamese boats had torpedoed U.S. Navy vessels in the same waters. The reports were featured in news articles on the front pages of the *New York Times* and the *Washington Post* on August 5. Historians have now established that the incident was knowingly falsified by the U.S. government. The first U.S. ship attacked in the Tonkin Gulf was not on routine maneuvers but was supporting an assault by South Vietnamese forces against the North that had been going on for six months with covert American assistance. The second attack on the U.S. fleet never happened at all. The report of it was apparently inspired by a nervous sonar operator who might not have understood his readings, followed by firings from his ship that disturbed and confused other U.S. ships in the area. President Johnson himself said of the second attack that the U.S. ships might have been Navy ships "shooting at whales." Nevertheless, the next day Johnson demanded that Congress grant him extraordinary powers to pursue a war in Vietnam based on North Vietnam's purported aggression against the U.S. Navy. Without adequate investigation of what had happened in the Tonkin Gulf, Congress acquiesced.

Within a year, two hundred thousand U.S. troops were in Vietnam. Bombing campaigns eventually reduced North Vietnam and much of South Vietnam to a wasteland. In 1968, as Johnson considered running again for the presidency, the pace of the war was intensified. Escalation resulted from North Vietnam's "Tet Offensive" (because it occured at the lunar New Year] of 1968, in which a change from guerrilla tactics to conventional warfare was attempted with simultaneous assaults on various cities held by the American or South Vietnamese forces, particularly the capital of Saigon. Massive casualties on both sides resulted before the assault subsided without gaining control of any new cities. But continuous and rising levels of exposure of the violence in the American press raised American and European awareness of the extraordinary costs of the stalemate in Vietnam. Demonstrations in the United States protested the continuation of the war—and particularly of the draft. Johnson's credibility was so badly damaged that he withdrew from the presidential race, and by the end of 1968, Richard Nixon, a Republican, had been elected president.

During 1968, political demonstrations became well established as a global phenomenon. Demonstrations against racism, for gay liberation, for women's equality, for better labor conditions, and for prison reform had taken place all around the world. The single most widespread inspiration for the demonstrations in 1968 and 1969, however, was opposition to the American prosecution of the war against North Vietnam. Nixon hoped to quiet public wrath in the United States by withdrawing ground troops gradually from South Vietnam. He and his advisers intended to pursue the war with bombing campaigns, assuming that an air war would mean fewer American casualties and that American fear of the draft would calm. In 1969, the bombings were extended to Cambodia and Laos without notifying Congress or making any public announcement. But Nixon had miscalculated. In May 1970, news of the bombings broke, along with the revelation that U.S. ground troops were in Cambodia.

Popular reaction in the United States was instant and widespread. Spontaneous public outrage at the news of the Cambodia bombings combined with the general acceptance of demonstrations to bring many thousands of participants to the colleges and universities, and also to public squares and parks. On many university campuses, authorities called in the local police to prevent students from vandalizing property or obstructing traffic. In some states, governors mobilized the National Guard to dispel demonstrations at state universities. This led to tragedy at Kent State University in Ohio, where the National Guard opened fire on students and killed four, two of whom were not involved in the protest. Shock and outrage at this event fueled even greater and more vigorous demonstrations on campuses, where students now occupied buildings, using the upper stories as grandstands from which to give speeches against the war and against the suppression of dissent in the United States. In New York, Philadelphia, Chicago, and Los Angeles, street fighting broke out as groups of construction workers or motorcycle gangs set upon demonstrators. On May 9, 1970, tens of thousands of protesters gathered at the Lincoln Memorial in Washington, D.C., where Nixon himself put in an appearance, hoping to mollify the crowds.

As in 1968, urban tensions combined with immediate political passions to sustain a general movement against "the system": capitalism, racism, the CIA, the military-industrial complex, and ecological devastation, all of which were now characterized by dissidents as mutually reinforcing elements of the bipolar system of global dominance. On May 14, 1970, students protesting the war and local racism at Jackson State College in Jackson, Mississippi, skirmished with police, with the result that two students were shot dead at close range and twelve others were wounded by scattered gunfire. By the end of May, nearly four hundred fifty campuses had been disrupted, some of them shut down completely. The general upheaval of college campuses and urban centers in May 1970 was followed by a marked shift in the political culture of the United States.

In the 1960s, protest against traditional values, against segregation and racism, and against the war had been associated with young people and, increasingly, with African Americans. But the steady stream of demoralizing news coverage from the war, the increasing casualties, the revelations in 1969 of the 1968 massacre of civilians in the village of My Lai, and the intense experiences of May 1970 produced a decline in the glamour of violence and extremism. The damage to campuses and city centers from fires, fire bombings, and occasional gunplay had produced enough rubble and repair bills that popular patience with mayhem had evaporated. Radical leaders who had promoted or permitted violence in their movements, whether white "Yippies" or commanders in the Black Panthers, were being indicted and imprisoned, and were increasingly being treated in the popular media as criminals. Violent factions such as the Weathermen (or Weather Underground, a reference to a Bob Dylan song) and the Symbionese Liberation Army were on the run, sought by the FBI and not supported by a sympathetic public. The public was weary of self-styled revolutionaries and undisciplined public displays, but it was also indignant at the brutality of the repression of the students in Ohio and in Mississippi. Skepticism about not only the war but the Nixon administration was widespread.

During 1970 and 1971, U.S. President Richard M. Nixon and his adviser, Henry Kissinger, came up with the apparently extraordinary idea of going to

China to talk directly with Mao Zedong about helping to end the Vietnam War. The plan was a confused one. China was a supporter of the North Vietnamese guerrillas, but it was not as important in that role as the Soviet Union. Whatever help the Chinese could provide to the United States in ending the war would be marginal. Nevertheless, official communications with China would be unexpected news in the United States and would possibly divert attention from the U.S. war in Vietnam and the Nixon administration's deepening political troubles. It would certainly discomfit the Soviet Union. China would undoubtedly demand something in return for this help, and that demand was expected to be that the United States reverse its entire China policy.

Up to that time, the United States had recognized the Republic of China government in Taiwan as legitimate and had claimed that the People's Republic of China (PRC) government was an illegitimate illusion. Not surprisingly, Mao and China's premier Zhou Enlai welcomed the idea of the U.S. president coming to Beijing and in practice recognizing the PRC as real. They were always eager to gain leverage against the Soviet Union, and the prestige of having the American leader coming to pay homage to Mao was overwhelming. Moreover, since Mao claimed that only the U.S. government and not the American people was an enemy, there would be a way for him to reconcile his reception of Nixon with his ideology by recognizing him as a representative of the American people. In the end, the public relations advantages for both sides of having the meeting were irresistible, regardless of whether real political change resulted. In 1972 Nixon and Mao met in Beijing and agreed to the "Shanghai Communiqué." It stated that there was "one China" and that U.S. policy would always recognize only one China.

The political meaning of the Shanghai Communiqué was nil, but the effects for the rest of the 1970s were dramatic. Ping-pong matches between Chinese and American players promoted travel exchanges and extensive media coverage. The giant pandas Hsing-hsing and Ling-ling were presented by China to the National Zoo in Washington, D.C., and became international media stars. Britain and Canada recognized the PRC as the government of China within a short time after Nixon's visit, and the groundwork was laid for the eventual recognition of the PRC by the United States under President Carter in 1979. For Taiwan, of course, the effects of the Nixon visit were initially devastating. In anticipation of PRC recognition, Taiwan lost its seat as China in the UN and its place in the Olympic games. By the end of the 1970s, the dictatorial government of Taiwan had a credibility crisis of its own, with a rising movement among the Taiwanese for political independence and overthrow of the immigrant militarists of Chiang Kai-shek's Nationalist Party who had seized power in 1947.

To understand the importance of the change in U.S.–PRC relations in the 1970s, the role that the PRC had played in the international cultural politics of the 1960s must be examined. Although China had positioned itself in the 1950s as champion of the Third World, it was only during its aggressively pursued and aggressively publicized economic reorganization campaigns of the late 1950s that it began to play the role of a model for nations pursuing self-reliance. Beginning in the late 1950s, Mao had argued that the best defense against a possible nuclear strike from one of the two superpowers was total decentralization. If every agricultural commune had its own fields, factories, hospitals, and schools, the destruction of the major urban centers would not bring the country to a standstill. Mao also promoted high birthrates, claiming that a developing economy could accommodate an unlimited number of workers, and that a dense but evenly distributed population would best survive a new world war. Finally, he argued for complete exploitation of the environment. To seek the best life, the people must be ready to mine every mineral, use every tree, draw all the water, and if necessary pollute the air in order to advance. Nature, Mao felt, was limitless.

Nixon went to China in 1972 to encounter the fantasy, and to co-opt it if he could. His visit certainly achieved a warming of all China's international relations and opened the path to a far more realistic way for the United States to deal with China in the future. It also meant that the Third World countries were not merely nations where the United States and the Soviet Union competed for influence and privileges, but were themselves competitors with the superpowers for influence in other nonaligned nations. As we saw in Chapter 11, India had enjoyed steady success since 1948 in improving agriculture and living conditions, as well as in managing stable democratic institutions. But with no enormous publicity machine working on its behalf, and with the glamour of the Green Revolution wearing thin, Asia's other giant was put in the shade of the Cultural Revolution's energetic publicity campaign. Indeed, global knowledge of and fascination with China's Cultural Revolution was so strong that the youth-oriented upheavals that marked North America, Europe, and Japan all identified themselves with the rhetoric of China's Cultural Revolution.

Flexing of the American Pole

So long as the Vietnam War continued, international abhorrence of the destruction of Vietnam's natural environment, the shattering of its economy, and the mass killing of millions of its people were held against the American government, and particularly against Richard Nixon and his adviser, Henry Kissinger. During the 1960s and 1970s, the willingness of Americans to disparage, satirize, peacefully and violently protest, and finally force the resignation of the president created an international withdrawal from the anti-Americanism of the 1950s and late 1960s. Though the bipolar system would survive for years, U.S. rigidity was seen by foreign editorial writers and diplomats to dissolve into a more complex and flexible structure during the rest of the 1970s.

Nixon and Kissinger Seek a Conclusion

The mainstreaming of opposition to the war was not less threatening to Nixon, but more threatening. His opponents were now not radical pacifists and violent anarchists but the great mass of the American middle class, the "silent majority" that he had previously claimed as his loyal supporters but whose support he now felt to be wavering. From the time he began to campaign for the presidency in 1968, Nixon had intended to withdraw U.S. troops from Vietnam. But he believed that this had to be done gradually, and he blamed Johnson's lack of political realism for the former president's unpopularity. Soon after his election, Nixon appointed Kissinger as national security adviser and had him engage in secret negotiations with representatives of the North Vietnamese government. The talks would buy time in which the United States could attempt to solidify the government of South Vietnam and to eradicate the last vestiges of Communist infiltration of the South.

The talks did not go well. Between 1969 and 1971, Kissinger was often in Paris meeting with his counterpart, Le Duc Tho, but the talks were complicated by many factors, including the refusal of South Vietnam president Thieu to cooperate. As time wore on and the 1972 elections approached, Nixon and Kissinger turned to tactics that were both more ruthless militarily and more flexible diplomatically. In 1972, Kissinger and Le reached an agreement assuring the sovereignty and independence of both North and South Vietnam. The agreement was publicized, Nixon won reelection in 1972, and Kissinger and Le were awarded the Nobel Peace Prize in 1973. But the bloody work of ending the war was still in the future. In December, the United States conducted its most destructive bombing campaigns ever against the North, seeking to force the North Vietnam government to enact the final peace provisions. American troops were withdrawn (and Thieu immigrated to the United States) just before Congress ended funding of the war on August 15. An invasion of the South by the North followed the American troop withdrawal.

Watergate and the Final Collapse

Before a conclusion was reached in Vietnam, Nixon confronted a political impasse at home that forced him to become the only U.S. president to resign his office under threat of impeachment. The origins of the drama probably lay in the increasing exposure, after 1968, of illegal decision making regarding the conduct of the war in Vietnam. Nixon and Kissinger suspected that leaking of the unflattering information came from some kind of conspiracy among the press, the Democratic Party, certain members of the State Department, and even members of the military. They were driven to act in 1971 when the *New York Times* published classified Pentagon documents—the "Pentagon Papers." The documents revealed that in the Johnson administration, and continuing in the Nixon years, Congress and the public had been repeatedly and deliberately misled about the reasons for the war, the amount invested in it, and the actual theaters of engagement. The Nixon administration attempted to prevent the newspaper from continuing to publish the documents, but it lost its case in the Supreme Court.

Thereafter Nixon decided that since they had no legal means of preventing such material from being published, they would have to find the individuals who were leaking the information and persuade them, by either bribery or black-mail, to cease. In the hunt for the leaks, his staff employed espionage mercenaries to burgle, bug, and bully those whom they suspected. In time their operatives were arrested (some at the Watergate Hotel in Washington), and new means had to be found to keep them quiet. Congress, already alarmed by the popular opposition to the war, turned on Nixon when the misdeeds of the "Watergate" scandal were gradually revealed. On August 9, 1974, Nixon resigned rather than face impeachment and probable conviction. He was succeeded by Congressman Gerald T. Ford. It was under President Ford that U.S. forces evacuated the South Vietnamese capital, Saigon, in 1975. Vietnam was finally reunified.

The cost for Vietnam was about two million deaths, a generation of massively wounded young, an environment that had been devastated by the effects of bombs and the defoliant chemical Agent Orange (used to destroy hiding places for the guerrillas), the great cities of Hanoi and Saigon reduced to rubble, and the countryside littered with unexploded land mines that would continue to maim for generations. For U.S. society, the cost had been very high too. Billions had been spent on the war, and 58,000 Americans had died in the conflict. One president had withdrawn from candidacy, another had been driven from office by the indirect effects of attempts to silence war critics, a generation of young men and their families had been affected by the trauma of war service (or imprison-ment or exile for refusing to serve), the economy was distorted by the effects of inflation, and the populace was disgusted with government deception. To many around the world, the differences between domestic politics and international affairs had been exposed as illusory. Whether for a superpower or for a small nation struggling for economic and political independence, the global effects of interconnection could not be avoided.

International Dislocations and the Dependence on American Policies

Between 1968 and 1973, the idea that an international communist conspiracy to control the world must be opposed at every location, lest nations would fall like "dominoes" into Communist hands, had no credibility in a world that was ideologically and politically diverse. There was no longer a bipolar situation in which countries were in either the communist or the capitalist camp. On the contrary, the nationalist movements in the Third World were promoting independence and self-sufficiency, without being in the shadow of either of the superpowers.

By the early 1970s, U.S. isolation had become as serious a problem as it had been in the early 1950s. In Europe, France had led the way to a repudiation of U.S. policy in Asia, recognizing the People's Republic of China in 1964. Popular opinion in Western as well as Eastern Europe, especially among students and young workers, ran heavily against the American intervention in Vietnam. In the crisis year of 1968, demonstrations, riots, and bombings in Paris were heavily focused on opposition to the United States, as well as on labor rights and govern-ment education policies. The French government, still under de Gaulle, was able to use the anti-American sentiments in France and Germany to propel a plan for a European Economic Community that would finally move Europe out of the American sphere and onto a path of local commercial power and shared political interests.

In Japan, too, U.S. prestige and credibility had been seriously damaged by the involvement in Vietnam. Though the occupation had ended in 1954 and Japan had entered the UN in 1956, it still played the role of helper in U.S. foreign policy and in the U.S. military presence in East Asia. Japan was also an important listening post for American intelligence, being only five miles from Soviet territory in the Kurile Islands, 150 miles from Korea, and 400 miles from China. In various ways, this was all a boon to Japan's economy, but Japanese born after World War II also regarded it as a serious wound to their national pride. Public protests against U.S. policy in Asia began as early as 1960 when students and workers demonstrated against the new security treaty, ANPO, that made Japan a staging area for American military action throughout East and Southeast Asia. In May 1968, and again in 1970, there were massive student demonstrations in Tokyo and other large cities, protesting extension of the American bombings. Like their European counterparts, Japanese political leaders wished to avoid a situation in which they would be forced to choose between remaining viable at home and supporting United States policies in Asia.

While facing the protests over its relations with the United States, the government of Japan had dealt with what was becoming an increasing and very threatening phenomenon: domestic political violence. Unlike most of the developed countries, Japan had had an intense experience of right-wing violence in the 1930s, part of its disastrous movement toward the Second World War. In the 1960s and 1970s, Japan was still not free of right-wing violence. In fact, the growing American influence on Japanese popular culture was as deeply resented by the Japanese right wing as the military occupation had been. This was shockingly demonstrated in 1970 when the internationally acclaimed writer Yukio Mishima led a small army of followers in an attack on a military office, then publicly committed suicide by self-disembowelment while a follower cut off his head.

This amazing but brief episode did not prevent Japanese political leaders from realizing that the greatest continuing threat was from left-wing violence. This was centered in the Red Army Faction, which had been known in the earlier 1960s but demonstrated its dedication to international terrorism at the Tel Aviv airport in Israel in 1972, machine-gunning twenty-six people to death and wounding eighty more. All over the world, democracies were dealing with outbreaks of relatively organized, very violent groups. The Red Brigade, which was active in Italy and Germany, was involved in bombings, kidnappings, and murder. Britain was vulnerable to attack by bombs and guns from the Irish Republican Army and its offshoots. Peru was troubled by a Maoist guerrilla group, the Shining Path. In the United States, the Weathermen periodically planted bombs to attempt to destabilize the U.S. government.

CONCLUSION

In the late 1960s and 1970s, a variety of factors contributed to major changes in popular culture and political attitudes in the United States, Europe, and Japan. By 1968, some of these changes had found expression in massive civil demonstrations, mostly but not exclusively involving university students protesting against American involvement in the war in Vietnam, against racism, and against what were regarded as the repressive intelligence policies of the United States and its international allies. In the United States, Britain, and France, these movements came to be deeply skeptical about government relationships with industry and finance, and about the use of the CIA to enforce the interests of multinational corporations. The political activism of 1968 progressed in the context of horrifying events: the bloody Tet Offensive in Vietnam in the spring of 1968, the murder of Martin Luther King Jr. in April, and the murder of Robert F. Kennedy in August.

Throughout the developed and developing world, an enthusiasm for casting off the cultural and social patterns of the Cold War was evident. Much of the rhetoric and imagery for this came from the richly tumultuous group of societies of the Third World. The great theme of their leaders—self-reliance—struck a chord with young people in many parts of North America and Europe. Self-supporting communes in which residents grew their own food, made their own clothes, and educated their own children became popular, at least as an experiment. Many idealized the Indian *ashram*, the traditional self-reliant communities that Gandhi (see Chapter 4) had championed as a means to Indian independence. Images of revolutionary self-reliance were glamorized, and revolutionary heroes became international cultural icons.

As we saw in Chapters 10 and 11, the early 1960s was both a period in which a new meaning of youth came to the fore and a time when global media permitted the rapid dissemination and standardization of youth culture. The emphasis on youth was in part a result of the postwar baby boom, which produced an unprecedented number of young people in the early 1960s. In addition, as the older generation of World War II leaders retired or died, younger people assumed positions of real power. However, large sectors of American and European society regarded politicians and vote casting as ineffectual or hypocritical. And for most of the world outside of the United States, Canada, Australia, and Europe, genuine transformation of the political and social systems could be achieved only through radical and perhaps even violent action. What distinguished them from the rebel heroes of the 1950s was that they were praised for taking public action against oppressive or constraining institutions.

Outside of the industrialized societies, politics in these times was also tumultuous and also strongly featured youthful activists, but the concerns and the assumptions were quite different. American, European, and Japanese youth were profoundly cynical about government in general. Their emphasis was on a search for idealistic "alternative"s—new choices in religion, in medical thinking, in social organization, in morality, and in politics. But in China, India, Chile, Nigeria, and many other parts of the developing world, suspicion was directed toward interference in local affairs by the government of the United States or the Soviet Union and their intelligence agencies, while people retained a great hope that honest nationalist governments could bring empowerment and economic development.

For Further Reading

John Lee Anderson, *Guevara: A Revolutionary Life* (New York: Grove Press, 1998). The only English-language book-length scholarly study of Guevara to date.

S. Johns Davis and R. Hunt Jr., eds., *Mandela, Tambo, and the African National Congress: The Struggle Against Apartheid, 1948–1990: A Documentary Survey* (Oxford and London: Oxford University Press, 1991). An important primary resource.

Mary L. Dudziak, *Cold War Civil Rights: Race and the Image of American Democracy (Politics and Society in Twentieth-Century America)* (Princeton, NJ: Princeton University Press, 2002). An important interpretation of this era's very strong connection between African American and African issues.

Todd Gitlin, *The Sixties: Years of Hope, Days of Rage* (New York: Bantam Books, 1987). An engaging and enduring overview of this period.

David Howard-Pitney, *Martin Luther King, Jr., Malcolm X, and the Civil Rights Struggle of the 1950s and 1960s: A Brief History with Documents* (Boston: The Bedford Series in History and Culture, 2004).

Stanley Karnow, *Vietnam: A History*, 2nd ed. (New York: Penguin USA, 1997). The best known single work on the Vietnam war.

Martin Luther King, *A Call to Conscience: The Landmark Speeches of Dr. Martin Luther King, Jr.*, Kris Shepard and Clayborne Carson, eds. (New York: Warner Books, 2002).

Tom Lodge, *Mandela: A Critical Life* (Oxford: Oxford University Press, 2006). The most thoroughly researched and objective treatment of Mandela.

Devin McKinney, *Magic Circles: The Beatles in Dream and History* (Cambridge Mass.: Harvard University Press, 2003).

Malcolm X and Alex Haley, *The Autobiography of Malcolm X* (New York: Random House, 1975). A classic of American literature, co-written with the author of *Roots*.

Mike Marquese, *Redemption Song: Muhammad Ali and the Spirit of the Sixties* (London: Verso Books, 1999). A contemporary study of sports, popular culture, and the impact of Ali.

Don Oberdorfer, *Tet* (New York: Avon, 1972; reprint, with a new preface, Baltimore: Johns Hopkins University Press, 2001). A war correspondent's account of the Tet Offensive and its aftermath.

Elizabeth Perry et al., *Proletarian Power: Shanghai in the Cultural Revolution (Transitions—Asia and Asian America)* (New York: Westview Press, 1997). A prominent historian of modern China focuses her review of the radical period on China's most dynamic and international city.

Jonathan D. Spence, *Mao Zedong* (Penguin Lives Series) (New York: Viking Penguin, 1999). A concise and absorbing biography of Mao.

David J. Whitaker, *The Terrorism Reader* (London: Routledge, 2001). A well-organized source book on the historical origins of many modern movements.

Related Websites

Kate Doyle, "Tlatelolco Massacre: Declassifi ed U.S. Documents on Mexico and the Events of 1968"
  http://www.gwu.edu/-nsarchiv/NSAEBB/NSAEBB10/intro.htm
African Biography on the Internet
  http://www.columbia.edu/cu/lweb/indiv/africa/cuvl/afrbio.html
The Biography Project (Che Guevara)
  http://www.popsubculture.com/pop/bio_project/ernesto_che_guevara.html
World History Archives: The Black Panthers
  http://www.hartford-hwp.com/archives/45a/index-be.html
The Rivonia Trial of Nelson Mandela
  http://www.thirdworldtraveler.com/Human%20Rights%20Documents/Mandela_RivoniaTrial.html

CHAPTER 13

Détente to Disarray: The Breakdown of the Bipolar World, 1969–1981

Those who know what happened to Salvador Allende are not talking about it. Allende, the president of Chile, died shortly after his government was overthrown by a military junta in 1973, perhaps by his own hand or perhaps by execution.

The coup was not entirely unexpected. Allende's political base had been weak to begin with. He had won a narrow electoral victory in 1970 against a divided opposition, polling only 36 percent of the total vote. Allende, a former professor with socialist views, aroused intense enthusiasm in Chile's powerful labor unions, but conservatives viewed his election as a fluke, made possible only by their own divisions and a slump in Chile's economy.

Indeed, Chile was facing a combination of economic stagnation and inflation, later dubbed stagflation, that would soon afflict most of the industrial West. While in office, Allende had tackled this problem and broader issues of social inequality with controversial measures: a freeze on prices, mandatory wage increases, an acceleration in the land redistribution begun by a predecessor, and the nationalization of copper mines and other large industries, which were often owned by foreigners. Although winning plaudits from organized labor and socialists at home and abroad, Allende made implacable enemies among Chile's elites and U.S. investors, who feared that Chile was on the path taken by Cuba in 1959.

Salvador Allende was a charismatic leader but a poor economist. Government-ordered wage increases stimulated consumer demand for goods while price controls restricted the growth of supply, resulting in shortages and black markets.

Weak international prices for copper, Chile's main export, reduced income from abroad as costs increased at home, and Chile's struggling central bank found it impossible to borrow from foreign lenders who doubted Chile's will or capacity to repay. Middle-class housewives in Chile's capital, Santiago, took to the streets, banging pots to protest rising food prices. Independent truckers, squeezed by price controls and rising costs, tied up transportation in a nationwide strike. The U.S. government, dismayed by Allende's seizure of American-owned property and outspoken friendliness to Castro, amplified Chile's difficulties by denying the country credit and by pumping funds into conservative opposition parties.

The precise role that the United States played in toppling Allende's regime is still uncertain, but the American president, Richard Nixon, and his secretary of state, Henry Kissinger, had made no secret of their distaste for Allende's politics. They quickly offered the new military government, led by General Augusto Pinochet, the diplomatic and financial support they had withheld from Allende. Pinochet, for his part, returned the industries that had been seized by Allende to private control, lowered tariffs, and renewed warm commercial ties with U.S. banks and business firms.

Yet despite its pro-American leanings, the new regime soon proved an embarrassment to Washington. Pinochet was determined to eradicate Marxism from Chile by any and all means. The new regime imposed draconian controls on political life, suspended Chile's democratic constitution, outlawed political parties, and filled prisons with those it suspected of leftist sympathies. In the end, the Pinochet government became infamous for its torture and execution of opponents, many of whom simply "disappeared" without warrant or trial—a technique that would soon be emulated on a larger scale by a military junta in Argentina. Fearing another Cuba, the United States had midwifed a brutal police state.

The 1970s: An Overview

Making change is often dangerous. But the tragic history of the Allende government also offers a parable about the seam between the 1960s and the 1970s. The most remarkable feature of the 1960s was the number of people, across the world, who entertained extravagant hopes for a better future. In North America, utopians dreamed of a colorblind society without poverty or war, an Age of Aquarius in which evils would dissolve in a sea of spontaneous love and harmony, or more prosaically, a future of ever-greater abundance and leisure. Western Europe, heartened by years of rapid growth, looked forward to the sustained extension of middle-class prosperity and social welfare benefits. Nation builders in Africa and Asia eagerly planned takeoffs into economic development, and in Latin America the Cuban revolution and the Alliance for Progress offered competing—but equally rosy—visions of the future. Even in the Soviet bloc, citizens saw hope that a warming of relations between East and West, soon to be called détente, might allow some of the long-postponed promises of communism to be realized. Neither the ongoing war in Vietnam nor the periodic crises in such hot spots as

The young Salvador Allende addresses a meeting of his Socialist Party in Santiago, Chile, July 1, 1959. Allende became a hero of the left in Latin America and globally not so much for what he accomplished in a three-year term as Chile's president as for dying for the cause of socialism.

Keystone/Getty Images

Berlin and Korea deterred optimists from imagining that a new and better world was in the making.

The disappointments of the 1970s were as remarkable as the hopes of the 1960s. In Latin America, the new decade belonged not to the socialists or to progressive reformers but to strongmen. It often looked that way in other regions as well as authoritarian governments took charge in much of Africa and Asia. Democratic institutions were subverted or suspended in the Philippines, Pakistan, and India. South Africa's white government intensified controls on the black majority, imprisoning and murdering black leaders and censoring or exiling critics. Meanwhile, in the rolling hills of Rhodesia, white supremacists struggled to retain power against an even larger black majority. Especially gruesome abuses of power occurred in Uganda, where an unpredictable dictator, Idi Amin, humiliated and terrorized his people, and in Cambodia, where a Marxist regime extinguished approximately a million lives in the name of ideological purity. In those regions where autocratic government had long been the norm, such as Eastern Europe, citizens suffered less egregious but nonetheless brutal forms of intimidation and repression.

Local circumstances and personalities shaped these conditions, but so, too, did global political and economic conditions. Despite improved bilateral relations, neither the United States nor the USSR could refrain from viewing the world as an arena of struggle, and regional conflicts such as the one in Chile continued to draw their involvement. The superpowers could embolden partisans, moving them from violent words to violent deeds. Regional contests, in turn, strengthened the hand of Cold War warriors in Washington and Moscow by confirming their doubts about the intentions of the other side. Détente was among the casualties. By the end of the 1970s, relations between the two giants were more acrimonious than they had been at any time since the Cuban missile crisis of 1962.

Economics displayed much the same reciprocal relationship between local and global as did politics. In Chile, the main nexus was copper. The country's arid northern provinces held about a quarter of the world's known reserves of this industrially important metal. The rich deposits lured foreign investment, but they also tied Chile's economy to fluctuations in international prices of that one commodity, creating a volatility that had broad political effects. Other nations had similarly critical resources. Zaire (the former Belgian Congo) had 60 percent of the world's cobalt, along with abundant uranium and copper; South Africa had about half the world's gold resources; and Southern Rhodesia (later Zimbabwe) held a significant fraction of the world's chromium. These critical materials gave outside powers strong motives to deal with governments that could promise stability, even at the cost of human rights, and afforded these nations a status in global politics out of proportion to their size.

No natural resource was more critical to industrial economies than oil, which had powered much of the world's postwar economic expansion. Swelling demand focused attention on those parts of the world that had it, and no region had more than the Middle East. Long a scene of international disputes because of its strategic location and its significance to three major religions, the region now became crucial to the global economy. Twice during the 1970s, upheavals in the Middle East disrupted global energy markets: a war between Israel and its neighbors in 1973 triggered an Arab-led oil boycott of Israel's Western allies. In addition, a revolution in Iran at the end of the decade drastically reduced exports from the world's second largest oil producer. By constricting the supply of oil, these events drove energy prices far beyond the levels anyone had anticipated at the beginning of the decade. The higher prices touched lives around the world by pushing the cost of living higher, reducing rates of economic growth, and shifting huge amounts of capital from oil-importing to oil-exporting nations.

The economic turmoil of the 1970s had political consequences. In North America and Western Europe, many voters became disillusioned with liberal governments, which seemed helpless to remedy economic malaise, and turned rightward at the end of the decade. In poorer nations, rising energy costs derailed development plans, fed uncontrolled inflation, and undermined political stability. Even the Soviet bloc, which was largely insulated from global trade, felt the aftershocks as the states of Eastern Europe had to borrow money and tighten budgets to meet the higher prices charged by the Soviet Union, which was eager to capitalize on its petroleum riches.

Nor did oil importers alone suffer the consequences of rising prices. Blessings had a way of turning into curses. The oil-exporting nations, the main economic winners in the 1970s, experienced exhilarating booms, but these often led to excesses of spending that were no less destabilizing than the poverty of their oil-poor neighbors. Only in the Pacific, where Japan proved remarkably resilient to economic malaise and political upheaval, were some of the hopes of the 1960s realized. The Japanese economy steamed ahead despite oil shortages, pulling many other Asian nations in its wake.

The 1970s, then, were hardly what the 1960s had aspired to. Instead of sustained economic growth, there was widespread economic stagnation. Instead of constructive cooperation between the superpowers, there was renewed enmity. Instead of an Age of Aquarius, there was a proliferation of dictatorships, atrocities, and repression.

What general themes run through this welter of disappointed hopes? The broad answer is that economic and political changes were making many of the patterns of the postwar world obsolete. The long postwar economic expansion, fed at first by reconstruction projects and later by expanding markets for consumer products and higher defense expenditures, came to a temporary halt in the 1970s. The interruption tested assumptions that had prevailed since the war in both East and West. Neither Soviet Marxism nor the liberal democracies of the West seemed to have an elixir that could restore robust economic growth. By the end of the decade, Marxist states were turning to free enterprise, while the United States and Western Europe explored a variety of remedies, some homegrown and others influenced by the singular economic health of Japan, but most of them decidedly more business-friendly than the policies of the 1960s. The era of big government and command economies was not over, but the economic setbacks of the 1970s chastened all those who believed that growth could be readily managed by central economic planners.

The 1970s also provided a second economic lesson: The North Atlantic was no longer the undisputed center of global economic activity, as it long had been. This was apparent not only in the huge capital flows from Europe and the United States into the Middle East and other oil-producing areas but also in the more gradual but still stunning economic growth of Japan and the economies most directly linked to it. The Pacific Rim, including South Korea, Taiwan, Hong Kong, Singapore, and the west coast of North America, was coming to rival the North Atlantic in trade, investment, and manufacturing and showed much faster and steadier growth. These shifts in economic power, from energy consumers to energy producers and from the economies of the Atlantic to those of the Pacific, posed difficult challenges to an international system of trade and finance that was built on cheap energy, stable currencies, and the dominance of the U.S.–Europe axis.

The 1970s saw the beginnings of a reorientation of world politics that was no less important than the reorganization of the global economy. The United States and the USSR remained the world's dominant military powers, but they were beset with political and economic troubles at home and shrinking leverage abroad. Not only could China and Western Europe challenge the superpowers diplomatically, as they had for over a decade, but regional powers became increasingly adept at playing the superpowers off against each other in contests for local advantage. The pressures of this new world, with its many competing and overlapping fields of influence, gave the United States and the USSR new reasons to talk and new reasons to argue. At the same time, other forms of conflict—religious, ethnic, and economic—competed with the old Cold War issues for center stage.

The bipolar world had imposed a crude sort of order on global politics. As that world evolved into something more complex—a hope that had long been nourished in many regions—conflict didn't end; in fact, it often intensified. Neither the democracies of Western Europe and North America nor the Communist regimes of Eastern Europe and Asia were prepared for the change. The fragile democracies in Latin America and the nations evolving from Europe's old empires were even less prepared. The economic and political turmoil of the 1970s toppled many governments in the industrial West and undercut Communist regimes in the East, but it spelled disaster for large parts of the developing world.

Regional Rivalries and the Decay of Détente

After an enormously expensive effort, the Soviet Union attained rough parity with the United States in strategic nuclear forces during the 1970s. Each side possessed more than ten thousand nuclear weapons, including many that were a hundred times more powerful than the Hiroshima bomb. Each had two to three thousand missiles or bombers of intercontinental range. Many of these were armed with multiple warheads. Most were protected from attack. Some bombers were airborne at all times, and others were on fifteen-minute alert. Missiles were concealed under the sea on silent and wide-ranging submarines or housed in dispersed underground silos. Both superpowers had also equipped their armies and navies with tactical nuclear weapons—explosives carried by artillery, torpedoes, short-range rockets, or short-range aircraft. These huge nuclear arsenals gave each superpower the capacity to obliterate the other, even after suffering a first strike—a standoff called "mutually assured destruction," or MAD for short.

Despite the seeming absurdity of building forces that neither side could safely use, the rough equivalence in nuclear weapons created new opportunities for arms control. Previously, neither the United States nor the USSR had seen much advantage in bargaining. The United States enjoyed a superiority that it would not negotiate away, and the USSR refused to accept second-class status. Now, both parties stood to gain. Moscow was spending over 15 percent of its gross domestic product (GDP) on defense, a level that it sustained only at great sacrifice to other sectors of the economy, notably agriculture and the production of consumer products. Although Washington could match Soviet spending by devoting only about 5 percent of its much larger GDP to defense, even that level troubled economists and voters. Liberals believed that tax dollars could be much better devoted to schools or public health; many conservatives maintained that taxes were better left uncollected so that individuals and firms could invest the money more productively.

The Politics of Détente

Recognizing a mutual interest, Soviet and American diplomats opened talks focusing on limiting strategic nuclear weapons soon after Richard Nixon and his top foreign policy adviser, Henry Kissinger, entered the White House in 1969. The talks proceeded against a broader backdrop of easing tensions, or détente, between East and West. Both Washington and Moscow had come to the sober realization that a nuclear exchange would be mutually disastrous; neither any longer harbored expectations about the imminent collapse of its adversary. Talk of a rollback of Soviet forces from Eastern Europe had all but ended in the United States in the late 1960s, as had Soviet predictions of the imminent collapse of capitalism. "Peaceful coexistence," a slogan of the 1950s, became a shared premise.

Détente, however, was not just about the United States and the USSR; it also involved dynamic new centers of power in Europe and the Far East. The bipolar postwar world was becoming a game with many players, in which diplomacy might be more important than rhetoric or the size of nuclear arsenals. Thus, while Soviet and American negotiators painstakingly discussed arms control, West Germany, under Chancellor Willy Brandt, signed a nonaggression pact with Moscow in return for Soviet recognition of its statehood, trade concessions, and freer movement of East Germans across the wall. While Brandt practiced this "*Ostpolitik*" or "politics of the east," Mao's foreign minister, Zhou Enlai, was negotiating warmer Sino-American relations with Kissinger. Their talks culminated in a visit by Nixon to Beijing and the normalization of Sino-American relations.

A rigid bipolar world served the interests of neither the Europeans nor the Chinese. Their diplomatic maneuvers, in turn, amplified pressures on the superpowers to reach mutual accommodations. Soviet leaders wanted to forestall collusion between the United States and China. The Americans wanted to quell criticism from their European allies, who desired better trade relations with the East. Détente, in short, was driven by the bilateral interests of the United States and the USSR, but also by calculations involving other powers.

Despite the economic and political pressures moving the United States and the USSR toward détente, agreements were slow in coming and narrowly drawn. The first round of Strategic Arms Limitation Talks (SALT) produced a treaty, signed in 1971, that merely imposed constraints on the pace of future arms increases rather than actually reducing stockpiles. Both parties agreed to limit the number and payload of delivery vehicles to roughly the levels that were then prevailing. More important, both agreed to refrain from building full-scale antiballistic missile (ABM) systems, which were then in the early stages of deployment. These antiballistic missiles were intended to destroy incoming warheads in the upper atmosphere by detonating their own nuclear warheads. Both sides were preparing to spend tens of billions of dollars to shield their cities and missile fields with these ABMs, although neither knew if they would prove effective. The SALT I agreement had the great merit for both sides of preventing, or at least postponing, an enormously expensive escalation of the arms race.

In the early 1970s, the United States and the USSR reached other agreements governing trade, scientific cooperation, immigration from the Soviet Union, and the control of chemical and biological weapons. The two parties also commenced a second round of SALT negotiations aimed at extending the first SALT treaty to include reductions in offensive weapons, as well as talks aimed at reducing the levels of conventional forces in Europe. Perhaps the high point of détente arrived in 1975, when, after two years of negotiations, the United States, Canada, the USSR, and thirty-two European nations signed accords in Helsinki that acknowledged the legitimacy of existing European borders and committed the signatories to a common statement regarding human rights.

The agreement could be seen as ending two eras of conflict. By validating the borders imposed by the Allies in 1945, it constituted the long-postponed settlement of the war against Germany. East and West Germany renounced any ambitions to recover lands that had been lost in the two world wars. At the same time, the Helsinki accords appeared to resolve one of the long-standing issues of the Cold War by recognizing Germany's division into two states and the paramount Soviet influence over Eastern Europe. Acknowledgment of these political facts reassured the Soviet leadership and further eased the way for the opening of its trading bloc to Western goods and capital—an opening that all parties had come to see as economically desirable.

The Superpowers and Regional Conflict

The very fact that the United States and the USSR were negotiating and finding common ground was a marked change from the 1950s and 1960s when serious diplomatic exchanges were few and far between. Diplomatic progress, however, barely concealed enduring mistrust. Some of these suspicions were justified. The Soviets did not live up to the Helsinki statement on human rights and continued to harass, imprison, and exile political dissidents. Recent revelations by former Soviet officials also reveal that Moscow continued to produce potent biological weapons long after signing a 1972 treaty outlawing them. More significant, however, was the enduring reflex of both sides to contest the other's position in regional conflicts. Indeed, clashes involving clients of the two superpowers were at least as numerous in the 1970s as they had been in the two preceding decades. Wherever political conflicts became intense, the leaders of both superpowers tended to see the hand of their rival at work, as was the case in Chile. And, as in Chile, factional leaders in civil wars, coups, and border disputes were quick to appreciate the advantages of enrolling one superpower or the other in their cause.

Both Moscow and Washington used the ideological terms of the 1950s and 1960s to justify these engagements. Soviet leaders defended socialist comrades against reactionary forces or assisted progressive forces in struggles of national liberation. Their counterparts in Washington, meanwhile, backed freedom fighters against communist aggression or helped legitimate governments contend with communist subversion. But the ideological rhetoric often bore only a distant relationship to the reality. Age-old balance-of-power considerations drove policy.

Ultimately, the ideological slogans of the Cold War mattered even less to the participants in these struggles than to their distant patrons.

Some of the worst conflicts occurred where decolonization had left a legacy of uncertain borders, weak institutions, economic dependency, and bitter ethnic and religious divisions. Nowhere was this legacy clearer than in Africa. Only a handful of states in sub-Saharan Africa maintained their equilibrium through the 1970s; many, including the two largest and richest, Nigeria and Zaire, fell into destructive civil war. Swelling populations, declining agricultural productivity, decaying infrastructure, and volatile commodity prices overwhelmed governments that could call on neither deep financial resources nor broad public support. Impoverished and ill-educated people migrated by the thousands from villages that seemed to offer no future into slapdash cities that promised more but often delivered less. There they became easy prey to hucksters and criminals, not the least of whom were political leaders ready to exploit office for personal gain. Propped up by their control of armed militias, political parties, and outside powers, these kleptocrats and petty dictators squeezed wealth from their impoverished peoples, exploiting whatever tools came to hand—ideology, ethnic loyalties, and the greed of willing henchmen.

The grand geopolitical ambitions of the superpowers repeatedly intersected the local politics of sub-Saharan Africa during the 1970s. These intersections sometimes had beneficial results. Agile African diplomats, for example, could parlay votes in the UN into development assistance from the United States or the USSR. And in a few cases, the great powers found opportunities for productive cooperation, as in an ultimately successful effort to eradicate smallpox through mass vaccination. But at least as often, the superpowers' subventions and military assistance became tools in brutal struggles for political power that both damaged U.S.–Soviet relations and wreaked havoc across wide swaths of the continent. Such was the outcome in two of the bloodiest and most chaotic wars of the 1970s, one between several factions seeking control of the former Portuguese colony of Angola and the other a border fight between Ethiopia and Somalia.

Civil War in Angola, War Between Ethiopia and Somalia

The war in Angola commenced in 1974, when Portugal, itself undergoing a difficult transition from dictatorial rule to democracy, abruptly announced that it was dissolving its African empire. Three groups, each with its own regional and ethnic strongholds, promptly laid claim to control of this prized colony, rich in minerals and oil. One group, the Progressive Movement for the Liberation of Angola, or MPLA, occupied the capital, Luanda, and secured recognition from both the Soviet Union and a number of African states. Other factions established control of regions in the north and south of the country and took what aid they could get from China, South Africa, the United States, and Zaire (see Map 13.1). A civil war ensued, in which rebels backed by the United States and South Africa first seized the initiative and then lost it as Soviet aid and seventeen thousand Cuban troops tipped the balance decisively toward the MPLA government. For the Ford administration, support for Angolan rebels was a way both to check the expansion of Soviet influence and to counter conservative critics at home who saw détente as a Soviet plot. For Brezhnev and his colleagues, it was equally important to demonstrate to Marxist hard-liners at home and abroad that détente did not mean stasis.

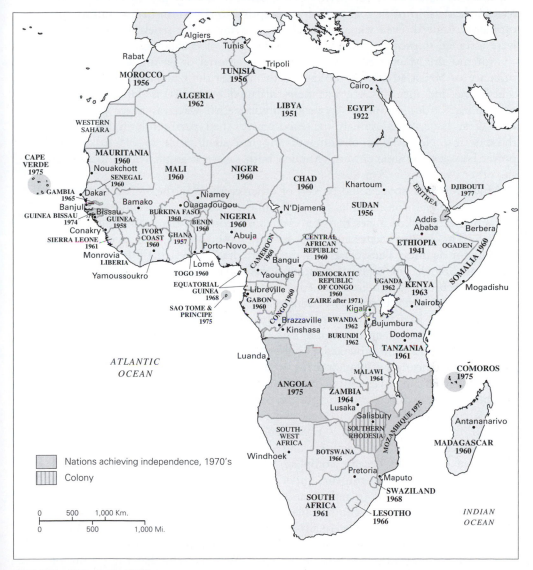

Nations achieving independence, 1970's

Colony

MAP 13.1 Africa in the 1970's.

The collapse of the Portuguese Empire in 1975 added half a dozen new states to the United Nations and all but ended the era of formal European colonial rule in Africa. Nevertheless, the former colonial powers continued to exercise economic and political clout in their former colonies, and South Africa and Southern Rhodesia remained under the control of their white minorities for a few more years.

By the end of 1976, the MPLA had consolidated its power in most of Angola. Cuban troops had stiffened the government's army. At the same time, Democrats in the U.S. Congress, uneasy about American sponsorship of a rebellion with uncertain prospects, had voted a cutoff of U.S. aid to the rebels. The outcome appeared to be a victory for Soviet policy, but this quickly proved illusory. The Marxist leadership of Angola proved as receptive to American investment as any capitalists. Indeed, even when U.S. aid was flowing to the rebels, Cuban troops were assigned to protect U.S.-owned oil wells from rebel sabotage.

Nor did the Marxist government remain enamored of having a large Cuban presence or Soviet advice. By the end of the 1970s, the Cuban troops had been sent home and the MPLA government, alarmed by Soviet meddling, had distanced itself from its former sponsor. Angola's civil war was never purely an East-West issue, even though the superpowers had persistently framed it in those terms. Nor was its outcome of any real significance to the balance of power between the superpowers, although both saw in it ample reason to suspect the other's motives.

Much the same thing could be said of other episodes in the 1970s. A coup in Ethiopia in 1974, for example, triggered another confrontation between Soviet- and American-backed forces that was even more complex than the free-for-all in Angola. The United States had lent Ethiopia modest economic and military support for decades. The Soviets, for their part, had cultivated Ethiopia's eastern neighbor, Somalia, in hopes of securing a naval base near the strategic shipping lines between the Persian Gulf and Asia. The 1974 coup at first seemed a victory for Soviet interests because it brought a self-proclaimed Marxist, Colonel Mengistu Haile Mariam, to power in Ethiopia, thereby giving the U.S.S.R. dominant influence throughout the region. But Mengistu's brutal efforts to consolidate power in Ethiopia soon provoked a civil war in its arid southeastern province of Ogaden where nearly a million Somalis lived. In July 1977, hoping to take advantage of Ethiopia's internal turmoil, Somalian forces marched into the Ogaden.

The invasion created a dilemma for the Soviet Union. After an effort to broker a peace collapsed, the Kremlin threw in its lot with the larger nation, Ethiopia, and airlifted equipment and Cuban troops to support Mengistu. Somalia promptly ejected its Soviet advisers and closed its ports to Soviet vessels. The reversal of alignments became complete when Somalia requested U.S. aid and an alarmed American government, under President Jimmy Carter, arranged arms transfers to Somalia from friendly Arab states in the Middle East.

Neither superpower was comfortable with its new ally. Mengistu's ruthlessness chilled his Soviet sponsors; the equally brutal methods of Somalia's military dictator, Mohammed Siyad Barre, made open American patronage impossible. But, as in Angola, the lingering dynamic of the Cold War dictated that the enemy of your enemy must be a friend. And, also as in Angola, none of the parties reaped lasting benefit from the political maneuvers and violence. Ethiopia, having checked Somali advances with Soviet aid, denied Moscow a naval base to replace the facilities the Soviet Union had lost in Somalia. The United States, having lost all influence in Ethiopia, proved unable to exert much control in Somalia. Futile combat over the Ogaden sputtered on until a peace was signed in 1988. By then, both belligerents had all but disintegrated amid rebellions and factional strife. Coups overturned Mengistu in 1990 and Barre in 1991. The greatest losers, however, were the unfortunate citizens of Ethiopia and Somalia, who were cursed by recurring drought, famine, epidemic, and leaders who placed their political ambitions above human needs.

Tilts on the Subcontinent: India Versus Pakistan

The tragic wars in Africa had their counterparts in Latin America and Asia. Although these wars often drew in the superpowers and sometimes had ideological overtones, most were fueled by more traditional motives: territorial ambition, religious and ethnic hatreds, and the common tendency of weak rulers to seek power at home through victories abroad. All three motives were on display in 1971, when Pakistan and India fought a two-week war over issues that had been accumulating for more than two decades.

India and Pakistan were divided by religion, a disputed border, and a history of suspicion reaching back to their violent partition in 1947. That partition had left Pakistan itself a divided state. A wedge of Indian territory nearly a thousand miles wide separated its mostly arid western half, which was almost entirely Muslim and home to the nation's capital, from its tropical, densely populated, and religiously diverse eastern half. Divisions between the two halves grew during the 1960s, as Pakistan's government gave top priority to the arms race with India and the economic development of West Pakistan. By the late 1960s, demands for regional autonomy in the much-neglected East led to the imposition of martial law.

Civil unrest only grew as a vastly outnumbered army struggled to maintain control of a civilian population that was increasingly bent on independence. Riots provoked repression, and during the spring and summer of 1970–1971 nearly ten million refugees fled across the border into India. Indira Gandhi, India's prime minister since 1966, no doubt found some satisfaction in the disintegration of a long-time adversary, but she was also dismayed by the burden of feeding and housing the refugees. In August 1971, perhaps with an eye toward an eventual war with Pakistan, Gandhi signed a friendship pact with the USSR. India needed Soviet military and diplomatic support, especially since Pakistan enjoyed close relations with both the United States and China.

Pakistan's leaders, seeing their control over their eastern provinces slipping away and anticipating an Indian attack, launched a preemptive strike on India in December 1971. It was futile. The Indian army was larger, better equipped, and united rather than divided. Pakistan's tanks made limited headway in the west before being repulsed; in the east, Indian and secessionist forces quickly forced the Pakistani army to capitulate. The fighting was over in twelve days.

A new nation, Bangladesh, emerged from the former East Pakistan, and India and Pakistan found new reasons to nurse their mutual suspicions. But the war also had effects in more distant areas. The Soviet treaty with India reawakened Western anxieties about Soviet designs on warm-water ports on the Indian Ocean. After

World War II, the United States had sought to make Turkey, Iran, and Pakistan sturdy sentinels against Soviet expansion southward. A blow to Pakistan was a strike against this cordon, and hence the U.S. government made a well-publicized tilt toward Pakistan during the war, going so far as to order a naval battle group to the waters off India. As far as the Soviets were concerned, America was meddling along its borders and using Pakistan as a base for espionage and propaganda campaigns. Moscow was especially concerned with joint U.S.–Pakistani efforts to stir up ethnic and religious separatism among the largely Muslim peoples of the USSR's southern republics. In short, both superpowers read events on the subcontinent through the lens of Cold War politics.

Neither the war on the Indian subcontinent nor the conflicts in Africa engaged the vital interests of the United States or the USSR, as the earlier crises over Berlin and Soviet missiles in Cuba had done. Nor did the troops of either superpower play a direct role, as they had in Korea and Vietnam and in the suppression of revolutions in Hungary and Czechoslovakia. But these regional crises again and again brought Soviet and American diplomatic goals into collision. They formed a steady background noise to negotiations over arms control, giving each side reason to be suspicious of the motives of its partner.

Equally important, they provided American and Soviet critics with evidence to support hardline policies. In truth, the government of neither superpower viewed détente as a full settlement of their differences or a resolution of their rivalry. For Moscow, détente promised Western recognition of the legitimacy of the Soviet empire, equivalency to the United States in international councils, and an opportunity to break through the walls of containment and obtain access to much-needed Western technology and goods. It did not mean that the Soviet Union would cease to support revolutionary movements in developing nations or to extend its influence in the developing world. For Washington, détente promised Soviet cooperation in restoring peace to troubled regions and new markets but also an end to Soviet support for wars of national liberation and an opportunity to penetrate the Iron Curtain with Western ideas. Both parties wanted to avoid direct confrontation, but neither was willing to give up all hope of undermining the other's international position. Détente, then, was not a fundamental shift in U.S.–Soviet relations but rather a tactical adaptation to new conditions, most notably parity in strategic weapons and the growing capacity of third parties, such as China and West Germany, to influence international events.

The Yom Kippur War, 1973

The Middle East posed the most dangerous threat to international stability during the era of détente (see Map 13.2). Once critical because it straddled trade routes between Europe and Asia, the region was now vital because of what it produced: petroleum. Saudi Arabia, Kuwait, the string of Arab emirates along the western shore of the Persian Gulf, Iraq, Iran, and Libya were all major producers of oil and natural gas. Together, these nations, all Muslim although not all Arab,

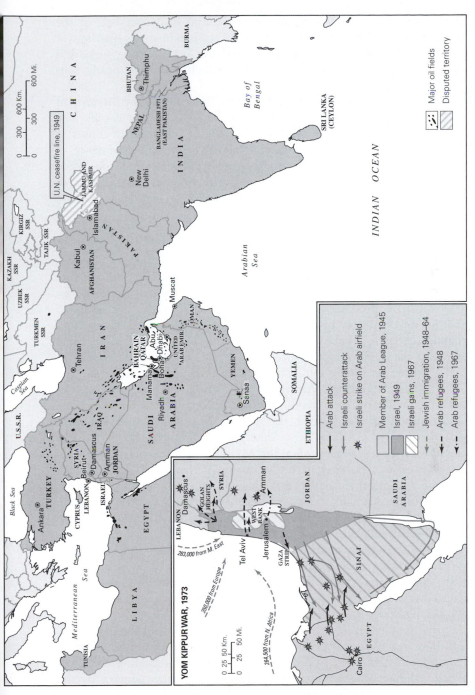

MAP 13.2 South Asia and the Middle East in the 1970s.
The swath of land from Libya to Bangladesh was the scene of frequent conflict in the 1970s, including the war between India and Pakistan in 1971 and the Yom Kippur War between Israel and its Arab neighbors in 1973. The region's oil resources ensured that local political and religious tensions would have international repercussions.

produced a third of the world's petroleum in 1970 and held over half of the world's known reserves. Their oil had powered the vast industrial expansion of Western Europe and Japan in the postwar era and was even coming to have a modest but significant role in the United States, which had been nearly self-sufficient in oil until the 1950s.

The strategic significance of oil made the Middle East vital to the interests of the industrial West, and this made it significant for the Soviet Union as well. The Soviets did not need Middle Eastern oil; Soviet territories held reserves almost as great as those of Saudi Arabia. But they understood that political dominance of that oil-rich region could be parlayed into economic influence over the West. Indeed, it was the one part of the nonaligned world that was truly crucial to Western interests.

Sources of Instability

To speak of the Middle East as a single region is to greatly simplify a complex reality. The Middle East was a palimpsest of old and new. Mullahs and socialists preached to the young. Monarchs ruled beside military strongmen and democratically elected politicians. Engineers built oil refineries beside Bedouin tents. In Iran, a shah who ruled courtesy of a CIA-sponsored revolution used oil revenues to try to rebuild the ancient Persian Empire of Cyrus the Great, while in Israel Jews from around the world sought to restore the biblical state of Solomon. In Jordan, a king trained at Britain's military academy, Sandhurst, accepted CIA funds while publicly denouncing America's ally, Israel. And throughout the region, there were deeply religious Muslims who looked to atheistic Moscow for help in destroying other "peoples of the book": Israeli Jews and Lebanese Christians.

The turmoil of the postwar years, when the Middle East threw off colonial rule and the state of Israel was founded, gave way in the 1970s to an era of yet more destructive conflict. Terrorists, better armed and more numerous than ever before, made bombings, plane hijackings, and cross-border mortar attacks routine features of Israeli life. Lebanon, an island of constitutional government and prosperity in the 1960s, disintegrated as extremist factions of Christians and Muslims went to war with one another, with support from Israeli, Syrian, and Palestinian allies intent on advancing their own interests. Assassinations of political leaders afflicted all the lands of the Middle East, and states throughout the region struggled to balance extravagant military spending with the needs of economic development and social welfare.

The unresolved problem of Palestinian refugees was one root of the instability. Hundreds of thousands of Arab Palestinians, displaced by the expansion of Israel, grew increasingly bitter as years passed and their hopes of regaining their lost lands dwindled. Ignored by Israel, they were treated as stateless refugees by the rest of the world, including fellow Arabs. Many lifted themselves out of poverty by education and hard work, their children becoming the engineers and accountants who managed the refineries and investments of oil-rich sheikdoms. But many others became eager disciples of extremists preaching violence. Their refugee camps became states within states; their political organizations, of which Yasser Arafat's Palestine Liberation Organization had become the largest, organized their own militias, often with Soviet bloc aid.

Whereas the leaders of Arab states publicly vowed unity with Palestinians, they privately saw Palestinian refugees as a burden and a danger to their own societies. Indeed, the common desire to repatriate these troublesome refugees fueled hostility to Israel. So long as Israel existed, its neighbors believed that they would have a Palestinian problem. Vocal support for the Palestinian cause was a moral necessity for Arab leaders, but it also reflected self-interest.

Uneven economic development was a second root of instability in the Middle East. Israel had the financial and human resources to compensate for its meager natural endowments. It enjoyed large-scale aid from Western states and Jewish philanthropies; its citizenry was far better educated than the peoples of neighboring states, giving it a greater capacity to harness science and engineering for both economic development and defense. Alone in the Middle East, Israel had the know-how to design and build advanced fighter aircraft and radar equipment— and, by some accounts, nuclear weapons.

The oil-rich states along the Persian Gulf could buy expertise and weapons abroad, and some were financing liberal social services for their populations. But despite their wealth, the oil sheikdoms had only begun to take steps toward diversified economic development by the early 1970s. Those states that lacked significant oil reserves, such as Egypt, faced many of the same problems that plagued many parts of Latin America and Africa: growing populations that were concentrated more and more in bloated cities, chronic underemployment, shortages of capital for investment, and corrupt government.

A third root of conflict was the religious and political fractiousness of the Muslim world. An ancient schism divided Muslims between the Sunni and Shia communities, with the latter tending to favor a broader role for religion in government than the former. Shiites, a minority in most Arab states, also tended to be poorer than their fellow Muslims. Poverty and suspicion of secular authority disposed Shiite youth toward religious radicalism and solidarity with the dispossessed Palestinians. It also made them a growing threat to moderate politicians across the region.

The colonial adventures of European powers had generated additional layers of suspicion and hatred. While some ruling families, notably those of Jordan and the Arabian Peninsula, owed their thrones to former colonial masters, elsewhere political revolutions in the 1950s and 1960s had shifted power to nationalists with military support and socialist leanings, such as Gamal Abdel Nasser in Egypt. Some of those revolutions had come at the expense of monarchs related by blood to the royal families of the more conservative Arab states. The military officers who took control of Iraq in 1958, for example, ousted members of the same Hashemite clan that governed Jordan.

Ethnic divisions further scrambled the politics of the Middle East. While both Turks and Iranians might feel solidarity with fellow Muslims, they had distinct histories, languages, and national interests. Ottoman Turks had ruled the Arab world long before the era of European control, and Turkey still controlled the headwaters of the rivers that supplied Iraq and Syria with water essential for irrigation. To the east, Iran's megalomaniacal shah, Mohammad Reza Pahlavi, spoke openly of restoring the regional dominance enjoyed by Persia in ancient times. His ambition and his arsenal of U.S.-supplied weapons alarmed Arab neighbors all around the Persian Gulf. Both Turkey and Iran relied on U.S. diplomatic and military support as a counterweight to their powerful neighbor to the north, the Soviet Union.

War's Consequences

The bitter dispute between Israel and its neighbors was but one element in a tapestry of Middle Eastern conflicts. The complexity of the fabric helps explain why a peaceful settlement between Israel and its neighbors was so difficult. Major changes of any kind had secondary effects that were hard to anticipate or control. Arab governments understood that any recognition of Israel might precipitate internal disorder and political isolation. Israeli governments feared that concessions on land or Palestinian rights would jeopardize the very existence of their state. The 1967 war had made a settlement even more difficult. Israel's easy victory and enlarged borders bred complacency with the status quo and cemented the already strong ties between the United States and Israel. The Arabs' embarrassing defeat reinforced old angers and made any negotiations appear to be a form of surrender.

Unwilling to negotiate from a position of weakness and unable to accept the status quo, Syria and Egypt, Israel's main adversaries, accepted huge Soviet loans and thousands of Soviet advisers in an effort to rebuild their war-shattered armies. New regimes had taken power in both states and were consolidating their power. Hafez al-Assad, who assumed the presidency of Syria in 1970, was the shrewd but unproven leader of a party committed to Arab nationalism and socialist modernization, the Ba'ath or Resurrection Party. Anwar Sadat, widely viewed as a placeholder, succeeded to Egypt's presidency when Nasser suffered a fatal heart attack in 1970.

While Assad strengthened Syria's links with the USSR, Sadat experimented with a new policy. In hopes of loosening the U.S. alliance with Israel or at least securing some U.S. aid, Sadat dramatically ejected tens of thousands of Soviet military and economic advisers from Egypt in 1972. But the move produced little change in U.S. policy and appears to have left Sadat with the lesson that Arab states would have to go to war to change the status quo.

After careful planning, Sadat and Assad launched an attack on Israel on October 6, 1973. It was Yom Kippur, a holy day of the Jewish calendar. The size, suddenness, and intensity of the assault immediately threw Israeli forces into retreat, both in the south, where Egyptian forces vaulted across the Suez Canal and into the Sinai desert, and in the north, where Syrian armor reclaimed much of the Golan Heights, which had been lost to Israel in the 1967 war. The stunning Arab advances soon ended, however, as Israel mobilized its reserves and counterattacked. Within a week, the Israeli army had regained the initiative. Within two weeks, it had retaken lost territory, surrounded the main Egyptian army west of the Suez Canal, and was poised to strike toward Cairo and Damascus, the capitals of both its adversaries. Both Syria and Egypt were forced to seek a truce.

The truce appeared to reaffirm the situation prior to the start of the war. Israeli armies were once again in control of the lands occupied in 1967, and the Arab states had suffered staggering losses. But the Yom Kippur War had a far different effect on morale than had the war of 1967. The early victories of Arab arms had exposed Israel's vulnerability and bolstered Arab confidence. Even in their subsequent defeats, Arab armies had retreated in good order rather than panic. Both sides now had new reason to bargain. Israel no longer felt itself invulnerable, and its adversaries no longer felt powerless.

The war also moved the Middle East to the top of the U.S. government's diplomatic agenda. No U.S. administration could ignore Israel, a state with a democratic government and a people that were closely linked to Americans by blood and history. Until 1967, however, the United States had generally followed a passive strategy in the Middle East, giving Israel firm support while hoping that the Arabs and Israelis would find their own way toward a settlement. The war stimulated a much more aggressive policy, not only because Israel itself was now disposed to talk, but also because Arab–Israeli relations impinged on American interests in new and more vital ways.

The United States and the USSR had both airlifted ammunition to their clients during the desperate fighting of October. During the final days of the war, tension between the superpowers had briefly threatened to get out of hand. After Israel had won the initiative on the battlefield, Brezhnev sent Nixon a note that raised the possibility of Soviet intervention to impose a cease-fire. Brezhnev was eager to halt the Israeli armies that were threatening Cairo and Baghdad. Nixon was determined to keep Soviet forces out of the Middle East and to demonstrate his toughness. Citing intelligence reports that Soviet airborne troops might be preparing for action, Nixon ordered a worldwide alert of American forces, including units armed for nuclear war. The scare evaporated when the Soviets disavowed unilateral intervention, but the episode illustrated the potential for Middle Eastern conflict to expand into superpower confrontation.

The Yom Kippur War also had economic and political consequences for the United States that mandated active diplomacy. The renewal of fighting inflamed anti-American sentiments throughout the Arab world, and in many non-Arab Muslim countries as well. Vitriolic rhetoric by Arab leaders escalated into attacks on U.S. embassies. Yet more ominous, Arab producers of oil, including the conservative sheikdoms of Arabia, imposed a boycott on the sale of oil to the United States and other nations supporting Israel. That support had long been an obstacle to warm relations between the United States and the Arab Middle East, despite their other shared economic and political interests. The war eclipsed all other issues and turned what had been a fissure into a deep chasm. The only way to restore American influence in the region (and to limit Soviet influence) would be to bring Israel and its neighbors to a settlement. This became the Holy Grail of U.S. diplomacy in the region for the next three decades.

And so, whereas the Six-Day War of 1967 had hardened divisions in the Middle East, the Yom Kippur War created opportunities for diplomatic movement. Sadat had won new respect for Arab arms; Israel was shaken by its losses; and the United States had new reasons to wield promises of economic and military aid to facilitate a peace. Building on a series of agreements that disengaged the combatants and a stunning trip by Sadat to Israeli-occupied Jerusalem, Egypt and Israel signed a peace treaty in Washington in 1979 that restored the Sinai Peninsula to Egypt in exchange for Egyptian recognition of Israel. The settlement relieved Israel of the threat of attack from its most populous neighbor while giving Egypt much-needed U.S. economic help. At the same time, the agreement served American interests not only by reducing the likelihood of another war but also by demonstrating to conservative Arab states that the United States could deliver what the Soviets could not: Israeli-occupied lands.

The war and its aftermath had other consequences. Despite the influence of U.S. arms and wealth, evident both in the Israeli victory during the war and in the American-brokered peace between Egypt and Israel, the region's problems ultimately demonstrated the limits of U.S. power. The U.S. diplomatic offensive failed to resolve many critical issues, including the status of Palestinian refugees, the ultimate disposition of Jerusalem, and the Israeli occupation of territories seized in the Six-Day War. Syria's Assad refused to follow Sadat's lead and remained hostile to both Israel and U.S. interests, and Israel, having neutralized one adversary, felt no urgent need to negotiate with another.

One reason for Assad's intransigence was popular anti-Israeli sentiment, both at home and throughout the Arab world. Neither a truce nor a treaty could extinguish passions that had been decades in the making. Palestinians and fundamentalists alike feared that secular Arab leaders were betraying their interests in return for U.S. dollars and Western approval, and some sought to derail the process through terrorist acts that intimidated Arab leaders and stoked Israeli anger and anxiety. Indeed, extremist groups grew stronger and more active while the negotiations went on. Their growth represented a dilemma for diplomats. Peacemaking seemed to demand an American midwife, but the larger the U.S. role, the greater the popular suspicion of the process and the greater the threat to the stability of those regimes engaged in negotiations. An assassination in October 1981 illustrated the risks. Egypt's Sadat fell victim to soldiers of his own army, members of one of the many fundamentalist Islamic groups that had come to see him as a traitor to his people and his faith.

Oil Embargo and Economic Change

The erosion of the bipolar political system coincided with the emergence of a new, more complex international economic order. The United States remained

Egypt's President Anwar Sadat, U.S. President Jimmy Carter, and Israeli Prime Minister Menachem Begin after signing the Camp David Accords, September 17, 1978. The Accords became the basis of a formal peace treaty between Egypt and Israel, signed the following year, and cemented the position of the United States as mediator and power broker in the Middle East.

the world's largest economy during the 1970s, but it no longer held unchallenged supremacy in industry, banking, and agriculture. The economies of Western Europe had grown at stunning rates since being jump-started by American reconstruction aid and the formation of a Common Market. By the early 1970s, Western Europe had attained parity with the United States in trade and production, although not as yet in personal income or technological innovation. Even more dramatic was the long-term boom in Japan, where growth rates during the 1950s and 1960s had often been double those of Western Europe and triple those of the United States. By 1969, Japan's GDP had surpassed that of West Germany, Britain, and France and was fast overtaking that of the much larger USSR.

Growth of the European and Japanese economies obscured a broader shift in economic power. The Pacific was gradually supplanting the North Atlantic as the crossroads of world trade. The trend had been under way for some time, but it became increasingly evident in the 1970s, not only through Japan's dramatic economic growth but also by the migration of jobs, wealth, and population from America's East and Midwest to the shores of the Pacific. The volume of trans-Pacific trade grew by leaps and bounds as Japanese ceramics, steel, TVs, and automobiles moved east to Seattle, San Diego, and Long Beach, and U.S. lumber and commercial aircraft moved west to Yokohama.

The growing trans-Pacific commerce had many repercussions, not least of all for Japan's neighbors. Deficient in most raw materials, Japan had to import in order to thrive, and that meant orders for Australian iron, zinc, and bauxite; Indonesian nickel and oil; and Malaysian tin and rubber. Trade boomed as Japan's suppliers in turn became consumers of its textiles, bicycles, and radios. Later, as wages in Japan grew, Japanese firms looked to low-wage neighbors such as South Korea and Taiwan as sites for assembly of labor-intensive items such as circuit boards and auto parts. Other forms of investment, in banks and real estate, followed trade. By 1970, Japan had become the hub of a large and expanding region of industrial development, thereby achieving a commercial version of the regional dominance that had been its aim in 1941.

Pacific trade also had consequences for U.S. politics. Increasingly sophisticated Japanese products, often made better and at lower cost than their U.S. counterparts, undercut many sectors of American manufacturing and created a backlash of resentment against Japan. At the same time, growing trade created interdependence and an economic interest in the enlargement of commerce. While U.S. automakers and autoworkers complained about unfair Japanese competition, dealers of Japanese cars in the United States enjoyed year after year of record sales and profits.

The debate between protectionists and free traders was as old as the U.S. republic, but it had fallen silent during the postwar decades when few Americans saw foreign competition as a threat to their jobs or their profits. But as international accounts in the United States fell into deficit in the 1970s, the debate revived. It would remain a central element in U.S. politics and a destabilizing factor in world politics for the rest of the century. While free traders maintained control of U.S. policy, any hint of ambivalence aroused intense concern among America's trade partners. American demand had fueled postwar growth in Japan and Europe; U.S. leadership had been vital in lowering international trade barriers and building institutions to manage the international flow of goods and payments. An uncertain commitment by the United States to the free movement of goods and money therefore seemed to jeopardize the entire structure of world trade that had evolved since 1945.

The Economics and Politics of Petroleum

The extended boom of the postwar years had depended on more than U.S. hunger for foreign products and the expansion of trade. Energy was an essential factor in the production and distribution of goods, and in the postwar decades energy prices were both low and stable. The United States remained essentially self-sufficient in petroleum until the late 1950s; Western Europe and Japan met their growing needs through the exploitation of the huge oil fields of the Middle

East, North Africa, and Indonesia. But through most of the 1950s and 1960s, demand was expanding faster than supply.

Sales of automobiles soared in North America, and more and more of the well-to-do were taking to wheels in Western Europe, Japan, and Latin America. Where the affluent didn't drive, they flew. As jet-powered aircraft replaced piston-driven models, the miles flown by passengers doubled and redoubled, as did the consumption of fuel. Oil was steadily supplanting coal as a source of heat and power because it was inexpensive, relatively clean-burning, and easy to transport. It was also finding new uses in the chemical industry, where it was a starting point for products ranging from plastics to synthetic fibers. By the early 1970s, this unrelenting growth in consumption had eliminated most of the world's excess capacity for oil production. There were still abundant reserves in the ground, but the world's wells, pumps, and pipelines were working near their maximum. In such a situation, even modest reductions in supply can have large effects on prices, and the Arab-led oil embargo of 1973 was much more than a small reduction. By 1972, Saudi Arabia was supplying 13 percent of the world's oil.

The cessation of sales of oil to the United States and other supporters of Israel in October 1973 created chaotic conditions in world markets. The price of crude oil quadrupled, rising from under $3 a barrel (42 gallons) at the beginning of the year to nearly $12 at the end as consumers bid against one another for the much-reduced supply. Panicky drivers in the United States waited in line for hours to fill their gas tanks, corporations broke commercial ties with Israel to curry favor with Arab oil producers, and some nations, including France, agreed to sell advanced weapons in exchange for long-term supplies.

Oil prices stabilized when the boycott ended early in 1974, but at levels far above those of the early 1970s. The United States, which as late as the 1950s could crank up production from its own wells to balance supply and demand, no longer had sufficient reserves to meet its own needs, never mind those of the rest of the industrial world. That power now resided in the member states of the Organization of Petroleum Exporting Countries (OPEC), an organization formed in 1960 to protect the interests of oil producers in a market that then favored buyers. Now, with the tables reversed, OPEC used its control of supplies to set prices at levels far above those that would have prevailed in a free marketplace.

Member states maintained, with some justice, that the price of oil had long been manipulated by Western oil companies and that higher prices would better reflect the true value of a nonrenewable resource. Consumers, by contrast, saw such reasoning as little more than a thin veil for greed. Justified or not, OPEC had derived a clear lesson from the 1973 oil boycott: If oil producers could agree to limit sales, consumers would pay extraordinary prices to ensure supplies.

The Oil Needy and the Oil Rich

After the embargo ended in 1974, oil started to flow again, but the effects of the boycott continued to ripple through the global economy. Inflation was one such effect. Petroleum prices affected the costs of almost all goods and services, and

GLOBAL
Technologies

Nuclear Power

The shortages of the 1970s prompted intense work on alternatives to OPEC's oil in countries around the globe. South Africa built massive plants to convert coal to oil using technologies pioneered in Germany during the world wars. In the Rocky Mountains, firms built pilot plants to squeeze petroleum from oil sands in Canada and from oil-containing shale in the U.S. Multinational oil firms rushed to bring new wells into production, especially on Alaska's North Slope and in Europe's North Sea, where rich reserves had been found in the late 1960s. Meanwhile, utilities converted oil-fired plants to other fossil fuels that were in more plentiful supply—coal, natural gas, and even wood.

Oil, natural gas, coal are all fuels derived from decaying organic matter. Their abundance reflects our planet's long history and remarkable fertility. Scientists differed (and still do) about how best to estimate reserves of fossil fuels, but all recognized that supplies were finite. Nuclear power was the most plausible alternative to such fuels in the early 1970s.

Research on the first atomic bombs had opened doors to the use of nuclear energy for the generation of power. In both a bomb and a nuclear power plant, energy is produced by a self-sustaining chain reaction in which decaying atomic nuclei release neutrons that go on to split other nuclei. The fissionable material is either a rare isotope of uranium with an atomic weight of 235 or plutonium, an element that itself is created as the byproduct of neutron bombardment of the more common uranium isotope with an atomic weight of 238. The cleavage of either type of atom is accompanied by the release of tremendous energy. In an atomic bomb the fissionable material is very nearly pure U-235 or plutonium, and energy is released almost instantaneously upon detonation. In a nuclear reactor, fuels have lower percentages of neutron-producing U-235 and plutonium, and neutron-absorbing moderators, such a graphite or deuterium (heavy water) are used to slow the chain reaction so that the fuel will release energy over a period of months or years. That energy, mostly released in the form of heat, is then used to produce steam for turbines much as in a conventional plant burning oil or coal.

both the taxi driver and the international conglomerate raised prices to recoup their higher costs. A second effect was unemployment. The long gasoline lines of late 1973 gave way to long unemployment lines in 1974 as Europe and North America suffered the worst economic downturn since the depression decade. The recession hit older manufacturing regions in Britain and the United States especially hard because they were already feeling the effects of competition

The U.S. built experimental nuclear reactors during World War II as part of its atomic bomb project; by the late 1950s, nuclear power stations were coming on line in the United States, Britain, the Soviet Union, and France. Some scientists believed that nuclear power would prove the most important application of nuclear physics. Nations with an advantage in the production of energy have long enjoyed economic leverage out of proportion to their size or other assets. In the nineteenth century, England's huge coal reserves gave it a significant advantage over states such as France that had fewer and less productive coal mines. Later, North America's abundant coal, oil, and natural gas powered American industry to global dominance. In the 1950s, it seemed that nuclear power would become the new prime mover, prompting speculation about "electricity would be too cheap to meter."

The enthusiasm waned in the 1960s, as experience showed that nuclear power plants had very significant costs. It was expensive to mine and enrich uranium, to build multiple tiers of safety equipment into plants, and to dispose of the radioactive byproducts of their operation. But the oil embargo of 1973 altered both the economics and the politics of the industry. Higher oil prices made electricity from nuclear plants more competitive; at the same time big oil consumers grew eager to reduce the vulnerability of their oil supplies. In the U.S., where the first large-scale civilian nuclear power plant had been commissioned in 1957, electric utilities ordered forty-one new nuclear power plants in 1973 alone. In that same year, France's government declared a goal of producing the nation's entire electrical needs from nuclear energy, an undertaking that required construction of scores of nuclear power plants by the end of the century. Germany, Britain, the Soviet Union, and Japan likewise invested heavily in a nuclear future.

That future did not arrive not in the form the nuclear optimists had projected. In 1979, operators lost control of a reactor at the Three Mile Island nuclear power plant in Pennsylvania, leading to the release of modest amounts of radioactive materials and panic among the millions living in its vicinity. Although the accident had no discernable effect on public health, it scarred the image of nuclear power. Far more serious incidents occurred in 1984 at Chernobyl in the Soviet Union and in 2011 at Fukushima in Japan. In both cases, runaway nuclear reactions led to extensive environmental contamination and injuries, leaving many to wonder if power too cheap to meter had become energy too risky to use.

from the more efficient plants of West Germany and Japan. Even after a recovery began, the combination of economic stagnation and inflation persisted. And just as the Western economies were beginning to regain their footing at the end of the decade, a revolution in Iran provoked a new round of oil price increases that again threw the major economies into recession. By 1981 the price of oil was touching $40 a barrel, more than ten times the level prevailing a decade earlier.

Owen Franken/Corbis

The Yom Kippur War precipitated a shut-off of oil from Arab states to the West and triggered both gasoline and oil shortages and the economic recession of the mid-1970s. This photo was taken beside a road in Connecticut in 1974.

The stagflation of the 1970s jeopardized the well-being of nearly all social groups. Those who were living on fixed incomes (pensions, for example) saw the purchasing value of their income erode. Where labor unions were comparatively weak, as in the United States, workers found it hard to bargain for better wages. Where organized labor was stronger, as in Western Europe, wages generally kept up with inflation, but often at the expense of employment and productivity. Britain's economy grew at an average rate of less than 0.5 percent a year between 1973 and 1981.

These economic pressures had effects on behavior. The young found it harder to establish independent households. The growing costs of child rearing led to smaller families. Declines in the real income of wage earners led to unprecedented increases in the number of young mothers in the labor force as more and more families found it impossible to get along on one salary. Government welfare programs mitigated the worst effects of this stagflation in the industrial West, but even so, poverty grew. The percentage of Americans living below the official poverty level, for example, expanded steadily from the early 1970s into the early 1980s, reversing many of the gains made during the 1960s.

Higher energy prices struck harder in poor regions of the world and where economic development was uneven. Nations without scarce commodities or internationally competitive industries had to cut budgets, shelve development projects, and slice spending on health care, education, and infrastructure. The one hundred million inhabitants of Bangladesh, for example, had to make do with a national income that averaged only a little over $100 per person; they could ill afford higher prices for kerosene, which was still used for lighting and power in rural areas, or for the petroleum products that were essential to urban life. Bangladesh, parts of west and equatorial Africa, and many small island republics in the Pacific and the Caribbean became increasingly dependent on the charity of foreign governments and nongovernmental organizations to bridge the growing gap between essential needs and resources.

Developing nations that had significant reserves of oil and minerals fared better, at least during the early stages of the global recession. Mexico and Brazil, for example, became favorite customers of lenders who were seeking faster growth than seemed possible in the struggling economies of Europe and North America. But heavy borrowing left these nations dependent on their earnings from commodities to meet loan payments; when prices began to fall in the 1980s—in part as a result of new oil production in such areas as the North Sea and Alaska—they found themselves saddled with impossibly high debt service. By 1983 developing nations around the world, including seventeen in Latin America alone, were in or near default on their international loans. This debt crisis paved the way for intervention by the World Bank, which imposed drastic terms on borrowers as the price for loan extensions. The resulting austerity measures, including sharp reductions in imports, cuts in social services, and currency devaluations, erased a decade of gains in living standards.

While most of the globe struggled to pay for energy, the major exporters of oil faced another sort of challenge: absorbing windfall profits. The dramatic increase in oil prices had shifted huge amounts of money from the accounts of oil-consuming nations to those of oil producers. Saudi Arabia's income from the sale of petroleum, for instance, grew from about $6 billion in 1972 to $102 billion in 1981. Awash in petrodollars, Saudi Arabia, Iran, and other major producers went on shopping sprees, building armies and infrastructure at home and investment portfolios abroad.

Iran, second only to Saudi Arabia as an oil exporter, illustrates the benefits and risks of the sudden windfall. Intent on making Iran the dominant power in his region, the shah purchased $10 billion of advanced weapons, roads, ports, and railroads; a modern telephone system; and ambitious new oil refineries. Palaces and schools, office buildings and apartment houses rose up in Iran's cities, and in the countryside the government purchased the estates of absentee landlords for redistribution to peasants. Billions more went for health care and education, and the new schools were opened to women, who were granted broad new political and economic rights as part of the larger project of modernization.

Yet the sudden and massive changes also created hardships, anxieties, and grievances. Traditional elites—the merchants of the marketplace, the Muslim clergy, and many landowners—saw their influence and authority being eclipsed by professionals and bureaucrats. Western styles of dress for women and women's new legal rights violated traditional ideas and customs. Boom-driven inflation consumed workers' wage increases, and the excesses of the shah's court disgusted many of the civil servants upon whom the regime depended.

Ultimately, the pressures generated by the shah's top-down program of economic and social change overwhelmed the state's rickety political institutions.

Too much the autocrat to compromise and too much the reformer to make all-out war on his people, the shah fled when a coalition of conservative clerics and merchants, led by the Islamic leader Ayatollah Ruholla Khomeini, challenged him with a series of ever-more massive street demonstrations in 1978 and early 1979.

Iran's cycle of economic boom and political bust was exceptionally dramatic, but it illustrates tendencies visible among other oil exporters. Petrodollars often proved destabilizing. They overturned existing economic relationships, threatened traditional elites, and quickened the pace of social change. They could also lead to corruption and exacerbate political tensions between as well as within states. The clans that governed Saudi Arabia and the oil-rich states along the west coast of the Persian Gulf, including Kuwait and Bahrain, were intensely conscious of the vulnerability of their thinly populated nations both to predatory neighbors and to social upheaval. Their policies reflected these concerns. At home, they combined liberal profit sharing with the preservation of Islamic laws and practices; abroad, they showed solidarity with other Arab states in opposing Israel and supporting Palestinian statehood, while privately seeking assurances of American military support against potentially dangerous neighbors, including Syria, Iraq, and Iran. Contradictory as these policies sometimes seemed, they worked well enough to sustain order.

Japan, Inc.

Only one industrial nation rode out the oil shocks and stagflation of the 1970s: Japan. The Japanese economy shuddered briefly in 1974, but then resumed its extraordinary growth, suffering none of the unemployment and little of the infla-tion that dogged other nations during that decade. While steel mills in Pittsburgh and Manchester shut down, those of Tokyo and Osaka prospered. As Detroit's automakers stumbled, Japan's advanced from one record year to another. By 1981 the value of Japanese investments in the United States exceeded the value of American investments in Japan, a stunning reversal of conditions that had prevailed only a decade earlier.

Several factors account for the remarkable buoyancy of the Japanese economy in the 1970s. Energy had long been more expensive in Japan, which lacked sig-nificant domestic sources of oil and natural gas, than it was in the resource-rich United States. Consequently, Japanese firms had invested more heavily in energy conservation than their U.S. counterparts. In addition, they made products, such as automobiles, that were much stingier energy users than those made by their U.S. rivals because that was what the Japanese domestic market demanded. The sudden worldwide shortage of oil put a worldwide premium on these products.

Japanese business also showed a more realistic attitude toward shortages than their American counterparts. Power plants shifted quickly from oil to coal and natural gas. Firms concentrated on designing more efficient engines and electric motors, lighter vehicles, and methods for conserving power in housing, mass transportation, and household appliances. Japanese oil imports actually declined by 25 percent between 1973 and 1987 as the Japanese economy doubled in size. By contrast, the slower growing U.S. economy consumed more foreign oil in 1987 than it had when the first oil shock struck in 1973.

Frugality and agility were important factors in the Japanese response to the oil shock of 1973, but so, too, were other strengths that had helped propel postwar Japan from the brink of economic collapse to a position as the world's second largest economy. The government worked closely with corporations, providing them with guidance about what to expect in the future and incentives to help them better adapt to changing conditions. Such incentives (tax concessions for investment in fuel-saving equipment, for example) also appeared in the United States, but only after bruising public battles. Cooperation between industry and government aroused deep public suspicions in the United States, whereas in Japan it was routine—as it had been going back to the late nineteenth century when government worked with business to begin the process of industrialization. This close cooperation sometimes degenerated into corruption, but when the interests of big business and the state largely coincided, as they did during Japan's postwar reconstruction and its response to the oil crisis, it could produce growth that seemed almost friction-free.

A second key to Japan's economic success was its skill at making incremental innovations in technology. Japanese automakers, for instance, fine-tuned the fuel efficiency (and cleanliness) of engines by making modest improvements in cylinder design to improve fuel combustion. Here, the Japanese were drawing on an old tradition. Japan had commenced industrial development in the late nineteenth century by systematically studying such foreign products as locomotives, seeking to adopt the best designs and adapt them to local needs. When Japan reentered world markets after World War II, it once again found itself playing catch-up with Western technology.

Lacking the resources to undertake pioneering research, Japanese firms instead licensed foreign patents, subcontracted with overseas producers, and reverse-engineered imported products. Beginning in the 1950s, Japanese industries did this in sector after sector. European steel mills became the model for even more efficient Japanese mills. The British sports car became the model for a much more refined Japanese two-seater. German cameras became the points of departure for smaller and less expensive Japanese models. And experience in the production of optical equipment prepared the way for entry into a fast-growing copier market that was at first dominated by U.S. firms. Consumer electronics became a special strength. Japanese firms were among the first to purchase licenses to manufacture transistors from U.S. giant AT&T, and they promptly used them to miniaturize radios. Building on this base, they went on to dominate world sales of television sets and audio equipment by the early 1970s. United States firms had assumed the high costs of developing new products, such as color television receivers and videocassette recorders, but Japanese firms had quickly improved on the early models by paying meticulous attention to design, reliability, and production costs.

Competitors often dismissed their Japanese rivals as imitative, but in so doing they underestimated the significance of incremental engineering improvement for market success. They also underestimated the importance of Japanese innovations on the factory floor. Japanese businesses not only emulated and improved foreign products but also improved on foreign techniques for managing workers and the flow of materials. As in other respects, the postwar scarcity fostered frugality and painstaking attention to detail. Japanese manufacturers in the 1950s had a much smaller domestic market than did American firms. They could not expect buyers to snap up hundreds of thousands of identical units, and so they had to incorporate techniques for achieving flexibility into their production lines. This agility meant gains in productivity. Production of smaller quantities of a wide variety of products also created incentives to work with smaller inventories of parts. By the 1970s Japanese automakers had developed "just-in-time" methods for bringing components to the site of final assembly—methods that eliminated the need for large warehouses, placed a premium on minimizing defective parts, and further reduced the lead time for product changes.

Flexible and efficient production depended not only on machines and their arrangement, but also on human labor. Here, too, Japanese methods were different from those prevailing elsewhere. Many workers in Japan's large conglomerates, or keiretsu, felt that they had lifetime commitments from their employers and gave them lifetime loyalty. Corporations invested heavily in training workers to be versatile and multiskilled—an investment that many U.S. firms were reluctant to make in their more mobile workforce. Workers on the floors of Japan's factories had greater responsibility for the operation of the production line and greater influence over its arrangement than their U.S. counterparts. The benefits here were many: more stability in labor-management relations, faster feedback from the factory floor to the engineering laboratories, greater flexibility in work assignments, and greater worker involvement in quality control.

Japanese workers were also exceptionally diligent savers, putting away on average double and triple the percentage of their income that Americans saved during the 1960s and 1970s. These funds were typically deposited in low-yielding savings accounts, which could supply abundant capital to expanding business firms at low interest rates. So, when Nippon Steel borrowed money to build a new mill, it could often obtain the funds at a much lower rate than its competitors in the United States, where the savings rate was much lower and interest rates on borrowing tended to be correspondingly higher.

The high savings rate in Japan reflected the insecurities of individual workers and investors, who carried vivid memories of the poverty of the war and the immediate postwar years. They also reflected government policy, which was to restrict investment alternatives to encourage savings as a way to mobilize resources for industrial expansion. Here as elsewhere, government often worked hand in glove with big business to shape a society in which industrial efficiency was the highest value.

The formidable power of the Japanese economic engine became obvious in the 1970s through the growing market share of Japanese producers of steel, autos, ships, electronics, and other industrial products, and the growing financial clout of Japanese banks and insurers, not only in Asia but in the Americas and Europe as well. Foreign observers were both impressed with and intimidated by the successes of Japan, Inc., a society that seemed to have overcome both the economic challenges of the turbulent 1970s and many of the social tensions that bedeviled Western industrial democracies.

The social costs of Japan's economic boom were less visible, at least to outsiders. Cozy relations between businesspeople and government officials sometimes led to lax regulation of environmental hazards. Protectionist barriers to imported goods, sustained long after Japanese firms could compete internationally, kept the prices of many basic agricultural and consumer products artificially high. Tax laws and banking regulations discouraged investment in housing, and so most Japanese families occupied apartments and homes that were a fraction the size of those common in the United States and Europe, despite their rapidly growing incomes.

Labor no less than consumers paid a price for rapid growth. While unions in the United States and Western Europe often represented workers in many firms, Japanese unions typically represented the workers in a single company. Officials in these company unions cooperated closely with employers, sometimes in ways that undercut workers' interests. Most Japanese workers had no union at all. Behind the huge assembly plants of Japan's keiretsu stood thousands of much smaller workshops, often family-owned, that made parts under contract to larger firms. Here workers often put in irregular hours at piece rates dictated by their powerful customers, shared little in profits, and enjoyed no assurances of long-term employment. By subcontracting to this army of small producers, giants like Toyota and Mitsubishi could expand or reduce their production without incurring large capital and employee costs. In busy times, captive suppliers had to drive their workers and machines harder and expand at their own risk; in slower times, they had to reduce the workforce and tighten their belts. The plenty and the hardship were often shared by members of a household because many of these small businesses were family-owned and family-run.

Even as Japan's wealth grew, some Japanese found themselves wondering whether the social discipline that had yielded the marketplace triumphs of Sony and Toyota might fetter the creativity that yielded breakthroughs in technology and science or the vital renewal of political and social thought. Nevertheless, it was hard to gainsay the economic progress that had been made since 1945, and the Japanese model of industrial capitalism exerted growing influence as other industrial nations saw their economies falter during the turbulent 1970s. Whereas Japanese businessmen, engineers, and economists had once looked to the United States and Europe for guidance, more and more Americans and Europeans now looked to Japan for solutions to the problems of their own economies. And the Japanese model proved even more influential among the capitalist societies of East Asia (Taiwan, South Korea, Hong Kong, Thailand, Malaysia, and Singapore), which hungered to achieve some of the economic growth that Japan had known since the 1950s.

The Hollowing Out of the Soviet Empire

Readers of Western newspapers in the 1970s saw ample evidence of the relative decline of the United States. Photos of the chaotic evacuation of American citizens from Vietnam before advancing Communist armies and of U.S. diplomats held hostage in Tehran were vivid reminders of the limits of American military and diplomatic power. The dependence of the U.S. economy on oil imports was plain to see from the gas lines of 1973 and 1979. Shuttered steel mills and auto assembly plants testified to the decay of the old industrial region stretching from New England through the Midwest, which was coming to be known as the rust belt, while the swelling numbers of Japanese cars and TVs in U.S. households were daily reminders of the dynamism of the Japanese economy. The dissolution of the Nixon government amid scandal in 1974 shook confidence in American institutions at home and abroad, and neither the short-lived Ford administration nor the vacillating Carter administration could restore that confidence. The architect of American foreign policy in the first half of the decade, Henry Kissinger, spoke openly of the nation's need to adapt to a world in which it would be one among several competing centers of political, economic, and military power. President Carter, at the end of the decade, advised voters that they would have to tighten their belts, turn down their thermostats, curb their cars, and become accustomed to lower expectations in an age of limits.

The challenges facing the USSR were less evident, but more serious. Acutely sensitive about the shortcomings of the Communist system, Moscow's leadership made secrecy a fetish. Bureaucrats doctored published budgets and economic data to mislead foreign observers and its own citizens; even maps were systematically edited to conceal entire cities devoted to production of military goods. This secrecy sometimes served the state well. When the Soviets negotiated their first grain contracts with the United States in 1972, few Westerners realized how desperately the Soviets needed food and silage, and so Soviet buyers were able to lock in bargain prices. Much to the embarrassment of the Nixon administration, Americans ended up paying higher prices for U.S. cereals than their Russian customers. The commissars had outfoxed the Yankee traders.

Shortcomings of the Command Economy

Such occasional successes obscured more serious failures, as the grain shortages themselves suggest. Fifty years of Soviet agricultural policies had turned a food-exporting nation into the world's largest importer. The reasons were many. Stalin's use of force to drive peasants onto mammoth state-owned farms had generated enduring mistrust between Soviet farmers and their government and destroyed incentives for hard work. Grandiose land reclamation efforts under Krushchev had poured resources into districts where climate and soil made harvests risky at best. Both Stalin and Krushchev had placed agricultural research under the influence of a poorly educated agronomist, T. D. Lysenko, who purged Soviet research institutes of a generation of geneticists and wasted resources on hopeless experiments based more on folklore than on science.

By the 1970s, Soviet leaders were repairing some of these problems—by giving peasants rights to small plots to encourage greater productivity, for example, and by relieving Lysenko's disciples of authority over research. But the tinkering did not address the greatest problem of all: crippling mismatches between the systems for producing and for distributing food. A fifth of the Soviet harvest never even reached market. Grain rotted because collective farms lacked access to paved roads or railheads. Fruits and vegetables spoiled in transit because factories built too few trucks and boxcars with refrigeration equipment. Tractors and combines rusted for shortages of spare parts and mechanics.

Agriculture was not just a matter of forming big farms and mass producing tractors. It was a system of many components that had to mesh smoothly and respond together to altering conditions. The Soviets' highly centralized command economy was too slow and clumsy to integrate the many parts successfully. As it responded to one crisis, another would already be rendering its solutions obsolete. And so the system lurched from one shortage to another, never quite able to find the right combination to ensure sustained growth.

Such mismatches were endemic in the Soviet economy. The goods that factories produced were dictated by quotas rather than the immediate calls of the market. Raw materials were delivered according to inflexible schedules—sometimes to destinations where they could not be used for lack of labor or equipment. Machines were sent to unfinished factories, to rust on rail sidings or loading docks. Universities turned out engineers on the basis of long-term projections that failed to take into account changing technological conditions. Innovative ideas and designs often went unexploited for lack of contact between research institutes and production facilities. The more complex and diversified the economy became, the greater the difficulties that central managers faced. The result was a society of recurring shortages and excesses.

Amplifying this fundamental problem was a second: The Soviet command economy had the tools to recognize quantity, but not quality. The system rewarded managers and workers who met the quotas, whether or not their products proved to be durable. Slapdash work might affect sales very little because consumers had few choices in the state-controlled marketplace. Only where the bureaucracy could focus intensively, as in the critical defense industry, did managers and workers suffer consequences for poor craftsmanship. This helps explain why the Soviet economy, despite its great size, failed to find export markets for much besides its raw materials and military equipment. As barriers to trade with the West began to fall in the 1970s, the Soviets paid for their grain imports not by selling tractors, telephones, or televisions but by exporting tanks, gold, and oil.

By the 1970s, these problems were familiar to every taxi driver in Moscow. But Brezhnev and his allies in the Soviet leadership showed little interest in reform. To question the wisdom of collective farms or state ownership of industry was to question the Marxist foundations of the party's authority. The Soviet leadership of the 1970s had grown to maturity during the era when farming and industry had been socialized at great human cost. The system had achieved undeniable successes—creating heavy industry, defeating Nazi Germany, and attaining parity with the United States in nuclear weapons and space exploration. These achievements inspired confidence in the wisdom of central planning and created bureaucracies that had a vested interest in maintaining the status quo. Whether or not the system was efficient, it gave the Communist Party unchallenged authority over wages and prices, the allocation of resources, and the conditions of labor, housing, schooling, and the mass media. Those who enjoyed such power were reluctant to contemplate change.

Market Reforms in China and Eastern Europe

The other great communist power, China, suffered many of the same illnesses as its Soviet neighbor, as was plain to see in the gap between its economic performance and that of its traditional rival, Japan. Not only was Japan out-producing China, but its people enjoyed higher wages, longer lives, better food, and greater opportunities for education and travel. Japanese consumers could choose among products with a quality and variety unknown to their Chinese counterparts. Even the Red Army, upon which Mao lavished nearly 15 percent of his nation's GDP, had to make do with copies of obsolete Soviet aircraft and tanks while Japan's tiny self-defense force could afford the latest American jets. The Soviet Union could muddle through years of economic malaise. China, with unsettled institutions and a population four times that of the USSR, could not long live with failed experiments.

Mao, who had built a Soviet-style command economy, showed no more interest in market reform than his Soviet counterparts. Increasingly dogmatic with age, Mao tried to make a virtue of necessity by praising manual labor and decrying the dangers of excessive wealth. But during Mao's senescence and immediately following his death in 1976, an open struggle occurred between ideological purists (including Mao's third wife, Jiang Qing) who remained committed to a highly centralized economic system and pragmatists who urged the decentralization of agriculture and light industry. The pragmatists, led by Deng Xiaoping, won this struggle, in part by playing on the widespread fear that the radicals wished to renew the violence and confusion of the Cultural Revolution and in part by appealing to the ruling bureaucracy's self-interest. The Communist Party had to deliver food and goods to the people if it was to maintain legitimacy; it had to find ways to meet the challenge of technological change to avoid being hopelessly outclassed by foreign adversaries.

Deng was an unlikely reformer. A septuagenarian and a veteran of Mao's Long March, he was as dedicated to the supremacy of the Communist Party as his radical opponents, dubbed the Gang of Four. But he had little use for ideologues, having himself been humiliated by radicals during the Cultural Revolution. Above all, he was committed to enlarging the influence of China, and this depended on maintaining political order and robust economic growth. He saw no better way to achieve such growth than by establishing stronger incentives for productivity, and no better way to reward productivity than through the market.

Provincial leaders had already begun to free up parts of the market on a piecemeal basis. Peasants in some districts were being offered long-term leases on state-owned land; in others, laws regulating commercial activity were being relaxed to allow small businesses to buy raw materials, hire workers, and sell their products for profit. Deng offered the movement official protection and encouragement. The Communist Party maintained a monopoly on political power and control over heavy industries, but it opened the country to foreign investors and small-scale private entrepreneurship. The new hybrid system had many problems, not least of them a resurgence of graft and corruption. But it also produced amazing economic growth. Exports grew by leaps and bounds, especially to new markets for textiles, tools, and inexpensive consumer products in North America and Europe; farm production soared. By 1986 market reforms had moved so far that the government authorized formation of a stock exchange in Shanghai to permit greater concentration of capital and the partial privatization of some state-owned industries. Wall Street, long the target of Communist scorn, had come to China.

And not just to China. Indeed, some of the socialist states of Eastern Europe had instituted market reforms a decade before China. Yugoslavia, which had jealously guarded its independence from Moscow since the end of World War II, was in many ways the leader. Dominated by the popular former partisan Marshal Tito, Yugoslavia had nationalized major industries and broken up big estates, but it had never embraced collectivized agriculture or shared Stalin's obsessive fear of private initiative. In 1965, Tito's regime liberalized its already permissive laws on the ownership of property to encourage small-scale private enterprise and profit sharing among employees of state-owned enterprises. By the early 1970s Yugoslavia had a bustling trade with the West and living standards that made it the envy of its Communist neighbors. Similar reforms occurred in Hungary in the late 1960s, although there, as elsewhere in Eastern Europe, change was tentative.

There was no lack of interest in reform. The top-down command economies that the Soviets had imposed on their satellites after World War II simply did not generate the productivity gains and growth of capitalist societies. The system could meet basic needs, but improvements in living standards came at a glacial pace. The shortcomings of Soviet-style communism became increasingly obvious in the 1960s and 1970s, not just to foreign observers but to the peoples of Eastern Europe, who encountered evidence of Western wealth in television transmissions, print advertising, and the firsthand accounts of friends and relatives living in the West. The disparity between standards of living in the East and the West was especially damaging to a political system that had made material well-being central to its legitimacy. The Communists had promised workers heaven and delivered a kind of limbo.

Market reforms threatened the authority of ruling Communist parties, the livelihoods of bureaucrats, and the interests of the Soviet Union, which viewed central economic planning as a powerful tool for maintaining political control of Eastern Europe. Decentralization of economic power could lead to the emergence of new institutions—businesses and trade unions, for example—that could challenge the Communist Party's monopoly on political association. It could also redirect trade and travel from the East to the West, creating new partnerships and dependencies that would displace the Soviet Union from the hub of Eastern European commerce.

As a result, market reforms spread slowly across Eastern Europe and were carefully calibrated to local political conditions. Hungary, which was governed by a regime that the Soviets deemed reliable (having imposed it by force in 1956), enjoyed more latitude in economic affairs than Czechoslovakia, which had only recently been the scene of aborted political reform. East Germany, whose leaders were second to none in Marxist dogmatism, did not countenance capitalist activity but nevertheless borrowed freely from Western banks and decentralized decision making from central economic planners to the managers of state-owned enterprises. Romania's autocratic dictator, Nicolae Ceausescu, found central control of the economy too appealing to sacrifice even while pursuing diplomatic openings to the West.

Poland, which had a strong Roman Catholic Church, a tradition of anti-Russian nationalism, and a history of close relations with the West, posed an exceptionally complex problem both for its domestic Communist leadership and for Moscow. Its Communist leaders saw economic progress as essential to domestic tranquility and borrowed heavily from the West in the 1970s to maintain standards of living and to modernize antiquated industries. But Poland's Communist political leaders were too insecure to follow Hungary's lead in tinting socialism with capitalism. Their reluctance to experiment with market reforms was shared in any case by Moscow, which kept a close watch on Poland both because of its size and its strategic position between the Soviet Union and East Germany. Consequently, Poland had the worst of both worlds in the 1970s, racking up huge debts to the West while laboring under an oppressive economic bureaucracy.

The Soviet Invasion of Afghanistan

While Soviet leaders worried about unrest in Eastern Europe, global competition with the United States, and their broken relationship with China, a new crisis emerged in an unexpected quarter. Afghanistan had been a backwater in the politics of the Cold War. Isolated and deficient in natural resources, industry, and wealth, the country had long been ruled by Muslim clansmen who were essentially indifferent to international politics but sufficiently canny to accept aid from both East and West. Conditions shifted suddenly in 1978, however, when the People's Democratic Party of Afghanistan, a Marxist group with a secular reform agenda, seized power.

The new government's program of land reform threatened long-established rural elites, and its promotion of secular education and greater rights for women offended Muslim clergy. Within months, revolts broke out among tribal leaders, and the regime itself disintegrated amidst vicious intraparty fighting. Soviet leaders watched these developments with a mixture of hope and anxiety. Afghanistan could evolve into a Marxist state with friendly relations to Moscow—a buttress against growing Islamic fundamentalism in the tier of nations along the USSR's southern border—or it could swing to the right and become an outpost of American or Islamic influence adjacent to Soviet districts with sensitive military installations and large Muslim populations. Seeing Afghanistan as within their sphere of influence, Soviet leaders opted to risk military intervention. In the final days of December 1979, a Soviet army entered Afghanistan, put its favored faction in control of the government, and took charge of the campaign against rebels in the countryside.

The war in Afghanistan invited comparison with the war in Vietnam. In both cases, a superpower committed its forces to assist a friendly regime against guerilla insurrections that enjoyed strong rural support. And in both cases the superpower underestimated the strength of its adversaries and overestimated the power of its allies. Like the Americans in Vietnam, the Soviets could not translate superior weaponry into durable advantage. The more men and equipment they poured into the conflict, the weaker their allies became, as the very presence of foreign troops turned a civil war into a war of national liberation. The Soviets, like the Americans, found themselves destroying the villages they sought to pacify, demoralizing the allies they sought to assist, and alienating the people whose hearts and minds they sought to win. Both superpowers ultimately paid high prices for their miscalculations. Intervention alarmed neighboring states, discomfited allies, and invited regional and global adversaries to assist guerrilla forces with covert aid. The prices paid by the peoples of Vietnam and Afghanistan were much higher. Within two years, a fifth of Afghanistan's population had fled, most to neighboring Pakistan.

Soviet troops fought in Afghanistan for ten years and experienced many of the frustrations that U.S. forces had felt in Vietnam: ambushes along remote roads, surprise mortar and rocket attacks on bases, assassinations of off duty soldiers, and inconclusive skirmishes with an enemy that seemed to grow in strength despite frequent defeats in the field. But the war had broader repercussions. It mobilized opinion in the Islamic world and gave rise to networks of support for the Afghan rebels, some sponsored by governments and others by wealthy individuals. The war gave thousands of volunteers from the Islamic world experience in the organization and conduct of guerrilla operations. Some would later apply these lessons against Israel, in Muslim Bosnia's war with Serbia, and, ironically, in terrorist operations against the United States, which was a major supporter of the Afghan rebels.

The war also ate away at the self-confidence, the self-respect, and, ultimately, the political integrity of the Soviet Union. Mounting casualties shocked the Soviet people, as did the discovery that some Soviet troops were returning home with an addiction to Afghanistan's cheap heroin. Many found it hard to understand why a progressive Afghan government should require so much Soviet help to survive. The disparity between official claims of imminent victory and the realities of grinding combat further eroded the Soviet government's threadbare credibility with its citizens. Its brutal disregard of the claims of religion and national identity renewed old memories of Bolshevik repression under Stalin. It was easier for some Catholic Latvians or Islamic Tajikistanis to sympathize with the Afghan resistance than with their own government's policies.

These consequences of the war became apparent only gradually. Diplomatic repercussions were more immediate. Relations between Moscow and Washington had been unsettled even before Soviet troops entered Afghanistan. The long string of conflicts of the 1970s had all but driven the word détente from the superpowers' official vocabulary. Yet some of the forms of détente persisted into the late 1970s even after the spirit was gone. Cultural exchanges, trade, cooperation in space, and talks on strategic arms limitation continued. Indeed, despite bitter disputes over regional issues, Carter and Brezhnev met in Vienna in June 1979 and signed a second SALT treaty that modestly reduced nuclear arsenals.

The Soviet invasion of Afghanistan put an end to any pretense of goodwill between the superpowers. Fearing that the Soviet invasion was the first move in a grand strategy for securing a land route to the Indian Ocean and the Middle East, the Carter administration struck back. It canceled grain sales to the Soviet Union and suspended nonessential contacts, including U.S. participation in the 1980 Olympic games being hosted by Moscow. It also increased military spending, funneled new military aid to Pakistan, and provided money, arms, and advice to the strugglers, or mujahideen guerillas who were fighting Soviet forces in Afghanistan. The Soviets responded in kind, reviving vituperative rhetoric about anti-Soviet conspiracies, limiting emigration of its citizens to Israel and the West, and clamping down on domestic dissidents. A decade of efforts to improve the tone of Soviet–American relations had come full circle.

The Turn to the Right

The failure of détente, which was clear for all to see in the U.S.–Soviet impasse over Afghanistan, had repercussions for domestic policy in both East and West. The conundrum of Afghanistan tied the Brezhnev government in knots. Brezhnev had invested his personal prestige in détente; his policy was now in tatters. The Soviet system did not allow for quick popular expression of disappointment. But the war in Afghanistan would eventually contribute to the dissolution of the Communist Party's monopoly on power.

In the West, the Soviet invasion of Afghanistan stimulated a turn toward the right—a movement toward larger defense expenditures, more aggressive condemnations of the Soviet system, and a more outspoken commitment to the principles of free enterprise. Jimmy Carter's policies in the late 1970s reflected this movement. But its most forceful American spokesman was Ronald Reagan, an actor turned Republican politician. Condemned as an extremist in a failed effort to wrest the Republican nomination from Gerald Ford in 1976, Reagan found a more receptive audience when he returned to national politics in 1980 and won the White House from Jimmy Carter.

Stiff anti-Communist rhetoric was only part of Reagan's appeal. The United States had never shaken off the effects of the 1974 recession and was facing the worst inflation since the end of World War II. Americans were demoralized by the political scandals of the Nixon era and the ongoing captivity of U.S. diplomats in Tehran, seized by radicals after the overthrow of the Shah in 1979. Many also found it hard to understand why such grand undertakings of the 1960s as the war on poverty had yielded little fruit. Reagan knit these disappointments and anxieties into a broad and powerful argument for political change. Government needed to become smaller and less ambitious. Taxes should be lowered and made less progressive to encourage private entrepreneurship and economic growth. More resources should be focused on defense so that the United States could stand tall against a Soviet empire that exemplified the evils of big government.

Reagan's victory in 1980 was only part of a broader movement to the right that was under way in the Western world. Between 1979 and 1984, conservatives took control from left-of-center social democrats in Britain, West Germany, and Canada. France seemed to buck the trend, electing a socialist president in 1981, François Mitterrand. But after entering office, Mitterrand himself gradually shifted rightward until he came to embrace many of the positions of his conservative opposition. The breadth of this conservative trend owed less to the renewal of tensions between the United States and the USSR than to social and economic pressures that were at work across the industrialized societies of the West.

Britain, which was in the vanguard of this movement, illustrates both the nature of these pressures and the political response. Governed by the Labour Party through all but four of the years since 1964, Britain had suffered a steady erosion in the competitiveness of its industries, the purchasing value of its currency, and its share of international production, consumption, and trade. Powerful trade unions often resisted new technologies and methods of production out of fear of job losses or loss of control over the workplace. Steeply progressive taxes discouraged savings and investment. Orders for steel, ships, and textiles went to lower cost producers elsewhere in Europe or in Asia, and few new industries appeared to take their place. Trade imbalances undermined the value of the pound, making foreign goods more expensive for British consumers and stimulating inflation. Unemployment trended upward, putting ever greater pressure on government welfare agencies. Spending on social welfare programs seemed to expand inexorably, from 16 percent of GDP in 1965 to 24 percent in 1981.

Efforts by the Labour government to reverse these trends often seemed to do more harm than good. Uncompetitive industries that were nationalized to avert their closure became drains on the public purse. Efforts to focus government investment in new industries, such as the production of computers, miscarried as the new firms often proved less agile than their competitors abroad or unable to command sufficiently large markets to sustain expansion. Economist Joseph Schumpeter had described capitalism as a system of creative destruction, but Britain's mixed economy seemed to have the destruction without the creativity. Stunning increases in the cost of petroleum during the 1970s pushed the already fragile economy close to the breaking point, precipitating strikes and bankruptcies, and budget and balance of payment crises.

Government, labor unions, and business management all had a role in making Britain's economy dysfunctional in the 1970s, and some of Britain's problems were simply beyond control. But many British voters, rightly or wrongly, placed the blame on the Labour Party. In general elections held in 1979, the Conservative Party won a healthy majority.

Wally McNamee

Ronald Reagan and Margaret Thatcher, seen here at the White House, led a turn to the right as the 1970s ended. In the United Kingdom, "Thatcherism" came to mean the curtailment of public services and reassertion of British power overseas. In the United States, "Reaganism" was associated with lower taxes, monetarist economic policies, and a renewed aggressiveness against the Soviet Union.

Whereas Reagan clothed a firm message in genial storytelling, the leader of the British Conservatives had a manner that matched her message. Margaret Thatcher, "the Iron Lady," sternly demanded reductions in social services, the privatization of government-owned industries, and tax incentives for private investment. Labour governments, she charged, had eroded Britain's competitiveness through harmful meddling in the marketplace. Like Reagan, Thatcher celebrated the creative potential of free enterprise and turned a skeptical eye on central economic planning. And much like Reagan, only more forcefully, Thatcher insisted that the Western powers should defend their national interests aggressively when those interests were threatened.

She showed exactly what she meant in 1982 when the military junta ruling Argentina occupied a barren and thinly settled chain of islands six hundred miles off Argentina's Atlantic coast. Called the Falklands by the British and the Malvinas by the Argentines, the islands had been in British hands since the early nineteenth century. Despite skepticism about Britain's capacity to conduct a war over great distances, Thatcher responded with a lightning campaign that retook the islands in a matter of months. The stunning reversal precipitated the collapse of military rule in Argentina. It also propelled Thatcher's Conservative Party to another mandate at home—a clear-cut victory in the general elections of 1983.

Britain's economic woes were worse than those of other industrial nations in the West, but they were hardly unique. Milder versions of many of the same problems afflicted the United States, France, and Canada. Even West Germany's spectacular postwar expansion stuttered during the 1970s as energy costs rose, productivity growth slowed, and unemployment and inflation rose to levels not seen since the 1940s. And while the turn toward the right was nowhere quite so dramatic as in Britain, the disappointments of the 1970s provoked debate everywhere over the optimum size and role of government. Confidence in the managerial role of government in the economy, undermined by years of stagflation, yielded to a new skepticism about the capacity of politicians to make wise choices regarding investment.

The shift reflected the changing opinion of many economists. Keynesian theory gave government fiscal policy a crucial role in smoothing out economic growth. Wise leaders would lower taxes and increase expenditures during economic slowdowns to quicken economic activity and create jobs; they would increase taxes and limit expenditures during boom times to forestall inflation. But Keynesian prescriptions seemed inappropriate for the combination of inflation and unemployment that plagued the Western economies in the 1970s. Another school of thought, which had been percolating among economists for over a decade, came to supplant or at least supplement Keynesian orthodoxy by the late 1970s. Called monetarism, the new school emphasized the role of the money supply in determining economic growth and de-emphasized the role of government spending policy.

The trouble with using fiscal policy to regulate the economy, the monetarists argued, was that it was a slow and clumsy instrument, prone to misuse for political purposes and often too feeble to much affect overall levels of economic activity. By the time new taxes or spending policies took effect, the conditions prompting them had often been resolved through the natural workings of the business cycle. Rather than tinker with taxation and spending, the real aim of government ought to be to expand the supply of money at a rate commensurate with sustainable growth in production. So long as the supply of currency stayed in balance with the needs of the economy, growth would occur naturally and without violent spasms of inflationary boom and deflationary bust.

The key instrument for adjusting the growth of the supply of money was the rate that central banks charged other banks for borrowing money. This was the true tiller of the economy. Increases in the interest rates charged by central banks for loans would restrict growth in the supply of money, reduce the level of borrowing by consumers and businesses, slow growth, and wring inflation out of an economy. Decreases in interest rates would pump new money into an economy, encourage borrowing for everything from houses and autos to the construction of new factories, and thereby reduce unemployment and promote expansion. By applying the brake when the supply of money exceeded the needs of the economy and the accelerator when it lagged, central banks could, in principle, smooth out the business cycle.

To work effectively, however, such policies were best pursued in markets that were free. Monetarists generally decried wage and price controls for distorting the efficient flow of capital and labor, criticized high taxes for penalizing private savings and investment, and condemned Keynsian deficit spending because it led governments to compete with private industry for credit. The new economics, in other words, prescribed the sort of retrenchments in government that politicians such as Thatcher and Reagan were advocating.

CONCLUSION

During the early 1970s, it had been fashionable among political writers to argue that the Soviet and American systems were converging on some intermediate model, perhaps exemplified by the mixed socialist/capitalist economies of Scandinavia. By the beginning of the 1980s, that viewpoint seemed absurd. With conservative economists running central banks and conservative politicians running governments, the watchwords in the West had become privatization, entrepreneurship, free markets, and lower taxes. The new leadership had contempt for what it saw as failed experiments in socialism and an unshakeable conviction that state-managed economies bred not virtue but vice: the concentration of power in the hands of self-serving elites, a subordination of the rights of the citizen to the needs of the collective as interpreted by those elites, a decay of individual initiative, slovenliness in thought and work, and a preoccupation with redistributing rather than creating wealth. This message reverberated with voters in the United States, Britain, and other parts of the North Atlantic community, sometimes even among the very workers whose interests liberal governments had sought to promote.

The confluence of conservative politics and conservative economic thought halted a trend toward state-managed capitalism that stretched as far back as the New Deal in the United States and even farther in Europe. The election of Reagan also seemed to end any hope that détente, which had been all but shattered by the bitter dispute over the Soviet invasion of Afghanistan, could ever be restored. When seen against a backdrop of market reforms in China, the dissident movements of the Soviet bloc, the phenomenal economic growth of Japan, and swelling business activity in the Pacific Rim more generally, it seemed as though much of the globe was under renovation. The decade of the 1970s had dashed most of the hopes of the 1960s and had replaced them with others that might be less idealistic but were, perhaps, more realistic.

For Further Reading

William L. Cleveland, *A History of the Modern Middle East* (Boulder, Colo.: Westview Press, 2000). Especially good on the internal politics of Middle Eastern nations.

Raymond L. Garthoff, *Détente and Confrontation: American-Soviet Relations from Nixon to Reagan*, rev. ed. (Washington: Brookings Institution, 1994). Richly detailed; critical of U.S. policies.

Marshall I. Goldman, *Gorbachev's Challenge: Economic Reform in the Age of High Technology* (New York: W. W. Norton, 1987). Treats the economic problems of the Soviet Empire in the 1970s and early 1980s.

Henry Kissinger, *White House Years* (Boston: Little, Brown, 1979), *Years of Upheaval* (Boston: Little Brown, 1982), and *Years of Renewal* (New York: Simon & Schuster, 1999). Self-serving, but useful when read with Garthoff.

Mark Mazower, *Dark Continent: Europe's Twentieth Century* (New York: Knopf, 1999). Learned and provocative.

Stephen McCarthy, *Africa: The Challenge of Transformation* (London and New York: I. B. Tauris & Co., 1994). Both realistic and hopeful.

Walter McDougall, *The Heavens and the Earth: A Political History of the Space Age* (New York: Basic Books, 1985). A lively narrative and a provocative interpretation of Soviet-American competition in space and on earth.

Mohsen M. Milani, *The Making of Iran's Islamic Revolution: From Monarch to Islamic Republic* (Boulder, Colo.: Westview Press, 1994). A well-balanced synopsis.

William K. Tabb, *The Postwar Japanese System: Cultural Economy and Economic Transformation* (New York: Oxford University Press, 1995). A balanced treatment of Japan's rise to economic power.

Daniel Yergin, *The Prize: The Epic Quest for Oil, Money, and Power* (New York: Simon & Schuster, 1991). A lively history of the petroleum industry in its larger political and economic context.

Related Websites

A well-designed site that includes abundant links to Cold War documents and sources
http://legacy.wilsoncenter.org/coldwarfiles/index.html

Links to many excellent websites on the Cold War and U.S. foreign policy
www.mtholyoke.edu/acad/intrel/coldwar.htm

This link to Harvard University's Project on Cold War Studies provides access to recently declassified documents pertaining to the Cold War
http://www.fas.harvard.edu/~hpcws/index2.htm

PART IV

Emergence of New Global Systems from 1981

CHAPTER 14

Reconfigurations of Power, 1981–1991

I n 1988, critics of Communist rule in Czechoslovakia decided to mark the twentieth anniversary of the Russian invasion of that country with a meeting to discuss recent Central European history. But before it began, the Czech government arrested its hosts and hauled foreign guests into a police station, accusing them of provocative, antisocialist behavior and threatening nasty consequences. Rather than being intimidated, the well-known journalists and writers in attendance quickly informed the international press, which broadcast the story in Europe. The BBC and Voice of America promptly beamed it back into Czechoslovakia. The writers complained to their ambassadors and marched to the headquarters of the Communist Party to protest their treatment, all carefully captured on film for later broadcasting. Not only did nothing happen to them, but the imprisoned Czechs, once released, continued their defense of human rights and pressed for greater freedom. By the late 1980s, the media informed citizens not only of multiple challenges to Communist rule but also of the ineffectual treatment of dissidents.

Between 1989 and 1991, an increasingly drab and obsolete Communist system abruptly disintegrated in Europe and northern Asia, collapsing under the weight of its own incompetence and corruption. By that time, the Budapest branch of MacDonald's had more enthusiastic local fans than did Karl Marx. Moreover, one-party governments, whatever their ideological trappings, yielded ground to demands for elections and wider representation. The issue of how to establish and maintain democracy supplanted the choice between economic systems as the central international issue because capitalism became the only game in town.

Electoral regimes also had problems to solve as their societies became increasingly complex and well organized. The difficult issues of corruption, political accountability, and the influence of the media undermined confidence in politicians. Rising ethnic and religious consciousness undermined unitary national identities. Formally democratic political cultures found themselves challenged by their citizens to live up to their professed principles.

Political tensions took place against a background of economic restructuring. International divisions of labor continually changed as companies outsourced functions and shifted production sites. Instability became an inescapable fact of economic life as globalization of capital and labor markets continued. The multi-centered world economy, unified by the World Wide Web, undermined the protective barriers erected by nation-states.

The Collapse of Communism

The repressive activities of the Soviet and Chinese states had long since revealed the hollowness of Communist promises of a just, egalitarian society. Whatever the appeal of communist ideology in the abstract, it had clearly been flawed in practice, and history had falsified Marx's predictions that capitalism would impoverish all workers. As a result, interest in orthodox Marxism plummeted after 1970 among European and American intellectuals, and the Communist parties in non-Communist states shrank into insignificance. But Communist regimes had built powerful protective shields for themselves in the armies and parties that ran their states. Offering jobs and social security in return for at least public obedience, Communist leaders retained power despite their shortcomings.

The compromises that had suited an earlier era fell apart in the 1970s and 1980s. Growing numbers of city dwellers wanted better housing and food, higher wages, and greater professional opportunities. Their governments were unable to supply these things. Confidence in the communist solution evaporated, but no one foresaw the extraordinary outcome: the dissolution of the Soviet Union and its European and Asian empires.

Challenges Within Eastern Europe

In 1975, new international standards for political behavior were established when the Soviet Union and thirty-three European countries signed the Helsinki accords. In addition to freedom of thought and religion, these nations pledged to grant their citizens an unnamed set of civil, political, economic, and human rights and to give minorities equality under state laws. Even without instant or total enforcement, this declaration of universal human rights proved to be a powerful tool in the hands of democratic activists.

Poland was the first Communist country in which demands for reform acquired a mass following. Despite state control of the media, it was impossible for Communist governments to shield their citizens from knowledge of a wider world. When citizens could see on TV and through travel how wide the gap between their living standards and those of other industrialized states had become, they began to demand more. The technologies of modern communications and transportation could work to undermine repressive governments as well as to keep them in power.

In 1980, striking Polish shipyard workers formed Solidarity, an independent trade union that soon became a national party with several million members who called for change. Through Solidarity, citizens created a means of political participation, at least until it was banned in 1982 and martial law imposed. But the union was revived in 1988, when thousands of workers went on strike to protest rising prices and poor economic conditions. Led by Lech Walesa, a militant shipyard worker and a devout Roman Catholic, Solidarity negotiated with the Communist government for new economic policies and for an independent election, which Solidarity-backed candidates won. Within two years, the Polish Communist Party had voted itself out of existence, and Walesa became president of the country. When challenged by its citizens, the Communist regime had proved to be a paper tiger.

Communism in other parts of Eastern Europe fell even more quickly and easily. In Hungary, communism had lost its cultural and social hold long before it became politically obsolete. During the 1980s, the Hungarian economy had been partially reformed along free market lines, and incomes had risen as a result. When Erno Rubik patented Rubik's Cube and became a socialist millionaire, he joined a growing group of super-rich Hungarians, most of whom were businessmen and real estate owners. Although under a Communist government, Hungary had become a quasi-capitalist society. Shopping centers ringed Budapest, which also acquired a Hilton hotel and a McDonald's.

To the casual visitor, Hungary resembled its Western European neighbors despite its politically restrictive government. Criticism of the regime by reformist politicians mounted, and by 1989 these reformers felt bold enough to end the required teaching of Russian in the schools and to open their borders with Austria and permit free migration. Within a few months, elections brought democratic reformers into office. One-party rule also ended in Czechoslovakia in 1989, and Vaclav Havel, the playwright and a leading critic of the regime, was elected president.

Within the German Democratic Republic, which was neither democratic nor a republic, citizens took advantage of spreading enthusiasm for revolutionary change to organize and demand elections and power sharing. Civil society, in the form of organizations independent of the Communist Party, was reborn virtually overnight. Thousands of people took to the streets nightly, marching peacefully and demanding democratic rights, and thousands of others voted with their feet and took off for Western Europe via Hungary. Unable either to cope or to change their ways, the government simply resigned and threw open the borders to the West. The Berlin Wall literally came tumbling down, and thousands danced on its ruins. Within a year, the GDR itself ceased to exist, and its territories were

GERARD MALIE/AFP/Getty Images

On November 9, 1989, the Berlin Wall, which had divided the city for almost thirty years, was opened. In this picture, West Berliners watched East Berlin border guards as they cut through the concrete barrier to open a new crossing point.

incorporated into the German Federal Republic. The two halves of Germany were reunited. As miraculous as these changes seemed to people at the time, more surprising still were the decisions by leaders of the Soviet Union, who refused to use their troops to defend the existing regimes.

Glasnost and the USSR

The key to the speedy and generally peaceful revolution in Eastern and Central Europe lay in the Soviet Union, whose government had intermittently permitted limited dissent since the mid-1950s. Once Nikita Khrushchev had destroyed the myth of Soviet infallibility by criticizing Stalin, others had also found the means to do so, whether in private conversations or in informally circulated writings. By the mid-1970s and 1980s, eminent critics, such as the novelist Alexander Solzhenitsyn and the physicist Andrei Sakharov, were sent into exile rather than to labor camps or prison, and their books and speeches continued to be read. Even if private mutterings could not bring down a regime, they ate away quietly at the foundations of its support.

In any case, many of the disasters that befell the Soviet Union during the 1970s and 1980s could not be hidden given the penetration of the USSR by the European media. Its armies, which had invaded Afghanistan in 1979, did badly against the Islamic guerrillas supported by Pakistan and the United States.

Mounting casualties produced opposition at home, and escalating costs took needed resources from domestic projects. As a Soviet version of the Vietnam War, the conflict in Afghanistan magnified popular hostility to the Soviet government and unleashed widespread criticism.

Domestic problems compounded the impact of foreign misadventures. A meltdown at the aging nuclear power plant at Chernobyl sent clouds of radioactivity all over Eastern Europe in 1986 and forced the evacuation of large areas of the Ukraine and Belarus. In an environmentally conscious age, this pollution of air, land, and water symbolized the massive failure of Soviet technology and government. Incompetence was compounded by official dishonesty and an inability to fix mistakes. The Soviet economy looked ever weaker. Growth rates and per capita real income declined during the 1980s. By 1990 real output was also falling, and there were shortages of consumer goods, food, and basic industrial materials. The command economy, in which planners set prices and output targets and distributed supplies of raw materials, could not reform itself. The general loss of confidence and lack of cooperation by the workers made a bad situation worse. A common joke was, "We pretend to be working, and they pretend to be paying us!" By the 1980s the isolation that in the 1950s and 1960s had blocked comparison shopping by Soviet citizens had ended. Images of Western affluence were easily spread via VCRs and European television, intensifying the wish for reform.

Mikhail Gorbachev, who became first secretary of the Communist Party in 1984, saw the need for economic modernization, but he decided to follow indirect means for achieving it. He retreated from an aggressive foreign policy, withdrawing from Afghanistan, recommending change in Eastern Europe, and negotiating arms reductions with the United States. Peace and a slower arms race would free resources for economic development, or so he hoped. He then recommended a policy of openness (*glasnost*) to replace the secrecy that had characterized Soviet rule in the past. His plans for restructuring (*perestroika*) embraced not only the economic but also the political sphere, where he called for democratization. Citizens who were newly freed from the tight oversight of the state would, he hoped, revitalize the Soviet system and permit real reform. Step by step, Gorbachev pushed the government toward greater freedom of speech, of publication, and of religion. Contested elections took place in 1989, and reformers expected a multiparty system with an independent legislature to be established soon.

Instead of strengthening the Soviet regime, Gorbachev's policies produced a massive destabilization of the Soviet state and an abandonment of its ideology. The party soon lost whatever legitimacy and authority it had left. Revolution from above soon became revolution from below because Gorbachev and his associates had radically underestimated the ability of the state to contain the forces of an emerging civil society.

In many ways, the Soviet Union had long since ceased to be a unified society. Its constituent republics, which had their own bureaucracies and educational systems, had developed strong ethnic identities. Rather than seeing themselves as good Soviet citizens, people identified themselves as Armenians, Uzbeks, or Kazaks. Leaders of non-Russian areas saw that pluralism and tolerance in the center could mean independence for the periphery, and they seized their opportunities. Estonians declared their republic independent in 1988, and mass demonstrations for independence erupted in Georgia in 1989. Boris Yeltsin, the president of the Russian Federation, became the voice of the Russian minority, eager to defend its rights and to claim independence from the wider union. When attempts by the Soviet army to contain popular protests failed, other republics quickly moved against the Soviet state. The empire was dying.

The end of the Soviet Union came quickly. Hard-core Communists, appalled at the results of reform, attempted a coup against Gorbachev in August 1991, putting him under house arrest. Boris Yeltsin led resistance to the coup in Moscow, bringing thousands of supporters into the streets to protect the Russian parliament. Denounced by politicians around the world and given little support at home, the coup soon failed, and Gorbachev returned to Moscow a free man. But his political power had been weakened and demands for independence mounted. Ironically, Gorbachev, who had wanted to reform and modernize the Soviet Union, in fact succeeded in destroying it. In December 1991 he announced that the USSR had ceased to exist. Europe's last great territorial empire had collapsed, to be replaced by fifteen successor states (see Map 14.1).

The Cold War's Last Stand

Although Communist parties had lost power in Eastern Europe and the Soviet Union, they did not disappear but regrouped and were renamed. Experienced politicians and bureaucrats found new identities and roles in the states of Central Asia and the Balkans. Moreover, communism remained very much alive in several corners of the world. Communist regimes in Cuba, Vietnam, North Korea, Laos, and Albania managed to isolate their populations from the comparisons and contacts with capitalist countries that had weakened the party-led states in Europe. In these tiny backwaters, Communist leaders clung to old ways during the 1980s and maintained Soviet-style closed economies long past the point where they had been abandoned elsewhere.

Under the leadership of Fidel Castro, Cuba maintained its commitment to a socialist revolution that had slowly turned into a Caribbean variant of communism. In the constitution adopted in 1975, the Communist Party was given authority over all aspects of Cuban life, and Cuba became a long-distance client, dependent on Soviet economic aid. This linkage only deepened U.S. hostility, driven both by the strongly anti-Communist Cuban community in Miami and by Cold War fears. Isolated from North American markets by a U.S. trade embargo, the country supported itself by selling its tobacco and sugar to the USSR and receiving cheap oil and credits in return, which it used for needed medicines, fertilizers, and machinery. Castro offered Soviet leaders military and political support in return. Cuba sent technical and military help to several revolutionary regimes and dissident groups in Africa.

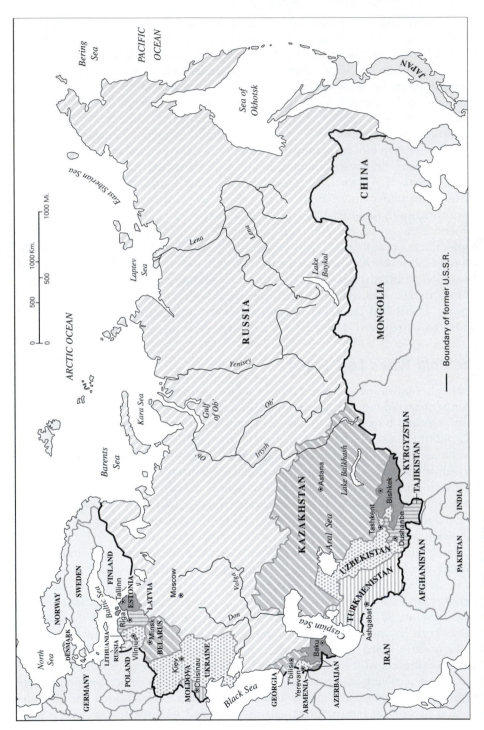

MAP 14.1 Successor states of the Soviet Union.
Because of its size, natural resources, and military might, Russia continues to dominate its region. Most of the southern circle of new states, which border on Middle Eastern countries, have large Muslim minorities, and they have experienced continued ethnic conflict.

During the 1970s, Cuba invested relatively large sums in health care and education. For a time, Cuba led Latin America in literacy and rates of infant survival because of its effective social welfare policies. During the later 1980s, however, harder times came: Depression hit the Caribbean, and the Soviet Union scaled back its subsidies. Under pressure, Cuban authorities permitted some free market reforms, opened the country to tourism, and scaled back their African adventures. Communism in Cuba fused with nationalism and anti-Americanism, giving the revolution many sources of ideological support. Even after the Cold War had ended in Europe, it remained alive in the Straits of Florida.

Communism Reconfigured in China

While Soviet officials chose political reform as a path to economic development, Chinese leaders opted to modernize the economy while refusing to make political changes. The party rejected democratization and the toleration of dissent, cracking down hard on those it claimed were calling for "bourgeois liberalism." While they were prepared to flirt with capitalism, China's leaders were not prepared to retreat from their monopoly of political power.

The Chinese state had established a Soviet-style command economy in the 1950s by nationalizing industry and foreign trade, setting prices, and collectivizing agriculture; inefficiency and low growth resulted. China had channeled too much economic energy into the production of steel and chemicals and paid too little attention to consumer goods and food. Seeing the need for change, Zhou Enlai, the premier of China until his death in 1976, pushed for increased trade and the importation of Western technologies.

After Mao's death in 1976, reformers gained more power and began more active restructuring of the economy. Deng Xiaoping, a masterly politician who became head of the Central Advisory Commission, slowly moved the party toward economic reform. Once they were allowed to contract out of their agricultural communes, peasants deserted them in droves, working as family units and selling their surpluses in private markets. Output and rural incomes rose, stimulating rural industry. As trading companies under local control multiplied, foreign contacts expanded and foreign investment poured into the country.

Although state industries continued in their inefficient ways, a new private sector boomed in southern coastal areas, particularly Guangdong and Fujian. Taiwanese and Hong Kong entrepreneurs shifted their manufacturing of shoes, clothing, and electronics to the Chinese mainland during the 1980s, bringing millions of new workers into a global economy. By the early 1990s, more than four hundred special enterprise zones existed where quasi-capitalist systems of production and trade operated. In the coastal cities, access to television, Western music, and fashionable clothes transformed daily life. Women began to wear makeup and get their hair permed. The information gap between urban Chinese and their overseas relatives lessened under the impact of telephones and travel. In a gesture of liberalization, the government permitted its citizens to listen to foreign radio broadcasts, and soon the BBC and the Voice of America became favorite programs.

Rural inland areas were left far behind. Public investments in irrigation and industry remained low, as did prices for grain sold to the state. Remote villages continued to lack roads, electricity, and running water. Moreover, in many areas population growth threatened to outstrip resources and encouraged migration into the cities. Although provinces had yearly baby quotas as part of the state's one-family, one-child policy, people in the countryside found these quotas easier to evade.

By 1990 China had in effect a triple economy: family-run farms, inefficient state-run industry, and dynamic, privately owned manufacturing located in the export zones and larger cities. Although standards of living in rural areas rose markedly during the 1980s and 1990s, the gap between urban and rural incomes widened. The government accepted increasing inequality as one of the prices of change. Moreover, government and party employees enriched themselves and their families, creating a large property-owning privileged class. In response, the demand by ordinary citizens for better housing and social services grew, along with the desire for greater participation in governing. Trading economic modernization for political consent proved not to be as simple as the government had hoped. However, the Chinese example shows the capacity of a Communist regime to abandon the command economy and to turn toward a market-driven system.

Problems of One-Party Rule

The difficulties of governing through political monopoly extended to far more than Communist countries. One-party regimes existed in states all around the world. All of them faced the issue of legitimacy. In whose name did the single party rule? Communists, of course, equated the party with workers, whose right to rule had been asserted by Marx and Lenin. Democratic political theory located the right to rule in the people more generally, which created a need to decide how the voice of the people could be expressed. In the twentieth century, political parties came to embody that voice. In theory, in democratic countries, multiple parties contend for power and then govern either singly or together according to the verdict of the ballot box. Of course, this political form covers many different political realities.

Elections take on the characteristics of the political culture that surrounds them. Whatever lip service is given to democratic ideals, no state maintains a completely free and open electoral process in which all adults participate. In some countries, presidents or prime ministers rig elections to ensure victory, jailing opposition candidates or barring them from the ballot. Married women require their husband's permission to vote in several Islamic states. Restricted access to citizenship denies a vote to immigrants in many societies.

Moreover, universal adult suffrage does not guarantee representation in the political process. In North America, many citizens neglect to vote, leaving decision making to a minority. Despite its democratic constitution, Mexico continues to struggle with the problem of how to distribute political power fairly. Until 2000, the governing party, the PRI (Institutional Revolutionary Party), had won every presidential election and held the lion's share of governorships and seats in the Congress. Nationalist appeals and dishonest elections gave the PRI, despite much evidence of corruption and inefficiency, a quasi-monopoly on politics. During the 1970s and 1980s, Mexico belonged in the camp of the one-party states despite its formally well-functioning democracy. Politics remained a lucrative profession there, and loyalty to the PRI was the path of entry.

The demand for wider representation and for open, freer elections gained strength during the 1980s. Reconfigurations of power took place as groups that had been excluded from the political process insisted that they be heard. Women marched in Argentina demanding news of their kidnapped and murdered children, the "disappeared." In North Africa, Muslim Brotherhoods used social welfare programs to challenge secular regimes. In Kenya and Malawi, church groups became centers of resistance against single-party rule. In Nigeria multiple human rights groups agitated against the country's military rulers. In many states, the growth of civil society, as shown by active nongovernmental organizations, made it increasingly difficult for a single party to maintain a monopoly on political power. States, whatever their form or ideological loyalties, had to recognize internal divisions and multiple centers of power.

Pro-Democracy Movements in Asia

During the 1980s, a growing number of Chinese students and workers spoke out in favor of a more open political system, despite the hostility of the Chinese ruling elite to political reform. Looking back to Nationalist demonstrations in 1919 and to the huge protests against Mao and the Gang of Four in 1976, they used slogans from the past to legitimate change in the present. Moreover, corrupt officials made easy targets, and Western news broadcasts gave dissidents alternative sources of information. Posters pasted on "Democracy Wall" in Beijing and similar sites in other cities called for respect for human rights and curbs on state power. Writers quoted the Declaration of Independence and demanded that the government grant democracy. Activists sold crudely printed underground journals, claiming freedom of speech and of the press. Feeding the process, Western reporters picked up interesting arguments and actions, then beamed them back into the country via radio, increasing their audience to millions.

The heyday of Democracy Wall was brief. The police clamped down on the underground press and arrested the regime's most vocal critics. In 1980 Deng

Xaioping asked that the right to put up wall posters be stripped from the Chinese Constitution because it was being abused by reactionaries who were eager to undermine Chinese unity and stability. A quiet struggle between hard-liners and tepid reformers within the party continued for several years, with Deng managing to fend off critics from both the right and the left. Although he successfully defended his economic reforms, he held the line against opening up the political system.

Dissent did not disappear, however. Resentment against public officials raking in riches grew. The issue of Chinese rule in Tibet proved a constant thorn in the official side, as Tibetan Buddhist nuns and monks led intermittent protests against Beijing's rule and as the Dalai Lama, the spiritual leader of the Tibetan population, defended their rights before an international audience.

In May 1989 thousands of students and workers gathered in Tiananmen Square, the capital's premier public space, to demand political reform. Soon supporters rallied in at least twenty other cities, and the international press directed the attention of the world to the protesters' demands. The demonstrations gave conservatives an excuse to crack down hard on dissent, which they did brutally. Deng, in consultation with the army, called out troops and brought them to Beijing. In June the military attacked the unarmed demonstrators, sweeping them out of the square and shooting resisters. Thousands were arrested, and an unknown number died. Some who escaped continued to demand political reform, but they did so from abroad or from hiding. One-party rule remained in force in China.

In the late twentieth century, political conflicts had an international audience. The media helped to spread a demand for more effective democracies in Europe, the Americas, Africa, and Asia. E-mail and the Internet doomed the efforts of authoritarian governments to close national borders to international influences.

South Asia

In the pluralist societies of India, Bangladesh, and Pakistan, support for democratic rule has to take into account loyalties to family, community, religion, and language, which are often in conflict with national norms. The wish for representation for one's own group has not translated automatically into tolerance for the fair representation of other groups. Although India was founded as a secular state committed to social equality, both its political and social system operate on the basis of acknowledged differences. The lack of a common language has weakened the construction of an Indian nation. In addition, not all citizens are treated equally by the law: Muslims and Dalits, or "untouchables," have special rights, and many Hindus would like to have privileges granted to members of their group. Not only are all citizens not equal in India today, but many would fight against that principle.

State-making in the region has been an ongoing process that has sometimes been contested violently by minorities. Individual characteristics often matter less than group membership or family identity. The political power of families such as the Bhuttos in Pakistan, the Nehrus in India, and the Zias in Bangladesh has been so strong that when there has been no suitable male heir, wives and

Kapoor Baldev/Sygma/Corbis

Indira Gandhi, Prime Minister of India, speaking to Congress-party supporters during her 1977 campaign for reelection. At that time voters rejected her attempt to remain in power after her declaration of a state of emergency, but they reelected her in 1980.

daughters have inherited normally male political roles, despite cultural norms restricting women's public activity. During the 1980s and 1990s, women served as prime ministers in Pakistan, Bangladesh, India, and Sri Lanka, as well as heading political parties. Their gender mattered less than their family name.

Unfortunately, often power has had much more appeal than due process. The army-dominated regimes that have controlled Pakistan have produced a constitution that gives little power to legislatures and parties, and they have sometimes felt free to cancel potentially threatening election results. Since the courts often follow the prevailing political winds, law can be an easy weapon against opposition politicians. India, in contrast, has had a well-functioning parliamentary regime with regular elections and an independent judiciary. But Indian democracy has co-existed with party and family monopolies, neither of which consistently played by constitutional rules.

From independence until 1977, the Congress Party controlled the Indian central government, dominated the bureaucracy, and used patronage to solidify its influence in the states. Three generations of the Nehru family—Jawaharlal, his daughter Indira Gandhi, and her son Rajiv—maintained an almost unbroken lock on the office of prime minister from 1947 until Rajiv's assassination in 1991. When threatened by the courts and a growing opposition movement,

Indira Gandhi declared a wildly unpopular state of emergency and ruled by decree. In 1984 her manipulation of state governments to benefit the Congress Party and her repression of opponents in Kashmir led Sikh militants to assassinate her. One-party rule in India collapsed as a result of its leaders' mistaken decisions and practices.

To varying degrees, the tension between authoritarian methods and democratic structures has troubled all the states of South Asia.

South America

The winding down of the Cold War also had repercussions in South America, where military regimes had garnered support in the 1970s through anti-Marxist rhetoric and hostility to socialist economic programs. In Argentina, Brazil, Chile, Peru, and Uruguay during the 1970s, generals ran national security states in which domestic order was their primary goal. They promised economic growth while restricting civil rights. Along with the powerful military dictatorships arose armed guerrilla movements dedicated to their ouster. Students, opposition politicians, trade unionists, and journalists soon became prime targets in campaigns of repression, death, and torture.

Both the military and their armed adversaries paid little attention to legality or evidence; thousands suffered in the crossfire. For years the United States offered military aid to the generals, trained their officers, and sold them arms because it feared the expansion of communism in the Western Hemisphere. But by the 1980s Marxism was a toothless tiger in the Americas, and the generals had long since discredited themselves by their inability to deliver sustained economic development. As ideological differences became less threatening, bread-and-butter issues came to the fore.

One by one, the national security states crumbled as popular opposition widened and mobilized. In the end, the combination of incompetence and brutality doomed military rule in much of Latin America. After General Leopoldo Galtieri's government provoked and then quickly lost a mini-war with Great Britain over the Falkland Islands in 1982, the humbled Argentinean military called an election in which voters decisively rejected them. The Brazilian military came under increasing attack for human rights abuses. By the early 1980s, the ruling generals opted for a slow transition back to parliamentary government. In 1985 the Brazilian legislature chose a centrist politician as president, reestablishing a democratic regime.

In Chile, General Augusto Pinochet ruled virtually unchallenged after ousting President Salvador Allende in 1973, despite his identification with the dirty domestic war, which had curbed civil rights and political freedoms. But in 1988, when he turned to the electorate to ratify his remaining in power, Pinochet was voted out of office. The Peruvian military also left office in disgrace, having proved incompetent to stop either the Shining Path (*Sendero Luminoso*) guerrillas who opposed them or a slide into steep economic decline. New regimes, led by younger, populist leaders who promised reform and used television effectively to get their message across to voters, came to power throughout Latin America.

As political realms democratized, economic ones became more open. Interest in free trade zones mounted, and regulations on businesses and on investments were eased. Latin America moved closer to its northern neighbors both in political and in economic practices. Economic and political justice proved elusive, however. None of the newly democratized states solved the problem of political accountability. Despite vocal demands for information and for prosecution of death squads, the new governments did not have the political capital to take their predecessors to court. At the same time, economic inequality intensified. Neo-liberalism proved a better remedy for the wealthy than for the masses, who voted populist. Even without the issue of communism to divide the electorates, Latin American states entered the 1990s with a mass of unsolved social and political problems.

Africa

The ending of the Cold War also had an impact on African states. Some of them had allied themselves with one of the superpowers, exchanging ideological support for aid. Several authoritarian regimes in Africa (Angola, Ethiopia, Congo, Mozambique, and Madagascar) took on a Marxist-Leninist identity in the 1980s, and others (Zaire, Malawi, and South Africa) made opposition to Marxism one of their justifications for rule. But in no case were these ideologies much more than skin deep, and they were easily jettisoned at the time of the Soviet Union's collapse. Communism helped to justify single-party rule in Africa, but it had little to do with the fundamental conflicts that undermined political and economic life on the continent.

During the 1980s, authoritarian or military governments ruled in most of sub-Saharan Africa. Nelson Mandela remained in prison on Robben Island, the (South) African National Congress was still a banned party, and majority rule for South Africa was a shadowy goal. In Angola, Mozambique, and Sudan, long-running civil wars devastated large regions. Nationalist leaders justified one-party rule at the end of the colonial period in the language of national unity and then stayed on with their followers to dominate the new states. By the 1980s the young agitators had become elderly dictators, clinging to power along with their followers and families. Politics became an avenue to wealth and patronage, benefiting the few. Preferring an existing state, however bad, to unknown alternatives, the richer nations kept dictators afloat with loans and gun sales.

The future of democratic government looked dim in Africa during the 1980s. Nevertheless, civil society in the form of churches, professional organizations, and ethnic and communal groups became increasingly powerful. Although some states were so fractured by religious, tribal, and linguistic differences that loyalty to the nation commanded little enthusiasm, interest in fair political representation grew.

The rapid shift from autocracy to contested politics in Africa during the early 1990s shows how widespread an interest in political participation had become. One regime after another abandoned monopoly politics for pluralism as its effective support waned. In South Africa, the ANC won the first elections held under conditions of universal adult suffrage, leading to a peaceful transfer of power from the defenders of apartheid to the supporters of majority rule. The ending of the Cold War coincided with a transformation of African politics toward greater openness and representation, which was pushed from below.

Economic Restructuring

The shifts toward democracy and multiparty rule in Eastern Europe, Russia, Latin America, and Africa took place during a period of rapid economic restructuring that undermined the ability of poorer governments to provide for their citizens. Deepening inequalities, both among individuals and among nations, helped fuel political transformations. By the 1980s the world economy had moved well beyond the phase of U.S., European, and Japanese domination.

With the aid of computers, production was decentralized and management was centralized in a handful of global cities from Tokyo to New York and London. The Internet provided instant communication within and among firms, who traded information as well as goods. The world economy was reshuffled during the 1980s under the pressures of international finance and international business. Entrepreneurs, whatever their country of origin, found they had to outsource, offshore, and stay online to remain competitive. The world in which they operated became increasingly complex, as regional and supranational organizations helped to drive economic globalization.

The Four Little Tigers

Over a century ago, Theodore Roosevelt predicted that countries on the Pacific Rim would rise to power and present an effective economic challenge to Western Europe and eastern America. The history of East and Southeast Asia since the 1950s has proved him right. Japan and the "four little tigers"—Hong Kong, Singapore, South Korea, and Taiwan—have joined the ranks of the world's strongest economies. They rode the wave of high investment in the 1950s and 1960s to launch economic growth and industrial enterprises.

Taiwan and South Korea built steel mills and shipbuilding yards, Hong Kong established textile factories, and Singapore turned to oil refining and petrochemicals. All four produced electronic goods for export, relying on their ample supply of well-educated but low-paid workers to attract entrepreneurs. By the 1980s, Hong Kong and Singapore functioned as centers of global finance and business services, and Japan became the world's largest exporter of capital. These countries' rapid rise into the ranks of rich, industrialized states killed forever the myth that only Western nations had the skills to launch an industrial revolution.

GLOBAL Technologies

The Internet

The Internet connections that many of us now take for granted depend on the integration of many technologies: cable, microwave, and satellite transmission systems; video displays; desktop computers and servers; software to route messages and maintain security; and innumerable conventions covering details from error checking to transmission speeds. Some parts of the system predate the twentieth century—the QWERTY layout of a keyboard, for instance, became conventional soon after typewriters first appeared in the nineteenth century. Others, such as Web browsers, date only to the 1990s.

The idea of networking is very old. Amateur radio enthusiasts, for example, were building networks of their own before World War I. Communicating freely across long distances, they formed the equivalent of user groups and chat rooms by agreeing to meet on the air at certain hours and frequencies. Networking via computer, however, emerged in the 1960s and 1970s, largely as the result of research sponsored by the U.S. Defense Department, which was eager to give scattered laboratories common access to specialized programs, data, and equipment and to build a flexible network for the command of worldwide forces in an emergency. With new software developed in the 1960s, it became possible to connect different operating systems and applications.

By 1971 several centers for computer research were linked by high-speed telephone lines into a network called ARPANET (the acronym for the Defense Department's Advanced Research Projects Agency). By the early 1980s, other large organizations— universities, corporations, and government agencies in the United States and abroad—had responded to a growing demand data-sharing services by creating their own networks. The Internet was born when these networks adopted ARPANET protocols for transmission and addressing, so that they could be interlinked via ARPANET's backbone of hubs, routers, and transmission lines.

The appearance of inexpensive desktop computers in the 1980s accelerated the growth of these interconnected networks dramatically. Whereas only about two thousand computers, almost all of them in North America and Britain, had access to the emerging Internet in 1985, the number had reached a hundred fifty thousand by 1989—about 20 percent of them located outside the United States.

How did these states transform themselves so quickly? Japan, of course, had begun its industrial revolution in the late nineteenth century and had emerged as the leading economic power in East Asia by the 1920s. Although Japan had to reconstruct its economy after World War II, it had entrepreneurs, a history of multinational businesses, an elaborate infrastructure, and a model of government-sponsored growth. The cases that need to be explained are those of the four little tigers: two tiny city-states, an island dominated by failed Chinese generals and refugees, and the southern half of a war-torn peninsula. All seemed unlikely candidates for economic development.

To be sure, times were favorable for change. World War II had wiped out the power of conservative social elites, and the Korean and Vietnam wars had brought large numbers of foreigners and lots of business into the area. In the ideology of the Cold War, Asia was on the frontline in the battle against communism, and it had to be secured for the free world. The way was paved for transfers of technology and expertise. In any case, the governments running these small states felt great pressure to modernize for their own survival. None of them had sufficient resources to support their populations without trade. If they did not export, they would die, or would at least run the risk of being swallowed up by their neighbors. Japanese state-led development proved an effective model, and these states invested heavily in education, infrastructure, and industrial development.

The New Europe

Globalization has encouraged regionalization. In the free-wheeling international economy, most individual states are too small to have much bargaining power, but by linking together they can create larger, protected markets and pool resources. Moreover, many believe that economic ties bridge political rivalries. Europe, which had been torn apart by two world wars and the communist-capitalist confrontation, moved to heal itself through the device of the European Economic Community (EEC).

The EEC was created in 1958 to dampen conflict between Germany and its neighbors and to foster economic development. This regional organization, head-quartered in Brussels, was a free trade zone, within which its members pledged to harmonize their social and economic policies while they worked toward political integration. The new united Europe was tiny: Only six states joined initially, the rest being uninvited or unwilling. But the EEC soon became a club to which all wished to belong. During the 1960s, its spectacular economic growth proved an irresistible attraction, leading the United Kingdom, Ireland, and Denmark to ask for and then accept membership in 1973. Greece, Portugal, and Spain entered during the 1980s, and Austria, Sweden, and Finland joined in the mid-1990s. The EEC, renamed the European Union (EU), became a global superpower, supplying 21 percent of world exports and buying 22 percent of world imports in 1990.

The EU has redefined Europe, eliminating many internal barriers, dampening inequalities, and encouraging a common identity. Free migration and the right to work throughout the EU have lured the unemployed from peripheral rural areas into the sleek cities of northwestern Europe. A new European bureaucracy working in Brussels has regulatory power over large areas of economic and social policy. But an insider-outsider distinction is carefully maintained. The EU now includes some formerly Communist states in Eastern Europe, but whether it will admit Turkey is an important unanswered question.

Europe's regionalization encouraged a similar process in other areas. Limited agreements binding together clusters of states for economic cooperation have emerged on virtually every continent. West African states formed an economic and monetary union in the early 1970s, and groups of central and southern African countries have also done so. The Persian Gulf states created the Gulf Cooperation Council after the outbreak of war between Iran and Iraq. In the Americas, Caribbean nations, as well as different combinations of Central and South American states, have signed regional agreements.

In 1992 Canada, the United States, and Mexico signed the North American Free Trade Agreement (NAFTA), the most important of these pacts. It opened each of these national markets to the goods, investments, and services produced by the others, eliminating tariffs and other barriers to exchange. Long before it was adopted, NAFTA was controversial. Opponents in North America feared the loss of manufacturing jobs as factories shifted south into Mexico, where wages and benefits are low. Supporters point to the new jobs generated in each country as exports rise. Caribbean countries resent the taxes and quotas that still block their goods from North American markets, and NAFTA has not slowed illegal Mexican immigration to the United States as it was predicted to do.

Although regionalism has become a common tactic for nation-states that are trying to survive in a global world, it has had varying degrees of implementation and success.

Deindustrialization and the World Cities

By the late 1980s, twenty years of deindustrialization in Europe and North America had left their mark. Steel plants had shut down in Essen, Sheffield, and Pittsburgh. Although some companies simply fired their workers and closed, others sent production or assembly abroad to the Philippines or Mexico. Clothing, automobiles, and electronics became footloose industries, moving from low-cost to lower cost areas. International geographies of production shifted, leaving capital-intensive, high-tech industries in the older industrialized countries and moving labor-intensive, poorly paid jobs to the developing world. Unionized labor in Europe and North America lost out as services replaced manufacturing.

When the assembly of complex goods went global, so did the organization of businesses. Keeping track of it all, selling shares, and financing foreign investment took on added importance, giving new status to accountants, advertising agencies, bankers, and, of course, lawyers with multinational connections and skills. Moreover, with computers ready to hand, there was no need for management and finance to decentralize to match production, and in fact there were major gains from not doing so.

Paradoxically, the same changes that doomed the industrial cities of advanced economies launched the capitals of those economies into a new realm of prosperity and dominance. By the later 1980s, New York, London, and Tokyo, assisted by Hong Kong, Frankfort, and Singapore, emerged as command posts for the global economy. Capital and foreign exchange moved through the banks and investment firms of those cities, which also housed the headquarters of most of the world's major corporations. The world economy developed a small urban core that reached out to a global periphery.

Oil and Debt

Modern economies run on oil. Transformed by machines into gasoline and electricity, oil frees people from the powerful constraints imposed by nature. Without oil, daily life would literally come to a stop, go dark, turn cold, or remain intolerably hot. Much of our ability to cheat nature in the modern period comes from oil. Pumped from underground and undersea, sent via pipelines and tankers to refineries around the world, oil is the lifeblood of today's economic body.

Both the United States and the USSR derive great economic advantages from their oil reserves, as did Britain and the Netherlands in the colonial era. With the ending of empire, however, Europe's ability to command world oil reserves decreased sharply, even though its large international companies continued to operate in its former colonies. With the founding of the Organization of Petroleum Exporting Countries (OPEC) in 1960, the oil states moved to use their collective bargaining power to raise their share of oil profits and to challenge the ability of the big multinationals to dictate terms. Several states nationalized their oil industries, bringing vast revenues into the hands of government bureaucrats.

In the 1970s, when oil prices shot upward, so did the national incomes of Venezuela, Nigeria, Saudi Arabia, Libya, and Iraq. Oil became better than gold, creating petro-millionaires. The small states of the Arabian Peninsula could now afford health care and advanced education. The Saudis air-conditioned much of their desert land; the Yemenis imported foreigners to do manual labor. Oil was the tempting bait that led Iraq to invade Kuwait in 1990 and the United States and its allies to counterattack.

The losers in this vast transference of wealth were the oil-importing countries, many of which took on huge amounts of debt during the 1970s to pay for the energy they needed to power their growing cities and manufacturing plants. By the 1980s most countries in Latin America and Africa had borrowed beyond their means. When oil prices had gone up, the agricultural products that these states exported could be exchanged for less. More and more of these countries' national budgets went to pay off loans contracted in better times. Local investment stagnated.

In countries where a large percentage of the population lacked basic health care and education, heavy debts blocked investment in human capital. The 1980s saw a widening of inequality both among nations and within them as the life chances of rich and poor diverged more sharply. The unskilled, wherever they lived, found their relative position worsening, while highly educated elites could use skills that were valued in international markets to increase their incomes.

Ed Kashi/Corbis

Oil drilling in 1983 at Port Harcourt in the Niger Delta. Pumping petroleum in Nigeria generates revenues for the government and foreign oil companies while degrading the local environment.

Identities and the Nation-State

On maps, states have tight boundaries and homogeneous populations. France seems to be filled with French and Brazil with Brazilians. But a closer look turns many countries into patchwork quilts of social difference. Brazil, China, Indonesia, Canada, the United States, the former USSR, and Yugoslavia have particularly complex ethnic geographies, as does South Africa (see Map 14.2). When new states formed in sub-Saharan Africa, they took on the boundaries of the colonial past, which were the result of conquest and had been developed for convenience, not because of the cultural affinity of the people within them. In virtually every country, people recognize strong social divisions based on ethnicity, race, and religion.

During the twentieth century, prevailing theories on how to deal with minorities changed. The International Labor Organization, which compares working conditions globally and monitors them for fairness and legality of treatment, moved from supporting the assimilation of indigenous and tribal peoples to recommending the preservation of their social identities and traditions. The United Nations, which had been an important defender of national unity and had fought wars to preserve the integrity of its member states, now supported some forms of self-determination to help minorities remain intact. The pluralist, multicultural society became a goal as well as a social fact.

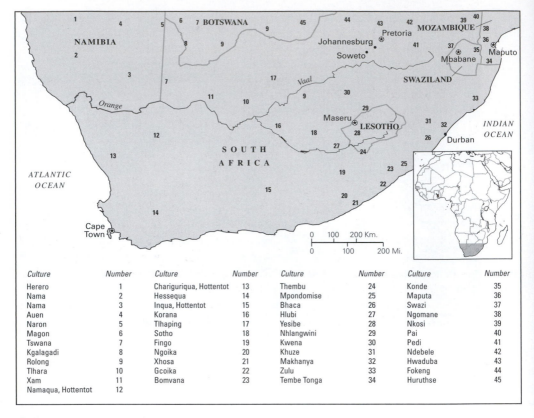

MAP 14.2   Ethnic divisions in Southern Africa.
Each of the region's states contains multiple ethnic groups. Their different languages and geographic movement across borders complicate local political life and the task of building national educational systems.

A State of One's Own

Since Woodrow Wilson promised the right of self-determination to the world's peoples, ethnic identity has been a rallying cry for hundreds of self-proclaimed "freedom fighters" eager to translate cultural difference into political independence. However, what counts as a "people"? Who has the right to nationhood? Governments, understandably, defend unitary nations and the integrity of historically created states, whether their origins date to 700 or 1970. Minorities, particularly in democratic states, push for the right to choose or, in more extreme cases, for the right to secede even without majority approval.

During the 1980s, the Québécois, whose Catholicism and French language distinguish them from Anglo-Canadians, demanded (and then voted down) a referendum on independence. The Palestinian Liberation Organization campaigned for a Palestinian state. Tibetans mounted major demonstrations against Chinese rule. In 1993, the United Nations counted more than forty ongoing civil wars and guerrilla campaigns over issues of ethnic rights.

One common solution to demands for ethnic rights has been decentralization of political power into a federal system. Grants of regional self-government defused much of the pressure for independence in Canada, Belgium, and India. In the late twentieth century, ethnic demands in the name of nationalism undermined state authority around the globe. Although some states contained nationalist pressures by granting additional rights to minorities, others lapsed into civil war when their leaders could not, or would not, negotiate a compromise.

The Problem of the Guest Worker

Economic growth and the need for labor in the postwar period led the richer nations to ease entry requirements. By the 1980s, hundreds of thousands of Latinos and Southeast Asians had moved into the United States. Turks flocked into West Germany, and North Africans into France. Arabs and South Asians moved in droves to the oil states of the Gulf. Most of these people became unskilled laborers or domestics, although over time increasing numbers found their way into skilled and professional positions. Originally invited as "guest workers", these migrants came as young men but then settled and stayed. Wives and siblings followed, creating distinctive ethnic communities in the major cities of Europe, North America, and the Middle East. Temporary soon became permanent, changing the ethnic mix of the host societies.

Economic integration proved far easier than social or political assimilation, however. Although the host societies wanted migrant labor, few of them successfully confronted the problems of discrimination and racism. Moreover, most states restrict migrants' political rights, limiting or barring their participation in politics. The process of becoming a citizen varies widely from country to country; the United States and Canada set rather low hurdles, whereas Switzerland, Kuwait, and South Africa normally set quite high ones.

Because most countries grant migrants' locally born children citizenship or relatively easy access to it, the second generation has had a much more secure place than its parents. Social and cultural acceptance requires more than legal changes, however, and the ethnic mixing of populations produced by the global economy has triggered conflicts that are not easy to solve.

Even more complex than the legal issues raised by migration are cultural ones. Who is included in imagined national communities? The task of reconfiguring national identities in a global era had only begun in the 1980s.

Different Sorts of Citizens

Identities can be constructed in multiple ways, and ethnicity is only one of many dimensions. Awareness of gender, religion, race, and, in some societies, caste shapes individuals' sense of themselves. But at particular times and places, some elements of identity become politically charged and aggressively defended.

In the late twentieth century, women in many regions became more assertive of their rights. International Women's Year in 1975 helped to legitimize feminist demands for equality in developing societies and intensified discussions of women's disabilities. Campaigns for legal reforms guaranteeing women equal rights in family law and in economic status widened. Feminists in India publicized cases of bride burning, and African women argued against genital mutilation of females.

Discussion of what cultural, social, and political norms were appropriate for women gained in intensity after the Islamic revolution in Iran in 1979 ordered females to veil themselves once more. Islamic states made different decisions on questions of women's rights; in some states women could drive, could go to school, and could take jobs outside the household. In others, such activities were regulated or not permitted.

In South Asia, caste and religious divisions continued to shape identity politics and trigger conflict. During the 1980s, parties in both Sri Lanka and India used religion and ethnicity to mobilize voters, subverting the idea of national unity. Militant Hindus organized against Muslim privileges. Dalits, long stigmatized in India as untouchables, demanded and received increased preferential treatment.

In other parts of the world, too, awareness of difference has bred fierce antagonisms. Lebanon erupted into civil war after 1975, pitting Christians against Muslims, each with complex sets of allies. In Sudan, fighting between the armies of the Christian north and the animist south continued. In both of these countries, group identities far outweigh national loyalties.

Racial identity dominated South African politics and society through the 1980s, with rights of residence and political participation defined on the basis of racial categories. Despite years of federal enforcement of civil rights laws and anti-discrimination legislation, racial identities continued to shape social behavior in the United States and Britain. In the United States, dozens of ethnic groups coexist more or less peacefully, but the press and the U.S. Commission on Civil Rights regularly bring local racial conflicts and inequities into the spotlight. Even where strong legal protections are in force, racial discrimination still can undermine social practice. In the 1980s nationalism could not cover over multiple fissures in the social body.

CONCLUSION

When communism collapsed in Eastern Europe and the Soviet Union, it not only ended the Cold War but also brought immediate economic and political changes. The command economy died along with one-party rule, posing the problem of what to put in its place. Struggles for power convulsed Eastern Europe and western Asia, newly released from the Soviet Empire. In many parts of the world, the retreat from communism gave demands for democracy new energy. In Latin America and Africa, military rulers handed over power to elected leaders, and opposition parties began to function relatively freely. Restraints on civil society lessened. The political realignments of the 1980s and early 1990s in Europe, Africa, and the Americas gave many groups more political space to define their identities and their aims. The results were chaotic as well as exciting.

During the 1980s, the world's economic system became increasingly multi-centered as globalization continued. Poorer countries in the Middle East, Africa, and Latin America organized regionally to protect themselves somewhat from the pressure of global markets. This strategy has so far had limited results. Poverty has remained a central social problem in much of the world. Moreover, desires for an improved environment and better health care have mounted, as has resistance to change on the part of particular countries and interest groups. In a world where TV and films translate global inequalities into graphic images, many people have chosen to migrate to areas where they will have better access to resources. Why stay at home and starve when jobs and wealth might be found in a distant city? Growing ethnic diversity and consciousness has resulted.

In many countries, demands for democracy have been hard to translate into stable political institutions. Moreover, the growing layer of international organizations complicates issues of responsibility and control. A continued clash of individual, national, and international interests presents politicians and citizens with difficult choices. Under what circumstances should international organizations or coalitions of states be able to violate national sovereignty and national borders?

In a world where the UN depends on its member countries for money and soldiers, the issue of just how to enforce international opinion is an open question. How can the authority of the UN be balanced against that of the United States or of regional organizations? During the 1990s, it would prove difficult to maintain peace within a multicentered world in which many states have invested in nuclear weapons and advanced military technologies. The end of the Cold War substituted one set of political problems for another.

For Further Reading

Leslie Bethell, ed., *Cuba: A Short History* (Cambridge: Cambridge University Press, 1993). Political and economic change in Cuba during the modern period.

Paul R. Brass, *The Politics of India Since Independence*, vol. 4, pt. 1 of *New Cambridge History of India* (Cambridge: Cambridge University Press, 1990). Analysis of the Congress Party and other Indian political movements after 1947.

Alexander Dallin and Gail W. Lapidus, eds., *The Soviet System: From Crisis to Collapse*, rev. ed. (Boulder, Colo.: Westview Press, 1995). Analysis of events in Russia during the 1980s and 1990s.

Thomas A. Friedman, *The World Is Flat* (New York: Penguin, 2006). A leading advocate of globalization, Friedman examines ways in which technology and markets have helped to diminish international differences.

Han Minzhu, ed., *Cries for Democracy: Writings and Speeches from the 1989 Chinese Democracy Movement* (Princeton, N.J.: Princeton University Press, 1990). Statements by dissidents in China in 1989 explaining their aims and hopes for political change.

Mark Mazower, *Dark Continent: Europe's Twentieth Century* (New York: Knopf, 1999). Discussion of European politics in the last century, linking the themes of war, instability, and democratic transformation.

Panikos Panayi, *An Ethnic History of Europe Since 1945: Nations, States, and Minorities* (Harlow, England: Longman, 2000). Discussion of the complexities of ethnicity and its links to nationalism since World War II.

Saskia Sassen, *The Global City: New York, London, Tokyo* (Princeton, N.J.: Princeton University Press, 1991). Analysis of the ways in which global cities direct the world economy and the consequences for residents of New York, London, and Tokyo.

Ron Gregor Suny, *The Revenge of the Past: Nationalism, Revolution, and the Collapse of the Soviet Union* (Stanford, Calif.: Stanford University Press, 1999). The importance of ethnicity in the Soviet Union and its contribution to the disintegration of the Soviet Empire.

Peter Winn, *Americas: The Changing Face of Latin America and the Caribbean* (Berkeley: University of California Press, 1992). History of Latin America and the Caribbean Islands in recent decades.

John A. Wiseman, *The New Struggle for Democracy in Africa* (Aldershot, UK: Avebury, 1996). Discussion of recent African politics and attempts to replace one-party rule with democratic regimes.

Related Websites

Documents of the Cold War
    http://www.mtholyoke.edu/acad/intrel/coldwar.htm
The European Union
    http://europa.eu/abc/history/index_en.htm
Indira Gandhi's assassination
    http://news.bbc.co.uk/onthisday/hi/dates/stories/october/31/newsid_2464000/
    2464423.stm
African National Congress in South Africa
    http://www.anc.org.za/

CHAPTER 15

Global Society in the New Millennium

T he meeting at the United Nations in 2003 was the most momentous since October 25, 1962, when American Ambassador Adlai E. Stevenson confronted USSR Ambassador Valerian Zorin publicly over the evidence of newly-emplaced Soviet missiles in Cuba. Now, on February 5, 2003, U.S. Secretary of State Colin Powell was before the UN claiming evidence of newly-emplaced weapons in Iraq. "The gravity of this moment is matched by the gravity of the threat that Iraq's weapons of mass destruction pose to the world," Powell intoned. The threat ranged from nearly completed nuclear bombs to anthrax. Powell held up before the assembly and the worldwide television audience, a small vial of white powder, which he said corresponded to the amount of anthrax that had shut down the U.S. Senate during the terrorist attacks of September 2001. Yet, he added, the amount of anthrax Iraq was suspected to possess amounts to many thousand times the volume of the small vial displayed.

Powell's presentation was intended to gain widespread international support for a U.S. invasion of Iraq to disarm the nation's dictator, Saddam Hussein. The effect was not as intended. Soon after Powell's presentation, and for months and years afterward, international journalists, security analysts, and academics disputed and eventually disproved all of Powell's allegations. The United States invaded Iraq without UN support on March 20, 2003, but no weapons of mass destruction were ever found.

The invasion's effects remains a profound turning point in global political dynamics. After the invasion of Iraq and reduction of its society to chaos, radical Islamic movements accelerated in some parts of the Middle East and Asia. Leftist candidates opposed by the United States such as Hugo Chavez in Venezuela and

Evo Morales in Bolivia enjoyed electoral success. Perhaps most significant for the second decade of the twenty-first century, the expense of wars in Iraq and Afghanistan, in combination with military actions in Pakistan and Libya, became part of a mounting U.S. deficit that produced a downward spiral of economic recession that came to affect Europe and Asia deeply. Global military spending would rise by nearly 50 percent between 2001 and 2011, with half of that spent by the United States alone. Global public debt, which had increased at a steady rate of roughly a trillion dollars a year in the late twentieth century, was sharply affected by the U.S. dive into major war expenditures in 2003, after which global debt began to accumulate at a rate of about 3 trillion dollars a year; in 2011 it reached about 43 trillion dollars, of which about a quarter belonged to the United States. By 2011, these dynamics had joined with debt crises in Europe and in Japan, as well as slowed markets for goods from exporting countries such as China and the Philippines, to create a global economic crisis. The effects were economic constriction in the developed countries, and lost opportunities for growth in developing countries.

Two Worlds on One Earth

In the industrialized areas of North America, Europe, Australia, and parts of Latin America and East Asia, the condition of human life changed dramatically during the twentieth century. At the beginning of the century, the industrialized world was connected by telegraph wires, rudimentary telephones, and steamboats and steam engines. By the end of the century, diesel engines, the automobile, electric trains and trolleys, jetliners, digital communications, and space shuttles had transformed this world. Public sanitation and water management was already well developed by 1900 and continued to be refined. Fertilizers, insecticides, and mechanized farming produced surpluses of varied, nutritious foods.

In the industrialized world, epidemic disease had been vanquished before a third of the twentieth century had passed. Great advances had been made in ameliorating common heart diseases and in curing or controlling some cancers. By the end of the century, the entire human genome had been mapped, opening the possibilities of technological intervention to end certain genetic defects or to use genetic material to cure disease. Industrialization had reached a point—particularly in North America and Europe—where workers enjoyed unprecedented productivity, safety, and convenience, with lower working hours, high wages, and retirement benefits. Housing was sufficient and safe. In this world, there had been an information revolution. Computers, high-speed phone lines, and wireless and satellite communications permitted all but the poorest inhabitants to have constant access to news, educational information, personal contacts, and entertainment. Most important, this world continued to generate capital for further investment and for research and development. Its plentiful educational institutions assured continuing dissemination of new knowledge and continued application of new technologies.

But a large portion of people sharing the earth did not live in this world. They lived in a world in which human and animal labor were still the basis of agriculture, and electricity and motor vehicles were unusual or unreliable. In their world water supplies were contaminated by bacteria, and sanitation systems were rare or poorly managed. The same infectious diseases that had been all but banished from the industrialized world still killed a majority of humans in this other world in the same way and at the same rate as they had done centuries before.

Agriculture in much of this world was inefficient or uncertain, particularly in times of drought. Telephones were available, but not on a universal, personal basis as in the industrialized world. Entertainment was limited to broadcast television or the occasional cinema. When wage work was available, the pay was very low and the hours were unregulated. A majority of children between the ages of five and fourteen were working for money needed for their or their family's survival. There were few—sometimes no—laws requiring safe working conditions or safe construction of houses. When earthquakes, floods, or fires occurred, casualties were ten or twenty times higher than they would have been if houses had been built to withstand catastrophe. And this was a world without capital. In times of famine there was relief from international agencies, and sporadically there was foreign aid for agriculture or education. But most often the gift that came from the industrialized world was a modern rifle or antiaircraft weapon, given in the interests of the giver.

Class Stratification in the Global Society

Historically, societies have handled questions of class inequality in different ways. Successful societies have mitigated the ability of elites to prey upon and eventually destroy weaker or poorer majorities. They have also maximized access to greater rewards for all in the society, so that the most talented and most creative will be able to make timely contributions to shared problems or opportunities. The least successful societies have permitted those who were born at the top to retain their privileges through contrived barriers to competition or ruthless exploitation of the majority. How the global society will behave in the twenty-first century is unclear. It might appear that the international organizations that are promoting global economic stability and limiting environmental deterioration would produce a generalized improvement of life in all regions, whether they are rich or poor, powerful or weak. But in the twentieth century, gross disparities in well-being between societies, nations, and regions grew sharper after the middle 1970s, and the gap continues to widen in the twenty-first century.

Mapping Disparities

In 1980 the Brandt Report, sponsored by the World Bank, underscored a strong global division between the North (North America, Europe, and industrializing Asia) and the South (Central and Latin America, equatorial and sub-Saharan

Riot police in Athens, Greece, confront protestors massed on the steps of Parliament in June 2011. Widespread, prolonged riots across Greece protested demands from the International Monetary Fund and the influential nations among the European Union—primarily Germany and France—that Greek social programs for health, education, and support of the unemployed be gutted. The debts of Greece are mostly foreign-owned, and some have been commoditized by international firms. The EU and the IMF continue to work to avoid a Greek default, partly by demanding further cuts in Greek social programs.

Africa, and Southeast Asia). The North was agriculturally productive, technologically advanced, and healthy, with good literacy rates. The South often struggled to eat, had few modern conveniences, suffered from epidemic disease, and had low literacy. Brandt quantified the difference in a way that is now famous: One-fourth of the world's population lives in the North, but they have four-fifths of the world's income.

In a general way, the North/South dichotomy still exists (if one excludes Afghanistan and Bangladesh from the North and Australia from the South). But it is probably more practical to realize that there are a small minority of the global population who not only control most of the world's income and investment but also have a standard of living that is centuries apart from that of some other people. Most important, this stratum of the global society does not necessarily follow the contours of nation-states. In most of the wealthiest nations there are pockets of poverty where the standards of living are not greatly different from those in the majority of the world's poor countries, just as in some generally poor societies there are pockets of great wealth. The real issues are the factors that control quality of life, length of life, access to education, leisure, and support in old age. As a general rule (though there are exceptions), wealthier societies do better at providing higher levels and more widespread availability of these benefits. For this reason, the distribution of wealth in the world is important to understand as a background to understanding other disparities.

Defining Wealth and Poverty

The World Bank has established an international poverty line. This is based on Purchasing Power Parity (PPP), which means that instead of translating income into an absolute currency unit (such as U.S. dollars), the income is weighed against local prices and rates of inflation. An individual is poor, in the World Bank's view, when his or her annual income could buy less than what about $500 could buy in the United States at present. Since prices tend to be low in the developing countries, this is calculated as being about $456.25 a year, or $1.25 a day. The percentage of the present global population that falls below that annual income line has been falling since 1990, primarily because of the economic development of China, Indonesia and the Philippines. But it is still about one-fifth, or about 1.4 billion of the world's 7 billion people. In case this standard should be considered too conservative, the World Bank also calculated a more generous poverty standard, in which PPP was about $650. Redrawing the line, slightly under half of all living people fell below it. The corresponding average for all nations considered to be in the upper income ranks (thirty-three nations plus Hong Kong in the World Bank's study) is $26,000. This means that the total income of the world's poorest one-fifth is equal to 0.33 percent of the total income of the top fifth. Overall, about one-seventh of the people on earth receive 80 percent of its income, with a middle group sharing the remaining 20 percent, and the poorest one-fifth having essentially no income at all.

Accumulated wealth is a different issue from income: Wealthy people are able to save and invest money, whereas poor people must spend all or most of their income to survive. In 2000 the United Nations collected its first comprehensive data on world wealth accumulation, and when the results were released in 2006 they produced shock. The top 10 percent of the world's adults controlled 85 percent of its wealth, and the top 1 percent alone controlled 40 percent of the wealth. In contrast, the poorest half of the world's adult population controlled only 1 percent of its wealth. The greatest collection of wealthy individuals was in the United States, where accumulated wealth averaged $181,000. In India the average wealth accumulation per adult was $1,100, and in most of Asia and Africa adults owned nothing at all.

There is a loose correlation between national wealth averages and the number of spectacularly wealthy individuals in any given society. There are about seven billion people on the earth, of whom a thousand are worth more than one billion dollars. Half live in the United States and Canada, while the rest are divided between Europe and Eastern Asia. Individuals worth more than $50 million number about 80,000 worldwide, and there are about 24 million people whose wealth amounts to between one million and 15 million dollars. About 330 million have a net worth of between $100,000 and one million dollars. This means, globally, about 360 million people on the earth have wealth of more than $100,000. At the other end, three billion people have accumulated wealth of less than $10,000 each; of those, 1.1 billion have less than $1000 of accumulated wealth. But these figures do not precisely describe levels of well-being within national societies. India, for instance, has 170,000 individuals with wealth between one million and fifty millions dollars, but it also has 307 million people who have accumulated wealth of less than $1000. The United States, which has the highest number of billionaires, today is far outranked in average adult wealth by Switzerland, Norway, Australia and Singapore. The figures suggest that societies like India and the United States are marked by extreme disparities in the distribution of wealth.

Is the gap—globally and within societies—in income between the wealthiest and the poorest becoming worse or better? This is difficult for historians to reconstruct, but studies suggest that over the course of the last two hundred years, the trend has been in one direction only. In 1820 the global income ratio between the richest fifth and the poorest fifth was estimated at 3 to 1. In 1870 (that is, after the initial industrialization of Western Europe and the United States) it had risen to 7 to 1. In 1913, before the disintegration of the European empires, it was 11 to 1. In 1960, after the United States, Europe, and Japan had largely recovered from World War II, it was 30 to 1. In 1990, it was 60 to 1; in 2000 it was 75 to 1. These figures relating to imbalances in income can be considered in light of the following regarding the human condition of the majority: Of the 7 billion people on earth, 3 billion do not have modern sanitation facilities. About 2 billion do not have access to electricity in their homes. About 1 billion have unsafe drinking water and inadequate housing. Slightly under 900 million have no medical care, and slightly under 800 million are chronically malnourished.

Attempts at Global Coordination

From the 1990s, "globalization" as a way of describing unprecedented fluidity in the movement of people, money, and ideas around the globe has become a cliché. The origins of globalization lay in the institutions of finance and economic development put in place as the Second World War came to a close. The programs not only made capital and expertise available to nations emerging from the ravages of war or imperialism, but also established rules that allowed failing nations to be disciplined by an international consortium. Over time, these institutions led to the redistribution of capital and the lowering of barriers to trade. The late twentieth century experienced significant economic stimulation from theses changes, but in the twenty-first century another side of the changes is being experienced: Economic crises in one society can be quickly transmitted around the world, while competition for markets and profits tends to drive living standards in the direction of huge, poor majority.

The Militarized United Nations and Unpopular Dictators

Since its declaration in favor of universal human rights in 1948, the United Nations has maintained a policy of humanitarian intervention, which has consisted primarily of the movement of food and medicines into areas of crisis, and help in the care and resettlement of refugees. Apart from a small security force, however, the United Nations did not maintain troops in its early phase. Certain international military interventions, such as that in Korea during 1950 through 1953, could take place under the temporary aegis of the United Nations. Such an arrangement was invoked after the leader of Iraq, Saddam Hussein, decided to invade and occupy the neighboring kingdom of Kuwait in 1990 (see Chapter 14). The United Nations officially approved of a military coalition to drive the Iraqi army out of Kuwait. The United States took the lead role, and the U.S. Congress made its own declaration of war against Iraq. Nevertheless, the Persian Gulf War was technically a war of the United Nations allies against Iraq.

Soon after the conclusion of the war in September 1991, a similar coalition attempted to resolve the ongoing civil war in Somalia to prevent millions from starving. This operation was not a success, and U.S. President William Jefferson Clinton withdrew U.S. forces in 1993. But secretary-general of the United Nations Boutros Boutros-Ghali made the extension of humanitarian intervention to military action official United Nations policy in 1992. Soon after, a conflict of international proportions broke out in the territories of the former Yugoslavia. In 1991 the state had in practice disintegrated, and the leader of Serbia, Slobodan Milosevic, attempted to bring all regions of the former Yugoslavia under Serb domination. The UN forwarded a very limited military intervention which depended on cooperation with Serbian forces to restore the peace. For three years Bosnia and neighboring regions were ravaged by the fighting, until political leaders of the factions agreed to a peace settlement in 1995 that awarded generous portions of Bosnia to the Serbian forces. When the same general conflict spread to Kosovo a few years later, the UN tried air strikes to force Milosevic to withdraw his forces. When this did not succeed, the UN committed a substantial troop presence, but negotiations concluded in 1999 with most Muslims and Albanians driven from Kosovo, as Milosevic had intended.

UN military forces were mobilized again in 1999 to intervene in the worsening situation in East Timor. In 1975 East Timor had declared independence from Indonesia. The UN endorsed independence, but the United States repudiated it, wary that a communist government might be established. With U.S. endorsement, the Indonesian govern invaded East Timor and crushed the independence movement. Under subsequent Indonesian rule, state terror and corruption were common. In 1999 the armed UN oversaw a referendum among the East Timorese who voted for independence. Thereafter the UN governed East Timor as it made the transition to "special autonomy" within Indonesia.

Subsequently a vote among the East Timorese again confirmed the popular preference for independence, and in May 2002 East Timor became the world's newest—and instantly its poorest—nation. It was also the first nation in history to gain its independence from the United Nations rather than from an empire or former occupying nation-state.

The two experiments with armed intervention by the UN had conflicting results. Serbian aggression under Milosevic produced most of the results he desired—"ethnic cleansing," or the removal of non-Serb populations from central Yugoslavian lands—and a great deal of death and destruction before the combined military and political interventions of the UN stopped the fighting. On the other hand, Milosevic himself did not prosper. In 2000, he was voted out of the presidency and was extradited by the UN for trial at the international criminal court in The Hague, in the Netherlands. He died in custody in 2006 before his trial for war crimes and genocide could conclude. In East Timor, however, refugees who fled the fighting before UN intervention have returned and there is no fighting. The country remains dependent on Australia for its economic and industrial development, particularly management of its underwater oil reserves.

The end of meaningful UN militarization came in March 2003, when U.S. President George W. Bush led a campaign—not endorsed by the UN and steadfastly opposed by key members of the Security Council—to destroy the government of Saddam Hussein. Though the United States acted in conscious disregard of the United Nations, the administration of President Bush was careful to construct an ostensible coalition that included Britain and Australia and many more symbolic partners as fellow combatants, and to repeatedly declare that Iraq was being punished for its refusal to disarm as it had been instructed to do by the United Nations. Thus even a national action that seemed to represent an assertive unilateralism was necessarily represented as a coalition on behalf of the United Nations. The result was that the UN and its military forces became metaphorical rather than real.

The absence of UN military intervention and discrediting of unilateral U.S. action in the guise of an international coalition makes the twenty-first century markedly different from the twentieth century when it comes to unpopular dictators after Milosevic and Hussein. In the summer of 2011, popular protests against political corruption, heavy police control and economic stagnation across North Africa and the Middle East led to the downfall of the governments of Tunisia and Egypt. The Egyptian case was particularly dramatic. Hosni Mubarak, who had assumed the presidency of Egypt in 1981, was regarded internationally as a heir to Nasser's legacy of secular government. He maintained peace with Israel and was generally a supporter of the policies of the United States and the United Kingdom. But at home, he was regarded as a corrupt supporter of international corporations, indifferent to Egypt's high unemployment rates, and reliant on military repression. Less than a month after protests against Mubarak broke out in early 2011, leaders of the military forced him from office. He was later tried individually for economic crimes such as shutting down the Internet, and he and his sons were tried together for murder of protesters in Cairo.

The pattern of the Mubarak overthrow was distinctly different from the pattern of the late twentieth century. Neither the United Nations nor the United States intervened either to stop the public mayhem or to effect "regime change" in the style of Iraq. And though he had been a supporter of U.S. policy, Mubarak was not offered safe exile by the United States, as in the case of the Shah of Iran in 1979. Instead, the public contest between Mubarak and his public ran its own course, and Mubarak was left to suffer whatever fate the new military government decided to impose upon him. The change in dynamics was not unnoted by government leaders such as Muammar Gaddafi (who was killed by victorious rebels in October, 2011) in in Libya or Bashir Assad in Syria, both of whom prosecuted prolonged civil war against their domestic opponents—some of whom are Muslim radicals—in the absence of UN or U.S. intervention.

The IMF, the World Bank, and the Costs of Discipline

In the latter twentieth century, the United States, Britain, France and Germany were acutely aware of the need for economic development in nations who could not float a domestic debt big enough to address their needs, and could not be considered good credit risks by other nations. This was the origin of the International Monetary Fund (IMF) and the World Bank, both chartered in 1944 (see Chapter 9). The primary purpose of the IMF is to certify nations as worthy borrowers. After loans are granted, the IMF provides oversight—or "surveillance" as it is officially called—of the ways in which borrowers manage the exchange rates of their currencies and their balance of payments. It attempts to keep currency values orderly, and to prevent lenders from suffering catastrophic losses if a borrowing nation should collapse. During the first decade of the twenty-first century, IMF loans—mostly to nations in Africa, Latin America, and Eastern Europe—dropped to a low of $28 billion in 2006, but in 2011 the amount committed to loans is roughly $280 billion, and the largest debtors are, for the first time in decades, Western European—Greece, Portugal, and Ireland.

In the 1960s and 1970s the World Bank became an important participant in financing plans for agricultural development in Asia and Africa. The funds made available, particularly by the United States, increased sharply, and in 1979 they rose above $10 billion for the first time. This coincided with the energy crisis of the 1970s, in which many poorer countries that did not produce oil were squeezed by extraordinary energy costs. By the middle 1980s, the World Bank had become a major consideration in the politics and policies of many nations. The leading investors in the bank—the United States, Britain, France, West Germany, and Japan—were concerned that many debtor nations were not managing their economies wisely, and as a consequence would default on their loans. Through IMF surveillance and direct pressure from the World Bank, debtors were pressured to discipline their economies to raise their credit ratings. Measures for discipline were called Special Adjustment Programs (SAPs), and they usually featured devaluation of the currency to make the country's products attractive abroad and increase the repayment time of domestic loans; raising interest rates to decrease domestic indebtedness and encourage savings; trimming social programs for health, housing, and education or making them private enterprises; cutting back on environmental protections that tend to raise the cost of resources or restrict access; and financing industry as the first priority of the government.

All nations undergoing SAPs have suffered some discomfort, whether from damage to the environment, the effects of devaluation on savings for education or retirement, or sharply increasing private costs of education and health care. In some cases, these discomforts have been absorbed without widespread suffering and without destroying existing national governments. In other cases the effects of IMF and World Bank interference have been catastrophic and even deadly. Ecuador, for instance, was a promising economy in the late 1970s because of its oil. But officials of Ecuador's oil companies mismanaged and misappropriated the income from the oil industries. The IMF required that the Ecuadorian public assume responsibility for the international loans upon which the oil executives had defaulted. Ecuador was forced to lay off hundreds of thousands of workers and to nearly double oil prices. At the end of the twentieth century, Ecuador had regained neither economic prosperity nor political stability. In a similar case, loans provided to Tanzania in 1985 by a consortium of international lenders were conditional on an IMF program demanding open trade, lower wages, and extreme cuts in health care and public sanitation. By the end of the twentieth century, Tanzania's per capita income had dropped by a third, and the country had shot to the top of the list of countries facing massive deaths (in Tanzania's case, over 1.5 million) from AIDS.

In 2000 Argentina was required by the IMF to institute an SAP after it defaulted on debt payments. Like Ecuador, the Argentine government was required to pay off debts contracted by business executives. The Argentine government agreed to cut its budget deficit by 20 percent in a single year, and the same percentage cuts were made in government assistance programs to the unemployed (whose numbers were ballooning under the new austerity program). When the public lost confidence in the economy and tried to withdraw money from the banking system, the Argentinean government imposed strict rules on withdrawals that left large numbers of citizens with no cash and companies unable to meet payrolls. The country experienced its worst rioting since a political crisis of 1989. There were repeated turnovers in the government leadership through the spring of 2002, when Argentina defaulted again on its international debts. From 2003 on, the Argentine economy has been improved by domestic development programs and devaluation of its currency, and has experienced a high rate of growth. But the economy has little depth to weather international crises, and in 2009 its growth rate fell to 0.8 percent.

Recent history suggests that the discipline imposed by the international system can be helpful in getting some nations out of destructive patterns of corruption, unsecured debt, and lavish government spending. Examples such as Poland in the middle 1980s and South Korea in the early 1990s show that countries that become unable to secure foreign credit because of their internal policies can, under international pressure, redeem themselves with strong policies and again become participants in the global system. But some nations cannot respond successfully to the pressures of that system. Many economists doubt the long-term wisdom of permanently destroying the economic viability of a large segment— perhaps ultimately a majority—of the world's population. More important, the specter of loan default has shifted from Asia, Africa and Latin America to Europe and North America, raising new pressure for changes in the international finance discipline that has prevailed since the Second World War.

Free Trade: Globalization Arrives

Like the IMF and the World Bank, the General Agreement on Tariffs and Trade (GATT) was created after the Second World War to ensure that no nation would attempt to protect its economy by erecting trade barriers. Instead, the majority of global trade was to be conducted in accordance with the principles of open markets and free competition. The aims of GATT were controversial in the 1960s and 1970s when nationalist sentiments were strong and many developing nations were attempting to protect their young industries from foreign competition by restricting or heavily taxing foreign imports. It was not until the 1990s that GATT experienced a sharp increase in its visibility and influence. This was partly due to the establishment of GATT-like free-trade zones in Europe (the European Economic Community, subsequently the European Union) and in North America (NAFTA). In those instances, the GATT principle of open markets was considered likely to enhance prosperity globally. Both the EU and the NAFTA signatories had used GATT rules to force Japan to open its markets to foreign products. At the same time, the collapse of the Soviet Union in 1991 and the decrease of centralized economic planning during the early 1990s in China created more venues for GATT policy and increased the number of aspiring GATT members.

In 1995, the World Trade Organization (WTO) was created to ratify and enforce the GATT regulations. In 2001, China was admitted as a member. In theory, this means that China's markets will now be open to foreign goods and that foreign investment will not be subject to special rules. According to the regulations, wages, housing prices, and the value of Chinese currency should be determined by global factors, not by government policy. In fact, China has artificially kept the value of its currency low, enhancing its exports.

The WTO has the power to enforce the rules and to punish nations that do not conform to specific instructions. It runs a system of closed courts—tribunals—in which member governments can sue other members for breaking the rules. Defendants who lose their cases must either change their laws as the WTO requires or reimburse the plaintiff for the amount determined by the court. Two-thirds of cases are settled by negotiation. Nations that refuse to comply can have trade restrictions imposed upon them by the WTO or can be expelled from the organization. The WTO courts are busy (they normally have more than 300 cases pending at any particular time), and they require a bureaucracy of administrators, lawyers, judges, economic monitors and advisors.

The combined effects of the IMF, the World Bank, and the WTO on the global economy are critical. At the end of the Second World War, the average tariff levied on imports into Europe or the United States was 40 percent. By 1990 it had fallen to 6.3 percent. During the 1990s it again fell dramatically, to less than 4 percent, which partly explains the burst of international trade and development in the last decade of the twentieth century. Overall, low-tariff policies promote worldwide access to goods that many societies otherwise either could not acquire or could not afford.

Effects of Globalized Trade and Finance

In the twenty-first century many nations, including the United States and China, are again using import tariffs on selected goods to protect home industries as a method of dealing with unprecedented long-term economic crisis. This is only one aspect of the global management system that is being altered in response to new conditions, in which the world's leading economic powers experience problems that in the late twentieth century were limited to developing nations.

The Specter of Competition: Wages, Specialization, and Advertising

In areas where wages are comparatively high, as in the United States, Canada, Europe, Australia, and Japan, the cost of goods can be high. In such circumstances, foreign products that compete with domestic products may be much cheaper because the workers producing them have lower wages. Before the 1980s, governments tended to offset this advantage of foreign goods by imposing a high tariff on imports. This kept domestic products competitive and wages high, but protectionism was strictly outlawed after creation of the WTO in 1995.

Now, domestic and foreign goods must compete in the same markets. If domestic companies produce goods efficiently enough to compete with foreign goods made by low-wage workers, then the domestic wages must fall or the goods must be manufactured in another country where wages are lower. For the developed nations during the 1990s, this meant a tendency to specialize. Goods that could be made or grown cheaply elsewhere—many electronic products, clothing, certain fruits and vegetables—either were not produced domestically or were produced only in small quantities. Instead, the economies of Europe, North America, and Japan focused on the development of high-cost essential goods, which still permitted paying high wages to the workers who made them. Automobiles and aircraft, military weapons, computers and surveillance systems, pharmaceuticals, and high-end medical equipment were produced almost exclusively in the most developed countries. As the twenty-first century began, however, China was transforming this system, as it grew from a supplier of low-wage labor for basic goods to a producer of high-end weaponry, computers, and ultimately automobiles, bringing a new dimension of competition to the most developed nations and undermining the last haven of high wages in the developed countries.

Many of the industries of the developed nations reserved huge portions of their operating budgets—often more than 50 percent—for advertising to the population at large, lobbying for government contracts, and making special appeals to target audiences rather than relying on low prices to make their products competitive. This was particularly true of firms providing medicines, weapons and security. In other cases, companies—particularly selling computer software—learned to control the terms of development and marketing so completely that prices could be virtually dictated by the seller. Instead of using the market attraction of quality goods at low prices, these companies used the cultural attraction of modern media and the economic ploys of limited competition to maintain their profits. This helped them survive in the ecology of international trade where tariff barriers to the exchange of goods were no longer permitted. But it also meant that in order to spread the appeal of their products, they had to spread the culture that supports them, so that cultural or religious conflict often became inseparable from other aspects of global competition. As the twenty-first century develops, the efficacy of these strategies is waning, and the question of products whose quality and reliability can transcend cultural assumptions must be confronted.

Globalized Debt

Debt is a normal part of global financial life and of national economic management. Wars, expanded agricultural or commercial sectors, and systematic modernization of industry or education have normally been the cause of governments going into debt. Historically, governments in need of money turned to the banking system, where private investors had accumulated capital that could be loaned to the government at profitable rates. But in the twentieth century, some of these patterns changed. The Great Depression of the 1930s, particularly, changed the historical relationship between government and banks. In that period, it was the banks that were in need of help, as the stock market and credit market crashes left them with sudden obligations and little cash. Beginning in that era, the governments of the United States, the United Kingdom, and France became the guarantors of the banks, and to avoid future troubles banks were carefully regulated regarding the proportion of their assets they could extend in loans, the conditions under which loans were made, and the speed with which interest rates could rise or fall.

Governments could function as rescuers of the banks, if necessary, because they could float their own debt—"sovereign" or government debt—to their own publics, in the form of bonds. Proceeds from the maturation of the bonds would go back to the public, stimulating the economy. If the government should have difficulty making its payments on time, it had the power to print money to cover the shortfall. This would lower the value of the nation's currency, lower the prices on its goods, and increase its exports. The result would be inflation. But, if not prolonged, inflation might do no permanent harm. To attract investment, the government might raise interest rates on its bonds, which would in turn raise interest rates on other loans. In the short run this, too, would have no serious effect. But if prolonged it would strangle credit, though lessening the burden on debtors (including the government). Inflation and rising interest rates would ultimately transfer equity from the creditors who bought bonds to the government itself, restoring the balance and allowing the government to continue to guarantee the stability of the banking systems.

These patterns pertained through most of the twentieth century, and became valuable tools in the 1970s, when the industrialized economies were staggered by a sudden rise in oil prices (see Chapter 13) and an inflationary spiral that impeded growth in Japan, Europe and the United States. After resolution of this extended stagnation, many banks and governments began, in the 1980s, to reassess the relationship between governments and banks. In this era of early globalization the notion of sovereign debt management struck many as obsolete. The former pattern of governments regulating banks while guaranteeing their solvency was based upon a premise that a loan was a closed system. The money was loaned to one party by another, and the debtor was expected to pay it back to the lender. But, it was argued by some economists, it should be possible to redistribute the dangers of lending by allowing the original lender to sell his asset to one or more parties. If the credit was thus made into units and distributed, it would spread the risk among many parties and permit many parties to participate in interest profits.

In response to these arguments, the 1980s and the 1990s were an era of "deregulation" across the developed world. President Reagan in the United States, Prime Minister Thatcher in the United Kingdom, and other heads of state argued that extensive government oversight of finance and manufacturing was inefficient, costly to the public, and encouraging to a mentality of public dependence upon the state. There began a process, lasting nearly a quarter of a century, of removing regulations that had previously controlled prices, investment policies, some safety regulations, and rules for protection of the environment. The result in some industries, such as the airlines, was the emergence of new companies that competed with the older ones, driving down prices and extending the availability of the product. In other industries, particularly manufacturing, loosened rules of investment and labor management permitted the transfer of jobs to countries with lower wages, lowering the cost of goods and raising profits dramatically. Together with the lowered tariffs of the era, these produced a flood of international trade, bringing investment to developing nations such as China, India, Indonesia, Vietnam, Mexico, and Poland, while creating new opportunities for export for nearly all manufacturing nations.

In the United States, Europe, Japan and South Korea, innovations in finding new ways of floating loans and redistributing debt brought rapid profits to banks and to international investment firms. Globally debt rose, but in most countries remained in a healthy relationship to national gross product, in the range of 5 to 20 percent. At the same time, global wealth was increasing, and people in many widely separated places enjoyed an increase in their income levels. Rises in investment, and in disposable income were made possible primarily by the ready availability of credit. This ability to keep cash flowing—to keep liquidity up—was regarded as the key to having resolved the great economic crises of the 1930s and the 1970s. Credit itself, in the forms of credit cards, mortgages, and home equity loans, was one of the most rapidly expanding businesses in the world. Some nations even had their public debt managed by the international firms who specialized in commoditization of private debt. Under such conditions, the standards for making loans—the primary form of profit—gradually fell. Expectations of income, reliability, and equity investment were lowered to such a degree that many loans became unlikely to be repaid. However, agencies that were expected to assure the quality of the loan commodities were ineffective, and many unsound loans were sold at high prices to unsuspecting purchasers around the world.

Global Credit and Liquidity Crises

This worldwide debt bubble burst in 2008 when U.S. real estate—the foundation of the global debt industry—fell in value. When Barack Obama was elected president of the United States in November, he was set to inherit a unique convergence of unsecured war debt, a financial world wasted by lack of regulation, and spreading international economic troubles. In the United States, major firms that were regarded as hugely wealthy were suddenly revealed to few no meaningful assets. The loans they held directly or indirectly could not be repaid. Very large failing firms turned to their insurers for help, and many insurers who were contractually bound to aid their clients also began to fail. The impending collapse of gigantic firms of global reach threatened a worldwide loss of liquidity and cessation of investment. To avoid these consequences, the governments of the United States, Canada, the United Kingdom, France, Germany, China and Japan all extended financial aid to their banks and investment firms. An immediate global financial collapse was prevented, but most countries were left with little margin for raising capital to further stimulate their economies or rescue huge numbers of workers whose savings, including retirement funds, had evaporated in the crisis.

The majority of nations in Europe were in a special situation. The European Union had, beginning in the 1980s, begun to introduce a new currency, the euro. The original plan was that all members of the European Union—most European countries except Switzerland, Norway, Croatia, Serbia, and Iceland—would eventually give up their own currencies and use the euro. Some nations were quick to do so, while others, notably the United Kingdom, delayed, or introduced the euro as a second currency beside their sovereign currency. Because Germany is the dominant exporter in Europe (and is the third exporter in the world after China and the United States), it had the greatest influence over the euro value.

A nation's relationship to the euro turned out to be a critical factor in their options for responding to the crisis of 2008. Those nations still using a sovereign currency had the immediate option of devaluation, lessening the value of existing debts and likely increasing exports. Those nations relying on the euro had no such option, and were dependent upon the leading EU nations—Germany, the United Kingdom and France—to either devalue the currency or provide loans to allow the governments to meet their domestic obligations. In either event, the ability of any euro nation to protect its own products from German competition was severely compromised. The worst-hit nations as of 2011 were Greece, Portugal and Ireland. In the case of Greece, austerity measures imposed by the IMF and the European Union had contracted the economy by more than five percent, and debt had risen to 140 percent of annual gross domestic product (GDP). In such circumstances it is impossible for a country to keep up payments on its loans. Its creditors suffer a loss, and its citizens become subject to more deprivation as a result of foreign demands.

Under the patterns of globalization, crises cannot be contained. As the situation in Europe endangers the credit-worthiness of an increasing number of countries, the United States is caught in the combined effects of the burst real-estate bubble of 2008, government aid to failing banks and investment firms, its ongoing obligations to social support programs, and its huge spending on a series of foreign military engagements since 2001. As a result the United States cannot come to the aid of Europe, or any other failing economic zone, as it had done in the last half of the twentieth century. As of 2009, the United States for the first time entered the category of nations whose public debt is 60 percent or higher of its annual Gross Domestic Product (GDP)—although the total debt is only one quarter the total wealth of the country, and 60 percent of the debt is domestically owned. Unlike Greece, the United States has a sovereign currency which if necessary can be printed to pay any debt obligation, and thus is not in danger of default. Nevertheless, there is fear that self-imposed austerity measures in the United States could impoverish a majority of Americans and dampen global trade. China, Germany and Japan are particularly vulnerable, since their economies are export-driven, and the U.S. market is crucial to them.

The relative debt position of the United States can be illuminated somewhat by comparison. In most cases, war expenditures are a factor in worsening a national debt. But Japan, a country with minimal military expenditures, leads the world for indebtedness. The oil crisis of 1974–1977 hit Japan very hard, and for the first time since the Second World War the country assumed a significant debt to sustain social services and attempt to stimulate employment. Though Japan remained a leading exporter, its political system in the 1980s and 1990s proved unable to resolve the economic problems, due in significant part to political corruption and legislative gridlock. As debt rises, paying the ongoing interest on the debt becomes a larger and larger part of the national budget; countries which borrow to pay this interest experience a very steep rise in their indebtedness. This has happened to Japan, especially since 1995. In March of 2011 Japan also suffered the catastrophes of a tsunami and subsequently nuclear meltdown at the Fukushima nuclear facilities. This destroyed much of the productive capacity of northeast Honshu Island and incurred mountainous expenses for medical care, rehoming, and reconstruction. As of 2011–2012, the national debt was believed to have reached 170 to 225 percent of GDP, the highest ratio by far in the world. Japan leads the list of countries whose debt is more than 100 percent of GDP—the others being the Federation of Saint Kitts and Nevis, Lebanon, Zimbabwe, Greece, Iceland, Jamaica, Italy and Singapore.

Despite the global proportions of the crisis that began in 2008, most of Asia and Africa are in good shape with respect to their debt as a percentage of GDP. Russia has a reported national debt of less than 10 percent, China under 20 percent, India is under 60 percent. Yet it is easy to over-estimate the importance of debt in a country's overall economic health. Japan's huge debt has not significantly raised its interest rates on government bonds, because the debt is domestically owned. So long as the national debt is primarily domestically owned, indebtedness is not necessarily a determinant of any country's national fortunes. The Greek debt, mostly foreign-owned, has driven bond prices above 15%, and brought huge international pressure for austerity. Historically, U.S. debt was domestically owned, but in the first decade of the twentieth century a slide began toward predominant foreign ownership. Nor does debt on its own determine collective national income. Despite high indebtedness Singapore ranks in the top five of the world's countries in terms of annual income per person—the United States is number 7, Italy is 23rd, Japan is 24th. On the other hand, Libya and Uzbekistan have perhaps the lowest rates of national indebtedness, but rank 43rd and 134th respectively in terms of income per person.

Management of Energy and the Environment

Investment and debt are now distributed worldwide, but environmental features such as air and water have always been global issues. Yet global systems for the management of trade and finance are now half a century old and are fully supported by the leading industrial nations, while the emerging organizations for management of the environment are young, weak, and not fully supported by all the industrial nations. Pollution of the atmosphere, damage to the ozone layer, and global warming are the most frequently invoked new dangers. But there are related and equally alarming problems with pollution of the oceans, over-fishing, deforestation generally and destruction of the rain forests in particular, soil erosion, and depletion of aquifers. Even space pollution is recognized as a problem; eight thousand separate items of space debris were identified as orbiting aimlessly around the planet, occasionally colliding with satellites and the International Space Station.

Pollution and Global Warming

The industrialized and industrializing nations produce far more than their share of greenhouse gases that contribute to global warming, as well as damage to the ozone layer that protects the earth's surface from ultraviolet radiation. The United States alone, with 4 percent of the world's population, produces nearly a quarter of the world's greenhouse gases. With effort this percentage can be lessened, and the United States had some success with this in the late 1970s following the oil crisis. Cars became smaller and more fuel-efficient, and Americans turned their thermostats down in the winter and up in the summer. But these measures were abandoned when the price of oil fell, and the U.S. contribution as a percentage of world pollution has increased steadily since that time.

Although the United States remains the greatest producer of greenhouse gases on a per-person basis, China is the single greatest producer among nations. China is still heated largely by coal, the dirtiest of all fuels. Its automobile use is increasing. Its industries do little or nothing to decrease the amount of pollutants they release into the air or water. Health problems in China caused by mismanagement of human and industrial wastes are common. Yet the position of the Chinese government has been that antipollution measures are expensive and would be a brake on China's pace of economic development. Indeed, the Chinese government in 2006 denounced demands that China decrease its pollutants as "environmental imperialism."

In 1992 the United Nations sponsored a meeting on climate change at Rio de Janeiro, Brazil. A convention signed by 155 nations established the goal of keeping the emission of greenhouse gases at 1990 levels for ten years. Compliance was voluntary, and few nations have complied. Instead of staying at 1990 levels, emissions rose 14 percent between 1990 and 2000. The result of subsequent climate change meetings was a complex agreement designed to accommodate the specific circumstances of individual countries, to allow wealthy nations to buy the right to pollute, but to lower the global emission rate by more than 5 percent by 2012. The treaty also called for the creation of an international authority to monitor emission levels and sanction nations that were not abiding by the agreement.

The controversies of subsequent global warming summit meetings demonstrate the contradictions in current development patterns. The European Union and Japan have consistently been the foremost advocates for drastic cuts in pollution rates. Gasoline is heavily taxed by both, and nuclear power is the preferred method of generation of electricity. The European Union and Japan were joined by the Alliance of Small Island States, which includes Jamaica, Singapore, and many nations of the Indian Ocean and the Pacific and Atlantic. One effect of global warming is rising sea levels, and some of these island nations may actually disappear if global warming does not abate. Indeed, the country of Tuvalu in the Pacific was completely evacuated in late 2001 because of rising sea levels, making it the first national casualty of global warming. Since then, Tuvalu has attempted to hang on, despite the fact that rising sea levels will eventually destroy it completely.

Opposing this group were the OPEC nations (see Chapter 13), all of whom are dependent on oil export for their incomes. They were joined by the industrializing nations of China, Indonesia, Russia, and Ukraine, who argued that the cost of pollution control would cripple their economic progress. Making a similar argument, some developed nations—particularly the United States, Canada, and Australia—claimed that although they could afford the cost of pollution controls, these costs would cut disposable income in their societies by as much as 10 percent, unfairly burdening the poor, slashing their consumption of foreign goods, and dampening economic progress around the globe. In the end, the U.S. proposal that pollution rights be bought and sold (so called "cap and trade") was accepted, along with exemptions for industrializing nations.

Energy and The Atmosphere

Political problems connected to improvement of the atmosphere are aggravated by the critical importance of oil production and consumption. The United States consumes more than 25 percent of the world's petroleum but produces less than 3 percent of the world supply. China, once an exporter of oil, is now the country with the most rapidly rising demand, and will soon rival the United States and the European Union as a consumer. The economic and political hierarchies of oil production and refining are determined not only by production rates but also by the quantity of oil still left to be processed. In general, environmental scientists estimate that by about 2004 approximately half of all the oil that was originally stored in fossil reservoirs beneath the earth's surface had been used.

In such a situation, the distinction between actively producing oil for the world market and reserving it for later use is important. In 2006, Russia surpassed Saudi Arabia in oil production, more than doubling its output in the previous five years. As a result, Russia has fallen in rank as a possessor of oil reserves. By contrast, Saudi Arabia has been producing oil for nearly a hundred years but still has a claimed reserve of nearly 280 billion barrels. Experts project that Saudi Arabia could continue its present rate of production for at least a hundred years without exhausting its supply. Thus Saudi Arabia is the leading power within OPEC, and it will continue to be a critically important player in many areas of world politics despite the fact that it is not a world leader in any important index of quality of life or international military significance. But Venezuela, a relatively new producer, has a proven reserve of nearly 300 billion barrels, making it the most oil-rich country in the world. How long Venezuela will be able to keep its reserve without dissipating it through consumption or exports is unknown.

Iran, Iraq, Kuwait, Saudi Arabia, and Venezuela can expect to continue production for many decades. But the most populous members of OPEC—Nigeria, Algeria, and Indonesia—have limited reserves. As a group they will continue to produce for decades at most, and Indonesia has nearly exhausted its known reserves. For these nations, maximizing production and maximizing returns (regardless of environmental consequences) are indispensable to their continued economic development. They must also seek some alternative source of income once their oil is gone.

Of the newly emerging oil producers, Mexico—which will be the last oil source in North America—has enough known resources to produce for a significant period of time. Most important will be the area where known reserves have hardly been exploited but will be eagerly sought in the twenty-first century: the Caspian–Caucasus–Central Asian lands of Azerbaijan, Uzbekistan, Turkmenistan, and Kazakhstan. But there will be an important difference for new producers. Saudi Arabian oil, like most oil in the Persian Gulf, is relatively near the surface and has been cheap to access. Central Asian oil is relatively difficult to access and will require major international investment. As a consequence, it is not likely that the Central Asian producers will become influential as individual nations the way Saudi Arabia has. As for alternate fossil fuels, Russia is already using its huge reserve of natural gas to great profit in supplying Europe and parts of Asia. Iran and Qatar will also be powerful in any natural gas market. The United States, India, China, Australia, and South Africa, by contrast, have the world's major reserves of coal, whose use with present technology would be devastating to the world's natural environment.

Water and Disease

The health of a majority of the world's population is directly tied to access to adequate clean water. In the twentieth century, great advances were made in the control of some epidemic diseases, such as smallpox and polio. But epidemic disease remains the primary cause of death in humans because a majority of the global population still live in conditions in which universal vaccination and improvement of public hygiene are not practical due to polluted or inadequate water supplies. Controlling epidemic disease is not extraordinarily expensive or complicated, but it is nevertheless beyond the capacity of many national governments. In the developed countries, deaths from diseases such as malaria, cholera, dengue fever, yellow fever, or tuberculosis are rare—less than 1 percent of all deaths. But as many as 16.3 million people in the developing nations died of epidemic disease in 1993, and about 15 million in 2010—over 40 percent of all deaths. In the late twentieth century, three million babies born each year in the developing nations did not survive one week.

The spread of HIV/AIDS is an important element because AIDS weakens the immune system and causes a ballooning in the number of deaths from infectious diseases. As of 2006, global health authorities estimated that forty million people are infected with HIV, about 65 percent of them in sub-Saharan Africa. Unlike earlier epidemics, AIDS is not inexpensive to treat or easy to defeat. In the United States, new drugs have been developed that mitigate the damage AIDS can do to an individual's body, and scientists claim they are close to a medical cure. While this represents an advance, it has come at a tremendous cost. During the 1990s the United States spent more research money on AIDS than on any disease except cancer. Many more people in the United States are afflicted by heart disease, for instance, but the long-term threat of AIDS proliferation has given this research a high priority. A concerted effort by international drug companies and governments could allow medicines necessary to maintain the health of HIV-positive patients to fall from a cost of $1,500 a month to as little as $300 a year. The World Health Organization of the UN subsidizes the world's poorest countries in purchasing some HIV/AIDS drugs, but countries that are developing but still relatively poor do not qualify. Mexico, for instance, has an average per capita annual income of $6,790 a year and is too wealthy to receive aid, but it would cost a Mexican HIV/AIDS patient $8,000 to purchase the drugs, even under the UN subsidy rules.

AIDS is clearly most severe in countries with compromised public hygeine, and the primary causes of epidemic diseases other than AIDS are a lack of safe drinking water and inadequate facilities for human waste. As antibiotics and other drugs are introduced into those countries to combat the epidemics, resistant strains of the bacteria and viruses responsible for them evolve, presenting a danger of boomerang infections in the industrialized nations where these diseases are under control. But the major problems are water sources and water processing. Although global warming raises water levels, it does nothing to increase the amount of water available for agriculture, drinking, or bathing. Indeed, flooding has always represented a major health hazard, spreading bacteria associated with dead bodies and waste products into areas where they can immediately affect human health. When this is taken in combination with the desertification of North China and Central Africa, which is certainly due to global warming, climate change is dramatically lowering humanity's supply of water.

Supplies of fresh water can be increased or redistributed through the use of dams, canals, desalination, and above-ground reservoirs. A nation's need for water is calculated by considering its population and its reliance on agriculture. Some countries have adequate supplies of water, but fewer have adequate means of making it safe for use in irrigation, drinking, and cooking (see Maps 15.1 and 15.2). Of the regions recently surveyed by a United Nations group, only North America, Europe, Russia, Iran, Saudi Arabia, Australia, and portions of North Africa and Central Asia had both adequate supplies of water and fully adequate means of processing it for safe use. Several very populous countries, including India, China, and Mexico, had nearly adequate supplies of water but cannot make much more than half the water safe. Africa above the Sahara Desert is overwhelmed by both scarce supply and virtually no means of processing what is available for healthful use.

Global warming is a less immediate problem for industrializing countries than for countries still heavily dependent on traditional agriculture. The desertification of Eastern Africa and northern China is advancing rapidly each year, causing the movement of populations into already crowded areas where agricultural production is still possible. The current rate of global warming is estimated at 1 degree centigrade per decade. Many nations in the temperate zones of the Northern Hemisphere are experiencing a pleasant lengthening of their growing seasons, but there is also an increasing threat from diseases such as malaria that thrive in warm damp environments. Tree species that need a minimum period of dormancy in very cold winters are weakening under the warmer conditions, and roads, railway beds, and large buildings that depend on firm ground in Scandinavia and Russia are sinking as the permafrost melts. If the rate of warming continues, rising sea levels will produce major migrations and refugee problems

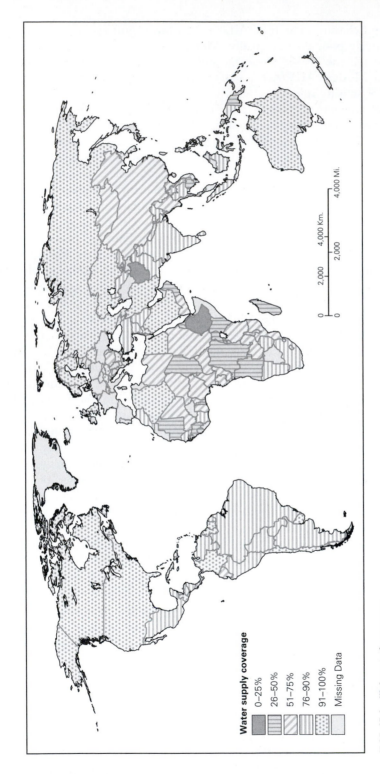

MAP 15.1 Water supply coverage.
It is to be expected that regions nearer the poles will have more plentiful water sources and those nearer the equator would have less. But recent data indicates China, Mongolia, parts of Central Asia and southern Africa, and other temperate zones are experiencing worsening water shortages due to climate change.

Water supply coverage

- 0–25%
- 26–50%
- 51–75%
- 76–90%
- 91–100%
- Missing Data

0   2,000   4,000 Km.

0   2,000   4,000 Mi.

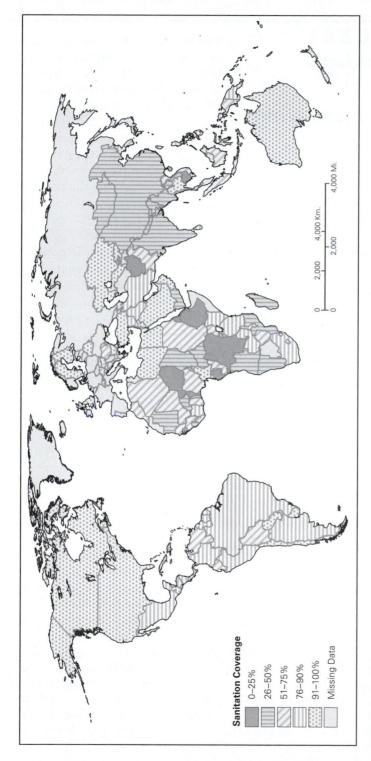

MAP 15.2 Sanitation coverage.
Environmental experts estimate that the current global population has about 80 percent of the water it needs and about 60 percent of the necessary sanitary water supplies. These maps show the differences, by national boundaries, between raw water supplies and sanitary water supplies.

Sanitation Coverage
0–25%
26–50%
51–75%
76–90%
91–100%
Missing Data

GLOBAL Technologies

Genetic Engineering

Since the beginning of genetic science in the middle nineteenth century, many have dreamed of being able to control the genes that seem to control so much of human destiny. At the end of the twentieth century, scientists were taking their first steps toward successful and practical manipulation of genes. This sometimes involves the insertion of genes (which are strings of protein in the nucleus of the cell) of one species into another, sometimes the deletion of genes, and sometimes advising humans to be aware that they carry genes that could be harmful to their offspring.

So far, humans have benefited in various ways from these projects.

The earliest and perhaps widest applications involved the manipulation of some crops to introduce genes to make the plants resistant to disease. In the United States, the use of genetically altered strains of corn, soybean, and cotton has been enthusiastically adopted. The United States accounts for far more than half of the world's production of genetically manipulated, or GM, crops. Argentina is a distant second. Even though the benefits of healthy plants without the use of pesticides is attractive, many fear that such procedures can introduce unknown variables that may threaten the health of neighboring crops or humans who eat them. At the very least, the prospect of scientifically altered plants suggests that in future large corporations may attempt to patent and monopolize basic crops.

Similar techniques have been used to produce healthier meat.

in Asia, as it already has in Africa. The waters of the Ganges and the Mekong, for instance, could rise by as much as a meter by 2020, driving away millions of inhabitants. On the other hand, some experts estimate that China's Yellow River could run dry in the middle twenty-first century without dramatic intervention by the Chinese government.

It is tempting to assume that prolonged, devastating famine may be a result of global warming and poor water resources. History shows that famines are not natural disasters, but are caused by a failure of governments to respond to changing environmental conditions. Before the twentieth century, governments attempted to prevent floods by keeping dams, dikes and irrigation systems in good working order. They responded to droughts with supplies of stored grain, construction of temporary housing, and other ways of supporting or relocating affected populations and getting agricultural land back into production. These are still the primary tools of modern governments responding to famine or threats of famine. But in the twentieth century there emerged clear instances

Pigs have been altered to produce high levels of healthy fatty acids normally found in fish. But many modifications are unrelated to healthy eating and only make animal products easier to process, such as cows that produce milk more resistant to heat and chickens that can remain healthy while eating cheap or contaminated feed. In related developments, animals from dwarf hamsters to pigs and horses have been bred to produce hormones and proteins needed for human medicine but otherwise impossible to obtain.

Although genetic engineering has unlimited potential applications, a primary goal of research has been the prevention or cure of cancer. In August of 2011, evidence seemed to confirm that a patient's blood could be genetically re-engineered by the targeted insertion of a patient's DNA into his own T-cells—programming them to not only seek and kill existing cancer cells, but to continue to monitor and eradicate new cells. Such research needs much further advancement before being a practical medical tool, but it is exemplary of the possibilities of genetic engineering.

Researchers warn that the function of all genes depends on the complex biochemical environment in which genes are naturally surrounded, and that learning to identify and manipulate genes does not produce complete control over their action. The possibility of unintended products that could enter and replicate within the gene pools of humans, animals, and plants is ever present. There have indeed been rare deaths of human subjects in gene therapy experiments, due to inadequately-understood variables. Knowledge must advance fast enough to keep abreast of the cultural and economic demands for improvement of our environment and our health.

---

of governments deliberately depriving their rural citizens of food in order to supply the military or urban populations. This happened in China during the Great Leap Forward (see Chapter 10) and is a regular occurrence in North Korea; perhaps 600,000 people starved in North Korea in the late 1990s, and famine still recurs there in the twenty-first century.

In some other regions governments have failed entirely. They are unable to prevent soldiers from appropriating food from starving populations, or to prevent the destruction of farmland through warfare. When refugees congregate, there may be nobody to provide them with water, food, or medical care. Dramatic incidents of this sort have occurred after 2000 in Afghanistan, Ethiopia, Niger, Guatemala, and Myanmar. The most tragic examples of such suffering in the early twenty-first century have arisen at Darfur, Sudan (where more than a hundred thousand people may have died between 2003 and 2010) and the ongoing conflict in Somalia. In the case of Somalia, a civil war raging since 1991 has destroyed roads, farmland, forest, and grazing areas. When drought hit the area in 2010, troops deliberately

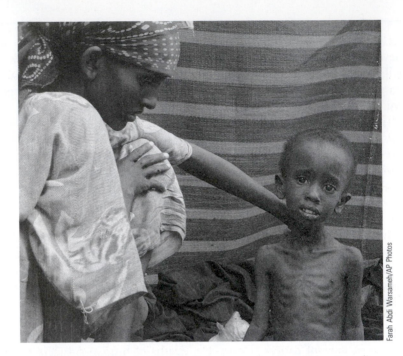

A starving child is bathed in a refugee camp in Mogadishu, Somalia. Since 1991, civil war has destroyed agriculture and transportation, putting some 11 million people at risk of death. International agencies provide inadequate help as the difficulties of food distribution increase in the country, and economic crises in Europe and North America discourage increased foreign aid.

prevented the migration of starving people. Refugees attempting to reach Kenya, Uganda, Yemen and other neighboring areas (which are also suffering from the drought) often die of the hardships of travel. The United Nations, no longer able to mobilize troops to help populations caught in these situations, attempts to coordinate international aid. Several European nations have reneged on promised funds, and aid that actually arrives is often stolen by soldiers or pilfered by corrupt officials. Somalia is a classic case of intense human suffering arisen from the inability of governments to respond to environmental challenges.

Economists estimate that providing basic medical care (including vaccinations), elementary education, safe water, sanitation, and basic nutrition to those who lack them would cost less than 4 percent of the combined wealth of the 225 richest single individuals in the world. The cost to the world's wealthiest nations would be negligible. Why is it not done? Many middle-or lower-income nations in the world attract foreign investment, but they are not the poorest countries. They are countries that have sufficient education, political stability, and infrastructure to support industries, many of them foreign-owned. Their low wage levels attract the investment, which creates more jobs and more incentives to improve education. Money does flow from the industrialized countries to these nations (such as Mexico, the Philippines, India, South Africa, and Vietnam). It generates new wealth both locally and in the investing countries. But the unindustrialized world has inefficiencies of its own, particularly an undeveloped or missing infrastructure for education, transportation, and communication, but also political instability and corruption. No single corporation or nation can profit from paying for basic health improvements in a country that is wracked by civil war (as in the cases of Sudan and Somalia) or chronic food shortages, or where educational levels are so low that most people have no understanding of disease, hygiene, or technology. If there is hope for improvement in the poorest countries, it probably lies in two trends. The first is wage creep in the developing nations. As countries such as China, Mexico, and the Philippines draw closer to the industrialized nations in living standards, the profitability of their labor will decrease. The search for cheap labor will inevitably raise the question of expanding investment in the very poorest nations.

CONCLUSION

History shows that gross disparities in well-being (usually resulting from gross differences in income) between classes are destabilizing. The issue is not inequality itself, but inequalities so extreme that people in the same society are living in different worlds—long-lived and short-lived, educated and uneducated, homed and homeless, invested in the society or alienated from it. It is a disturbing trend that the industrialized world is moving toward sharper skewing of the income distribution. Economists and political scientists usually quantify the destabilizing potential of inequalities through the Gini coefficient (named for Italian economist Corrado Gini), also called the Sustainable Government Index. A map of Gini coefficients shows that countries with a low ratio (greater equality of income distribution) are politically stable, with few incidents of public disorder, efficient and credible legal systems, and good continuity of representative government.

Twenty years ago, such countries included Japan, all of Europe and North America, northwestern Africa, India, Australia, Vietnam, Central Asia, and parts of eastern Africa. But developments of the last twenty years have brought instability to previously stable societies such as Greece and the United Kingdom, both of which were afflicted with widespread riots and looting in 2011. Subsequently, Europe, the United States, Canada and parts of Asia saw the spread of peaceful, broadly-based movements opposing government subsidization of huge corporations and shifting of debt burdens to the middle class and the poor. The United States and the United Kingdom both rank at 2.5 out of 5 on the Gini scale, but trend toward 3.5, where are found Georgia, Niger, Pakistan, the Philippines, the Russian Federation, and Turkey. Myanmar, the country with the highest Gini coefficient, is a mere twelve slots above the United States. There is no precise correlation between Gini ratios and political destiny. It is, however, an important indicator for trends and developmental issues relating to industrial innovation, market vitality, social integration and political stability. In an age of global protests decrying political corruption, high unemployment, and failure to relieve public misery, political analysts and historians will be examining the general problem of the Sustainable Government Index for some time.

For Further Reading

Studies relating to the content of this chapter in both print and digital media are flourishing, and we encourage you to pursue areas of interest. The suggestions here are well-established or unusually comprehensive sources.

Marq de Villiers, *Water: The Fate of Our Most Precious Resource* (New York: Mariner Books, 2001). On the basis of science gathered by major international agencies, this study presents the problems and suggests some policy options.

Teresa Hayter, *The Creation of World Poverty: An Alternative View to the Brandt Report* (London: Pluto Press, 1981). A reply to the arguments in the report.

Akira Iriye, *Global Community: The Role of International Organizations in the Making of the Contemporary World* (Berkeley: University of California Press, 2002). A leading historian of U.S. relations with the world considers the impact of nongovernmental organizations on the present and near future.

J. R. McNeill, *Something New Under the Sun: An Environmental History of the Twentieth-Century World* (New York: W. W. Norton, 2000). The most comprehensive and accessible discussion of environment issues by a historian.

Report of the Independent Commission on International Development Issues, North-South: A Program for Survival (Cambridge, Mass.: M.I.T. Press, 1980). The "Brandt report," a discussion of the causes of and remedies for global inequities.

Peter Unger, *Living High and Letting Die: Our Illusion of Innocence* (Oxford and New York: Oxford University Press, 1996). The most famous comprehensive view and ethical interpretation of these problems.

Gavin Williams, "Brandt Report: A Critical Introduction," *Review of African Political Economy,* vol. 7, no. 19 (Winter 1980), pp. 77–86. A reply to the arguments in the report.

Carmen M. Reinhart & Kenneth S. Rogoff, *This Time is Different: Eight Centuries of Financial Folly,* (Princeton University Press, 2009). A well-researched introduction to the history of bubbles and credit crises.

Related Websites

Virtual Library on International Development
    http://w3.acdi-cida.gc.ca/virtual.nsf
Sustainable Africa: Water Energy, Health, Agriculture, Biodiversity
    http://sustainable.allafrica.com/
Global Environment Outlook 2000 (United Nations Environment Programme)
    http://www.grida.no/geo2000/index.htm
Goddard Institute for Space Studies: Education: The Global Warming Debate
    http://www.giss.nasa.gov/edu/gwdebate/
HungerWeb (Brown University)
    http://www.brown.edu/Departments/World_Hunger_Program/

Index